# LITERARY HISTORY
## OF THE
# UNITED STATES

# CONTRIBUTORS

RANDOLPH G. ADAMS

CARLOS BAKER

RICHARD P. BLACKMUR

BRAND BLANSHARD

HAROLD BLODGETT

DAVID BOWERS

SCULLEY BRADLEY

HENRY SEIDEL CANBY

WILLIAM CHARVAT

GILBERT CHINARD

HENRY STEELE COMMAGER

ALEXANDER COWIE

MALCOLM COWLEY

MERLE CURTI

RALPH H. GABRIEL

MAXWELL GEISMAR

ERIC F. GOLDMAN

GORDON S. HAIGHT

HAROLD F. HARDING

ARTHUR PALMER HUDSON

EVERETT L. HUNT

THOMAS H. JOHNSON

HOWARD MUMFORD JONES

ADRIENNE KOCH

JOSEPH WOOD KRUTCH

LEWIS LEARY

HARRY T. LEVIN

TREMAINE MC DOWELL

LUTHER S. MANSFIELD

F. O. MATTHIESSEN

H. L. MENCKEN

JOHN C. MILLER

KENNETH B. MURDOCK

ALLAN NEVINS

HENRY A. POCHMANN

J. H. POWELL

CARL SANDBURG

TOWNSEND SCUDDER

ODELL SHEPARD

HENRY NASH SMITH

ROBERT E. SPILLER

WALLACE STEGNER

GEORGE R. STEWART

WALTER F. TAYLOR

HAROLD W. THOMPSON

STITH THOMPSON

WILLARD THORP

FREDERICK B. TOLLES

CARL VAN DOREN

JOHN D. WADE

DIXON WECTER

GEORGE F. WHICHER

STANLEY T. WILLIAMS

LOUIS B. WRIGHT

MORTON D. ZABEL

# LITERARY HISTORY
# OF THE
# UNITED STATES

*Editors*

ROBERT E. SPILLER · WILLARD THORP

THOMAS H. JOHNSON · HENRY SEIDEL CANBY

*Associates*

HOWARD MUMFORD JONES · DIXON WECTER

STANLEY T. WILLIAMS

00263

*VOLUME II*

1949

THE MACMILLAN COMPANY · NEW YORK

# CONTENTS

# CONTENTS

# EXPANSION

*. . . new perspectives*

# 38. THE WIDENING OF HORIZONS

AMERICAN literature to the end of the Civil War, the literature of the First Republic, presents a pattern of growth, maturity, and decline. By the seventies the Golden Day was dwindling to the mild glow of the Chautauqua Institution; and although the official standards of culture and "ideality" remained ostensibly dominant to the very end of the century, they came to seem more and more irrelevant in the face of the violent, crude, and formless energies generated by American society—in the westward movement across the continent, the development of mechanized industry, the attraction of immigrants from every corner of Europe.

The First Republic had been agrarian, with a few scattered commercial centers; the Second Republic, that was created by the Civil War, was focused on an industrial economy moving rapidly toward integration. The First Republic had been a relatively unimportant member of the community of nations occupying the shores of the North Atlantic basin. The Second Republic was different in scale and in geographical orientation; by 1900 it had emerged as a major world power and was on the point of becoming a First American Empire, dominant in the Caribbean and expanding into the Pacific.

If the transforming forces of the nineteenth century destroyed the tradition on which the First Republic had been based, at the same time they widened cultural horizons and laid the foundations for a new flowering of American literature in the twentieth century. It will therefore be expedient to depart from chronology at this point in our survey in order to glance at some of the expansive influences that were brought to bear upon the American people.

The famous portrait of American society in 1800 which opens Henry Adams' *History of the United States During the Administrations of Jefferson and Madison* emphasizes the conservatism and inertia which were all but universal. The South had of course produced its statesmen, but despite the influence of Jefferson interest in science and letters had declined since the time of William Byrd. New England was dominated by an alliance of clergy and magistrates who feared nothing so much as new ideas. "From 1790 to 1820," asserted Emerson, "there was not a book, a speech, a conversation, or a thought" in Massachusetts. Even in Philadelphia, which in Franklin's time had been the most enlightened and tolerant city in America, Joseph Dennie's *Port Folio* devoted most of its efforts to reproducing the attitudes of England a generation before. Among American men of letters, Philip Freneau, Charles Brockden Brown, and Hugh Henry Brackenridge indicated that some fresh viewpoints were struggling against convention; but they were isolated and on the whole ineffectual figures. The dominant tradition was one of provincial narrowness and sterile intellectual orthodoxy.

2

Yet forces were already at work that were destined to revolutionize American society. The first of these to make itself felt was physical expansion. Even before the Revolution, the frontier of settlement had begun to press against the Appalachian barrier. With the end of hostilities the first great wave of westward migration began to pour through the Cumberland Gap. Kentucky, with one hundred thousand inhabitants, was admitted to the Union in 1792. In 1820 there were three million people west of the mountains, and the frontier had crossed the Mississippi to advance two hundred miles up the Missouri. By 1848 the frontiersmen had pushed all the way to the Pacific Coast, occupying Texas and Oregon in their stride, and had rounded out substantially the present boundaries of the United States.

In the vast area between the Appalachians and the Pacific there appeared, as the frontier advanced, a society with fewer ties to bind it to the mother country. The Westerner, as contemporary observers described him, was restless, enterprising, and devoted to money-making. He had a pathetic desire for culture, in the abstract, coupled with a scarcely veiled contempt for impractical and effete representatives of older civilizations. He considered himself aggressively democratic, but his democracy often took the form of a refusal to acknowledge superiority of any kind. Eastern observers called Westerners barbarians; and from a certain point of view the charge was justified, for despite the efforts of pioneer men of letters in rising centers like Lexington and Cincinnati the West had lost contact with the cultural tradition of Europe and had not yet developed a civilization of its own. Yet it was the West that held the balance of power in the sharpening contest between North and South. In Jackson and Lincoln it furnished the only strong Presidents between the gentlemen of the Virginia dynasty and Grover Cleveland.

When the pioneer reached the end of the Overland Trail on the Pacific, he found that numerous other Americans had been there before him. Fur traders had come by sea to the Puget Sound area before 1800, and the droghers, or hide-trading ships, on one of which Richard Henry Dana sailed before the mast, had frequented the California coast in the twenties and thirties. As soon as the establishment of independence freed American mariners from the restrictions of the monopoly granted by Britain to the East India Company, they had set out for the Orient. *The Empress of China,* of New York registry, anchored off Macao in 1784. By 1790 the *Columbia,* of Boston, had explored the Northwest Coast, discovered the river that bears the ship's name, and begun the development of a complicated but profitable trade route from Atlantic ports around Cape Horn to Puget Sound, thence by way of the Sandwich Islands to Canton and home by way of the Cape of Good Hope.

Overseas trade charted paths which missionaries soon followed. The American Board of Commissioners for Foreign Missions began its work in Bombay in 1812 and in Ceylon in 1816. By 1840 it was maintaining 283 foreign missionaries, including some fifty in twenty-nine Oriental stations, from Bombay to Macao. These evangelists showed little interest in the civilization of the Far East, but they did set about learning the Oriental languages so that they might translate the Scriptures into the speech of their mission congregations. The joint effect of commercial and religious activity in the Orient was to keep at least a fraction of the American people aware of the strange and remote countries beyond the western sea.

American familiarity with the Pacific was also increased by the whale fishery. Many seamen followed the missionaries into the islands of Polynesia and Melanesia, and by the forties Melville was able to draw upon an extensive literature of Pacific travel and exploration in his *Typee* and *Omoo.* The needs of the whaling industry led in 1838 to the United States Exploring Expedition under the command of Charles Wilkes, U.S.N., which touched at Tahiti, Samoa, and Australia, engaged in Antarctic exploration, and visited the Oregon coast before returning home by way of the Philippines, Singapore, and Capetown. The acquisition of Oregon and California intensified the desire for the development of trade with the Orient and dictated the series of efforts to penetrate Japan which culminated in the Perry expedition of 1852–1854 and its commercial treaty. But the fifties represented a peak of interest in the Orient which was not reached again until 1898. The Civil War, the decline of the American merchant marine, and the absorption of the nation's energies in the West and in industrialization led to almost complete neglect of the far Pacific.

The decades following the war were, in fact, a period of introspection, during which the reunited nation seemed to be taking account of itself. For the national reading public, there were two domestic frontiers to be explored—not only the Trans-Mississippi, which was going through its greatest boom in the seventies, but also the South, which had been isolated from the North during the bitter decades of antislavery agitation and was now for the first time opened up to the forces making for economic and social integration under Northern leadership. The discovery of the South by hundreds of thousands of soldiers in the invading Union armies was reflected both in the popularity of factual narratives like Edward King's *The Great South* (serialized in *Scribner's* with numerous illustrations in 1874) and in the surprising Northern vogue of fiction and poetry elaborating the myth of the Southern plantation.

### 3

Even more important than expanding frontiers in transforming American society and altering perspectives were the related phenomena of industrialization, the rise of great cities, and immigration. Beginning with the use of steam power in transportation and manufacturing, which reached a significant scale in the thirties, the technological revolution went forward at a rate never before equaled. By the sixties, when the Atlantic cable was put into commercial operation, the characteristic rhythms of modern life were established: mass production of basic commodities, instant transmission of news, rapid and relatively cheap transportation on land or water.

The swiftly developing economy of the United States drew across the Atlantic millions of European peasants and artisans who saw in the New World a Utopian hope of economic betterment. During the first half of the nineteenth century the principal European immigration came from distressed Ireland and the Rhine provinces of Germany. By 1840 Irish peasants were crowding into Boston cellars and displacing the farmers' daughters who had made up the first labor force of the New England textile mills. The slum as a constant feature of urban society quickly came to seem inseparable from the idea of the immigrant. Faced with conditions having no precedent in the United States, leaders like Theodore Parker were forced to improvise or to adapt from British experience the modern techniques of case work and social service.

The German immigrants before the Civil War tended to move toward the Middle West, where they gathered in the growing cities, or, more often, bought out the improvements of American pioneer settlers and established compact, stolid, hard-working farm communities. Many of them, proud of the culture of their homeland, sought to preserve it in the New World through German-language schools and periodicals; and in the Midwestern cities they established beer gardens, *Turnvereine, Männerchore,* chamber-music societies, and even an occasional symphony orchestra. Another illustration of German influence in the West was the group of Hegelian philosophers who founded the *Journal of Speculative Philosophy* in St. Louis in 1867.

During the early decades of the century, Americans were usually proud to conceive of the Republic as a haven of refuge for the oppressed subjects of European monarchs. This attitude bore some relation to the chronic shortage of labor; it was especially marked in the West. In 1839, for example, the *Hesperian* (of Columbus, Ohio) proclaimed that "the gates of our entrance are never shut against the stranger and the foreigner; but stand wide open forever for the persecuted of every nation and tongue under heaven." Yet even as the West was welcoming foreign immigrants, the crowding of the Irish into cities of the Atlantic seaboard had begun to arouse opposition to them. Hostility to the Irish was increased by religious differences: the Know-Nothings, who advocated restrictions on the naturalization of immigrants, charged that the Pope was conspiring with the House of Hapsburg to overthrow American republicanism. Furthermore, the fact that, both before and after the Civil War, most immigrants settled in the North and West led Southerners to include the immigrant in their condemnation of Northern society.

Know-Nothingism disappeared as a political force in the realignment of the fifties, and eventually the rural immigrant vote, mainly German and Scandinavian, went over to the Republican Party. This made assimilation easier. The absence of a language barrier and inherited anti-English feeling in the United States similarly helped the Irish to gain acceptance in some parts of the country. But the industrialization which followed the Civil War created a new state of affairs. Although many European farmers were sent by railroads and land companies to the Western plains, by far the greater part of the "new" immigrants became factory workers and formed compact colonies in the great industrial cities, where they played an important if indeed not a dominant role in the increasingly class-conscious labor unions. After 1880, furthermore, most of the immigrants came from areas in Southeastern Europe whose languages and cultural traditions were much more remote from the American pattern than had been those of the earlier immigrants from Northwestern Europe. The unfortunate result was that toward the end of the century immigrants came more and more to be thought of as a distinct class, a well defined and perhaps unassimilable segment of the industrial proletariat. A protracted debate concerning the problem of "Americanization" and the "melting pot" occupied increasing space in magazines and newspapers; a cult of "Anglo-Saxon" superiority appeared, especially after 1890; and many of the contributors to the discussion revealed an irrational fear of the newcomers which was to find expression in the restrictive laws of the twentieth century.

It is not easy to determine exactly what effect these successive waves of immigration had on American thought and culture. The cosmopolitan character of the large cities was already pronounced by the end of the century. One factory in Chicago, in 1909, numbered among its forty-two hundred employees representatives of twenty-four nationalities; and in 1900 there were almost a thousand foreign-language periodicals and newspapers in the United States, published in twenty-five different tongues. Altogether, some twenty million aliens entered the United States during the nineteenth century. The census of 1900 showed more than ten million "foreign-born" in a total population of about seventy-six million. If persons whose parents were foreign-born were included, this number would perhaps be doubled, and would amount to more than one-fourth of the whole population.

From artists and scholars to illiterate peasants, all the immigrants brought with them an invisible baggage of cultural tradition: folklore, crafts, religions, patterns of the family and the community, foods and drinks. Much of this cultural baggage disappeared in the process of Americanization, but much of it was absorbed into the American way of life. Especially in the arts has the role of the immigrants and their descendants been important. It is worth noting also that the presence of many groups with a vital interest in European problems helped to offset the isolationism and provincial nationalism that were so powerful in nineteenth century America.

4

Such social and economic influences widened the cultural horizons of American society by adding increments of experience and proposing new topics of concern. But the century also brought many explicitly intellectual stimuli to bear upon the United States, just as it did upon Europe. The American people shared in all the major transformations of man's realm of ideas which took place during this period.

The first of these was the discovery of the past, the growth of the historic sense. Irving and Cooper early showed what richness of overtone could be added to familiar landscapes by weaving about them historical legends. Cooper's demonstration of the narrative interest of the American Revolution coincided with the growing spirit of nationalism, which in sanctifying the Revolution gave rise to the first efforts at systematic investigation of the American past. Around 1830 two Washington journalists began publishing collections of source materials for American history: Jonathan Elliott's *Debates* (in state and federal conventions on the Constitution), published 1827–1845, and Peter Force's ambitious *American Archives* (nine volumes, 1837–1853), comprising a documentary history of the British colonies in America. Thirty-five local and state historical societies were established between 1820 and 1850. (Only three, Massachusetts, New York, Pennsylvania, had been established before 1820.) In the same period collectors like John Carter Brown of Providence and James Lenox of New York began to form libraries of Americana. The fruition of these stirrings of interest in the American past came in the group of distinguished historians who dominated the mid-nineteenth century: George Bancroft, Jared Sparks, Richard Hildreth, and Francis Parkman.

The development of historical writing owed much to Americans who had studied in Germany during the first half of the century and had participated in the renovation of German scholarship that followed the nationalistic uprising against Napoleon. The new "philosophical" approach to classical antiquity, especially to Greece; textual criticism of the Scriptures; scientific study of the literatures of modern Europe—these enterprises drew a brilliant company of young Americans to German universities. Not only Bancroft's *History of the United States,* but George Ticknor's masterful *History of Spanish Literature,* John L. Motley's *Rise of the Dutch Republic,* and Longfellow's *Hyperion* and *The Golden Legend* developed out of impulses received at Göttingen and Heidelberg and Berlin.

But there was more in the transaction than scholarship. It was an important moment in the history of American culture when young Ticknor, the son of a wealthy Boston merchant, made a pilgrimage in 1817 to Wetzlar and experienced the emotions which he recorded in his journal as follows:

On the way I imagined that we passed the valley where the scene between Werther and Charlotte's distracted lover happened, and the chilly wind which blew as we went through it gave me a sensation of sadness such as I have seldom felt. I was still quite alone. A little farther on, I mounted the rocks, where Werther passed the dreadful night after he had left Charlotte—and in the village itself, I needed no guide to show me the red church—the lime trees—the burying ground, and the village houses which [Goethe] has described with such fidelity. On returning to the city, I stopped again on the rocks—read the description of his despair and stayed until the departing sun had almost descended behind the hills.

The American cult of Goethe, of which this is one of the early evidences, not only introduced a new generation to the complicated emotions of the *Sturm und Drang,* but led to a prolonged controversy on the subject of morality in art which helped to undermine the genteel tradition and to prepare the way for the eventual acceptance of realism in literature. German thought reached America more circuitously but with equal force in the transcendental philosophy transmitted to Emerson and his circle by Coleridge and Carlyle. The dimension of the self, of subjectivity, which transcendentalism set out to explore, was often described by critics of the movement as a morbid German invention.

Closely associated with transcendentalism, although not identical with it, was the ferment of social reform in New England during the thirties and forties. If all established institutions and usages were to be called before the bar of intuition and made to give an account of themselves, there was likely to be a great holocaust, as Hawthorne perceived. The young men and women of Brook Farm considered that they had come out from civilization, which they found too confining, and were engaged in building the society of the future on the principle of association. Together with Fourierists and Icarians and Owenites and Perfectionists scattered from New Jersey to Texas and Wisconsin, they were exploring the dimension of utopianism, and although presently the movement to free the slaves swallowed up many of the other reforming crusades that had flourished in the forties, there remained a leaven of willingness to experiment which never wholly disappeared from American life. A generation glorying in its gospel of "the Newness" had made it impossible for any future conservative to oppose change merely on the score of the wickedness of all "innovation."

5

While transcendentalists and reformers were voyaging strange seas of thought and tampering with the institutional foundations of American society, less radical writers and thinkers were undertaking an inventory of the actual conditions of life on the American continent, especially in the vast interior that had been so recently occupied by white settlers. The most striking symbol of the non-European factors in the new environment was the Indian. Although there was a tradition of exotic interest in the red man dating from the time of Columbus, the accounts of missionaries were the most reliable factual reports available when Cooper began his Leatherstocking series in the twenties. But the scientific impulse to collect and organize data was soon to yield tangible results. Beginning with Lewis Cass' criticism of Cooper's depiction of the Indians during the late twenties, the *North American Review* established a policy of publishing in almost every volume at least one solid article on the subject; and Albert Gallatin in his old age contributed to the *Transactions* of the American Antiquarian Society (1836) a "Synopsis of the Indian Tribes . . . in North America" which virtually created the science of American linguistics.

Less disciplined projects were going forward at the same time—perhaps because Andrew Jackson's policy of forcing the Eastern tribes beyond the Mississippi dramatized the Indians as a vanishing race. George Catlin, a Pennsylvanian who deserted the law for painting, began in 1832 a series of journeys that took him to every part of the United States, from Florida to the Yellowstone, where he might observe and paint the natives. His gallery of Indian portraits and his collection of costumes, weapons, and ritual objects were exhibited to large audiences in American cities of the East and in Europe. Catlin's *Manners, Customs, and Condition of the North American Indians* (1841) is strongly primitivistic in flavor, but it contains valuable accounts of the author's travels. Henry R. Schoolcraft married an Ojibway wife and lived for thirty years among the Indians of the Great Lakes region. His numerous books (published from 1839 to 1857, sometimes with subventions from the federal government) represent a design even more far-reaching than Catlin's to set down everything that could be learned about the aborigines. Schoolcraft's work provided the "source" for *Hiawatha,* but it was too unsystematic to endure as a scientific influence. Lack of method likewise impairs the sumptuous collection of Indian portraits with biographical sketches compiled by Thomas L. McKenney, Superintendent of Indian Trade in the War Department, and the Cincinnati writer James Hall, which was published in three folio volumes, 1836–1844.

During the forties the American Ethnological Society (founded in 1842 under Gallatin's leadership), and after 1848 the Smithsonian Institution, gave consistent attention to American ethnology; and by the seventies the discipline was assuming its modern form. Frank Hamilton Cushing, who lived from 1879 to 1882 in the pueblo of Zuñi, wrote a series of articles on his experiences for the *Century* (1882–1883) which are a landmark in the sympathetic yet accurate study of American Indian cultures. John Wesley Powell, after securing the establishment of the Bureau of American Ethnology in 1879, issued an important series of reports prepared by a professional staff. An equally enthusiastic student of the Indian was John G. Bourke, an officer of the regular army who fought in campaigns against the Plains Indians in the seventies. In addition to a pioneer monograph on the Snake Dance of the Hopi (1884), he wrote many scientific papers, and a half-dozen books designed for a more popular audience. The first half-century of work on the Indians was synthesized in H. H. Bancroft's *Native Races of the Pacific States* (1876–1882). American archaeology, in its early stages hardly to be distinguished from ethnology, had meanwhile been placed on its modern footing through the pioneer investigations of the Swiss-American Adolph Bandelier, whose classic papers on the art of war, land tenure, and social organization of ancient Mexico appeared between 1877 and 1879.

Like the study of buried American civilizations, the growing interest in folklore enriched men's understanding of the possibilities of life in the New World. British and Continental efforts to collect the tales and songs of the uneducated folk were not imitated immediately in the United States, perhaps because there was no obvious equivalent for the European peasant traditionally attached to the soil. But there were nevertheless some minority groups, isolated from the main currents of American life, which had retained

or developed an authentic folklore. In the Southern Appalachians were mountaineers who had preserved into the nineteenth century the social patterns of
the eighteenth; as collectors discovered with delight in the eighties, they sang
ballads which their ancestors had brought from the British Isles. Interest in
ballads had been aroused in the United States through the efforts of Professor
Francis J. Child of Harvard, who had begun his study of the English and
Scottish ballads before 1850; his great work eventually appeared in five volumes from 1883 to 1898. Appropriately, Professor Child became the first
president of the American Folklore Society in 1888.

The richest find of the collectors was the songs of the Southern Negro,
first recorded for publication by Northern Abolitionists and officers during
the Civil War. James M. McKim of Philadelphia and his daughter Lucy
(later the wife of Wendell Phillips Garrison) encountered spirituals among
freed slaves of the South Carolina Sea Islands in the early sixties, and T. W.
Higginson collected songs in the same area from soldiers in his colored regiment. In his pioneer article on "Negro Spirituals" in the *Atlantic* (1867),
Higginson says that he was drawn to the project because he had been "a
faithful student of the Scottish ballads, and had always envied Sir Walter the
delight of tracing them out amid their own heather, and of writing them
down piecemeal from the lips of aged crones." But the Northern collectors
also wished to create cultural prestige for the Negro. This purpose is evident
in the first book setting down words and music of the spirituals, *Slave Songs
of the United States*. Published a few months after Higginson's article, it was
compiled by Lucy McKim Garrison, Charles Pickard Ware, and William
Francis Allen, a Northern teacher who went South to help the freed Negroes
during the war. The same influence appears in the career of the Fisk University student singers who began touring the North in 1871 to raise funds for
their school. Joel Chandler Harris' Uncle Remus stories in the Atlanta *Constitution* in 1879 were the first significant notice of Negro folk tales.

6

Despite the importance of the forces already mentioned, the most drastic
changes in American thought during the nineteenth century came from
another source, the impact of natural science. Geological speculation concerning the age of the earth, in the early part of the century, and the Darwinian
theory of organic evolution in the latter part, called in question the infallibility
of the Scriptures and weakened the widely prevalent faith in the governance
of the universe according to an intelligible divine plan. The result was a
lessening of emphasis upon the supernatural aspects of religion with a corresponding growth of interest in its ethical and especially in its social implications. As the supernatural conception of sin lost force, evil was projected

from the individual soul into the environment. Here it was attacked by men who sought to apply a "social gospel" to American society as a remedy for urban poverty and for the tensions between employers and laborers that had resulted from the growth of large-scale industry. The social gospel was being discussed as early as the seventies, and its influence was eventually felt in every Protestant denomination—although of course with varying intensity. But if the idea of organic evolution thus indirectly strengthened humanitarianism in the evangelical churches, it could also have a contrary effect: the notion of the survival of the fittest was often interpreted as giving scientific sanction to the fierce competitive struggles of the closing years of the century.

The emphasis on adaptation to environment implicit in evolutionary biology influenced literature by calling attention to the varieties of man's efforts to accommodate himself to terrain and climate. Not only in the flood of travel books which described the various regions of the country—especially the Far West—but even more strikingly in the local color fiction which flourished in the eighties was evident an insatiable curiosity concerning the land and the people of the different parts of the United States. This new preoccupation with the physical conditions of life in the New World, with the unpredictable novelties of American experience, played a great if not easily definable part in the reorientation of American literature after the Civil War.

One of the most tangible evidences of the new point of view is the changing attitude of writers toward language. In the twenties Americans had been delighted to hear Irving's elegance of diction and avoidance of Americanism praised by the British, but much of the best writing of the period after the Civil War shows little regard for "correctness." The revolution had been prepared by the humorists of the thirties and forties—by books like A. B. Longstreet's *Georgia Scenes* and T. B. Thorpe's *The Hive of "The Bee Hunter,"* with their loving attention to the illiterate dialect of the frontier. Even the Brahmins of the great period had done their share to bring the vernacular into literary use. As George Philip Krapp remarks:

How tantalizingly near this rustic native speech [of New England] lay to the cultivated speech is evidenced by the use of the native speech which was made by writers like Holmes, Lowell, and others, who endeavored to express homespun character in homespun speech. Though this native speech was felt to be vigorously expressive, may even have been felt to be the real speech of New England, yet it was always used with a reluctant admission that the reality was not good enough for the highest purposes. It is doubtful, however, if Lowell ever expressed himself more sincerely than he did in the *Biglow Papers,* and time and again in Holmes, when he good-humoredly permits himself to forget the literary pose, glimpses of the essentially local, provincial New Englander, wise, kindly, and simple, show in the language he uses.

The intrusion of the vernacular into consciously literary usage had been preceded by a linguistic discussion dating from the eighteenth century. Noah Webster, asserting that "a *national language* is a band of *national union*," protested in 1789 that an "astonishing respect for the arts and literature of their parent country, and a blind imitation of its manners," were preventing Americans from establishing their intellectual independence of England. He predicted that American speech would grow entirely away from English. Although Webster was a Federalist, most conservatives in politics were opposed to the acceptance of Americanisms. The *Port Folio,* for example, reprinted with approval a pseudonymous attack on Webster's project for an American dictionary which took the familiar position that "it is incumbent on literary men, to guard against impurities, and chastise, with the critical lash, all useless innovations. . . . Colloquial barbarities abound in all countries, but among no civilized people are they admitted, with impunity, into books."

Official prejudice against the use of the vernacular in literature continued strong for more than half a century. As late as 1878 a critic in the *Atlantic* objected to a historical novelist's use of "the dialect supposed to have been spoken by the rude forefathers of the New England hamlets" on the score that the "wanton distortion of sounds and a hardy disobedience to grammar," characteristic of the speech of "the unrefined," were "wholly base." It was not until the appearance of Bret Harte after the Civil War that a writer could be generally praised for capturing "the robust vigor and racy savor of the miners' vernacular."

Whitman, however, had already advanced far beyond Harte's attitude toward the native speech. Whereas Harte continued to exploit his gambling and mining terms for comic purposes only, Whitman used the vocabulary, if not the rhythms, of American oral speech for the most elevated occasions.

American writers are to show far more freedom in the use of words [he declared in the late fifties].—Ten thousand native idiomatic words are growing, or are to-day already grown, out of which vast numbers could be used by American writers, with meaning and effect—words that would be welcomed by the nation, being of the national blood—words that would give that taste of identity and locality which is so dear in literature.

*Leaves of Grass* thoroughly bears out Whitman's theory; indeed, so important did he consider the question of diction that he once described his work as "only a language experiment . . . an attempt to give the spirit, the body, the man, new words, new potentialities of speech." But it was Mark Twain, in *Huckleberry Finn* (1885), who proved to America at large that the vernacular was adequate to meet any demand a serious writer might make on it.

As the quotation from Whitman suggests, the use of American English was closely bound up with the choice of vividly localized characters and incidents. Despite frequent exhortations by critics who urged the use of native materials, American writers during the first half of the century found it difficult to disentangle themselves from the notion that "low" scenes and characters could appropriately be dealt with only as comic. The humorists who created Major Jack Downing and Sam Slick and the Davy Crockett of the almanacs made an important transition from the conventional contempt for illiterate characters by endowing their creatures with an engaging shrewdness and a vein of poetry growing out of the folk experience. As Walter Blair points out, their work reached a wide and enthusiastic audience, although most critics, and for that matter the humorists themselves, would have been astonished to learn that posterity would consider their tales as the starting point of a truly American literature. Longstreet's *Georgia Scenes* went through twelve editions between 1835 and 1894; Benjamin P. Shillaber's *Life and Sayings of Mrs. Partington* sold fifty thousand copies within a few weeks of its publication in 1854; and William T. Thompson's *Major Jones's Courtship* went through thirteen editions between 1844 and 1855. The popularity of the *Biglow Papers* was a part of the same trend: no one could doubt, by 1860, that strongly localized characters had an appeal for the American public.

Closely related to the native humorous tradition, but more self-conscious and more superficial, was the local color movement. The demand for an American literature had often been understood to mean no more than the use of peculiarly American materials. As *Hiawatha* and *Evangeline* indicate, the writer's duty was taken to be simply the application of traditional techniques to native scenes and characters, usually of the past. The principal change evident in the local colorists after the Civil War was the use of contemporary "regional" materials. These writers had an astonishing vogue. Within ten years after Bret Harte's original success in 1869 the reading public was familiar with a long list of specialists, each of whom had identified himself with a given locality, from New Orleans to the Maine coast. By the end of the eighties no literate American can have failed to become acquainted with a score of formerly isolated and self-contained regions.

In the course of the nineteenth century, a variety of expansive forces completely altered the scale of American life and thought. The new national culture was in many respects raw and crude, but it had great vitality, and despite the variety of social patterns embraced within the national synthesis the parts were related to one another in a whole. In the future, although regional cultures would become increasingly significant, it would be impossible for an important writer to deal with his own area of experience in isolation from that of the entire society.

# 39. LITERARY CULTURE ON THE FRONTIER

IN recent years, it has become conventional to attribute these cultural changes to the "frontier." Nathaniel Ames, with an almanac maker's gifts of prophecy, foretold as early as 1758 that "Arts and Sciences will change the Face of Nature in their Tour from Hence over the Appalachian Mountains to the Western Ocean." While the settler was destined to transform the frontier, it was clear from the start in an equally real sense he would be transformed by it.

These interactions happened at successive times and places—as white settlement after the Revolution flowed first into the great meadows of Kentucky and the fertile wilderness of the Ohio Valley, then early in the new century pushed on to the Illinois country and began to explore the vast Mississippi Valley, while another tongue from Virginia and the Carolinas thrust itself into the then Southwest frontier of Georgia, Alabama, and Tennessee. Eddying around points of earlier settlement like New Orleans and St. Louis, the wave of migration that had surged so promptly into the territory of the Louisiana Purchase—the "choice country with room enough" promised by President Jefferson—began before long to encroach upon Mexican dominion in Texas and later in the Far West, until both vast regions had fallen to the Federal Union by 1848. Meanwhile in 1846 the United States, by treaty with Britain, gained undisputed title to that Pacific Northwest which for a decade had been the journey's end of the famous Oregon Trail. This, in brief, is the story of the frontier, whose march rounded out the continental expanse of the nation before the nineteenth century was half done—although areas and pockets of unsettled land remained for many decades, and the frontier was not declared officially closed until the Census of 1890. The cultural institutions and tools which shaped the mind of this frontier, through printing, reading, and writing, deserve examination.

Within a few years after the winning of independence, hosts of settlers —carrying seeds, a few tools, and one or two indispensable books like the Bible—had begun to cross the Alleghenies toward "the meeting point between savagery and civilization," as the historian Frederick J. Turner called the frontier. It has been defined as that zone, facing the trackless public domain, where fewer than two persons lived per square mile. Socially and culturally, it was a laboratory of mixed races and folkways from the start. Success came to the young and vigorous, rather than to the heir of wealth and prestige. Even book learning mattered less than brawn, daring, and the earthy lore of soldier, woodsman, and farmer.

In those early days, the valves of influence opened chiefly westward. Receiving from the Eastern seaboard almost all the culture it knew, the frontier gave little or nothing in return. Once a settler made the western traverse, he rarely went home. The mind of the East, in general, felt little more than casual curiosity about the rude frontier, save as a terra incognita of romantic novelists. Soon after the dawn of the nineteenth century, travel grew easier, thanks to the building of turnpikes into the West, and the steamboats that pioneered its great rivers, and the canals that linked its waters. In the thirties and forties came the first railroads, and conquest was assured.

Over these roads and watercourses eagerly streamed the advance agents of civilization. One such courier was the itinerant revivalist, missionary, or circuit rider. He helped break the shell of frontier loneliness, as the grim homiletics of Cotton Mather and Jonathan Edwards gave way to the warmth of backwoods exhorters like Lorenzo Dow and Peter Cartwright. "When I hear a man preach," said Lincoln, "I like to see him act as if he were fighting bees." Emotional oratory from the pulpit, and reading matter like missionary tracts, henceforth became a powerful element in frontier culture, shaping its imagination and daily idioms. From the preacher, also, much backwoods education stemmed. As early as 1800, the Methodist General Conference made its circuit riders agents for books published under direction of the church; the greatest of its Western missionaries, Bishop Francis Asbury, shortly became an evangel of popular education. The Baptists, who shared with Methodists the primacy on the frontier, presently followed suit. From early days, Presbyterians and Congregationalists, whose Yankee traditions demanded learning in the pulpit and literacy among the flock, tended the vineyard of knowledge. Biblical scholars like Lyman Beecher and Calvin Stowe—father and husband, respectively, of Harriet Beecher Stowe—transplanted their educational interests, with powerful effect, to the Ohio country.

Secular education in the West owed most to that hardy perennial, the wandering schoolmaster. The first historian of Kentucky and introducer of Daniel Boone to the world, in 1784, was a Pennsylvania pedagogue, John Filson. On the frontier, this profession was no sedentary calling; the first master of a log-cabin school at Lexington, Kentucky, began one day's tasks by strangling with his bare hands a wildcat in the schoolroom. First in the South, later in the Southwest, the New England schoolmaster grew proverbial for qualities of enterprise, rather than for the cloistered pursuit of knowledge.

He charged what he could get, and boarded around, while holding classes in a cabin of mud-daubed logs, where boards served for desks and shingles with bits of charcoal for slates and blackboards. Little beyond "readin', writin', and cypherin' to the rule of three" was expected of him. Nevertheless, he inducted his charges into the mystery of the printed word—chiefly by means of those aggressively American textbooks that came after Independence, like Noah Webster's blue-backed speller, Jedidiah Morse's geography, and Nicholas Pike's arithmetic ("more suitable to our meridian than those heretofore published").

Such books, and others on law, medicine, surveying, biography, history, and fictional subjects, were carried into the West by that humble pollinator of culture, the itinerant peddler. Like the greatest of his tribe, Bronson Alcott, this type was commonly Yankee. That New England wrote, published, taught, and sold the majority of books on the frontier, in the first generation of settlement, is a fact of much significance in the shaping of the western country's neo-Puritanism.

Free education was one of the pioneer's cherished ideas. The Land Ordinance of 1785 set aside section sixteen in each township for public schools; that of 1787 promised, "Schools and the means of education shall forever be encouraged." As a matter of sober fact, the dream of a great public educational system in the West did not come close to realization until the 1830's, when the taxes necessary to its support were at last levied.

Colleges, however, made early headway. Transylvania Seminary in Kentucky, the pioneer west of the Alleghenies, started in 1785 as little more than a grammar school; it began to confer degrees in 1802, amassed an important library, and grew to considerable prestige before sectarian quarrels sapped its usefulness. Ohio University at Athens, set up by act of the state legislature in 1804, drew sustenance from federal land grants. It bred a notable generation of schoolmasters in the New England tradition. Its president during the Van Buren era was William Holmes McGuffey, whose Eclectic Readers taught three generations of Americans good English and sound morals. Most pioneer colleges, by the yardstick of modern times, were poor in books, scholarship, and mental stimulus; but their spirit, like that of the region itself, fed upon hope. Naturally enough the fount of intellectual America remained in the East, whence came the best educators, and where backwoods sons with ambition and luck were prone to gravitate. Thanks to the religious orthodoxy of the frontier, the shadow of Yale, in the land of steady habits and Trinitarianism, and likewise that of safely Presbyterian Princeton, loomed larger across the Ohio Valley than did the influence of more liberal, heretical Harvard.

Mechanics' institutes, local lyceums, lecture and study courses, museums featuring exhibits and talks, all promoted Western education upon the adult level. Moreover, here and there, nuclei of utopian communities—such as New Harmony, Indiana, on the lower Wabash, which drew the English socialist Robert Owen, the feminist Frances Wright, the French naturalist Charles Lesueur, and others who taught in its school—served as intellectual beacons on the prairie, even though geographically the radius of their light was small.

Under great handicaps—indeed with an appetite whetted by privation— the westering pioneers cherished the crumbs of book learning and culture. In an address in 1859, Henry Ward Beecher picturesquely described these emigrants: "They drive schools along with them, as shepherds drive flocks. They have herds of churches, academies, lyceums; and their religious and educational institutions go lowing along the western plains as Jacob's herds lowed along the Syrian hills."

## 2

Subscription libraries sprang up before public ones. Amid the isolation of the frontier, books were prized for their rarity as well as their companionship. One Ohio pioneer, subscriber at $10 a share to the Belpre Farmers' Library, tells how he regularly made the twelve miles' round trip necessary to borrow books, and usually spent the winter evenings reading aloud by the light of pine knots, while his wife carded or spun. In the same state, Ames township in 1803 started its famous "Coonskin Library," whose members paid their dues in furs and skins which the factor sold in Boston to buy books. Free libraries began to develop in the next decade. Louisville gained its public library in 1816, while smaller settlements were grasping the idea. Henry R. Schoolcraft, student of the Indians, following the Wabash in 1821, found at Albion "a library of standard books, accessible to all, and much attention is paid to the improvement of the mind as well as the soil." That astute young Frenchman, Alexis de Tocqueville, exploring the backwoods in the early thirties—and discovering in a typical pioneer's cabin "a Bible, the first six books of Milton, and two of Shakespeare's plays"—reflected upon the paradox of the frontiersman:

Everything about him is primitive and wild, but he is himself the result of the labor and experience of eighteen centuries. He wears the dress and speaks the language of cities; he is acquainted with the past, curious about the future, and ready for argument upon the present; he is, in short, a highly civilized being, who consents for a time to inhabit the backwoods, and who penetrates into the wilds of the New World with the Bible, an axe, and some newspapers.

The printing press, carried in the wake of the pioneer, made the frontier more self-reliant. Although Filson in 1784 had to journey back to Delaware with his manuscript about Kentucky, in the lack of a single printer's shop west of the mountains, two years later the trans-Allegheny country produced its first newspaper, the Pittsburgh *Gazette*—sometimes printed on cartridge paper borrowed from Fort Pitt. Its publisher, John Scull, in 1793 printed the first book west of the Alleghenies, the third volume of H. H. Brackenridge's novel *Modern Chivalry*. Meanwhile a printing press, carried from Philadelphia by wagon and boat into Kentucky, in 1787 enabled John Bradford to start the second Western newspaper, the *Kentucke Gazette*. Copies stowed in the saddlebags of postriders penetrated far into the wilderness; staleness of news mattered little, and neighbors often gathered around a stump to hear the paper read aloud. In 1810, as the Postmaster General reported, Western newspapers made up less than a tenth of the total published in the nation; but by 1840 they comprised more than a quarter of the total.

Dearth of news, national and international, often proved to be a boon for literature. Amateur essayists, still under the spell of Addison and Steele and Dr. Johnson, revealed the timidity of a consciously bookish culture on the frontier. Also popular was the local poets' column, styled "The Parnassiad," "Seat of the Muses," or "Poetical Asylum," where fledglings attempted the flights of the English Augustans, and a little later Scott or Byron. Those two absorbing passions of the frontier, politics and religion, sired a great deal of verse, partisan and pietistic, which seldom rose above mediocrity, but encouraged the habit of versifying.

More exclusively the preserve of literature was the magazine. The pioneer in the West was Daniel Bradford's *The Medley, or Monthly Miscellany,* which lasted but one year, 1803, at Lexington, Kentucky. After the lapse of sixteen years, a successor appeared on the same spot, in William Gibbes Hunt's *Western Review*. History, biography, sentimental fiction, poetry, synopses of English novels, and an important series on science by Constantine S. Rafinesque, made up the bill of fare. (The work of that naturalist, along with the still more important findings of John James Audubon and Alexander Wilson, stirred keen interest upon a frontier which loved the outdoors and knew its natural history to be so largely unique.) If the purely literary complexion of these magazines seems pallid, beside the daily adventure of life in the West, at least the aspiration was in the making. Timothy Flint, romantic Yankee missionary who launched another *Western Review* in 1827, and Judge James Hall, planter of two literary magazines in Illinois in the next decade, both were fierce champions of Western culture against the effete East. Yet, significantly enough, the most distinguished magazine to come out of the West in this era, the *Western Messenger*—begun in 1835 by the Reverend James Freeman Clarke and other intellectual Unitarians—drew most of its sustenance from the taproot of Concord and Boston. Liberal and transcendental, it was the first periodical to publish Emerson's poetry; and thanks to George Keats, brother of the poet and a citizen of Louisville, John Keats' "Ode to Apollo" first appeared in its pages. Breasting strong currents of anti-Unitarian prejudice, the *Messenger* never made much headway in the West, and expired in 1841. In fact, most magazines in this region died young, after struggling against local poverty, the scarcity of gifted contributors, and competition for subscribers with imported Eastern and British reviews.

In forms less professedly literary, the printed word did flourish. The firm of Truman & Smith, founded in Cincinnati about 1830, presently became the largest schoolbook publisher in the world—in the first decade of its existence turning out more than 700,000 copies of texts like the McGuffey Readers, Ray's Arithmetic, Miss Beecher's Moral Instructor. Also in heavy demand were songbooks sentimental or patriotic, and almanacs, specially the comic almanac which salted its weather forecasts with funny stories about frontier favorites like Mike Fink, king of Mississippi keelboatmen, and Davy Crockett, that ring-tailed roarer of the woods. Humor in fact became the great medium for home-grown literature and art in the back country. Joke books, comic balladry, black-face minstrels, and the tall tales men told at frontier outposts or around the campfire, to beguile time and solitude—all added something to an art of humor that reached perfection upon the lips of such true frontiersmen as Abe Lincoln and Mark Twain.

This art flourished with special flavor in the Southwest. Its frequent appeal to slapstick, horseplay, and belly laughter should not lead one to hasty conclusions. Aside from the autobiography purported to be written by Davy Crockett and published in 1834—in which the hero's lack of book larnin' is somewhat proudly displayed—the most representative specimens of this humor did not spring from illiterate men. Augustus Baldwin Longstreet, a Georgian educated at Yale, and future Methodist clergyman, published in his small-town newspaper, the Augusta *Sentinel,* many of the droll sketches later collected as *Georgia Scenes* (1835). In the midst of such backwoods crudities as gouging matches and gander pullings, the author steps aside to quote Horace, or dress in classical mythology his account of a fox hunt. The sketch called "The Debating Society" suggests another cultural resource of the frontier, which enlivened Fourth of July barbecues and political campaigns, produced its finest flower in the oratory of Henry Clay, and led a wag to observe that speakers kept the American Eagle so constantly in flight that his shadow wore a trail across the Mississippi Valley. Another minor classic of the old Southwest, *Flush Times in Alabama and Mississippi* (1853), was written by Joseph G. Baldwin, a lawyer steeped in history and classical literature, who yet could savor the brawling and practical joking of the buckskin frontier.

The old Southwest, from Georgia to the Mississippi, was in fact a frontier with its own hallmark—settled by a more homogeneous population, largely Virginians and Carolinians, than that of the Northwest, and hence strongly molded by Southern influences, whether in the love of outdoor sports or in its code of honor. Culturally, its most characteristic instrument of education was the "academy" on the Southern plan, a secondary school somewhat more democratic than the Latin schools of the larger New England towns, but less so than the high schools which developed later. Sometimes this institution was called a county academy, and looked to the state for support; more often it was maintained by a religious denomination, private subscription, and tuition fees. With almost fanatic zeal, the South and the old Southwest trimmed the lamp of eighteenth century scholasticism in the lonely backwoods. They clung to Latin and Greek as the essence of gentlemanly discipline, supplemented by a smattering of mathematics and English grammar, while literature and history went begging. Rude in equipment and poor in staffing, the frontier academy still served as the chief implement of organized education in a region where elementary schools as well as colleges were still exceedingly sparse. But that no very vigorous thinking or writing, or even much constructive reading, sprang from that thin, derivative culture is not surprising. Sport, politics, gossip, and conviviality were the chief fruits of leisure in the old South, as the minor Georgia poet Henry R. Jackson observed plaintively in 1840, adding:

> As compared with the North, there are with us more individuals of leisure not engaged in the busy avocations of life. . . . Nature has given them temperaments demanding strong excitement! Unaccustomed to seek it in the more ennobling pursuits of literature, they too often resort to the short-lived stimulus of the intoxicating cup.

## 3

A cultural map of inland America, in the first half of the nineteenth century, would show "islands" of more exotic and sophisticated tradition. For, flowing west, the Anglo-Saxon tide first met the French culture of the Mississippi Valley, and then flowed on to encounter the Spanish influence of the new Southwest and the Pacific slope.

Catholic folkways differed from Protestant in the indulgence of a gayer Sabbath and pre-Lenten carnival, in the Latin passion for warmer colors and franker delight in the senses. From Canada to the Gulf, the *voyageur* carried his boat songs and folklore, and his French speech. That tongue won considerable popularity among the new schools and academies of Ohio, Indiana, Illinois, and Missouri. St. Louis, founded by French trappers, remained the insular center of Gallic culture in America; and its leading educational institution, St. Louis University, chartered by the Jesuits in 1832, from the start influenced the intellectual life of this region and drew students even from Mexico and South America. But the heart of France *in partibus infidelium* was New Orleans, whose gentry prized their Epicurism and courtly manners and education founded upon Continental and parochial models—for, until the Constitution of 1845, common schools were unknown in Louisiana. Most Anglo-Saxons who settled there were insensibly wooed by the charm, the apparent paganism, of the place, and those who came to convert often remained to conform. The effect of the Crescent City upon such tarrying birds of passage as Walt Whitman and Lafcadio Hearn, or upon a native son of alien stock like George W. Cable, proved of high import to literature.

In the westward current of empire, other whirlpools of culture appeared. German immigrants into Illinois after 1848, and Scandinavian settlers in Wisconsin and Minnesota in the middle years of the century, brought with them new languages, cultures, and nostalgias to the cabins and sod houses of the prairie. Foreign-language presses turned out many newspapers and a few books. Most such immigrants were sturdy, simple, hard-working folk rather than artists or scholars; but literacy ran high among them, with a craving for advancement, of which "the America fever" (as Selma Lagerlöf called it) was symptomatic. Among groups of old American stock, but sharply set apart from their neighbors by mores and theology, the Mormons drew most attention. Finding their promised land, after trials and tribulations, in the basin of the Great Salt Lake, the Saints fabricated a life of their own that culturally was somewhat bleak, but typically American in its accent upon enterprise and self-improvement—notably in the decree of compulsory education for all children, in secular schools that were tuition-free to the poor.

The Spanish civilization of the Pacific coast was too thin in population, too indolent, to make a concerted stand against the Anglo-Saxon. Within a short time it underwent absorption into the cultural complex of the New West—along with Southern New England, Midwestern, European, and Oriental elements—while lending the mass some of the richness of its pigment. Spanish language newspapers, sermons in Spanish and a few quaint remains of liturgical drama, and the inflow of a modest quota of books from Mexico City and Spain, were persistent enclaves in the midst of a speedy English-speaking conquest. The cultural history of the frontier beyond the Rocky Mountains, therefore, was written anew after Manifest Destiny turned the page.

When Americans began seriously to think about pushing the nation's western boundary to land's end, two main trails led from the middle border into the West. The older was the Santa Fe Trail, from the Mississippi Valley through Kansas into the highlands of New Mexico—a path of trade rather than of folk migration, at least prior to the California Gold Rush. Younger but of greater importance was the Oregon Trail, from the woodlands of Missouri northwestward across the Great Plains and mountain passes to the forests of Oregon and northern California. Its ground breakers, the preacher Samuel Parker and the medical missionary Marcus Whitman, had been sent to work among the Nez Percés and Flathead tribes. Lean years following the Panic of 1837 sent legions of dispossessed men and their families over the Oregon Trail. Though traveling light, many carried a few of life's amenities. Joel Palmer, off to Oregon in 1845, wrote in his journal while encamped on the Trail:

At two of the tents the fiddle was employed in uttering its unaccustomed voice among the solitudes of the Platte; at one tent I heard singing; at others the occupants were engaged in reading, some the Bible, others poring over novels.

To west-coast ports at this time, sizable shipments of books from New England and New York were already being brought around the Horn, in the course of the hide and tallow trade. While the almost bloodless deliverance of California from Mexico was being won, other cultural developments appeared. The *Californian,* first newspaper in that state, appeared at Monterey in August, 1846, but shortly moved to San Francisco to merge with a junior rival as the well known *Alta California.* The Public Institute, an educational enterprise, opened in San Francisco's Portsmouth Square on the eve of the Gold Rush; in 1849 the new state constitution promised free education to all.

Discovery of gold forced the early flowering of northern California. (As a touch of bookishness worth remark, the finders of ore in Sutter's millrace carefully read the article on gold in the *American Encyclopedia* before believing their luck.) Now the Pacific trek began in earnest. President Everett of Harvard might exhort Boston emigrants to go "with the Bible in one hand and your New England civilization in the other, and make your mark on the people and country," but influences here were too diverse to permit any such distinctive impress of culture as New England had left upon the early Ohio Valley. This was a novel kind of frontier. Footloose and ambitious men from all the states, and most nations, flocked to the diggings. The intelligent and sophisticated mingled with the rough and ready. The unsuccessful were apt to lay aside pick and pan, to try their hand at trade, politics, journalism, literature. The Civil War and its aftermath sent thousands more to California, in a passage from the East that the years had made successively easier by clipper ships, the Nicaragua passage, the overland stage and pony express, and finally the transcontinental railway in 1869.

Unlike earlier frontiers, that of northern California enjoyed both the wealth to patronize art and the cosmopolitan spirit to create it. In literature, for instance, the best talents seemed to spring from young expatriates of staid communities and various brands of provincialism: Sam Clemens from Hannibal, Missouri; Bret Harte from Albany; Joaquin Miller from Liberty, Indiana, by way of Oregon; Ambrose Bierce from Horse Cave Creek, Ohio; Edward Rowland Sill from Windsor, Connecticut, and rural Ohio; Charles Warren Stoddard from Rochester, New York; Prentice Mulford from Sag Harbor, Long Island; George Horatio Derby ("John Phoenix") from Dedham, Massachusetts, and Ina Coolbrith from Illinois, by way of Los Angeles. Flung into the heady life of the frontier, they were immensely stimulated—often reaching powers they never attained before or afterward. Reading and writing flourished on a scale never before seen in any frontier environment. As early as 1850, San Francisco was keeping fifty printers at work. By the middle of that decade the city boasted more newspapers than London, more books published than all the rest of trans-Mississippi put together. Magazines of belles-lettres—the *Pioneer, Golden Era, Hesperian, Californian, Overland Monthly* —sprouted, flourished, and even in dying left a literary humus from which successors sprang. Here also the average newspaper, metropolitan or rural, favored high-flown essays, humorous skits, and "Poets' Corners" to which tradesmen and brokers alike contributed. Around the Comstock Lode, red-shirted miners (especially when in their cups) loved to hold hot argument over the merits of rival bards like Joe Goodman and Rollin Daggett, or solemnly ballot in a poet-of-the-day contest. The first slim collection of California verse, *Outcroppings* (1865), made by Bret Harte, recognized only nineteen poets and overlooked so many "thousands" that it caused a literary riot. A sequel, *The Poetry of the Pacific* (1866), extended the list to seventy-five and, among writers of repute, omitted only Harte.

Moreover, a bent toward practicality so characteristic of all frontiers fostered in the West many types of writing other than "mere literature." At their best they are represented by Clarence King and John Muir on geology and natural science, Henry George on economics and social reform, and Hubert Howe Bancroft on California records and history; at their mediocre bulk, by innumerable political speeches, orations, legal works on mining and riparian rights, and the early propaganda of the booster.

Other instruments of culture were not neglected. Seven years after the start of the Gold Rush, San Francisco was supporting three public libraries, twenty-four public grade schools, and one public high school; outside this orbit of new wealth and population, Los Angeles had no free library, and only one public school of elementary level, in addition to parochial schools. The College of California, soon to become the University at Berkeley, was founded in 1855. The system of public support, assured for technological and agricultural education by the Morrill Act of 1862, rapidly became the keystone of all higher education in the Midwestern, Rocky Mountain, and Far Western regions. Lacking the colleges and universities of private endowment traditional in the East, the West built its collegiate and university structure, for cultural and vocational training, upon the base of state and federal aid. While certain amenities were missing, the gains for democracy were evident.

San Francisco's gilded age witnessed an almost frenzied enthusiasm for the drama, opera, and music. Lectures—given in theaters, churches, billiard saloons—were vastly popular. The effect of certain visiting celebrities upon the style of Western humor and sentiment, and the development of young journalists like Mark Twain and Bret Harte, proved notable. A passion for entertainment and culture radiated from the Bay region into remote mining camps. Miners supported a lively theater circuit from Rabbit Creek to Mariposa, and drew the best that gold dust could buy. On Sundays, miners held their own debating societies. Often, of course, the yearning of the parvenu was naïvely earnest—among a generation of provincials who had sometimes heard, and resented, the sneers of Mrs. Trollope and Charles Dickens. Wealth meant a new stake in gentility. It is reported that the first miner to strike gold at Gregory's Gulch in Colorado, in 1859, flung down his pick with the exclamation, "Thank God! Now my wife can be a lady—and our children can have an education!"

A tincture of social vanity, mingled with a sincere wish for the good life, set the tone for aspiration on this Western frontier. If the prospector, mountain man, or cattle king be scorned because he reckoned culture by weight and bulk, or recognized beauty only when certified by convention, it must be added that he was faithfully striving for better things. By the building of schools and colleges and free libraries, the West was trying, according to its lights and with admitted future success, to enhance the cultural perception of its children.

# 40. THE AMERICAN LANGUAGE

I<small>T</small> was the great movement to the West that finally fixed the character of the American language, preserving as it did the Elizabethan boldness which characterized the speech of the first settlers. "Our ancestors," said James Russell Lowell in his "On a Certain Condescension in Foreigners," "unhappily could bring over no English better than Shakespeare's." This, of course, was mere rhetoric, and its aim was only to confute the English chauvinists who for more than half a century had been howling against American speechways. As a matter of record, not many of the colonists who stumbled ashore during the seventeenth century were steeped in the poetical glories of the Elizabethan age, and four-fifths of them, in all probability, had never so much as heard of Shakespeare. But if we dismiss the exact meaning of Lowell's words—often a safe plan in dealing with a literary critic—and consider rather their underlying drift, it turns out that a good deal of truth was in them. The newcomers to the wilderness, if they lacked both information and taste, were at least Englishmen, and they shared with all other Englishmen the enormous revolution in the national language, as in almost every other cultural trait, that had gone on during the forty-five years of Elizabeth's reign.

Those years saw the disappearance of the last trace of medieval resistance to change. The English, once predominantly insular and introspective, became an eager and expansive race, full of strange curiosities and iconoclastic enterprises. They began to investigate the world beyond the sky rim; they made contact with outlandish and inexplicable peoples; they looked with sharp and disillusioned eyes upon many of the ideas and ways of life that had sufficed them for centuries. All this ferment of fresh concepts and unprecedented experiences had its inevitable effect upon the language in which they expressed their thoughts, and it began to burgeon in a manner truly amazing. The last of the bonds that fastened it to the other tongues of the Indo-European family were loosed, and it settled into a grammatical structure so slipshod that, in more than one detail, it suggested less the related German, French, Latin, and Greek than Chinese. Simultaneously, there was a sudden increase in its vocabulary, with new words and idioms coming in on all levels, from that of the street boys of London to that of the court poets and university illuminati. The contribution of Shakespeare himself, whether as inventor or as introducer, was heavy, and in part at least it was lasting. Not infrequently, to be sure, he failed to find a market for his novelties, as when he launched *to happy, to child,* and *to verse,* but his successes were quite as numerous as his failures, and it would be hard to imagine English today without some of the terms he introduced, e.g., *to fool, disgraceful, barefaced, bump, countless, critic, gloomy,* and *laughable*; or without the swarming coinages of his contemporary poets and dramatists, e.g., *dimension, conscious, jovial, rascality, scientific, audacious,* and *obscure.*

All these locutions are now universally accepted, and no one apparently has ever challenged them. But as Tudor license began to succumb to Puritan dogmatism, there was a tightening of the whole English *Kultur,* and the language did not escape its effects. Grammarians arose, and efforts were made to break English to the patterns of Latin. All novelties in speech were received hostilely, and the doctrine was launched that there were enough words already, and no more were needed. The Restoration had but little corrective effect upon this foolishness, and it went roaring into the eighteenth century when Samuel Johnson became its chief fugleman. No man who ever undertook to write a dictionary knew less about speechways. He was all theory— and nine-tenths of his theory was nonsense. It may seem incredible today, but it is nevertheless a fact, that he tried to put down *touchy* and *to coax*; what is more, *stingy* and *to derange*; what is yet more, *chaperon* and *fun.* Nor did he battle alone; for example, Jonathan Swift had frowned upon *banter* and *sham, bubble* and *mob, bully* and *to bamboozle.* Under such attacks English became again a highly policed language, and lost almost altogether its Elizabethan hospitality to novelty. The writer who thought of a new word kept it to himself, for the penalty of using it was infamy. The tony English style became an imitation of Johnson's quasi-Latin, and no term was countenanced by the elegant that was not in his dictionary. Thus the old libido for word making went underground, and there it has remained in England, to this day. Ardent neologists, of course, have arisen since Johnson's time—notably Thomas Carlyle—but they have had but little influence upon the language, and a good three-fourths of the novelties it has adopted in our own time have come from the United States, and have been on the level of the vulgar speech.

Why the people of America, despite their general subservience to Puritan ideas, have preserved the Elizabethan boldness of speech remains a bit mysterious; perhaps it is mainly because the life they have led has continued to be predominantly Elizabethan. They had, during their first two centuries, an immediate and menacing wilderness to subdue, and the exigencies of their daily lives did not favor niceness, whether in language or otherwise. It was not until the early years of the nineteenth century that the influence of English purism began to be felt here, save only upon the higher levels, and by that time the great movement into the West had begun—a movement that seems to have fixed finally the character of American speech. Moreover, it is not to be forgotten that, to the immigrants who swarmed in during the century following, life in the United States continued to be a sort of frontier life, even in the East, and that niceness was beyond their powers, even if they were aware of it. Whatever the chain of causes, American English refused to be policed, and it continues in a kind of grammatical, syntactical, and semantic outlawry to this day. The schoolma'am has tried valiantly to bring it to heel, and only too obviously in vain. Most of the native grammarians of any sense have long since deserted her, and the rules they now propagate tend to be more and more inductive. If she continues to war upon *ain't, it's me,* and the confusion of *will* and *shall,* it is only because most of the supergogues who train her are apparently unaware of this collapse of the old-time grammar. New words and idioms swarm around her in such numbers that she is overwhelmed, and her function as an arbiter of speech withers away. In this great free Republic the verdict of life and death upon a neologism is not brought in by schoolma'ams, whether in shorts or step-ins, but by a jury resembling a *posse comitatus,* on which even schoolboys sit. In brief, the American language is being molded by a purely democratic process, and, as on the political level, that process is grounded upon the doctrine that any American is as good as any other.

2

The first Americanisms, naturally enough, were nouns borrowed from the Indian languages, designating objects unknown in England. Some of them reached the present bounds of the United States by way of the older colonies to southward or northward, e.g., *tobacco, canoe,* and *potato,* but the great majority entered the colonial speech directly, and nearly all the earlier ones came from the Algonquin dialects, e.g., *hickory* (1634*), *hominy* (1629), *moccasin* (1612), *opossum* (1610), and *pone* (1612). The colonial chronicles are full of such loans, and though many of them survive mainly in place names or have become obsolete altogether, e.g., *cockarouse* (1624), *sagamore* (1613), and *tuckahoe* (1612), others remain alive in the general American speech, e.g., *moose* (1613), *persimmon* (1612), and *raccoon* (1608). Not a few, indeed, have been absorbed by standard English, e.g., *tomahawk* (1612)

* The dates here and hereafter are of the earliest examples found by the searchers for the *Dictionary of American English.*

and *squaw* (1634), and even by other languages, e.g., *totem* (1609). "The Indian element" in American English, said Alexander F. Chamberlain in 1902, "is much larger than is commonly believed to be the case. . . . In the local speech of New England, especially among fishermen . . . many words of Algonkian origin, not familiar to the general public, are still preserved, and many more were once current, but have died out within the last one hundred years." *

At later stages American English was destined to receive many loans from the languages of non-English immigrants, especially the Dutch, French, Spanish, and Germans, but before 1700 they seem to have been relatively small in number. *Portage,* from the French of Canada, has been traced to 1698 and is probably somewhat older, but *bureau, chowder,* and *rapids* are not recorded until the time of the French and Indian War, and many other familiar French loans, e.g., *prairie* and *gopher,* did not come into general use until the Revolutionary era. The same time lag is observed when Spanish loans are investigated, and there was no appreciable infiltration from the German until the middle of the eighteenth century. Even the borrowings from Dutch, save in New York, were very few before 1700. *Scow* is traced to 1669, and *hook* (as a geographical term) to 1670; but most of the loans now familiar are later, e.g., *sleigh* (1703), *stoop* (1755), *span* (of horses, 1769), *cooky* (1786), and *coleslaw* (1794). It was not, indeed, until after Yorktown that there was any considerable infiltration of Dutch into the common speech, and some of the loans now known to every American are surprisingly recent, e.g., *spook* (1801), *cruller* (1805), *waffle* (1817), *boss* (1818), and *Santa Claus* (1823). John Pickering omitted all these save *scow, sleigh,* and *span* from his pioneer *Vocabulary* of 1816, but by 1859 John Russell Bartlett was listing *boss, cooky, hook, stoop,* and *cruller* in the second edition of his *Dictionary of Americanisms. Yankee,* perhaps the most conspicuous contribution of Dutch to American English, was at first applied to the Dutch themselves, and it was not until the years immediately preceding the Revolution that it came to signify a Northern American.

Of far more importance than these loans were the new words that the colonists made of English materials, mainly by compounding but also by giving old words new meanings. *Snowshoe* is traced by the *Dictionary of American English* to 1666, *backlog* to 1684, *leaf tobacco* to 1637, *statehouse* to 1662, *frame house* to 1639, and *selectman* to 1635. By the middle of the eighteenth century the number of such neologisms was very large, and by its end they were almost innumerable. Many were invented to designate natural objects not known in England, e.g., *bluegrass* (1751), *catbird* (1709), *tree frog*

* *Journal of American Folk-Lore,* XV (1902), 240. The best account of such loans is to be found in the etymologies by Joseph Coy Green in *Webster's New International Dictionary,* 1934.

(1738), *slippery elm* (1748), *backwoods* (1784), *salt lick* (1751), and *garter snake* (1775), and others were names for new artifacts, e.g., *smokehouse* (1759), *ball ground* (1772), *breechclout* (1757), *buckshot* (1775), *shingle roof* (1749), *sheathing paper* (1790), *springhouse* (1755) and *hoecake* (1755). But not infrequently, as if delighting in the exercise, the colonists devised novel appellations for objects that were quite well known in England, e.g., *broomstraw* (1785), *sheet iron* (1776), *smoking tobacco* (1796), *lightning bug* (1778), and *bake oven* (1777), and almost as often they gave old English names to new objects, e.g., *corn, shoe, rock, lumber, store, cracker, partridge,* and *team.* Some of the latter were extended in meaning, e.g., *rock,* which meant only a large mass of stone in England, and *barn,* which meant only a building for storing crops, with no accommodations for cattle; others were narrowed, e.g., *corn,* which indicated any kind of edible grain to the English, and *boot,* which indicated any leather footgear; and yet others underwent a complete change in significance, e.g., *freshet,* which the English applied to a small stream of fresh water, and to which the Americans gave the meaning of an inundation, and *partridge,* which the English applied to *Perdix perdix* and the Americans to *Bonasa umbellus, Colinus virginianus,* and various other birds.

By 1621 Alexander Gill was noting that some of the new words bred in America were coming into recognition in England, by 1735 Francis Moore was denouncing one of the most vivid of them, to wit, *bluff,* in the sense of a precipice or escarpment, as "barbarous," and by 1754 Richard Owen Cambridge was suggesting that a glossary of them would soon be in order. But so far as the studies of such philological historians as Allen Walker Read, M. M. Mathews, and W. B. Cairns have revealed, there was no attempt at an orderly treatise upon them until 1781, when John Witherspoon printed a series of papers on the subject in the *Pennsylvania Journal and Weekly Advertiser* of Philadelphia.* This Witherspoon was a Scots divine who came out in 1768 to be president of the College of New Jersey (Princeton). When the Revolution shut down his college he took to politics, was elected a member of the New Jersey Constitutional Convention, got promotion to the Continental Congress, and signed both the Declaration of Independence and the Articles of Confederation. But though he was thus ardently for independence as a political idea, he was outraged by its appearance in speech, and denounced not only the common people for daring to exercise it, but also the bigwigs who showed signs of it "in the senate, at the bar, and from the pulpit." His animadversions, in the main, were only echoes of the pedants then flourishing in England, and they had but small effect. Thus

---

* They appeared under the heading "The Druid." They are reprinted in full in **M. M.** Mathews, *The Beginnings of American English*, Chicago, 1931.

when he protested against the peculiar American use of *to notify,* as in "The police were notified"—"In English," he said, "we do not *notify* the person of the thing, but the thing to the person"—he roared in vain. The politicians, lawyers, clergy, and journalists of the time paid little heed to him, and the generality of Americans never heard of his attempt to improve their speech.

Of much more potency were the English reviewers who began, after the Revolution, to notice American books. They were, with few exceptions, bitterly hostile to the new republic, and their hostility often took the form of reviling Americanisms. Thomas Jefferson was one of the first victims of this crusade, which went on violently for almost a century and is not infrequently revived in our own time. When he used the verb *to belittle*—apparently his private invention—in his *Notes on the State of Virginia,* the *European Magazine and London Review* showed as much dudgeon as if he had desecrated Westminster Abbey, and during the years following nearly all the other contemporary American writers were attacked almost as savagely, notably John Quincy Adams, John Marshall, Noah Webster, and Joel Barlow. It would be too much to say that all this fury had any substantial effect upon the national language, but it undoubtedly shook some of the national literati. Even Noah Webster was influenced more or less, and in his earlier writings he was extremely polite to English opinion. As for Benjamin Franklin, he yielded to it with only the faintest resistance.

3

This complaisance was broken down at last by the War of 1812, but there were still signs of it in the first formal study of American speech—the before-mentioned *Vocabulary* of John Pickering. Pickering was no dilettante like Witherspoon, but a diligent and learned student of language, and Franklin Edgerton has described him as "one of the two greatest general linguists of the first half of the Nineteenth Century in America." * His observations on Americanisms first appeared in a paper he read to the American Academy of Arts and Sciences of Boston in 1815. This paper attracted so much attention that in 1816 he expanded it into a book that is still well worth study, for it is admirably documented and contains a great deal of valuable matter. Unhappily, it is mainly devoted to the objurgations of the English reviewers, and even more unhappily, it shows a lamentable tendency to yield to them. Though he might produce some English authority, says Pickering, for many of the Americanisms he lists, "yet the very circumstance of their being no-

* "Notes on Early American Work in Linguistics," *Proceedings of the American Philosophical Society,* July, 1943, p. 27. The other was Peter Stephen Du Ponceau.

ticed by well-educated Englishmen is a proof that they are not in use at this day in England, and of course ought not to be used elsewhere by those who would speak correct English." This position was fatal to any really rational discussion of them, and in consequence Pickering's book probably did more harm than good. Its influence hung over the discussion of the national speech for a long while, and is not altogether thrown off today. A number of American writers, during the thirty years following its publication, dissented sharply from its thesis, notably James K. Paulding; but many more acquiesced, and it was not until 1848, when Bartlett brought out the first edition of his *Dictionary of Americanisms,* that American English found an anatomist willing to take it for what it was, without any regard for what Englishmen or Anglomaniacs thought it ought to be.

Pickering was thoroughly the scholar, and showed some of the deficiencies that occasionally go with that character. His outlook was rather narrow, and he was more than a little cautious. He omitted all mention of Indian loans from his *Vocabulary,* probably because they were predominantly uncouth, and he dealt only gingerly with the common speech. The great movement into the West was already under way as he wrote, and was already coining the gaudy neologisms that were to give color to the national language, but he seems to have been either too pained to deal with them or unaware of them altogether. By Bartlett's day they were everywhere visible; indeed, they were so numerous after 1840 that all novelties in speech came to be called Westernisms. Bartlett not only listed hundreds of them; he obviously relished them, and he found the same relish in a large number of readers, for his *Dictionary of Americanisms* had to be brought out in a revised and expanded form in 1859, again in 1860, and yet again in 1877, during which time its bulk doubled. It is still on the shelves of most public libraries, and copies often turn up in the secondhand bookstores. Bartlett, unlike Pickering, was not a schooled philologian; but he had a fine feeling for language, and in his preface to his fourth edition he discussed the sources of Americanisms with great perspicacity. Most of them originated, he noted, in the argots of the more raffish trades and professions, and entered the common speech as slang. There they entered upon a struggle *à outrance* for general acceptance, with no assurance that the fittest would survive. Some of the best succumbed, and some of the worst gradually took on respectability, were passed by lexicographers, and became integral parts of the language. Such was the history, for example, of *to lynch, squatter, to hold on,* and *loafer.*

There were various other writers on American speech in the period between the Revolution and the Civil War—for example, Jonathan Boucher, David Humphreys, Charles Astor Bristed, James Fenimore Cooper, Robley

Dunglison, and Adiel Sherwood—but their studies were fragmentary and not of any importance.* Noah Webster, though he was an ardent reformer of spelling and believed in the future autonomy of American English, gave relatively little attention to Americanisms, and did not list them in any number until his *American Dictionary* of 1828. The first discussion of them on a large scale by a man trained in language studies was in Maximilian Schele de Vere's *Americanisms: The English of the New World* (1871). Schele was a Swede educated in France and Germany, and was brought out to the University of Virginia to profess modern languages. He arrived in 1844, and save for four years in the Confederate Army, held his chair until 1895. In his book he attempted a classification of Americanisms, and was the first to give adequate attention to the loan words among them. After him there was a hiatus until 1889, when an Englishman, John S. Farmer, published *Americanisms, Old and New,* a useful compilation but not altogether free from English prejudice. A year later the American Dialect Society was formed, and the publication of *Dialect Notes* was begun. The ostensible field of the society was narrow, but it soon branched out into wider studies of the national speech, and there is a vast richness of material in the files of its journal. Its projectors included many philologians of sound distinction—for example, Charles H. Grandgent, E. S. Sheldon, E. H. Babbitt, J. M. Manly, and F. J. Child; and in the course of time it attracted the interest and collaboration of many younger scholars of ability, including especially Louise Pound, who became the first editor of another valuable journal, *American Speech,* in 1925. But the Dialect Society, though it had a profound influence, flourished only feebly, and the publication of *Dialect Notes* was often delayed by lack of money.

Next to the appearance of *Dialect Notes* the event that had most to do with putting the study of American English on a scientific basis was the publication of Richard H. Thornton's *American Glossary* in 1912. Thornton was an Englishman who migrated to the United States in 1874. He was a lawyer by training, and died in 1925 as dean of the Oregon Law School, but a good part of his leisure of half a century was given over to an attempt to produce a really comprehensive dictionary of Americanisms. Pickering, Bartlett, and Farmer before him had introduced the practice of illuminating the subject by dated quotations, but he went much further than any of them. Among other things, he seems to have read the whole file of the *Congressional Globe,* along with a multitude of early newspapers. The result was a work of wide range and very high merit. There were a few slips in it, but not many. Unhappily, no American publisher would venture to publish it, and

---

* Humphreys, Cooper, Dunglison, and Sherwood are reprinted by Mathews in *The Beginnings of American English.*

Thornton had to turn to a small firm in London.* He continued his researches afterward, and between 1931 and 1939 the printing of his posthumous materials went on in *Dialect Notes*. His work was not only valuable in itself; it also paved the way for the much more comprehensive *Dictionary of American English,* edited by Sir William Craigie and published between 1938 and 1944 by the University of Chicago Press. Meanwhile, a *Linguistic Atlas of the United States and Canada* was begun in 1939 under the supervision of Hans Kurath.

## 4

"For some two centuries, roughly down to 1820," said Craigie in 1927,† "the passage of new words or senses across the Atlantic was regularly westward; practically the only exceptions were terms which denoted articles or products peculiar to the new country. With the nineteenth century, however, the contrary current begins to set in, and gradually becomes stronger and stronger, bearing with it many a piece of drift-wood to the shores of Britain, there to be picked up and incorporated in the structure of the language." This eastward current, at the start, was resisted with the utmost violence, partly because of the lingering English suspicion of all neologisms, but mainly because of an increase in the political hostility that had begun with the Revolution. From the turn of the century until after the Civil War, the Americans, to all right-thinking Englishmen, were the shining symbols of everything infamous. "They have," wrote Southey to Landor so early as 1812, "acquired a distinct national character for low and lying knavery; and so well do they deserve it that no man ever had any dealings with them without having proofs of its truth." To which the Very Reverend Henry Alford, Dean of Canterbury, added in 1863:

Look at those phrases which so amuse us in their speech and books . . . ; and then compare the character and history of the nation—its blunted sense of moral obligation and duty to man; its open disregard of conventional right when aggrandisement is to be obtained; and I may now say, its reckless and fruitless maintenance of the most cruel and unprincipled war in the history of the world.

The literati—for example, Dickens—were in the forefront of this fray, for they had a special grievance: to wit, the refusal of the United States to make a copyright treaty with Great Britain, and the consequent wholesale piracy of their works by American publishers. But there were also deeper and

* The J. B. Lippincott Company of Philadelphia brought out 250 sets of the London sheets in 1912; but they sold slowly, and there was never a genuinely American edition.
† *The Study of American English* (S.P.E. Tract No. XXVII), Oxford, 1927, p. 208.

more general considerations. The population of the United States had gradually overtaken that of the United Kingdom during the first half of the century, and in the fifties it went bounding ahead. American commerce and manufactures began to increase at a rate which offered an alarming menace to English world trade, American agriculture and mining developed in almost geometrical progression, and the discovery of gold in 1848 and of oil in 1859 gave promise of new and almost illimitable floods of wealth. Thus the English, once only contemptuous, began to view the republic with a mixture of envy and dread, and it is no wonder that most of their chosen augurs hoped (and predicted) that the Civil War would wreck it.

The insular hostility to American ways of speech hardly needed any fresh fillip; it had been active and violent, as we have seen, since the palmy days of the English reviewers. But now it was augmented by a gathering sense of futility. What could be done to stay the uncouth novelties that so copiously barged in? Apparently not much. Every returning English traveler brought them in his baggage, and every American book bristled with them. In 1820, at the precise moment fixed by Sir William Craigie for the turn of the tide, Sydney Smith could still launch his historic sneer at American literature; but only a few years later Cooper and the early American humorists were beginning to break down the English barrier, and they were soon followed by authors of greater heft and beam. The English purists, of course, did not surrender without a bitter fight. Moreover, they had some successes, especially against such shocking Westernisms as *gone coon, semioccasional, to scoot, to skedaddle, to stay put,* and *to shell out*. But when they encountered the more decorous and plausible American novelties, e.g., *outdoors, telegram, anesthetic, presidential, to belittle, to progress, reliable, mileage,* and *caucus,* they objected in vain. These words were sorely needed, and England itself had nothing to offer in place of them—nothing so logical, so apt, so good. The Elizabethan gift for bold and vivid neologisms had been transferred to this side of the water, and here it has remained. The dons of Oxford, perhaps, still make some show of clinging to the waspish precepts of Johnson, but the English plain people, ever since the Civil War era, have exhibited an increasing and, in late years, overwhelming preference for the novelties marked "Made in America."

It was the American movie, of course, that gave the final impulse to this revolution. When the first American-made films reached England, in 1907, they were too few and too crude to attract the attention of the guardians of the national speech; but this age of innocuousness did not last long. By 1910 the English newspapers began to print an increasing spate of letters from Old Subscribers protesting against the new words and phrases that the silent legends were bringing in, and during the fifteen years following, the protest gradually mounted to a roar. In 1927 legislation was adopted limiting the influx of American films, and it was hoped that the onslaught might be stayed. That hope was renewed on the advent of the talkie, for most authorities declared that the patriotic English people would never tolerate the abomination of American spoken speech. Even the American movie magnates seem to have been of that mind, for they showed a considerable perturbation in the talkie's early days, and even got out English versions of their masterpieces, manned by proper English actors. But within a short while they had trained their native performers to give a tolerable imitation of English speech, and soon afterward they began to discover that English audiences really did not object to what remained of the Yankee twang. By the middle thirties a wholesale imitation was in progress, and on December 14, 1930, a woman contributor to the London *Evening News* was writing:

An American, coming over to England for the first time, was struck by the fact that English children in the streets of London and elsewhere talked exactly the same as children in the United States. An American impresario came to this country to make films. He was anxious to secure a crowd of English-speaking children, but he utterly failed to find English children who could talk English, and he had to abandon that part of his programme.

To which D. W. Brogan, of Cambridge University, added in 1943:

There is nothing surprising in the constant reinforcement, or, if you like, corruption of English by American. And there is every reason to believe that it has increased, is increasing, and will not be diminished. If American could influence English a century ago, when the predominance of the Mother Country in wealth, population and prestige was secure, and when most educated Americans were reverentially colonial in their attitude to English culture, how can it be prevented from influencing English today, when every change has been a change of weight to the American side? *

5

There was a time when most Americanisms originated in the Western wilds, but by 1940 their source was mainly among city sophisticates, many of whom were devoted professionally to inventing them. They appeared in the compositions of gossip columnists, comic-strip artists, sporting reporters, press agents, advertisement writers, and other such subsaline literati, were quickly gathered into the movies, and were then on their way. They were first adopted in England, as at home, on the lower levels of speech, but if they had the requisite pungency they gradually moved upward. It is curious to note

* "The Conquering Tongue," London *Spectator,* Feb. 5, 1943.

that the very few Briticisms that enter American take a different route: they appear first on pretentious levels, and then sink down. But not many of them ever really survive. English speech seems affected and effeminate to the 100 per cent American, and he would no more use *civil servant, liftman, luggage van*, or *boot shop* than he would stuff his handkerchief into his wristband.

American spelling and pronunciation, like the American vocabulary, have departed considerably from English standards. Efforts to simplify and rationalize the spelling of the language were begun in English so early as the sixteenth century, but it remained for Noah Webster, the American, to work the first effective reforms. It was he who induced Americans to drop the *u* in the *-our* words, the redundant consonants in *traveller, jeweller,* and *waggon,* and the final *k* in *frolick* and *physick*; and to change *gaol* to *jail, plough* to *plow, draught* to *draft, barque* to *bark,* and *cheque* to *check*. In the first flush of his enthusiasm Webster advocated a large number of other reformed spellings, including such bizarre forms as *bred, giv, brest, bilt, relm, frend, speek, zeel, laf, dawter, tuf, proov, karacter, toor, thum, wimmen* and *blud,* but by the time he came to his first dictionary of 1806 he had abandoned them. To the end of his days, however, he had a weakness for *cag* (keg), *hainous, porpess,* and *tung,* and it remained for other lexicographers to dispose of them. Two pets of his later years were *chimist* and *neger,* but they never got a lodgment. Perhaps his partiality for them arose from a desire to change the common American pronunciation. *Neger,* which seems to have been borrowed by the early colonists from some Northern dialect of English, survived until the nineteenth century, though *negro* had been challenging it from the start, and *nigger* has been traced to 1700.

The Simplified Spelling movement, which was launched by Francis A. March, W. D. Whitney, F. J. Child, and other eminent philologians in 1876, languished until 1906, when Theodore Roosevelt, then in the White House, gave it his imprimatur and Andrew Carnegie financed it. In its heyday, during the fifteen years following, it brought out long lists of proposed new spellings, including *corus, giv, stomac, brekfast, harth, bluf, activ, hostil, giraf, ar,* and *wer*; but the country would not have them, and after 1919, when both Roosevelt and Carnegie died, it ceased to trouble. Its efforts, however, succeeded in reducing words of the *programme, catalogue,* and *quartette* classes to their *program, catalog,* and *quartet* forms, and in giving *tho, thoro,* and *thru* a certain amount of countenance. It also promoted the exchange of the last two letters in words of the *theatre* class. In England the reform of spelling at the turn of the century was chiefly furthered by the brothers Fowler. Their *Concise Oxford Dictionary,* which first appeared in 1911, retained the *-our* ending; but it abandoned the English *-ise* for the American *-ize,* and the *y* in *cyder* and its analogues for *i*, and made various other concessions to American practice.

The first Englishmen to observe American speechways all reported that there were no dialects in this country. This was an exaggeration; but it remains a fact, as John Witherspoon wrote in 1781, that "there is a greater difference in dialect between one county and another in Britain, than there is between one state and another in America." More painstaking investigation has revealed three major speech areas. The first includes the New England states, the second the South, and the third all the rest of the country. These areas are divided into subareas more or less narrow, and the speech of Boston differs from that of New England in general just as the speech of the Southern tidewater differs from that of inland regions. But these differences, which mainly have to do with the pronunciation of *a* and the treatment of terminal *r*, are not important, and even on the most ignorant levels an American of one speech area readily understands an American of another. Noah Webster based his recommended pronunciations upon the cultivated usage of New England, and for many years this practice was inculcated by the school-ma'am; but it has been losing ground since the Civil War, and most authorities seem to believe that what is commonly called General American or Western American will eventually prevail everywhere. It is, on all counts, an admirable form of English, and its great superiority to the Oxford form fashionable in England is manifest. A great many educated Englishmen, indeed, denounce the Oxford form as affected and absurd, and it shows no sign of spreading hereafter. General American is much clearer and more logical than any of the other dialects, either English or American. It shows a clear if somewhat metallic pronunciation, gives all necessary consonants their true values, keeps to simple and narrow speech tunes, and is vigorous and masculine.

# 41. THE MINGLING OF TONGUES

So rich and diverse is the great body of writing by Americans who use tongues other than English that it is difficult to generalize about it in any precise terms; yet, when it is examined in detail, certain recurrent patterns emerge. Prior to 1870 the immigrants to America, however different their backgrounds and the impulses which moved them to migration, underwent in the United States similar emotional experiences and found similar means for their expression. The pattern bears close resemblance to that of the English colonists when they first settled on the Atlantic seaboard, and it was repeated again and again in the westward movement of the frontier.

There was first a pioneer period of diaries and letters. The departure from the old country, the crossing of the ocean, the first steps on the new soil seemed to each traveler an experience of special significance; it demanded to be recorded.

Next came the expression of ideas, religious and political—advanced ideas most of them, though the preponderant immigrant influence has been steadily on the side of conservatism; the majority of the newcomers were democrats only in the sense that they considered the American brand of government best suited to the acquisition and maintenance of property and position. The organizers of communistic experiments, on the other hand, and the intellectuals, sent out by the abortive European revolutions of the early nineteenth century, though few compared to the multitude of laborers, peasants, and artisans, were earnest and articulate social crusaders, journalists, or litterateurs. They were determined to avoid a repetition in the new land of the stresses and suppressions that had driven them from the old. They wanted a perfect America. Each of these men with a mission, as soon as he set foot in the United States, bought a press or secured access to one, and Volume I, Number 1, appeared. Many of these journalistic ventures barely survived their launching; others drifted along for years; a few are prospering today.

The reading class of each racial or national group—of the Germans in Milwaukee, the French in New Orleans, the Mexicans in San Antonio, the Poles in Chicago, the Chinese in San Francisco, the Jews in New York—soon had its own monthly, weekly, or daily paper. Even the smaller and scattered groups had their periodicals. It was not uncommon to find the publisher of an English paper willing, sometimes eager, to allow a German or Norwegian to use his shop to print a sheet that would not compete with his own. The small capital outlay and the scissors and paste-pot editorial method in common use made these foreign language journals practicable if not always of first-rate quality, and they served a dual purpose, giving recently arrived immigrants news from the homeland while offering them opportunities to record their new experiences or express their views. Gradually the space devoted to the news of the mother country and clippings from European periodicals decreased, but the distant continent was never wholly forgotten. Marcus Lee Hansen reminds us that in the years before 1914 the American citizens best read in international affairs were probably the older generation of immigrant farmers in the Middle West. The gradual process of Americanization can be traced, almost measured, by the lengthening columns of American news and the increasing space devoted to the local activities and interests of each immigrant group.

Clumsy and crude as the early attempts at journalism often were, they fostered a taste for expression among both readers and contributors. Simple letters or reminiscences soon developed into memoirs and histories. Essays and polemics followed, and then came the third stage of immigrant writing: stories, novels, and plays, usually with a strongly romantic cast and obviously imitative of Scott, Irving, or Cooper.

2

After 1870 the literary patterns changed. The vast increase in the number of immigrants—nearly a million arrived each year—caused them to concentrate in urban areas where they suffered sharper pains of readjustment than their predecessors of the earlier decades, the majority of whom were absorbed by the land. The new immigrant writers, increasingly conscious of social and economic issues, began to criticize their environment in realistic novels, as the American-born writers of the period were doing.

An important change took place at the same time in the immigrant's attitude toward his native culture and his native tongue. During the nineteenth century he had subscribed to the melting-pot theory, assumed since the time of Crèvecœur and translated into a crusade by such men as Israel Zangwill and Theodore Roosevelt. The immigrant's native gifts and his language would, he had supposed, be distilled into the new American race that was being formed. By the time of the First World War it began to be apparent that no such assimilation was taking place, that the spontaneous play of natural social forces was not achieving the expected fusion of alien cultures. The older Americans took alarm and launched the strident Americanization movement which produced the Immigration Act of 1924. Designed to stabilize the foreign elements in the United States at their current proportions, the Act succeeded in virtually stopping all immigration. It succeeded also in allaying among the "natives" the fear of "foreigners" and in quieting the agitation against them.

Among the foreigners themselves its immediate effect was an intensification of racial and cultural pride. An attitude of mind that had long been growing among the more thoughtful now became general. The national groups ceased to feel that they must abandon as quickly as possible their native language and their native customs. They began to take pride in their racial characteristics, to exploit and cultivate their folklore and folk literature. The reading public in each foreign language increased. At the same time the writers began to translate their work into English so that it might reach a larger audience and America as a whole might come to understand their nation's special characteristics and contributions.

It was at this point, too, that novelists who, though American-born, had grown up in close proximity to one of the cultural islands began to write about their friends and neighbors. Such pictures as George Washington Cable's of the New Orleans Creoles, Willa Cather's of the Nebraska Czechs and Germans, and Harvey Fergusson's of the Spaniards of the Southwest bear eloquent evidence that the regional cultures have enriched American literature.

### 3

In the work of German-American writers, the most considerable body of non-English writing produced in the United States, many of the lines of the pattern of development we have indicated are clearly and easily discernible. Sooner even than the French in New Orleans, the Germans in colonial Pennsylvania and New York became articulate.

The first exponents of ideas were animated by religious zeal: Francis Daniel Pastorius, founder, in 1683, of Quietist Germantown, whose contribution to colonial literature deserves to be better known; Johann Kelpius, the hermit of the Wissahickon; Conrad Beissel and his monastic brothers and sisters in the Ephrata Cloister in Lancaster County, Pennsylvania, who composed and edited two large collections of hymns (1739, 1766). Benjamin Franklin printed hymn books for the Ephrata Dunkers as early as 1730, and Sauer's press, established in 1738, brought out later editions as well as a complete Bible in German and a German newspaper which reached four thou-

sand readers scattered from Pennsylvania to Georgia. Henry Miller, printer to
Congress, founded in 1762 the *Philadelphische Staatsbote* and published many
German books. German presses in the United States were soon able to handle
anything written here except voluminous works like the *Hallesche Nachrichten* (1787) of the Lutherans, the *Nachrichten* (1735-1752) of the Salz-
burgers, the diaries of the Moravian missionaries, or the travels of Mittel-
berger (1756), Achenwall (1769), and Schöpf (1788). Such books, too elaborate for the German-American presses, publishers in Germany were glad to
print.

In the second and third decades of the nineteenth century, when the
heavier flow of German immigration set in, a stream of travel literature began,
much of it designed to attract or direct immigrants. Some of these books had
considerable literary power; the immigrants not only studied them before
they crossed the ocean but reread them with pleasure in America.

Critical accounts of the New World began to appear at about the same
time. In the form of essays or fiction they ranged from extravagant idealization to fierce indictment of everything American, with attempts, by the
revolutionaries of 1848, to reshape the United States into something closer to
their dreams. Men like Heinzen, Hecker, and Weydemeyer joined with such
older liberals as Körner, Weitling, and Münch to form strong German-
American blocs bent on reforms which looked to their contemporaries "radical" and "subversive." Others, like Nicholaus Lenau, whose American
experience is the basis of Ferdinand Kürnberger's *Der Amerikamüde* (1855),
thought improvement hopeless and contented themselves with denunciation
of the "philistines of these hog-besotted States, scoundrels all, who in their
horrible vacuity cannot conceive that there can be any gods higher than those
struck in the mint." If they had circulated beyond the German reading
public, books like *Der Amerikamüde,* Karl Büchile's *Land und Volk der
Vereinigten Staaten,* and Friedrich Gerstäcker's *Nach Amerika!* (all published in 1855) would have roused quite as much anger as Dickens' *American
Notes.*

Somewhere between the extremes of delight and disillusion stood Charles
Sealsfield, the first important German-American writer to devote himself to
fiction. He was an enthusiastic republican, ready to overlook some cultural
deficiencies in the United States because he believed in the rugged virtues
which he saw pushing on the construction of a new social order. He was also
the sworn enemy of oppression in any form, a fiery defender of liberty, who
would swing into action his full battery of satire, ridicule, and abuse whenever he encountered human slavery, political corruption, or commercial
opportunism.

Sealsfield cloaked his true identity so effectively during his lifetime that he kept the editors and critics of two continents guessing as to his true nationality. When he died in Switzerland in 1864 his last will and testament revealed that "Charles Sealsfield," "C. Seatsfield," and "C. Sidons" were all of them Karl Anton Postl, a runaway monk from a Bohemian monastery. In 1823 he landed in New Orleans as a German immigrant and traveled extensively through the Mississippi Valley region and the Southwest, possibly as far as Mexico City, gathering experiences and impressions which went into a long shelf of books, essays, and stories published in Germany, in Switzerland, and, sometimes simultaneously, in London, Philadelphia, and New York. In the United States, Sealsfield made Kittanning, Pennsylvania, his headquarters; but he shuttled back and forth across the Atlantic, maintaining precarious connections as a newspaper correspondent and a private political agent in London and Paris. Hobnobbing with people as various as Lord Palmerston, Joseph Bonaparte, and Stephen Girard, he had a hand in a variety of picturesque international intrigues. His books were widely translated and reprinted (with and without his permission), adapted, imitated, and plagiarized, and he enjoyed a considerable international reputation before he was much read in America outside German-American circles, where he was popular from the first. He acquired and proudly maintained American citizenship and, while carefully preserving his anonymity, claimed to be "America's Most Famous Author."

His earliest works were *The United States of North America As They Are,* published in 1827 in Stuttgart and in London, and a book on Austria which attacked the reactionary policy of Metternich. His first novel, *Tokeah, or the White Rose* (1829), recast in *Der Legitime und die Republikaner* (1833), though a rather wooden performance, was a prototype of the genre at which he became so successful—the "ethnographic" novel, where the hero is a whole people. The characters are typical shapers of the new republic, frontiersmen and pioneers. They are portraits, Sealsfield insisted, from life, and they move against a background of magnificent scenery described in realistic detail.

From 1834 to 1841 Sealsfield produced in quick succession a series of novels based on American themes. He grouped them under such collective titles as *Lebensbilder aus beiden Hemisphären* or *Transatlantische Reiseskizzen.* The setting is usually the Southern or Southwestern states, where he was most at home, and where the panorama of river and plantation life, racing, fishing, hunting, and adventures in forest, swamp, and prairie gave his powers of observation and imagination ample scope. The best of these collections is *Das Cajütenbuch* (1841), stories told by a company gathered at a retired sea captain's house (built in the shape of a ship's cabin, hence the title). The tales are most of them dramatic incidents of the Texas War of Secession. "Die

Prairie am Jacinto," with which the book begins, is considered to be Seals-field's best piece of work.

The later books are inferior to the earlier, partly because, during his absence from the United States, Sealsfield lost touch with the rapidly chang-ing American scene, partly because he began to blur his realism with clouds of romantic phantasmagoria. He came to believe that it was impossible to write realistically of a society that no longer existed; so he burned the manu-script of an autobiography together with all his memoirs and personal papers, and retired to Switzerland, poverty, and seclusion.

In addition to his popularity with readers in Europe and the United States, Sealsfield put his impress on American letters through his influence on native American writers. Longfellow spent entire evenings reading his "favorite Sealsfield" and reread the Louisiana portions of the *Lebensbilder* while he was working on the second part of *Evangeline*. A. B. Faust has shown that William Gilmore Simms borrowed a telling episode for *Guy Rivers* from *Ralph Doughbys Brautfahrt,* that Helen Hunt Jackson's *Ramona* bears striking resemblance to *Tokeah,* and that the third, and best, part of Mayne Reid's *Wild Life* is filched outright from Frederick Hardman's trans-lation of *The Cabin Book*.

There were other popular novelists who, like Sealsfield, made literary capital out of their own picturesque adventures in the New World. Friedrich Armand Strubberg was a hunter, soldier, rancher, merchant, physician, and entrepreneur of German colonization ventures before, at fifty-two, he began to turn out, under the pseudonym "Armand," sensational novels with such titles as *Sklaverei in Amerika* (1862) and *Der Sprung vom Niagarafalls* (1864). He was quite uninfluenced by Sealsfield or anyone else, and his unliterary straightforward prose gives his wildest tales an air of authenticity. His *Carl Scharnhorst: Abenteuer eines deutschen Knaben in Amerika* (1872) was long one of the most popular German stories for boys.

Friedrich Gerstäcker, after adventures that led him through both Amer-icas, produced some hundred and fifty books of travel and adventure, half fictional, half true, to become, during the fifties, the most popular of German-American novelists. His best known and in some respects his best work is *Nach Amerika!* (1855), a realistic account of the fortunes of a shipload of German immigrants who land in New Orleans and make their way up the Mississippi.

More skillful as a writer—his best *Erzählung* is *Der Pedlar* (1857)—was Otto Ruppius, who came to the United States as a refugee in 1848 and worked as a journalist in New York and St. Louis until 1861, when the Prussian proclamation of amnesty permitted his return.

Heinrich Balduin Möllhausen, sometimes called the German Cooper, came to seek not political refuge but adventure. He served as artist and topographer for the Smithsonian Institution on expeditions charting transcontinental railway routes across the mountains, and turned his experiences into some fifty novels and travel books which were translated into English, French, Dutch, and various other languages.

Though all these writers returned eventually to their native land, they are to be considered not German travelers but actual German-Americans. They shared the hazards of migration and the hardships of the frontier, and their point of view is always that of the immigrant and settler, never of the European observer merely.

More brilliant as a writer than any of the adventure novelists was the German-born polemicist and poet Robert Reitzel. He was educated for the ministry but turned freethinker. In the United States he wandered about the country lecturing, writing, and lending a hand to any agitation fomented in the Midwest by German radicals. He propagandized for *Sozialdemokratie, Weltbürgertum, Materialismus, Arbeiterbewegung, Turnerei, Freimännerei,* defying arbitrary power wherever he met it and loving truth even to a pose. In 1884 his friends and admirers set him up in Detroit as editor of a weekly literary paper, which he named *Der arme Teufel,* and into which he poured, for the remaining fourteen years of his life, his wit, irony, and fierce philippic. He recognized revolutionary spirits when he found them and by excerpt and translation did much to familiarize readers on the frontier with the ideas of Emerson and Thoreau.

The nineteenth century German-Americans were of course prolific writers of lyric verse. Thousands of poems chant praise of the adopted home or sigh for the distant fatherland, and the range beyond these obvious themes is wide. There is a considerable body also of German-American epic poetry, and there are some interesting poetic narratives based on immigrant and frontier experience. The poets tried valiantly, too, to familiarize their countrymen with the poetry which was being read by their new fellow citizens. German translations were made of *Evangeline, Hiawatha,* "The Raven," *Snowbound,* and *Leaves of Grass,* as well as of the English poets most popular in the United States. Chicago was long the poetic capital: at least half the High German poetry written in America was published there.

The German theater in America began in New York in 1840, and by 1854 the city had two houses devoted entirely to German plays. The famous Germania Theater opened in 1872; the Thalia in 1879; and the Irving Place in 1888. Philadelphia, Milwaukee, Chicago, St. Louis, and Cincinnati also had important theaters, and in at least a dozen other cities with large German populations the drama flourished. With rare exceptions the plays presented were classics of the German stage, for the actors were far more interested in

performing great roles like Wallenstein and Hamlet than in encouraging new
playwrights, but there are a few notable instances of plays by German-
Americans reaching and holding the boards. Those plays that succeeded best
had such titles as *Ein lateinischer Farmer* and *Der Corner Grocer aus der
Avenue A,* though, unlike the novelists, most of the playwrights sought to
dramatize events of grand proportions or to tell romantic stories against
exotic backgrounds.

After 1870 the use of German in speech and writing declined. The once
popular *Erzählungen* survived only in the moralized tales of church periodicals; by 1900 the German theater had almost disappeared; and lyric poetry
grew weak and thin. By the twentieth century not more than two or three
writers of importance were using High German. Literature in German
dialects, on the other hand, especially Pennsylvania German, increased
steadily as cultural pride and racial consciousness grew. The dialects lent
themselves readily to humor, and popular verse appeared in Hessian, Swabian,
and Palatinate as well as in *Plattdeutsch.*

Less defensible linguistically, though amusing to a larger audience, were
Karl Adler's *Mundartlich Heiteres* (1886) and Charles Godfrey Leland's
*Hans Breitmann Ballads* (1856–1895), written in a kind of *Kauderwelsch,* a
mixture of broken English and German dialect, not to be confused with
Pennsylvania German. Hans is a huge, bearded, good-natured rogue, who
gorges and guzzles his way through a roistering and checkered career, speaking a tongue and portraying a character which German-Americans say is a
libelous caricature. Much later, in the twenties and thirties, Kurt M. Stein
succeeded in amusing both Americans and Germans with the same sort of
linguistic exaggerations.

### 4

Pennsylvania German, or Pennsylvania Dutch as it is often called, is more
nearly a language than a dialect. It is the tongue of the emigrants from the
Palatinate and the upper Rhine who settled in Pennsylvania in the seventeenth and eighteenth centuries. During the long colonial period, Pennsylvania German literature, most of it religious, was written in literary German,
but there was a decade between 1830 and 1840 when dialect stories, poems,
and columns filled the newspapers and magazines. After the Civil War, High
German receded while English advanced, but the trilingual Pennsylvania
German clung tenaciously all the while to his vernacular. The language
ceased to be funny, and men like Henry Harbaugh and Henry L. Fisher used
it to preserve "in simplicity, dignity, and loveliness" all phases of life from the
cradle to the grave and beyond. Legends, tall tales, anecdotes of rural and

small-town life, huskings, apple butter bees, and quilting parties, gentle satire of pretenses, and superstitions are the common themes of Pennsylvania German poetry. More and more dialect was written as the century wore on; probably nowhere else in the United States were so many average citizens trying to express themselves in verse. Newspaper letters were followed by newspaper columns and then by dialect radio programs. The dialect short story flourished. Also, like the High Germans, the Pennsylvania German poets translated for their audiences the currently popular American poems. Toward the middle of the twentieth century, as knowledge of the written language waned, dialect plays became increasingly popular.

Exploitation of the Pennsylvania Germans in American literature began as early as 1869 in the novels of Mrs. Phebe Gibbons and has continued ever since. Most widely read of the exploiters is Mrs. Helen Reimensnyder Martin, whose *Tillie: A Mennonite Maid* (1904) went into twenty editions. She followed it with a score or more of novels and short stories, some of which were dramatized and others made into movies. The Pennsylvania Germans themselves think Mrs. Martin's pictures defamatory, and generally prefer those of the even more prolific novelist Elsie Singmaster (Mrs. Elsie S. Lewars).

## 5

French literature did not begin to blossom in Louisiana until that region had been separated from the mother country for more than half a century. Starting timidly when Louisiana was transferred to Spain in 1762, it grew vigorously only after the annexation of the territory by the United States (1803). Scarcely any of the work of the early period survives, and what importance it has is not literary but historical.

After 1820 the number of French writers in Louisiana is large. Edward Larocque Tinker's bibliography lists three hundred fifty in a population of less than a quarter of a million Creoles, as the descendants of the original French and Spanish settlers were called. The ability to write either prose or verse was a necessary accomplishment for a Creole gentleman whatever his occupation, and leisure for writing increased when the admission of the territory to statehood (1812) and successive waves of immigration from the North brought a rise in land and slave values. The Creoles now had means for travel and study abroad, generally Paris, which strengthened their cultural ties with France. At the same time, as the number of Anglo-Saxons about them multiplied, the Creoles became more aggressively conscious of their language and culture, and more determined to preserve them. It was in this period, from 1840 on, that the most significant French works appeared, Gayarré's histories, the lyrics of the Rouquette brothers, Canonge's plays, and Testut's historical novels.

Charles Etienne Arthur Gayarré was a Creole whose ancestors had for generations been prominent in the colony—his maternal grandfather was host to the Duke of Orléans during his visit to Louisiana in 1798. Educated in New Orleans and trained at law in Philadelphia, Gayarré entered politics and held several important elective and appointive positions, including that of United States Senator in 1835, an office which he resigned for reasons of health soon after his election. Very wealthy, he was able to spend eight years of travel in Europe collecting material and documents for his history of Louisiana. His first survey was the *Essai historique sur la Louisiane* (1830) which, enlarged and documented, became *Histoire de la Louisiane* (1846–1847). Later he published in English several series of lectures which, collected into four volumes, formed his *History of Louisiana* (1866).

Gayarré was ambitious also to become Louisiana's Walter Scott. He wrote novels and one play, and in his histories took some poetic liberty with strict fact. He took care also in the course of his historical narrative to point out good subjects for fiction, such as the expedition of the Chevalier Saint-Denis into Mexico in 1714. His suggestions were seized upon by a number of novelists and playwrights. Charles Testut drew on Gayarré for two of his three historical novels; so did Louis-Armand Garreau for his *Louisiana* (1849), a tale of the anti-Spanish conspiracy of 1768. That same conspiracy inspired a poetic tragedy by Auguste Lussan and a prose drama by Louis-Placide Canonge. Canonge, the best of Louisiana dramatists, was the author of *Le Comte de Carmagnola* (1856), which is said to have had a run of one hundred performances on the Parisian stage.

The only Louisiana poetry of importance was written by the Rouquette brothers, sons of a French father and a Creole mother, who idealized the noble savages of the St. Tammany forest near New Orleans. Their admiration of the Indians was no mere product of theory and imagination, like that of their French contemporaries. As small boys they perpetually ran away from home to live with the Choctaws, and each of them spent a large portion of his mature life in the woods.

François-Dominique Rouquette, the elder and the better poet of the two, was educated in New Orleans and Paris and, as long as the family fortune permitted him to live as he pleased, alternated residence in Paris with sojourns in St. Tammany. Forced eventually to support himself, he engaged in a variety of unsuccessful ventures ranging from the direction of a *lycée* in New Orleans to the running of a grocery store in Arkansas. He finally ceased to worry about practical affairs or to feel any obligation to society, while he extolled in his poetry the simple primitive life of the Indians and

Negroes, the beauties of solitude and of nature. His *Meschacébéennes* (Paris, 1839) was praised by Hugo and Béranger, and *Fleurs d'Amérique* (New Orleans, 1857) was also well received by Parisian critics. His social attitude is made plain in a Civil War poem: "If I don't fight, the State has me shot; and if I fight, Uncle Sam will hang me."

The younger Rouquette, Adrien-Emmanuel, had been so fascinated by the life of the Indians that when he completed his education in France, he went back to his Choctaws and, like a proper romantic, fell in love, from reports of her beauty, with an Indian chief's daughter whom he had never seen. (She died of consumption before their marriage.) Like his brother, Adrien-Emmanuel traveled back and forth between Paris and New Orleans, and it was in France that he published his first collection of poems, *Les Savanes* (1841). Barthélemy and Sainte-Beuve praised it; Brizeux hailed the author as "the American Ossian," and Thomas Moore called him "the American Lamartine." On his return to Louisiana, Adrien-Emmanuel entered a seminary and was ordained priest. For fourteen years he served as vicar-general of the Archbishop of New Orleans, longing always for the solitude of the forest and the society of the Indians, feelings he expressed in his prose work *Le Thébaïde en Amérique* (1852). Eventually he obtained permission to go as a missionary to the Choctaws, with whom he spent the rest of his life, identifying himself with them so completely that they called him Chahta-Ima, "One of Us." He died in 1887 while working on a dictionary of the Choctaw language. His books include *Wild Flowers* (1848), a collection of his English poems, and *La Nouvelle Atala* (1879), an Indian legend which was highly praised by his friend Lafcadio Hearn. He wrote also some delightful poems in gombo, the Negro-French dialect.

The Civil War was a fatal blow to the French language and French literature in Louisiana. It ruined the Creoles, like the rest of the wealthy South, and cut the umbilical cord that had connected them with France; they could no longer afford Parisian travel and education. During the Reconstruction period, also, there was strong government hostility to French culture, partly because it was alien, partly because of the uncompromising loyalty the Creoles had shown to the Confederacy. In 1868 it was decreed that laws and documents in Louisiana must be published in English only; and the teaching of French was forbidden in elementary and frowned upon in secondary schools. Children of Creole families speaking the French they had learned at home were taunted by their schoolmates as "kiskeedees" ("Qu'est-ce-qu'il dit?"). Older writers like Gayarré and the Abbé Rouquette continued for a time to publish in French, but few young men rose to take their places and carry on their work.

Most important of the small group who fought the losing battle was Dr. Alfred Mercier, who combined novel and poetry writing with his medical practice. With eleven other intellectuals he founded in 1876 the Athénée Louisianais, a cultural association, whose bulletin, the *Comptes Rendus,* was for a time the sole medium of publication for French writers in Louisiana. Dr. Mercier himself contributed more than sixty items. One of the later contributors, Alcée Fortier, made the first attempt at a survey of French literature in Louisiana and composed also a *History of Louisiana* (1914), which equals Gayarré's in importance.

Twentieth century scholars have made interesting studies of the interplay of French and American culture, and in both the nineteenth and twentieth centuries the Creole has furnished material for American fiction. The best pictures of French New Orleans are in the novels and stories of George Washington Cable, Kate Chopin, Lafcadio Hearn, and Grace King.

6

During the period of Spanish exploration and conquest of the American Southwest and during the Mission period that followed, reports, histories, diaries, and memoirs were written by government officials and by members of the religious orders. Some of these were published in Spain or Mexico and were later printed in English versions by American historians.

The literature that survives today among the descendants of the early colonists is an oral literature of plays, songs, ballads, and folk tales brought from old Spain. In 1598 missionary priests in New Mexico began to perform religious mysteries and pantomimes as a way of teaching Christianity to the Indians, and the tradition has survived. Every year at the recurrence of certain festivals, especially during the Christmas season, local casts in most of the Spanish settlements produce religious dramas. Most popular of these are *Los Tres Magos, Los Moros y los Christianos, Los Pastores, La Aparición de Nuestra Señora de Guadalupe,* and *Los Comanches.*

Of other writing there was little. The theocratic rule of the Mission period was hostile to profane knowledge. Scientific books were sometimes publicly burned, and not until 1833 was a printing press brought to California. Then it published almost exclusively official documents. The first volume printed in Texas, in 1829, was in English by an American immigrant. The secularization of the Missions (1833–1834) might have created an atmosphere more favorable to literature, but it was accomplished only a few years before the annexation of California. The Gold Rush followed almost immediately, bringing a large American immigration and a period of lawlessness which impoverished the Spanish settlers. The rancher class could not acquire the wealth and leisure with which to do for Spanish literature what the Creole planters of Louisiana had done for French.

In the twentieth century, Spanish-American culture, both early and contemporary, furnished material to such American-born novelists as Gertrude Atherton, Willa Cather, Harvey Fergusson, and John Steinbeck.


### 7

Long before Italian immigrants came in large numbers to America, Italian explorers, political exiles, and adventurers visited or settled in the United States. Their number was small—3,645 in 1850, 16,766 in 1870—not large enough to form a reading public, and the literary men among them wrote consequently in the languages spoken by the people with whom they lived— English, French, Spanish—rather than in their native tongue. One of the few early works in Italian is a series of articles on the political problems of the colonies in 1774, written by the physician, trader, farmer, and diplomat Filippo Mazzei. It was translated into English by Thomas Jefferson and published in Pinckney's *Virginia Gazette*.

The political exiles who came to America between 1815 and 1861 either published in English or had their Italian works published in Italy. The only notable exception was Lorenzo Da Ponte, author, before he came to America in 1805, of many librettos, including Mozart's *Le Nozze di Figaro* and *Don Giovanni*. Settling in New York, he became the first professor of Italian at Columbia University and published numerous Italian works in prose and verse, most of them ephemeral. His only surviving book is an autobiography, republished several times in Italy and translated into French and English.

After 1880 the huge increase in Italian immigration created an American market for Italian writers, but, since most of the immigrants were of humble origin, their literary requirements were satisfied by the daily and periodical press and the propaganda literature published by labor groups and the Protestant churches who tried to evangelize them. The better writers soon began to use English as well as Italian, partly to reach the American reading public, and partly because the majority of the children of the immigrants were unable to read Italian.


### 8

Scandinavian culture in the United States is nineteenth century history, but its pattern of development bears close resemblance to those of the earlier migrants from Southern Europe. More easily than the Germans or Latins, the Norwegians, Swedes, and Danes adjusted themselves to the new land. They had had at home some schooling in democratic processes; they had not been much hampered by class distinctions; and they gravitated toward the broad expanses of the American Northwest where they took natural and sturdy root. Their numbers increased with such rapidity that there were, for example, more Norwegians in the United States at the end of the nineteenth century than there had been in Norway at its beginning. The Swedes, too, are numerous and have to their credit a considerable body of literature in the United States. The earlier writers were either journalists or ministers, but a professional literary class developed toward the end of the nineteenth century, producing a great quantity of work in the familiar forms, some of it excellent in quality. But no Swedish-American author emerged of the stature of the American-Norwegian Rölvaag.

The growth of Scandinavian-American literature is closely associated with the vigorous development of the Scandinavian periodical press, but before long the writers were using English even when treating Old World themes. The first Norwegian-American novel, Hjalmar Hjorth Boyesen's *Gunnar*, was written in English and published (1873) by William Dean Howells in the *Atlantic Monthly*. The material is all Norwegian. It is the story of a little goatherd and a mermaid, and the trolls play important parts. Some of the later novelists wrote successfully in two languages, but most of them used English whether they were dealing with Scandinavian themes or with pioneer struggles against Indians and the wilderness.

In the twentieth century the social novel became a distinctive feature of this literature. It reached its highest point in O. E. Rölvaag's novel of Norwegian-American life, *Giants in the Earth* (1927). Rölvaag, who was born of Norwegian fisherfolk, came to America in 1896 when he was twenty years old. He worked for three years on his uncle's farm in South Dakota and then determined to get an education. Without funds, with scant knowledge of English, struggling against illness, he put himself through three years of school and matriculated at St. Olaf College in Northfield, Minnesota. His determination, his ability, and his fine integrity of character endeared him to his professors who, after his graduation in 1905, made possible for him a year of graduate study in Norway and then called him back to St. Olaf to teach Norwegian.

Rölvaag found the transition from the Old World to the New difficult, but exciting and rewarding. He analyzed the process thoughtfully and became convinced that, to make a good American, a Norwegian must be surely rooted in his own culture. He believed that the United States needs the stability and mature richness of the old civilizations. All his life—it was cut short at fifty-five—he taught this doctrine with passion, in his classroom, on the lecture platform, in societies organized in the Northwest for the preservation of Norwegian culture, and in the many novels he wrote in Norwegian from *Amerika-Breve* (1912), so autobiographical that he published it under a pseudonym, to *Peder Victorious* (1929) and *Their Father's God*, published in

1931, the year of his death. Most effective of all was *Giants in the Earth* (1927), which, translated like most of his work and widely read in both Norway and the United States, fulfilled the ambition Rölvaag had cherished from his college days to become the spokesman of his people, to tell the story of the immigrant's part in the making of the great new nation.

## 9

Jewish-American literature, one of the richest products of the mingling of tongues, has developed in some respects in ways similar to those followed by the Latin, German, and Scandinavian. In other respects the divergence is sharp, for Jewish immigration derived from all parts of the world, and each Jewish immigrant brought with him not only the racial and religious traits which united him with other Jews but also many of the manners and customs of the people among whom he dwelt before migrating. Thus the Jews in the United States form not one composite group but rather a congeries of many groups, at once individualistic and generic. Hebrew, traditionally the national language of the Jew, is spoken by relatively few of the Jews outside Palestine, while Judaeo-German, commonly called Yiddish, as the mother tongue of some seven million, is the nearest approach to a Jewish language. German and French, Greek and Syrian Jews often spoke the language of their fellow nationals, while Russian and Polish Jews, hedged about by restrictions in the old country, spoke mainly Yiddish. Many a Jewish immigrant, landing in the United States, had to submit to a double process of assimilation: first to find his place in the ghetto, and then to make his way in the New World. In spite of these handicaps and other difficulties, Jews, who in 1825 numbered only 16,000, increased until a century later there were more than 4,000,000. Approximately half this number lived in New York City, making it the largest Jewish community in the world.

The literature of the Jews in the United States, as in almost all European countries, began with Hebrew writings of a religious nature and branched out either into the special national dialects used by the Jews among themselves or into Yiddish. They have considerable bodies of literature not only in Hebrew and Yiddish but also in German, English, French, Spanish, Portuguese, Italian, Dutch, and Russian. Sharply divided by factions, often splitting on one issue while combining on another, they are subject not merely to linguistic cleavages but also to such a variety of social, religious, and economic strains and stresses that valid generalizations are hard to make.

The love of Zion, which found early supporters in America in individuals like Mordecai Manuel Noah, Emma Lazarus, and Henrietta Szold, has always been indissolubly linked with religious orthodoxy and the Hebrew language. The plight of Jews in Europe shortly before and after 1900 won support for "political" Zionism from many Jews in America hitherto untouched by the Zionist program; and after the First World War Zionism, under Louis D. Brandeis, appealed to a larger American following than ever before. Brandeis approached Zionism through Americanism, explaining that, to be good Americans, Jews must be better Jews; and, to be better Jews, they must become Zionists.

The movement was marked from the beginning by a fervent faith and high idealism; but faith and idealism were not enough to attract and hold the masses, who were moved by social forces in the ghetto, by hard working conditions, and by the struggle for existence to look for leadership to the labor unions and the radical Yiddish press, both of which were largely antireligious and anti-Hebraic.

Then there were many who, holding to the melting-pot theory of social-racial assimilation, broke with their cultural heritage and sought, by obliterating the Jewish element within them, to become altogether "American," or tried, by the annihilation of all national differences, to promote an unrealistic internationalism or an impossible cosmopolitanism. Between these extremes were all possible variations and gradations, so that no racial or national group in the United States presents a greater range of conflict and complication than the Jewish.

The literary import of this complexity is indicated by such a compilation as A. S. W. Rosenbach's *An American Jewish Bibliography* . . . [*to*] *1850* (1926). The complexity is increased by the remarkable activity, first of the Yiddish writers following the great Jewish migration from Eastern Europe that began in 1881, and second, by American Jews writing in English, from Mordecai Noah and Emma Lazarus to Waldo Frank and Ludwig Lewisohn or George Jean Nathan and Elmer Rice (Reizenstein), to say nothing of Jewish personalities in the related fields of the cinema and the radio. In many instances the American Jew who expresses himself in English has written, consciously or unconsciously, in a manner to make his product almost indistinguishable from the main stream of Anglo-American literature. This tendency on the part of Jews who write in English has become so marked that one prominent Jewish critic, Ludwig Lewisohn, has insisted that whatever the medium or the subject, a book is Jewish only when it is written by a Jew who "knows he is a Jew." But even this simple distinction fails to identify satisfactorily all books produced by Jews. It classifies Abraham Cahan's *Rise of David Levinsky* (1917) as "Jewish," though written in English, but it does not dispose as patly of Mary Antin's autobiography, *The Promised Land* (1912), a lyric, ecstatic apostrophe to America as the golden land of opportunity for the persecuted immigrant child from the Pale of Settlement.

One of the strongest forces in arresting the assimilative process of the Jew has been the ancestral language, which, in turn, was kept alive even during the darkest days of Jewry by the fact that Jewish religious observance remained largely identified with the Hebrew language. As might be expected, the earliest Hebrew books produced in the United States were almost exclusively rabbinical works like "responses" on disputed points of religious law or practice, commentaries on parts of the Talmud, and homilies. Of strictly literary books in Hebrew virtually none appeared until after the profound effects of the First World War quickened popular interest on the part of American Jewry in the Hebrew movement. Where earlier periodicals had seldom survived beyond a year or two, the new Zionism aided in the establishment and maintenance of new journals, notably the monthly *Hatoren* (founded in 1913), the *Miklat* (1917), the *Hadoar,* a Zionist weekly (1921), and the *Bitzaron* (1939), a monthly of high standards. The establishment of the Histadruth Ivrith, or Hebrew Organization, which serves as a central agency for the dissemination of Hebrew culture in America, aided in the founding of the *Hadoar.* This same organization, through its publishing company, has issued some fifty books and pamphlets, including an anthology of American-Hebrew poetry. While not devoted exclusively to the propagation of Hebrew, the Jewish Publication Society, taking as its motto "More Jewish books in Jewish homes," has reinforced the work of the Hebrew Organization. It encourages authors to devote their attention to Jewish subjects. It has published some two hundred titles. In 1940 it sold 52,844 volumes to numerous persons throughout the country, including many of its 6,357 members. It is estimated that through its efforts three and a half million copies of Jewish books have reached the homes of Jews and of Gentiles interested in Jewish knowledge.

There is a considerable body of Hebrew poetry, and there are a few novels, short stories, and essays, but American-Hebraic writings are still primarily rabbinical, and the writers are still essentially East-European immigrants. The development of a genuine American-Hebrew literature, indigenous to the country and rooted in American soil, remains contingent upon the crystallization of an American Judaism and an American Jewish tradition.

Yiddish, or Judaeo-German, literature in the United States began slowly. The educated refused to recognize Yiddish as a literary language, and the masses, driven by toil and grinding poverty, bought few books. But with the rapid increase of immigration, the gradual recognition of Yiddish as a legitimate vehicle for literary expression, and the establishment of periodicals, Yiddish authors began to find support. By 1916 the Yiddish daily press in New York was reaching 537,982 readers; after that it hovered between three and four hundred thousand. In Chicago, Philadelphia, Cleveland, and other cities, Yiddish periodicals flourished.

It was Abraham Cahan of *Vorwärts* (*Forward,* founded 1897) who did most to make newspapers the principal literary outlet and source of support for Yiddish writers. By consistently maintaining high standards for the fiction and poetry published, he raised the level of literary appreciation among Yiddish readers; and he was as assiduous in discovering new talent as in maintaining established writers. Such men as Sholem Asch (whose *Kiddush Ha-Shem,* 1926, is usually considered the greatest Yiddish novel), Abraham Weissen, and Jonah Rosenfeld were contributors to the paper. While doing the normal daily chores of newspaper work, they were permitted to create what they pleased in whatever way they pleased. Metropolitan editors and editors in other cities followed Cahan's leadership in this respect, so that the rise of Yiddish literature has been closely identified with the development of Yiddish journalism. This relationship is one of the important reasons for the use by Yiddish writers of the *Skitze* and the short story rather than the full-length novel. Most important of *Skitze* writers are Solomon Libin (Israel Hurewitz) and Solomon Rabinowitz (Shalom Aleichem), sometimes called the Jewish Mark Twain.

Yiddish writers, who made almost no progress in the drama while they were in Europe, found in America the conditions they needed for developing their talents. Their earlier and crude dramatic workmanship underwent a reformation at the hands of the producer Jacob Gordin, who, while not himself a playwright of the first class, recognized excellence when he met it in the work of others. By the end of the nineteenth century he had lifted Yiddish drama from cheap popular entertainment to the dignity of legitimate art. His insistence that acting was an art, demanding serious study and hard work, did much to raise the level of dramatic performance and undoubtedly contributed to the preeminence which the Jews have enjoyed in the twentieth century American theatrical world. The Yiddish theater in America, which began as early as 1883, reached its high point in the twenties with the organization of the Yiddish Art Theater under, successively, Emmanuel Reicher, Ben-Ami, and Maurice Schwartz.

The study of other foreign literary cultures in the United States—of such groups as the Icelanders, Finns, Poles, Czechs, Portuguese, South Americans, and Asiatics—has only just begun, but it is evident that the patterns they follow are similar to those that have been examined in detail. Something of the nature of this cultural amalgamation may be discovered by following the leads suggested in the bibliographical essay on "The Mingling of Tongues." The early desire to cast the Old World into a mythical melting pot has given place to a conviction that the immigrant serves his adopted country best when he is steeped in the traditions of his fatherland; that various and lively regional cultures increase the vitality of the culture of the United States.

# 42. THE INDIAN HERITAGE

NOT until the nineteenth century was well on its way did Americans begin to look upon the Indian as a cultural asset. The English colonists on the Atlantic seaboard usually felt that the best Indian was a dead Indian, and whole tribes were extinguished without any record of their inner life. If Indian traditions became known, they were romanticized and dressed up in cultural-white literary modes.

Interest in the Indian, even on the part of Cooper, was more in the individual than in his traditions or arts. It was not until the time of Henry Rowe Schoolcraft that any adequate attempt was made to gather the tales and songs of any American Indian tribe.

Schoolcraft was a good workman, and in the 1830's he collected a large amount of authentic traditional lore from the Ojibwa tribes around Sault Ste. Marie. But he lived in a romantic age, and there seems to be little doubt, in the light of more recent collections, that he not only changed and prettified, but actually invented some of his material. He certainly mixed the traditions of various tribes. In spite of all this, however, he did a fine service in bringing to the American public some acquaintance with the interesting legends of our Indians. It is also fortunate, of course, that Schoolcraft's work should have fallen into the hands of Longfellow at a favorable moment. For it is through *Hiawatha* that most Americans even now learn what little they know about the American Indian story.

The remarkable group of ethnologists who worked in the last decades of the nineteenth and the first of the twentieth century achieved at last an adequate record of Indian life and lore. They set themselves at all times an ideal of verbal accuracy in reporting, and they tended increasingly to take material down in the original language. With the perfection of phonograph recording it became possible to preserve not only words and phrases but also the actual tone and emphasis of oral delivery; thus it is as an oral art that American Indian song and tradition must be considered.

There is really no such thing as a written literature among the Indians of the United States. Such picture writing as appears on rocks and on birch bark or skins is nothing more than a kind of sign language, sometimes serving as a crude historical record and sometimes as a device for remembering the details of ceremonial. The most ambitious "literary" production of the Indians of the United States is a historical record of the Delaware Indians known as the Walam Olum. The text, apparently taken down by dictation, is accompanied by illustrative pictographs. Its value is entirely linguistic and historical, not actually literary.

All traditions of artistic value among our Indians are oral. These are handed down by word of mouth and are retained by individual and collective memory. Such expression is analogous in many of its details of form and substance to the genres familiar to students of European literatures. It serves and has served for a very long time the same needs for its unlettered folk as the literature of manuscript and printed page has served for its readers.

Somewhere among American aboriginals examples of nearly all of the familiar literary patterns are to be found. The lyric, always as a song; the chant; the incantation; the myth; the fairy tale; the humorous anecdote; occasionally even the riddle and the proverb—all these have been widely practiced from the time when we first meet the Indians shortly after the Discovery. The small amount of change observable in their traditions suggests that many of these patterns must be very old. We read tales in the Jesuit Relations of the 1630's and find them told three centuries later with insignificant change. But there has also been a continual importation of the new and an adoption of material from neighboring tribes, and the far traveler has always carried alien material and transplanted it in distant regions. This folk literature of the natives of the United States is therefore a complex structure, the result of the mingling of many influences and of centuries of ripening and refining.

It is not possible to consider the Indians of the United States in complete separation from those of the rest of the continent. Our present political boundaries have no practical bearing upon the traditions of these people. The coast tribes of Washington and British Columbia form a unit, while those of Oregon and California do not. Our Pueblo culture extends far into Mexico, and the Blackfeet are equally at home in Montana and Alberta. A thorough study of the American Indian must be made with the whole continent as a background. We may well assume that the high culture of the Incas in Peru and the Mayas in Yucatan produced their correspondingly fine myths and ceremonial songs, and perhaps other literary forms. But, except for some poor fragments preserved by early Spanish colonizers, this literature has perished and left no trace in tradition.

2

Both because of the wealth of available collections and the wide geographical distribution which they display, myths and tales have always been given more attention than other aspects of American Indian folklore. In contrast to the students of a half-century ago, recent scholars no longer expect to find hidden meanings, symbolism, or dream interpretation in them; nor are they concerned with determining just what is tale and what myth. They find that these narratives not only are interesting in themselves, but afford an excellent opportunity for studies of the distribution of narrative material from one culture area to another and for a comparative examination of narrative patterns. Any reader of American Indian tales becomes impressed with a certain uniformity in the story plots throughout the continent; but further examination always brings out significant differences dependent not only upon geography but also upon many obscure facts of history. For the nine well recognized culture areas north of Mexico present not only their characteristic tale patterns but interesting differences in stylistic emphasis and in the social milieu of story-telling.

In accordance with the definition of mythological tale here suggested, a considerable number of the stories coming from all these regions can be thought of as myths. They give accounts of origins, and their action lies in a world different from the present. As for the actual myth of creation, it is hardly present at all. Perhaps the nearest approach to it is to be found in California and the Southwest. A number of the small tribes still surviving in California have rather elaborate accounts of the formation of the earth and its features and of the beginnings of human culture. But the "creator," usually conceived of in animal form, already floats about on a primeval water and sends down one animal after another to bring soil from the bottom. When the muskrat or some other animal succeeds in bringing a little soil, the creator works upon it and makes the earth. But the initial problem of where the primeval water and the muskrat came from, as well as how the creator himself came into being, remains as unanswered by these people as by our own theologians.

Somewhat less naïve, though perhaps even more difficult for the mind to grasp, and somewhat similar to traditions of other Southwestern groups, is the account of beginnings reported from the Zuñi of New Mexico. Here the world is considered as an emanation of the creator's thought. As Cushing has it, he "thought outward in space, whereby mists of increase, steams potent of growth, were evolved and up-lifted." * This vague world-stuff was consolidated by easy stages and through many cataclysmic changes into the earth as we now know it.

In other parts of the continent all the so-called creation myths assume the existence of the earth and are concerned primarily with the origin of the tribal culture hero or demigod, and with the ways in which he changes shapes and

* *Report of the Bureau of American Ethnology*, No. 13, p. 379.

conditions of objects and animals on the earth. We thus find the Iroquois telling how the mother of their twin gods fell from the upper world onto the backs of water birds, and how the earth originally rested upon the shell of a great turtle. Much of this tale is shared by the Algonquian peoples around the Great Lakes. In the Plains and Plateau the interest is primarily in the transforming activities of the culture hero, and this is true to an extent among the Northeastern tribes. But with the latter the hero is almost completely humanized instead of being essentially an animal. The nearest approach to an origin myth in the Southeast is usually an elaborate history of migrations of the tribe from some fancied original home. These migration legends are also present in Southwestern mythology, usually consisting of the ascent of the people from a series of lower worlds.

If well integrated mythologies are rare, it does not follow that our aboriginals in general are uninterested in explanations. Every tribe has a number of separate stories used to account for particular phenomena. Especially widespread over the continent are the tales of the thefts of light and of fire. In spite of some superficial resemblances to the Prometheus myth, these stories are certainly indigenous. They are especially popular in the western half of the country. As ordinarily told, the animal culture hero learns of the presence of fire in possession of some monster. By some trick he is able to steal it. The whole point of the story usually consists of an elaboration of the trick employed. Sometimes, for example, he turns himself into a particle and is swallowed in water by the monster's daughter. He is magically reborn and, as a child in the house, succeeds in stealing the fire. Other well known mythical incidents concern the regulation of the seasons, the origin of death, the placating or conquering of monsters or of some unruly natural forces— strong winds, high tides, floods, or the like.

No sharp line can be drawn between such explanatory tales and the large number of simple anecdotes to which explanations have been added almost at random. Earlier scholars were inclined to overestimate the importance of these explanatory tags and to assert that they were the essential part of the anecdote. More recent studies have shown, however, that it is the anecdote rather than the explanation which has permanence in tradition. There is no one story about how the chipmunk got his stripes, though that explanation has been appended to several different anecdotes. Some tribes do have the habit of sprinkling explanatory remarks at many places in the tales, appropriate and inappropriate.

In nearly all parts of the continent a considerable portion of the native narrative repertories deals with situations thought of as humorous by both teller and audience. These are usually known as trickster tales, since the point of the anecdote is nearly always some clever act of a half animal, half human being, conveniently referred to as a trickster. From region to region his name and nature vary. On the North Pacific Coast he is Raven or Blue Jay or Mink, according to the location of his tribe. By far the most widely known of all tricksters is Coyote, whose cleverness and foolishness are celebrated from the Eastern Plains to the California coast. With such tribes as the Ojibwa the culture hero and the trickster are the same person. In religious contexts, at initiation ceremonies and the like, Manabozho (Longfellow's Hiawatha) is the bringer of culture and livelihood to his people. But in everyday gatherings the stories told about Manabozho are much the same as the trickster tales related farther west concerning Coyote. The ducks that the trickster lures into dancing blindfold so that he can kill them, or the race which he wins by pretending lameness and getting a handicap—these illustrate the simple tricks which show him in his clever aspect. But the same trickster on other occasions is a buffoon or dupe. He buries his feast in the sand while he climbs a tree in order to stop the limbs from rubbing each other. Then he is caught between the limbs and looks on helplessly as the ducks are stolen.

These trickster incidents are humorous. Many of them are distributed over half or two-thirds of the continent, and they are probably known to more individual tale-tellers than any other kind of story. Their inconsistencies seem not to matter. Coyote is at one moment an animal, at the next he is obviously a person; Manabozho appears at one moment as a demigod, at the next as a buffoon; and all tricksters are uncertain mixtures of cleverness and foolishness.

As in our own culture, these humorous or near-humorous anecdotes are usually short and have little narrative elaboration. At their best they are witty and pointed; at their worst, silly and stupid. The only way in which they are given any length is by the process, familiar to all story-tellers, of stringing independent incidents together into an acceptable sequence.

Our aborigines do, however, have a number of stories of substantial compass. Some of these take a half-hour in the telling, and they are usually recited on more formal occasions than the trickster anecdotes. Of the longer tales, many are widely known, sometimes from ocean to ocean. Others belong to one or two culture areas. Rarely does an elaborate story remain in a single tribe unborrowed by neighbors. The process by which the rather elaborate tales have spread over the American continent is extremely interesting to the folklorist. For here he sees the principle of diffusion of oral narrative freely at work without interference from writing and literature.

Of the more popular of these longer stories among the American Indians there are some forty. About a dozen can be spoken of as "hero" tales, since they recount conflicts between a hero, often weak and unpromising, and a monster or at least a frightful adversary. Some of them remind one of the

European cycle in which the father-in-law puts the son-in-law through almost impossible ordeals. Another series, known as Lodge-Boy and Thrown-Away, current primarily in the Plains, has fortuitous resemblance to the medieval romance of Valentine and Orson. A woman is killed by a monster who takes twin boys from her body, leaves one in the lodge and throws the other into the bushes. Eventually Lodge-Boy and Thrown-Away find each other and go together on heroic adventures.

Frequently the hero tales come as a sequel to events which have taken place in the upper world. These other-world stories are not numerous, but they are among the most popular and best told of all our native tales. Particularly well known is "The Star Husband," which recounts how a girl goes to the star world, marries a star, is forbidden to dig, but disobeys and is overcome by longing to return home. Sometimes she has borne her supernatural husband a son. In any case, she makes a rope, and on it begins a descent to the earth. In some versions she succeeds in returning, but in others it is only the son who survives. Among the Plains tribes this boy becomes the hero of an elaborate series of adventures.

A tale like "The Star Husband" must be old. It has had time to develop three different characteristic forms, each with a clear-cut geographical distribution. It is known from Alaska to Nova Scotia, from California to Alabama.

A detailed account of American Indian stories is impossible in a short sketch. But even a cursory acquaintance shows that they have about them a considerable degree of narrative skill, a rather wide range of interest, and large scope for the imagination of both story-teller and audience. Most tribes recognize certain individuals as especially endowed with the gift for narrative. The stylistic resources of such artists, their repertories, their social status, and their relation to other gifted persons—all of these remain largely unnoticed in the available collections; but folklorists are becoming increasingly aware of the importance of learning more about such problems.

3

To the person with a background of European or white American culture, the tales of the North American Indians are, for the most part, interesting and clear, even in fairly literal translations. But this is not true of some of the other literary forms. The riddle and proverb are present but are scarce, and when approached through translation they lose much of their point. We know also that there have been many renowned Indian orators, and several of their orations have become famous. Students of American history are familiar with the remarkable oration attributed to the Mingo chief Logan after the massacre of his family in 1774: "There runs not a drop of my blood in the veins of any human creature. This called on me for revenge. I have sought it—I have killed many—I have fully glutted my vengeance. For my country I rejoice at the beams of peace; but do not harbor the thought that mine is the joy of fear. Logan never felt fear. He will not turn on his heel to save his life. Who is there to mourn for Logan? Not one." Yet it is extremely difficult to know just what the chief actually said, since it appears that the speech as we have it was composed only from rough notes. Something of the original in this and other orations doubtless remains, but it is natural that, in the excitement of debate, no one would think to record the orator's exact words.

Though they are not a part of literature themselves, the ceremonials of many American Indian tribes have served as a framework for several literary forms, particularly for the myth and the song. Intimately connected with both is the religious dance. In many groups the ceremonial life is so important as to be the mainspring of practically all artistic activity. This is especially true of the Southwestern group, which has a tendency to draw everything into the ritualistic pattern. The externals of such ritualism are clear and interesting to the observer, even to the casual traveler, but the esoteric significance of the dances and songs remains hidden, and of course unappreciated.

Generalizations about the poetry and songs of the American Indian are difficult, for these vary considerably from tribe to tribe. It is a long way from the elaborate chanted ritualistic poems of the Southwestern peoples to the short and often inarticulate miscellaneous songs of the Plains. In the latter particularly, the actual words seem unimportant in comparison to the music. Frequently there is little more than a succession of meaningless syllables, and always an excessive repetition. The musical idiom varies, but it almost never becomes pleasant to the unaccustomed ear unless profoundly modified by some professional composer. The range of subject matter of the songs is considerable and it varies with their use: for particular parts of a ceremonial, for dances, for gambling, for magic incantations, for war, for children's games, for love making, for lullabies, or for other events of ordinary life.

The ritualistic chants of such peoples as the Navaho or Iroquois, though they are naturally filled with repetition, usually fourfold, and are likely to tire the listener from outside the group, often contain excellent imagery and in their proper setting are truly impressive poems. An adequate appreciation of their literary value is only now becoming possible with the publication of the more extended texts. It is certainly going too far to assert, with Mary Austin, that these elaborate poems have had any profound influence on the rhythm of American poetry.

Perhaps the best opportunity which the American Indian had for the exercise of an individual poetic gift is in the short magic song. These songs are usually alleged to have been learned in a dream, and they are undoubtedly a combination of suggestions received from poetic patterns already well known with an observation or emotion of the moment. In such songs we find described a situation such as the singer wishes it to be. He expects by singing the song to bring this about. Thus in a song from the Papago of Arizona, preserved by Ruth M. Underhill, the corn is encouraged to come up:

The corn comes up;
It comes up green;
Here upon our fields
White tassels unfold.

The corn comes up;
It comes up green;
Here upon our fields
Green leaves blow in the breeze.

Blue evening falls,
Blue evening falls;
Near by, in every direction,
It sets the corn tassels trembling.

Or the rain is called down from the clouds after the long desert drought:

Where stands the cloud, trembling
On Quijotoa Mountain,
The cloud trembling,
There lies my heart
Trembling.

Within Quijotoa Mountain
There is thunder.
I looked through it and saw
In every direction
Light!

Wind came, clouds came.
I sat above them.
Underneath, the mirage glittered.
Rain fell,
The mirage was gone. . . .

At the edge of the world
It is growing light.
The trees stand shining.
I like it.
It is growing light.

At the edge of the world
It is growing light.
Up rears the light.
Just yonder the day dawns,
Spreading over the night.

The oral literature of the Indians of the United States has served for these peoples in much the same way as the written literature has contributed to the civilization of Europe. In the contact between Indian and white these traditions have largely remained unassimilated and even unknown by the dominant group. But they were here long before the whites came and they remain, even in an age of books and radio, the artistic outlet for our increasing Indian population.

# 43. FOLKLORE

THE same stirring of the historic sense which turned attention to the lore and culture of the American Indian began, by the middle of the nineteenth century, to stimulate exploration of the riches of American folksong and folklore. The Negro spiritual was "discovered" in the North at about the time of the Civil War. The collection of folk tales was seriously undertaken in 1888. By the twentieth century, scholars were at work in delighted earnest collecting, collating, and comparing.

Strictly speaking, folklore is that congeries of knowledge (beliefs, customs, magic, sayings, songs, tales, traditions, etc.) which has been created by the spontaneous play of naïve imaginations upon common human experience, transmitted by word of mouth or action, and preserved without dependence upon written or printed record. Practically, since printed matter has become cheap and easily accessible, and reading and writing have become commonplace accomplishments, folklore is not easily distinguishable from "popular" (or oral) literature, and vice versa.

In 1849 thousands of men trekked across the continent in the Gold Rush, encountering danger and hardships, suffering disappointments. Folklore handles the historical fact in the ballad of "Joe Bowers," humorously recounting the fate of a Forty-niner who left Pike County, Missouri, to raise a stake for his Sally. Who composed the song—whether one of the Argonauts and his pals, on the trail, or a professional comedian—no one can say with certainty. But it was sung on the stage of a San Francisco theater, spread to the mining camps, was brought back to the South to become a favorite of Confederate soldiers in the Civil War, and eventually achieved almost nation-wide diffusion. Today, nearly a century later, it is still sung in many variants throughout the United States. It has become folklore—current for a considerable period of time among the people, owing its preservation and circulation to word of mouth, not the printed page, and existing in numerous variants.

Thus folklore has its origin in an imaginative attempt to relate events, express feelings, and explain phenomena according to a graphic and rememberable pattern. This attempt, normally begun by an individual, is transmitted to other individuals by word of mouth or by action. Through repetition and unconscious variation, it loses its original individual traits, if it has any, and becomes a common possession of a group.

The group best qualified to make and keep folklore is one that "has preserved a common culture in isolation long enough to allow emotion to color its forms of social expression." Examples are the Southern Highlanders, once cut off from the rest of the country by difficulty of communications; the Pennsylvania Germans and the Louisiana French, with linguistic and cultural heritages different from those prevailing around them; and cowboys, sailors, lumberjacks, and miners, unified by occupations. In a sense that may still be true of most European nationals, the people of the United States are not a folk, and "traditionalist" folklorists have therefore denied that there is an American folklore. But such theorists have minimized or left out of account the culturally unifying memories of several profound experiences peculiar to the American people. Most of these are embraced in the frontier heritage. Though for millions of the foreign-born and the urban-dwelling this is not a memory, still it is an inescapable tradition, coloring manners, speech, song, story, and social attitudes. To an important degree it has produced a likeness of mind, a homogeneity of character, and an accent of expression which constitute the real test of a folk. Furthermore, regional consciousness, the ties of a common occupation, and other integrating principles have shaped our people into groups capable of preserving folklore, and have tended to stimulate the creation of it. Obviously, too, whatever folklore is imported into a country remains folklore *in* that country as long as it is remembered. The extent to which the people of the United States have created a considerable body of folklore will appear from examination of types and examples of what has been preserved.

Folklorists recognize four main types. Three of these circulate by word of mouth: the "literary," including folk poetry and such varied prose forms as legend, myth, and tale; the "linguistic," including speech, proverb, and riddle; and the "scientific," including cures, prophecies, witchcraft, weather lore, and other forms of belief. The fourth, circulating by action or practical imitation, includes arts and crafts, custom, dance, drama, festival, game, and music. For obvious reasons, this chapter is chiefly concerned with the literary and the linguistic, leaving, however, some of the categories, speech and myth, to other more appropriate chapters, but noting a few action types—e.g., drama and games—in their relation to song and story. The scientific and most of the action types will be passed by as belonging more to scientific folklore, anthropology, sociology, and general cultural history than to literary history. Although the subject matter of folksong and ballad frequently overlaps that of the folk tale, verse and prose forms will be treated separately.

2

The framework and the patterns of our folklore are in the main British. The linguistic medium by which it has largely been preserved and transmitted is English. The types thus established are those closest to the experience of our people and most intimately related to our print-recorded literature. For these reasons, aside from incidental references and comparisons to the other three largest pockets—the French, the German, and the Spanish—the illustrations will be taken from folklore of British types and type modifications expressed in the English language as spoken in the United States.

The first type of "Relics of Old English Folk-Lore" named by the first editor of the *Journal of American Folk-Lore* (1888) as an object of research was "old ballads." "The prospect of obtaining much of value," he wrote, "is not flattering." At that time Francis James Child of Harvard had been collecting the English and Scottish ballads for over thirty years, chiefly from British sources, and was in process of publishing his monumental work. The harvest of over fifty years of collecting in the United States has proved that the "prospect" was greatly underestimated; more than one-third of the 305 ballads in Child's *The English and Scottish Popular Ballads* (1882–1898) have been found in oral tradition among the people of the United States.

These old ballads, stories told in song, are the bluebloods of folksong in the United States. Their narratives illustrate all the major themes of ancient balladry. The favorites are romantic love stories like "Barbara Allen," "Lord Thomas and Fair Annet," "The Maid Freed from the Gallows," and "The Gypsy Laddie." Domestic tragedies are well represented by "Edward," "Babylon," "The Two Sisters," and "Lord Randal." Riddles and wit contests are exemplified by "Riddles Wisely Expounded" and "Captain Wedderburn's Courtship." Medieval romance is echoed by "The Marriage of Sir Gawain" and "Thomas Rhymer." Saints' legends and sacred stories are recalled by "Sir Hugh, or, The Jew's Daughter," and "The Cherry Tree Carol"; jests and fabliaux, by "Our Goodman" and "The Wife Wrapt in Wether's Skin"; the Robin Hood cycle, by nine pieces. The supernatural is impressively handled in "The Wife of Usher's Well" and "Sweet William's Ghost." Two superb sea ballads are "The Sweet Trinity" and "Sir Patrick Spens," the latter found of late in Virginia and Tennessee.

Such ancient song stories, couched in language and style of an archaic flavor and set to the older musical modes, ministered to the need in the New World for a view of the romance, the tragedy, the comedy, the heroism, the adventure of life shaped into easily remembered patterns. That they have been remembered so well is due to continuation of that need in isolated and socially undeveloped sections of the country, as well as to the inertia of folk memory. Yet they are far from being an exclusive possession of the ignorant and the illiterate. Many of the best texts have come from educated and locally prominent people who learned them in the traditional way. Great Americans outside the ranks of literary scholars—John Randolph of Virginia, Abraham Lincoln, Woodrow Wilson—have been fond of them and have sung them. The metrical patterns have been well preserved. Though most of the ballads have deteriorated by transmission, a few have been improved. Unfamiliar words have been corrupted or lost, names of persons and places changed, strange customs or beliefs dropped or rationalized, feudal possessions exchanged for homely goods. One editor has remarked that these old ballads have been made as thoroughly American as anything not Red Indian can be. They are aristocrats in homespun.

Of foreign ballads known to oral tradition in the United States, those most comparable to the group just discussed are Spanish *romances* of the Southwest. About a score of these, dating from the sixteenth and seventeenth centuries, have been found in New Mexico. Most of them belong to the novelesque type, treating of love, honor, fidelity and infidelity, war, legends originating in Arabic traditions, and religious emotion. They have undergone little change since they were transplanted. Among them are "Delgadina," telling the old Apollonius of Tyre story of an incestuous father; "Gerineldo," relating the love of Emma, daughter of Charlemagne, and Eginhard, the Emperor's steward; "Un Angel Triste," describing the intervention of the Virgin to save a condemned soul; and "Estaba el gato prieto," a burlesque story of a lovesick cat. The French ballads "Le Prince d'Orange" and "Le Prince Eugène" have been sung in sections contiguous with French Canada, and "Malbrough," "Montez, la Belle," and "Sept Ans sur la Mer" are known in Louisiana.

Referring to the old traditional legendary and romantic ballads, the editor of the *Journal of American Folk-Lore,* previously quoted, complains: "In the seventeenth century, the time for the composition of these had almost passed; and they had, in a measure, been superseded by inferior rhymes of literary origin, diffused by means of broadsides and song-books, or by popular doggerels, which may be called ballads, but possess little poetic interest." It may have been such "foolish songs and ballads," hawked and sung in every town, that annoyed Cotton Mather. As a matter of fact, even today these pieces, of later and more plebeian rise, and other comparable types like the Irish come-all-ye's, are more current than the legendary and romantic ballads. Not all of them, however, are distinctly inferior. Exception must be made for such as "The Babes in the Wood," described by Addison as "that darling song of the English common people," and almost equally a favorite in America; "Shooting of His Dear," "The Yorkshire Bite," "The Pretty Fair

Maid," "The Bugaboo," "Foggy, Foggy Dew," and nursery favorites like "Cocky Robin" and "The Three Jolly Huntsmen." More typical of the broadside are "The Butcher Boy" (an American amalgam of two or three British broadsides), "The Bramble Briar" (naïvely relating an analogue of Keats' "Isabella," previously treated by Boccaccio and Hans Sachs), "The Drowsy Sleeper," "The Silver Dagger," "The Sheffield Apprentice," and "The Wexford Girl"—the last three gory murder stories that established a pattern for many native ballads on that theme. In their relations to the older balladry and in their inferior quality, such pieces are paralleled by Spanish ballads of the Southwest like "La Esposa Infiel" and "Lorenzo Gutiérrez" (a murder ballad), by French ballads of Louisiana like "On a resté six ans sur mer," and by the Pennsylvania German "Wie ich von Frankreich komm" (perhaps an old Huguenot ballad transformed into an accumulative song), and "Der Tod von Basel."

Many of the nursery songs known in this country are perhaps as old as the ballads, and most of them are likewise traceable to British or Irish origin. Of such, besides "The Babes in the Wood" and "Cocky Robin," are "The Jolly Miller," "The Miller and His Three Sons," "The Carrion Crow," "Shule Aron," "Three Jolly Welshmen," and "The Frog's Courtship." The English-derived "Paper of Pins," "Billy Boy," and "Sleep, Baby, Sleep," have their counterparts, respectively, in "Te donnerai un papier d'aiguilles" and "Charmant Billi," sung by Louisianians of French descent, and the Pennsylvania German

> Hei-yo Bubbeli schlof,
> Der Dawdy hüt die Schof.
> Die Mommy hüt die rote Küh,
> Un kummt net heem bis Morge früh.

Bound up with the ballads in origin and transmission are the game songs and rhymes. The oldest of these early found use in such children's games as "Here Comes a Duke," "Green Gravel," "King Arthur Was King William's Son," and "Ring Around Rosie." Out of these games and the square dance, with its songs and calls, developed the unique American social fête known as the play party. Deemed an innocuous substitute for the square dance, which was interdicted by Protestant religious sects, the play party took over many of the old children's game songs and developed new ones, giving them an American flavor. Favorites have been such songs as "All Down to Sleep," "Hog Drovers," "Buffalo Girls," "Circle Left," "King William Was King James's Son," "Miller Boy," "Shoot the Buffalo," and "Skip to My Lou."

3

Of early native American ballads few have survived in popular tradition. "Lovewell's Fight," narrating an Indian fray of 1725, was remembered into the nineteenth century. Perhaps "Springfield Mountain" (originally a dolorous story about the death of a young New Englander from the bite of a rattlesnake, gradually burlesqued into a nursery tale) is the oldest and sole survivor from colonial times. The incident on which it was based happened in 1761, but there is "no evidence that the ballad is of earlier date than the second quarter" of the nineteenth century. From the period of the Revolution, "Yankee Doodle," "The Bombardment of Bristol, R.I.," and a few others, mainly of broadside origin, survived to some extent in oral tradition. It is known that there was one on Shays' Rebellion, but it has been lost. The War of 1812 produced "The Constitution and the Guerrière," "James Bird" (connected with the Battle of Lake Erie), "Andrew Jackson's Raid" (celebrating the campaign against the Creek Indians in 1813–1814), and "Ye Hunters of Kentucky" (known to a few folk singers of the present century). Regardless of their exact origins, "Springfield Mountain" and "Young Charlotte" (by Seba Smith), are perhaps the best exhibits of native balladry, their chief rivals for popularity being the later "Jesse James" and "Casey Jones," and a flock of low-life ballads, of which "Frankie and Albert" is the prize piece.

Other types of folksong may be characterized without regard for origins or strict distinction between ballad and lyric. The arbitrarily drawn distinction between these two genres is that the ballad tends to be narrative, romantic, and impersonal; the lyric (without story content), to be emotional, passionate, and personal, more often than not on an amatory theme. Folk singers are not conscious of the difference. A better principle of classification, for the remainder of what is to be said on the subject, is the functional relationship of folksongs to the singers' interests and activities.

Functional classification, however, convenient as it is for exposition, to some extent distorts the facts of relationship. Practice of the folk-singing art is closely interwoven with all the actions, interests, and moods of everyday life, not merely with its ordinary avocations. A few incidents from collectors' field experiences will illustrate the point. In a Virginia cabin, Maud Karpeles listened to the singing of "The Green Bed" by a mother of thirteen children, all present in the room. "Then almost as though impelled by some unseen power" the children "softly joined in the singing of this beautiful air . . . the haunting loveliness of their young voices subdued to an overtone so as not to disturb their mother's singing." A Mississippi informant said she had learned "Sir Hugh" as a lullaby sung by her mother. An Alabama family, father, mother, and son, sang "The Gypsy Laddie" dramatically, in character. Cecil Sharp found among the Appalachian mountaineers that aspect of "an ideal society" in which every child developed the inborn capacity for song and sang the songs of his forefathers "in the same natural and unselfconscious way in which he now learns his mother-tongue." Folk singing functions spontaneously in most of the singer's relations to himself and to his fellows. All folksongs are broadly "social."

A large body of songs have to do with the events and movements of American history. Besides the historical ballads already mentioned, a few, like "Plains of Mexico" and "Buena Vista," adaptations of earlier songs, relate incidents of the Mexican War. During the Civil War songs in the folk idiom, like "John Brown's Body," were modeled on more stately pieces, like the "Battle-Hymn of the Republic," and old favorites like "We'll All Take a Ride" were adapted into such pieces as "The Union Wagon." "Grafted into the Army" was perhaps the first of many comic treatments of conscription. "I Would Not Be Alone" is a more scornful handling from the point of view of a high-spirited Southern woman. "Come in Out of the Draft" may be the first pun on the word. "Tenting on the Old Camp Ground" and "Just Before the Battle, Mother" achieved wide circulation on both sides of the line, but not "Marching Through Georgia." On their side the Confederates sang "Dixie" in the folk version, not in the words of Albert Pike's "bastard Marseillaise," revamped "Wait for the Wagon," and started "The Bonnie Blue Flag" and its tune sharer "The Homespun Dress" on careers that practically made them folksongs. "The Southern Oath," composed perhaps by Rose Vertner Jeffrey in 1862, was still traditionally known in Missouri as late as 1906. The gaiety of Southern spirits was best expressed by "Goober Peas," "The Captain with His Whiskers," and "The Rebel Soldier" ("I'll eat when I'm hungry"). Finally, the "unreconstructed" spirit of the South proclaimed itself in "I'm a Good Old Rebel." From the Spanish-American War emerged "There'll Be a Hot Time in the Old Town Tonight" and a few picturesque pieces about the girl-kissing naval hero Hobson, but no songs achieved long or extensive circulation. The First World War produced several soldier songs, of which "Hinkie, Dinkie Parlez-vous (Mademoiselle from Armentières)," indubitably composed communally, on the model of the British Army "Skiboo," is *facile princeps*.

The stirring presidential campaigns of the forties were marked by extensive use of political songs in the folk style, published in *The Harrison and Log Cabin Song Book, The Clay Minstrel, The Polk Songster, The Rough and Ready Songster,* and the like. The Harrison campaign song "What Has Caused This Great Commotion?" was sung to the tune of "Little Pig's Tail." "Frémont Campaign Song" has a stanza beginning, "Old Ten-Cent Jimmy is no go." "Henry Clay," sung to the tune of "Old Dan Tucker," survived in Mississippi as late as the 1920's—

> Henry Clay came riding a jack,
> He rode on his belly to save his back;

and "Harrison Campaign Song," celebrating the farmer who left his "tidy log cabin" to drive out the occupants of the White House, and "When the Old Hat Was New," praising Harrison and Clay, were known in Missouri in 1912. These are early illustrations of an American political tradition continued in the transient popularity of such songs as "Happy Times Are Here Again" and "The Sidewalks of New York," and climaxed by the use of hillbilly music and song in state campaigns in Texas and Louisiana during the late 1930's and the early 1940's.

One of the most characteristically American bodies of songs, in content if not in originality of form and style, is that reflecting the Old West. Three groups of these may be illustrated.

The Gold Rush of 1849 and the conditions of life in the mining towns produced a considerable number of songs. "The Dying Californian" was modeled on an older tear-jerker, "Ocean Burial." "Joe Bowers," alluded to at the beginning of this chapter, has a less tragic conclusion. After enduring hard work, privations, and perils for his Sally, Joe received a letter from brother Ike stating that Sally had married a butcher with red hair—

> And what was worse than that—
> I almost wisht I was dead—
> That Sally had a baby,
> And the baby's hair was red.

The companion piece to "Joe Bowers" is "Sweet Betsy from Pike":

> Oh, don't you remember sweet Betsy from Pike,
> Who crossed the big mountains with her lover Ike,
> With two yoke of oxen, a large yellow dog,
> A tall shanghai rooster and one spotted hog?

Several romantic and circumstantial accounts of the origin of "Joe Bowers" have been published, from which the most probable fact seems to be that the singing of the ballad at the old Melodian Theater in San Francisco, in 1849, by a comedian, John Woodward, member of Johnson's Minstrels, gave impetus to its currency. The origin of "Betsy from Pike" seems to be unknown. Similar pieces, sung to folk and popular tunes, were broadcast among Californians by songsters, of which John A. Stone's *Put's Original California Songster* (1854) is an example. Among the favorite pieces with folksong antecedents are "An Honest Miner," "Days of Forty-nine," "Sacramento Gals," "Hog Eye Man," and "What Was Your Name in the States?" Two or three of these are still traditionally known. "The Dreary Black Hills," relating to the gold strike in Wyoming in the sixties, is a pendant to these ballads of the Forty-niners.

A second major contribution of the West is the cowboy song. In John A. Lomax's and most succeeding collections, there are two types. Songs transmitted by purely oral tradition are exemplified by "The Old Chisholm Trail," "Git Along, Little Dogies," and "Old Paint." What Howard Thorp describes as "songs originally printed, clipped from a local paper or magazine, fitted to a familiar air, and so handed down from one cowboy to another, becoming genuine folksongs in the process," are exemplified by "The Glory Trail" (reshaped and sung as "High-Chin Bob"), "The Cowboy's Christmas Ball," and "The Texas Cowboy." Among the best and most memorable modeled upon older songs are "The Dying Cowboy" ("Oh, bury me not on the lone prairie"), based upon "Ocean Burial"; "The Cowboy's Dream," on "The Sweet By-and-By"; and "The Cowboy's Lament," on an Irish broadside, "The Dying Rake." Comparable Mexican pieces known in Texas are exemplified by "La Corrida de Kiansas," relating the heroic death of a vaquero. However the cowboy songs may have originated, they were adapted to the needs of the lonely men who rode night herd, drove the steers from range to range or to market, and forgathered around campfires, in the ranch houses, or at the saloons. They have a distinctively American accent, and they splash the palette of American folksong with bright colors.

A third group of Western songs describes pioneering. "Starving to Death on a Government Claim" and "Dakota Land" typify the usual themes. These are supplemented by a considerable number of Norwegian emigrant songs and ballads.

Songs of the sea, the canals, and the rivers are variously adapted to the work, the interests, and the sentiments of men whose business has sent them upon the waters. The chanteys flourished in the glorious era of American shipping following the War of 1812, and their heyday coincided with the supremacy of the clipper ships. Though some of them are traceable to the Elizabethan period, the first description of chantey singing on an American ship is said to be R. H. Dana's, written in 1834. Critical opinion awards equal merit to British and American sailors for developing them. The true chanteys, directing the movements of sailors at work, followed a definite pattern in which solo and chorus were adjusted to the practical purpose in hand. Four types are represented in standard collections: the short-drag, exemplified by "Haul Away, Joe"; the halyard, by "Whisky Johnny" and "Blow the Man Down"; "any song with a long 'chorus' and swing," by "Shenandoah" and "Santy Anna"; and the "Forecastle Song," by old traditional English ballads like "The Golden Vanity," and broadsides of the War of 1812 such as "The *Constitution* and the *Guerrière.*" The whalers sang both the chanteys and a number of ballads and songs especially related to their experience. Among these were "Reuben Ranzo," the success story of a tailor who "shipped on board a whaler" and made up for his landlubberly deficiencies by marrying the captain's daughter; "Jack Wrack," a moralistic piece on spreeing; and "Blow, Ye Winds" and "Greenland Whale Fishery," describing the hardships and perils of whaling.

The mingling of the waters by the construction and operation of the canals resulted also in the mingling of folklores. Besides scattering the Irish laborers and their songs and tales from Rome to Buffalo, the Erie Canal became a five-hundred-mile folk festival. "Paddy on the Canal" describes the digging of the ditch. Other ballads celebrate races and fights, and numerous songs issue warning about the business end of a mule, satirize the hotels, and detail the accommodations of jails. "The Raging Canal" is a rhymed tall tale on the perils of navigating a four-feet-deep ditch. "Boatin' on a Bull-Head," however, describes a real danger—"The bowsman he forgot to yell, 'Low bridge, ducker down!' " The classic is "Low Bridge, Everybody Down" (I've got a mule and her name is Sal), called by Sandburg "the Volga Boat Song of America."

Of even greater variety than the songs of the sea and the canals are those sung by paddlers of canoes and bateaux, polers of keelboats, steersmen of flatboats and steamboats, pilots, roustabouts, and passengers on the river. The "rouster" and the "soundings" songs are the closest river counterparts of the sea chanteys. These and sprawling song narrative like *"Katie* and the *Jim Lee* Had a Little Race," and bits like "The Gold Dust Five," are the most distinctive river pieces. "Steamboat Round the Bend," dating from the Civil War, is known throughout the length and breadth of the land. Except for fragments about such steamboats as the *Stacker Lee,* the *Lovin' Kate,* and the *City of Cairo,* most of the river songs are remembered only by the river people. Like the cowboy songs, they are local and topical in content, loose and rambling in structure.

As the lumber industry moved westward from the Atlantic seaboard toward the end of the eighteenth century, the industrial woodsman (lumberjack, raftsman, sawmill hand) began to appear. The invention of the circular saw and the demands of the West for building material brought on the golden age of the industry in the North Central states and produced the shantyman as an industrial and folk type. By 1900, when the industry spread

to the South, most of the romance and glamour had disappeared as the
Irishman, the Scotchman, and the French Canadian gave place to the native
hired hand in the woods. It was during the years between 1850 and 1900 that
most of the songs of the shantyboy were composed and first sung around the
deacon seat. Most popular of all was "The Jam on Gerry's Rocks." "Jim
Whalen" relates a similar story of death in a log jam. "Shanty Boy and
Shanty Girl" and "The Little Eau Plaine" develop romantic episodes. "The
Little Brown Bulls" is a delightful yarn of a pulling contest between ox
teams. Paul Bunyan, the mythological hero of the lumberjacks, is celebrated
in a few ballads, but these are overshadowed by the tall tales about him.

Railroad construction produced the Negro hero John Henry, who looms
gigantic in a cycle of ballads. The functional aspects of this ballad, setting the
rhythm for hammer or pick, are complemented by a host of other work songs
most fully developed by Negroes. But accidents and disasters incidental to
operation supply the most dramatic and picturesque themes. The best ballads
of train wrecks have come out of the South and West. "Casey Jones," for
instance, was probably composed on older models by a Negro roundhouse
worker, Wallace Saunders, about John Luther Jones, engineer of the Cannon
Ball Express, who died at the throttle in a collision at Vaughan, Mississippi,
in 1900. The ballad owes much of its present form and wide diffusion to
vaudeville rehandling of the earlier song by Saunders. "The Wreck of Old
'97" is well known in Virginia and the Carolinas.

Linked to the balladry of the nation's canals, lumber camps and railroads,
but dashed with a Celtic infusion, are songs growing out of the mining
industry. The best of these have come from the anthracite region, where
Irish and Welsh immigrants, with their old-country songs and tunes and
their communal gatherings on the green, a part of every "mine patch," developed their own minstrelsy. Some of the pieces recall the troublous days
of the Molly Maguires, Irish laborers who terrorized the anthracite region
in the seventies; but the most characteristic treat of mine work, disasters, and
strikes: "Pat Dolan" and "Thomas Duffy," two Molly Maguire ballads; "The
Shoofly" and "Down, Down, Down," on the fears and hopes, the hardships
and mishaps, of the industry; and "My Sweetheart's the Mule in the Mines."

4

Realization of the varied wealth and cultural significance of religious
folksongs in the United States is comparatively recent and is still somewhat
confused by controversy. Curiously enough, the story begins in the forties
with minstrel-show capitalization of plantation melodies. Stimulated by this
interest, Northern writers during the period of the Civil War "discovered"

the spiritual. Allen, Ware, and Garrison's *Slave Songs of the United States* (1867) is a landmark. It was followed by other books devoted to spirituals. In the seventies the Negroes themselves at Fisk University and Hampton Institute, with their far-journeying troupes of singers and their published collections, began to take a hand in exploitation of the spirituals. Until recently it was generally assumed that the Negro originated the spirituals; but it is more probable that he "borrowed themes, song patterns, and tunes from the white man, and adapted or reshaped them, investing them with his own mental, emotional, and vocal mannerisms." Thus, each race has an honorable and 'not necessarily invidious claim: the white, for primacy of the spiritual as a folksong type; the black, for the distinctiveness of the Negro spiritual.

As a result of almost a century of collecting and a quarter-century of controversy over origins, we do not have agreement among the scholars, but we do have a great and beautiful host of spirituals from both the blacks and the whites. Examples of songs shared by the two races, the white versions being the older, are "Old Ship of Zion," "When the Stars Begin to Fall," "Roll Jordan," "Old-Time Religion," "Poor Wayfaring Stranger," "Swing Low, Sweet Chariot," "Go Down Moses." In time-hallowed association and power of emotional evocation and expression for millions, the spirituals have no serious rival among the types of American folksong.

Vying with the spirituals in distinctiveness are several other types of Negro songs. First to attract the attention of the whites were the plantation songs, like "Zip Coon" and "Ole Virginny Nebah Tire," which were sung all over the country by such companies as the Ethiopian Serenaders and the Virginia Minstrels. "Massa Had a Yaller Gal," "Uncle Ned," "Oh, Susanna," and "Run Nigger Run" are examples of pieces ultimately traceable to plantation melodies but adapted to minstrel use by white composers, and given a currency still persistent in both Negro and white oral tradition. Recent collections of Negro folksongs recognize and abundantly represent a large variety of work songs, including those of pick and hammer sung by labor gangs, and those sung in farming and miscellaneous other types of work. Besides these occupational songs, there are those that have to do with animals, recent events, and sex relations. As a result of a mayoralty campaign in Memphis, Tennessee, in 1909, in which W. C. Handy, a Negro singer, played a prominent part, the blues began to sweep the country. In contrast with the spirituals, which are communal and choral, the blues are individual and lyrical. Their common themes and moods are best described in their own phrases—"a good man feelin' bad," "a woman on a good man's mind," and

> De blues ain't nothing
> But a poor man's heart disease.

As with the ante-bellum plantation songs and as with the "coon songs" a half-century later, commercialization and popular fad have made the blues a dubious expression of the Negro folk mind. But they and the other Negro song types are among the most characteristically American contributions to folklore.

## 5

From the beginning of American literature through the Romantic Period, connections between art poetry and folk poetry were incidental and more or less consistent with British precedent. Until well into the nineteenth century broadside and newspaper ballads were staple provender. Franklin and, later, Bryant and Cooper wrote ballads used by newspapers and itinerant singers and peddlers. Royall Tyler's "Ode Composed for the Fourth of July" (1796) gives a gusty list of folk customs, including game songs and dances. Freneau occasionally used folksong patterns, as in the come-all-ye "Barney's Invitation" and the ballad "The Battle of Stonington." Bryant, as in "Song of Marion's Men," and Poe, as in "Annabel Lee," show general influences of the literary vogue of popular poetry; but in Longfellow and Whittier treatment of American material in the ballad goes somewhat beyond the conventions established by British Romantics. "The Wreck of the Hesperus" and "Paul Revere's Ride" are authentic in their traditional form and in their native substance. Both qualities are less pronounced in Whittier's idyllic "Maud Muller" and "Telling the Bees," but more so in "Skipper Ireson's Ride," with its tarry and salty folk speech. Oliver Wendell Holmes would have relished the irony that his "Ballad of the Oysterman," parodying the pseudo-ballads of the time, has been adopted by the folk themselves. Form and mannerisms characteristic of folk poetry, well known to Lowell, as well as Yankee dialect and shrewdness, help to explain the raciness of *The Biglow Papers*, especially in pieces like "The Courtin'." "I hear America singing, the varied carols I hear," declared Whitman. He showed a passionate awareness of folksong, and its refrains and rhythms pulsate in his orchestration; but it did not exert a strong formal influence. Author of one of the most eloquent tributes to the old ballad, Sidney Lanier wrote at least two fine imitations, "The Revenge of Hamish" and "A Ballad of Trees and the Master." His dialect pieces, like "Uncle Jim's Baptist Revival Hymn" and "Thar's More in the Men Than Thar Is in the Land," though inferior, are closer to current American folksong.

With Bret Harte and John Hay, vernacular poetry in the United States plants its feet solidly on the ground of American folksong. Tickled by "Joe Bowers," they established the vogue of the Pike County ballad with such pieces as "The Heathen Chinee" and "Jim Bludso." Shortly after this innovation, Irwin Russell, a young Mississippian, showed the possibility of a more authentic poetic treatment of Negro life and character than had hitherto appeared in pseudo-Negro poetry, even at its best in the songs of Stephen Collins Foster. Such poems as Russell's "Christmas Night in the Quarters" owed a part of their effectiveness to their undertones of Negro song and dance. Dialect verse exhibiting the inspiration of folksong and affinities with it constituted an important part of the local color movement. Among the chief practitioners were Will Carleton, James Whitcomb Riley, Eugene Field, and the Canadian Robert W. Service.

The quiet simplicities of folksong, and frequently its forms, appear in much twentieth century poetry. Edwin Arlington Robinson's ballad "Miniver Cheevy" is an early example. Robert Frost has played with both folk material and form in such pieces as "Brown's Descent, or the Willy-Nilly Slide," characterized by Louis Untermeyer as "a tart New England version of 'John Gilpin's Ride,'" and "Paul's Wife," a bit of apocryphal Bunyaniana. Nursed on *Uncle Remus*, Negro songs, and pioneer traditions, and later roaming the country as a minstrel, Vachel Lindsay reflected his heritage in such poems as "The Congo," "General William Booth Enters into Heaven," "My Fathers Came from Kentucky," "The Statue of Old Andrew Jackson," and "Preface to 'Bob Taylor's Birthday.'" Carl Sandburg, singing minstrel, distinguished folksong anthologist, owes little to the form but much to the feeling and the phrase of folk poetry. The best illustrations of the influence of all elements are to be found in the poetry of Stephen Vincent Benét. "The Ballad of William Sycamore" is the incarnation of the pioneer spirit set to a perfect American transposition of the old ballad music. "The Mountain Whippoorwill . . . (A Georgia Romance)" is a capital ballad on a fiddlers' contest. Echoes of spirituals and dance songs and the exquisite ballad beginning "Love came by on the river smoke" enrich the harmonies and color the texture of *John Brown's Body*. Both American folksong and Benét's poetry show how irrepressible the American spirit is:

> They tried to fit you with an English song
> And clip your speech into the English tale.
> But, even from the first, the words went wrong,
> The catbird pecked away the nightingale.

"Folk-songs," remarked Constance Rourke, "have been set like rosettes on the surface of plays and novels." In early American drama and fiction this use was decorative, as Miss Rourke's simile suggests: chapter tags from the old ballads, as in the Waverley novels, an occasional song by one of the characters in a play or novel, *entr'-acte* singing. Many of the famous old actors—

e.g., Edwin Booth and Joseph Jefferson—grew up singing folksongs. The development from vaudeville solo to duet, duet to dialogue, dialogue to play is characteristic of the history of the theater in America. *Old Lavender* (1877), "growing out of a vaudeville sketch [about a] genial drunkard" is an illustration. The capital examples of dramatic use of folksong occur in the 1930's— Marc Connelly's *Green Pastures,* woven of religious fantasies and spirituals of the Negro; such operatic pieces as DuBose Heyward's *Porgy and Bess*; Lynn Riggs' *Green Grow the Lilacs,* which flowered into *Oklahoma.* A study of the use of folksong in fiction descriptive of the Southern scene shows that between 1923 and 1932 thirty-one writers (among them James Boyd, DuBose Heyward, Elizabeth Madox Roberts, Thomas Wolfe) utilized over two hundred folksongs in more than twoscore novels and short stories. The songs afforded bright threads for the tapestry of history, primary colors for genre painting of folk scenes, and character-revealing high lights and shadows for the chiaroscuro of individual personality; thematic and choral music to suggest the moods and signalize the stages of dramatic action; and the spirit and substance of action itself. Fiswoode Tarleton, in "Curtains," and Olive Tilford Dargan, in *Call Home the Heart,* handled climactic episodes by representing the process and the results of communal composition through the characters.

## 6

The collecting and preserving of folktales in the United States was not seriously undertaken until 1888, when W. W. Newell declared that scarcely a single nursery tale had been recorded in America. He was hopeful, however, that something might be done to save from oblivion the great store of fairy tales, beast fables, and jests still alive within the memories of nurses and mothers only a few years before the time of his writing. During the next fifty years Newell's hopes were abundantly fulfilled. In addition to thousands of examples of the types he named, other richly illustrated types were discovered and collected. Among these are legends transplanted and naturalized, new legends invented, and, notably, the tall tale. The latter has the strongest claim to being an indigenous American invention. It exhibits a tendency toward cyclic evolution around representative American heroes which approaches the familiar pattern of Old World cultural myth.

The store of collected Old World *Märchen* remembered in the United States is now large. Examples in English from white people are "The Wolf and the Pigs," "Bluebeard," "How Jack Went to Seek His Fortune," "Johnny Cake," "Lazy Maria," "The Three Brothers and the Hog"; adaptations of the ancient Mak-the-sheepstealer episode; and a whole cycle of "Jack Tales" (giant killing, dragon quelling, and the like). Congaree River Negroes in

South Carolina have stories explaining why jaybirds are not to be killed and why the skin of the ox is used to whip the mule. Gullahs on the Sea Islands tell traditional versions of Rumpelstilzchen, of "Rescue of the King's Daughter," and of the doings of Ber Rabbit, Ber Fox, Ber Wolf, and the rest of the hierarchy of the Uncle Remus stories. Independent versions of many of the last-named cycle have also been recovered from Mississippi and published in a delightful book, *The Tree Named John*. Louisiana French tales, early collected by Alcée Fortier, include Compair Lapin's exploits with animals, fairy stories, and vaudevilles of song and prose story. An extensive collection from a pocket of French-speaking people in Missouri falls into somewhat similar categories; Compair Lapin is an important figure, and there is also the French Canadian hero P'tsit Jean. Collections made in the Southwest illustrate the range of the Spanish folktale. Almost every major Old World tale type, including such international examples as "The Tar Baby" and others in the Uncle Remus cycle, is exemplified in American folklore.

Of the other prose narratives falling within the classical folklore categories, the legend is also well represented. Literary treatment of legendary material by Irving, Hawthorne, and Cooper called attention to its existence in the East. It has since been found to be widespread. Stories of treasure hidden by Captain Kidd, Blackbeard, Teach, and other pirates have been recovered from Money Cove, Maine, to the North Carolina Banks. On Chappaquiddick, Martha's Vineyard, have been found stories of the Phantom Ship, the Blue Rock Treasure, the Haunted Hollow, and the Little Man. In the Bayou country of Louisiana flourish stories of Jean Lafitte, of the Acadians, and of old plantation houses. Among the people of the Middle West have sprung up countless legends like "The Lone Tree" (commemorating the birth of a baby to a pioneer Iowa couple), "Providence Hole" (relating the escape of a child from Indians), and "Lovers' Leap" (a story, current in many versions throughout the country, of a death pact kept by tragic lovers). The most characteristic and widely diffused legends of America are those about seekers after treasure and wealth. The Southwest abounds in these tales of lost mines and hidden, sometimes forgotten, hoards.

Tending also to be localized are tales of witches, ghosts, devils, and phantoms. In number, popularity, and variety, they form one of the most considerable groups of folktales. They also reflect some of the most ancient and deep-rooted superstitions of the American people. "De Witch 'Oman an' de Spinnin' Wheel" from Louisiana, "Old Skinny" from North Carolina, and "Out of Her Skin" from South Carolina Gullah Negroes illustrate the belief that witches slip out of their skins in order to do mischief. "The Bell Witch of Tennessee and Mississippi" combines the vampire and the poltergeist in a story of the supernatural persecutions visited by the "witch" of a murdered overseer upon a North Carolina family who moved to the lower South early in the nineteenth century. Dating from the eighteenth century and localized in New Jersey, "The Leeds Devil" relates the horrendous acts of a witch's offspring. "The Death Waltz" from the Southwest exemplifies the return of the ghost of a dead lover to interrupt the wedding of the surviving mate. Traffic with the devil motivates "Jack-o'-My-Lantern," a Maryland tale of a clever Jack who outwits the Evil One. The impulse which created tales of the supernatural is still alive. Automobile accidents on lonely roads have given rise to a widespread story of a traveler who picks up a beautiful hitch-hiker, to discover in the denouement that she is the ghost of a girl killed at the spot where he was accosted.

"Skitt's" (H. E. Taliaferro's) *Fisher's River Scenes and Characters,* published in 1859 but containing North Carolina stories said to be current in the twenties, is perhaps a fair sampling of pioneer tales. These include hunting yarns by Uncle Davy Lane, who "became quite a proverb in the line of big story-telling"; tales about panthers, bears, horn snakes and buckmasters, frontier fights, and eating exploits; anecdotes about greenhorns and local characters; and a localization and vernacularization of Jonah and the whale. Such stories, also preserved in old newspapers, almanacs, county and church histories, personal memoirs, and the like, and still current where memories of the frontier linger, are largely anecdotal.

Pioneer yarns and anecdotes began early to cluster around two types of the folk character—the hero as philosopher and the hero as man of action. The evolution of the first includes the Yankee, recognized in Royall Tyler's *The Contrast* (1787), and Seba Smith's *Jack Downing* (1834); the backwoodsman; the Irishman, the Negro, and the Jew; and the old farmer. It is an exaltation of homely wisdom and shrewdness applied to comment upon men, manners, and events. The other type, beginning with the backwoodsman, develops the epic or mythological hero. Its chief narrative medium has been the tall tale, defined as "an exuberant combination of fact with outrageous fiction."

Already shaped by oral tradition, the backwoodsman was publicly recognized in 1822 at a theater in New Orleans, when Noah Ludlow, a comedian, sang "The Hunters of Kentucky" to a pit full of flatboatmen. The "half horse, half alligator" described in the ballad at once suggested the Gamecock of the Wilderness. Davy Crockett, who best personified the type, was apotheosized in stories about him and in his own writings and speeches. "Cradled in a sap trough, clouted with a coonskin," he became "the yaller blossom of the forest . . . all brimstone but the head and ears, and that's aquafortie. . . . I'm that same David Crockett, fresh from the backwoods, half-horse, half-alligator, a little touched with the snapping turtle; can wade the Mississippi, leap the

Ohio, ride a streak of lightning, slip without a scratch down a honey locust; can whip my weight in wildcats—and if any gentleman pleases, for a ten dollar bill, he may throw in a panther,—hug a bear too close for comfort, and eat any man opposed to Jackson."

The man who thus declared himself became the "coonskin Congressman" from Tennessee, figured prominently in the politics of the Jacksonian period, led in the conquest of the West, and died in glory at the Alamo. It has been averred that the Crockett myth was deliberately fabricated in Washington for frankly partisan purposes. On the other hand, no one has identified the inventors or connected them with the almanacs published by Crockett or under his name between 1835 and 1856. In these, as in the tales that flourished in the Old Southwest and still linger in Tennessee, Texas, and the Ozark country, the Indian fighter and hunter, with his long rifle Betsy, his dogs Grim and Soundwell, and his bear Death Hug, grins coons out of trees, wrings the tails off comets, thaws and greases the frozen axis of the earth, and returns to his neighbors with a piece of sunrise in his pocket.

A contemporary and rival in fame, who appeared in Crockett's *Almanac,* was Mike Fink, King of the Mississippi Keelboatmen. Early printed tales about him dating from 1828 are close to oral tradition. Gigantic in stature and strength, the peer of Crockett as a marksman, and a whimsical roisterer, Mike lined up in his sights a deer and a pursuing Indian and killed both with one bullet, shot the scalp lock off a brave, and raised shindies at Natchy-under-the-Hill.

Similar stories began to appear in print in Porter's *Spirit of the Times,* a sporting journal published in New York between the thirties and the sixties; in numerous Southern and Western newspapers; and in books like *The Big Bear of Arkansas* (1845).

Meanwhile, new types, both comic and heroic, were emerging. From authentic folk manners and characters the theater and the minstrel show created Jim Crow and Old Dan Tucker. In the logging camps the Paul Bunyan legend, crossing over from Canada, was burgeoning. Loggers of the United States later gave Paul the Blue Ox (who was "forty-two ax handles and a plug of chewing tobacco between the eyes"), the mythical logging camp, and many of his associates. They set him up as inventor, orator, and entrepreneur. They devised a chronology and a meteorology—the Winter of the Blue Snow, the Spring that the Rain Came from China. Wisconsin raftsmen told stories about a hero of their own, Whisky Johnny, who once worked for Paul but left camp to escape a monotony of prunes, and who practiced his own version of the Crockett coonskin trick. American sailors laid the keel of Old Stormalong, "fourteen fathoms tall," deep-water sailor-man and whaler. His greatest feat was sailing the *Courser,* which was too big to turn around in the North Sea. Out of dialogue, tale, and tune was woven around the swamp squatter the cycle of "The Arkansas Traveler."

Anecdotes and tall tales arising from later economic and social conditions have polarized about new folk types and modified the older ones. Blood brother to Paul Bunyan was Pecos Bill, a creation of the cowboys. He was a "killer of the bad men . . . taught the bronco how to buck . . . staked out New Mexico and used Arizona as a calf pasture." The Southern Negroes developed the saga of John Henry, the steel-driving titan, localizing his birthplace, his *enfances,* and his exploits all the way from Cape Fear to the Mississippi Delta, and celebrating, in ballad and tale, his triumphant death in competition with the steam hammer. Texas oil workers imported Paul Bunyan to the pipe line, and American soldiers brought him to the fighting fronts of the Second World War. A twentieth century hero is Joe Magarac, the Slav steel man of the Pennsylvania mills.

Folk fancy has created now the saint, now the bad man. Parson Weems' inventions about Washington, the beautiful pioneer legend of Johnny Appleseed, some of the yarns (dashed with humor) about Lorenzo Dow and other pioneer preachers, and the elaborate myths about Lincoln gathered by Lloyd Lewis illustrate the hagiological impulse at work in the New World. The opposite impulse has found expression in tales about such ogres as the Harps of the Old Southwest, the Murrell gang, Quantrell, and the Daltons. Most of the technically bad men, however, like Jesse James, Billy the Kid, and Wild Bill Hickok, have been heroized as expressions of the innate American admiration for courage and violence. One of the recent discoveries in literary history is that the ultimate source of the humorous writings that emerged from the East and the South in the thirties was such popular oral narratives as have just been noted, especially anecdotes and tall tales. While conscious literary exploitation of this material was going on, it was being purveyed, often in more naïve form, in such periodicals as Porter's *Spirit of the Times* (1831–1861) and such books as *The Big Bear of Arkansas* (1845), T. B. Thorpe's *The Mysteries of the Backwoods* (1846), T. A. Burke's *Polly Peablossom's Wedding* (1851), and the Philadelphia firm Carey & Hart's Library of Humorous American Works.

The influence of this indigenous material upon the form and substance of twentieth century American literature has already been noted by critics and historians of our culture. Among the examples cited are Wayman Hogue's *Back Yonder,* autobiography grounded on folklore and folkways; Lloyd Lewis' *Myths After Lincoln,* showing "the primitive myth-making faculty at work among us"; and Roark Bradford's *John Henry,* "a little epic, half fantasy, stripped to the core of tragedy." H. W. Odum's *Rainbow Round My Shoulder* and Opie Read's *I Remember* show interesting variations of the folklore foundation for autobiography, imaginative in the one, factual in the other. Stephen Vincent Benét's *The Devil and Daniel Webster* and Wilbur Schramm's Windwagon Smith stories illustrate the refinement of the tall tale, and such stories as William Faulkner's "The Bear" and Marjorie Kinnan Rawlings' *South Moon Under* demonstrate the effectiveness of the hunting yarn.

## 7

Englishmen coming to America in the colonial period brought their folk plays and continued to act them for several generations. The old St. George Christmas Play was as familiar to Bostonians of the eighteenth century as it was to Thomas Hardy's Wessex peasants. A Mummers' Christmas Play and a Plough Monday Play were remembered by Kentucky mountaineers as late as 1930. The most elaborate example of folk drama in the United States is *Los Pastores,* a dramatic representation of the birth of the Savior, enacted by the inhabitants of the Lower Rio Grande, in Texas, as late as 1907. Native examples of folk drama are few and rudimentary. The best, perhaps, is *The Arkansas Traveler,* little more than a skit. A more elaborate but less definitive example is *Easter Rock,* a pagan rite "clothed in Christian symbolism," of choral and dramatic nature, traditionally practiced by Negroes in the lower Mississippi Delta.

The chief, if not the only, purely native American dramatic entertainment is the minstrel show. Its basic character was, of course, the Negro, in person or impersonated. Although the Negro had appeared on the stage as early as 1795, it was not until 1828 that the minstrel type exploiting folklore was successfully presented. Thomas D. Rice, a popular actor of the period, having observed an old and deformed Negro singing and dancing "rockin' at de heel," learned song and dance, introduced Jim Crow to a Louisville, Kentucky, audience, and entered upon a career that won for Jim Crow international fame. From this innovation, Rice proceeded, by collecting Negro melodies and weaving them into medleys, to develop "Ethiopian Opera." These "operas" were the elaborate precursors of the sketches which became characteristic of the minstrel shows established during the forties. *Bone Squash: A Comic Opera,* by Rice and Charles White, is a good example.

The first public presentation of the minstrel show as such is thought to have taken place at the Bowery Amphitheater in New York in 1843. The priority of companies rests between Christy's Minstrels and the Virginia Minstrels. Other early companies were the Kentucky Minstrels, the Ring and Parker Minstrels, and the Congo Melodists. These stereotyped the minstrel-show form. The heyday of the minstrel show was the period 1850–1870. It has been estimated that in the eighties thirty companies carried this form of dramatic entertainment by wagon, stagecoach, steamboat, and railroad train to practically every center of population in the United States. Until the movie developed, it remained the most popular form of indoor public entertainment.

Though indisputably originating from Negro folksong and folkways, often incorporating genuine Negro songs, the minstrel show cannot, of course, be regarded as pure folklore. Yet it continued to utilize many of the folklore types—dance, song, spiritual, folktale, tall tale, proverb, riddle, jest. It "created a *genre* which cannot be regarded as a folk-song, although it has the folk-song feeling, nor as an art-song, nor yet merely as popular ballad." Its reflex effects upon folksong have been considerable. While the minstrels made their entertainments out of folksongs, the people also made folksongs out of what had originally been minstrel compositions by known individual authors. Foster's "Oh, Susannah," and Rice's "Ol' Virginny Never Tire" have histories illustrating the cycle.

During the fifty to sixty year span of its popularity (about 1870–1930), American vaudeville drew more largely upon urban folklore and folkways than did the minstrel show. Yet vaudeville bills show considerable folk stuff of racy rustic origin. For example, in the eighties the Chicago Clark Street Museum put on a black-face song-and-dance act entitled "Arkansas." As with the minstrel show, so with vaudeville—banjo music, dance, and songs were standard. In "The South Carolina Home," a rheumatic old darky interpolated banjo music and a song about " 'mancipation proclamation" into a dialogue with a plantation owner about the ol' Marster, who was suddenly revealed sitting in his privy. The "racial comics" of the eighties (Negro, Irish, German, Italian, etc.) resembled those of the minstrels. Some of the songs sung in them (e.g., "The Roving Irish Gents" and "The Lackawanna Spooners") touch upon occupations. "Drill, Ye Terriers" has gone into folklore as far south as Florida. The comedian J. W. McAndrews impersonated the old Southern darky in dress, speech, and action in a way that made Southerners nostalgic. Goss and Fox, a famous blackface team of the eighties, used plantation and camp-meeting melodies almost exclusively. In general, however, the stuff of the later variety programs was urban and sophisticated, treating such topics as politics, baseball, the Army and Navy, trades and professions, and immigrant types.

In legitimate American drama of the twentieth century, artistic use of other types of folklore than songs is so common that a few examples will suffice. In *Lightnin'* (1918), the hero tells a tall tale about driving a swarm of bees across the prairie in dead winter without losing a bee, but—"got stung twice." Percy MacKaye's *This Fine-Pretty World* (1923) presents the Kentucky mountaineer Sprattling, the "lie-swearer who follies the Oninvisible and the Onbeheerd-of" and runs afoul of the law into seventeen jail sentences. *Ile,* treating with dramatic intensity the material found in whaling folklore, and *The Emperor Jones,* utilizing motives like the beat of the tomtom, the chorus, the silver bullet, and the "boogers" of superstitious terror, illustrate Eugene O'Neill's notable practice. Jack Kirkland's dramatization of Erskine Caldwell's *Tobacco Road* exhibits an intimate knowledge of folkways and folk speech of Georgia Crackers, dedicated to the purpose of shocking and spicing a jaded popular appetite. A sharp contrast in point of view is afforded by *Porgy and Bess,* the folk opera shaped out of Dorothy and DuBose Heyward's *Porgy,* a moving and sympathetic dramatization of the life of Catfish Row in old Charleston.

More sympathetic exploitation occurs in the work of what might be called a school of folk drama. Early in the 1920's appeared Lula Vollmer's *Sunup* and *The Shame Woman,* plays about mountain folk. In similar vein were Hatcher Hughes' *Hell-Bent fer Heaven* (Pulitzer Prize play for 1923–1924) and *Ruint* (1925). While these plays were enjoying success as regular theatrical productions, a fundamental program was established at the University of North Carolina. This had a twofold aim: first, to discover the stuff of drama in the lives of primitive folk removed from urban and sophisticated centers and to shape it into simple plays; second, to take folk drama to the people. The leader was Frederick H. Koch; his instruments were his classes in folk drama and the Carolina Playmakers. The early plays dealt in the main with the North Carolina scene—the fisher folk on the Banks, the mountaineers, Piedmont tenant farmers and mill hands, moonshiners, outlaws, picturesque or romantic character types among the Negroes and the Croatans. The plays were first produced at Chapel Hill and then taken on tour to all quarters of the state and to large centers in near-by states. Since then, Koch's pupils have extended the scope of quest for material and of treatment by writing folk plays representative of life in more than half of the states and in all of the major regions of the nation. One pupil, Paul Green, who began in the Carolina Playmakers' tradition, has transcended it in plays which have won for him a national reputation. Others, as actors, playwrights, and teachers, have disseminated the idea of a people's drama throughout the nation.

8

Of the "linguistic" types of folklore current in the United States, the proverb records common human experience most pungently. It has been extensively collected from several language groups—English, German, Spanish, Yiddish, etc., but no extant collection can claim to be nationally representative. The collections we have show that most of our proverbs came from Great Britain. For example, "An apple a day . . ." is traceable to the English

> Eat an apple on going to bed
> And you'll keep the doctor from earning his bread.

Of one collection of 199 proverbs from the Northeast, 70 per cent were in use in England two hundred years ago. A few, however, are definitely American in origin, e.g., "A sitting hen never grows fat," "Don't kick a fellow when he's down," "It pays to advertise," "The bigger they are, the harder they fall," and "Paddle your own canoe." Most of the proverbs collected from the various foreign-language groups originated in the Old World.

Since the time of *Poor Richard's Almanack,* American public speakers and writers have salted their discourse with homely proverbs. Two Presidents have given currency to possible American coinages: Lincoln with his figure about swapping horses in midstream; Franklin D. Roosevelt with his allusion, in a war-bond address, to "an old saying about sticking to the plow until you have reached the end of the furrow." Mark Twain used proverbs freely in his works. The dialect humorists have cultivated the homely aphorism and invented new ones, as, for example, Josh Billings (Henry Wheeler Shaw) in his *Allminax* and "Kin" (Frank McKinney) Hubbard in *Abe Martin, Hoss Sense and Nonsense.* Some of these have become folklore. E. W. Howe's similar predilection earned for him the epithet "the modern Poor Richard." Platform humorists and columnists like Will Rogers have used the proverb as stock in trade. In Carl Sandburg's *Good Morning, America* (1928) it became art.

With a few exceptions, the minor linguistic types of folklore, great stores of which have been gathered, have only slight significance for literature. Because of its pert tone and compact form, the riddle has been well preserved in parts of the country where riddling, the oldest extant form of humor and intel- lectual exercise, is still a fireside amusement. It exists in simple forms like

> Runs over fields and woods all day,
> Under the bed at night sits not alone,
> With tongue hanging out,
> A-waiting for a bone;                    [shoe]

and

> De dia con la boca llena de carne
> y de noche con la boca al aire.          [*zapato*—shoe]

A more elaborate form frames the riddle in a story relating how a condemned man saves his neck by riddling. North Carolina mountaineers have sought to cure burns, and the Pennsylvania Germans to keep off bumblebees by the use of charms. The counting-out rhyme, characteristically traditional and rural or small-townish, sometimes shows distinctly urban traits, as in this one:

> The people who live across the way
> At nineteen-eighteen East Broadway—
> Every night they have a fight,
> And this is what they say:
>
> Icky-bicky soda cracker,
> Icky-bicky boo,
> Icky-bicky soda cracker,
> Out goes you.

One of the most delightful bits of urban folklore is the street cry, heard in Charleston, New Orleans, New York, and other of the older cities, and even in some of the new ones. A Louisiana Negro was heard chanting this cry on a Chicago street:

> Watermelons fresh and fine,
> Watermelons right off the vine.
> Come and get your nice, sweet watermelons,
> Only a dime.

## 9

This account of types of folklore in the United States has made incidental mention of various modes of transmission and diffusion. For folklore in its purest state, the individual singer, story-teller, or speaker is of course the primary medium. Often his calling gives him preeminence in this function. Before the development of the railroads the wagoner was frequently a spreader of songs and tales. So have been the peddler, the fruit-tree seller, the sewing-machine agent, the canal worker, the railroad man. But these natural and spontaneous agencies were supplemented by print and by professional entertainers. The broadside continued to be commonly printed well into the nineteenth century; it is still occasionally struck off by country presses. In the nineteenth century hundreds of songsters and almanacs that flooded the country gave currency to folksongs as well as recent hits. More important than the almanacs were newspapers. Even city editors followed the practice of the country sheets in devoting columns to old songs and stories. All this printed material worked side by side with the minstrel shows, the Negro college spiritual singers of Fisk, Hampton, and Tuskegee, and the professional singers like the Continental Vocalists and the Hutchinson Family, in making nationally popular folklore that might otherwise have been confined to one region or locality.

In the twentieth century the phonograph, the radio, and the sound movie enormously multiplied the means of diffusion, so that a story or a song like "Praise the Lord and Pass the Ammunition," inspired, it is said, by a chaplain in the Pacific during the Second World War, might overnight become, for a few weeks at least, a sort of national folk possession, and the millions of a continent might share an experience comparable to that of a Scottish Border community learning for the first time one of the old riever ballads.

Folklore in the United States is a massive, vital, and portentous heritage. At first the unreflectively possessed memory of an ancient mother and an antique land, it has begun to achieve an unselfconscious expression of the experience of a continent that has wrought deep changes in human habits, attitudes, and outlooks. In its relations with literature it has been both borrower and lender. Indeed, present-day means of communication and record are so swift and so nearly universal that they tend to sweep away the criteria of differentiation. Phonograph, radio, and sound movie now expand indefinitely the range of oral transmission. At the same time, with universally accessible print intelligible to a literate people, they diminish the need for memory. Folklore may instantly become literature, and literature may speedily travel the road to folklore. Their interaction may threaten to invalidate the "traditional" folklorist's criteria, but it will be beneficial for both. Thomas Mann makes Mai-Sachme, Joseph's wise and humane jailer, say: "There are, so far as I can see, two kinds of poetry: one springs from folk-simplicity, the other from the literary gift in essence. The second is undoubtedly the higher form. But in my view it cannot flourish cut off from the other, needing it as a plant needs soil."

# 44. HUMOR

MORE effectively even than folklore—from which it has persistently borrowed—American humor from colonial days to the present has acted as a catalytic agent for the changes in our expanding nation and its mingled peoples. It has been said that humor is born of incongruities—and of these we have always had plenty. But at every stage of our awkward and uneven growth, our humorists have spoken to our extravagances and helped us appreciate our common humanity. In their writings are often to be found the most distinctively American strains in our literature.

It is the recognition of unity amid differences, the addition of imaginative sympathy to a sense of reality, the acceptance of a common denominator in a people of innumerable origins and widespread regions that makes American humor important, not only for a student of what Whitman called "These States" but for the student of mankind.

That there are differences between American humor and that of other nations, in subjects and in technique, has been recognized at home and abroad for more than a century. As long ago as 1838, a puzzled Englishman in the *London and Westminster Review* wrote, "The curiosity of the public regarding the peculiar nature of American humor seems to have been early satisfied with the application of the all-sufficing word exaggeration." Evidently burlesque and the tall tale then seemed the principal types; then as now, exaggeration was regarded abroad as our funniest gift to literature.

But from whom did we learn to exaggerate? Lucian, a Syrian-born wit writing Greek in the second century after Christ, composed a preposterous *True History* about a trip in a Mediterranean whale, and Rabelais could have held his own on the deacon seat of any American lumber camp. And it is probable that in the past century Americans have owed as much to the Baron Munchausen as to any English drawer of the long bow. That suave and poker-faced master of lies represents the cosmopolitan sources of one brand of American fun. By 1835 twenty-four American editions of the Baron's adventures had been published—according to a title page of that date. An early New York edition includes a tour through the United States in the year

728

1803, and this transatlantic trip appeared also in the Philadelphia edition of 1832; so Munchausen was a welcome immigrant. Many of his stories have been collected (and sometimes published) by American folklorists from New England to New Mexico; others appear with changes that somewhat disguise the original narrative. The favorite, the story of the stag shot with cherry pits and later growing a cherry tree from his antlers, has at least fourteen American variants; doubtless scholars will uncover many more. What Americans have done with the Baron is to improve upon his stories by adding local settings and dialect, and by expanding short comic tales into richly humorous yarns of our oral tradition.

What has been suggested regarding "American" exaggeration could also be applied to other favorite devices or forms. The trickster is found in the Yankee hero of the nineteenth century down to the hoss-trading David Harum, but he is also a favorite with the Red Indians as Manabozho or Coyote, with the Negro as Br'er Rabbit or Jack, with the Jew as Herschel or Motke. An essay could be written on the fable from Aesop to George Ade and James Thurber. How much have we borrowed? Nobody knows. Certainly Americans are not necessarily sharp dealers because they like tricksters, or childish because they like their wisdom in fables; but in folklore and in humor they are as certainly the heirs of all the ages.

Even though there is this continuity in our humor, there is also a difference between its early and late forms. Artemus Ward and Clarence Day are of different ages. Some time between 1860 and 1875, American humorists began to draw less upon the incongruities of an expanding nation and more upon those of a heterogeneous people struggling with internal problems of adjustment. The story may therefore be roughly divided by the pivotal work of Abraham Lincoln and Mark Twain into a first phase which developed mainly out of frontier conditions as civilization moved from the Atlantic to the Pacific, carrying the memories of the Old World with it, and a second phase which gave expression to the absorption of immigrant strains, the progressive industrialization and urbanization of our society, and the increasing complexities of modern living. No single generalization can therefore describe the American brand of humor. We laughed as we grew.

2

The distinguishing characteristics of the first phase of "American" humor were already defined by the time of the appearance of the professional humorist in the second quarter of the nineteenth century. In it were combined —in a combination distinctively American—the traditional satire of the learned sophisticate with the traditional exaggeration of the folktale and hero legend. The idea that it is exclusively "Western" has been pretty well dispelled. Such types as the "crackerbox philosopher," the "Yankee," and "Gamecock of the Wilderness," and the Negro minstrel are symbols of the national character. More accurate is a broader classification into main groups and types, such as the humor of the New England crackerbox philosopher, of the frontiersman, of the Old Southwest, and of the literary comedian.

Our first coastal frontier set the patterns. Even in Massachusetts, gaiety was not entirely lacking. The anti-Puritan Thomas Morton, with his maypole at Ma-re Mount, sang his "songe" beginning, "Drinke and be merry, merry, merry boyes," and lampooned Miles Standish as "Captain Shrimp." Here we have the humor of contrast with a vengeance. There is plenty of humorous incongruity also in the Puritan diaries, especially that of Master Samuel Sewall at the opening of the eighteenth century, with his autumnal, parsimonious, and ineffectual wooing of Madam Winthrop, as well as in the comments of Mistress Sarah Kemble Knight, who in 1704 took an October junket from Boston to New Haven, jotting down in her journal the whims and perils of the way. In Virginia we find the best example of the Queen Anne wit in the person of William Byrd II, master of Westover. Byrd was an aristocrat but an easy one with interest in all classes and races. He is perfectly willing to apply his satire to his own class, as when he gives a summary of the history of his colony and of the early settlers, who were "most of them reprobates of good families." He loves folktales like the one about a North Briton who found his way out of the great swamp by the aid of a fat louse from his collar, or his stories of comical adventures with bears. Perhaps he started the traditional jests about the men of Lubberland, the poor whites of North Carolina; but they sound like folklore too.

With the Revolution came an outburst of political satires, for which the way had been prepared by such earlier works as Ebenezer Cook's *The Sot-Weed Factor,* which had much of Byrd's gusto and a command of Hudibrastic rhyme. When political issues finally broke into open war, American ridicule, sarcasm, and irony poured forth in newspapers, periodicals, broadsides, and pamphlets in every literary form known to a surprisingly literate lot of writers. More than three hundred satires in prose and verse have been studied, a third of them never reprinted. The most humorous seem to have been modeled upon ballads and popular songs, or upon *Hudibras* or periodical essays or fables. Swift, Dryden, Pope, Churchill are the inspiration from English literature, but Aristophanes, Juvenal, Horace, Claudian, and Rabelais are easily traced also; in other words, our urban wits like Benjamin Franklin and H. H. Brackenridge knew both their folk and their classics.

Similar use of folk material or manner is found in the numerous songs that parodied "Chevy Chase," "Hearts of Oak," "The Vicar of Bray"—not to mention the jovial "Yankee Doodle" in all its variants. An example of the blending of folk tradition with urban humor is "The Battle of the Kegs" by the variously gifted signer of the Declaration, Francis Hopkinson, who was also the composer of several love songs that Arne might have signed. In this case the tune used may have been "Yankee Doodle," as the opening stanza will show:

> Gallants, attend, and hear a friend
> Trill forth harmonious ditty;
> Strange things I'll tell, which late befell
> In Philadelphia city.

John Trumbull's burlesque epic, *M'Fingal,* now almost forgotten except for a Hudibrastic epigram or two, in its day evidently seemed the apex of American satire, and we are still amused to find the rough-and-tumble of colonial Connecticut resembling frontier humor of later days. As Sir Walter Scott explained to Washington Irving, the character of a nation is to be found in its plain people—the gentry are much alike everywhere. One must turn, therefore, not to such city wits as Irving and Holmes, but to the plain people of post-Revolutionary days to find humor that can be called characteristically American.

Trumbull's kinsman, Governor Jonathan Trumbull of Connecticut, is sometimes given credit for furnishing the name of the first important typefigure in American humor, the Yankee Jonathan, though Yankee Doodle of the song had suggested the comic rustic ignorance sometimes found in this type. New Englanders in the eighteenth century and thereafter enjoyed a rich local lore about greenhorns as well as about smart tricksters and assorted "originals," and the Yankee's humorous wisdom was a staple of New England's second bible, the almanac. The Yankee peddler became a familiar figure, not only in the Northeast but also in the South and the Middle West, where he gained a reputation for being not only brisk and funny but a master of sharp business methods, a vender of wooden nutmegs, pit-coal indigo, and "Yankee notions." Jonathan made his first appearance on the American stage in the middle of the second act of Tyler's *Contrast* (1787) and thereafter furnished the chief fun in a thoroughly sentimental and patriotic play.

For some years his imitators continued to play minor parts on the stage, while dialect poems filled the newspapers, often in celebration of comic Yankee love—as Lowell knew when he later wrote "The Courtin'." Actors like G. H. (Yankee) Hill recited monologues between the principal play and the farce, just as actors sang Negro songs before the days of the minstrel shows. Finally in 1825 Jonathan Ploughboy in Samuel Woodworth's *The*

*Forest Rose* showed that this Yankee type could furnish forth a principal role; and thereafter such actors as Hill, Marble, and Silsbee starred in similar parts.

Washington Irving was too busy building the comic figure of the Dutchman to contribute very much to the characterization of the Yankee for whom, as a Yorker, he used rather contemptuous satire in his *Knickerbocker History*; but Ichabod Crane shows that the amorous type was certainly within his acquaintance. Similarly Cooper was much more interested in the frontiersman of New York than in Yankees, though he shows some of them unsympathetically in *The Pioneers, Lionel Lincoln,* and *The Last of the Mohicans.* If the type did not fare well in more pretentious fiction, by 1830 it was famous in folklore, in almanacs, in newspapers, and on the stage.

Other type-characters were slower of development and never reached the stature of the Yankee and his lineal descendant, the frontiersman. The only funny fat man of the era was the Dutchman of Washington Irving, whose *Knickerbocker History,* as a burlesque, was compelled to feature the humor of exaggeration. Irving gave his own native mood of good-natured indolence to Governor Wouter Van Twiller, and later, minus the burlesque exaggeration, created a village counterpart of the type in Rip Van Winkle. The minstrel Negro was the Northern white man's conception of the happy-go-lucky "darky," who was comical in love and in retort but at the same time was a singer of sentimental nostalgia. Later the combination of humor and pathos was to be a staple of local color tales and the movies; in the case of the minstrels the ever-present burlesque blurred the pattern. Thus the basic types of American humor are discoverable well before the West was opened to settlement.

3

At this point enters the "crackerbox philosopher," introduced by Seba Smith, creator of the Jack Downing Papers, which date from 1830 in the era of Jacksonian Democracy. Descended from English immigrants of the seventeenth century, Smith was born in a log cabin in Maine and, in true Yankee fashion, left school early to work in a grocery, a brickyard, a foundry, and a little school—all this before he managed to graduate with honors at Bowdoin at the age of twenty-six. Literary historians think of him as a journalist, but folklorists remember him as the author of a ballad still widely known and sung about "Young Charlotty," the girl frozen on the way to a dance. He won from Poe the title of "worst of all wretched poets" when he composed a lively broadside ballad about Sam Patch, a folk hero from Rhode Island who in 1829 jumped 120 feet from Goat Island into the eddy below Niagara Falls and later killed himself in the attempt to leap the Genesee Falls at Rochester.

"Some things can be done as well as others," was Sam's motto, and it might well have been Jack Downing's.

The first of the Downing letters were written for the Portland *Courier*, founded by the young Bowdoin graduate as an independent journal. In Letter I, Jack comes down to Portland from his native Downingville with a load of ax handles and his mother's cheese for market, but he blunders into a session of the Maine Legislature (which first met in Portland) and reports in rustic wonder the struggle to organize a government. Fired by political ambitions, he fails to obtain a nomination for governor but resolves to try his luck at Washington where, he is informed, the Cabinet has "blown up." He finds that people carry on in Washington "like old smoker." After showing his mettle in dispersing a turbulent crowd which "marches away as whist as mice," he is commissioned a captain, and after freeing (without bloodshed) some American prisoners on the northern border, he is made a major. "I and the President" (Jackson) see their country through the threat of Nullification, though at times the major is "wamble-cropt" with fear at the idea of military action. "I'd sooner let nullification go to grass and eat mullen," he says. He attends the President on a grand tour to the North, assisting as a handshaker:

I took hold and shook for him once in a while to help him along, but at last he got so tired he had to lay down on a soft bench, covered with cloth, and shake as well as he could; and when he couldn't shake, he'd nod to 'em as they came along. And at last he got so beat out, he couldn't only wrinkle his forehead and wink. Then I kind of stood behind him, and reached my arm around under his, and shook for him for about a half an hour as tight as I could spring.

In similar fashion Artemus Ward was to interview Lincoln after his first election, and Will Rogers was to describe his visit to the White House in the Presidency of Calvin Coolidge. All three humorists show how "common" and how comically harassed the Chief Executive can be. The result is the sympathy of democratic humor.

Between 1833 and 1847 there is a gap in the genuine Downing Papers of Smith, though other journalists borrowed the hero's name. (At one time he said he knew himself only by the scar on his left arm.) Then we find the major in the reign of Polk, struggling with the problem of annexation during the Mexican War. Jack has a dream in which Polk, as captain of a ship, decides to take Europe and Asia and Africa—"don't stop for bird's-egging round among the West India Islands; we can pick them up as we come back along." Manifest Destiny was never more genially displayed.

There is folk wisdom also in the parable that Jack tells to show that peace has not really been won. When they were boys the major and Bill Johnson undertook to conquer a hornets' nest, expecting to get lots of honey. Bill smashed the nest with a club but found that it "wasn't conquered, only scattered." "Darn it all," says he, "if I hain't got no honey, I knocked their house to pieces; I've got that to comfort me."

Curiously enough, the comic New England character that ranked close to Major Downing in popularity for a score of years was the creation of a Nova Scotian judge, Thomas Chandler Haliburton. Still more curious is the fact that the creation of Sam Slick of Onion County, Connecticut, was the result of the Judge's desire to contrast Yankee industry and inventiveness with Blue-Nose indolence and indifference. Inasmuch as Haliburton's ancestors on both sides came from New England, he probably knew something about Yankee ways; but he owed quite as much to print as to observation, and he never had the sure touch of Seba Smith.

The first series of *The Clockmaker,* which appeared in 1836 (Halifax), introduces Sam as a tall, thin peddler with hollow cheeks and twinkling black eyes, riding upon a fast stepper called Old Clay. Sam boasts to a Nova Scotian squire (the author): "I guess we are the greatest nation on the face of the airth, and the most enlightened too. . . . We are a 'calculatin' people, we all cypher." Yankees are "actilly the class-leaders in knowledge among all Americans." Sam attributes his own success to that knowledge of "soft sawder and human natur" which enables him to dispose of a clock worth six dollars and a half for forty dollars. He mollifies the cross hostess at a tavern by praising and kissing her children, who have "mamma's eyes." "Any man that onderstands horses," he says, "has a pretty considerable fair knowledge of women, for they are jist alike in temper, and require the very identical same treatment. *Incourage the timid ones, be gentle and steady with the fractious, but lather the sulky ones like blazes."*

Sam's wise saws and modern instances are derived principally from the folk; he says: "Brag is a good dog, but Hold-fast is a better one"; "A nod is as good as a wink to a blind horse"; "Power has a nateral tendency to corpulency." He likes such proverbial comparisons as "deff as a shad"; he and his countrymen are "spry as a fox, supple as an eel, and cute as a weasel." He has a vivid set of figures such as, "I'll send your tongue a sarchin' after your teeth." He knows folktales such as the one about the Yankee's wooden nutmegs, and folk heroes like Sam Patch. All these features amused millions on both sides of the Atlantic; in *Portraits of the Sixties,* Justin M'Carthy said, "I can remember the days when Sam Slick was as well known in England as Sam Weller." Old Walter Savage Landor addressed verses to the "witty head of Haliburton,"

> Wherein methinks more wisdom lies
> Than in the wisest of our wise.

Like the boasters of the frontier Sam is said to have claimed, "I'm half fire, half love, and a little touch of the thunderbolt!" He has the best shooting rifle in all Virginia and declares himself to be a "free and enlightened nigger-whipping Peddlar as ever was raised, and no soft-sawder." Evidently the English were acquainted with more than one type of American humor and liked to have all varieties at once.

In his later years Haliburton had some theories regarding varieties. In the preface to an anthology which he called *Traits of American Humor* he observed that the humor of the middle states, like that of the English, is "at once manly and hearty, and, though embellished by fancy, not exaggerated"; humor of the West is like the Irish, "extravagant, reckless, rollicking, and kind hearted"; that of the Yankees is like the Scotch, "sly, cold, quaint, practical, and sarcastic."

Both Sam Slick and Major Downing owe much to the earlier tradition of the type-Yankee, but Jonathan realized his full possibilities only when Lowell embodied him in Hosea Biglow. Until 1846 the humor of the Yankees had never been recorded with any great range except in folktales which got into print, and had never engaged the talents of a first-rate writer. Then Lowell started the First Series of his *Biglow Papers* during the Mexican War and later continued his success during the Civil War in a Second Series. Like Seba Smith he was a true Yankee himself, reared in Cambridge in days when that little university village was set in farming country. In an Introduction written for the complete Papers he said of the Yankee dialect:

When I write in it, it is as in a mother tongue, and I am carried back far beyond any studies of it to long-ago noonings in my father's hay-fields, and to the talk of Sam and Job over their jug of *blackstrap* under the shadow of the ash-tree which still dapples the grass whence they have been gone so long.

This homely speech Lowell had found "fuller of metaphor and of phrases that suggest lively images than that of any other people I have seen." In his Introduction he follows this remark with a series of proverbial sayings and comparisons that have the sap of humor in many of them. As for exaggeration, thought to be typical of American humor, it seemed to him "that a great deal of what is set down as mere extravagance is more fitly to be called intensity and picturesqueness, symptoms of the imaginative faculty in full health."

For his wartime satires Lowell required more than a single Yankee. In creating Hosea Biglow, he says, "I imagined to myself such an upcountry man as I had often seen at antislavery gatherings, capable of district-school English, but always instinctively falling back into the natural stronghold of his homely dialect when heated to the point of self-forgetfulness." Parson

Wilbur was added to express "the more cautious element of the New England character and its pedantry"; he was to be "the complement rather than the antithesis of his parishioner"—there would be a humorous element in the "real identity of the two under a seeming incongruity." Birdofredum Sawin was to be the clown of the puppet-show: "I meant to embody in him that half-conscious *un*morality which I had noticed as the recoil in gross natures from a puritanism that still strove to keep in its creed the intense savor which had long gone out of its faith and life." He was to be the incarnation of "Manifest Destiny," of national recklessness as to right and wrong. In presenting these three characters, moreover, the satire was to be generalized so far as was possible.

The humor of Parson Wilbur derives from learned sources and has had few successors except in the familiar essays of capering professors. The humor of Birdofredum, the unmoral trickster and rascal, has deep origins in folklore and appears often in the Southwest. It depends for effect not only upon characterization through monologue but also upon Sawin's actions as he goes to the Mexican War, which he finds as disillusioning and uncomfortable as all our war humorists have done down to Bill Mauldin; as he loses one leg, one eye, his left arm, and four fingers on his right hand; as he fumbles with the idea of becoming a politician; and, in the Second Series, as he spends some time in a Southern jail for a crime of which he is innocent. At the end he is freed, joins the Southern cause, marries the Widder Shennon—for whose sake he would like a divorce from his Yankee wife—and settles down comfortably.

> An' here I be ez lively ez a chipmunk on a wall,
> With nothin' to feel riled about much later'n Eddam's fall.

He may, as some have thought, show moral degeneration, but after all there was not much of the moral nature to degenerate, and he has earned his place among America's most amusing rogues.

Hosea likewise shows some development of opinion and character from the radical idealism of the forties to the sad mellowness of Civil War days when his creator lost many relatives in a war which he did *not* call murder. The poet and humanist in Lowell replaced the witty zealot; like Hosea, he could say:

> I sometimes think, the furder on I go,
> Thet it gits harder to feel sure I know . . .

Men of good will who wish for unity in the nation and in the world may regret some of the sharp propaganda inevitable in wartime satire, but the fundamental sympathy for human rights is forever valid. We cannot neglect the humor which opposes those who say,

> I *don't* believe in princerple,
> But O, I *du* in interest.

So *The Biglow Papers* are the high point of Yankee humor, solidly based upon principle and folk wisdom. Lowell added to the Second Series his "The Courtin'," a poem which has nothing to do with war and everything to do with sincere though comical love; the addition was in a long tradition and it was a happy symbol.

### 4

After the Yankee, a second type-figure, that of the frontiersman, embodied American humor. The most famous exemplar, Colonel David Crockett of Tennessee, was taught to look upon the people of New England as "a selfish, cunning set of fellows, that was fed on fox ears and thistle tops," though when he visited them he changed his mind. When need arose at home, he managed to trick a "gander-shanked Yankee" into selling him ten quarts of liquor for a single coonskin which Davy deftly stole between quarts.

To find the first examples of this second type we must go back to those famous Injun-killers of New York State and Pennsylvania whose more romantic features were used by Cooper for Leatherstocking. There was, for example, Tom Quick, the Avenger of the Delaware, who cut his teeth on an arrowhead and shortly after his death made up the tally of a hundred Indians whom he had aspired to kill in vengeance for his slain father; Tom's body was dug up and sent in pieces to various villages of red men who did not know that he had died of smallpox. He was a trickster; like Daniel Boone he is said to have caught seven Indians in a cleft log which they generously agreed to help him split before putting him to torture. Tom just knocked the wedge out while Indian hands were pulling. There was also Tim Murphy of Morgan's Rangers and the York militia, who bent his gun to shoot an Indian chasing him around a boulder, and who made leggings of Indian skins. There was Nat Foster the trapper, who is said to have called himself Leatherstocking long before Cooper wrote; he referred to his killings as "taking the filling out of a blanket." When the Yorkers laughed at exploits of Colonel Crockett in the twenties and later, they had the pleasure of identifying him with sons of their own, all of whom shared the opinion of Artemus Ward that "Indians is pizen wherever found."

Long before Davy published his autobiography in 1834 or furnished material for the narrative of his tour of the North, the War of 1812 had glorified those "Hunters of Kentucky" in whose honor a popular song to the tune of "The Old Oaken Bucket" was first sung in 1822 at New Orleans, the scene of their greatest battle. "Half man and half alligator" was the subtitle of the Boston broadside version of the song, and for these dashing frontiersmen other names were devised—"the gamecock of the wilderness," "the ring-tailed roarer," "the yaller blossom of the forest." Mighty deeds as well as names were invented; after his death at the Alamo, Crockett of popular almanacs was made into the tallest myth before Paul Bunyan. The thirties saw exaggeration enthroned.

Davy's autobiography is still read with delight, not only for its comical self-portraiture and its tallness but for the gift of oral narrative and humor that he had learned from the folk. He is full of proverbs: liquor is like the Negro's rabbit, "good any way"; in making love he practices "salting the cow to catch the calf"; he escapes from Indians "like old Henry Snider going to heaven, 'mit a tam tite squeeze"; when he wins an election he remembers, "A fool for luck, and a poor man for children"; he reminds corrupt financiers that "what is got over the devil's back, is sure to be spent under his bellie"; he thinks that the denizens of a city's slums are "too mean to swab hell's kitchen." Perhaps the Scots-Irish strain in such frontiersmen as Crockett, Boone, and President Jackson explains their love for the picturesque as well as occasional supernatural fantasy. What Davy likes is "a regular sifter, cut-the-buckle, chicken-flutter set-to." He always sees pictures: "I didn't think that courage ought to be measured by the beard, for fear a goat would have the preference over a man."

The tall tales and high boasting lived on in the legend of Mike Fink and in Mark Twain's boatmen; for that matter, you can hear them from almost any Adirondack guide. Crockett's rather thin vein of romance filled a number of plays that held the boards in the memory of men now living. Hamlin Garland saw Frank Mayo play the title role in Frank Murdoch's *Davy Crockett, or, Be Sure You're Right, Then Go Ahead*. Paulding is thought to have had the Tennessean in mind when he invented Colonel Nimrod Wildfire in *The Lion of the West*. The Yankee actor, Dan Marble, won applause in *The Gamecock of the Wilderness*. Much more important, some of Davy's funny traits were fused with the humor of the Old Southwest.

## 5

This humor of the Old Southwest (Georgia, Tennessee, Missouri, and the Deep South) deserves to be called a third principal type, though it was never embodied in a single picturesque figure like that of the Yankee or the frontiersman. Americans visualized for the Yankee a figure and costume which have survived in our cartoons of Uncle Sam; for the frontiersman they saw a "gamecock" in deerskin shirt and coonskin cap. Perhaps the "cracker" of 1835 was as close to a single type as the Southwest achieved, but even for the cracker there was no single stereotype. Certainly the shiftless, pasty-faced, "dirt-eating" cracker does appear, but he is not in the majority. Major Jones, one of the most popular heroes of Southwestern humor, is represented in one volume as wearing the striped trousers and swallow-tailed coat of Uncle Sam, but so, for that matter, are certain Negro minstrels depicted on the covers of sheet music a century ago. No, the Southwest did not furnish a single picture but rather a number of individual portraits whose humor shows certain common traits.

Its writers usually found publication in local newspapers, but for a national audience they were deeply indebted to William Trotter Porter, a Vermonter who lived in New York and often visited the South. Brought up in a family that owned much land and many horses, he was a lover of sports—angling, hunting, horse racing, and even cricket. The *Spirit of the Times,* which he edited from 1831 for a quarter of a century, was a sports magazine that became the receptacle for masculine anecdotes and humorous sketches sent from every part of the country. At times he gathered these contributions into such books as *The Big Bear of Arkansas* and *A Quarter Race in Kentucky,* and most of his principal contributors brought out books of their own. The quality of their humor has already been suggested by the word "masculine"—the humor of sports and those circuit courts where Lincoln polished the great art of oral anecdote. The trickster and the practical joker are much in evidence. Most of the writers were men of varied professional experience; for example, Augustus B. Longstreet, a Georgian of Yale's class of 1813, was in turn a lawyer, a legislator, a judge, a Methodist minister, and the president of two colleges (Emory and Centenary) and of two universities (Mississippi and South Carolina).

Longstreet's *Georgia Scenes* (1835) had for its subtitle *Characters, Incidents, &c., in the First Half Century of the Republic*; in other words, his tales are of less civilized times in the back country. "They consist," he said, "of nothing more than fanciful *combinations* of *real* incidents and characters. . . . Some of the scenes are as literally true as the frailties of memory would allow them to be." The remark applies to nearly all the other writing of this type; here realism found its most entertaining expression before the Civil War, and the realistic charm of oral narrative is what keeps this kind of humor alive. The first "scene" in Longstreet's book tells of a young man who practiced all alone the frontier art of gouging while he shouted the emotions of two contestants. The most spirited of the narratives concerns a fight started by one Ransy Sniffle, a dirt-eating cracker, between two champions who bite noses, ears, and cheeks to the vast entertainment of a vividly realized crowd. Other sketches include a gander pulling, a militia drill, a fox hunt, a horse race, and a shooting match. (All these subjects are duplicated in current folklore of New York State.) Before the Civil War the Negro played small part in Southern fiction; but Longstreet does use him occasionally, with careful reproduction of dialect; he even satirizes the attitude of a lady who remarks, after seeing a Negro rider killed in a race, "I declare, had it not been for that little accident, the sport would have been delightful."

The softer side of life in back-country Georgia is found in Major Jones, the creation of William T. Thompson who had some of his early experience as a journalist with Longstreet on the Augusta *States Rights Sentinel*. (Later he handed on the leadership in Southern humor to the creator of Uncle Remus when Harris worked on a Savannah newspaper.)

*Major Jones's Courtship,* the first and best of three books about this hero, shows the folkways of kind and fun-loving people in a back country that still existed in 1843; the major himself is an amiable innocent who woos and wins, presenting himself as a Christmas gift in a large bag at his sweetheart's door. Before his marriage the best scene shows him tricked at what folklorists call a play party; with the aid of his fiancée he turns the tables on his tormenter, who falls into a tub of water. Thereafter we see the cares of a young father and the humors of domestic life. In *Major Jones's Sketches of Travel* the hero makes a tour to Washington, Baltimore, Philadelphia, New York, Boston, Lowell, Niagara Falls, and Canada, falling into such embarrassments as various generous men of feeling had endured in eighteenth century novels. The epistolary form helps build up the character of a Southern innocent at home and on his travels in such a way that a Northerner feels the humor to be not narrowly local but sympathetically American. Loyal Georgian as he was and defender of slavery, Thompson was born in Ohio of a Virginian father and an Irish mother, and, like Joel Chandler Harris, he was a lover of Goldsmith, whose *Vicar of Wakefield* he dramatized.

The best example of the genus rogue in Southwestern humor, and the most spirited before Twain and H. T. Lewis, is *Some Adventures of Captain Simon Suggs,* by a lawyer and journalist named Johnson J. Hooper, who was to be Secretary of the Provisional (Confederate) Congress. Hooper was born a Tarheel but migrated to the Gulf States when twenty and identified himself with Alabama. Leader of the "Tallapoosy Vollantares," more accurately known as the Forty Thieves, his Simon had a single principle, "It is good to be shifty in a new country." In a series of picaresque tales, remarkable for gusty dialogue and a rowdy humor that Smollett would have enjoyed, Suggs cheats his own father at cards to get a horse, and thereafter dupes everyone

whom he meets. Perhaps the most famous chapter tells how he gets religion—
and the collection—at a camp meeting where, under the inspiration of the
Reverend Bela Bugg, the crowd exhibits all the ecstasy of emotional religion,
shouting,

> I rode on the sky,
> Quite ondestified I,
> And the moon it was under my feet.

Some readers would prefer Simon's tearful trick to escape from a prison
sentence, or his adventures at a faro game. Almost as amusing is a later sketch
in which Simon does not appear, called "Taking the Census," a remarkable
piny-woods study in genre.

If Simon Suggs is the rogue par excellence, the prince of coarse practical
jokers is the hero of *Sut Lovingood's Yarns.* The author, George W. Harris,
was born in Pennsylvania, was apprenticed to a jeweler, was captain of a
river boat, worked in metals, and after the Civil War was the superintendent
of a small railroad in Tennessee, the scene of his yarns. His first full-length
sketch for the *Spirit of the Times,* in 1845, was "The Knob Dance," which
shows the gusty loving and fighting then popular in the Great Smokies.
"I'm agoin to marry Jule, I swar I am, and *sich* a cross! Think of a loco-
motive and a cotton gin! Who! Whooppee!" That is the tempo of Sut
Lovingood also, the bad boy who attended Sicily Burns' wedding, where he
jerked the handle of a basket over a bull's horns with violent and confused
results when the critter backed "agin the bee-bainch." Beside his somewhat
sadistic practical jokes and rough fighting Sut enjoys sniggering about sex, a
subject taboo in nearly all other American writings of the period. "Rare Ripe
Garden Seed," a fabliau about a first baby that arrived too soon, would be
considered too broad by almost any modern magazine editor.

Many other humorists of the Old Southwest are worth reading for a story
or two. T. B. Thorpe's "The Big Bear of Arkansas" is a masterpiece of oral
narrative, tall and imaginative, supposedly told on a Mississippi steamboat.
Henry T. Lewis, in "The Harp of a Thousand Strings," parodied a ranting
sermon in a manner which inspired imitations. Joseph G. Baldwin, whose
*Flush Times of Alabama and Mississippi* appeared in 1853, would have made
his boastful Ovid Bolus, Esq. much funnier if he had not tried to be an
essayist recapturing the faded elegance of the eighteenth century.

6

In the decade before the Civil War the most popular humorous writers
were the literary comedians, authors and lecturers whom it is convenient to

group together as a fourth general class. Some of them were as well known to the public as the heroes of comic strips or the leading radio comedians of today. Most of them conducted columns in newspapers, but all preserved the qualities of oral address. To the techniques of predecessors they added certain literary devices or brought them into greater prominence: dead-pan solemnity, meandering stream of consciousness, burlesque, anticlimax, puns, bad spelling, and skillful timing. Manner was more than matter; the grand aim was to entertain—not to record types or vanishing manners. Each writer adopted the character of an eccentric individual.

It was from the writings of Artemus Ward that President Lincoln is said to have read before presenting to his Cabinet the draft of the Emancipation Proclamation. The creator of Ward, Charles Farrar Browne, was "born in the State of Maine of parents." (Imagine the pause after the word Maine.) He learned the printer's trade and got on so fast that at twenty-three he was city editor of the Cleveland *Plain Dealer,* in which the first Ward letter was published three years before the Civil War. Four years later *Artemus Ward: His Book* was as huge a success as the lectures which brought a telegraphed message from San Francisco, "What will you take for forty nights in California?" The reply was, "Brandy and water," and Browne had plenty of that spirited beverage when he met young Sam Clemens and other local humorists in Virginia City, Nevada. It was Artemus who helped Mark Twain get a hearing in the East with his "Jumping Frog." The English enjoyed Browne so well that he sailed in June, 1866, to lecture and contribute to *Punch*; but less than a year later Fate played its cruel "goak" on him and the admiring public when he died of tuberculosis.

Browne's creation, Artemus Ward, was a Yankee crackerbox philosopher with a difference, a mixture of apparent simplicity and shrewd showmanship which suggests the great P. T. Barnum, who had opened his American Museum of curios in 1842. Artemus operated on a smaller scale, of course, with a few "Wax Statoots" and certain "Sagashus Beasts" which included "three moral Bares" and a "Kangaroo (a amoozin little Raskal)." His motto was, "Cum the moral on 'em strong." A feature of his written style was comical spelling; for him a critic was a "cricket" and Boston was the "modern Atkins." He had trouble with his verbs: "I asked her if we shouldn't glide in the messy dance. She sed we should, and we Glode."

Politically Artemus was slyly neutral, as the entertainer for the entire country needed to be: "My perlitical sentiments agree with yourn exactly. I know they do, becawz I never saw a man whoos didn't." He was, however, decidedly unsympathetic toward "Our Afrikan Brother" whom he regarded as "a orful noosance." At the opening of the war his "Interview with Lincoln" ridiculed the job hunters and advised the President to fill his Cabinet with showmen who would know how to cater to the public. During the course of the war, Artemus satirized not the South principally but the rascals at home in the North—the hypocrites who whooped about enlisting, the sixteen able-bodied citizens who bought a stage line because stage drivers were exempt, the young patriot who sold disabled cavalry horses as beef—and throughout was loyal to the core. To be sure, at the outbreak of the war, Artemus had a "narrer scape from the sonny South" after a struggle with a Secesher who "put his nose into my mouth." In May, 1865, he went to Richmond and found a remarkable amount of alleged Union sentiment:

> I met a man to-day—I am not at liberty to tell his name, but he is a old and inflooential citizen of Richmond, and sez he, "Why! we've bin fightin' agin the Old Flag! Lor' bless me, how sing'lar!" He then borrer'd five dollars of me and bust into a flood of tears.

However, Artemus was equally irreverent at Washington: "The D.C. stands for Desprit Cusses, a numerosity which abounds here, the most of whom persess a Romantic pashun for gratooitous drinks."

Any popular butt he was safe in attacking—the Shakers, the Spiritualists, the Free Lovers, the contenders for Women's Rights, the "Mormins," and even the necessary harmless college students. Of Harvard he wrote, "This celebrated institootion of learnin is pleasantly situated in the Bar-room of Parker's, in School Street, and has poopils from all over the country." Even in the best of the interviews, such as the one with Brigham Young, there is such flat "goaking" as talk about the "Scareum," though nobody else would have thought to ask so mildly upon learning of the Prophet's eighty wives, "How do you like it, as far as you hev got?" Nobody else would have repulsed an offer of Mormon marriage with the cry: "Awa, you skanderlous femaile, awa! Go & be a Nunnery!"

A thoroughly partisan literary comedian was Petroleum Vesuvius Nasby, the creation of an upstate New Yorker, David Ross Locke. The son of Abolitionist parents, he was editor of the Toledo *Blade* at the opening of the war. His Nasby is a rogue in the tradition of Suggs and Birdofredum. At home in Ohio he is a Copperhead who, when drafted, escapes to Canada and then to the South. When drafted there, he escapes again to found churches in the North until the close of war, when he manages to get the postmastership of "Confedrit X Roads" in Kentucky. Later he tries running a grogshop in New York, fails because he drinks too much, and finally retires to Kentucky.

When drafted in the North, Petroleum finds ten reasons why he should be exempt, including:

1. I'm bald-head'd, and hev bin obliged to wear a wig these 22 years.
2. I hev dandruff in wat scanty hair still hangs around my venerable temples.

One of the sharpest of these satires is dated from Saint's Rest in New Jersey and begins: "The nashen mourns! The hand uv the vile assasin hez bin raised agin the Goril—the head of the nashen, and the people's Father hez fallen beneath the hand uv a patr—vile assasin." If this seems crude, like all the rest of Nasby, we might remember that according to Charles Sumner, Lincoln had said of Nasby, "For the genius to write these things I would gladly give up my office." Lincoln just did not talk that way—the rhythm is wrong, but he certainly enjoyed Petroleum, as Grant and Lowell did. After all, he was attacking cowards and traitors and rogues in the North.

On the Southern side there was one effective literary comedian, the Bill Arp of a Georgia lawyer, Major Charles H. Smith, son of a Massachusetts father and a South Carolina mother. The tone reminds the reader of Major Jones; except for its references to "niggers" the letters are restrained, reasonable, and toward the close rather plaintive but not unmanly. The first epistle to "Abe Linkhorn" in April, 1861, asks for a little more time before obeying his proclamation—the boys in Rome, Georgia, are in a sizzling mood: "A few days ago I heard they surrounded two of our best citizens, because they was named Fort and Sumter." Bill politely asks that the President "let us know whereabouts you intend to do your fitin." At the end of the war, Arp writes to Artemus Ward to remind him, "If we ain't allowed to xpress our sentiments, we can take it out in *hatin*; and hatin runs hevy in my family, shore. I hated a man so bad onst that all the har cum off my hed, and the man drowned himself in a hog waller that nite." The whites "aint a shamed of nuthin"; as for the blacks, "Sumboddy have drawed the elfant in the lottery, and dont know what to do with him."

The last of the important literary comedians of Lincoln's era was Josh Billings. When an Englishman was preparing to bring out a British edition of Josh, he guessed that the author might be Hosea Biglow or Horace Greeley, but was solemnly assured that it was President Lincoln himself. The honor properly went to Henry Wheeler Shaw, a native of western Massachusetts, whose father and grandfather were both members of Congress. In later years young Shaw used to say, "Hamilton College has turned out a good many fine men—it turned me out." The tradition is that Shaw left because he stole the clapper of the chapel bell, but a roving disposition is the better explanation; at any rate another alumnus is right in saying, "Thus, at the age of fifteen, Josh had much more than most men acquire in a lifetime—a sense of humor and a year's schooling at Hamilton College."

Shaw was forty when he abandoned farming, steamboating, and varied wandering to settle down as an auctioneer at Poughkeepsie. In the following year he wrote his essay on the mule, beginning, "The mule is haf hoss and haf Jackass, and then kums to a full stop, natur diskovering her mistake," and ending, "I herd tell ov one who fell oph from the tow path, on the Eri kanawl, and sunk as soon as he touched bottom, but he kept rite on towing the boat tu the nex stashun, breathing thru his ears, which stuck out ov the water about 2 feet 6 inches; i didn't see this did, but an auctioneer told me ov it, and i never knew an auctioneer tu lie unless it was absolutely convenient." Generously appreciative of a rival's talent, Artemus Ward helped secure a publisher for *Josh Billings, His Sayings* in 1865, at which date Josh was already a national figure.

Not unexpectedly Shaw was a successful lecturer in the dead-pan style; in some seasons he spoke as often as eighty nights in the wandering, solemn manner so acceptable. He made a greater hit with his annual *Farmer's Allminax* for the decade following 1870 when Bret Harte and Mark Twain were the other most popular humorists. Anyone acquainted with almanacs will enjoy the burlesque upon that American perennial, but the "affurisms" are the enduring part, with their blend of folk wisdom and mellow irony:

Most people repent ov their sins bi thanking God they aint so wicked as their nabers.

There may cum a time when the Lion and the Lam will lie down together—i shall be az glad to see it as enny boddy—but i am still betting on the Lion.

Dont never trust a man at the rate ov 50 cents on a dollar—if you kant confide in him at par let him slide.

Josh knew that "yu hav tew be wise before yu kan be witty," and he went on interspersing his wisdom of middle and old age between daft little "characters" of men and such critters as "The Frequent Fly," or his receipts, riddles, advice about planting, and prophecies about "windy winds" and "liquid rains." He died in 1885 while sunning himself on a hotel veranda in California. With him passed the last great literary comedian whom Lincoln had enjoyed.

## 7

Lincoln appreciated these comedians because he was a humorist at heart himself. The wisdom that directed a people through a civil war was close kin to wit. In him and in Mark Twain our early types of humor matured and formed a tradition; for both of these men realized that, as Mark Twain said, "humor is not enough."

As they understood the era that was passing, so likewise they sensed the forces that were at work in the era that was to come. Lincoln died before he could put all of that knowledge into expression, but Mark Twain lived on and wrote. Master of the oral tradition, both Negro and white, his early

LITERARY HISTORY OF THE UNITED STATES

humor was radiant with youth. It is first as the poet of childhood's unsearched possibilities that he is to be remembered in comparing him to other humorists. When he and the era grew older and more disillusioned, it is to him again that we turn for comparison with the more ironic and sophisticated wit of a later day.

Perhaps it was the success of *Tom Sawyer,* perhaps there are deeper reasons for the vogue of humorous childhood stories in the latter years of the century. Six years before Mark Twain's classic was published, Thomas Bailey Aldrich explored the humors of childhood in an autobiographical book called *The Story of a Bad Boy* (1869). Tom Bailey, who is of about the same age as Tom Sawyer and Tarkington's Penrod, lives in the "rusty, delightful old town" of Rivermouth (Portsmouth, New Hampshire) where he and his companions engage in such pranks as burning an old stagecoach and firing off a battery of old cannon. There is an amusing club called the Rivermouth Centipedes; there are theatrical performances such as delighted Penrod; instead of the dogs so comically important to Tarkington's boys there is a pony, and instead of the companionable, funny Negroes of Twain and Tarkington there is the droll sailor Ben Watson who woos Kitty Collins, a maid descended from Irish kings. The girls of Primrose Hall play minor parts, and Tom has a short season of love for Miss Nelly, aged nineteen. "It was a great comfort to be so perfectly miserable and yet not suffer any." Except for the tragic loss of one boy at sea the tone of realistic comedy is well sustained, though the author shows a didactic preference for the sort of manly lads exhibited thirteen years earlier in *Tom Brown's Schooldays* by the Englishman Thomas Hughes—to whom Aldrich refers as the author of "one of the best books ever written for boys." Of course there is a bully, properly and comically trounced by the hero.

Stephen Crane's *Whilomville Stories* (1900) carried on the tradition of Aldrich and Twain, though in the author's somewhat dour style. To Crane, children often seemed "little blood-fanged wolves," just as their mothers were a "company of latent enemies," infatuated by affection for their offspring. He realized that "in the jungles of childhood . . . grown folk seldom penetrate," but he had insight into the psychology of boys sore beset by ridicule, humiliation, and hostility. Again there is a genial and companionable Negro servant; there is also comical gormandizing and showing-off. The harassed father, the Angel Child daughter, and the screaming mob of children with their damnable iteration were hints for the more genial Tarkington.

More in the spirit of Tom and Huck is Booth Tarkington's Penrod. When well-born Tarkington graduated from Princeton, he went to live in that mildly Bohemian New York of the nineties whose young writers looked upon Crane with awe—but not for his humor. After success as a writer of romance

Tarkington finally came home from Paris to the "tranquil, friendly life of the people," in this case the people of his home town, Indianapolis. There in the year in which the First World War broke out, he found himself as a humorist and wrote *Penrod*. From his autobiography, *The World Does Move,* we know that he regarded war itself as a "herd mania . . . one of the adolescent disorders of undeveloped mankind"; we know also that he was as suspicious as Sinclair Lewis of "the tremendous universal respect for respectability"; but in his best humorous books he accepted the world of his own youth in which, as the milkman told him, "Pretty much everybody is either a church member or at least abiding." As a consequence, in recent years owlish historians of literature have regarded him as a *farceur,* whereas he was one of the two American humorists who have seen farthest into our childish hearts.

For his three most durable studies of childhood's humors—and there are several others—Tarkington chose a boy in his eighth year as the hero of *Little Orvie*; one in his twelfth for *Penrod*—about the same age as Tom Bailey, Tom Sawyer, and Crane's Whilomville set; and a high-school adolescent, Willie Baxter, for *Seventeen.* Each age has its special trials and humors, carefully discriminated. "Look how I do! Haw Poot!" is the slogan of Orvie and his destructively buoyant peers; what makes him comically puzzling to adults is the simple fact that "not many older people transform all their impulses into action."

Penrod Schofield has reached the romantic age of adventure; he is the ardent author of "Harold Ramorez the Roadagent or Wild Life among the Rocky Mountains." He has moments of soaring reverie and can extemporize tall tales of embarrassing realism. Lovely Marjorie Jones can give his heart a squeeze, but he is so far from the Court of Love that "little gentleman" is the most abusive of epithets. His world is still so separate from that of adults that punishment and clemency are alike inexplicable.

Willie Baxter is at the age of romantic posturing, with a sense of his own picturesqueness, a fear of derision, and devastating love for Miss Pratt, "a howling belle of eighteen who talked baby-talk even at breakfast." He lives by a code that is not without dignity and decency; his griefs are real enough to answer the charge that Tarkington is incapable of humor deeper than farce.

Tarkington's three heroes are surrounded by a variety of companions individually characterized. They inhabit a world of well-to-do midlanders in the last tranquil period of American history, they are true of American children everywhere. Though they may not seem so elemental as Mark Twain's boys and certainly lack his grandly romantic setting, they are as prophetic of the adult human comedy. Like all great humorous creations they reconcile us to other men by reminding us that we are all comical—and on the whole decent—boys.

8

As Mark Twain moved from the study of a small boy to that of his world, and salted the whole Midwest with his humor, so his contemporaries like Bret Harte, Edward Eggleston, and Joel Chandler Harris exploited local customs, dialects, and other regional characteristics in story and verse. "Local color" was humorous as often as it was serious in the decades following the Civil War, and when developed in a racial idiom like that of the Negro, the Irishman, or the Jew, as well as in the idiom of a region, it provided the dominant tone of the literature of the post Civil War period.

Most successful in combining sentimental with humorous interest in the local story was Joel Chandler Harris. His *Uncle Remus: His Songs and His Sayings* (1880), was the first of eight notable volumes that gave America one of its half-dozen finest humorous characters and its best example of artistically treated folklore, "befo' de war, endurin' de war, en atterwards."

He insisted that his own stories of the "old-timey" Negro were "uncooked," that he aimed only at "honesty, sincerity, and simplicity" in their telling. A shy man himself, though fond of pranks and practical jokes, he took easily to animal tales in which the trickster element is almost always prominent. He also had, possibly from his Celtic ancestors, a fondness for myth, the supernatural, and the picturesque proverb. He liked such funny language as "How does yo' copperositee segashuate?" He had the wisdom to know that "You er what you is, en you can't be no is-er." Once again the shrewd American views life, this time through the eyes of a benevolent, aged Negro who instructs the world in such humorous tales as "The Story of the Deluge." For Harris as for Mark Twain, humor was not enough; but unlike Twain he did not despair of the "damned human race." He went on sanely in the Remus tales, and in such other books as *The Chronicles of Aunt Minervy Ann,* always instructing through laughter.

The first Negro American to learn the literary lessons of Harris was Paul Lawrence Dunbar, who was equally skillful in dialect, having studied it in the white Hoosier poetry of James Whitcomb Riley, an Indianapolis journalist whose *The Old Swimmin'-Hole and 'Leven More Poems* came out three years after the first Remus book. Five years after Riley's poems had taken the nation's favor, Dunbar was born at Dayton, Ohio, the son of former slaves. After graduating from high school he sold his own first volume to passengers on an elevator which he operated for four dollars a week. Two years later, in 1895, his second book of verse, *Majors and Minors,* was reviewed by Howells, who appreciated the value of humorous folkways found in such poems as "The Party." When *Lyrics of Lowly Life* came out in the following year, Dunbar's poetry took first place in Negro literature. Like James Weldon Johnson of later fame, he realized that humor and pathos are the "two stops" of dialect; but instead of leaving those stops undrawn, as Johnson and Countee Cullen did, he mingled their sweetness in verses about children (white and black), love making, frolics, and religion. If he occasionally permitted himself such tragic notes as "We Wear the Mask," he was usually content to be the sympathetic humorist of the folk.

In the third and fourth decades of the twentieth century, three young Negro poets showed that laughter was still not drowned in tears or wrath. Countee Cullen's *Color* includes such sharp epigrams as "To a Pessimist," "For a Mouthy Woman," and "For a Lady I Know." As he said of Dunbar,

> Born of the sorrowful of heart,
> Mirth was a crown upon his head.

While Cullen avoided dialect, Langston Hughes used it for poems often in traditional folk form, such as his "Po' Boy Blues." As folklorists have observed, the mood of the blues is a curious mingling of humor with self-pity. In *Southern Road*, Professor Sterling A. Brown of Howard University tried further experiments with the blues and other folk rhythms; he also started a series of humorous poems about the adventures of Slim Greer, a wandering Negro whose odyssey is full of tall tales and sly satire. In verse Brown proved himself the most accomplished Negro humorist since Dunbar, partly because of his sympathetic vision and wide range.

In prose depicting the humor of Negro life the outstanding writer of her race is Zora Neale Hurston, an anthropologist as well as a creative writer. Her *Mules and Men* (1935) was called by Alan Lomax "the finest single book in American folklore"; one of her novels, *Jonah's Gourd Vine,* is equally full-blooded in humor. When she describes the life of colored people in Florida, she never loses humanity and zest in the quest of science.

If the Negro has given unique turns to American humor, others not of the old English stock have also made their mark. "The last one over" has always been cause for mirth, like the new boy in any school. Before the Civil War the Irishman was already a comic figure on the stage, and after the great immigration of the "famine forties" books of humorous Irish songs were popular. The first really great Irish figure, however, did not appear until Finley Peter Dunne triumphed in the late nineties with Mr. Dooley, the most popular literary comedian and crackerbox philosopher between Artemus

Ward and Will Rogers. Born of Irish Catholic parents in Chicago, Dunne started newspaper work at the age of sixteen, was a city editor at twenty-one, thereafter was one of the first baseball reporters, and by 1898 had held good positions on every Chicago paper except one. From two of his colleagues, Eugene Field and George Ade, he may have learned tricks of journalistic humor, but from the time when he started to write Irish pieces for the *Sunday Post,* he broke ground for himself.

For his early articles he created the character of McNeery, suggested by a saloon-keeper named McGarry; but when McGarry objected to the rather obvious identification, the name was changed to Dooley and the saloon was moved to "Archey Road." To ask Dooley questions and to represent the prejudices of an ignorant day laborer, the character of Hennessey was added. In 1898 a volume of sketches in which the two cronies had appeared was published with the title of *Mr. Dooley in Peace and in War*; in the next year this was followed by *Mr. Dooley in the Hearts of His Countrymen,* with a dedication to the English publishers who had pirated the first book. Other books appeared annually through 1902, and the five volumes represent the best of their author's writing, though he continued to publish for a long time. In all, Dunne wrote more than seven hundred dialect essays, about a third of which were republished in eight books.

Though some of the early essays contained a considerable amount of Irish sentiment and pathos, those remembered now are nearly all political commentaries by a "scourge of princes" who satirized affectation and corruption at home, toadying and imperialism abroad. Most of our crackerbox philosophers have been famous for common sense; when his own prejudices were not involved, as in the case of Woodrow Wilson, Dunne wrote from the uncommon sense which derives from intelligent and humane principle. Before the *Maine* disaster Dooley tells Hennessey: "Ye cud niver be a rale pathrite. Ye have no stock ticker in ye'er house." After Dewey's victory at Manila, the Irish sage announces that the Admiral is a member of his own family and prophesies that he will be king of the Philippine Islands, "Dooley th' Wanst." Dunne paraphrases Lodge's slogans as "Hands acrost th' sea an' into somewan's pocket" and "Take up th' white man's burden an' hand it to th' coons."

The most amusing of the early sketches is a review of Theodore "Rosenfelt's" account of exploits of the Rough Riders: "'Tis th' Biography iv a Hero be Wan who Knows! . . . But if I was him I'd call th' book 'Alone in Cubia.'" Great politician that he was, Roosevelt thereupon invited Dunne to pay him a visit. It is said that President McKinley used to have Dooley's remarks read at weekly meetings of his Cabinet, evidently forgiving such barbs as occur in an account of the President's visit to Chicago: "Th' proceedin's was opened with a prayer that Providence might remain undher th' protection iv th' administhration."

At the time of the Boxer insurrection in China imperialism was castigated again and again. To Hennessey's smug observation that the "Chinnymen" would be civilized by the war, Dooley replies: " 'Twill civilize thim stiff. An' it may not be a bad thing f'r th' rest iv th' wurruld. Perhaps contack with th' Chinee may civilize th' Germans." If Americans consider themselves anti-imperialists, we may owe more to Dooley in this regard than to the rage of Mark Twain and the noble indignation of William Vaughn Moody.

Comments on domestic problems were equally frank and pungent, particularly at the time of the anthracite coal strike in 1902 when a winter without fuel threatened. "The rich can burn with indignation, thinkin' iv th' wrongs inflicted on capital, th' middle or middlin' class will be marchin' with th' milishy, an' th' poor can fight among thimsilves an' burn th' babies." When Hennessey asked Dooley what he thought of a man in Pennsylvania who said that the Lord and he were partners in a coal mine, Dooley asked, "Has he divided th' profits?" When the twentieth century's perennial suggestion for a "business administration" was first heard, Dooley agreed ironically: "We must injuce th' active, conscientious young usurers fr'm Wall Street to take an inthrest in public affairs." When Hennessey defended high tariffs on the ground that the foreigner paid the tax anyhow, Dooley said, "He does, if he ain't turned back at Castle Garden." He described the elder Rockefeller as "a kind iv a society f'r th' prevention iv crolty to money. If he finds a man misusing his money he takes it away fr'm him an' adopts it." In the era of muckrakers he deplored the American method of cleaning a house by burning it down, "but I want to say to thim neighbors iv ours, who're peekin' in an' makin' remarks about th' amount iv rubbish, that over in our part iv th' wurruld we don't sweep things undher th' sofa."

Of the other national strains that have had interpreters in humorous dialect, none has produced a philosopher of the stature of Uncle Remus and Mr. Dooley; but the Jews have fared well in sympathetic characterization. Before the twentieth century they were usually presented as tricksters and money grabbers; but a devoted schoolteacher in New York, Myra Kelly, showed them and children of other immigrants in more amiable light when, at the opening of the century, she wrote her *Little Aliens* and *Little Citizens*. Adults have always enjoyed the books for their dialect and for the humorous contrasts in civilizations. In 1910 Montague Glass, an English-born Jew who knew intimately the cloak-and-suit trade of New York, began a series of books about Potash and Perlmutter and other businessmen who were both as sharp and as kind as David Harum, the Yankee Yorker. These stories reached both the popular magazines and the stage. In 1937 the *New*

*Yorker* published a series of sketches later collected in a book called *The Education of Hyman Kaplan*. The author, Leonard Q. Ross (Leo C. Rosten), took for his hero a puzzled, genial, and patriotic member of an "American Night Preparatory School for Adults." Part of the fun derives from Kaplan's struggle with the English language, but more of it is due to the creation of an enthusiast who is a real person. As the author says, there was "something sacrilegious in trying to impose the iron mold of English on so unfettered an intelligence." He is perhaps the most amusing immigrant in our literature and one of the most amiable.

Funny German dialect appeared in the Hans Breitmann ballads of Charles Godfrey Leland, a Philadelphian who studied at Heidelberg and Munich. "Hans Breitmann's Barty" started the series in a magazine in 1857, and a collection was made for a volume as late as 1914. In the 1930's the radio comedian Jack Pearl popularized again the Baron Munchausen in a program not entirely limited to tall tales. As for the Italians, T. A. Daly of Philadelphia wrote sympathetically humorous verses in their immigrant dialect from the year 1906, when his *Canzoni* was published; in prose the important book is *Mount Allegro* (1943) by Jerre Mangione, who writes about the gusty folkways of Sicilians in Rochester, New York.

Meanwhile humorous figures bearing English names have found places in the American gallery. In what has been called the "B'Gosh School," a favorite is David Harum, hero of the single novel published at the turn of the century by Edward Noyes Westcott. Member of a prominent family in Syracuse, New York, the author began his book after tuberculosis had compelled him to leave the world of finance. Though a friend has declared that David is a composite portrait, his character is undoubtedly based upon that of David Hannum, a small-town banker and horse trader in Homer, New York. Certainly he is as true to the type of central New York Yankee as Irving Bacheller's Eben Holden is to the North Country hired man of the same era. Part of the time David is a crackerbox philosopher whose sayings have become proverbial: "Do unto the other feller the way he'd like to do unto you, an' do it fust." "A leetle too big's about the right size." "A reasonable amount o' fleas is good fer a dog—keeps him from broodin' over *bein'* a dog, mebbe." Part of the time he is a trickster, but secretly he is a generous man of feeling.

A Southern counterpart of Harum in the twentieth century will be found in *Back Home* (1912) and Irvin S. Cobb's other tales about a Confederate veteran, Judge Priest. Cobb himself, the sage of Paducah, was a "character," and his funny face was as welcome in a movie role as at a banqueting board. Such rambling essays as *Speaking of Operations* are proofs that Cobb was one of those numerous "columnists" of his generation who always knew what would make his countrymen laugh. So did Frank McKinney ("Kin") Hubbard of Indiana, whose "Abe Martin" ran in syndicated columns and collected volumes for almost forty years before 1930. Abe was a crackerbox philosopher who reached out from Hoosier land to almost all the country.

Of course the philosopher who has held highest place since Dooley is Will Rogers of Oklahoma, inheritor of Cherokee Indian blood and proud of it. He was born bowlegged, "so I could set on a horse," and knew that life of the range which was popularized at the end of the nineteenth century by *Wolfville* (1897) and other tales of Alfred Henry Lewis, as well as by John A. Lomax's great collection of cowboy ballads in 1910. After touring the world in Boer War days as a rider and rope thrower, Rogers progressed through vaudeville to the Ziegfeld Follies. Thereafter he played in silent movies, then in the "talkies," in which he was starred as the Connecticut Yankee and David Harum. From 1919 he published a number of books, including *Letters of a Self-Made Diplomat to His President.* His syndicated newspaper column was said to reach 40,000,000 readers; his talks certainly were heard by everyone who owned a radio.

Will's mottoes were, "We are all ignorant, but not about the same things," "All I know is what I read in the papers," and "I'm always agin the party that is up." As he said, "There is no credit in being a comedian, when you have the whole government working for you. All you have to do is report the facts." He insisted that there were 120,000,000 in the American kindergarten, and he addressed these infants in a slow, friendly drawl that usually carried over into his books and columns. The irreverence of the Southwest sometimes shocked the well bred, as when he referred to the Supreme Court as "nine old men in kimonos" or when he wrote for a popular magazine a burlesque account of his visit to President Coolidge. The older comedians all lived again in him; he reminded the American people that "there is a big country west of the Hudson River."

9

By the turn of the century, American humor was no longer a reflection of a nation in the making. It had gained a sophistication, an urbanity, of native origin. It was wit, not humor. One thing that had happened west of the Hudson and elsewhere in America after the Civil War was the shift of population to the cities, with a consequent change in our humor. As early as 1879 humor of the suburbs appeared very successfully in *Rudder Grange* by Frank R. Stockton, who was born in Philadelphia and spent most of his writing life in suburbs of New York. His most popular story was suggested by the sight of a family living on a ruddered canal boat in the Harlem River;

its most entertaining character, Pomona, was patterned after an orphan maid who had worked for the Stocktons. Pomona is incurably romantic before her husband takes her on her honeymoon to a lunatic asylum where she meets people whose imagination has carried them a little further than she is willing to go. The competent hero and his wife Euphemia are the sort of pleasant young married people whom Howells was using for his "parlor farces" and are not unlike those whom Christopher Morley was to make so agreeable in all his early works. The style is as well bred and felicitous, though not so original, as Morley's; and like Morley the earlier author is able to mix fancy with realism. At least once again Stockton got his mixture right in the following decade, when he wrote *The Casting Away of Mrs. Lecks and Mrs. Aleshine.*

Much of the urban humor of the late nineteenth century appeared in three weeklies: *Puck* (1877–1918), of which Henry Cuyler Bunner was editor from its second year until his death in 1896; *Judge* (1881–1939), founded by seceders from *Puck*; and the older of two magazines called *Life* (1883–1936), started by two young Harvard wits, J. A. Mitchell and E. S. Martin. Bunner composed familiar verse and parodies which included a clever set on "Home, Sweet Home"; he also wrote stories collected in *Short Sixes* and other volumes.

Oliver Wendell Holmes and John G. Saxe had written admirable light verse in the mid-century, but Bunner, John Kendrick Bangs, and a host of others made *vers de société* even more popular in the nineties. This form of urban humor continued and had a greatly increased vogue again in the 1920's, when its irony and frequent tone of comic depression complemented the angry disillusion of the novelists. Any collection of such verse might well include all of the following books and more: Guy Wetmore Carryl's *Fables for the Frivolous* (1898); Franklin P. Adams' *Tobogganing on Parnassus* (1911); Arthur Guiterman's *The Laughing Muse* (1915); *A Few Figs from Thistles* (1920), by Edna St. Vincent Millay in the flippant mood of Greenwich Village; Samuel A. Hoffenstein's *Poems in Praise of Practically Nothing* (1928); Dorothy Parker's *Not So Deep as a Well* (1936), collected from three earlier volumes; Christopher Morley's *Poems* (1931), including some of the best sayings of the character called the Old Mandarin; Morris Bishop's *Spilt Milk* (1943); and Ogden Nash's *The Face Is Familiar* (1940), selected from earlier volumes. Practically all these writers are Horatian in some degree; all have gaiety, irony, and a command of technique that ranges from Guiterman's flashing triple rhymes to Nash's deliberately bad and funny ones. All have the tang of New York.

In prose certain individuals have stood out for some special theme or themes which the twentieth century found funny. George Ade's *Fables in*

*Slang* (1899) vied in popularity with Mr. Dooley. To be sure, Ade's had been preceded by many comical or satirical fables from the day of Franklin and had to compete in 1899 with the mordant *Fantastic Fables* of Ambrose Bierce, whose *The Devil's Dictionary* (1881–1906) is an American masterpiece of cynical wit. (We still remember that "positive" means "mistaken at the top of one's voice.") But it was the slang that gave Ade preeminence, as it did O. Henry's stories a little later, a slang that gave America a common speech in those days before the radio.

Don Marquis caught the dafter features of the twenties. His *The Old Soak,* from which a popular play was made, is the comic monument to the Prohibition Era. In the persons of a cockroach and an alley cat his *archy and mehitabel* satirizes the frustrations of the little man and the gay sexual amorality of the "liberated" woman. Almost as funny are his *Hermione and Her Little Group of Serious Thinkers,* his *Sonnets to a Red-Haired Lady,* and the book of verse entitled *Noah an' Jonah an' Cap'n John Smith.*

The gold-digging "babes" of the same period are exploited in Anita Loos' *Gentlemen Prefer Blondes* (1925) and its sequel, *But Gentlemen Marry Brunettes.* The illiteracy of these ladies is matched by that of the baseball players in Ring Lardner's *You Know Me Al* (1916) and by that of various other conceited and inarticulate people who are castigated in other volumes of the same author down to the time of his death in 1933. No other American humorist except Bierce, Mark Twain in his last years, and H. L. Mencken in his Booboisie period has shown such contempt for those whom he satirized; few have equaled Lardner's savage mimicry and the slang which was nicknamed "Lardner's Ringlish." The more genial tone returned with the work of another sports writer, Damon Runyon, whose *Guys and Dolls* in 1932 was the first of several volumes which told in illiterate, imaginative slang about the adventures of gamblers and other sporting characters of the big city.

A New Yorker from a very different social stratum was Clarence Day, educated at St. Paul's and Yale, a writer who began the fashion of accounts of ebullient parents, told from the point of view of their offspring. As early as 1920 he had published *This Simian World,* in which the types of mankind were broken down into their animal resemblances and the irony completed without pointing a moral. In the same decade he began to publish his famous studies of a financier and his family that afterwards became known as *Life with Father* in the most successful play of the turn of the forties. *God and My Father* and *Life with Father* were published in book form in 1932 and 1935. His unformed but mordant drawings in illustration of his text set a style which James Thurber developed toward fantasy.

Day, who began his career in *Harper's Magazine* and the *Literary Review* of the New York *Evening Post,* became one of the valued contributors to the

*New Yorker,* founded in 1925 by Harold Ross, who gathered the most notable group of urbane writers since the early years of the *Atlantic Monthly* and the Saturday Club. Of them, Ring Lardner was the most influential in setting the sophisticated tone with undernotes of an irony which was often savage. These writers included E. B. White, Alexander Woollcott, Robert Benchley, Dorothy Parker, James Thurber, and many others who could properly be called the New York Wits. Their urbane knowingness was often accompanied by an almost naïve wonder at their mad and beautiful city. The style of all was deliberately easy and conversational. As writer and actor for the screen, Benchley specialized in the sort of nonsense which only literates achieve; *My Ten Years in a Quandary, and How They Grew* is a typical example of his titles. Woollcott's wit, arrogance, sentiment, and wonderful command of an audience made him the First Gentleman of the Radio; even the best of his books, *While Rome Burns* (1934), and the book of his letters would give an imperfect idea of his flashing personality if he had not found the perfect biographer in Samuel Hopkins Adams. Mrs. Parker, in the humorous verse already mentioned, specialized in the comically woeful war of the sexes; in such prose sketches as *Laments for the Living* (1930) and *After Such Pleasures* (1933) there is still plenty of mordant wit but also such penetration into the grief of being woman that she is obviously a good deal more than a pert humorist.

E. B. White, who was a chief contributor to the *New Yorker* at the beginning, and again much later to its editorial section called "The Talk of the Town," was known for his *One Man's Meat* (1942), a collection of essays published elsewhere, but indicative of the best qualities of his anonymous editorial writing. Here was an ironic mind holding up the mirror of Nature and her simplicities, which he loved, to the noisy, thoughtless life of the metropolis, where the rush for publicity and profits had warped the desirable values of living. He was, indeed, a sophisticated Thoreau come to preach Concord to the town, and by many of his contemporaries he was regarded as the best essayist, the best writer of prose of this kind in a time when the personal essay as a literary form had almost disappeared. It is noteworthy that from the beginning, but particularly in the heavy years of the Second World War, his unsigned leaders in the editorial section, light in style but deeply incisive and with powerful emotional undercurrents, performed the same function as the commentators who had overshadowed the editorial writers of the newspapers. His comments were unsigned, but his style made them personal. Many were republished in *The Wild Flag* (1946).

James Thurber brought to the *New Yorker* another strain of American writing, but transformed almost out of recognition. A Puckish genius, his skits and stories depended upon burlesque and exaggeration for their impact;

but, as with Mark Twain, a whimsical realism (in his case often fantasy) sheathing a deadly satire, gave them quality. He was as much in love with contemporary life as Mark Twain was with the Mississippi Valley; but where Mark's rancor against human inconsistency finally broke into tragic despair Thurber was content if all would see, either in word or in picture, that his world was more mad than bad. He is best represented in *The Thurber Carnival,* a cumulative collection made in 1945, and in his later work, *The White Deer* (1945).

The wits and essayists mentioned in the paragraphs above evidently belong in that marginal area which can be called either journalism or literature, or both. Yet in many instances, as, for example, the light verse of F. P. A., the ironic and affectionate character sketches of Don Marquis, the subtle period studies of Clarence Day, or the essays and skits of E. B. White and James Thurber, the end result is clearly a literature of sophisticated humor. Not news of events, which is the staple of journalism, but news of life prepared for the discriminating reader, and addressed to his imagination, defines this literary journalism, especially in its creative period in the early 1920's.

So our national humor, which began with university wits, has strength- ened itself on folklore and various emerging types, often crude but nearly always sympathetic and kind and wise, until it has returned to the wits of the city. On the way it has joined arms with the Yankee, the frontiersman, the Southwesterner, the children, the Negroes, the Irish, the Jews, the Italians, and such genial folk heroes as David Harum, Judge Priest, and Will Rogers. It has taken innumerable literary forms, from the fable and the anecdote and the tall tale and the trickster story to the parlor farce, light verse of the wits, and the playful retelling of classical legend. It has recorded all our follies, especially those of politics but also Prohibition, the snares of the gold digger, and the cantrips of the underworld. It has gone deep into satire of the kind of human nature shaped in our society. It has not been afraid of dialect or slang; it has glorified them. And always it has been democratic; it has made us one.

# 45. WESTERN CHRONICLERS AND LITERARY PIONEERS

THUS in language and ethnological change, in folklore and humor, can be traced the widening horizons of culture as the United States grew from a confederation of former British colonies to a cosmopolitan and continental nation. The record of this growth is further and more explicitly manifested in the literature of the frontier itself—or rather, the two literatures, one written on the ground, the other from the point of view of the East. The present chapter picks up this story where an earlier chapter on "Reports and Chronicles" (Chapter 3) left it, and describes a representative selection of some two dozen books written by explorers and travelers in the frontier West, or by literary pioneers who made the earliest efforts at artistic use of Western materials. Because these books are important primarily for the experiences they record, they group themselves naturally according to the phases of the westward movement: the Franco-British struggle for empire; the American agricultural advance into the trans-Allegheny; early exploration of the Louisiana Purchase; American contact with New Spain in the Southwest; the great lunge across the Plains and over the Rocky Mountains to Oregon and California; and the integration of the West with the nation in the period following the California Gold Rush.

2

The chronicle literature dealing with the Mississippi Valley during the first six decades of the eighteenth century reflects the dramatic contest between France and Britain for control of North America. The French point of view is well represented by a young Parisian Jesuit named Pierre François Xavier de Charlevoix who, sent out in 1720 on a tour of inspection by Louis XV, traveled from Quebec to New Orleans along the well established highways of Bourbon imperialism. In the course of time he pieced out his own notes with descriptions of the flora, fauna, and native inhabitants drawn from such sources as the Jesuit Relations. The resulting *Journal of a Voyage to North America,* published in Paris in 1744 as part of an ambitious *History of New France,* shows a clear intelligence and a gift for style. Charlevoix's comments on the Indians are almost devoid of religious dogmatism and are even tinged with a respect for natural man that hints at the coming Enlightenment. In the French-Canadian colonists he discerned many traits that came to characterize the English settler in the New World: love of danger and hardship, and of a wandering life; an "excellent genius for mechanics"; an impatience of discipline even in war, combined with a general capacity for "managing the greatest affairs." Yet, like the British administrators whom Burke criticized on the eve of the Revolution, Charlevoix failed to read the lesson offered by the character of the colonists, and proposed to direct the settlement of the Mississippi Valley through a centralized administration in Paris. He could not foresee that the advance of European settlers into the great wilderness would shatter all efforts at control from a remote metropolis.

Although of course he did not know it, Charlevoix was writing the end of a chapter in the history of the West. The future of North America belonged to the British. Twenty years after the urbane Jesuit floated down the Mississippi an advance guard of fur traders from South Carolina was firmly established on the eastern bank of the river. Among these was James Adair, a younger son of a Scotch-Irish baronet who left a unique record of the southern Mississippi Valley before the Revolution in a book published in London under the title *The History of the American Indians, Particularly Those Nations Adjoining to the Mississippi, East and West Florida, Georgia, South and North Carolina, and Virginia* (1775).

Although Adair wastes a regrettable amount of energy in trying to prove that the American Indians are descended from the Jews, his discussions of Indian ritual, government, oratory, and modes of warfare are still valuable sources of ethnological data. He took an aristocratic delight in wilderness life, fighting and all, and had a backwoodsman's contempt for city-dwelling officials. Into the mouths of the Indians he puts a scathing satire of the "young, lazy, deformed white men, with big bellies," idling their time away in Charleston. With its love of the forest, its stern warrior's ethics, and its rejection of the norm of "civilization," Adair's *History* is the first important book written from the point of view of the American frontier.

Jonathan Carver's journey westward to present Minnesota in 1766–1768 was made during the brief interval between the destruction of French power in America and the outbreak of the Revolution. Carver was a subordinate of the famous, or notorious, Robert Rogers, sometime commandant of Detroit, whom Kenneth Roberts has celebrated in *Northwest Passage*. But the *Three Years Travels through the Interior Parts of North-America* (London, 1778), which went into more than thirty editions, made Carver better known than his superior officer.

The New England traveler viewed the trans-Mississippi in a grandiose mood. Proclaiming that the seat of Empire moves toward the West, he predicted that stately palaces and solemn temples would one day adorn the wilderness where at that time only the savage's hut gave evidence of the handiwork of man. But the most noted part of his book is his long essay "Of the Origin, Manners, Customs, Religion, and Language of the Indians," a compendium of information, much of it secondhand, that gained for the *Travels* a greater international reputation than any other book of American authorship in the eighteenth century. Chateaubriand drew upon it for his *Voyage en Amérique,* and a German translation of 1780 furnished the source for Schiller's famous "Nadowessiers Totenlied."

### 3

With the settlement of Kentucky, a new phase begins in the history of the West. Charlevoix, Adair, and Carver had been primarily representatives of European empires, but the American Revolution divorced the problem of the American frontier from Europe. The two most important books dealing with the post-Revolutionary West, John Filson's *The Discovery, Settlement and Present State of Kentucke* (1784) and Gilbert Imlay's *Topographical Description of the Western Territory of North America* (1792), suggest how the Mississippi Valley was to be occupied during the next hundred years. The Daniel Boone of Filson's account already bears much of the significance with which the folk mind was to invest him during the next half-century: he is a Long Hunter, a woodsman, an Indian fighter who can beat his enemies at their own game. It is significant that the illiterate hero cannot write his own story, but must dictate his reminiscences to a schoolmaster who clothes them in stilted language. The "cutting edge" of the frontier has all but lost contact with the cultural tradition of Western Europe.

Gilbert Imlay, probably a native of New Jersey, served in the American forces during the Revolution. In 1784 he appeared in Kentucky as a land speculator and surveyor; he may have dabbled in intrigues with the Spanish. After a couple of years he left America for London. Here his *Topographical Description* appeared in 1792, and a novel laid in part in Kentucky, *The Emigrants,* in 1793. In that year he was in Paris, where he formed a temporary liaison with Mary Wollstonecraft. His subsequent career is obscure: he seems to have lived in Europe until his death in 1828.

Imlay's description of Kentucky is permeated by ideas of the Godwinian Enlightenment. In a state of exalted sensibility, he finds the beauty of nature bound up with political ideas:

Everything here gives delight; and, in that mild effulgence which beams around us, we feel a glow of gratitude for that elevation our all-bountiful Creator has bestowed upon us. Far from being disgusted with man for his turpitude or depravity, we feel that dignity nature bestowed upon us at the creation; but which has been contaminated by the base alloy of meanness, the concomitant of European education.

Passing over the tedious details of settlement, Imlay takes it for granted that within a hundred years the entire continent will be peopled by republicans and governed according to the highest dictates of reason. The ingredients of Manifest Destiny are already present.

But the occupation of the trans-Allegheny was not carried through by rhetoric alone. The often repeated phases through which the frontier passed as it moved steadily westward have been described by Frederick Jackson Turner: first the fur trader and Indian fighter; then the hunter-farmer who clears a small patch of the forest, puts in a crop or two, and moves on when the country begins to fill up; then the more substantial farmer who buys out the preemption rights and "improvements" of the first settler; and finally the "men of capital and enterprise," the first market towns, banks, a rudimentary industry, and so on.

Of the characteristic figures shaped by the successive stages of the frontier, only the fur trapper and Indian fighter seemed heroic and glamorous. As a result, pioneering experience in the trans-Allegheny has left its mark upon imaginative literature almost exclusively in fictional versions of the character of Daniel Boone. The most famous of these is of course Cooper's Leather-stocking, but even here the imaginative synthesis is incomplete: Leather-stocking is half Noble Savage and Forest Philosopher, half illiterate back-woodsman inferior in social status to the "straight" heroes and heroines of the novels. Writers in the Ohio Valley who tried to use frontier materials in literature were unable to improve on Cooper's formula. The *Legends of the West* (1832) of James Hall, a Philadelphia lawyer who settled in Cincinnati, were intended to celebrate "the gallant men who . . . conquered for us the country of which we are so proud." But although Hall occasionally makes valuable notes on what he saw around him—trappers from the Missouri, missionaries boating down the Ohio, camp meetings, border crime—his backwoodsman is as stilted and unreal as his genteel characters. The other early novelist of the Mississippi Valley, Timothy Flint, who came out in 1816 from Massachusetts as a missionary, was more ambitious than Hall but even less successful. With a valid perception of the literary opportunity offered by the early West, but with a notable lack of imaginative power, he wrote long, tedious, and now justly forgotten novels dealing with fur trapping in Oregon, the maritime trade of the Pacific Northwest, and Mexican revolutionary intrigue against Spain in the Southwest. Flint's rambling *Recollections of the Last Ten Years* (1826), despite some rather self-conscious passages of nature description in imitation of Chateaubriand, is a much more valuable record of the early West because of its first-hand observations of life along the rivers.

Only here and there in contemporary writing do we get a glimpse of the period when a semiagricultural population began to arrive in the footsteps of the Indian fighter. The most vivid reports are those of travelers like Henry R. Schoolcraft, who, as a youngster of twenty-four, came out from upstate New York in 1818 to make a geological exploration of the Ozarks. On the headwaters of the White River he encountered the Coker family, living within three miles of the farthest white settlement.

These people [Schoolcraft noted] subsist partly by agriculture, and partly by hunting. They raise corn for bread, and for feeding their horses previous to the commencement of long journeys in the woods, but none for exportation. . . . Gardens are unknown. Corn, wild meats, chiefly bear's meat, are the staple articles of food. In manners, morals, customs, dress, contempt of labour and hospitality, the state of society is not essentially different from that which exists among the savages. Schools, religion, and learning, are alike unknown. Hunting is the principal, the most honourable, and the most profitable employment . . . a man's reputation is measured by his skill as a marksman, his agility and strength, his boldness and dexterity in killing game, and his patient endurance and contempt of the hardships of the hunter's life.

A later stage of agricultural settlement is depicted in Morris Birkbeck's *Notes on a Journey in America, from the Coast of Virginia to the Territory of Illinois* (1817) and his *Letters from Illinois* (1818). Birkbeck was an English farmer (that is, an agricultural entrepreneur leasing a large tract of land). He brought to early Illinois a determination to set up in America something equivalent to the well kept farms he had conducted in Surrey. His freedom from frontier prejudices enabled him to see the advantages of prairie lands at a time when most backwoodsmen were convinced that land too poor to grow trees was worthless for farming. For the benefit of other Englishmen who, disgusted with political reaction at home, might be induced to join him in republican America, he presented an eloquent record of his expenditures and his profits, emphasizing the fact that within a few years he expected to have clear title to a valuable property.

With the advent of settlers who regulated agriculture by cost accounting, the trans-Allegheny was ready for the boom days of town planners, real estate brokers, lawyers, and promoters of wildcat state banks. The advance of the plantation economy into the Gulf Plains is described in two collections of sketches that are famous as landmarks in the development of American humor: Augustus Baldwin Longstreet's *Georgia Scenes* (1835) and Joseph G.

Baldwin's *Flush Times in Alabama and Mississippi* (1853), both rich in the local color of lawyers' circuits, frontier brawls, "groceries" (whisky), and tall tales. A similar period in the Old Northwest is depicted with less masculine gusto but with a feminine wit and an eye for detail by the New York mistress of a young ladies' seminary, Caroline Kirkland, who went out to southern Michigan in the 1830's and lived there for several years until her husband's venture in town promotion was ended by the panic. *A New Home —Who'll Follow?* (1839) is marred by obvious efforts to impose conventional plots on Western material; but the author had a sense of humor, and her notations concerning squatters and their wives, small-town society, and the imaginative finance of Western bankers constitute an all but unique historical record.

4

The acquisition of the vast area between the Mississippi and the Rocky Mountains through the Louisiana Purchase (1803) meant that the cycle of frontier advance had to begin again with exploration of country that was still almost a blank on the maps. Even before Napoleon's unexpected decision to sell Louisiana to the United States, Jefferson had planned an expedition overland to the Pacific with his secretary and fellow Virginian Meriwether Lewis at its head, and Lewis had chosen William Clark, a boyhood companion who had gone out to Kentucky, as second in command. The party was in camp on the east bank of the Mississippi near St. Louis when Louisiana was formally transferred to the United States on March 9, 1804.

Despite the fact that Jefferson had devoted years of study to the geography of the trans-Mississippi, Lewis and Clark had no more than vague conjectures about the country they were to traverse. Besides the two officers, the party consisted of fourteen soldiers, "nine young men from Kentucky," two French-Canadian *voyageurs,* an interpreter, a hunter, and Clark's Negro slave York. Blending the French and American traditions of wilderness travel with what they could learn from the Indians, Lewis and Clark at a single bound carried the advance guard of the westward movement to the Pacific Coast.

A series of misfortunes, climaxed by the mysterious and violent death of Lewis in the Tennessee forest in 1809, delayed publication of the narrative of the journey *(History of the Expedition Under the Command of Captains Lewis and Clark to the Sources of the Missouri, Thence Across the Rocky Mountains and Down the River Columbia to the Pacific Ocean)* until 1814. The book, prepared by Nicholas Biddle of Philadelphia from the manuscript journals, is one of the great travel narratives of the world. The editor had the good sense to let the hard, compact prose of the journals stand with a minimum of tidying up. The result is a day-by-day record of things done and seen, of physical toil and hardship, of the country and the Indians, of conjecture and increased knowledge. Only from the whole does the grandeur of the accomplishment emerge: the discovery of a new world in the Far West, by a party that never numbered more than fifty men.

The Lewis and Clark expedition immediately stimulated the fur trade up the Missouri. Within five years the river had become almost a thoroughfare, and a restless young man with literary ambitions could make a trip up to the Mandan Villages in present North Dakota simply as a tourist. Henry Marie Brackenridge, son of the author of *Modern Chivalry*, had grown up in Pittsburgh and was making gestures toward the practice of law in St. Louis. The journal of his travels with one of Manuel Lisa's fur-trading brigades appeared in 1814 as an appendix to a little book called *Views of Louisiana*, and was published separately in an enlarged version in 1816. It is a charming document. Exempt from either the labor or the responsibilities of the journey, the author was free to stroll along the bank thinking of Ossian, Fénelon, Ariosto, or the Arabian Nights Entertainments. He read *Don Quixote* in Spanish with Lisa's help. He set himself literary exercises in rendering the landscape—the sky "as clear as that represented in Chinese painting," "the flowery mead, the swelling ground, the romantic hill, the bold river." Or he picked up a local tradition and composed "Lines on an Unfortunate Female Maniac, Seen on the Missouri, Beyond the White Settlements." But Brackenridge was more than a sentimental poseur. He made shrewd notes on the Indians, and at this early date he perceived the role which the West would play in restraining the sectional bitterness of North and South.

While Lewis and Clark were wintering at the mouth of the Columbia, Captain Zebulon Montgomery Pike was in northern Minnesota carrying out another part of Jefferson's plan by trying to find the source of the Mississippi. Hardly had he got back to St. Louis when General James Wilkinson ordered him out across the Plains to the headwaters of the Arkansas in the Colorado mountains. Here Pike, according to plan, allowed himself to be arrested by Spanish troops and returned to the United States under guard by way of Texas.

Pike's journals, published in 1810 under the title *An Account of Expeditions to the Sources of the Mississippi, and Through the Western Parts of Louisiana . . .*, afford an attractive picture of a young and enthusiastic professional soldier. He carried with him Volney, Shenstone, and Pope, and occasionally remarked upon the picturesque features of a landscape. His flair for rhetoric not only gave an Elysian coloring to his description of the Kansas prairies, where his "warm imagination" pictured "the future seats of husbandry, the numerous herds of domestic animals, which are no doubt destined to crown with joy those happy plains," but also led him to exaggerate the sterility of the Great Plains farther to the West, which he compared to the Sahara so vividly as to establish the myth of a Great American Desert east of the Rockies.

The second major American effort to explore the upper Arkansas was made some fifteen years after Pike's expedition, under the command of Major Stephen H. Long, with an elaborate scientific staff. Setting out up the Platte in June of 1820, the party traveled out to the mountains and returned down the Arkansas. The voluminous narrative of the expedition, published in 1823, was compiled from several manuscript journals by Edwin James, a young Vermont physician and geologist. It touches upon portions of the Mississippi Valley as widely separated as Pittsburgh and the Royal Gorge in Colorado, and is filled with careful observations, especially concerning the public domain beyond the frontier. The scientists' opinion confirmed the gloomy report of Pike. James describes a "Great Desert at the Base of the Rocky Mountains" five or six hundred miles wide, stretching from north Texas to the Canadian border.

5

In Josiah Gregg's *Commerce of the Prairies* (1844) the American advance along the Santa Fe Trail toward the outposts of New Spain produced a work that ranks with the Lewis and Clark narrative as a literary monument of the westward movement. The author grew up on the Missouri frontier, but the life of the trails across the Plains became so thoroughly a part of him that even this primitive society came to seem overcivilized:

Scarcely a day passes [he wrote later] without my experiencing a pang of regret that I am not now roving at large upon those western plains. Nor do I find my taste peculiar; for I have hardly known a man, who has ever become familiar with the kind of life which I have led for so many years, that has not relinquished it with regret.

Gregg had little formal education, but he had the vocation of a scientist. The Plains and the strange Latin civilization lying beyond were his library and his laboratory; the keeping of his journal, his professional work. In form his book is an apotheosis of the familiar traveler's diary. Gregg calls it "The Journal of a Santa Fé Trader." But although he adopts the narrative framework to describe one trip out of Santa Fe, one southward to Chihuahua and Aguas Calientes, and one back to Missouri, the entries are enriched with the fruits of observations made during four trips out and back in his nine years in the trade. In addition, separate chapters discuss such matters as the history and government of Santa Fe, animals and plants, and Indian tribes. The effect is that of a systematic monograph devoted to the new Southwest that was rising over the American horizon.

In George W. Kendall's *Narrative of the Texan Santa Fé Expedition* (1844) the outlines of the coming war are plain, and the tone is quite different from that of Gregg's tranquil picture of the 1830's. The fantastic expedition which Kendall accompanied set out in the belief that the people of New Mexico would welcome Texan aid in securing their independence from Mexico, and that a trading route from Austin to Santa Fe could be developed in competition with the trail out the Arkansas from Missouri. But when the half-starved travelers reached the Rio Grande settlements the Mexican authorities arrested them as armed invaders, shot two of them, and marched the rest to Mexico City as prisoners.

The early part of the narrative offers gruesome evidence of the sanctions which the West could exact of travelers who tried to substitute enthusiasm and courage for the ancient skills of the fur trader. Their horses were stolen by Indians, they suffered agonies of thirst, their baggage was burned in a prairie fire, stragglers were scalped. Yet Kendall, who was editor of the New Orleans *Picayune,* maintained his professional poise and was capable of noticing the landscape of the Staked Plains or telling a tall tale in the midst of his sufferings. The book is an admirable expression of the society which was about to go to war as an outlet for its rhetorical expansionism, its contempt for ignorant Catholic Mexicans, and its young sublime confidence in the American (that is, the Western) idea.

The war, when it came, was not in all respects adequate to the rhetoric in which it had been conceived. But one campaign, Alexander W. Doniphan's march into northern Mexico, proved to be the all but incredible audacity which the Western imagination demanded. There are several journals of this venture, of which the fullest is John T. Hughes' *Doniphan's Expedition,* published in Cincinnati in 1847. Doniphan set out down the Rio Grande in December of 1846 with something less than a thousand of his Missouri volunteers. They cut themselves loose from any base of supplies, and after two battles occupied Chihuahua. Then the column turned eastward for the seven-hundred-mile march across the Bolsón de Mapimí to join Wool's army at Saltillo. No professional soldier would have risked his reputation by such foolhardy behavior, but the Missourians made it plain that they wanted nothing to do with professional soldiers. They threw sheep's entrails into the tent of a West Pointer who tried to get them to drill. Hughes describes them as they emerged from the desert.

Their dishevelled hair, their long-grown whiskers, their buck-skin apparel, their stern and uncouth appearance, their determined and resolved looks, and their careless and nonchalant air, attracted the gaze, and won the admiration of all people. Though they were somewhat undisciplined, yet they were hardy, unshrinking, resolute, independent, chivalrous, honorable and intelligent men.

It was the very ideal of the frontier made flesh.

The best book growing out of the exciting winter of 1846–1847 is Lewis H. Garrard's *Wah-to-yah, and the Taos Trail*. The author, a native of Cincinnati and a stepson of Justice John McLean of the United States Supreme Court, was only seventeen years old, but despite the war he persuaded his parents to let him make a trip out to the Rocky Mountains. He accompanied a Bent, St. Vrain & Co. caravan to Bent's Fort on the Arkansas in present southeastern Colorado and spent the winter with trappers and Indians. *Wah-to-yah* (the title is taken from an Indian name for the Spanish Peaks near Fort Bent) appeared in 1850, when the author was twenty-one years old. Garrard had a rare natural ability to record the rich metaphors of the trapper language, compounded as it was of Kentucky, Spanish, and Indian elements. A long passage describing John Hatcher's dream of his visit to hell is the richest single item in the lore of the mountain men. Garrard also remembered happy hours passed in a Cheyenne camp—"the bright faces of the girls . . . the dancing eye of 'Morning Mist,' . . . the low chuckle of the young men, as they gained a triumph in the favorite game of 'guess' "—and other pretty girls in Taos, smoking shuck cigarettes, "their magically brilliant eyes the meanwhile searching one's very soul."

6

Although the military invasion of the Pacific Coast in 1846 followed a southern route by way of the Gila River, American settlement of Oregon and California had begun earlier along the more northerly trail of the fur traders which went out the Platte and through South Pass. Wide public interest in the Oregon Trail dates from the report of Lieutenant John Charles Frémont on his trip to South Pass in 1842. Frémont's role in the history as well as the literature of the West was the outgrowth of his marriage to the daughter of Senator Thomas Benton of Missouri, who secured a Congressional appropriation for the mapping of the trail, caused Frémont to be selected as commander of the party sent out, and saw to it that the report (judiciously edited, if not in large part written, by Frémont's wife) received wide circulation as a government document. Frémont became a symbol, and the myth-making faculty of the people read into his Western journeys a vast extrinsic interest derived from the heightened public emotions of the period of Manifest Destiny.

The *Report of the Exploring Expedition to the Rocky Mountains in the Year 1842* (1843) seems to a modern reader somewhat routine. But thousands of Americans in the 1840's experienced an aesthetic glow upon reading such comments as:

My horse was a trained hunter, famous in the west, under the name of Proveau, and with his eyes flashing, and the foam flying from his mouth, sprang on after the [buffalo] cow like a tiger.

If this seems to derive too directly from Delacroix, there are other entries in the mode of Defoe, such as Frémont's description of how he made a new tube for his broken barometer from a powderhorn. The passages establishing the guide Kit Carson as a faithful retainer of the chivalrous hero made Carson the first mountain man to attain national celebrity. Like Filson's life of Boone, Frémont's report contributed a figure to the national folklore.

After the explorers came the settlers. To this group belonged Edwin Bryant, a Kentucky newspaperman headed for California. His skillfully written *What I Saw in California* (1848) records a typical covered-wagon journey across the Plains: the gathering of prospective travelers near Independence, Missouri, in April; ceremonies of farewell with the indispensable speeches; the election of officers and drafting of by-laws; the nightly corral; the bugle at dawn. With the arrival in California Bryant stops his journal in order to recount the ghastly fate of the Donner party of the emigration of 1846 who, caught in their late crossing of the Sierra by winter snows, were sealed up in a fetor of starvation and cannibalism that has remained the most revolting chapter in the history of the Overland Trail. Later, as a member of Frémont's California Battalion, and as alcalde of San Francisco under the American military occupation, he describes the comic opera of the conquest.

Bryant's book is a sufficiently vivid reminder that the American advance to the Pacific Coast did not begin with the discovery of gold. The Forty-niners merely swelled the number of emigrants on trails across the continent, and their narratives add little to the picture of the crossing available in earlier chronicles. Among contemporary journals of the Gold Rush, one of the best is Alonzo Delano's *Life on the Plains and Among the Diggings* (1853). Delano, a resident of Illinois, recorded the hardships of the 1849 migration which resulted from exhaustion of the limited supplies of grass, water, and game by the greatly increased traffic across the Plains. As emigrants had to lighten their loads they dumped food and other supplies by the side of the trail.

We . . . found sugar on which turpentine had been poured [wrote Delano], flour in which salt and dirt had been thrown, and wagons broken to pieces, or partially burned, clothes torn to pieces, so that they could not be worn, and a wanton waste made of valuable property, simply because the owners could not use it themselves, and were determined that nobody else should.

## 7

During the first half of the nineteenth century all observers regarded the trans-Mississippi as a region remote from the normal patterns of American society. But when the Gold Rush brought a large population to the Pacific Coast almost overnight, the Far West was suddenly recognized as the area within which lay the destiny of the American people. The narratives of Western travel between 1849 and 1869, when the Union Pacific Railway at last connected New York and San Francisco, accordingly emphasized the need for integration between West and East, or announced its achievement. Most of them were written by newspapermen who felt an obligation to interpret the West for a national audience.

The beginnings of the new attitude are evident in Bayard Taylor's *El Dorado, or, Adventures in the Path of Empire* (1850). Taylor, already a professional travel writer, was sent out by Horace Greeley to cover the Gold Rush for the New York *Tribune*. Traveling by steamer via Panama, Taylor reached San Francisco in July of 1849, and set out at once on mule back for the diggings. It was at the height of the boom, when miners were warming canned lobster over campfires and drinking champagne at tables made of packing cases. Taylor witnessed the spontaneous creation of local governments for mining camps and the first convention which met to draw up a state constitution. He also described the pistol battles, the gambling dens, the theaters, and the Stephen Foster songs that have ever since been associated with 1849.

Horace Greeley's *An Overland Journey, from New York to San Francisco* (1860), based on the editor's letters to his famous paper, devotes two or three chapters to the Pikes Peak rush of 1859, but gives greatest emphasis to Republican politics in Kansas and to agricultural settlement beyond the Mississippi. As a New England farmer's son, Greeley was interested in the Western soil and climate, and was distressed both by "the infernal spirit of land speculation and monopoly" and by the widespread frauds in the patenting of public lands. In California he saw the early stages of hydraulic mining and wrote the tribute to Yosemite Valley which was henceforth to be obligatory in all tourists' books. He also made a substantial contribution to the already vigorous California boosters' tradition by recording corn twenty feet high, squashes like brass kettles, and two-year-old steers larger than three-year-olds in the East.

The integration of West and North which Greeley so earnestly desired was cemented by the Civil War. When peace finally came, the triumphant Republican Party was aware that it had secured a vast theater for the expansion of Northern industry. Within six weeks of Appomattox, Schuyler Colfax, Speaker of the House of Representatives, set out on a triumphal tour beyond the Mississippi that symbolized the official commitment of the party to the development of the West. He was accompanied by Samuel Bowles, influential editor of the Springfield (Massachusetts) *Republican,* who described the trip in his *Across the Continent* (1865, reissued in 1869 with additions based on a later trip, as *Our New West*). Bowles was as confident as Gilbert Imlay had been that the West would undergo prodigious development. He saw in the trans-Mississippi, as Imlay had seen in Kentucky,

an aggregation of elements and forces that . . . will present on the North American Continent such a triumph of Man in race, in government, in social development, in intellectual advancement, and in commercial supremacy, as the world never saw,—as the world never yet fairly dreamed of.

# 46. THE WEST AS SEEN FROM THE EAST

BEFORE the Louisiana Purchase the people of the United States had little knowledge of that as yet foreign region which was to become the western half of their country; they lacked indeed any special reason for interest in it. Once that area had been acquired, interest sprang up quickly, but knowledge came more slowly. Gradually, however, some information was disseminated—by actual travel in the West, by word-of-mouth reports of such returned travelers, by fugitive articles in newspapers and magazines, and by books. Inevitably there was another lag before such information could be absorbed and reexpressed in writing which may be described as "the West as seen from the East."

The process of informing the East was gigantic in proportions. The book titles alone constitute a formidable list. The West was described to the East in numerous volumes based upon the notes of official explorers—Lewis and Clark, Pike, Long, Frémont. Many other notable accounts were written of the journeyings of travelers and unofficial explorers—Brackenridge, Catlin, Leonard, Gregg. Some highly interesting books, like James Pattie's *Personal Narrative* (1831) and D. H. Coyner's *Lost Trappers* (1847), lay along the line between fact and fiction. Other writers, such as Emerson Bennett, wrote novels or romances. Some of the interpreters of the West were not Americans at all. They might be British like Ruxton and Marryat; or from the Continent, like Sealsfield and Prince Maximilian of Wied.

The present chapter passes by these interesting but scattered writers, in order to concentrate upon a few of the most important literary figures. The work of such men has a double interest, being an interpretation both of the West and of the men themselves. In general, moreover, their attitudes toward the West show the variations characteristic of the less important writers and of the country as a whole.

Doubtless along the frontier the chief source of information about the farther regions was always actual travel and the talk of returned trappers and Indian traders. For the rest of the country, newspapers and magazines were perhaps most important. The literary men, however, were readers of books, and their ideas were largely shaped by such reading. In fact most of the sources of their writings about the West can be found in a few books. Of these the most important were Biddle's redaction of the journals of Lewis and Clark (1814), the narrative of Long's expedition (1822–1823), and Frémont's report (1843).

2

Among our early writers, the two who most strongly felt the influence of the West were Cooper and Irving. In addition, these two deserve first and fullest attention because their books in turn became strong influences upon later writers. The melodramatic tradition of Western fiction may be said to spring directly from Cooper.

*The Prairie* (1827) appeared at the height of Cooper's popularity. It was widely read by a public which as yet had little real information, and was therefore unable to separate fiction from actuality. The book can thus be set down as one of the most important single documents in producing a picture of the West in the American mind.

The novel itself shows that Cooper had read Biddle and the Long report, and perhaps a newspaper account of the Santa Fe trade. So far so good, for Biddle and Long were authoritative. From Biddle, for instance, Cooper took the names for his Sioux chiefs, Mahtoree and Weucha; Hard Heart and most of the other names were from Long. The trouble was that Cooper went no further, and seems to have read nothing else. He did not, like Irving, actually visit the West. Instead, with this slight smattering of knowledge, he merely let his romancer's imagination have free play. The result, however luring as romance, is a farrago of absurdities as a picture of the West.

For illustration, a single example of Cooper's method must suffice. In a romance, he needed heroes and villains. With his Indians, he had already worked out a formula. The Indians on our side shall be noble Red Men (Mohicans); the opposing Indians shall be Red Devils (Mingos). In *The Prairie* he cast the Pawnees as the heroes, and the Sioux ("Siouxes," he wrote originally) as the villains. In reality there was little difference between the two tribes; each had its good and bad points. (Curiously, in Irving's *Tour on the Prairies* the Pawnees have the villain role.) One detail of Cooper's traducing of the Sioux is his constant attribution to them of all the horrors of practicing torture upon their captives. Probably he did this because he assumed them to be like the Iroquois and some other Eastern Indians. The Sioux themselves, however, have vigorously denied the charge, and the fact apparently is that, being a primitive people, they killed their captives outright. Torture thrives among more sophisticated peoples who have learned artistic restraint, such as the Iroquois or the Italians of the Renaissance.

In one instance Cooper unconsciously made a remarkable prediction of the future by taking covered-wagon emigrants out on the plains. In 1827 only a few Santa Fe traders had traversed the plains with wagons. But in spite of this triumph of intuition *The Prairie* spread misinformation broadcast.

Fortunately the next important Eastern writer to approach the subject set a higher standard and subscribed to the sometimes forgotten principle that a writer should, when possible, collect some first-hand knowledge on a subject before setting himself up to write about it. In short, Washington Irving went to look at the West for himself.

There has been of recent years a tendency to sneer at Irving's Western writings. Many moderns, their own knowledge gained of necessity chiefly from books, seem to have forgotten that Irving learned about the Old West from actual sight and sound. He crossed the swollen Arkansas in a bullboat; he saw Sublette come home wounded from the epic fight at Pierre's Hole; he knew the terror of the cry "Pawnees!"

*A Tour on the Prairies* (1835) may be called a simple and factual record of an expedition across what is now Oklahoma. There is, of course, artistic omission and shaping. Critics point out that Irving suppressed some incidents which would have made him seem ridiculous, that he developed an unfortunate and unwarranted dislike for the half-breed Beatte, that his polished style is not cousin to the roughness of the Cross Timbers. But there is no traveler's narrative which does not show such distortions. Certainly Irving's narrative is much more detailed and interesting than the two others still extant upon the same expedition. In many ways it is more alive than any of his other works.

An actual background of Western experience must have given Irving confidence, and must have helped to make *Astoria* and *Captain Bonneville* the solid books that they are. Inspired, they are not; and yet they still remain the authoritative works on their subjects. The chief charge that can be brought against *Astoria* is that it is not what it purports to be. Irving in his Introduction mentioned "the journals, on which I chiefly depended," but listed also six published works of which he had availed himself "occasionally." Actually the reverse was true, and many parts of *Astoria* are nothing more than paraphrases of the accounts of Bradbury, Brackenridge, or one of the other earlier writers.

Granted, however, that his acknowledgments are not what they should be, Irving shows up well as both scholar and writer. Like many a modern professor, he hired a research assistant to do the spadework. Then from the half-dozen different accounts he drew his own conclusions as to what most probably had happened, and wrote a reasonably well unified and certainly a readable account. To produce solidity of background he had his own experiences, and he also culled information from such basic work as that of Lewis and Clark. *Astoria* is neither profound scholarship nor brilliant writing, but it is at least that somewhat rare combination of good scholarship and good writing.

*Captain Bonneville* is more difficult to appraise. It is perhaps not so well constructed or well written as *Astoria*. On the other hand, it is a much more original contribution, based upon now lost documents and upon conversation with Bonneville himself.

*Astoria* was the subject of a highly laudatory review by Poe in the *Southern Literary Messenger* for January, 1837. The book apparently stimulated Poe's interest in the West, and one may note, as details, that in the *Narrative of A. Gordon Pym* (1838) the hero selected for his reading "the expedition of Lewis and Clark to the mouth of the Columbia," and that his comrade Peters is described as a "hybrid" Upsaroka Indian.

Poe's only extended piece of writing about the West appeared in 1840. He saw fit to masquerade the "Journal of Julius Rodman" as "an account of the first passage across the Rocky Mountains." Probably, however, it deceived few people. In writing it, Poe seems to have followed the Lewis and Clark narrative chiefly, but also drew material from *Astoria, Captain Bonneville,* and probably other works. Since *Astoria* itself often echoes the words of its sources, it is difficult to be dogmatic about whether Poe was borrowing from it or directly from the earlier books. In order to make the story more reasonable, he adopted the device of understatement—"in every point, Mr. R[odman]'s account *falls short* of Captain Lewis's." Such a method naturally did not produce an exciting story, and in the end Rodman, like Pym, merely petered out and left his story unfinished. The *Journal* is thus of little importance in itself, although it remains a document of some interest as another indication of the turn of attention westward near the end of the thirties.

3

The transcendentalists concerned themselves more with the Far East than with the Far West, although the mountain men indeed were skilled practitioners of self-reliance and really lived the kind of life which Thoreau played at living when he camped by Walden Pond. The practical or Yankee side of Emerson appreciated the expansive, go-ahead spirit of the frontier, but his earlier experiences with it and most of his scattered statements about it deal with Middle Western rather than Far Western conditions. He read Frémont, but his comment in his journal is a shrewd one upon the Pathfinder's own self-consciousness, not upon Western scenes or characters.

One might expect Thoreau to display an interest in the great opening

Western land. He seems rather, however, to have reacted by contraries. Extensive passages in his journal were devoted to the fur trade and the California Gold Rush. He conceived both primarily in economic terms, and made his judgments on what he would probably have called "moral grounds." There must always, of course, be an argument as to how largely the economic factors loomed in such frontier movements. Yet anyone reading a few of the genuine Western books can notice that hope of profit was seldom the sole motive, or even the first one. There were plenty of volunteers, for instance, to go with Lewis and Clark, but none of them could have expected to make money in addition to wages. Among the motives often mentioned in reminiscences are desire to go adventuring, to see strange country, and to live a free life removed from the restraints of civilization. Thoreau, however, saw in the mountain men only "the loafing class tempted by rum and money," and exclaimed, "What a pitiful business is the fur-trade!" He thought that the rush to California reflected "the greatest disgrace on mankind," and there is a hint of jealousy in his antagonism toward the West. The trappers were gloriously shooting the rapids of a hundred uncharted rivers while he floated upon the placid Concord; they made Homeric revelry and battle at Pierre's Hole, but he raised beans within the sound of the home-town dinner horn.

The poets also paid the West little attention. Bryant's famous "where rolls the Oregon" apparently sprang from his reading of the Biddle version of Lewis and Clark, as is shown by his use at first of the spelling "Oregan." * The next few lines beginning, "Yet the dead are there," were probably suggested by the vivid descriptions of Memaloose Island and the other Indian burial grounds along the Columbia. Bryant's "Prairies," although showing his familiarity with Far Western conditions, actually sprang from his own experiences in Illinois and describes scenery of that state. A few minor poems also show Bryant's continuing interest in the West.

Section IV of Part Two of *Evangeline* opens with a sweeping scenic passage:

> Far in the West there lies a desert land, where the mountains
> Lift, through perpetual snows, their lofty and luminous summits.

Most of its details can be traced to Frémont, even such a touch as the juxtaposition of "luxuriant clusters of roses and purple amorphas." Although well handled, the passage does not necessarily show much reading on Longfellow's part. Most of the allusions can be found in the first few chapters of the book,

---

* The Biddle volume appeared in 1814. But even if a version of "Thanatopsis" was written in 1811, there is no proof that the Oregan-Oregon passage was written very long before its first publication in 1817.

and the fine geographical coup d'œil with its place names is suggestive of the inspection of a map.

Two young New Englanders went to see the West for themselves. Richard Henry Dana, Jr., chose to call his book *Two Years Before the Mast* (1840), but it might equally well have been *A Year in California*. Francis Parkman, like Irving, took a trip upon the plains with a view to utilizing his experiences in writing. His *California and Oregon Trail* (1849) was misleading in title, for he never got near to either California or Oregon. Doubtless many a Forty-niner cursed the book as a worthless catchpenny, but it has survived as a juvenile.

Dana was an excellent factual reporter upon the West. Parkman was more likely to be carried away, and to interpret upon the basis of his own insufficient experience. Both the youngsters carried with them their Bostonian traditions. Dana had a raised eyebrow for frontier immorality; Parkman, although rejoicing in Western spaciousness, curled a snobbish Brahmin lip at uncouth covered-wagon emigrants.

This sketch of early writings about the farther West can naturally be brought to an end around 1850. By then the Gold Rush of '49 had stirred the whole country. In the new desire for information, *Two Years Before the Mast* was rescued from obscurity; Frémont gained thousands of new readers; because of the name California in its title, Parkman's little volume became a best seller; and dozens of now forgotten books about the West came sliding from the presses. Casual references to the West began to crop up everywhere. Poe wrote his "Eldorado." Melville adorned the pages of *Moby-Dick* with some half-dozen Western allusions—"the black bisons of distant Oregon." Even Hawthorne's dimly lit world of dream and allegory was not wholly insulated; the Introduction to the *Scarlet Letter* (1850) contains a reference to digging gold in California, and Chillingworth is stated to have "dug into the poor clergyman's heart, like a miner searching for gold."

4

Thus, by 1850, the Eastern writers all knew something about the Far West, or at least had some vague notions about it. What was this knowledge—or what were these notions? Most typically, they conceived the Far West as a very strange country. The American tradition, and the English tradition before it, assumed that a well watered and well forested country was the natural state of the earth as God had created it. (Actually, vast regions are desert or steppe, and only comparatively small areas are well watered and thickly forested; the misconception, however, is easily understood.) Early descriptions of the West emphasized again and again treeless plains unbounded as the ocean, bare rocky buttes like ruined castles, dry earth half encrusted with salt, endless buffalo herds that shook the prairie. The "scoriac rivers" of "Ulalume" could have been derived from some description of a Western lava flow. Certainly Julius Rodman described the scenery in not dissimilar terms; for example, "The whole descent towards the stream has an indescribably chaotic and dreary air. No vegetation of any kind is seen." There is no need to multiply examples; the strangeness of the country was notable then, by experience or through descriptions, just as it is still notable to any born and bred Easterner making his first transcontinental trip.

If this first acquaintanceship with the Far West had begun during the middle eighteenth century, no one can doubt that the new land would have been judged altogether hideous and repulsive. But even before the "perioques" of Lewis and Clark first cut the muddy current of the Missouri, the spirit of Romanticism was abroad in the land. People had begun to love deep romantic chasms and forests decaying but never decayed more than well trimmed sylvan parks and enameled meads. As Poe wrote of Julius Rodman: "He stalked through that immense and often terrible wilderness with an evident rapture at his heart which we envy him as we read." Such a sentence is almost a textbook demonstration of Romanticism, and it might also be quoted of Frémont, Jedediah Smith, and other actual Western explorers.

This rapture at the heart, sometimes combined with advertising zeal, led to the build-up of the West as a land of beauty. First perhaps the strangeness stirred the heart, and when the heart was stirred the eye saw beauty. Thus, by grace of Jean-Jacques Rousseau, our poets and novelists came to see the West as a strange but beautiful land of vast spaces where a man could live freely—and so, as dream and partially as reality, it has been ever since.

## 47. ABRAHAM LINCOLN: THE SOIL AND THE SEED

There is one man in whose words, spoken and written, the West of vast spaces and the East of many peoples are subsumed under one meaning. It is no accident that a hero myth has sprung up about the name and person of Abraham Lincoln as earlier such a myth grew about George Washington. In Lincoln the people of the United States could finally see themselves, each for himself and all together.

Abraham Lincoln had many styles. It has been computed that his printed speeches and writings number 1,078,365 words. One may range through this record of utterance and find a wider variety of styles than in any other American statesman or orator. And perhaps no author of books has written and vocalized in such a diversity of speech tones directed at all manners and conditions of men.

This may be saying in effect that the range of the personality of Abraham Lincoln ran far, identifying itself with the tumults and follies of mankind, keeping touch with multitudes and solitudes. The free-going and friendly companion is there and the man of the cloister, of the lonely corner of thought, prayer, and speculation. The man of public affairs, before a living audience announcing decisions, is there, and the solitary inquirer weaving his abstractions related to human freedom and responsibility.

Perhaps no other American held so definitely in himself both those elements: the genius of the Tragic—the spirit of the Comic. The fate of man, his burdens and crosses, the pity of circumstance, the extent of tragedy in human life, these stood forth in word shadows of the Lincoln utterance, as testamentary as the utter melancholy of his face in repose. And in contrast he came to be known nevertheless as the first authentic humorist to occupy the Executive Mansion in Washington, his gift of laughter and his flair for the funny being taken as a national belonging.

Three short pieces from his pen are kept as immemorial possessions of the American people, each keyed to a high tragic note. These are the Letter to Mrs. Bixby, the Gettysburg Speech, the Second Inaugural.

The War Department records showed a Boston woman to have lost five sons in combat actions. The number was less than five, as later research

778

revealed, but Lincoln spoke through her to all families that had lost a boy or man in the war. "Weak and fruitless must be any words of mine which should attempt to beguile you from the grief of a loss so overwhelming," he wrote. "But I cannot refrain from tendering to you the consolation that may be found in the thanks of the Republic they died to save." He poised his quill pen for the final sentence of the letter, he on whose initiative, action, and responsibility the war had begun and had been carried on for nearly four years, and he wrote: "I pray that our heavenly Father may assuage the anguish of your bereavement, and leave you only the cherished memory of the loved and lost, and the solemn pride that must be yours to have laid so costly a sacrifice upon the altar of freedom."

In a photographer's studio eleven days before delivering the speech at Gettysburg, Lincoln had held in his hands the lengthy address of Edward Everett, the designated orator of the day, the printed two-hour discourse covering nearly two sides of a one-sheet supplement of a Boston newspaper. To a young newspaper correspondent from California he said his own speech at Gettysburg would be "short, short, short"—as it proved to be, ten sentences spoken in less than five minutes. In its implicative qualities, it stands among the supreme utterances of democratic peoples of the world. "A new nation, conceived in liberty and dedicated to the proposition that all men are created equal"—for the perpetuation of this men were dying on battlefields, he said. And, having so died, they would be forgotten men and their deaths of no use unless the living dedicated themselves to the unfinished work for which the dead had given "the last full measure of devotion."

Virtually the Gettysburg Speech is one of the great American poems, having its use and acceptation far beyond American shores. It curiously incarnates the claims, assurances and pretenses of republican institutions, of democratic procedure, of the rule of the people, and directly implies that popular government can come into being and can then "perish from the earth." How he would have defined "a new birth of freedom," at length, must be sought elsewhere in the body of his utterance. No accusations, no recriminations, no lash of invective, not even a mild outspoken reproach of the enemy. Some have detected in haunting echoes of the Gettysburg Speech a quiet summons to those of the South reluctant to let go of national unity: Come back into the old Union of states and let us make of it what those Virginians, Washington and Jefferson, envisioned. Apart from its immediate historic setting it is a timeless psalm in the name of those who *fight* and *do* in behalf of great human causes rather than *talk,* in a belief that men can "highly resolve" themselves and can mutually "dedicate" their lives to a cause, in a posture of oath-taking that "these dead shall not have died in vain."

As one may delve endlessly into the restless implications of the Gettysburg Speech, so also one may ponder the Second Inaugural and the intricate derivations to be made from it. A cry for merciless and further war, so some took it, while others read it as a benediction, a prayer, and a fathomless hope set to music. How did the war begin? He would try to tell it in two sentences, one long and one short: "Both parties deprecated war; but one of them would make war rather than let the nation survive; and the other would accept war rather than let it perish. And the war came." The peculiar sobriety of judgments pronounced on both of the warring sections of the country has had wide discussion and keeps a permanent value:

Neither party expected for the war the magnitude or the duration which it has already attained. Neither anticipated that the cause of the conflict might cease with, or even before, the conflict itself should cease. Each looked for an easier triumph, and a result less fundamental and astounding. Both read the same Bible, and pray to the same God, and each invoked his aid against the other. It may seem strange that any men should dare to ask a just God's assistance in wringing their bread from the sweat of other men's faces; but let us judge not, that we be not judged. The prayers of both could not be answered—that of neither has been answered fully.

In like pitch and key was the often quoted passage from the First Inaugural four years earlier:

Suppose you go to war. You cannot fight always; and when, after much loss on both sides, and no gain on either, you cease fighting, the identical old questions as to terms of intercourse are again upon you.

The Bixby Letter, the Gettysburg Speech, the Second Inaugural, these were widely reprinted and went to increasingly large readerships as decades passed. Yet there was another utterance of Lincoln that did not come to any immense audience until the Second World War. This consists of passages from the President's Message to Congress, December 1, 1862. In this message, Lincoln was using to the limit his powers of persuasion to get the Congress to enact legislation enabling "compensated emancipation," the Federal government to buy the slaves and set them free. Also in this message he presented the cause of national unity in new phases.

A nation may be said to consist of its territory, its people, and its laws. The territory is the only part which is of certain durability. "One generation passeth away, and another generation cometh, but the earth abideth forever." It is of the first importance to duly consider and estimate this ever-enduring part. . . . Our national strife springs not from our permanent part, not from the land we inhabit. . . . Our strife pertains to ourselves—to the passing generations of men;

and it can without convulsion be hushed forever with the passing of one generation.

Having presented his plan for compensated emancipation he appealed for united action as between Congress and Executive:

We can succeed only by concert. It is not "Can any of us imagine better?" but, "Can we all do better?" Object whatsoever is possible, still the question occurs, "Can we do better?"

Then came his pleadings wherein it is seen that he was sensitively aware of how momentous was the hour and of the need for each man to make his personal record such that it would stand the scrutiny of remote generations:

The dogmas of the quiet past are inadequate to the stormy present. The occasion is piled high with difficulty, and we must rise with the occasion. As our case is new, so we must think anew and act anew. We must disenthrall ourselves, and then we shall save our country.

There have been long-time students of Lincoln who place among his sublime passages the one that closed this 1862 message:

Fellow-citizens, we cannot escape history. We of this Congress and this administration will be remembered in spite of ourselves. No personal significance or insignificance can spare one or another of us. The fiery trial through which we pass will light us down, in honor or dishonor, to the latest generation. . . . We shall nobly save or meanly lose the last, best hope of earth. Other means may succeed; this could not fail. The way is plain, peaceful, generous, just—a way which, if followed, the world will forever applaud, and God must forever bless.

That the Congress paid little heed, that it balked at the legislation suggested, that it had a low or indifferent opinion of Lincoln's language and persuasions, is part of the record. That the Congress, save for a remnant of two or three members, had any dim vision that possibly eighty years later, in another national crisis of world scope, there would be global circulation of sentences from this message of Lincoln, there is little or no indication. Not until the Second World War did there come wide circulation, in print and in radio broadcasts and in musical composition, of cadenced declarations from this message. A grim fighting insistence was found in such lines as, "The fiery trial through which we pass will light us down, in honor or dishonor, to the latest generation."

Lincoln, it would seem, practiced his mind in private, rehearsed by himself the method of the abstruse, lofty, cogent reasoning he would apply to the materials of public discussion. Among memoranda written about the time of the debates with Douglas is the following piece of dialectic:

If A can prove, however conclusively, that he may, of right, enslave B, why may not B snatch the same argument, and prove equally that he may enslave A? You say A is white, and B is black. It is *color,* then: the lighter, having the right to enslave the darker? Take care. By this rule, you are to be slave to the first man you meet with a fairer skin than your own. You do not mean *color* exactly? You mean the whites are *intellectually* the superiors of the blacks, and therefore have the right to enslave them? Take care again. By this rule, you are to be slave to the first man you meet, with an intellect superior to your own. But, say you, it is a question of *interest*: and if you can make it to your interest, you have the right to enslave another? Very well. And if he can make it his interest, he has the right to enslave you.

The ancient cry, "Against stupidity even the gods struggle unavailing," had a manner of paraphrase from Lincoln before a Midwest audience.

If a man will stand up, and assert, and repeat, and reassert, that two and two do not make four, I know nothing in the power of argument that can stop him. I think I can answer the judge so long as he sticks to the premises; but when he flies from them, I can not work an argument into the consistency of a maternal gag, and actually close his mouth with it.

2

The tragic note, the fateful event at hand or to come, the screen of mist and cloud behind which Providence wrought his designs, the drama of man in shadowy and portentous deeds, this enters in the Bixby Letter, the Gettysburg Speech, the Second Inaugural, and other instances given. Of another color are Lincoln's many forensic passages where his purpose is the achievement of inexorable and unanswerable logic. The most celebrated example of his style in this field is his letter in the summer of 1862 to a New York antislavery editor who continuously attacked Lincoln as slow, indecisive, and vacillating in emancipation policy. In clarity and as a definition of political and military aims in the turmoil of civil war, the letter has curious dignity and the self-possession that cheers adherents.

The editor had addressed a vehemently critical letter to Lincoln, and without sending a copy of it to him had published it in his newspaper. Lincoln's reply began:

If there be in it any statements or assumptions of fact which I may know to be erroneous, I do not, now and here, controvert them. If there be in it any inferences which I may believe to be falsely drawn, I do not, now and here, argue against them. If there be perceptible in it an impatient and dictatorial tone, I waive it in deference to an old friend whose heart I have always supposed to be right.

Of his policy he would not leave anyone in doubt, wrote the President, as he proceeded:

I would save the Union. I would save it the shortest way under the Constitution. . . . If there be those who would not save the Union unless they could at the same time save slavery, I do not agree with them. If there be those who would not save the Union unless they could at the same time destroy slavery, I do not agree with them. My paramount object in this struggle is to save the Union, and is not either to save or to destroy slavery. If I could save the Union without freeing any slave, I would do it; and if I could save it by freeing all the slaves, I would do it; and if I could save it by freeing some and leaving others alone, I would also do that.

Equally fateful, and as widely known and discussed at the time of its delivery, was the House Divided Speech of 1858. This was the preliminary to the nine debates with United States Senator Stephen A. Douglas that year, from which Lincoln emerged a national figure, and the Cooper Union Speech of February, 1860, which dramatized Lincoln as a possible presidential candidate. Out of the tumult and troubled horizons of '58 came the tall Illinoisan with his relentless, "If we could first know where we are, and whither we are tending, we could better judge what to do, and how to do it." The slavery agitation would not cease, he declared as his opinion, until a crisis should have been reached and passed. He quoted, "A house divided against itself cannot stand," and proceeded, "I believe this government cannot endure permanently half slave and half free. I do not expect the Union to be dissolved—I do not expect the house to fall; but I do expect it will cease to be divided. It will become all one thing, or all the other."

Perhaps nothing else that Lincoln ever wrote or spoke brought so many inquiries as to what he meant as did the House Divided Speech. Some construed that he favored war, wanted war. Before he became President and afterward, these queries came. He intended to be plain-spoken, he would reply to these questioners, and the speech meant what it said. To one puzzled correspondent he wrote, after quoting the opening paragraph of the speech: "It puzzles me to make my meaning plainer. Look over it carefully, and conclude I meant all I said, and did not mean anything I did not say, and you will have my meaning." His final counsel in this letter ran: "If you will state to me some meaning which you suppose I had, I can and will instantly tell you whether that was my meaning."

Plain reasoning to reduce the opponent's position to absurdity was often

Lincoln's aim and method as writer and speaker. Into grim fantasy could he carry it, as in 1856 when he sketched a cultural apparatus arrayed and a climate of opinion generated toward the chattel slave:

All the powers of earth seem rapidly combining against him. Mammon is after him, ambition follows, philosophy follows, and the theology of the day is fast joining the cry. They have him in his prison house; they have searched his person, and left no prying instrument with him. One after another they have closed the heavy iron doors upon him; and now they have him, as it were, bolted in with a lock of a hundred keys, which can never be unlocked without the concurrence of every key—the keys in the hands of a hundred different men, and they scattered to a hundred different and distant places; and they stand musing as to what invention, in all the dominions of mind and matter, can be produced to make the impossibility of his escape more complete than it is.

### 3

Thus we have considered, or touched in degree, the brooding and speaking figure of Lincoln in the human Tragedy. How he moved and spoke as part of the human Comedy became vivid mouth-to-mouth folklore while he was alive, and his quips and drolleries went beyond his own country and began the process by which he was internationally adopted by the Family of Man.

A paradox was seen. Year by year came the stream of photographs reporting the face of the Chief Magistrate in the Executive Mansion. Camera craft had developed. The carte de visite was more than a vogue. Millions came to know the Lincoln face as though they had seen it in life. There it was, gaunt, fissured, melancholy, tragedy scrawled over it as on no other that had moved with authority among the doors and rooms of the Executive Mansion. "A Hoosier Michel Angelo," wrote Walt Whitman. And yet this man was the source and wellspring of a current of folklore and humor that widened and grew, that still exists and has its periodic accretions of newly found authentic material and its apocryphal and gratuitous contributions.

Among ten-cent books in paper covers published in the latter half of Lincoln's administration, one was titled "Old Abe's Joker" and another "Old Abe's Jokes—Fresh from Abraham's Bosom." It could be taken as part of a trend in American literature. The horse-laugh school of American humor had come into its own with its preeminent pen names of Orpheus C. Kerr (Robert H. Newell), Artemus Ward (Charles Farrar Browne), and Petroleum Vesuvius Nasby (David Ross Locke), vulgarians all, with their potshots at pomposity, and a meat ax for frauds, hypocrites, and snobs. Friends and compatriots of the President, they supported him and his cause with their satire and gibes. It was a country and a people warmly receptive of these jesters, whose persiflage often carried a razor edge, that gave its response and understanding to the byplay and humor that came to be known as "Lincoln stories."

Several facets had the Lincoln humor. His generation and his kinsfolk had their story-tellers who could "spin a yarn" to pass the time and to brighten the pioneer corners where they lived. He could tell a story for the sake of merriment, a medicine to his bones. Or again he would use a story as illustration of an argument or point of view, or as fable and allegory. Or again what he was saying could be veiled in a delicate irony. And there were phrasings and pithy utterances that came to be known as "Lincoln sayings," such as, "You can fool all of the people some of the time and some of the people all of the time, but you cannot fool all of the people all of the time." Or: "It is not best to swap horses while crossing the river." And: "Broken eggs can not be mended"; "Bad promises are better broken than kept"; "We shall sooner have the fowl by hatching the egg than smashing it"; "A jury too frequently has at least one member more ready to hang the panel than the traitor"; "No man knows so well where the shoe pinches as he who wears it."

Of the authenticated stories that Lincoln used for illustration, one seemed to have been reported by callers and visitors more than any other. Often his duties required him to be furtive and secretive beyond what he liked in political affairs. And he would tell of the Irishman in the state of Maine, where the sale of alcoholic liquor was prohibited. Having asked a druggist for a glass of lemonade and having the glass as ordered set before him, the Irishman whispered, "And now, can ye pour in just a drop of the creeter unbeknownst to me?" In a discussion of his use or misuse of constitutional prerogative Lincoln once said, "I am like the Irishman, I have to do some things unbeknownst to myself."

To make a point, Lincoln could mention, in passing, the two gentlemen who met and fought themselves out of their overcoats, each into the other's. To the query of an old neighbor from back home, "How does it feel to be President of the United States?" he could answer, "You have heard about the man tarred and feathered and ridden out of town on a rail? A man in the crowd asked him how he liked it, and his reply was that if it wasn't for the honor of the thing, he would much rather walk." One verbose man had the rating, "He can compress the most words into the smallest ideas of any man I ever met." A rural orator from the Southwest "mounted the rostrum, threw back his head, shined his eyes, and left the consequences to God."

The Lincoln vocabulary ranged from the plainest of street vernacular to hoary and archaic Anglo-Saxon terms. The enemy had "turned tail and run," he told a crowd on the White House lawn in 1865, to the dismay of various purists. And again he would trust to be understood in the ancient form of the noun "burthen" or the verbs "holden" and "disenthrall." His influence on the styles of other speakers and writers has been vast. The extent of it is incalculable. His use of the gift of laughter has been better emulated than the depths of his desire to mislead no man by act or word. This latter lay at the root of his counsel to the Congress in the 1862 Message:

> In times like the present, men should utter nothing for which they would not willingly be responsible through time and in eternity.

Human solidarity, unity of action and feeling, may rise from a leadership knowing somewhat of both soil and seed; a leadership knowing somewhat of the dynamics Lincoln believed he could see at play among men and political states and civil factions when in 1862, he wrote to a New Orleans man:

> I shall do nothing in malice. What I deal with is too vast for malicious dealing.

# THE SECTIONS

*--- tradition and experiment*

# 48. THE SECOND DISCOVERY OF AMERICA

THE defeat of the Confederacy in the Civil War preserved the Union, but at the same time transformed it from a federal aggregate of sections into a national state dominated by the industrial and financial power concentrated along the axis Boston to New York to Chicago. After the opposition of the Southern plantation class had been eliminated, the leaders of the Republican Party were to carry through their program with only minor concessions to the rapidly developing agrarian West. Beginning with the Pacific Railway subsidies and the National Banking Act during the early years of the war, the Republican majority in Congress enacted a remarkable series of laws designed to aid finance and industry. The tariff was increased, the war debt was manipulated in the interest of investors, and the greenbacks were redeemed at par. Even the public-land system, ostensibly intended to favor the penniless settler, was administered in such a way as to transfer vast portions of the public domain to mining, lumbering, and stock-raising corporations.

In this favorable environment, the scale of business enterprise rapidly increased. Principles of management which had been developed in order to maintain the Union armies were applied to private undertakings of comparable scope. Improved transportation enabled raw materials to be carried great distances and made markets accessible for the mass-produced goods of the new factories. Technological improvements, like the introduction of the Bessemer process for making steel and the use of refrigeration in meat packing, revolutionized traditional types of manufacturing; and new major industries were developed on the basis of petroleum and electricity. Industrial expansion created the modern cities: by the 1890's New York, Philadelphia, and, miraculously, Chicago had grown beyond a million inhabitants each. New York, with three millions, had outstripped Paris and Berlin and had attained half the size of London.

These and similar factors determined the main trends of American literature during the thirty years following the Civil War. Despite the work of Henry James and Mark Twain, it was an age of transition rather than of fulfillment. The prewar enlightenment which had so variously and richly expressed the insights of transcendentalism was fading; and although there was no lack of new ideas, none appeared that was capable of providing the impetus for a literature commensurate with the nation created by the war. The dominant American intellectual tradition had been a creation of New England. Explicitly theocratic in the seventeenth century, it had been secularized into a program of humanitarian reform by the middle of the nineteenth, and after the formal enactment of abolition it was left with no more than minor political goals like civil service reform. The civic zeal of former abolitionists was frustrated by their commitment to a Republican Party controlled by Roscoe Conkling, James G. Blaine and Mark Hanna. And since the official tradition with its emphasis on ideality took little account of economics, it was powerless to understand, much less to direct, a society which subordinated everything to business. Even such a well informed conservative as E. L. Godkin, editor for thirty years of the influential weekly *Nation,* who considered himself a political economist, could only resort to moralistic invective against critics of the business system who rejected his dogma of the automatic beneficence of free competition. Men like Godkin continued to invoke an ill defined code of values which they called Civilization, Culture or Refinement. But the code was based historically upon a theology, and their position became increasingly confused as the new deterministic ideas of Darwin and Spencer undermined the old supernatural sanctions and made necessary a restatement of all the accepted theological doctrines.

Here then were the problems which faced American writers during the decades after the Civil War: the New England tradition was to be transformed, or if necessary supplanted by ideas adequate to the task of interpreting a continental nation that embraced a South and a West—indeed, a succession of Wests—in addition to the regions from which had come the first flowering of American letters. At the same time, the Industrial Revolution was to be confronted. Attitudes derived originally from an uncentralized agrarian social pattern were to be replaced by attitudes relevant to an integrated society dominated by huge metropolitan centers. Values formerly based on supernatural sanctions were to be restated in terms of natural law or to lose their authority entirely. None of these problems was fully solved before the end of the century, but a beginning was made toward solving all of them. Literary interpretations of the South and the West were devised; a critique of Big Business was begun; and American literature was launched upon an exciting exploration of nontraditional materials, forms, and assumptions. The new realism, imported as a literary method from Europe, became the radical implement of interpretation for an expanding America; the old ideality became its unrelenting foe, the defender of all the threatened values and memories.

2

The inauguration of Hayes in 1877 symbolized the end of Reconstruction in the South. Democratic and Liberal Republican protests against the corruption of Grant's administration, which had forced the nomination of Hayes instead of Blaine or Conkling, were reinforced by the fact that the popular vote for the Democratic candidate Tilden had actually exceeded the Republican total. The carpetbag period was over, and Hayes quickly withdrew the remaining troops from the South. But it was still necessary to formulate the intellectual terms on which the South could be received back into the nation. This task was undertaken by a group under the leadership of the Atlanta editor Henry W. Grady, who adopted the slogan of the "New South."

Economically, the New South movement sought industrialization, with slogans and aspirations already familiar in Britain and the Northern states; a minor theme, emphasized by Sidney Lanier, was development of diversified farming to replace the single-crop system of the plantation. For literature, the New South movement implied a rapprochement with the Northern publishing houses and magazines which were creating and guiding the new national audience. The Southern writers of fiction who for a decade all but dominated the American magazines—George W. Cable, Joel Chandler Harris, Thomas Nelson Page, and to a less marked extent Mary Noailles Murfree—were committed to the New South point of view. The strategy was explained to them by J. G. Holland and his successor R. W. Gilder of *Scribner-Century*, who in many instances took the initiative in discovering and developing Southern writers. "A sane and earnest Americanism," a calculated desire "to increase the sentiment of Union" were the principles imposed upon the Southerners, and accepted by them, even to the point of editorial deletion of phrases or ideas that were not sufficiently reconstructed. Only by accepting the new order and the principle of integration did these writers achieve a national audience; but once this major position was established they found in the romance of a no longer dangerous South an inexhaustible storehouse of themes related to the prewar plantation for which readers all over the country showed an apparently insatiable appetite. To take a single example, the Negro, presented in fiction according to the Southern conception of an inferior race happily adjusted to a feudal class structure, became a stock literary character of the first importance. If the Southern writers conceded to the nation the fact of union, the nation conceded to the South its view of the race problem, and by the 1890's it was possible for such a former Abolitionist as T. W. Higginson to sit dissolved in tears over the death of a slave owner in Page's "Marse Chan."

3

If the South, during the twenty years from 1876 to 1896, seemed to be transformed from a menace into an opportunity for the industrial and financial metropolis, the West developed in almost exactly the opposite direction. From a numerous army of journalists who set out along the Union Pacific in the late sixties and seventies, Eastern readers learned to think of the trans-Mississippi as a boundless treasure house of natural resources waiting to be developed through the investment of Eastern capital. L. P. Brockett's encyclopedic *Our Western Empire* (1881), which compiled all available information in an apotheosis of the Emigrant's Guides of the first half of the century, adequately represents prevailing attitudes toward the "Goodly heritage, with which God has endowed this Nation." Brockett emphasized economic matters like the new bonanza farming, the cattle industry, mineral resources, railway construction, and the astonishing growth in population beyond the Mississippi. Yet he was apprehensive lest the innumerable Westerners of the future, forced to live "without opportunities of education, and far from civilizing influences," might fail to show proper "reverence for law and order" and might, through pride and fullness of bread, become easy victims of demagogues. The prophecy, although based on widely held opinions, was wide of the mark. When the demagogue did appear, to proclaim the abomination of free silver, he derived his power not from fullness in his hearers but from hunger. The inability of the East to perceive this basic fact about the Populist West had a great deal to do with the misunderstanding between the sections in the eighties and nineties.

The literary discovery of the Far West came soon after the Civil War in the widely acclaimed work of Bret Harte, Joaquin Miller, and Mark Twain. The sudden vogue of Harte, especially, suggests that the American audience was hungry for literary experience beyond the somewhat narrow confines established by current critical theory with its emphasis on ideality. Confronted with the fact of Harte's popularity, the critics at first were inclined to concede that his heart-of-gold formula was an adequate device for palliating the introduction of prostitutes, sluice robbers, and gamblers into fiction. His work, wrote a critic for *Putnam's Magazine* in 1870, showed "the capability of our American experience of an original and fine artistic treatment." With "the eye and the sympathy of genius" the Californian had been able to bring his characters and events, in themselves commonplace and often repulsive, "out of their vulgar relations, and transplant them into a realm of beauty." But as the original freshness of Harte's materials was staled by too constant repetition, and especially when a more sensational exploiter of Western materials appeared in Joaquin Miller, the doubts about morality which had lurked in the background again came to the fore. William Dean Howells predicted in 1882 that readers would not care for "the huge Californian mirth, when the surprise of the picturesquely mixed civilization and barbarism of the Pacific coast has quite died away." Harte dealt, after all, remarked James Herbert Morse in the *Century,* with "passion . . . in its original, natural conditions, released from the decencies of social restraint, and subject only to the instinctive laws of the heart." The *Atlantic* itself, which in 1871 under Howells' editorship had welcomed Harte to the East with the unprecedented offer of ten thousand dollars for his next year's work, had decided by 1882 that sentiment alone was the motive force in his stories; that his heroines had lost their honor, his men their principles; and that at best one could speak of his "unmoral treatment of immoral subjects." Joaquin Miller's more daring exploration of a sentimental, as opposed to a theocratic, code of ethics had already suggested the true leading of his precedessor's "easy optimism," as *Appleton's Journal* had perceived as early as 1876. Bret Harte's effort to find "something good even in the worst of men and women—gamblers, *roués,* border-ruffians, harlots, etc.," remarked the critic for this magazine,

is one thing; but it is quite another to laud these people as, by reason, apparently, of their very "primitiveness" and "savagery," an exceptionally praiseworthy species of the genus man. Mr. Miller makes a parade of condemning everything that civilized and decent men hold in respect; and his social code seems to be that men are "noble," and "grand," and "earnest," and "sincere," and admirable, in exact proportion to their barbarism.

An open and avowed sentimental ethics, then, was going too far. Conservative opinion, accustomed to finding literature heavy with explicit moral judgments, was not prepared to see the moral weight of fiction thrown into the scales on the side of clear violations of the social code. Yet a compromise was possible. If immorality could not be forgiven, certain other less central aspects of barbarism, such as incorrect speech, illiteracy, and uncultivated manners, could be condoned and even enjoyed as picturesque, provided the author demonstrated the inner moral purity of outwardly crude characters. In this milder version, the heart-of-gold formula became the stock in trade of the local-color movement and furnished the framework on which dozens of industrious authors could drape the representations of new landscapes, new provincial types, and new dialects that filled the magazines during what have been called "the local-color eighties."

The influence of the West was felt not only in the development of local-color fiction, but also in a reversal of the westward movement by small but significant numbers of back trailers, sons of pioneers who were impelled east-

ward by disenchantment with the epic dreams of the earliest frontiers and by
the broader opportunities of the metropolitan centers. Lincoln himself was a
back trailer, after a fashion. His election directly involved John Hay's translation to Washington and eventually to a diplomatic post in Paris from what
Hay considered a "dreary waste of heartless materialism" in Warsaw, Illinois;
and was indirectly responsible for sending the young Ohioan Howells, who
had written a campaign biography of Lincoln, to a consulate in Italy. Howells
presently emerged as editor of the *Atlantic* and close associate of the Cambridge Brahmins, while Hay moved into the charmed inner circle of "The
Five of Hearts" (the Henry Adamses, the Hays, and the geologist Clarence
King) in Adams' drawing room. Bret Harte and Joaquin Miller likewise
followed the back trail as far as Europe. Mark Twain settled in Hartford
and, like Godkin and Howells, married an Eastern wife. In other fields men
like John W. Powell, who had made their careers in the West, were climbing
paths of increasing authority and influence to positions comparable with
Powell's directorship of the United States Geological Survey. The name "Back
Trailers" is a creation of the Middle Westerner Hamlin Garland, who followed Howells' footsteps to Boston two decades later, returned for a time to
Chicago in a rather self-conscious effort to establish a literary center independent of the East, and when this effort failed migrated to New York.

Some of the Back Trailers managed to adapt themselves to the newer industrial America, as Howells did, and retained a certain sweetness and poise
as the century drew to a close. But some of them, like Garland, seemed unable to establish a satisfactory relation with either the East or the West; and
some, like Hay, despite successful careers, took over the gloomy social outlook
of leading Eastern intellectuals. The novelists E. W. Howe and Joseph Kirkland, who remained in the Middle West with their own kind of disillusionment at the failure of the high hopes of the first waves of settlement, prepared
grim reports of small-town life that contributed much to the consciously if
mildly antiromantic "realism" of the 1880's. A new literary mood was being
created.

4

The new mood was even more plainly evident in the protests against the
industrial order which were nourished both by Western farmers' resentment
of railroads and moneylenders, and by the growing awareness of poverty and
suffering in the cities. A significant if not a representative ex-Copperhead,
Henry Clay Dean of Iowa, whose nickname "Dirty Shirt" anticipated the
"Sockless Jerry" Simpson period of Populist spellbinding, declared in his impassioned *Crimes of the Civil War* (1868) that the East had used the Re-

publican party to "enslave" the Mississippi Valley under the pretext of freeing the Negro slaves, and pleaded for a union of West and South against the "eastern capital and manufacturing machinery." In the late sixties "Gentleman George" Pendleton, another former Copperhead leader, sponsored the Ohio Idea of repaying war bonds in greenback currency—the earliest of many Western inflationary schemes. A succession of third-party movements leading up to the Populism of the nineties tried in vain to bring about political cooperation between farmers and urban laborers. Humanitarian clergymen in the cities, appalled by conditions in the slums, developed a "social gospel" which proclaimed, in the words of the Congregational minister George D. Herron, that "the Sermon on the Mount is the science of society."

Such movements gave rise to a vast body of writing, both imaginative and expository, denouncing the plutocracy in the name of an older American equalitarianism. Henry George, the most influential critic of the existing order, constructed his single-tax theory in protest against the monopolies in land he had observed being formed during the sixties in California. The most important novelists of the dissident group—Edward Bellamy, the early Hamlin Garland, and William Dean Howells in his Utopian phase—different as they were in detail, were alike in their refusal to accept either the standards of value or the practical consequences of the economic revolution.

The critics of Big Business were unable to find support in the conservative New England literary tradition. The great Bostonians were gentlemen, well descended and almost to a man independently wealthy. Longfellow, Lowell, Holmes, Norton—such men belonged to an aristocracy that could hardly be called even middle-class, and it was difficult for them to conceive of a literature not produced in an atmosphere of refined leisure. The dominant literary figures of New York, such as Edmund Clarence Stedman, Charles Dudley Warner, and Richard Henry Stoddard, strove to keep literature unsullied from the world of politics and economics. "There were certain subjects," remarked Stoddard's literary executor, "which remained wholly foreign to the atmosphere of the poet's library. He lived in New York, but the omnipotent name of the stock market was never heard"—despite the fact that Stedman, one of Stoddard's most intimate friends, was head of a firm of brokers.

Nevertheless, the stock market existed, and in the last decade of the century, men who studied American society became increasingly aware that changes were under way whose end no man could see. The historian Frederick Jackson Turner's famous paper on "The Significance of the Frontier in American History," read in the year of the Panic of 1893, ominously announced "the closing of a great historical movement" with the imminent disappearance of the frontier of settlement in the West. In an essay on "Industry and Finance" contributed to the three-volume symposium *The United States of America* edited by the Harvard geologist Nathaniel S. Shaler in 1894, the economist F. W. Taussig noted the decline in the rate of growth in population since 1860 and predicted it would continue. Like Turner, he asserted that the good farming lands of the public domain were nearing exhaustion, and drew the inference that "The conditions of the future must be different from those of the past." Other contributors to the symposium alluded to the many problems that industrialization and urbanization had brought: the "new immigration" from Southern and Eastern Europe, the slum, the approaching exhaustion of forests and other natural resources, corruption in municipal government, trusts and monopolies. Dr. D. A. Sargent of Harvard, the noted expert on physical training, described the nervousness resulting from the pressures and stimuli of modern urban life and asked, "Can we stand it?" He believed that Americans would learn to adapt themselves to the new conditions, but the question itself would have sounded strange amid the optimistic predictions made at the opening of the Philadelphia Centennial Exposition of 1876, when Progress was the watchword and official spokesmen unanimously foresaw a new age which would outshine even the glorious first century of the Republic.

The somber tone of the early nineties was brightened somewhat by the success of another world's fair, the Columbian Exposition at Chicago. Here, in the white neoclassical columns and the majestic esplanades, was evidence both that the supposedly materialistic West had grown upward into aesthetic expression and that American art in general need no longer be called weak and pretentious in comparison with the best work of Europe, as it had so unmistakably seemed at Philadelphia two decades earlier. Even Henry Adams, who made two visits to Chicago and found there "matter of study to fill a hundred years," was willing to acknowledge that the West had at least known how to hire its art made for it. Sitting on the steps before Richard Hunt's Administration Building, he was tempted for a moment to wonder whether it was indeed as impossible as he had imagined for "the new American world to take this sharp and conscious twist towards ideals." "Chicago," he wrote, "asked in 1893 for the first time the question whether the American people knew where they were driving."

But on his return to Washington late in the summer, he found his answer in the repeal of the Sherman Silver Purchase Act. He interpreted the establishment of the gold standard as the final decision of the American people to abandon the past, the eighteenth century, the Constitution of 1789, the world of the Adamses, and to accept the leadership of business.

A capitalistic system [Adams continued] had been adopted, and if it were to be run at all, it must be run by capital and capitalistic methods; for nothing could surpass the nonsensity of trying to run so complex and so concentrated a machine by Southern and Western farmers in grotesque alliance with city day-laborers, as had been tried in 1800 and 1828 and had failed even under simple conditions.

If Adams overdramatized the year 1893, at least his analysis of the outcome of the Industrial Revolution in America suggests the future that faced the nation on the eve of the twentieth century: "Once admitted that the machine must be efficient, society might dispute in what social interest it should be run, but in any case it must work concentration." And concentration meant

the protective tariff; the corporations and trusts; the trades-unions and socialistic paternalism which necessarily made their complement; the whole mechanical consolidation of force, which ruthlessly stamped out the life of the class into which Adams was born, but created monopolies capable of controlling the new energies that America adored.

# 49. THE EDUCATION OF EVERYMAN

JAMES A. GARFIELD, last of the log-cabin candidates to sit in the White House, declared at Lake Chautauqua during his campaign in 1880: "We may divide the whole struggle of the human race into two chapters: first, the fight to get leisure; and then the second fight of civilization—what shall we do with our leisure when we get it." Sitting there in the lake breeze, his audience knew what Garfield meant, these prosperous farmers with leathery faces and gnarled hands, retired merchants and small-town bankers with palm-leaf fans, women who had left their summer canning and jelly making to come and hear about books and ideas. Most of them were middle-aged or over, for leisure had come late and dearly bought. Even so had success come to the speaker—scion of a poor pioneer family "hungry for the horizon," who had reversed their westward march to work his way through Williams College, and become schoolmaster and politician.

The setting of the speech was significant. In southwestern New York State in 1874 an experiment in adult education had begun. Lewis Miller, agricultural inventor and Sunday-school teacher, here joined forces with a onetime circuit rider, John H. Vincent, who as a youth had gone preaching with "a few very good books" in his saddlebags. These two Methodists started with the idea of a camp meeting for Sunday-school teachers. Thanks to their own inclinations and the link which bound the church to social life and serious entertainment in most middle-sized American towns, they soon found themselves sponsoring a cultural program called the Chautauqua Assembly. Lectures on the Bible and Palestinian geography quickly expanded into study courses in history, literature, science, art, and music. In 1878, gratified by the popular demand, Dr. Vincent extended "the Idea" to include a winter's program of reading at home, the Chautauqua Literary and Scientific Circle. The circle offered a four-year study course, like that of the regular colleges, appealing to middle-aged women for whom the establishment of Vassar, Smith, and Wellesley had come too late. Members studied European and American history, classical civilization, and modern science. Those who persevered to the end won a diploma and marched on Recognition Day through the Golden Gate, while flower girls strewed their path—in a quaint blending of academic with nuptial pageantry. By 1892, one hundred thousand were currently enrolled in the circle. The advent in 1883 of William Rainey Harper, future president of the University of Chicago, as educational director, attracted to Chautauqua some of America's best university lecturers, such as the historians John Fiske and Herbert B. Adams, the economist Richard T. Ely, the psychologist G. Stanley Hall. William James might stand appalled before these "earnest and helpless minds," but his Harvard colleague George Herbert Palmer saw the colony of summer tents and tabernacles as the expression of a folk impulse, idealistic, hopeful, bizarre, but vital, comparable to the Crusades or the Greek Mysteries.

From the shores of this lake the Idea spread far and wide in the eighties. Hosts of local Chautauquas each summer drew their hundreds of thousands, sending them home to study over the winter months, to earn "seals" for their diplomas. The ranks of those who "wanted to know" were swelled by young men and women seeking bonds of acquaintance, housewives and shut-ins, pastors and congregations, a myriad farm and village families caught in the doldrums of loneliness between the husking bee and house-raising of frontier days and the undiscovered future of motorcar, radio, and movies. Above all, in this generation Chautauqua helped allay the thirst of those middle-class Americans who had had too little book-learning in the rude schoolhouses and poor libraries of their youth, and now felt an urge to come within hailing distance of their children. The gospel according to Chautauqua proclaimed that study was no longer drudgery, but radiant opportunity; that education did not end when a boy went to work or a girl got married, but persisted forever. It also asserted that knowledge was no closed preserve or class monopoly, but lay open to squatters' rights by Everyman.

The breaking of barriers between scholar and common citizen, scientist and mechanic, specialist and layman, is a corollary of that Jeffersonian democracy which needs many generations to work out all its implications. But no era in American history saw more speeding of the process, in the diffusion and popularization of knowledge, than the seventies and eighties. The Civil War and Reconstruction had been distracting to adults of military and business age, even though education for the young had advanced steadily. The Panic of 1873 induced, if not an about-face to plain living and high thinking, at least some inkling of values more durable than Wall Street stocks. Even more important in the long run was a growing mass awareness of the new science and its miracles—if not Darwin and Huxley, then the visible wonders of chemistry and electricity—with the consequent stirrings of curiosity in many, hostility among a few. Moreover, this same science purchased freedom from toil and a broader margin of leisure, for farmer as well as city dweller.

And finally, the technique of publishing had begun to bombard the average citizen with the printed word. From newspapers he might pass tentatively to the cheaper magazines and paper-backed novels, thence to books of better quality, until he began imperceptibly to educate himself. From the other side of the barrier, seeking to make easy his ingress into the garden of knowledge, were both the idealists, like Chautauqua's founders, and entrepreneurs like James Redpath the lecture agent, Thomas J. Foster the founder in the eighties of the International Correspondence Schools at Scranton, and a little later Elbert Hubbard the author of chapbooks inspirational and informative.

Popularization had a dark and a bright side. On the one hand, it often meant a cheapening of standards that spread from adult mass education into other compartments of American life, such as schools, colleges, and pulpits. A smattering took the place of scholarship, while intellectual distinction faded in the glare of novelty and notoriety. On the other hand, it helped keep the savant from isolation and intellectual snobbery, and the common man from sullen suspicion of these mysteries. The Wisconsin novelist Zona Gale called the phenomenon of the eighties "a homely renaissance, not of learning, but of study." Whether for good or ill, it helped to make us the greatest popularizers of knowledge on earth. Our shrewdest observer, Lord Bryce, recognized this fact in 1888, reporting in his *American Commonwealth* that "the average of knowledge is higher, the habit of reading and thinking more generally diffused, than in any other country."

Kindred symptoms, in the post-Appomattox period, had antedated Chautauqua. The women's club in America began in 1868 with the Sorosis in New York and the New England Women's Club in Boston; by 1889, when the nation-wide General Federation of Women's Clubs was organized, uncounted thousands of women were conning Robert's *Rules of Order,* or preparing papers on English flower gardens and the poetry of Robert Browning. Also in 1868, the journalist Redpath from Boston revamped the old lyceum into a commercialized lecture bureau. Attended by greater publicity, and featuring more humor, color, and sheer entertainment, the Redpath Lyceum Bureau quickly raised the modest $25 and $50 fees for which Emerson and Thoreau had once spoken, to the $400 to $500 commanded by John B. Gough the reformed drunkard or Thomas Nast the cartoonist, or the $1,000 sometimes paid Henry Ward Beecher or Henry M. Stanley (just back from darkest Africa). Almost equal in popularity were Anna E. Dickinson the crusader and feminist, John L. Stoddard with stereopticon views of his travels, and funny men like Petroleum V. Nasby and Mark Twain. When some old favorites dropped out, and lectures began to pall, Redpath turned first to magicians, then to musical soloists and quartets, small opera companies, and programs verging more and more upon the domain of the circus. The edifying lecture, which had driven a wedge in Puritan America for opera and drama, slowly crumbled in the later years of the century, after long-continued profit from the quest for culture.

2

"I never made a success of a lecture in a church yet. People are afraid to laugh in a church," wrote Mark Twain to Redpath early in the seventies. But inspirational speakers easily bridged the chasm between lyceum and pulpit. One of the most celebrated was the Reverend Russell H. Conwell of Philadelphia, who delivered his "Acres of Diamonds" some six thousand times. "Opportunity is in your own backyard," was the theme. A religion of success, old as Cotton Mather and popular enough before the Civil War, now flourished with renewed vigor. Its great practitioner in fiction was Horatio Alger. A neurotic Unitarian clergyman, timid and solitary, he lived in a newsboys' hostel in Manhattan and wrote more than a hundred books of pluck and luck, beginning with *Ragged Dick* (1867) and *Tattered Tom* (1871), together with inspirational lives of Lincoln and Garfield. Like many exemplars of the success cult, these books were products of the author's own morbid awareness of failure. But beyond question they mirrored a naïve hopefulness, a passion for self-improvement, characteristic of the times. Their blend of morality with riches can be found in scores of nonfiction books throughout this period, all pointing the way to wealth and happiness.

In this age of many aspirations, the church found itself a house divided. Too often it yielded to the blandishment of riches, ultimately to lose prestige both as spiritual and educative force in American life. Some ground it recovered through the gospel of social service, trying to satisfy the query propounded in the nineties by Charles M. Sheldon's immensely popular novel *In His Steps*—"What would Jesus do?" The success of two other best sellers in this generation, *Ben Hur* (1880) and the Revised Version of the Bible (1881–1885), gauges the breadth of religious interest. More radical departures from orthodoxy appeared in the cult of Christian Science, stemming from Mrs. Eddy's *Science and Health* (1875), and flowering into churches, reading rooms, lecture courses, and literature of nation-wide distribution; the Theosophical Society, established in New York by Madame Blavatsky in 1875; and Dr. Felix Adler's Society for Ethical Culture, founded in 1876. Meanwhile, the rapid increase of Roman Catholic power, notably through the new immigration, stirred forebodings in rural Protestant minds and led to the foundation in 1887 of a secret order, the American Protective Association, which, like the Know-Nothing movement of the fifties, for a while aligned farm belt against city, Anglo-Saxon against Irish and Latin culture.

A more important battle front in the zone of religious loyalties lay between supernaturalism and science. Within a few years after the Civil War, the real impact of Darwin's theory regarding the descent of man was first felt in American thought. The New York *World* published John Fiske's Harvard lectures on Darwin and Comte; in 1871 James Freeman Clarke's popular *Ten Great Religions* introduced the public to the subject of comparative religions and myths; in this year Edward L. Youmans, a self-taught farm boy from upper New York State, established the International Scientific Series, to which Tyndall, Darwin, Huxley, and Helmholtz soon contributed, and in 1872 Youmans launched his *Popular Science Monthly*. The hypotheses of science found perhaps their ablest champions in the seventies in President Andrew D. White of Cornell, whose famous Cooper Union speech, "The Battlefields of Science," was embodied in the book *The Warfare of Science* (1876); and in Dr. John W. Draper, physicist, physician, and author of the widely read *History of the Conflict between Religion and Science* (1874). Almost from the first, certain liberal clergymen like Henry Ward Beecher proclaimed that geology no less than Genesis was a revelation of God's purpose, that the animal origins of *homo sapiens* no more impeached his dignity than did the "mud man" theory of Creation. Citadels of the old-time religion could not be expected to strike their flags in instant surrender. "Harvard's raid on religion" was fiercely resented in the Corn Belt; young Vanderbilt University in 1878 dismissed a professor of geology for "untamed speculation," and within the next six years similar purges occurred in at least three other academies in the South. More thoughtful men meditated an emergent paradox deeper than these conflicts—between survival of the fittest and the law of love and solicitude, with even science (cast in the role of healer) seeking to arrest the harsher operations of nature. As time went on, popular curiosity about the new biology and anthropology increased, reaching some kind of truce with the old dogmas of supernaturalism. When in 1893 a series of lectures on evolution by Henry Drummond was the feature of that Chautauqua summer, the *Nation* called it "a sign of the times which no observer can neglect."

3

Beside this harvest of new ideas, fruitful of debate, questioning, and final assimilation, one must set the more tangible instruments of culture which aided the sowing of those ideas through the Republic. Reading, writing, school teaching, travel, and bookmaking advanced in a manner befitting a literate and technical-minded democracy. For not even the Fundamentalists opposed the new efficiency of applied science.

In 1876 Alexander Graham Bell invented the telephone, a boon to communication and the breaking down of rural isolation, while doubtless contributing to the decay of letter writing as a fine art. Of vast import to the literary man and journalist was Christopher Sholes' invention of the typewriter in 1868. Mark Twain and a few other pioneers took it up with alacrity; most creative writers lagged behind businessmen in its adoption. Its ultimate effect upon literature—in promoting fluency and speed, while perhaps discouraging niceties of revision—can hardly be measured today, when most writers have become very centaurs of the machine age, half man and half keyboard. The practice of dictation, common in American business life after the spread of the Pitman system; popularity of the new Eclectic method in the seventies, and introduction of the Gregg system at the close of our period, appealed to only a few literary men—notably Henry James in his later years—and its effects upon style were consequently sparse. A greater aid to the average man came in 1884, with Lewis E. Waterman's invention of the fountain pen, enabling one to write wherever he went. Also universal were the innovations wrought in the reading and writing habits of Americans by the steady improvements in gas illumination through the seventies, and the final triumph of Edison's incandescent light early in the eighties. In the multiplication of books, no other achievement of modern times surpasses Ottmar Mergenthaler's invention of the linotype in 1885.

4

In general the phenomenal growth of the city during the quarter-century after Appomattox meant concentration of the demand for culture and amusement, bigger and possibly better newspapers, magazines, publishing houses, and bookshops. It also meant more local wealth for the taxgatherer's sickle, with correspondingly improved municipal art galleries, museums, concert halls, public libraries, and schools. Such interplay quickened the educative and creative spirit within the focus of city life.

Illiteracy declined from 17 per cent of our population in 1880 to 13 per cent in 1890, despite the influx from Ellis Island. Compulsory school laws, beginning in the North and West in the early seventies, embraced nineteen states at the start of the next decade. Free textbooks were first offered in New York City in the eighties, then spread to other cities, and were presently demanded for back-country schools by crusaders like Minnesota's Ignatius Donnelly. In the farm belt, groups such as the Farmers' Alliance and the Grange agitated for better schools; the Grange itself, through its circulating libraries and homely debates on politics and economics, built civic intelligence. In 1878 high schools numbered less than 800 throughout the nation;

twenty years later, 5,500 were reported. This increase in turn fed colleg attendance enormously, making higher education less a class luxury and mor the birthright of all Americans with ambition and ability.

Between the common school and the college, vocational education wa spreading its vast ramifications. In the wake of the Morrill Act of 1862, trad and technological schools in the East were prone to stress engineering; in the Midwest and the South, agriculture; in the Rocky Mountain and Fa West, mining and metallurgy. Other institutions fitted themselves for nev service. In the seventies the Young Men's Christian Association had begur to assume cultural as well as spiritual and recreational tasks; in the eightie it set up evening classes in crafts and skills which proved popular. This latte decade also saw the dawn of university extension courses, through lecture and correspondence methods, under the inspiration of British example and the labors of Herbert B. Adams from Johns Hopkins.

Among the universities, innovation flowed from the Harvard of Charle William Eliot. In the *Atlantic* in 1869 he had blown the reveille whose echoe sounded through the next generation: the elective system, shattering the ole predestined regimen of ancient languages and disciplines, giving play to free will. In consequence, modern languages and history, science, applied mathe matics, economics, and English literature came virtually to dominate the field. The new state universities, seeking broad programs of study, welcomed this change with as much alacrity as they showed respecting another inno- vation, coeducation. Women's work in the Civil War had accelerated rec- ognition of their rights in higher education and the professions, just as their services in a later war sped the award of the ballot. By 1880 the United States counted 154 mixed colleges and universities, in addition to those exclusively the property of women, pioneered by Vassar in 1865, and Smith and Wellesley ten years later.

Graduate study was another marked development of the times. At Yale and Harvard organized graduate work began about 1870, though a few doc- torates on the German model had been given in the sixties. Johns Hopkins opened in 1876 as an institution of purely graduate study. Private endow- ments, upon a scale of generosity hitherto unknown, led to establishment of new and powerful universities—of which Stanford, founded in 1885—is representative. The eighties also witnessed a flow of American students toward German universities, where Virchow, Mommsen, Harnack, and other teachers of world fame had set up the highest standards of research then known. An estimated two thousand American candidates for degrees were constantly in residence there throughout the eighties. By 1886, with due acknowledgment of past benefits, James Russell Lowell began to voice alarm lest Prussian pedantry widen the breach between mere erudition ("the new dry rot of learning") and true culture of the spirit. Men of his persuasion turned increasingly for their ideal toward Oxford and Cambridge, where a balance was held between extremes in a manner befitting the cardinal maxim of humanism, "nothing in excess." But just now, in an age of avid specialization, they found themselves outvoted.

## 5

For the great mass of Americans, the printed word remained their chief instrument of culture. A most significant development, therefore, was the burgeoning of public libraries. Subscribers' libraries, as has been seen, flourished from colonial times. In many a city, ambitious mechanics and laborers pooled modest resources for a common lending library. But free public libraries supported by taxation were comparatively late, beginning in communities of New Hampshire, Massachusetts, and Maine around the middle of the nineteenth century. In 1865 several other states began to follow, until the whole nation swung into line. By 1875 the number of free libraries owning upwards of a thousand books was 2,000; by the century's end it had grown to 5,400. Early arguments for the cause strike a modern mind as rather naïve: for example, that studious workingmen will absent themselves from "haunts of vice and folly," while the unemployed "are much safer with a book in the library than elsewhere." Thus, as if to appease a lingering scruple of Puritan capitalism, many Americans have always found hardheaded arguments for mass cultivation and recreation. Greatest of private benefactors was the steel king Andrew Carnegie. In 1881 he began to donate library buildings to those towns which would provide the site and promise maintenance. Before the end of this era, the continent was studded with Carnegie libraries. Meanwhile, to promote efficiency of cataloguing and other services, the American Library Association had been organized in 1876.

Magazines were growing in number from 200 at the outbreak of the Civil War, to 1,800 by the end of the century. Highest literary prestige still clung to the *Atlantic,* which in 1871 passed into the editorial hands of young William Dean Howells from Ohio. Boston Brahmins, like Holmes, who impressed him with solemn remarks about apostolic succession and the laying on of hands, had picked their man with much astuteness: Howells deferred to his "Holy Land of Boston" and its literary mores, while injecting into his job the earnest enthusiasms of the West. Despite all his efforts, the *Atlantic* was far outstripped in the race for circulation by *Harper's,* which prospered steadily under the editorship of Henry Mills Alden. The really spectacular successes were reserved for the *Century* under Richard Watson Gilder, which in 1885 topped 200,000, eventually helping to draw Howells himself to the brighter lights of New York; and on less literary levels, the *Ladies' Home Journal,* with 270,000 circulation in this same year, and the *Youth's Companion* with 385,000, as a record-breaker of all previous time. Artificial aids to circulation in these days were the news-stand traffic of organizations like the American News Company, and the awarding to new subscribers of premiums ranging from lithographs to sewing machines. Small but influential was the *Nation* under E. L. Godkin, begun in 1865, whose ideas were cribbed by innumerable liberal preachers, lecturers, and editors throughout the country. Thomas Nast's cartoons against the Tweed Ring and later corruptions buttressed the crusading prestige of *Harper's Weekly.* In 1877 *Puck* appeared, the first durably successful magazine of humor in America, fashioned somewhat on the model of the London *Punch*; *Judge* followed in 1881, and *Life* with more subtle satire in 1883. When set beside an ante-bellum specialist in misspelling and rustic horseplay like Shillaber's *Carpet-Bag,* such magazines reveal the coming-of-age of American tastes in comedy.

In the book trade, New York clearly overshadowed every other center of production, as early as 1865 excelling Boston and Philadelphia put together. In the eighties Chicago began to challenge these runners-up, with San Francisco continuing her prosperous regional business. Certain developments within the trade promoted the circulation of books. Rescued from the obscurity of certain back shelves in drug and mercantile stores, or casual newspaper racks, the bookshop declared its independence in scores of middle-sized American towns, and by window display sought to make its wares attractive. Circulating libraries, often as adjuncts of these shops, continued to multiply. With even greater enterprise, book agents became an increasingly common sight, canvassing from house to house in town and suburban communities, or jogging along country roads from farm to farm. They were the heirs of Parson Weems and the Yankee peddler of Bronson Alcott's youth, but unlike their forebears dealt almost exclusively in books. In the first years after Appomattox they vended encyclopedias, dictionaries, illustrated books about battles and leaders of the Civil War, and sets of standard authors. Soon they began to purvey series—like the Seaside Library, Standard Library, Leisure Hour Series, Library of American Humor, Town and Country Library, fiction and nonfiction, of variable quality, in cheap cloth and paper—which issued from presses in an unending stream. Foreign titles abounded, in the lack of international copyright. The obviously heavy profits for publisher, but small royalties to author, of a canvassing concern like the American Publishing Company of Hartford, led Mark Twain early in the eighties to set up his own firm, C. L. Webster & Company, and to achieve a dazzling success by selling over 300,000 sets of General Grant's Memoirs at $9 to $25 a set. Other ventures, like a life of Pope Leo XIII which Twain assumed all good Catholics would buy, proved far less lucky, and the ultimate crash of that firm is well known. Nor was the effect of "subscription sets" upon literature itself a very happy one. To take an example from the same author, Twain's *Life on the Mississippi,* written for James R. Osgood of Boston and his impatient canvassers, had been hurried along and padded out, to bring it up to cubic specifications, at the cost of inspired art.

The greatest disservice which publishing methods inflicted upon this generation of authors came from a lack of international copyright laws. Every author was likely to be without profit save in his own country, and even on native ground had to bear an unfair competition with foreign authors which did not even benefit them. In the sixties and early seventies a "courtesy of the trade" convention, among American publishers of European books, for a while curbed excessive reprints. But it collapsed in the latter seventies and eighties, as new firms multiplied and competition in paperbacks grew fiercer. Abroad conditions were no better. John Camden Hotten and other Britons flew no flag but the Jolly Roger. By 1878, as G. H. Putnam reported, one out of every ten books printed in England was an American book. Typographers, binders, and printing management in general opposed international copyright, masking their greed in pious words about the cheap dissemination of good books. Needless to say, the basis of their selection was not quality, but often quite the reverse. On their side, authors and magazine editors fought for new legislation, banding together in 1883 as the American Copyright League, to bring pressure in Washington. The Berne Copyright Convention in 1887 found the United States still isolationist. Not until 1891 was the first major battle won, when a workable law (though not so stringent as the Berne Convention) finally passed Congress.

Culturally this was a generation of parvenus—naïve, exuberant, in the main self-satisfied. Vastly impressed by the wonders of applied science and the material gains for which it thanked Edison and Bell, the average American was oblivious of Willard Gibbs and looked somewhat askance at Darwin and Huxley. Yet his awareness of economic and intellectual problems and dilemmas was not without significance, nor was the talisman, increasingly prized everywhere, of a college education and a nodding acquaintance with "the best books."

The primary stage of American culture, literacy, which had gone hand in hand with the primary era in our material production—of corn and cotton, coal and iron—had absorbed majority interest and effort prior to the Civil War. Now a secondary stage had begun. Upon the material plane industrialization of a once agrarian nation laid new stress upon manufactures, their technology and quantitative output. Meanwhile, in the sphere of mass culture, a more than literate citizenship sought to fuse the inspirational with the utilitarian, sensing in education and books the means to an end of worldly success and happiness. A tertiary stage—which might witness the emergence of fine craftsmanship upon the one plane, and a corresponding concept of quality upon the other—had hardly begun to develop.

# 0. DEFENDERS OF IDEALITY

BETWEEN 1870 and 1890, therefore, the lder tradition in American literature—the tradition which found its rigins in Franklin and Edwards, its fulfillment in Emerson and Melville and Whitman—seemed suddenly the articulation of a vanished era. Only its ideals urvived, but without their familiar bearings. Painfully the American writer nust start over again the gigantic task of national self-discovery and expresion, of reducing elemental experience to the discipline of art. The securities f Concord and Cambridge were gone, even though Longfellow and Lowell, Holmes and Emerson, lived on. Plainly the culture for which so much effort ,ad been expended, and which now seemed so close to perfection, must be ,reserved. Mark Twain and William Dean Howells, already becoming the pokesmen for the new realism, felt its power and hurried East on the morng of their first fame. The issue was sharply drawn: if one wished to write, ,ne must choose to defend the old order or to throw in one's lot with the ,ew. There was no easy blending of ideality with reality in these uncertain imes.

From the time of the Civil War until past the turn of the century, the vriting and the criticism of poetry were largely in the hands of a group of riends bound by many personal and literary ties. Presenting a united front to he materialism of the age, resentful of the claims of the realists, they self-:onsciously proclaimed themselves the champions of Ideality in literature. Their influence was so persuasive that when their control over editors and ɔublishers was broken by the writers of the newer generation, the naturalistic ɾevolt was the more violent because they had held it in check for more than ɑ quarter of a century.

At the center of the group were five close friends—Stoddard, Taylor, Boker, Aldrich, and Stedman. They had made their way up together, and during the early years in New York they were constant companions. They praised one another in their correspondence and occasional verse; they reviewed one another, dedicated books to one another, and cajoled editors to help along their common cause. Surrounding them were a dozen writers, obedient to the same canons of criticism and allied to them through friend-ship.

Their common denominator was Richard Henry Stoddard. New England born, the son of a sailor, as a boy and young man he was scarred by a poverty which left him the least sophisticated of their company. Not until he was over fifty could he support himself completely by writing. The meeting place of their company—"the band," as they called themselves—was Stoddard's house at the northeast corner of Fourth Avenue and Tenth Street. His ardor and sympathy and the critical acumen of his moody wife, whose forgotten novels show her to have been gifted with an imagination finer than that of any member of the group, were the ties that drew them to Dick and Lizzie.

The first to join Stoddard was Bayard Taylor, eventually the most widely known of their company. Taylor's first fame had come when he reported in Views A-foot (1846) how he made the European grand tour on less than five hundred dollars. His ambition was to be a great poet, and his published verse eventually filled a dozen volumes. But his insatiable public wanted from him only new accounts of exotic lands. In twenty years' time he surveyed the world. Between excursions he wrote three creditable novels on social themes, built himself a lavish house at his native Kennett Square, near Philadelphia, and served as secretary of legation at St. Petersburg. His friends could not have been surprised when, at the moment of his greatest triumph as newly appointed Minister to Germany, the body which ambition had pushed beyond endurance refused to obey his will any longer, and he died at fifty-three.

Even closer to Taylor than Stoddard was the handsome, aristocratic millionaire, George H. Boker, whose house at 1720 Walnut Street was the Philadelphia rendezvous of the group. Each moved gracefully in the company of European diplomats and writers. Boker had the means to indulge his connoisseurship of good living; Taylor did not have the means, but he lived well all the same and sometimes let Boker lend him the money. Less feverishly active than Taylor's, Boker's life was a crowded and useful one, in business, in literature, in the affairs of his native city, and in diplomacy.

Thomas Bailey Aldrich, the Tom Bailey of his Story of a Bad Boy (1870), was destined for Harvard, but his father's death forced him to try business in New York. Deserting Pearl Street for journalism, he flocked with the Bohemians at Pfaff's restaurant in the basement of 647 Broadway. Though he soon repudiated these early companionships, the attenuations of Boston life never effaced his early dandyism. Safely in New England in 1865, he was glad to forget the stridencies of New York; he wondered that he had got out with his English tolerably correct. The act was symbolic: he would be withdrawing the rest of his life—from his editorship of the Atlantic, from Boston, even, to the Maine seacoast and to the indolence of travel.

New Yorkers spent the month of October, 1859, laughing over "The Diamond Wedding," a poem in the Tribune which satirized the well advertised vulgarities of a courtship in what was called society. The poem brought the young poet, Edmund Clarence Stedman, the threat of a duel and a lawsuit, but it also made him a member of the band. Taylor, meeting him in the *Tribune* offices, invited him to the house which he and Stoddard were sharing. The next year, through Stoddard's connivance, Scribner's issued Stedman's first collection of verse. In time he would become the member of the group whose criticism most thoroughly expressed their ideals. He would evangelize for them in Philistia itself, for Stedman earned his living in Wall Street, and his contemporaries thought it a wonderful thing that a poet could also be a broker.

Around this loyal band of five, who thought and felt as one, must be grouped their outriders, if one is to gauge their influence. It is indicative of their early prestige that the Southern poet, Paul Hamilton Hayne, sought them out by correspondence in the late sixties in order that he might find his way back into the society of writers. As Hayne came into their circle, Thomas Buchanan Read, now remembered only for his "Sheridan's Ride," dropped out. By the late fifties he had forsaken poetry for portrait painting and wrote his friends condescendingly from London, where Patmore undid him by declaring that his "Closing Scene" was superior to Gray's "Elegy" and where the Brownings sat to him. In contrast, William Winter was their most faithful adherent. During the forty years he was dramatic critic on the *Tribune* he preached their law against the heresies of Ibsen. Exiled in California and later in Ohio, Edward Rowland Sill, who would not let editors print his name under his poems, reached Eastward for the advice of Aldrich: "I have no friendly sage at hand to help me judge of my things. . . . So I have to send and trouble you." Richard Watson Gilder, editor of the *Century*, 1881–1909, must be counted in this company. So should Louise Chandler Moulton, Boston poetess and dealer in discreet literary gossip, and Richard Grant White, a gentleman always, and a critic occasionally. This is only the beginning of the roll. The lesser names, or shall we say, the names of the less well known, the curious may find in the 1,292 pages which the official biography of Stedman requires to tell the story of his literary friendships.

The members of the band of five and their satellites were sure that they represented the continuing tradition in poetry and criticism, yet they saw that the Civil War was a great divide separating the older New England generation from theirs. In their efforts to renew the tradition and keep its aims high, they felt they were contending with the depravity of a public which for ten years had been fed on the literature of sensation and propaganda generated by the war. They had also to make their way against the continued popularity of Longfellow, Holmes, and Whittier, who still charmed but were now, so they said, "running in grooves."

Their attitude toward these elder poets is ambivalent. They were tied
them by many acts of kindness received at their hands. Aldrich acknowledge
that Longfellow made him a poet. Stedman wrote Whittier in 1890: "Y
have put your hands upon my head and blessed me." Taylor was grateful
Lowell for having been the first to give his poetry respectful criticism. Ev
Stoddard, who occasionally got out of line and wrote disparagingly of h
elders (the band was distressed by his irreverent review of Lowell's *Under t
Willows*), remembered the day when Hawthorne received him, an unknow
young poet, and took him up to himself as an equal and a friend.

In the band's relations with Lowell one begins to see that there were flaw
in this filial regard. They submitted meekly enough to his epistolary lecture
and time and again they humbly accepted honors first offered to him: Tayl
in 1876, when he took the commission of the Centennial Ode after Lowe
(as well as Bryant, Longfellow, Holmes, and Whittier) had refused it; Ste
man in 1891, when he delivered the first series of Turnbull Lectures on poetr
at Johns Hopkins in place of Lowell who had declined. But as their reput
tions increased, we can see from angry outbursts in their letters that the
chafed under this gentle domination by their elders—all except Aldrich, c
course, who was, as he said, if not genuine Boston, at least "Boston-plated.

This determination to assume their rightful place is evident also in thei
attitude toward their English contemporaries. They believed that at la
poetry and fiction were on the same level in the two countries. They accepte
the friendship of English writers with no trace of humility or bluster. Nc
even Aldrich who idled around Europe in his last years had anything of th
expatriate about him. Though they spoke constantly of the difficulty of thei
fight, they never felt, as did some of their later disciples, that it would be los
and that escape from American vulgarity was the only possible retreat.

Without possessing George W. Curtis' zeal for reform or Henry Adams
cosmic insight, they were appalled by the dislocations of American society
The holy show the *arrivistes* made of themselves from Nob Hill to Newport
the antics of what Stedman called the "champagne aristocracy," the preten
tiousness of its Fifth Avenue *palazzi*, its toadying to bogus titles of nobility
moved them to oppose to this vulgarity the ideal world of their poetry
Economically illiterate, as most intelligent Americans have been until recently
they could not fathom the changes in the nation's life. Even if they could have
followed the sinuous legal line by which, under the Fourteenth Amendment
the sacred American doctrine of individual rights had been twisted into sanc
tion for the unlicensed greed of great corporations, they would have rejected
the evidence. They saw nothing incongruous in their friendship with such
comparatively civilized plutocrats as Andrew Carnegie and Collis P. Huntington.

They proposed to reduce the fever of the age by means of a poultice of Ideal Poetry. What exactly they meant by the phrase is not easy to say since they used it passionately. All they disliked about the era of Grant they summed up under realism—its materialism, the extravagant rewards it offered men of action, its faith that science would soon answer all questions. From this world of immediate reality poets faithful to their noble calling must try to lure men to the ideal world of the artist's creation. Two stanzas in Boker's *Book of the Dead* sum up their position:

> We poets hang upon the wheel
>     Of Time's advancement; do our most
> To hide his inroads, and reveal
>     The splendors which the world has lost.

> Science and Avarice, arm in arm,
>     Stride proudly through our abject time;
> And in their footsteps, wrangling, swarm
>     Their own begotten broods of crime.

What happens in this ideal world? Who inhabit it? Obviously it is not the Platonic heaven of ideas; nor is it a spiritual kingdom, since these poets share in the passive agnosticism of their age. Stoddard, in his "Castle in the Air," locates it within the heart, but shows that he does not mean by his trope the complex consciousness of modern man. It is, evidently, the world of dreams in which the poet's spirit wanders, unfettered from the False and free to seek the (ideally) True. Here we have it. The ideal world of these poets can only be achieved in dreams from which all base desire, all action (except heroic action), all speculation have been purged. Stedman, as usual, most clearly shows us what they were aiming at. Speaking of Tennyson's "Lady of Shalott" and "A Dream of Fair Women," he calls them "those peculiar, delicious, ideal —*intensely ideal* and elevated productions."

When one understands that this is the kind of poetry they desired to write, it is easy to account for certain of their principles and prejudices. Their objection to dialect poetry, for example, is subsumed from their belief that the deeds and words of Harte's gamblers and Kipling's soldiers are not the stuff from which poetic dreams can be distilled. Or consider their stand on sex as a fit subject for poetry. The prevalent notion that they were prudes is, of course, absurd and is derived apparently from the editorial allergies of the squeamish Gilder who was not a charter member of their band. The youthful poetry of all of them is warmer than that of Keats who inspired it. Sex as the naturalists presented it they kept out of their later poetry, but not because they could not "abide carnation" (Boker, according to his biographer's surmise,

had three mistresses, *seriatim*). They kept it out because Love's dream but n
Love's act is admissible in ideal poetry.

Stedman's discussion of poetry and sex, in his study of Whitman (*Poe
of America*), will be found illuminating by any who wish to fathom the
view of this troublesome aesthetic problem. We should have to answer Stee
man that, in spite of his fine words about the idealization of sex, he reveals a
attitude which in the modern view betrays his whole argument. He accuse
Whitman of taking away the "sweetness and pleasantness of stolen waters an
secret bread. *Furto cuncta magis bella.*" Even to an enlightened Victorian, se
at best was illicit.

The aesthetic aims of the group explain in part such features of thei
humanism as their excessive idolization of the artist and the decline in thei
poetry of the earlier romantic enthusiasm for nature. The ideal world of th
poet is not revealed to him by contact with nature; it is not the natural worl
transformed. It obeys its own laws, which are aesthetic. The poet, as th
creator of this ideal world which men desperately need as an anodyne t
soothe the pain caused by Huxley, Tweed, and Zola, should be cherished b
society. The desire of these poets to be useful had something to do, too, witl
their adherence to what Stedman spoke of as "our Canon—the law of fidelit
to form in poetry." They wished to be influential not only in their own tim
but with posterity; and the "things that have lasted," Aldrich declared, "ar
perfect in form."

Although the aesthetic principles of the band prevailed by the end of th
century, at least in the criticism of poetry, they had not had things entirel
their own way in the earlier years. The strongly ethical but witty critical essay
of E. P. Whipple lightened the pages of the *North American Review* until hi
death in 1886. Even though Lowell's last years were largely given up t
diplomacy and after-dinner speeches, he wrote criticism in the eighties and
most readers would still have considered him the first of American critics
The name of Henry James, Jr., was frequently signed in the seventies and
eighties to critical papers, chiefly on French and Russian authors, in the
*Atlantic* and the *Nation*. In the camp of the realists, Howells and his Nor
wegian-born friend H. H. Boyesen, novelist and essayist, kept up a truceless
war against the criticism and poetry written by the band.

As the years went by, the connections which the group formed with
magazines and publishing houses multiplied until their names were spoken
and seen everywhere, and they formed a kind of literary interlocking direc-
torate. In time their influence infiltrated even into the colleges. There the
teaching of literature was still preempted by the last of the professors of belles-
lettres or had just passed to the alert young "scientific" scholars trained in
Germany and determined to substitute for the sweetness of Blair's *Lectures on*

*Rhetoric* the light of Sievers' *Angelsächsische Grammatik.* None of the band accepted an academic post, though Stedman in particular was wooed by the universities. But they were frequently honored visitors to academic lecture platforms, however, and in the next generation disciples like Woodberry of Columbia, Wendell of Harvard, and van Dyke of Princeton would challenge the philologists on their home ground.

2

Though Edmund Clarence Stedman was by no means a great critic he uniquely represents his generation and may here speak for it. His industry was prodigious. Despite the financial upheavals of his Wall Street life and the hypochondria which often kept him from attempting still huger tasks, Stedman signed his name so frequently to long reviews and thick books of criticism that there was no escaping his opinions. By constant study he became really learned in English and American literary history and in Greek poetry. Most unusual of his qualifications were his catholicity of taste and his courage. If his enthusiasms were rather too numerous, they were usefully contagious. Many readers were persuaded by his gusto to a just view of Poe and to an acceptance, at least, of Swinburne and Whitman.

Stedman developed for himself a set of critical principles that were, if not very original or profound, at least consistent and workable. He adhered to them in *Victorian Poets* (1875) and *Poets of America* (1885). His two poetry collections which served as companions to these works, the immensely popular *Victorian Anthology* (1895) and *American Anthology* (1900), were made with these principles as the guide. After several partial attempts at definition, he stated his principles fully in *The Nature and Elements of Poetry* (1892).

Stedman's eclectic method at first diverts the reader of his *Victorian Poets* from the fact that it was written to amplify, by illustration, his poetic beliefs. He liked to call himself a judicial or philosophical critic, and such he was, in the main. But since he was eclectic in his methods as well as in his ideas, he moves vigorously from the discussion of the historical background of literary figures to impressionistic rhapsodies stimulated by their work. Though he shifts his method constantly, he keeps his eye on his main objective, the illustration of his theories.

The book was of slow growth. Stedman summarized the story of it:

This book grew out of a study of R. H. Stoddard's "Late English Poets" [an anthology]—a review of which I contributed, at Mr. Lowell's request, to the *North American Review* in 1865 or '66. Five years later I made the study of Tennyson and Theocritus (see Chapter VI) which appeared in the *Atlantic Monthly.* The interest excited by it led me to write the other essays, mostly for *Scribner's Monthly,* which I afterwards revised and collected in "Victorian Poets." The *prefix "Victorian" had not previously become familiar.*

Stedman stated in a letter to Theodore Watts that his real purpose in both the *Victorian Poets* and *Poets of America* was "to give the author's *views* and *canons of poetry* and the *poetic art,* and to study a *poetic era* and *poetic temperaments."*

Stedman's tact and ingenuity were abundantly needed in writing *Poets of America.* Holmes, Lowell, and Whittier were still alive; Bryant, Emerson, and Longfellow, only recently dead. Though partisans faced him on all sides, he contrived to write a book which pleased his generation and survives in ours. He wished to demonstrate to Americans by means of his book that our ideal and intellectual progress, which was gaining speed, warranted less deference to Europe, and to assert, against such critics as Lowell and Richard Grant White, the "distinctive national character" of our poetry.

As in the *Victorian Poets,* Stedman applied his canons throughout the work; yet in contrast with the earlier volume there is much less technical criticism and more discussion of the "poetic temperament and the conditions that affect it; more of poetry as the music of emotion, faith, aspiration, and all the chords of life." Stedman may have pursued this method in order not to be too explicit in condemning certain works of poets who were admired in every American home. The reader is fascinated, nevertheless, in following the turns by which he managed to say what he believed, even when the truth was likely to shock. If we peel off his elaborate praise of the elder poets as kind neighbors and good citizens, we come, time and again, on the hard core of a valid judgment. In his essays on Poe and Whitman, Stedman was at his best, since, as a strategist, he preferred attack to defense. To praise Poe required some courage but no magnanimity on his part since Poe, like Swinburne or Rossetti, was to him a poet of the Ideal. His generous criticism of Whitman shows more clearly than anything else he wrote his superiority to the other critics of his time.

As has been said, Stedman's criticism of poets and schools was always guided by the principles he had worked out for himself. These he tentatively set forth in three systematic essays: "Elements of the Art of Poetry," "Genius," and "What Is Criticism." *

When in 1891 he was asked to be the first Turnbull Lecturer in poetry at Johns Hopkins, he took on the labor of preparing *Nature and Elements of*

* *Galaxy,* I, 408–415 (July 1, 1866); *New Princeton Review,* II, 145–167 (Sept., 1886); *Epoch,* I, 108–109, 131–132 (Mar. 11 and 18, 1887).

*Poetry* (1892) as a chance to do battle in the war of the Idealists against the corrupting influences of science, realism, and journalism. Poets are born with special insights and should rule by divine right. The age of economics and physics and prose fiction had forgotten this and should be made to acknowledge poetic sovereignty. The volume is not only a recapitulation of Stedman's leading ideas on aesthetics, but a history of poetry and poetic theory as well. Always inclined to overwrite, he felt the occasion to be so momentous that he sought to cover every conceivable idea and argument as thoroughly as he knew how. But when the digressions and excessive illustration are stripped away, the thesis of the book stands as the one complete defense of literary Idealism which the age produced.

What it owes to the Platonic tradition in criticism and to Poe and Emerson especially is evident throughout, but Stedman's awareness of how far on the defensive he and his friends had been driven by the new forces operating in men's lives compelled him to modify the tradition. He saw clearly that the discoveries in the physical, biological, and psychological sciences and the new positivism based on them had sapped the position of the Idealist in art as well as religion. Poetry's chief enemies were the realists who had capitulated to the spirit of the age. In his essay on "Genius," written five years earlier, Stedman had tried to take them into his camp by the genial method of convicting the best of them—Howells in particular—of unwittingly seeking the "ideal which is the truest truth, the absolute realism," which the poets also sought. But this maneuver by transvaluing values had not succeeded. In these lectures, therefore, he tried a different attack by which he might destroy the realists from a superior position.

The crux of Stedman's argument is found in his chapters on "Beauty" and "Truth." Beauty is ever the object of the poet's search—and, as well, of the transcendentalist's, the impressionist's, and the realist's. Beauty exists, though it cannot be measured: in the mind of the poet it is a "quality of his imagined substance." By an argument which owes much to Emerson, Stedman proceeds to equate beauty with truth, of which it is the "unveiled shining countenance." All natural things "make for" beauty, and the poet, having insight into the soul of truth (i.e., "natural things") expresses the beautiful. But a given truth, to be beautiful, must be complete. The fallacy of the realist is that he deals only with things that are seen; the rest which remains to complete the truth, he ignores. Hence he can never produce beauty.

At this point in his argument Stedman introduces an idea which shows how far he had come from his early Poesque aestheticism and the degree to which he had unconsciously yielded to the realistic and utilitarian spirit of the times. In essence his next argument is an assertion of the functionalism which has dominated American aesthetics from Emerson and Greenough (whose theories of art are more impressive than his sculpture) to Louis Sullivan and Frank Lloyd Wright. He concedes that beauty does accord somewhat with use; the essence of beauty, in fact, lies in conformity to the law and fitness of things. But Stedman draws back from a complete acceptance of the functionalist theory of art in time to save his idealism. His compromise here is instructive. That ideal beauty "lies in adaptation of the spirit to the circumstances" is true, but this adaptation need not always be to the "apparent material exigencies." It is a function of ideal needs rather than of mundane necessities.

Stedman's Turnbull Lectures must have comforted those who wished to believe the realists could be beaten back and the supremacy of poetry, the most ideal and comprehensive of the arts, reasserted. His own confidence that this could be done was supported by his belief that a new age of ideal poetry was about to begin. Genius, he had tried to make Howells understand, is a fact; the spontaneous poet is born when least expected. The poetry he brings into the world is of the highest kind, heroic in tone and dramatic in form. Stedman was sure that the signs indicated the advent in his time of this kind of poetry. He discerned it, remarkably enough, in the work of Swinburne and Whitman. He found it significant, too, that our poets had ceased to be landscape painters and were becoming figure painters, turning to "human life with its throes and passions and activity."

Stedman's hierophantic attitude toward poetry, which he shared, of course, with such Victorian critics as Arnold and Pater, ultimately repelled rather than attracted readers. In his zeal to claim all for poetry, he lost the ground he hoped to reclaim from the realists. The irony is that having made, as he thought, generous, even dangerous concessions to the claims of science and utility, he and his kind should have been reviled by the next generation as timid, genteel, and reactionary.

Though Richard Henry Stoddard wielded influence equal to Stedman's, his contemporary reputation as a critic is now difficult to understand. The reader who looks through the mass of his introductions to anthologies, scans his numerous literary biographies and his reviews will come on little which he can call criticism. In the preface to his most substantial volume of literary essays, *Under the Evening Lamp* (1892), Stoddard acknowledges that in these studies of authors who were "worsted by misfortune" he was more interested in their lives than in their writings.

Stoddard was chiefly responsible for the great popularity in the last quarter of the century of decently intimate pictures of poets and novelists at home. N. P. Willis was our first dealer in the table talk of literary celebrities, and the form into which much of this sort of writing was cast had been devised by the authors of the sumptuous *Homes of American Authors* (1854). Though he did not invent the "pilgrimage" to the "shrine" of the man of letters, Stoddard made the appetite which craved this sort of thing. His Bric-a-brac Series, anthologies of reminiscences of writers, sold over 60,000 copies in eighteen months.

When Stoddard occasionally ventured beyond anecdote and platitude, as a critic he could be disconcertingly incisive. He never publicly deflated any of his poet friends; he was a faithful member of the *Brüderschaft*. In his letters, however, one comes on acute judgments of his contemporaries, such as these remarks about Taylor's verse.

When [his poems] are only fairish or middling, they are always well written, and in their way, faultless. You will see his "Sunken Treasures" in Put[nam's] for Septr. I can't find any verbal fault with that piece, but somehow it don't leave any marked impression on my mind. It seems *built*; it wants simplicity; it is more artificial than natural. The artifice of rhetoric is second nature with Bayard.*

Such bull's-eye criticism makes one believe Stoddard could have taken the palm from Lowell and Stedman if he had cared to be a public critic.

### 3

Though the last of the chief defenders of Ideality had died by 1910, a group of their heirs carried the tradition into the age of Dreiser, Mencken, and Anderson. Three of them were professors of literature: George Edward Woodberry at Columbia, Barrett Wendell at Harvard, and Henry van Dyke at Princeton. The fourth member of the group, Hamilton Wright Mabie, literary editor of the *Outlook,* whose inspirational messages on ideals and literature comforted hundreds of audiences up and down the country, served the new naturalistic generation as a symbol of everything from which they scurrilously dissented.

Twenty years before his death, in 1930, Woodberry felt that the cause was lost. Toward the end he spent as much time as he could in his favorite Italy, venturing occasionally into the Western wilderness to lecture at the summer sessions of various state universities. Not even the admiration of the large circle of his one-time students reconciled him to modern America.

At first glance Woodberry's criticism seems to echo that of Stedman, Stoddard, and the others, but important differences appear. He worships beauty, as do they, but its pursuit eventually so obsessed him that only in the Greek past or the Italian present could he find it. The war which Stedman made on realism had been a vigorous counterrevolution. The plaintiveness of

---

* Quoted in Schultz, *Unpublished Letters of Bayard Taylor* (1937), pp. vi–vii.

Woodberry's protest shows how much narrower is his humanism than that of the earlier Idealists. In his criticism, refinement rather than Ideality is the key word.

In his attitude toward American literature Woodberry also stands apart from his predecessors. His first important work was his collaboration with Stedman in their edition of Poe, a by-product of which was his own biography of the poet (1885; revised 1909), and he had also written biographical studies of Hawthorne (1902) and Emerson (1907). But as time passed he grew doubtful of the status of our writers. As his disgust with the materialism of his native land increased, he spoke bitterly of the future of the arts in America. It was bad enough to have to admit that what we had produced was merely a backflow from Europe. Prospects for the future were even worse: they were rooted in Mark Twain and Missouri.

Immured by his Harvard professorship, Barrett Wendell saved himself from Woodberry's melancholy over the state of our national culture. A more robust spirit, he hedged himself from the new vulgarity by means of his New England lineage, his Tory prejudices, and his wit. Unlike Woodberry, who as a young man shared the nativism of the Idealist critics, Wendell at no time in his life thought very highly of the accomplishment of American writers. His depreciatory *A Literary History of America* (1900) tries them at the bar of the tradition of English letters and finds them guilty of so many literary crimes that the reader wonders why he wished to write the book at all. In the nineties he was already quite reconciled to the "provincial obscurity" into which his class and kind were vanishing; it cost him little pain to observe twenty-five years later that "this age of ours [in England as well as America] grows literally obscene—thrusting into sight everywhere the foulnesses which are better ignored."

The other two members of this group of latter-day disciples never gave up. Mabie rallied the supporters of the waning cause by overpraising his friends. His method of dealing with the new naturalistic literature was to ignore it. To the end, Dr. van Dyke of New York's Brick Presbyterian Church and Princeton, never missed a chance for a scrap—ecclesiastical, political, or literary. At the age of seventy-eight, when the international blue ribbon was pinned on the triumphant naturalists by the award of the Nobel Prize for Literature to Sinclair Lewis, van Dyke was ready for one fight more. Addressing the Germantown Business Men's Luncheon Club, he deplored the act as a backhanded compliment to America and so gave Lewis a chance to tell off the Idealists in his acceptance speech at Stockholm, by declaring that the American Academy of Arts and Letters, which the Idealists had founded and still controlled, represented only Henry Wadsworth Longfellow. Dr. van Dyke hit back, but the ring was empty.

4

None of the poets among the band and their associates—and nearly all of them attempted poetry—so ardently longed for literary fame as Bayard Taylor. From his correspondence one can see that he thought constantly of his "place" as a poet. His works are "slowly gaining ground"; his biography is wanted for a German *Konversations-Lexikon* ("That seems almost like fame, doesn't it?"); his appointment as Minister to Germany shows, at last, that "the world *does* appreciate earnest endeavor."

Taylor's instinctive doubts of his poetic talent, which these constant references to his reputation reveal, do him credit as a critic. Despite the novelty of his "California Ballads" and the popularity of his gushing *Poems of the Orient* (1854) and the hopeful labor he bestowed on *The Picture of St. John* (1866), despite the many poems in praise of the poet's calling, he was a verse-maker, as Stoddard said, and not a poet. His lines will not stick in the mind. Invariably, as one reads, a tolerable passage sinks to bathos. His gift for parody induced echoes of other poems in his verse. Even the "Bedouin Song," which some provincial soprano is carolling at this moment, is the offspring of Shelley's "Indian Serenade." It is significant that Taylor, unlike his friend Aldrich, rejected or revised little of his early poetry, but carried most of it along into later editions.

Of all his volumes of verse, Taylor's *Home Pastorals* (1875) alone is intrinsically as well as historically valuable. Here, for once, he lays aside his usual bardic disguises and speaks movingly of his predicament as man and artist, clear to him at last; the clearer perhaps because he had just finished his translation of Goethe's great metaphysical poem. Sated with visions, he pictures himself as one who wishes to come home after wandering over the world. His predicament is sharper than that of other American poets who, starved in the Present, are weary of singing only the Future. His Quaker neighbors, whose lives he wishes to poetize, are suspicious of him and his work. He cannot really be at home among them. Here, as in every other corner of America, "the form of Art abides as a stranger."

The *Home Pastorals* also reveals the struggle of a typical American intellectual of the time to find a tenable philosophical position. Taylor had earlier subscribed to the conventional romantic Nature worship, but Nature, the "indifferent goddess," no longer inspires him. He is glutted with physical beauty and Man is now more to him than the suns and rains and "the plastic throes of the ages." He repudiates boldly the various Victorian religious compromises and is satisfied to be shadowed by the Angel of Unfaith. These themes he carries over into his ambitious Faustian drama, *Prince Deukalion* (1878), in which the Prince and Pyrrha, guided by Prometheus, reject in turn the solutions of Medusa (Roman Catholicism) and Urania (Science), to accept the doctrine contained in the following lines:

> Seek not to know Him; yet aspire
> As atoms towards the central fire!
> Not lord of race is He, afar,—
> Of Man, or Earth, or any star,
> But of the inconceivable All.

These two poems show that the poetical maturity Taylor had longed for was at last evincing itself. He died a month after the publication of *Prince Deukalion.*

The kind of fame Taylor had so wistfully sought was his, actually, in December, 1870, when his translation of *Faust,* Part I, was issued by Fields, Osgood & Company in a volume uniform with Longfellow's *Dante* and Bryant's *Iliad,* the second part appearing in March, 1871. This great moment of his career was marked by Fields' ceremonial dinner at which the coveted praise of his New England masters was cordially given. There was, indeed, little dissent from their opinion that Taylor had made a handsome contribution to American culture. In Germany it was said that he had assimilated to himself the German "mode of thinking and feeling." Taylor's *Faust* still leads the procession of forty-four translations of Part I, and sixteen of Part II, and seems certain of permanence, in spite of passages which are neither German nor English in style and of occasional misinterpretations of Goethe's meaning.

Taylor's devotion to *Faust* was so great that without effort he came to know by heart almost all of it. A man without academic training, he had mastered the Goethe literature, extensive even at that date, and had made "lateral studies" to complete his comprehension of the drama. He industriously consulted German scholars and men who had known the poet. He was the first enthusiast in England or America to comprehend Goethe's intention in the second part of *Faust,* which even G. H. Lewes, his foremost English biographer and *Dolmetscher,* had called "an elaborate mistake." Particularly eager to counteract the prejudices created by the two "stupid translations" then existing, Taylor analyzed in his Introduction the development of Part II act by act, and correctly asserted the unity of the poem.

Taylor discussed his theory of translation in his prefaces to the two parts. Sensitively aware of how much of the *Stimmung* of the poem is communicated by its varied rhythms, he set himself the task of reproducing Goethe's meters. Though he did not always succeed, there is no doubt that his bold attempt gives his version scope and weight lacking in the work of his many rivals. Since he had wisely relied less on his intuitions of Goethe's meaning and more on the painstaking search for the exact word, no critic, paraphrasing Dr. Bentley, could tell him his *Faust* was a "pretty poem" but not Goethe. The translation is not a great poem, but it is still after seventy years as much of Goethe as a reader with small German can hope to have.

Like his friend Taylor, George Boker longed for poetic fame. "My theatrical success I never valued," he wrote Taylor. "I had not, nor have I, any ambition to become a mere playwright. . . . If I could not be acknowledged as a poet, I had no further desire, and no further active concern in literature." His poetry never caught on with the public, though one volume, *Poems of the War* (1864), was popular, fittingly enough, since he had founded the mother-house of the Union League Clubs and had exhorted his fellow poets to turn propagandists for the Northern cause. His longer poems, like "The Song of the Earth," "The Ivory Carver," and the autobiographical *Book of the Dead* (1882), written to answer the slanderers of his father, exhibit the defect most characteristic of the minor poetry of his time. The form revolves like the musical phrases repeated in the groove of a victrola record when the needle is stuck. The images change but the metaphorical dimension does not expand.

Taylor was the only one of Boker's friends who knew he had written a sequence of 313 love sonnets, probably intended for publication but not issued in his lifetime. Together with fifty-eight printed in his *Plays and Poems, II* (1856), the first 282 of these sonnets commemorate a prolonged and passionate affair with a "golden-brown beauty well known in his native city." The remaining thirty-one sonnets were inspired by two subsequent love affairs.

As it was Boker's misfortune that he wished to write Elizabethan dramas in a most un-Elizabethan time, so it will always be the fate of these love sonnets to invite comparison with Shakespeare's sequence. The echoes are troublesome. Occasionally, too, the modes of Victorian love-making interfere with one's pleasure in reading, although it is possible that these conventions may in time seem no more quaint than Petrarchan conceits. Yet unfinished and imitative as they are, these sonnets surpass anything written by the poets of Boker's generation. Sufficiently the artist to distinguish emotion from its communication, he worked to achieve the *parlante* quality which the sonnet form demands.

Of the poets of his generation Aldrich was the most conscientious artist. We may now find the emotions displayed in his verses decorative and their inspiration trivial, but we must admit that the trivia are his own. The shades of Chatterton and Keats, Tennyson and Hafiz loom over the early poems, and a devotion to Herrick is continuously evident in them, but Aldrich worked away from these masters to a recognizable idiom of his own. He eliminated the Victorian lumber from his lines and he is seldom guilty of the bathos of Taylor or the sentimental vulgarity of Stoddard. An exception must be made, of course, for the enormously popular "Ballad of Babie Bell," the tale of whose ethereal birth and gratuitous death made strong men in Western barrooms break down and weep, remembering home and mother But then no nineteenth century poet could be trusted with a baby.

Though Aldrich's forms and subjects are traditional, his interest in impressions conveyed through the clear image anticipates the later style of the Imagists of the generation of 1910. Either because he shrank from indecently exposing himself in his verse or because he was seldom deeply stirred, Aldrich worked as they did, on the surface. Even when the reader suspects the mood may be personal he finds it hidden behind a Persian or Italian or medieval pseudonymity.

From the beginning Aldrich rigorously educated himself to be a poet of the Ideal. His first volume, *The Bells* (1855), swoons and pulses with extravagant emotion. Aldrich never reprinted anything from this volume. From the next, *The Course of True Love Never Did Run Smooth* (1858), a perfumed tale of a Caliph who permits Giaffer to marry the Princess Abbassa but not to enjoy her, he saved a few of the chaster lines. This process of rejection and revision continued relentlessly from volume to volume until the canon was established in 1897.

What survives of Aldrich's poetry now that Time has completed his own winnowing? Not the picture poems and idylls which the taste of his age so much approved. Nor the society verse which his friends admired: "Pepita" and "In an Atelier" seem to this post-Freudian generation arch rather than daring. There is left a handful of lyrics of the kind the poet especially labored to perfect, the quatrains he called "Footnotes"—

> Four-line epics one might hide
> In the hearts of roses.

There is a place, too, for three fine elegiac poems on the Civil War dead: "December," "Spring in New England," and a sonnet, "By the Potomac." Aldrich thought topical poems were not worth the effort because they would not survive!

It is significant that most of Aldrich's remarks on the poetry of his time are condemnatory. When he became editor of the *Atlantic* (1881) he wrote to Stedman: "Our old singers have pretty much lost their voices, and the new singers are so few! My ear has not caught any new note since 1860." By 1900 he had grown completely despairing of the art. The vogue of dialect poetry and especially the enthusiasm for the unspeakable Kipling ("a narsty little brute") had completely vitiated all literary taste. The demand for mediocrity had given America a ragtime literature as well as a ragtime art. Worst of all, the dark night of realism was closing in and those who were still faithful to Beauty were twilight poets, groping alone.

> The mighty Zolaistic Movement now
> Engrosses us—a miasmatic breath
> Blown from the slums. We paint life as it is,
> The hideous side of it, with careful pains,
> Making a god of the dull Commonplace.
> —"Funeral of a Minor Poet"

5

Despite Aldrich's gloomy view of the state of poetry, contemporary readers and critics were in the main pleased with his *Friar Jerome's Beautiful Book* and Stedman's *Blameless Prince,* Stoddard's *The Book of the East* and Hayne's *Legends and Lyrics* and spoke of their verses as noble and elevated. One heretic in their midst, Elizabeth Stoddard, the "Pythoness" as the band called her, penetrated the grace and rhetoric of their poems to the emptiness within. Boker records a session in July, 1874, when Lizzie exploded the terrifying truth: "George, you, Dick, Bayard, Stedman, Aldrich, Read, the whole lot of you youngsters, have all been dreary failures as poets. . . . It was not time that you lacked . . . but poetic ability."

The situation was more complex than even she, wise woman though she was, could comprehend. It should be plain from what has been said in this chapter, that the band held firmly to a set of standards which permitted them to write only "ideal" poetry. They did not suspect how completely this literary asceticism had devitalized their imaginative powers and cut them off from the modern world. So disgusted were they with realists in verse like Harte and Riley that they suppressed what talent of this sort they had. Classical themes they had grown weary of. Because they were humanists and city men, they found little to inspire them in nature. Small wonder that Stedman, writing to Winter in 1873 about the discouragements of their literary generation, should conclude by saying: "You may be sure that whatever failure such men as you experience grows out of the *only* difficulty in our literary life—want of *themes* suited to *our* tastes and aspirations."

Inflexible in their belief that only the traditional forms of verse were suitable vehicles for the few themes which they found worthy, they were little interested in the experiments in free forms carried out in their time by Arnold, Whitman, Emily Dickinson, and Stephen Crane. Their reverence for the great masters made them deplore the vogue of ballads and villanelles and the preoccupation with form for form's sake which this vogue encouraged. All of them, except Boker, repudiated the romantic introspection of their early poetry, preferring, as Stoddard put it, "objective creation to subjective medita-tion in verse."

Forced deeper and deeper into a blind alley by these exclusions and rejec-tions, their imaginative scope narrowed until their poems became merely daydreams. For polite readers to whom poetry was an institution to be main-tained this dream poetry sufficed. To earnest folk perplexed in the extreme by the dilemmas of the age and to the more stalwart who were exhilarated by the prospects opened up by science and the material progress promised by the Corliss engine and the dynamo, their poems were, what Lanier called them, "dandy kickshaws of verse."

# 51. PILGRIMS' RETURN

THE historians have had much to say about the influence of the idea of the West on the American mind and imagination. They have neglected an equally powerful force operative during the years between 1850 and 1900, a force which, incidentally, helped to maintain the dominion of the "defenders of Ideality" in poetry and criticism. During this half-century Americans discovered Europe, with results which were culturally quite as significant as the discovery of the West.

In ever increasing numbers travelers returned home to record what they had seen and felt in the Old World. From this migration came a superlative travel literature and a new type of fiction, the "international novel." Ultimately this exodus was also responsible for a shift in attitude which, on the eastern seaboard and with the more literate classes, transformed the chauvinism of the forties into the cosmopolitanism of the 1900's.

The causes of this great exodus are not obscure. There was, of course, more money and more leisure for travel. After the *Great Western,* marvel of the age, made its first voyage in 1838, the terrors of the Atlantic were converted into pleasures, even for the invalids on their way to European spas. The revolutions of 1848 drew patriotic Americans to Italy and France that they might be on hand when monarchical Europe was republicanized. Though their hopes were betrayed, liberals continued to arrive in order to learn why the revolutions had been abortive. The various European countries wooed American tourists by providing them with special objectives for their holiday, such as the Great Exhibition at the Crystal Palace in 1851 and the Paris exhibitions of 1855 and 1867.

More powerful than any other persuasive were the books written by the pioneer generation of travelers. Irving's *Sketch Book* (1819) and *Bracebridge Hall* (1822), though they imaged an England which scarcely existed in actuality, inspired his countrymen to search for it. N. P. Willis' *Pencillings by the Way* (1844), his collected travel letters contributed to the New York *Mirror,* enchanted the subscribers to the five hundred newspapers which made excerpts from them. Longfellow's *Hyperion* (1839), Irving's *Conquest of Granada* (1829), and more factual but equally influential books, such as Silliman's *A Journal of Travels in England, Holland and Scotland* (1810), induced thousands of Americans to go in quest of the holy places of Europe these pioneers had so eloquently described. In the time of Irving and Willis the casual tourist, who was abroad chiefly to absorb as much as he could in a short time, was the exception. After 1850 he is the type.

2

Few Americans in the fifties went to Europe without a sense of the momentousness of their journey. They often apologized for leaving home, knowing that many of their countrymen believed that one's Americanism could be corrupted by foreign travel. It was possible to enjoy Europe too well, and a good American had to be on his guard. W. W. Story, an early expatriate, spent the winter of 1849–1850 in Berlin, which seemed to many Americans the most nearly like Boston of European cities, as a kind of expiation for his excessive enjoyment of Italy. As Henry James says of this visit, he had not yet burnt his ships; "he was to saturate himself . . . but he was somehow, by the same stroke, and in some interest to be felt better than named, to be protected against that saturation." Few of the apologists were so philosophical as C. A. Bartol in *Pictures of Europe, Framed in Ideas* (1855), which is more a transcendentalist treatise on the theory of travel than a book about Europe, but invariably, at some point in his narrative, the traveler in these earlier years reassured his readers that he had come home undamaged.

There was much to disapprove of in Europe: the power of the Roman Church, the beggars, the indifference to social reform of the British upper-classes, the evils of the land system in the Papal states, the lax morals of Parisians and Florentines, the absence of a "go-ahead" spirit. Some patriotic travelers were so disturbed by what they saw that they considered it their duty to indict Europe. Julia Ward Howe, for instance, decided that even art study hardly justified a prolonged residence abroad. "The Prometheus of the present day is needed rather to animate statues than to make them."

The professional humorists warned their countrymen against losing their native common sense among the ruins and becoming monarchists or aesthetes. The devotees of Artemus Ward, Petroleum V. Nasby, and Samantha Allen, of J. M. Bailey (the Danbury News Man) and Mr. Dunn Browne (of the Springfield *Republican*) were eager to hear such undeludable Americans inform against Europe. Unfortunately the calculated candor of the humorists seldom goes beyond a scornful paragraph on the battered noses of the Elgin Marbles or a tempered insult aimed at the British royal family. Their books are, on the whole, as mild as milk, possibly because they had a profitable public in England. Two or three, Locke's *Nasby in Exile* (1882) for example, comment shrewdly on European manners and morals, but the only master-piece of this genre is Mark Twain's *The Innocents Abroad*.

After the failure of the revolutions in the mid-century made Americans less sure that democracy was predestined to triumph everywhere and after our own Civil War had sobered their chauvinism, they were more open to the persuasions of travelers like E. C. Benedict, who asked them to believe, in his *A Run Through Europe* (1860), that an acquaintance with the Old World "must be of great value to our national character . . . letting some of the gas out of our conceit, and some of the hyperbole out of our vanity." Readers of G. S. Hillard's *Six Months in Italy* (1853), the most widely quoted of all the travel books, were at length ready to submit to his advice that they must leave notions of progress behind, and "learn to look on churchmen and church rites as a pageant."

The gradual aesthetic education of Americans during these earlier years is fascinating to watch. What they knew of European art they had learned from line drawings, engravings, bad copies in oil of Raphael and Guido, plaster casts of statuary in a few sepulchral galleries. Ruskin had taught them to admire Gothic art and to despise that of the High Renaissance. Some of them debated whether a preoccupation with aesthetic matters was not debili-tating. There was always a searching of the conscience when the tourist con-fronted the nudity of the Venus of the Tribune in the Uffizi and turned to gaze on her even more unabashed sister smiling from Titian's canvas across the room. This cabinet, remarked one traveler, might be called a public boudoir.

No one worked harder to diffuse artistic knowledge in America than James Jackson Jarves, world traveler, editor of the first paper published in Honolulu, art critic, connoisseur, and collector. Jarves is remembered now because he was forced in 1871, because of poverty, to relinquish his magnifi-cent collection of Italian primitives to Yale; but he should be known also as the author of four delightful European travel books (which will be discussed later in this chapter) and for *Art Hints* (1855) and three other pioneer works of this sort notable for their acuteness. In all these books his announced pur-pose was to convince Americans that their moral and utilitarian prejudices blinded them to what they had gone to Europe to see.

Equally independent are the aesthetic theories and judgments advanced by a Philadelphia amateur, Horace Binney Wallace, whose *Art, Scenery and Philosophy in Europe* was issued posthumously in 1855. One of the first to propose a functional theory of architecture, Wallace discusses in "The Law of the Development of Gothic Architecture," one of the best essays in his book, ideas which are far in advance of his time. In another chapter he describes with great perspicuity the aesthetic effect produced by various European cathedrals, an achievement which is not a little remarkable when one considers how firmly he held to the requirement of functionalism in architecture.

One is likewise interested to watch the progress in aesthetics of certain better known Americans. In all three of his travel books Edward Everett Hale shows an extraordinary open-mindedness. Possessing the usual prejudices in favor of the later Gothic style, he worked his way back, by study and contemplation, until he could enjoy primitive painting and Romanesque and Byzantine art. Hawthorne struggled with art while he was in Italy even though he was often weary and sometimes disgusted. He went back to certain pictures and statues time after time, trying to find—not what his friend Powers, the sculptor, told him was to be found in them—but what he might experience by himself. His *Italian Note Books* show him "improving" day by day. His persistence bore fruit in *The Marble Faun,* whole pages of which are observations from the *Note Books* transformed for the purposes of fiction.

These amateurs, indeed, often returned home better instructed than the scholars and critics whose profession it was to interpret European civilization. Charles Eliot Norton, Harvard's Professor of the History of Art from 1875 to 1898, was, for example, strangely limited by his American prejudices. As friend and disciple of Ruskin, a founder of the Archaeological Institute of America, the School of Classical Studies at Rome, and the *American Journal of Archaeology,* Norton might have been expected to comprehend and treat sympathetically various schools of painting and styles of architecture. Actually few American travelers in Europe were so narrow. His lifelong hatred of Catholic institutions—he once wrote Lowell that he thought he could roast a Franciscan with pleasure and that he would only need a tolerable opportunity to make him stab a Cardinal in the dark—constantly interfered with his aesthetic judgments. With a zeal worthy of a member of the Know-Nothing party (whose principles he approved) he sets forth his detestation of the Roman Church in his early *Notes of Travel and Study in Italy* (1860) and permits it to intrude on his observations about art.

### 3

There was scarcely a professional writer of this period who did not furnish his public with his impressions of Europe. Grace Greenwood (Sara Jane Lippincott) in *Haps and Mishaps of a Tour in Europe* (1854) satisfied her readers, for whom she was the arbiter in matters of sentiment, with long meditations inspired by famous paintings or historical scenes. Mrs. Stowe, celebrated as the author of *Uncle Tom's Cabin,* described in *Sunny Memories of Foreign Lands* (1854) her royal progress through the drawing rooms of England and the Continent. Bayard Taylor's fate was settled when his *Views A-Foot* (1846), the naïve raptures of a twenty-year-old boy, captivated the nation. Twenty editions were required in the next ten years. Taylor would be fifty before he could cease traveling up and down in the world as a professional weigher and gauger of culture for his countrymen. Year by year he pushed into new lands: Africa, Asia Minor, India, and Japan, the Scandinavian countries, Iceland. "I am led," he wrote, "into these wanderings without my will; it seems to be my destiny."

The less imaginative of the professional writers soon evolved a sort of standard pattern for the travel book. The author must begin with the excitements of the ocean voyage itself and devote at least a portion of a chapter to the thrill, so long anticipated, of setting foot on foreign soil. From this point on he should mix architecture and scenery with comment on philanthropies, skillfully work in a little history cribbed from Murray's guides, taking care to add a touch of sentiment or eloquence when the occasion permitted. If the essay or book required a little padding, it was always possible to retell an old legend or slip in an account of dangers surmounted in crossing the Alps.

Soon there would be interesting deviations from this pattern, but in the fifties and sixties the reader wanted a series of variations on a theme. It did not matter to him that he had read forty descriptions of the hallowed places —Shakespeare's tomb, the Burns country, Warwick Castle, and the Tower of London, the vale of Chamonix, and the Roman Campagna. He listened with delight to any new variations which Edward Everett Hale or Helen Hunt Jackson could compose.

In the sixties this predominantly sentimental approach begins to yield to the kind of book which offers chiefly information and advice. Tourists were in a hurry and they wanted to know how to get over the ground without wasting any time in unprofitable expeditions. The books such determined travelers found most useful were those represented by J. H. B. Latrobe's *Hints for Six Months in Europe* (1869) and C. C. Fulton's *Europe Viewed Through American Spectacles* (1874) which supplied, in addition to 310 double-columned pages of fact, an appendix of "Hints to European Tourists."

Soon the more sophisticated began to shun the spots where their meditations might be disturbed by the rushing hordes to whom such books appealed and fled to haunts whose charms had not yet been defiled. As early as 1852 W. W. Story complained to Lowell, "We must take some untravelled paths which the English have not spoiled, and go into the wildest fastnesses of the Abruzzi, perhaps to Sora." Eugene Benson, whose *Art and Nature in Italy* (1882) is caviar for the élite, traveled to Ferrara not for the sake of Tasso and Lucrezia Borgia whom the vulgar pursued there, but to seek out the work of an obscure painter named Scarscinello [sic]. It was a mistake to let such secrets out. Henry James knew well enough what always happened. Writing in 1903 of W. W. Story's *Vallombrosa* (1881), he lamented that the dense Etrurian coverts to whose secluded beauty Story had unwisely given publicity would by then be "scarred and dishonoured by the various new contrivances for access without contact and acquaintance without knowledge."

These books unlocking the secret charms of particular regions are sufficiently numerous to constitute a subdivision of travel literature, but the sophisticates who produced them were also responsible for another kind of book. This is the detailed study of some city already repeatedly described but never so minutely nor by a traveler so devoted and so learned. W. W. Story for example, knew Rome as few Americans have ever known it, and he found in Italy, and in Rome especially, an antidote to the ugliness of the rest of the world. It is not surprising therefore that some of the chapters in his *Rob di Roma* (1862)—on *villeggiature,* on games, ceremonies, and holidays—are unexcelled.

One book of this type, F. Marion Crawford's *Ave Roma Immortalis* (1898), possesses a distinction which almost makes it great. Son of the Italian trained sculptor Thomas Crawford, convert to Catholicism, after 1883 resident of Italy, Crawford was in every way fitted to write the perfect book about Rome. Accurate, swift, adroitly planned, heightened in the right place by a careful rhetoric, his *Ave Roma Immortalis* achieves the totality of impression which eluded scores of novices. Crawford's Rome is not the Rome of Garibaldi or of Pio Nono, but his description fulfills the ideal toward which many writers, baffled by the beauty and mystery of the city, had struggled. Here at last the glories of the fourteen "regions" and the immensities of St. Peter's are adequately reduced to words.

Before the century ended, the travel writers had devised yet another sort of book designed for tourists who went to Europe to escape. Too sophisticated to ration their days to the Blue Grotto at Capri and the castle at Heidelberg, and too well traveled to need hints and helps, they were in Europe in search of the picturesque. Stevenson's *Travels with a Donkey in the Cévennes* (1879) had delighted them, and for them the Pennells drew and wrote the series of "pilgrimages" beginning with *A Canterbury Pilgrimage* in 1885. F. Hopkinson Smith in *Gondola Days* (1897) describes the mood of these latter-day travelers.

In this selfish, materialistic, money-getting age, it is a joy to live, if only for a day . . . in a city the relics of whose past are the lessons of our future; whose every canvas, stone, and bronze bear witness to a grandeur, luxury, and taste that took a thousand years to perfect, and will take a thousand years of neglect to destroy.

All that had vexed the first generation of European visitors—ecclesiastical corruption, feudal survivals, filth, indolence—was now dissolved in a glow generated by acceptance. Smith, noting the toppling of jamb and lintel in Venice, is full of thanks to the little devils of rot and decay. They are, he says, really "the guardians of the picturesque."

### 4

Among the hundreds of Americans who attempted travel books, at least a dozen theorize about what they are doing and strive to give shape and character to their observations. In "Leaves from My Journal in Italy and Elsewhere" * Lowell wrote at length on modern travelers. They see nothing out of sight, are skeptics and doubters, materialists reporting things for other skeptics to doubt still further upon. With every step of the modern tourist "our inheritance of the wonderful is diminished," and year by year more and more of the world gets disenchanted. Lowell's own travel book was written in emulation of the elder navigators to whom the world was a huge wonder horn.

The young George William Curtis, returning from abroad in 1850, sought in his *Nile Notes of a Howadji* (1851) to re-create for his readers—and he soon had a host of them—the "essentially *sensuous,* luxurious, languid and sense-satisfied spirit of Eastern life." No one, he noted, had ever sought to do this. He accomplished his aim so successfully that his family was terribly shocked, especially by his voluptuous description of an Oriental dancer whose style descended from Salome's. The spirit of this book, Curtis wrote to his aggrieved father, is "precisely what I wish it. I would not have it toned down, for I toned it up intentionally."

Several later writers, determined to do more than furnish guidebook information colored intermittently a deep purple, throw a challenge to their readers. John Hay ironically warns in *Castilian Days* (1871) that he does not belong to the "praiseworthy class of travelers who feel a certain moral necessity impelling them to visit every royal abode within reach." Charles Dudley Warner in *Saunterings* (1872), the first of ten travel books, suggests to his audience that, as a compromise, "we shall go somewhere and not learn anything about it." Thomas Bailey Aldrich in *From Ponkapog to Pesth* (1883) complains of another restriction on the freedom of the travel writer. He is not vexed, like Hay and Warner, by the requirement that he be informative, but he does reject the convention which decrees that he may be "aesthetic, or historic, or scientific, or analytic, or didactic, or any kind of ic, except enthusiastic."

* *Graham's Monthly,* 1854; published in *Fireside Travels,* 1864.

Aldrich indulged in nostalgia rather than enthusiasm, but his chapter have a characteristic quality. This is compounded partly from his humorou picture of himself as a provincial American, awed though not cowed b Europe; partly from his conveyance of that disturbing desire which America travelers have always experienced, a longing to possess Europe, to stave of disenchantment, to carry home, in Signor Alinari's sepia photographs or b act of memory, some of the age and beauty of the Old World.

Because these authors took care to organize their impressions and to infec their readers with their discoveries, the travel books of Lowell, Curtis, Hay Warner, and Aldrich are still alive. But they do not reach the level attaine in the records left by Emerson, Hawthorne, Jarves, Twain, Howells, D Forest, and Henry James. The difference is not explained by simply notin; that the men in the second group are better writers. The point is that the were more concerned to find a valid answer to the question which was, i some degree, in the consciousness of all traveling Americans: What shall I, a an American, do about Europe?

The first of these records, in point of time as well as in absolute excellence is Emerson's *English Traits* (1856). The book gave him much trouble and di not appear until nearly ten years after his second visit to England. In hi anxiety to make it deep and accurate, he invited the young Clough to stay with him for two or three months at Concord to "answer a catechism o details touching England, revise my notes on that country, and sponge ou my blunders." This plan did not go through; but Emerson expended an unusual amount of labor on his book, and it was much on his conscience before the printers finally got the first chapter in October, 1855.

The first printing of 3,000 copies sold quickly, and a second printing of 2,000 was required within a month. Emerson's countrymen sensed that here, at last, was the true and perfect answer to the British travelers who for a half-century had sneered at the nascent American civilization. The liberal British reviews gave the book serious attention; the conservative journals conjured it away by ignoring its existence.

*English Traits* is less a travel book in the ordinary sense of the word than an essay in cultural anthropology, undertaken years before the science was named. Only a civilized man like Emerson who understands the interaction between ideas and institutions can judge wisely the faults and achievements of a civilization alien to his own. He had little to say about architecture and scenery, but much to say about the English character. He did not admire it with a whole heart, and though, as Richard Garnett observed, there is not a sneer in the book it is full of a wonderful irony England lacked, for Emerson, what the best civilization must have, spirituality; but England was a success, and he wished to know why. His proposition is stated in the first paragraph of the chapter called "Result."

England is the best of actual nations. It is no ideal framework, it is an old pile built in different ages, with repairs, additions, and makeshifts; but you see the poor best you have got. London is the epitome of our times, and the Rome of to-day.

A fact of such importance for the nineteenth century needed to be explained, and so Emerson probed his way through chapters on Land, Race, Ability, Manners, Truth, Character, Wealth, and pondered the influence exerted by the aristocracy, the universities, the Anglican Church, and the *Times*.

The marvel of the book is how much of it is still true, a tribute both to Emerson's penetration and to the unchanging characteristics of the English people. Page after page could be reprinted as the record of an observer living in our time. Admirers of English unity and courage during the desperate nights of 1940 understand what he means in saying, "In politics and in war, they hold together as by hooks of steel." Though it is now less true than it was in the fifties that "man in England submits to be a product of political economy," England's rivals, as Emerson noted, are still irritated because the English have found out how to unite success with honesty. What he has to say about England's dealings with other nations, particularly those she rules, still needs no amendment.

They assimilate other races to themselves, and are not assimilated. . . . The English sway of their colonies has no root of kindness. They govern by their arts and ability; they are more just than kind; and, whenever an abatement of their power is left, they have not conciliated the affection on which to rely.

Such is their tenacity, and such their practical turn, that they hold all they gain. Of these memorable judgments, none goes so far in explaining the equipoised character of English civilization as Emerson's conclusion to his chapter on "Literature." There are, he says, two nations in England, not Norman and Saxon, or Celt and Goth, but the perceptive class, and the practical finality class. These

are ever in counterpoise, interacting mutually; one, in hopeless minorities; the other, in huge masses; one studious, contemplative, experimenting; the other, the ungrateful pupil, scornful of the source, whilst availing itself of the knowledge for gain; these two nations, of genius and of animal force, though the first consist of only a dozen souls, and the second of twenty millions, forever by their discord and their accord yield the power of the English State.

While Emerson labored at the composition of *English Traits*, Hawthorne, his Concord neighbor, serving as our consul at Liverpool, was keeping a 300,000-word record of his impressions. The experiences of these years between 1853 and 1857 affected him profoundly. If his health had not failed, he would have transmuted them into a novel. It was mainly for this purpose that the *English Notebooks* (completely published in 1941) were compiled. In two abortive romances, *Dr. Grimshaw's Secret* and *The Ancestral Footstep,* he attempted to tell his story, the theme of which was the symbolic return to England of an American whose ancestor in Cromwellian times had violently broken his ties with the homeland. Fortunately, before his creative powers weakened, Hawthorne distilled the more significant passages from the *Notebooks* into *Our Old Home* (1863).

To one who knows something of Hawthorne's state of mind in his last years, his apprehension over the imminence of civil war in America, his struggle to find himself at home in England, the shift in his thinking from the belief that England and America might complement each other, the one supplying the deficiencies the other lacked, to the view, which was also Emerson's, that the two civilizations could not be reconciled and that the future lay with America; to one who perceives how these and related themes return again and again in the pages of *Our Old Home,* the book becomes the most moving autobiographical record left by any of the travelers.

His best chapters are built from the themes related to the all-engrossing question: How shall an American come to terms with England? In the chapter on Leamington Spa these themes emerge most insistently. The little resort city evidently attracted him because it is a "home to the homeless all the year round," though no man has reared a house there wherein to bring up his children. From this theme Hawthorne moves on to his disquiet in trying to picture the influence of hoar antiquity lingering into the present daylight; then to the theme of the illusion to which Americans are constantly subject in England, of having been there before, the result of the print of a recollection in some ancestral mind, transmitted with fainter and fainter impress, through several generations, to the descendant who returns to our old home.

5

James Jackson Jarves resembles Emerson as a travel writer in at least one respect: both men were concerned to describe only those particulars which illustrate general propositions. Because, either unconsciously or by intent, Jarves usually succeeded in going to the heart of the matter in his books about France and Italy, the modern reader who discovers them will be impressed with the significance as well as the prodigality of the details of life in Paris, Florence, and Rome which pour from his pages. His four books are valuable "documentaries."

*Parisian Sights and French Principles Seen Through American Spectacles*

(1852) takes us, in the fashion of the earlier travel books, to the favorite tourist haunts—the Morgue, Père-Lachaise, the Madeleine; but already Jarves evinces the wit and the independence of judgment which make his books the most amusing of the group now under discussion. He likes to begin a chapter with an informing idea, often epitomized by a symbolic building or a Parisian type, and then to describe the ceremony or process or institution or social class about which he has generalized. Occasionally the details swamp the generalization; but the reader is none the poorer, for he is permitted to see Paris as it was in 1852, recovering from the coup d'état by which Louis Napoleon undid the Second Republic, gay and splendid in its new boulevards, squalid in its attics and slums. Jarves has already begun to discuss freely subjects hinted at by other travelers. What, one wonders, did the family circle think of Chapter VIII, "Something Curious for Moralists"—an unsentimental account of prostitution in Paris and of the French code of extramarital behavior? In the second series of *Parisian Sights* (1855) Jarves even more consistently follows his own bent, poking his nose into dubious alleys and hitherto unvisited places.

In *Italian Sights and Papal Principles Seen Through American Spectacles* (1856) Jarves was again under the necessity of reporting on the usual tourist places. But he saw in his rounds so much more than any of his contemporaries that the reader's interest never diminishes. His incomparable chapter on Pompeii is a tour de force of historical reconstruction. As he went deeper into his subject, Jarves became increasingly reflective. Few Americans meditated with such profit, for instance, on the comparative influence of Romanism and Protestantism on the societies in which each predominated. He ridiculed the mummeries of Holy Week in Rome; but he was no bigot, and, as always, he told his fellow Americans what it was good for them to hear. In this early book, as in the later and mellower *Italian Rambles* (1883), he warned them against the false and meretricious, and encouraged them to carry home a desire to make a civilization in which the artist could exercise his function freely and fully.

Mark Twain's *The Innocents Abroad* (1869) was, in its day, the most famous of American travel books. At last his fellow countrymen, long deceived by the sentimentalities of the guidebooks, were to have the truth about the Old World fraud. He would convince them that the pictures they had rhapsodized over were now too dingy to be deciphered, and the tales of chivalry were actually records of cruelty and avarice. Some of his impieties were shrewdly calculated, but most of them sprang from a deep suspicion of Europe. A success Europe could never be, Italy least of all, for it is the "heart and home of degradation, poverty, indolence, and everlasting unaspiring worthlessness."

Everything Mark saw on his first trip abroad affected him too immediately to permit any historical or aesthetic detachment. Napoleon III, bowing to the plaudits of the crowd and watching everybody with cat's-eyes to discover incipient treason, was no nearer to him in time than the Medicis who required their hireling artists to drag pride and manhood in the dirt for bread. In funereal Venice thoughts of its hidden trials and sudden assassinations crowded out the splendor of St. Mark's. He hurried past frescoes and altarpieces because his anger was still hot from the sight of the gold hoard in the *trésor*.

In these satiric attacks on the easy, un-American acceptance of what is esteemed to be culture we find the Mark Twain we know in his other books: the hater of pretense, resentful of all forms of tyranny, defender of the Jews and other oppressed minorities, tender toward women, the extravagant admirer of what is new and progressive. One enjoys this book, chiefly perhaps, as one does *A Tramp Abroad* (1880), for these sudden fires kindled by the ardor of his prejudices. For the sake of them we indulge him in the crudities of his humor—his fondness for burlesquing venerable legends (a hint here of *A Connecticut Yankee in King Arthur's Court*), his tiresome fun with the intricacies of foreign languages, his set pieces of comic meditation, such as the doing-up of a spectacle in the Coliseum as a Barnum might have produced it.

As compensation for these barbarisms we receive passages which move us strangely, for Mark was not always without reverence. The monuments of Greece and of Rome (before it became Peter's seat) could stir him to write descriptive prose of an unexpected quality. His unlawful visit to the Acropolis by moonlight, the silence of the streets of Pompeii, which he peoples with the oblivious workaday citizens soon to be stricken, Damascus as the type of immortality, such sights and moments impelled him to drop his clown's false face.

The chapters on the new pilgrims in the Holy Land are the best of the book, though they must have pained many churchgoers in the seventies. This climactic episode in the *Quaker City* excursion was Mark Twain's meat. Ill at ease when confronted by a cathedral, he was specially created to satirize the grim willingness with which his pious countrymen endured heat and risked filthy diseases in order that they might follow in His steps. One gets more than delight from these chapters. In no other book is the psychology of the modern pilgrim so clearly exposed, his determination to find a Presbyterian or Baptist Palestine, his ruthless lugging off what of Judaea was not trampled into mud. As for Mark himself, if he had met the Queen of Sheba on the way to Solomon, he would have said to himself, "You look fine, madam, but your feet are not clean and you smell like a camel."

6

Remembering William Dean Howells as the novelist of social change in America, *Atlantic* editor, and convert to Socialism, we forget that he was from 1861 to 1865 our consul at Venice and that out of this experience came some of his first work in prose, *Venetian Life* (1866) and *Italian Journeys* (1867). Nor do these and his other travel books, *Tuscan Cities* (1886) and *A Little Swiss Sojourn* (1892), contain the sum of his impressions of Europe. In his early years he was as much an "international novelist" as his friend Henry James, delighting in contrasts between the fresh innocence of young American girls and the deviousness of Europeans. His first novel, *Their Wedding Journey* (1872), is more travel book than novel, and *A Chance Acquaintance* (1873) furnishes a better portrait of Quebec than of its heroine. He saw Europe as a novelist might be expected to see it. The life of Lucca in the past, the life of Venice in his years there—this is what he has his eye on. We notice before we have read far how frequently these sketches turn into fiction. The patriarch of Capri is as engagingly introduced as if he were to be the leading character in a novel; episodes blossom inevitably into dialogue. Passages from these travel books turn up, only a little transformed, in the novels themselves. (In the twentieth century Howells wrote six travel books.)

No travel writer of these years gives us a fuller sense of how it felt to be in Pisa in 1883, in Vevey in 1887. His attention soon loses its grip on church and statue, but, to our profit, it fixes on what the average tourist, nose down in Hare, would have thought trivial: the little steam tram snuffling through the Piazza Santa Maria Novella; his Holiness hawking into his handkerchief during Mass; the guide in the Baptistry at Pisa who could howl so ably that he has to perform twenty times a day for the tourists who have read about him in the guidebooks.

Howells' observations on architecture and painting are prejudiced, but at any spot where men have been moved to great actions, he was willing to be entranced. "At home," he says, "one may read history, but one can realize it, as if it were something personally experienced, only on the spot where it was lived." To effect this realization, Howells believed, was the prime use of travel. Henry James, the perfect travel writer, saw that the problem for the artist in this genre was to fuse the past and present, the monuments of unaging intellect and the politics of the moment. This fusion Howells could not effect; and he admits that he cannot. For him there was a "sweet confusion" in travel. When we try to lose ourselves in the past, our modern dreariness intrudes. Yet if we were less modern we should be the more indifferent to the antique charm. He cannot bring the two worlds together.

This division of interest between the present and the past is everywhere apparent in his books. *Venetian Life* concentrates on the present. Howells had resolved to tell as much as possible about the everyday life of the Venetians and to develop a just notion of their character. He studied the social structure of Venice and the effect of the weight of the past on its inhabitants. He penetrated every quarter of the city, festival, and gathering place where he might observe them advantageously. In the end he thought he took on a little of the Venetian tone himself, the dispiritedness and the sense of loss and helplessness. His method in *Tuscan Cities* accords with his equally compelling purpose as a traveler: the "experiencing" of history. He lounges in some memorable square or court until the thought of its great moment drives out all other impressions, and the story follows. In telling it he strives for the circumstantial minuteness, the air of simple truth he so much admired in the old Florentine gossipers, in whose tales "the passions are as living, the characters as distinct, as if the thing happened yesterday."

Howells' predilections as a traveler changed, as did those of his countrymen, between the sixties and the nineties. Beneath the ingratiating manner of *Venetian Life* one detects the seriousness of the generation of Americans for whom Europe was a problem to be solved. The tone of *A Little Swiss Sojourn* is very different. Howells is content now to escape for a time, imagining how pleasant life might be in a certain noble *château meublé à louer* by the Rhone. If one had daughters to educate or were wearing out a heavy disappointment, this great house would suit very well. For many Americans, as for Howells, Europe was becoming a château to be rented for a season of self-indulgence.

Like Howells, who was his admiring critic and sponsor, John W. De Forest first practiced the art of the novelist in his travel books. His *Oriental Acquaintance* (1856) is lifted above the usual accounts of the tour to the Holy Land by its descriptions of the antics of the enraptured tourists. An even better book is his *European Acquaintance* (1858). In his conversation De Forest, so he would have us believe, indulged in the usual banalities of tourists who felt it was their duty to compare the canvases of the Venetian painters to gorgeous sunsets; but his book is almost entirely about the wonderful eccentrics he met by the way. Twelve chapters are devoted to those who endured with him the savage water cure at Gräfenberg and the more effeminate wettings and purgings and freezings at Divonne, near the Swiss border. More valuable than Norton on Orvieto cathedral is his account of the horrors of the Curd Cure, and the Straw Cure, and, most terrible of all, the Wine Cure, so barbaric that patients and doctors, when the prescribed tortures were relaxed each Saturday, all got drunk together.

In the travel essays of Henry James, collected in three volumes—*Transatlantic Sketches* (1875), *Portraits of Places* (1883), and *A Little Tour in*

*France* (1884)—the genre attains its highest development. One thinks regret-fully in reading these neglected books of the misfortune of the hundreds of James' countrymen who carried their prejudices abroad in their baggage. And not Americans only. In a devastating attack on Ruskin's inadequate percep-tions (*Portraits of Places,* pp. 64–69), James defines by implication his own qualifications for this sort of writing. "Instead of a garden of delight, [Rus-kin] finds a sort of assize-court, in perpetual session. Instead of a place in which human responsibilities are lightened and suspended, he finds a region governed by a kind of Draconic legislation." For James travel was an immense pleasure. Perpetually going a journey, he was willing to permit the scene to take hold of him and "speak"—to use the word he often uses himself.

For each experience he returns a picture which is harmonious and com-plete. Having sorted out and related the multitude of separate impressions, he builds his essay around a dominant idea or object or mood, so that the reader may grasp the essence of the scene. At Lichfield his theme is the commonplaceness of the little city looked down on by the wonderful cathedral whose great towers overtake in mid-air the conditions of perfect symmetry; at Wells it is the perpetual savor of a Sunday afternoon. In Venice what most impresses one is the way one lives "in a certain sort of knowledge as in a rosy cloud," which "certain sort of knowledge" James exquisitely defines.

What moves him least is scenery. There is a limit to the satisfaction with which one can sit staring at a mountain. Even the liquid sapphire and em-erald of Leman and Lucerne suffer when compared with firm palace floors of lapis and verd-antique. He retreats in haste from literary shrines too much possessed by tourists. What pleases most is a great English country house like Haddon Hall, where the incommunicable spirit of the ghost-haunted scene strikes with almost painful intensity; or the brooding villas of Florence whose extraordinary largeness and massiveness are a satire on their present fate. For him a great building is the greatest conceivable work of art, because it represents difficulties annulled, resources combined, labor, courage, and patience. A great building has been, and still may be, inhabited by men and women, and James relishes above all a human flavor in his pleasure.

These essays fascinate for another reason than their superb art. Whether James is contemplating the façade of Rheims cathedral from his stage-box window at the Lion d'Or or abstracting the French character from the dis-play of bathing manners on the *plage* at Etretat, the scene is always, to him, a drama. "To travel," he says, is "to go to the play, to attend a spectacle." Sometimes the gestures and murmured conversation of actual persons supply the plot; sometimes it rises from the contrast between past and present, as when he is struck with the insufferable patronage of the culture-seeking tourists toward Young Italy, preoccupied with its economical and political

future and heartily tired of being admired for its eyelashes and its pose. Ofte〈n〉
it is the conflict of ideas implicit in the scene before him which transform〈s〉
it into a psychomachia. Thus, in the midst of his enjoyment of the tranqu〈il〉
grandeur of Rheims he is overwhelmed with the realization that the hierarch〈y〉
which erected this magnificent structure is now the go-between of Bon〈a〉partism. "How far should a lover of old cathedrals let his hands be tied b〈y〉
the sanctity of their traditions? How far should he let his imagination brib〈e〉
him, as it were, from action?"

If the modern world obtrudes in these sketches more insistently than on〈e〉
might have expected, the past is always there as a continuous present, mad〈e〉
palpable by the endless devices of James' art. He hated the restorers of th〈e〉
nineteenth century, professional vandals like Sir George Gilbert Scott an〈d〉
Viollet-le-Duc, the more, perhaps, because their licensed depredations de〈-〉
prived him of his chance to evoke and reconstruct. To James a great ruin wa〈s〉
a great opportunity. Mark Twain fled from ruins because he did not have th〈e〉
skill to make them speak. James was impelled to them by a kind of aestheti〈c〉
hunger. Though only a beautiful shadow remain (as he said of Leonardo'〈s〉
"Last Supper" and of the hoary relics of Glastonbury), that "shadow is th〈e〉
artist's thought." This thought was James' quest; it gave him each time new
proof of that most pertinent lesson of art, "that there is no limit to the amoun〈t〉
of substance an artist may put into his work."

# 52. DELINEATION OF LIFE AND CHARACTER

There was living substance in the land that spread in three directions from the New York of Stedman and James, but it was a substance largely unrefined and undisciplined. To discover and develop the values and the order within it required perhaps a greater tolerance, more empirical knowledge and a freer spirit of literary experimentation than the defenders of ideality could supply. Once again the old patterns were being repeated; once again a new literature was evolving spontaneously from close contact with new ways of life and new lands at the same time that familiar forms and modes were being put to fresh uses. This time, the new land was a continental nation, the literary modes were the modes of realism and romance. Those writers who so enthusiastically rediscovered the life of the old America of the East and South or the new America of the Middle and Far West might, like naturalists from William Bartram to John W. Powell, put it directly into descriptions of nature, or might like writers of romantic tales from Fenimore Cooper to Bret Harte, strive to find literary forms adequate to what they wished to say. If they chose to make short stories and novels and poems and plays of the new material, whether it be the life of the Southern Negro or that of the California prospector, realism and romance vied with each other to create satisfactory forms.

When Harriet Beecher Stowe published *The Minister's Wooing* in 1859, Lowell welcomed her return from the intersectional triumph of *Uncle Tom's Cabin* to her true literary ground, the delineation of New England life and character. No other writer, said he, was so capable of perpetuating, through the medium of prose fiction, the fast vanishing essence of Yankeeism: Mrs. Stowe confirmed her welcome with *The Pearl of Orr's Island* (1862), and although it was not flawless, it glowed in a warm light of native affection. Without visible effort, Mrs. Stowe showed that she was capable of sharp genre painting; she got the feel of Kennebec Island life among the Pennels and Kittridges; she proved once again the importance of localized environment to verisimilitude in fiction; and she got inside common people like Aunt Roxy and Aunt Ruey as if she had never left them for Topsy and Legree. *Oldtown Folks* (1869) was an even more deliberate study of village

843

character, manners, and social organization, this time in her husband's birt
place, South Natick. She took the task seriously. "It is more to me than
story," she said. "It is my résumé of the whole spirit and body of Ne
England." In the *Oldtown Fireside Stories* (1872) she used the dialect yar
of the philosopher-raconteur Sam Lawson to lighten the darker aspects of t
New England spirit, and her *Poganuc People* (1878), in which she condens
her recollections of girlhood in Litchfield, Connecticut, might have be
written to Lowell's order.

Mrs. Stowe's work reflects the limitations, as well as some of the positi
virtues, of the literary movement to which her name thus early lent prestig
Dedicated to the exploitation of the most anciently settled America, t
coastal plain and the adjacent mountains from Maine to Florida and alo
the Gulf to the Mississippi Delta, the movement gained momentum in t
East and South during the years of war and reconstruction. Under the doub
impact of foreign and Western influences it reached a production peak aft
the third quarter of the century, and continued, with various modificatio
and interruptions, as a prominent force in American writing for a good fif
years thereafter. Long before Mrs. Stowe's return to the New England scen
a democratic regionalist tradition had begun to take form and amass su
stance both in the North and in the Deep South. All the elements Mrs. Stov
employed were ready to her hand in the literary record: exploitation of rur
character and manners in the immediate or the colonial past, using dialec
local coloring, or any other devices which would produce, at the literary leve
the kind of realism represented in the visual arts by genre painting, where th
aim was to render truthfully, though always selectively, a picture of ordinar
life as it was being lived or had been lived in times not too remote. Partl
because of her own limitations as a writer, Mrs. Stowe fell heir also to th
main weaknesses of the tradition: structural deficiencies, labored histrionic
sentimental didacticism.

In the year of *Poganuc People* appeared books by two other Connecticu
Yankees. Rose Terry Cooke's *Happy Dodd* and Annie Trumbull Slosson
*China Hunters' Club* indicated that the tradition was not to be allowed t
languish. Mrs. Cooke's profound religious feelings and her love of the in
dustrious poor found expression in *Happy Dodd,* the life chronicle of a plai
little cripple. The ensuing years saw other volumes, of which the stories i
*Huckleberries Gathered from New England Hills* (1891) are among th
best. Mrs. Slosson reached full stature only with *Dumb Foxglove and Othe
Stories* (1898), studies in the psychology of religious emotion among th
lowly. If the three middle-aged ladies from Connecticut did not establish
school, they fixed upon the writing of the period the mark of their ow
gentle and generous personalities, and proved that in the proper hands th
democratic regionalist tradition was still capable of development.

Meantime a doctor's daughter in South Berwick ("a Maine borderer," she called herself) was quietly commencing what would become the most distinguished career among all the writers of regional fiction. Sarah Orne Jewett developed her gifts more rapidly, maintained them at a higher level, and employed them with greater dexterity and control than did any of her predecessors in the field. After a period of apprenticeship to children's magazines she entered adult fiction at twenty with a story in the *Atlantic* (December, 1869), and in eight years had accumulated enough others to take Howells' advice and collect them in her first book, *Deephaven* (1877). In that year Mrs. Stowe was sixty-five, Mrs. Cooke fifty, and Mrs. Slosson thirty-nine. Miss Jewett was only twenty-eight, and her youth may have had something to do with the fact that *Deephaven,* for all its faults, has a certain distinctive newness and brightness beside which *Póganuc People, Happy Dodd,* and *The China Hunters' Club,* all issued in the following year, seem dull and old-fashioned. But *Deephaven* was only a start. Through the next twenty years she published in the best monthlies, and then collected, a succession of stories which showed a steadily deepening insight into the complexities of human character, and a steadily growing technical skill. Her masterpiece, *The Country of the Pointed Firs* (1896), is the best piece of regional fiction to have come out of nineteenth century America.

Yet this great book is not her only claim to admiration. Nearly all the stories she wrote after 1880 show the distinctive quality of her work: that particular combination of deep and tender insight with technical resilience and toughness which none of her contemporaries in the field learned to match, chiefly because they were unwilling to work as hard as she. She took very seriously her own Arnoldian maxim: "Study the work that the best judges have called good and see *why* it is good." Occasionally she was capable of being deceived by her respect for men like Tennyson into thinking them greater than they were; but her letters repeatedly show the rightness of her judgments about Henry James and the French and Russian novelists. She read Balzac with discernment, admired Zola's "shrewdness of workmanship," borrowed two leaves from Flaubert as a counsel of perfection, and even grew to comprehend what Tolstoy, her antithesis in most ways, was attempting to do. Yet of Miss Jewett one might repeat what someone said of George Sand: although she had the deepest veneration for the aristocracy of the intellect, the democracy of suffering touched her more. Even as a child, making sick calls with her father, she had learned how to get in among the people of York, Wells, South Berwick, and the surrounding countryside, and when she became a writer they still received and trusted and confided in her—these "village people—not the new ones, but those to whom in their early days Berwick was the round world itself." The quiet towns and the weathered farms gave her all her best stories—"The White Heron," "Marsh Rosemary,"

"The Only Rose," and a great many others—and she felt only an occasional need to look farther afield. "People talk about dwelling upon the trivialities and commonplaces in life, but a master writer gives everything weight, and makes you feel the distinction and importance of it."

What gave her writing weight was her ability to combine a rightness of observation with an intuition that looked beneath surfaces. In the precision of her feeling for natural objects she resembled, and knew she resembled, Dorothy Wordsworth. The reader is often brought up sharp by the clean, poetic accuracy of her epithets: the westering sun, for example, is said to light up schooner sails, far on the eastern sea, like "golden houses." But Dorothy Wordsworth could rarely develop her scattered observations into a total pattern; whole stories of Miss Jewett have this quality of breathless delight, or display that equally compelling sense of thoughts that lie "too deep for tears." One recalls the picture of the deserted farmhouse in *Deephaven*:

that fireless, empty, forsaken house, where the winter sun shines in and creeps slowly along the floor; the bitter cold is in and around the house, and the snow has sifted in at every crack; outside it is untrodden by any living creature's footstep. The wind blows and rushes and shakes the loose window-sashes in their frames, while the padlock knocks—knocks against the door.

Miss Jewett's landscapes had always figures in the foreground, for people were always in the foreground of her consciousness. "You must write," she told Willa Cather, "to the human heart, the great consciousness that all humanity goes to make up. Otherwise what might be strength in a writer is only crudeness, and what might be insight is only observation; sentiment falls to sentimentality—you can write about life, but never write life itself."

To such ideas she had triumphantly adhered throughout her writing life, though not at first with so deep a sense of either tragedy or comedy, or so complete a dominance over her material. The growth between *Deephaven* and *The Country of the Pointed Firs* can be measured by seeing how observation has matured to insight, and how her attitude toward both her people and her art has subtly deepened. In the early book the narrator seems (though she was not) a summer resident in search of the quaint and unique; without looking down on the people she is never quite at one with them, and her experiments with scenes are sometimes tentative and unsure. By the time of the *Pointed Firs* and its epilogue-story *The Dunnet Shepherdess,* she knows how to understand and therefore how to present her people; she has learned the great trick of true realism: to combine depth of sympathetic involvement with artistic detachment, reaching unity through the establishment of a point of view. Deeply responsive to a look or a word from people like Almira

Todd the gatherer of pennyroyal, or William Blackett the taciturn islander, she can still see that look or word as only one thread in the fabric of her total impression. An emotional experience is thus never felt to be the end in view, but only an indispensable contribution to that end. One could cite among dozens of examples the farewell to Mrs. Todd, soon followed by the distant prospect of the same Antigone-like figure descending the profile of a hill as party to a walking funeral. One hears that Miss Jewett's was a limited and muted art. But the significant point—in an age of realism for social history's sake, or regionalism strongly dependent for its force on mere local color, where characters were sometimes embarrassed and stereotyped by being saddled with the responsibility of representing a particular region—is that her stories were works of art, and of a high order.

Two of Miss Jewett's contemporaries, Rowland Robinson and Celia Thaxter, showed what could happen to regionalism and local color when other motives than those of the serious artist were predominant. Robinson was a Quaker farm boy from Vermont who invented the fictional village of Danvis as a theater of operations for characters like Lisha Peggs, Sam Lovel, and the French Canadian, Antoine. According to its author, *Danvis Folks* (1894) "was written with less purpose of telling any story than of recording the manners, customs, and speech" in vogue in Vermont during the early nineteenth century. At the other extreme stood Celia Thaxter, whose deservedly popular sketchbook, *Among the Isles of Shoals* (1873), ran through seventeen editions in twenty years. Her subject matter is that of the poet-naturalist, and she writes as a pure local colorist determined to describe, in the closest detail, her own well loved region: the lonely islands, flower-studded and peopled with birds, the landsmell wafted eastward after rain, the cries of terns, the breathing sound of whales in the bay at night. The few Shoalers who appear in her pages are gingerly handled; her interest is in the setting.

If Robinson and Mrs. Thaxter are preoccupied with extensions of the exploitational idea, the work of Mary Eleanor Wilkins, a native of western Massachusetts, is close to the center of the tradition. Her best work was done before 1902, when she married and henceforth wrote as Mary E. Wilkins Freeman. At the top of her form, she was a finer artist than any of her contemporaries except Miss Jewett, and there was a sharpness of line and directness of purpose about her first two collections which even Miss Jewett could not match. The fifty-two short stories in *A Humble Romance* (1887) and *A New England Nun* (1891), represent about a quarter of her total short-story output. The locus of her interest is always the proud, reticent, stoical people. Descriptive passages are spare and apposite, and the local customs, like the local idiom, are used for high-lighting and never for substance. In these respects she resembles Miss Jewett, but hers is on the whole a more objective art. On one occasion the narrator in *The Country of the Pointed Firs* notices how "a narrow set of circumstances had caged a fine able character and held it captive." But Miss Jewett rarely stresses, as Miss Wilkins so frequently does, the caging environment, the captivity of circumstance, and there seems, accordingly, a larger measure of modern realism in the work of the younger writer. Yet her grimness has been overemphasized; she is not primarily the expositor of social conditions, the iconoclast of country codes, and if she has not the tenderness and humor of Miss Jewett, she has a saving sense of the comic. In "A New England Nun," where Louisa Ellis finds herself unable to admit her aging fiancé to the gentle rhythms of her spinster's domain, there is suggestion of hidden sublimations of which a Freudian might have made much. In the complex jealousies of "A Village Singer" or the inherent hardnesses of "A Village Lear," similar opportunities present themselves. Miss Wilkins' refusal to overplay her hand is a sign of control rather than lack of courage. Yet she was unable to sustain the high level thus early achieved in these stories, and later collections are far less admirable, although one observes, even in the first two volumes, that little effort has been made to distinguish the mediocre and repetitious from the fifteen or twenty stories which are her real contribution to the tradition.

2

The regionalist impulse in one form or another accounted for the emergence of almost every prominent writer in the Middle Atlantic states and the Deep South in the last quarter of the century. By 1887, fourteen years after Hayne had supposed that Southern literature could not survive, a score of young writers were vigorously engaged in the exploitation of native materials, for which many of them found a ready market in the section-conscious magazines of the North. When the reading public discovered, somewhat belatedly, an insatiable interest in prewar planters and country gentlemen, poor whites of mountain, piedmont, tidewater, and bayou, and the plantation Negro, whether enslaved or emancipated, the writers were ready to supply the demand, and the number of stories and articles about the South reached proportions formerly undreamed of.

That prominent driving force among the Northern regional writers, the desire to preserve in print a vanished or vanishing past, reappears most strikingly in the plantation literature of Virginia where it often leads to an idealization of former times far more marked than one finds in New England writing of the same period. The tendency was hard to resist, as was shown in the career of Dr. George W. Bagby. In 1859 this Lynchburg journalist had sought half seriously to accomplish what he called "The Unkind but

Complete Destruction" of that well known romancer, John Esten Cooke, who kept his eye steadily fixed on the glories of the Old Dominion. Bagby was tired, he said, of hearing his ancestors cracked up as the topmost top-sawyers of all creation, and he called for a man who could effectively paint the real Southern life around him. Bagby's own contribution was the "Mozis Addums" letters, where the common-man humor of overstatement, the slap-stick practical joke, and the barbaric spelling indicate that Mozis is another in the long queue of broadly humorous commoners, like Hosea Biglow, Jack Downing, and Simon Suggs. But nostalgia ultimately triumphed even over Bagby. The huge success of his lecture "Bacon and Greens," a lengthy and discursive panegyric on rural life in prewar Virginia, led him to undertake other similar experiments, of which his idealized and intensely localized por-trait of "The Old Virginia Gentleman" is a prime example. In a note to this lecture Bagby recalled that during the life of the Commonwealth he had been at pains to satirize its shortcomings. "But our Mother," he added, "is dead." Now, without shame, he could mourn the loss of that beauty, simplicity, purity, uprightness, cordiality, warmth, grace, and lavish hospitality which had undoubtedly distinguished country life in old Virginia.

Neither his good friend Cooke, whose romances he had satirized, nor the young lawyer Thomas Nelson Page took Bagby to task for this reversal of his former position. Page, indeed, saw in the old tidewater Virginia a mature and deep-rooted civilization upon which he was presently to draw. After Cooke, the gentleman cavalier tradition found its most articulate exponent and apologist in Page. The *Century* in 1884 accepted his "Marse Chan," a retrospective piece in the dialect of an aging Negro body servant who still loyally guards the dog of his late master, a gallant war casualty. This and five other tales form *In Ole Virginia* (1887), the success of which drew Page away from his Richmond law practice into the profession of letters. The Page formula is revealed in stories like "Marse Chan," "Unc' Edinburg's Drown-din," or "Meh Lady." Forlorn ex-slaves yearn for the good old times—"de bes' Sam ever see"—or worshipfully recall the great dark eyes and blushing cheeks of those goddesses in crinoline, the plantation ladies; or remember how they stood by as sympathetic servant-observers when dashing young soldiers left for the wars, or galloped back under cover of darkness to pluck a rose from the bush under milady's window. "That the social life of the Old South had its faults I am far from denying," says Page in a characteristic echo of Bagby's words. "But its virtues far outweighed them; its graces were never equalled. . . . It was, I believe, the purest, sweetest life ever lived." Page's faults—overidealization of character and melodramatic emphasis in his management of incident—are at least matched by his virtues: genuine descrip-tive skill, as in the lingering and loving account of a Christmas feast and dance in the plantation washhouse, or the sinister swamp atmosphere of "No Haid Pawn"; an eye for significant detail and an ear for the niceties of dialect which gave him in these respects a marked superiority over Cooke and Bagby; and enough appreciation of the realities of war and reconstruction to enable him to shrug off the charge that he was totally immersed in what Bagby had called "the golden patriarchal days that shall come no more."

By 1884, when Page was getting his start, James Lane Allen had decided to make a career of the central Kentucky plateau around his native Lexington, and to use the landscapes of this single neighborhood as the locale of all his work. But it was characteristic of him that he rejected the selective realism of the genre painters in favor of synthetic prose tone poems about Kentucky's "soil and sky and season"; and that he depended heavily, as Bagby and Page did not, upon a mannered and heightened style, designed to lift his work above the common run of localized writing. His first collection, *Flute and Violin* (1891), showed where his theories led in practice—to the bizarre heroics of Palemon, the insurgent Trappist monk; or the sacrifice of Sister Dolorosa, gone from Kentucky to die among Damien's lepers; or the idealization of the tramp King Solomon, redeemed from disgrace in a cholera epidemic. The sense of the actual flows away in this never-never land of Allendom. Nor is it totally regained in the famous and popular idyls, *A Kentucky Cardinal* (1894), and its sequel, *Aftermath* (1895). We should now apply differently the remarks of those contemporary reviewers who compared these books and *Summer in Arcady* (1896) to pressed flowers smelling faintly of lavender, exuding sweetness, moral fervor, and light. *The Choir Invisible* (1897), Allen's novel of late eighteenth century Kentucky, sometimes gets closer to reality. Yet its hero, John Gray, is too much the feudal knight in the garb of a frontier schoolmaster to seem more than remotely credible. What Allen missed, even in so marked an advance as *The Reign of Law* (1900), was that deep belief in the importance of earthy character which strengthened and sustained those regionalists who were in other ways his inferiors.

Yet Southern writers discovered other values than those of the plantation aristocracy, and with the appearance of Charles Egbert Craddock's *In the Tennessee Mountains* (1884), the Southern poor white, described here and there by earlier writers, began to look like a subject for exploitation. Little was known about the author of these sketches, except that this was probably not his real name, that he wrote a bold, black hand, and that he was apparently well acquainted with the regional idiosyncrasies of the hill dwellers in the Tennessee Cumberlands and the Great Smokies. "Possibly not since George Eliot's time," wrote Charles Coleman in 1887, "has there been so great a literary sensation as that created by the discovery" that Craddock was the pseudonym of a well educated, partially crippled Tennessee spinster named Mary Noailles Murfree. This young lady's love of mountain topographical features was such that huge blocks of scenic description were allowed to obstruct the flow of her narrative, and her desire to produce phonetically exact transcriptions of the local dialect was so strong that the reader, as with Rowland Robinson's Vermonters, must overcome his objections to the orthography before he can read the dialogue with any pleasure. A patience durable enough to survive these obstacles finds its reward in the generally realistic tales of moonshiners and posses, fist-fighters and hunters, pointed up with graphic accounts of courting, dancing, eating, drinking, plowing, and card playing among the human neighbors of brooding old peaks like Chilhowee. One finishes books like *The Prophet of the Great Smoky Mountains* (1885) and *In the "Stranger People's" Country* (1895) with an authoritative knowledge of backwoods life in Tennessee during the Reconstruction period.

Although Miss Murfree was among the earliest of the regionalists to gain fame through the fictional treatment of mountaineers, she had no corner on the Southern poor white. Henry Watterson's anthology, *Oddities in Southern Life and Character* (1882), showed that in the humorous writing of the old Deep South, particularly that which originated in Georgia and Alabama, there was a strong rural democratic tradition. Watterson's collection came late enough to include samples of the work of two Georgians, Richard Malcolm Johnston and Joel Chandler Harris, who plainly occupy the tradition of Longstreet, Hooper, and Thompson. What chiefly distinguishes their achievement from that of the raucous elder humorists is a combination of the rugged virtues of the old with a new and pervasive sympathy and a restrained use of sentiment.

Johnston was almost fifty when his Dukesborough stories first gained wide recognition and he had become an old man by the time people began to talk about the Uncle Remus stories of the young Atlanta editor, Harris. The antetype of Dukesborough was Powelton, Georgia, near which stood Johnston's plantation birthplace, "Oak Grove." By the time he died in 1898 he had published some eighty tales and three middling novels, all of them centered in or near the Georgia he had known as a plantation child, or as lawyer and educator among the villages of the state. A gifted raconteur in the leisurely manner, he brought both ebullience and charm to his accounts of Dukesborough school life, family feuds, and red-letter days in the village calendar, often employing the native idiom of a special narrator, old Mr. Pate. The accent was on a particular terrain, and the Dukesborough people: their suspicions of the local witch, their excitement over the weasels in the chicken house, the nervous mother's caution to her children when the World-

Renowned Circus parades through town: "Stay behind there, you Jack, and you Susan! You want to git eat up by them camels and varmints?"

Like his fast friend, Colonel Johnston, Harris had grown up among small planters and impecunious villagers from whose mode of life the grand manner was conspicuously absent. Like Johnston, too, he preferred to picture Georgia country life as it was, not as a lost paradise through which the rustle of angelic wings could be heard, but as a democratic society. This is not to say that Harris employed naturalistic techniques, or that he habitually painted Southern poor-white life as Caldwell and Faulkner were to do. But he contrived to show that the annals of the poor are neither short nor simple, and there is an air of complete naturalness about everything he wrote. His characteristic approach lay somewhere between that represented by Goldsmith's *Vicar of Wakefield,* his favorite novel, and the work that he regarded as the most characteristic American story thus far written, E. W. Howe's *The Story of a Country Town.* He shared the opinion (however one may disagree with it) which underlay all the best genre writing of the period: "No novel or story can be genuinely American unless it deal with the *common people, that is country people.*" And he held boldly forth against a strictly regional emphasis:

What does it matter whether I am Northern or Southern, if I am true to truth? . . . My idea is that truth is more important than sectionalism, and that literature that can be labeled Northern, Southern, Western, or Eastern, is not worth labeling at all.

That Harris' merits were not totally comprehended in the songs and sayings of Uncle Remus became evident in 1884, when he published the volume *Mingo, and Other Sketches in Black and White.* The struggle between the stalwart moonshiners of Hog Back Mountain in North Georgia and their inadequate foes the revenue agents, provides the substance of the novelette, "At Teague Poteet's," longest and best of the four stories in this volume. The gay mountaineer, his taciturn cracker wife, and his daughter Sis, whom Harris cannot resist idealizing a little, are all worthy to stand beside Uncle Remus. "Trouble on Lost Mountain" in the next collection, *Free Joe and Other Georgian Sketches* (1887), is a tragic variation on the same theme, less successful as a story, but excellent in the vitality of characters like Abe Hightower with his healthy and breezy but deep-founded affection for his daughter Babe. Among the lowlanders, one remembers especially Mingo's sour companion, the embittered Mrs. Blivins, cracker rebel against the shortcomings of her "restercrat" kinfolks; and the stoical yellow-faced Emma Jane Stucky, the piney-woods tacky of Harris' sandhill novelette, "Azalia." The most striking aspect of Harris' writing, the quality that destroys his often reiterated avowal that his work was valueless as literature, is the apparently effortless ease with which he convinces the reader of the truth of what is being read. If the Negro Balaam's wealthy master is a sensual good-for-nothing, Harris refuses to idealize him; if Colonel Flewellen was so much a gentleman that he was willing to live on what the ex-slave Ananias could steal for him, Harris gives the facts and lets the reader judge. Had he done nothing beside the stories in these and several later collections, Harris would still stand out as a minor master among the Southern genre writers.

Harris' picture of the Georgia Negro is his foremost achievement. Those who do not easily surrender to the charm of Uncle Remus or complain that there is too much honey and too little gall in the animal stories can turn for variety to the portraits of the dignified Mingo, the abject Ananias, the splenetic Mom Bi, Aunt Fountain, Balaam, Free Joe, or Blue Dave. Harris' characteristic respect for the truth, and his close knowledge of the Georgia Negro as he existed under slavery and reconstruction, gave his Negro stories an authority which few of his contemporaries could approach.

The Negro had need of Harris, if only to explain his variety. The slave Hector in Simms' *The Yemassee* (1835), Jupiter in Poe's "The Gold Bug" (1843), and Mrs. Stowe's Uncle Tom (1852) hardly presented an adequate composite picture of a minority group which in 1860 numbered close to 4,500,000. Nor were the songs of Stephen Foster of any great value in filling out the picture of what the Southern Negro was like. Not only was Foster a native of Pittsburgh, but he was also preeminently a showman, looking for marketable material, and lacking in what may be called the deeper literary motives. For all his enviable hold over the singing habits of a nation, in his own day and ever since, Foster had little first-hand knowledge of the Negro, and his songs merely perpetuate a stereotype of the melancholy plantation "darky." Closer to the real thing were the dialect poems of the Mississippian, Irwin Russell, who once remarked of *Uncle Tom's Cabin* that it gave no more true idea of Negro life and character than the Nautical Almanac. Russell's death in 1879 at the age of twenty-six was lamented throughout the reading South, and Harris stated, in introducing a posthumous edition of his *Poems* (1888), that Russell was among the first of the Southern writers to appreciate the literary possibilities of the Negro character, which he represented with great accuracy. Russell's poems are too few to make sound judgment possible. Yet the often praised "Christmas-Night in the Quarters" is certainly a minor triumph, a Southernized version of Burns' "The Jolly Beggars," which has all the vivacity Bagby could have wished. One of the recitativos, a localized retelling of the Noah story ("'Dar's gwine to be a' ober-flow,' said Noah, lookin' solemn") uses a method since widely popularized in the work of Roark Bradford.

Harris' *Uncle Remus, His Songs and His Sayings* (1880) was the first collection of Negro lore, plantation song, and country anecdote to reveal at all comprehensively the possibilities for genre painting inherent in the Negro life and character. One could best measure the value of Harris' contribution, said Professor William Baskervill, pioneer historian of Southern letters, by comparing Uncle Remus with the ideal Negro of "My Old Kentucky Home," *Uncle Tom's Cabin,* "Marse Chan," and "Meh Lady" or with the impossible Negro of the minstrel show. Beside such visionary types or clownish, plug-hatted caricatures, thought Baskervill, Uncle Remus stood out, largely because Harris knew whereof he spoke. His protagonist was a composite picture of old Uncle George Terrell and half-a-dozen other workers to whom Harris had listened during the early sixties when he was a youthful protégé of Joseph Addison Turner at the "Turnwold" plantation, not far from his birthplace in Putnam County, Georgia. After some years of newspaper work in Macon, New Orleans, and Savannah, Harris had settled down permanently in 1876 as a staff member of the Atlanta *Constitution,* and about a year later had begun to realize that his home-grown knowledge of the Negro was a valuable possession. Although Harris undoubtedly overworked Uncle Remus, and although he disclaimed literary pretensions, the ten Uncle Remus books which he (or his executors) published between 1880 and the First World War showed appreciable merit; a skillful variation of materials, a love of ironic implication, a mastery of the short dramatic form, and a sure grasp of humorous idiom and the natural rhythms of folk speech.

During the latter years of the century the most noteworthy followers in the wake of Harris were the Negro writers Charles Waddell Chesnutt and Paul Laurence Dunbar. Both happened to be Ohioans, but Dunbar's mother (to whom he owed the idea for his best known poem, "When Malindy Sings") was a native of Kentucky who had grown up in slavery, while Chesnutt's legal training involved a number of years in North Carolina. The *Atlantic Monthly* accepted several of Chesnutt's stories in the late eighties, and in 1899 he selected seven tales for his volume *The Conjure Woman.* These were unified through their common subject matter, Negro magic, and through the character of Uncle Julius McAdoo, an elderly colored man who suggests Remus, and is his closest rival. With his second collection, *The Wife of His Youth* (also 1899), Chesnutt forthrightly considered the tragi-comic implications of the "color line," and his career included also three novels which expose the consequences of racial prejudice.

Dunbar's early work in verse caught the attention of Howells, who wrote an introduction for *Lyrics of Lowly Life* (1896) in which he praised Dunbar's "refined and delicate art," his objective study of the Negro, and his conviction that there is or ought to be an essential unity among human beings which has nothing to do with skin color. Dunbar's first collection of short stories, *Folks from Dixie* (1898), employed dialect successfully, and although two or three of them follow too closely the lead of Page, others are original and apparently authoritative. Before his early death in 1906, Dunbar published four novels, three other collections of short fiction, and several more volumes of verse. If as writers of fiction he and Chesnutt sometimes derived suggestions from other analysts of Negro character, both brought to their work the stamp of their persuasive personalities, and both enriched that branch of nineteenth century literature which relates to the old-time Southern Negro.

### 3

Nowhere else in the literature relating to the older America does one find the particular flavor which distinguishes the regional writing of New Orleans. Elsewhere plainness and homeliness are the rule; New Orleans writing inherits from its setting an Old World patina. Elsewhere the stress is on the rural, the lonely; but the sprawling city of New Orleans teems with life. Elsewhere the Americanness of the characters is unmistakable; in New Orleans, even the eccentric "Posson Jone" (who would have been quite at home in Dukesborough) seems like a foreign interloper, that is to say, an *Americain*. Elsewhere one observes a certain unanimity of thought and language among the inhabitants of a particular region; in the polyglot New Orleans of George W. Cable, French, Spanish, Irish, and Dutch mingle with American boatmen from the upper reaches of the Mississippi, West Indian refugees, and sailors of fortune from every quarter of the globe; the quadroon demimondaine lingers on the edge of society; Choctaw women vend sassafras along the banquettes; the levels of thought and the details of action, like the divisions of speech, are as various as the tongues of Babel.

At the time of Cable's emergence, New Orleans and the delta region of Mississippi was in a sense virgin territory for fiction. A French literature had flourished in colonial and early nineteenth century Louisiana, and a few American writers had tentatively scratched the ground. But a full-fledged literature of New Orleans and the bayou country did not appear until the 1870's.

Cable's struggle for fame was long and arduous. He had gone to work as a boy of fifteen, served in the Confederate cavalry, and worked for a cotton wholesaler. But he remarked that although the cotton business was pleasant enough, he could not help striking higher, and "trying for an honourable profession." For a time it seemed that reporting for the New Orleans *Picayune* would do, but when the newspaper discharged him he was not sorry. "I wanted to be always writing," said he, "and they wanted me to be always reporting. This didn't work well . . . and I went back to bookkeeping." The books he began to keep in 1871 were those in the counting rooms of Black and Company, cotton factors, and for the next ten years he handled the firm's financial transactions with accuracy but without enthusiasm. At last he was able to tell Howells that he had resigned his secretaryship, closed his office and now stood armed with nothing "for offense or defense but my grey goose quill."

That goose quill had been busy for the better part of the preceding decade. During the sweltering days when the countingroom was ahead of schedule Cable used to slip away to the municipal archives. There he read hundreds of old newspapers, and soon knew more about the New Orleans past than anyone else in town. But he also found, among the yellowing items, stories that cried for fictional development. "It seemed a pity," he explained later "for the stuff to go to waste," and in off hours he tried his hand with three or four: " 'Sieur George," "Bibi" (later rewritten and incorporated in *The Grandissimes* as "The Story of Bras-Coupé"), and one or two more. When Edward King, on contract to *Scribner's Monthly* for a series of articles on the South, visited New Orleans in 1872, he met the slight, black-bearded book-keeper, read his tales, and enthusiastically recommended them to the Scribner editors, Holland and Gilder. Although they rejected half of the stories Cable submitted (they cared nothing for "Posson Jone" and found the subject of "Bibi," as they said, "unmitigatedly distressful"), they had accepted and printed four others by the spring of 1876, and Edward King's "discovery" was being mentioned as a coming name in Southern literature. By 1878 Scribner's had invited him to do a serial novel (*The Grandissimes*), and had agreed to bring out a volume which Cable thought of calling *Prose Idyls for Hammock and Fan,* but which bore, on its appearance in 1879, the familiar title, *Old Creole Days.*

American letters had previously seen nothing quite like these seven fresh though hardly faultless, stories—the old city of mellowed brick and mildewed stucco, with bustling streets over the wall from fragrant gardens; or, on the purlieus, doomed plantations like the Belles Demoiselles; or, in the French Quarter, the *Salle de Condé* where young bloods went to dance with well chaperoned quadroons; the languor, femininity, gaiety, or knife-wielding ferocity of the Creole caste, from General Villivicencio down to Mazzaro of the Café des Exiles; the invariably beautiful women, demure in bearing but strong in will, like Madame Délicieuse, or Madame John, 'Tite Poulette's guardian; misfits like Poquelin or Monsieur George; mild-mannered young men like Dr. Mossy or Kristian Koppig. The whole was projected poetically, with care for precision of simile, and a certain allusive richness; yet it carried too, a sly humor which touched with acid some of the Creole portraitures

Still, it fell short of first-rate writing. A certain desultory clutter inhibited the forward march of the narrative; the use of Creole dialect was overzealous; characters were often merely eccentric; and there was a fondness for the smash ending which soon dated the stories of 'Tite Poulette, Jean-ah Poquelin, and Madame Délicieuse. What one noticed as a leading quality was the gentle love of mystification, a diffusion—not of syntax but of total effect—which seems to be the chief source of Cable's charm.

This charm accounted partly for the success of *The Grandissimes,* a leisurely, discursive, densely populated, panoramic, high-colored, witty, and complicated novel which Cable brought out in 1880. The book had shape, movement, richness of texture, and a kind of subdued violence, and it was crammed with living portraits; the two Honorés (one a quadroon); Frowenfeld the German apothecary (another of those young foreigners whom Cable delighted to put into his books); the beautiful Nancanous, mother and daughter, on whom Cable lavished his best talents; Palmyre Philosophe, the fierce and unpredictable *voudou*; the fabulous Negro prince, Bras-Coupé, and a dozen others. The elements of romance were there in plenty: the simmering feud, the stolen inheritance, the half-brothers separated by the laws of caste, the triple love story, the visitation of yellow fever, the mob assault, the knife in the dark, the hamstrung slave, the trapped and screaming Negress in the cypress swamp, and behind all the slow spectacle of a proud Louisiana, sold over the heads of its citizens, blunderingly resisting Americanization. But there was also a strong infusion of the actual, and Cable knew how and when not to take himself seriously. The Creoles were the "Knickerbockers of Louisiana," relentless reactionaries who had called caste and slavery right, and then "sealed the whole subject." In reopening that subject, Cable did not hesitate to impale these dark butterflies, to borrow a phrase from Hawthorne, upon the iron rod of social ethics; but it was plain, in this and later books, that Cable loved the Creoles, too, and his laughter at their expense was not loud enough to conceal his admiration for their better qualities.

Succeeding years showed Cable's versatility and staying power. *Madame Delphine,* published in 1881 and added to later editions of *Old Creole Days,* was a deft novelette, a variation of the theme of " 'Tite Poulette," but more subdued and controlled, suggesting *The Scarlet Letter* translated to the New Orleans milieu. *Dr. Sevier* (1885) was another thronged and complex novel, more straightforwardly told than *The Grandissimes,* in which were detailed the struggles of a serious young married couple against poverty and despair in ante-bellum New Orleans. In the idyllic *Bonaventure* (1888), a trilogy of novelettes, the hero was a Creole schoolmaster, living among the Acadian peasants.

Despite his continued exploitation of Creole character, Cable lived in the

North for the last forty years of his life. When he collaborated with Mark
Twain on a series of lecture tours, he found audiences as ready for his stories
and songs as for Twain's drolleries. He denied the charge that he had fled the
South through social pressure arising from his Creole portraits and his ably
reasoned social essays on the predicament of the Southern Negro, and before
his death in 1925 he often happily revisited his native city, gathering more
material for stories about a region which he, more than any other writer, had
indelibly engraved upon the map of regional literature.

About the time Cable moved to Northampton, Massachusetts, Creole
enmity toward him was pronounced, and the allegedly injured group soon
found a genteel champion. Grace King, daughter of a New Orleans lawyer,
assured Gilder in 1884 that Cable had proclaimed his preference for colored
people over whites, and for quadroons over Creoles. Gilder icily suggested
that if Cable were such a traitor, someone had better try writing better. What
Miss King produced in response to the challenge was not spectacular, but it
was respectable. *Monsieur Motte* was a girlish, theatrical piece, but the four
long stories of Louisiana which she collected in 1892 as *Tales of a Time and
Place* displayed a distinguished style, a prose deliberate and cool, illuminated
with splashes of color, and filled at the end with climactic passages of action.
Both here and in later works Miss King carefully avoided controversial
matters, stepped softly, and sought everywhere to tone down the more garish,
but always more interesting, portraits which Cable had drawn.

The writing career of Kate Chopin, one of the shortest in the annals of
the ordinarily long-lived regional writers, began in 1899 with some indifferent
poetry and followed a meteoric course which ended a year or two before her
death in 1904. What she did in that time had, however, an intensity, courage,
vigor, and independence which sets her work in sharp contrast to the pale
antidotes to Cable which Miss King had chosen to offer. An exact contemporary of Miss King, Katherine O'Flaherty was born in St. Louis of Irish
and French parents, was graduated from a convent into the active life of a
Missouri belle, married Oscar Chopin at nineteen, entered New Orleans
society, bore six children, moved to a Red River plantation, saw her husband
die of swamp fever, returned to St. Louis, fended off several potential suitors,
and in 1890, at the age of thirty-nine, published her first novel. She subsequently wrote nearly a hundred short stories, about half of which were
collected in two volumes, *Bayou Folk* (1894) and *A Night in Acadie* (1897).
The best of these describe the Acadians in the mid-Louisiana parishes of
Natchitoches and Avoyelles, regions with which Mrs. Chopin had become
acquainted during her plantation days. Many of them (and there is possibly
a connection here with Mrs. Chopin's own mild unconventionality) turn
upon acts of rebellion: Zaida's attempted elopement during the Cajun ball

at Père Foché's; the refusal of Athenaise to settle into a dull marriage; young Polydore feigning rheumatism to escape work; Chicot, the *neg creol,* whose professed paganism contradicted his Christian practice. At their best the bayou tales displayed a clean economy of line, and were rounded off with a kind of Gallic finesse which suggested that Mrs. Chopin's study of Maupassant had not gone unrewarded. She knew, better than many of her contemporaries among the regionalists, how to begin, develop, and conclude a story without waste motion or observable self-consciousness. Her feeling for character was supported by an almost instinctive grasp of form and pace. Like Miss Jewett, she knew how to use dialect for flavoring; with her it never became an obstacle. Miss Murfree might have learned from her the art of subordinating environment to character. Like Harris and Johnston, she knew where sentiment ends and sentimentality begins. Yet many of her stories fell short of excellence because she wrote too swiftly and impulsively, leaned too heavily upon the suggestions of the moment, and impatiently shrugged off the burden of correction and revision. She rarely resorted to mere trickery, though it is a trick which mars her frequently anthologized (and not very typical) study in race relations, "Désirée's Baby," which satisfies the reader's sense of justice while disappointing him with a contrived conclusion. Even her failures are readable, and at her subtle and economical best, she challenges the workmanship of Mary Wilkins Freeman, analyzing the more exotic and passionate Cajun character or painting the humble romances of canebrake and cotton field with something of that control and candor which her Northern contemporary brought to her studies of New England nuns and village choristers.

4

The regional movement in the East and South, for all its scope and variety, produced few writers of the first magnitude. The best work of Miss Jewett and Mrs. Freeman, like that of Harris and Cable, shows a wholesome originality, a masterly dominance of difficult materials, a devotion to problems of structure and texture, a feeling for character and motivation, a love of the actual and a hatred of the artificial, the bathetic, and the cheap which raises it far above what one usually thinks of as run-of-the-mine local color writing. Many of the lesser writers succeeded often enough so that if a patient editor were prepared to read hundreds of sketches and short stories, he could select, even after applying the most rigorous standards, a group of two or three dozen short stories worthy to stand beside the best short fiction of the period, whether in America or abroad.

Modern critical opinion has divided sharply on the question of the value of regional fiction. One side of the argument is represented by Botkin's assertion that "regionalism marks a trend away from the belletristic—pure literature and absolute poetry—toward a social and cultural art." The other side would follow Tate in believing that regionalism at its worst leads to "a falsification of the creative impulse with the motives of social action." A fair judgment of the achievement of the genre writers would follow a middle path between these extremes. The limitations are clear enough, although they have been somewhat overemphasized: absorption with the picturesque for its own sake (as variously observable in Mary Murfree, James Lane Allen, Celia Thaxter, or sometimes in Cable); the curious pursuit of the unique idiosyncratic, or grotesque in local character (as *passim* in Ruth McEnery Stuart, Johnston, Mrs. Freeman, Mrs. Cooke, Miss Jewett, Mrs. Slosson, and others). One finds also a noticeable though not universal tendency to gloss over the uglier aspects of the human predicament; an occasional lapse into mere formula writing; a reactionary glorification and sentimentalization of a wealthy and powerful plantation *aristoi* (as in John Esten Cooke, T. N. Page, or sometimes in Bagby, Mrs. Stuart, and Grace King); an equally deplorable tendency to overdo the "common man" motif until one is led to the apotheosis of the mediocre. One could see, over all, an attempt to petrify and monumentalize that which in all classes and castes was petering out through its own internal weakness or decadence—the sort of effort which can usually be trusted to produce a negative and static art, unmoved from within and therefore unmoving. The predilection for dialect (it was then the fashion, however irritating it may be to modern readers), in which authors played at amateur phonetics under the mistaken impression that the use of heavily apostrophized contractions, barbaric misspellings, and other desperate expedients would be useful to future linguistic historians, is distressing, as is the tendency to introduce extraneous social detail, which sometimes led in practice to the refusal or failure to compress the sprawling sketch into the tighter limits of the bona fide short story.

The faults are probably outweighed by manifest virtues, whether one is a social historian, a student of literary history, or a plain reader in search of entertainment and instruction. The best of these writers, and even the worst, were aware of a usable past. They were deploying for the attack on the monster bulk of America, like their literary brethren in the Middle and Far West, and they were everywhere showing that earlier critics had been correct in believing in the richness, abundance, and variety of the American scene as a field for literary exploitation. They were proudly displaying and defending such native traits as individualism, ingenuity, sectional or clan loyalty, charity, humility, shrewdness, toughness, and stoicism. They were apologizing for, frankly deploring, explaining, or sometimes trying to explain away such prominent American vices as moral opportunism, social or economic inequality, slavery, racial prejudice, caste divisions, ignorance, indolence, shabby gentility, hypocrisy, mob law, and violence.

It is too easy to deride these writers for their preoccupation with the past, as if the backward look were necessarily a mark of reaction. Like most blanket condemnations, this one neglects the genuine liberalism of Harris and Cable, the forward-looking aesthetic of Jewett, Freeman, or Chopin, or the over-all democratic orientation of a movement deeply devoted to the common people, and to those fundamental integrities of mind and heart which in dangerous days have strengthened and saved the American republic. It is too easy to become supercilious over the "minor triumphs" of the "chroniclers of decay." Regional exploitation per se drove writers to deal with life as they directly knew or had known it. It has never been satisfactorily proved that the example of regionalist fiction was not as effective in the development of the short story and the American novel as the influence of foreign models. The occasional leavening of romance did not invalidate the rule that the movement was fundamentally realistic and that its basic attempt was the analysis of homespun character. Much effort was profitably brought to bear upon the correction of stereotypes—the shrewd Yankee trader, the shiftless mountaineer, the plantation darky, the Kentucky colonel—and what resulted was not another battery of types, but a series of highly individualized people whom one can classify as old maids and dewy maidens, moonshiners and mariners, crackers and sandhillers, Cajuns and Creoles, but who in practice are no more limited by these categories than Falstaff is limited by his resemblance to the *miles gloriosus* of Latin comedy.

Even without these achievements, the regionalists and genre writers of the East and South made their contribution to the history of American culture. At a crucial period in American history, when old faces, manners, customs, recipes, styles, attitudes, and prejudices were undergoing rapid change or total extirpation, they seized and perpetuated, through the medium of fictional character, the cultural landscape: the native idiom, the still unravished rural peace, the feel and flavor of things as they were, and would never be again.

# 53. WESTERN RECORD AND ROMANCE

$W$ESTERN literature in the generation after the Civil War was a literature of discovery. Peace released grand energies, scattered fortune hunters and land-hungry veterans westward, heightened the sense of national oneness, gave Americans their first real notion of what it meant to be a continental nation. The transcontinental railroad linked the social and cultural variants thus far formed in the West—the farming Midwest, the Mormon commonwealth in the Rocky Mountains, and the mining and ranching world of California—and tied not only them but the Indian and Spanish societies of the West into the national fabric. Now began the final filling-in of the continent westward from the Missouri and eastward from the Pacific. Now American writers began to explore their country; now Americans began to know themselves as a single people and at the same time a diverse people, one large pattern full of endless variations.

The literary exploitation of the West was simultaneous with that of the older sections of the country, but its spirit was very different. It was equally sectional, equally national, but the newness of the material made it more adventurous, more romantic. Picturesque sections of the continent were thrown open; all the sections were tied into one. And all through the period after the Civil War explorers and writers and travelers and geologists were enthusiastically recording their own versions of what life in the West came to.

There were in general two kinds of people who wrote this literature: those who knew what they were talking about, and those who did not; those who aimed to tell the truth, and those who aimed to dress it up. At their extremes, these two tendencies are represented on the one hand by the scientific report and on the other by romantic local color fiction. But it would be a mistake to assume that only scientists told the truth about the West and only storytellers glamorized it. The same new country, the same new experiences, were encountered by all sorts of people, and were reflected from different surfaces.

One may discuss these writings in either local or national terms. The two distinct schools of Western literature, one centered in Indiana and one in California, were distinguishable not only by geographical but by tempera-

mental qualities. Earthy realism more like that of the East, stemming from
Edward Eggleston, was dominant in Indiana; when Indiana writers strayed
into more romantic paths they were likely to take the way of folksy sentiment,
and a flavor of piety was in most of what they produced. The local colorists,
on the other hand, stemmed from Bret Harte; their piety, like their concern
for the truth of social patterns and customs, was less demanding, and both
their materials and their methods were altogether more gilded than those in
style in Indiana. Yet currents of cross-fertilization flowed back and forth.
Both Indiana and California were on the main street of America, and their
very localism gave them something in common. Between them, they produced not only two vigorous schools of regional literature, but a type of
American literature which derived strongly from native soil and native character. The scientific writings of the period can hardly be said to belong to
either school; they deal primarily with the more recently opened trans-
Missouri West, and thus have close links with California, but their objective
scientific approach is closer to the realism of Indiana.

The writer who knew both Midwestern and Western life most fruitfully
was Mark Twain. In him, various strains met and fused; but in the lesser
figures the same strains are observable separately or in other combinations.
It is the function of this chapter to detail who they were, what of America
they discovered, what literary tendencies they created or followed.

Their discoveries may be listed: They discovered first the romantic Past,
though antiquarian delvings produced more for Eastern and Southern imitators than for the Westerners themselves. There was a bloom over two areas
of the Western past—over the French settlements around the Great Lakes,
and over the drowsy Lotus Land of Spanish California. Both were exploited.

They discovered also the Present. A society with a character of its own was
forming in the Midwest, maturing first in Ohio and Indiana. It was not a
highly developed society: Maurice Thompson compared it to a boy whose
voice was changing. But it provided a succession of realistic writers from
Eggleston on with a chance to paint the unposed face of inland America.
The tradition that Eggleston began would flower later in other Midwestern
realists, in Garland and Dreiser and Cather and Sandburg and Lewis. And
what might be called its dialectic strain would become the homespun tradition
of sentiment and folksy philosophy, the subliterary but immensely popular
poetizing of Carleton, Riley, and Field.

At the other end of the West, Bret Harte, Mark Twain, and Joaquin
Miller also discovered a social order, a fleeting and picturesque one, in the
world of the frontiersman and miner. These characters had practically passed
before they broke into serious literature; and by that time they had acquired
the romantic patina of time. But for a brief moment in the fifties and sixties,

Angel's Camp and Red Dog were reality of a startling kind. Another heroic and almost as transitory society, that of the cattlemen, was later in finding chroniclers except on the dime-novel level. It was the end of the century before Andy Adams and Owen Wister and Alfred Henry Lewis made the cattle frontier the subject of serious fiction.

These discoverers were all literary men—poets and novelists and short-story writers. Quite as important in their way were a group of men whose primary interest was the country itself, the superb physical endowment of the nation. A good part of the best writing done in the West in these postwar years was done by geologists, explorers, surveyors, mountain climbers, naturalists. Sometimes, like George Horatio Derby (John Phoenix) of an earlier generation, they were geologists with one hand and writers with the other. Sometimes they blended geology and scenery with action and ideas and produced literature of a special kind, as did Clarence King, John Muir, John Wesley Powell, and Clarence Dutton.

There were also the frontiersmen of the mind, explorers of ideas. Henry George looked gloomily upon the Pacific Railroad, prophesying that it would bring wealth to a few, poverty to many, and out of his observations built a new economic philosophy. Major Powell studied the arid regions and told the nation explicitly how it would have to settle that country if it wanted to avoid erosion, droughts, floods, and the ruin of the land. And William Gilpin, who has been called the first geopolitician, dreamed mighty dreams of the global mission of the American people. Because people have gone on reading the books of these men, and because their ideas have been of incalculable influence, all three men deserve inclusion in any literary survey of the period.

Finally, the postwar discoveries must include the basic American, the common man. He had appeared in print before, but usually on the level of the sporting magazine. He was brother to the Hoosier and the poor white and cousin to the Yankee farmer or peddler; but in California his name was "Pike," and he dominated Western literature for almost two decades. He was named for Pike County, Missouri, but he came from Illinois, Arkansas, or North Texas quite as frequently: in practice, Pike County was as large and vague as Los Angeles County is today. At the eastern extension of his range, the Pike merged imperceptibly into the Hoosier and poor white of Indiana, Ohio, and Kentucky. His literary portraits show him as anything from the "acclimated man" of Mark Twain's *Gilded Age* to Abraham Lincoln; anything from the "Missouri Pukes" who massacred Mormons in the forties to Jim Bludso or Huckleberry Finn.

Bayard Taylor defined the Pike as "the Anglo-Saxon relapsed into semi-barbarism." But relapsed or not, his discovery by writers of the sixties, seventies, and eighties was something tremendous and wonderful for native literature. And when Pikes began *writing* books, we had for the first time a literature that mass America could feel in its bones. Ultimately, the biggest discovery of the whole period was the Pike, the common man.

2

A country and a people, a forming society in a newly opened land, were thus before the writers of the West, who fell upon both land and people as the gold seekers fell upon the placer sands of California's rivers. Neither scientific observer nor literary exploiter, realist nor romantic, had precedence. Discovery was simultaneous in several directions, so that when we look at the beginning of the seventies we find every major element already there. Bret Harte's first unheralded mining-camp story, "The Work on Red Mountain," which was to be rewritten as "M'liss," had come in 1860; and Twain's *Celebrated Jumping Frog of Calaveras County and Other Sketches,* in 1867. But with the linking of the rails in 1869 the stage was set for more spectacular things. Harte's "Luck of Roaring Camp" and "Plain Language from Truthful James" appeared in 1870. John Hay's *Pike County Ballads,* in the same dialect vein as Harte's poems, came in 1871, as did Joaquin Miller's *Songs of the Sierras.* The year 1871 also saw Edward Eggleston's *Hoosier Schoolmaster,* a realistic study of Midwest village life, and the first volume of Will Carleton's homespun verses. And in that same year came Clarence King's *Mountaineering in the Sierra Nevada,* in many ways the most delightful book of its decade, though written by a geologist.

None of these discoveries—local color, dialect, homely sentiment, realistic rural life, or the grandeur of natural scenery—was actually a discovery. Writers had done local characters and local dialects before, dug into the national past; for example, Theodore Winthrop's *John Brent* (1862). Though this Western country was new, it had been written about by Lewis and Clark, Pike, Frémont, Marcus Whitman, and others. The local scene in California had been exploited by newspaper and magazine writers from the time when Sam Brannan unloaded his boatload of Mormons and uncrated the press machinery for the *California Star* in 1846. Even before that, Dana's *Two Years Before the Mast* had told the world something of the Spanish towns strung from Yerba Buena to Guaymas. Earlier still, the wild life of the Mississippi and Ohio had been caught by Timothy Flint and James Hall. Even the Pike was no fire-new character. The *Alta-California* had advertised a romance, "Pike County Bill, or the Maid of the Mountains," in 1854, and by the next year the Pike was having his malarial phiz sketched by several newspaper humorists, including "Old Block," "Jeems Pipes from Pipesville," and "John Phoenix." Wagon trains were already rocking westward to the strains of "Sweet Betsy from Pike"; the ballad saw print as early as 1858 in *Put's Golden Songster.* The Pike was thus almost a stereotype in California before Harte ever took him up. Back of California there were earlier versions of the general type in the Beowulfian humor of the Mississippi, the nameless newspaper exchanges, the *Spirit of the Times,* the *Georgia Scenes* of Augustus Longstreet and the *Autobiography of Davy Crockett of Tennessee.*

Drawing more than they knew on traditions, a handful of innovators at the beginning of the seventies remade Western literature, and in a real sense the literature of the United States. Harte, Miller, Eggleston, Hay, King, and Carleton (and of course Mark Twain, who is discussed in a later chapter) gave the literature of a whole generation its directions.

3

Bret Harte was no Argonaut. He came to California from Albany, New York, in 1854 to join his mother, not to seek gold. Though he worked at several jobs—teaching school at La Grange in the gold country, setting type for the *Northern Californian* in the town of Union, compounding pharmaceuticals, contributing to and editing various journals, especially the *Golden Era* and the *Alta California,* and acting as secretary of the mint—yet he never quite became a participant. Essentially he was a civilized man, a bookish man. In San Francisco, by dedication and hard work, he made himself the leader of a brilliant group that at various times included Twain, Henry George, Ambrose Bierce, Prentice Mulford, Charles Warren Stoddard, Joaquin Miller, Clarence King, and Ina Coolbrith. His appointment in 1868 to the editorship of Anton Roman's new magazine, the *Overland Monthly,* was recognition of the position he had won. In the three years of his editorship he not only made the magazine the most brilliant of all Western periodicals, but made himself a national figure.

He had had triumphs of a minor and local kind, written occasional poems and Irvingesque sketches with legendary and Spanish themes, had parodied popular novelists in a clever series called *Condensed Novels* (1867). His first big success came with the *Overland's* second issue, which carried "The Luck of Roaring Camp." The stir was tremendous; the *Atlantic* wired extravagant offers for stories of the same kind, fan mail poured in. Harte followed "The Luck" with others, among them the best stories he was ever to write: "The Outcasts of Poker Flat," "Tennessee's Partner," "Miggles," "The Idyl of Red Gulch," and "Brown of Calaveras." He scored a second triumph as great as the first when he printed, rather dubiously, the dialect poem called "Plain Language from Truthful James." This was reprinted in magazines, newspapers, broadsides, and spread in store windows, all over the nation. Together with other "Pike" poems, it was reissued as "The Heathen Chinee" in 1871.

"The Luck of Roaring Camp" is the father of all Western local color stories; "The Heathen Chinee" begot a progeny of dialect poems. Both represented something new to sophisticated audiences: a romantic, picturesque world; characters as striking as the characters of Dickens and perhaps in part derived from Dickens; a trick of neat paradox that gave scoundrels Raphael faces and endowed bruisers and hard cases with a saving spot of sentiment; a method of story telling that was lean, unpadded, finely calculated. Harte had served a long apprenticeship. He was a finished writer by the time "The Luck" appeared. He was destined to have an influence as great as that of the greatest.

But when Harte left San Francisco in 1871, bound for Boston and the larger world, he had already done all his best work. Money pressures, the demands of a public that always wanted "more like 'The Luck,' " and perhaps a drying-up of his inspiration, forced him into a mold. He went on, the rest of his life, imitating himself. The last twenty-four years of his life he lived abroad, in Germany, in Scotland, and in London where he died. At the end he was a tired, skillful, dependable hack, turning out stories to order and adding a volume every other year or so to his collected works. The best of his achievement lay far back in the seventies.

Talent, Harte certainly had; but he lacked Twain's fecundity, and he was farther from reality. Reading through his twenty volumes, one has a feeling of deadly sameness. The characters are Dickensian types: never a gambler who is not Jack Oakhurst, never a stage driver who is not burly and "squar' " like Yuba Bill, never a miner who is not a rough soul with a vacuole of sentiment pulsating in him somewhere, like Tennessee's Partner or the heroically sentimental gift bringer in "How Santa Claus Came to Simpson's Bar."

Yet this last story, like earlier ones, illustrates Harte's strengths. Dick Bullen's wild ride is a masterpiece of dramatic action reporting. A story such as "Mrs. Skagg's Husbands," though ruined by an impossibly bad ending, has a beginning as sharp and clean and modern as John Steinbeck at his best might have written. Harte was no prude; he drew no morals and preached no sermons; he painted prostitutes and foul-mouthed children and drunken sots without apology. His children are always sympathetically and convincingly drawn. He had humor, a good ear, a style that was disciplined and clean. Yet through all, even his best work, runs a thread of something theatrical and false.

Hobos have a word for anyone who pretends fellowship in the fraternity of the road. Such an impostor they call a "scenery stiff." In spite of the trained brilliance of his best stories, Harte was a scenery stiff. It is safe to apply the same term to Joaquin Miller, who in the year of Harte's first success was in London peddling his poems to various publishers. Born in Indiana (as he said, "in a covered wagon headed West"), he had traveled the Oregon Trail with his family, had snatched a handful of education here and there had taught school, and had edited a newspaper which was closed for its Copperhead sympathies at the onset of the war. He had, so he asserted, lived and fought with the Modoc Indians, had begotten at least one little half-breed Miller, and finally had married an Oregon girl whom he left behind while he bore his poetic ambitions to San Francisco. There the literary were not impressed.

Neither were the London publishers impressed. Never one to be over-modest, Miller printed *Pacific Poems* at his own expense and sent them to the reviews. The result was startling: somehow the barbaric, uneven verses took the British fancy. W. M. Rossetti wrote a glowing review, the Pre-Raphaelites welcomed Miller to themselves. In cowhide boots and sealskin coat he dined with London celebrities; in red shirt and Stetson he knocked the eye out of Britishers eager to support a tame frontiersman. With help from Rossetti and others, Miller revised *Pacific Poems* and reissued them as *Songs of the Sierra.* When he went home to the United States the next year he was an international figure, self-made.

Except for his influence, which was not lasting, and his reputation, always slightly tainted with ridicule, Miller seems of little account today. His long verse dramas, his panoramic and tempestuous narratives of the Indian country, Nicaragua, the mountains, and the deserts, are mainly sound and fury. The poet's own posturing, his bald self-aggrandizement, made him a character, though he was only in flashes a true poet. He wrote through a long life many books, but a very large proportion of what he wrote is chaff. Of the dramas, only *The Danites of the Sierras* offers much to a modern reader; and of his prose writings, cluttered with incredible lies, there is nothing likely to live except *Life Among the Modocs,* a fragment of what he called auto-biography. Of his shorter poems, the anthologists neglect everything but "Columbus."

In the wake of Harte and Miller—especially of Harte—came a whole gen-eration of lesser local colorists mainly female. They are worth a summary statement, hardly more. In general, they approached local habits and local characters as a tourist would approach them. It is fair to say that as a group they avoided the commonplace, concerned themselves chiefly with the un-usual, were incurably romantic, obsessed with the picturesque, and accurate only to the superficial aspects of their chosen materials. The spirit of the West almost inevitably escaped them because they wrote from outside, not from within. Constance Fenimore Woolson and Mary Hartwell Catherwood dug industriously into the past and present of the Great Lakes settlements and the romantic history of New France. Alice French (Octave Thanet) exploited Davenport, Iowa, and Black River, Arkansas, though with a greater understanding and a stronger impulse to realism. Mary Hallock Foote brought readers back to the mining camps of Idaho and Colorado and to some of the materials first publicized by Bret Harte.

Though there are fine passages and fine single stories among these writers, especially in the work of Miss French and Mrs. Foote, their reputations are likely to dwindle further rather than revive. But one reputation will last. It is that of Helen Hunt Jackson, who after a prolific career of romantic hack writing became interested in the fate of the Indians and, in her honest indignation, wrote two books. One, *A Century of Dishonor* (1881), was a bitter indictment of the federal policies toward the Indian. The other, *Ramona* (1884), was calculated to be for the Indian what *Uncle Tom's Cabin* was for the Negroes, but wound up as a romance about the dying Spanish society of southern California. It is hard now to read *Ramona* and realize that Alessandro is Indian at all, or Ramona a half-breed. But people still read it; there is hardly a library in the land without several copies; it has hit the millions in Technicolor. Part of that enduring charm is in the principals and in the backgrounds and in the theme of thwarted love, but the greatest strength of the novel is the portrait of Señora Moreno, guardian of the old Spanish ways against the encroaching Americans. In her practice of duty without love, justice without kindness, she dominates the first half of the book. It is not so good a book when she leaves it.

It would not do to omit mention of the Indiana romancer Maurice Thompson, who began in his literary career with a volume, *Hoosier Mosaics* (1875), in the realistic vein of Eggleston, but quickly gave up realism for more colorful story telling. None of his books, either in poetry or in prose, achieved marked success until *Alice of Old Vincennes* (1900) crowned his career with a best seller. This romance about George Rogers Clark and the Northwest Territory served, with Mary Catherwood's New France novels, as a model for most of the later writers of historical novels. Yet, popular as they were in their day, these romantic local color writers are not the people to whom we would go for pictures of their own times. Rather we must consult the school of Edward Eggleston, which began, like most of the trends of the period, in 1871.

4

Edward Eggleston came to writing not by way of a long literary apprenticeship and a sense of dedication, as Harte did, but by way of the Methodist ministry and the editing of Sunday-school papers. Until he was well grown he had never even read a novel.

Yet he had had encouragement from his old teacher in Vevay, Indiana; and though his schooling had been irregular he had had access to his father's good library, and was well read in the Bible, history, and the classics. For a time he was a circuit-riding minister in southern Indiana: his health broke down in six months. After a period of settled pastorates in Minnesota he took the editorship of the *Little Corporal,* a Chicago children's paper, going later to the *Independent,* and finally to *Hearth and Home* which he made—as Harte had made the *Overland*—with his first contribution, a serial version of *The Hoosier Schoolmaster.* He justified his tale to himself and his employers on the ground that, though a novel, it contained valuable moral lessons.

Eggleston's method was quite different from Harte's. Led to picture local manners and local speech by his reading of Taine's *History of Art in the Netherlands,* he produced something as realistic as Dutch painting, touching with love and care the homely details of living. From his childhood and his experience as a circuit rider, he knew the Indiana backwoods intimately; and only a year after Harte had set a romantic fashion Eggleston turned the fashion back. He never changed his method, though he learned a great deal about writing novels after his first attempt; and even when in later life he turned to writing history he adopted the same aim and the same method as in his novels.

Mechanically *The Hoosier Schoolmaster* (1871) is a bad novel. Its villain is unmotivated, its incidents syncopate like a badly patched film, its style is lumbering, it preaches. Eggleston did better in *The Circuit Rider* (1874), *Roxy* (1878), and *The Graysons* (1888). He did much worse in *The Hoosier Schoolboy* (1883), a curious recession in style and tone. Altogether, he wrote seven novels of the West, as well as a good many juveniles and two solid volumes of history. Like Harte, he was the author of a philosophy of composition, the cornerstone of a school. It is a proof of the validity of his method that, even when he is clumsy, he can still be read without boredom.

Two other dialect writers, both poets, deserve a place beside Eggleston as early painters of the local. One is John Hay, whose *Pike County Ballads* (1871) numbered only six poems, tossed off in a hurry and regretted ever after. Probably they were stimulated by Harte's dialect poems, though Mark Twain thought they had been written before Harte's "Truthful James." Whether influenced by Harte or not, Hay tapped a purer vein than Harte. He had been born in the Midwest, had attended school in Pike County, Illinois, had read law in Springfield next door to Lincoln. As a result, his Pike poems have a ring that Harte's lack, a depth of character not all paradox and surprise. "Jim Bludso" and "Little Breeches" have become virtual folk possessions; and of the six poems only "Golyer," the tale of a no-good stage driver who redeems himself by shielding a child from robbers' bullets, is in the Harte vein. It is the worst of the six.

Hay's only other connection with Western literature comes through his collaboration with Nicolay on the ten-volume life of Lincoln; but the crude little ballads he was ashamed of are likely to prove quite as durable as the monumental biography. Jim Bludso was too real to die.

In the same year that Hay and Eggleston tackled real Midwestern themes and people, a Michigan poetaster, Will Carleton, published the first of a long series of volumes. Carleton's name is not usually spoken when the literary markers are counted, and there is no irresistible reason why it should be; yet he cannot be quite overlooked either. Limping as to meter and simple as to sentiment, his poems were widely read, and still are. He was the first "People's Laureate" in the Midwest, and poems like "Over the Hill to the Poorhouse" and "Gone with a Handsomer Man" have as solid a place in subliterary America as any of James Whitcomb Riley's. Tear-jerking situations, happy endings, the celebration of homely virtues, were the stock in trade of both Carleton and Riley, though Riley was both a smoother versifier and a better showman than his predecessor. Along with a grasp of the plain emotions of plain people (which in literature often means the stereotyped emotions of stereotyped people) Riley had a wit, an aptness of phrase, an acuteness of observation, that give his work for all its conventionality a frequent lift. Though he was in many ways, like Carleton, completely unrealistic in his pictures of Midwestern farm life, also like Carleton he was triumphantly common; and commonness has been part of a magic formula for popularity for a long time, at least in America.

The "Hoosier School" begun by Eggleston, forwarded by Thompson's *Hoosier Mosaics,* and modified by the work of Carleton and Riley, went on producing writers pretty much according to its original patterns. Eggleston's uncompromising realism did not flower until later, and farther west; but his influence touched every Midwestern writer. Booth Tarkington and Meredith Nicholson both exhibited in curious ways the mixture of realistic, romantic, and commonplace that went into the making of the earliest Indiana literature. In *Monsieur Beaucaire* (1900) Tarkington was as romantic as Thompson; in *The Gentleman from Indiana* (1899), *The Magnificent Ambersons* (1918), *Alice Adams* (1921), and other novels he exhibited the moral earnestness and seriously realistic intent of Eggleston; in the Penrod series he showed the sharp eye, the humor, the delight in the commonplace that distinguished Riley. In the same way Nicholson swung between romantic and realistic, between *The Port of Missing Men* (1907) and *A Hoosier Chronicle*

(1912), between *The House of a Thousand Candles* (1905) and *The Poe* (1914).

Something of that same blending of realistic and romantic is to be found in the best of the cowboy novelists. Least romantic of these was Andy Adams whose solid, Defoe-like books are so underplayed and accurate that they pass for history. The best of them, *The Log of a Cowboy* (1903), is really the synthesized record of the many cattle drives Adams took from the Texas range to the cattle country of Nebraska and Montana. Others, equally honest are *The Outlet* (1905), *Reed Anthony, Cowman* (1907), and *Cattle Brand* (1906), a collection of short stories.

Another cowboy writer, Alfred Henry Lewis (Dan Quin), is notable as the author of the whole series of Wolfville novels, the first of which was published in 1897. Probably one of that series is enough for the average reader but the literary flavor of the cowboy West has not been fully sampled without at least one of the Old Cattleman's drawling yarns.

Lewis as well as Adams had been a cow hand, and wrote of what he knew inside and out. But the most readable of all cowboy novels was written by a visitor from Pennsylvania and Harvard. Owen Wister began with short stories of ranch life, collected in *Lin MacLean* (1898) and *The Jimmyjohn Boss* (1900), and followed them with *The Virginian* (1902) which, in spite of some romantic goings-on that Adams would have scorned, has held its place as a literary milestone. It is still immensely readable, full of action and humor, and the ring of authenticity. Wister's ear for lingo was unusually keen, and he had apparently absorbed ranch life through his pores. "When you call me that, smile!" is still standard for young Americans playing cowboy, and the situation between the buckaroo and the schoolmarm has become stock equipment for horse opera. But the book from which many horse operas derive has a dignity and strength not shared by its imitators. Adams, Lewis, and Wister made the cowboy a respectable character for serious literature. Though their lead has been followed since by Eugene Manlove Rhodes and others, their performance has not yet been bettered. All came when local color as a coherent movement had about played itself out; all owe as much to the honest realism of Eggleston as to the flossy melodramatics of Harte.

5

The authentic cowboy writers and the novelists of Eggleston's school had one great virtue in common: they knew what they were talking about. So did the geologists and nature writers who all through the last three decades of the nineteenth century were busy building a literature out of observation and facts. The taste for that literature was national. In a career that lasted fifty years, John Burroughs was establishing it in the East as a writer of essays that mingled the philosophy of Emerson and Whitman with careful observation of the birds, trees, and flowers of the Catskill Mountains. His readers shared in the work, reporting their observations in letters and in pilgrimages to "Slabsides."

The first of the Western nature writers, Clarence King, was for a short time a member of the *Overland* group in San Francisco, and in 1871 his *Mountaineering in the Sierra Nevada* sketches were sharing the *Atlantic*'s pages with Bret Harte's writings. It is not customary to give King credit as an innovator or source of anything; yet *Mountaineering in the Sierra Nevada* was very widely read and has been persistently reprinted, and he had dozens of friends, among them Hay and Henry Adams, who admired him extravagantly. He was the first Western nature writer to find a public.

*Mountaineering in the Sierra Nevada* is a completely charming book, exciting, gay, vigorous, witty, and written in polished and perceptive prose. If he had chosen, King could probably have been a major writer; but, even though he wrote only the one book outside the geological field, his reputation will last. In the chapter "The Newtys of Pike" he gives us a Pike family with an odd, sidelong sympathy, one of the best and subtlest portraits of the Pike in our literature. A romantic chapter like "Kaweah's Run" does the Bret Harte sort of thing as fluently as ever Harte did it. In "Cut-Off Copples's" he paints a hilarious portrait of a self-taught, garrulous Pike artist. And the core of the book, concerned with climbs up Tyndall, Shasta, and Whitney, is personal experience narrative and nature description of top literary quality. The short story "The Helmet of Mambrino," so cherished and overpraised by King's friends, has no connection with Western literature except that it was written as a letter to a friend in San Francisco.

Of all the men who followed King in writing about Western scenery, John Muir is unquestionably the most important literary figure. Though ten years of residence in Yosemite identified him with that spot, he knew the continent as few did, had walked over it lengthwise and crosswise and cornerwise, had explored the Alaskan coast and the Sierras and the Great Basin ranges and the Midwest and Florida. When he talked about North America, he knew whereof he spoke.

Though he seems never to have met King, their histories are entangled. Muir's first paper, a piece of Yosemite glaciers, appeared in the New York *Tribune* in 1871, while King's mountaineering sketches were running in the *Atlantic*. Maintaining that the Yosemite was glacier-formed and not formed by cataclysmic splitting, as King and his chief Whitney had supposed, Muir started a controversy that ended in Whitney's complete discomfiture. Muir knew glaciers had formed the valley: he had followed their tracks all over the range.

During the course of an energetic life Muir established himself, without academic or governmental aids, as an authoritative geologist and naturalist. He was invited on the Harriman Expedition to Alaska and toured the nation's forests with eminent scientists. Emerson, Theodore Roosevelt, the great of the world, beat a path to his door in Yosemite. To his understanding and love for natural things we owe much of our national forest and national park program. Busy as he was, he wrote many articles and kept voluminous journals; but most of his books were put together in later years, and his journals did not appear until 1938, when a selection was published. Between 1894 and 1918 he wrote nine books which have become a part of our literature—among them *The Mountains of California* (1894), *The Story of My Boyhood and Youth* (1913), and *Travels in Alaska* (1915).

On the strength of these writings Muir must rank as the very best of the nature writers who followed the paths earlier explored by Thoreau. Indefatigable, dedicated, enthusiastic, single-minded to the point of bullheadedness, he wrote only what echoed the freedom and delight of his life. His writing is full of exclamations and glad shouts, and though he wrote slowly and his ideas are not, on examination, of extraordinary variety, yet his words have an air of the most sprightly spontaneity. They bubble and dance; occasionally, as in the essays on conservation in *Our National Parks* (1901), they are hot as flying sparks. A kindly, friendly, open-souled man, Muir made friends by the score and won many to the wilderness he loved. As the years pass he will win more.

Not every one of our areas of stupendous scenery has its *genius loci,* as Yosemite had its Muir. But the Grand Canyon of the Colorado has two, both geologists and explorers. One, the last great explorer of continental America, was a one-armed veteran of Shiloh, Major John Wesley Powell, who in 1869 and again in 1871 ran the Colorado River by boat from Green River Crossing, Wyoming, to the mouth of the Grand Wash, just above the present Boulder Dam. The account of the first trip, which took from May until the end of August and covered over a thousand miles of wild and terrible river sunk in canyons sometimes more than a mile deep, was published for the Smithsonian Institution, which had sponsored the expedition, in a cumbersome quarto, *Exploration of the Colorado River of the West* (1875). It is one of the best adventure stories in American literature.

As director of the United States Geographical and Geological Survey of the Rocky Mountain Region, and later as the second director of the United States Geological Survey (succeeding Clarence King), Powell gathered around him a corps of able men, one of whom, W. H. Holmes, is an unpublicized

Western painter for someone to discover. Another, Captain Clarence E. Dutton, was assigned through more than a decade of field work to most of the grand parts of the West—first to Utah, then to the Grand Canyon, then to the extinct volcanoes of Oregon and the desert near Mount Taylor in New Mexico. Of Dutton's books and monographs, two deserve reading not merely as geology but as nature writing of a fine and sensitive sort. *The Geology of the High Plateaus of Utah* (1879–1880) and *The Tertiary History of the Grand Canyon District* (1882) are not likely to attract readers either by their ponderous format or by their formidable titles, and neither has been reprinted. Yet both are delightful and rewarding books, the geological exposition livened constantly by powerful descriptions. In country so bizarre that orthodox notions of color and form were inapplicable, Dutton learned to know and love what has merely startled most observers. His descriptions of the Grand Canyon and its surrounding plateaus and canyons are certainly the best that have appeared in print—and literally hundreds of writers have essayed the task of getting that chasm into words. Both Muir and Burroughs leaned heavily on Dutton when they came to write of the Grand Canyon, and Charles Dudley Warner borrowed freely and without enough quotation marks. Within the canyon Dutton is remembered by the dozens of names he gave to amphitheaters and buttes; but his two books about that region deserve far wider reading than they have had.

6

Midwestern and Western life—the developing farms of Indiana and Ohio and Illinois and Iowa, the fleeting world of miner and cowboy, the past of the Spanish and the French black-robes—were reflected with varying degrees of accuracy in the literature from 1870 to the end of the century. But there were attempts at forecasting the future, and those too are of literary importance. It is appropriate to close a discussion of this period with the stargazers.

One of these, Henry George, is discussed at length elsewhere in this volume. His observation of the ways in which land ownership in a new country patterned itself led him to the writing of *Progress and Poverty* and to economic conclusions that have brought him millions of readers in the past sixty years. He prophesied the slow revolution which has concentrated land ownership into fewer and fewer hands, and as the burning advocate of the single-tax system he became a figure of international importance.

Another, William Gilpin, who visited the Northwest with Frémont's expedition in 1842 and got the continental vision earlier than most Americans, never became an international figure; but he thought in international terms. An officer of the Missouri Volunteers in the Mexican War, first territorial governor of Colorado, and the man who saved Colorado for the Union, he spent much of his life developing one big dream, foreshadowing the geopolitical thinking of Mackinder and others of a later time. Within what he called the Isothermal Zodiac, Gilpin thought he had found the area where all high civilizations must develop. Most of the United States lay within that straggling belt, and because of this and the favorable unifying influence of North American topography, America must become the first and best example of peace and prosperity and unity, and must teach those lessons to the world. Full elucidation of Gilpin's theories would take pages; those theories were both extravagant and prophetic. Many of the things he said in *The Central Gold Region* (1860—reprinted, 1875, as *The Mission of the North American People*) and in *The Cosmopolitan Railway* (1890) have been verified by later geopolitical studies. Even his pet notion of intercontinental railways linking America and Asia by way of Bering Strait, and Europe and Africa by way of Gibraltar, was in its way perfectly logical. The opening of the West, which both George and Gilpin lived through, was a mighty explosion of forces; it is appropriate that it should have produced not merely a new theory of property and a new economic philosophy, but the first geopolitical theorizing, the first global thought.

Modern geographers are not likely to go back to Gilpin's books as to a bible, interesting as they are. But modern regional planners have gone back again and again to Major Powell's *Lands of the Arid Region* (1878). An innocent-looking government report on land and irrigation surveys in the West, this book contained the germs of far weightier things. Though the program recommended in it, including a sharp revision of the public-land system in the arid belt, never won out against the opposition of Western Congressmen, these surveys were the first step in the formation of the Reclamation Service which has remade whole sections of the West. Moreover, from his own studies of Western land and resources, Powell knew that the whole American pattern of settlement would have to be altered if the arid lands were to be settled without disaster. The homestead laws were inapplicable, size of farms had to be enlarged, probably government had to control what and how much land was to be plowed up. The whole region had to be opened carefully, with long-range planning. Powell demonstrated methodically the effects of breaking sod where there was scant rainfall; he showed the effects of overgrazing, water wastage, and destruction of timber and grass on the watersheds. Earlier than almost anyone else, and more thoroughly than any, he sensed what colossal engineering, both social and mechanical, would be necessary if we were to prevent large parts of the nation from becoming deserts as bleak as Palestine. He prophesied dust bowls, foretold floods and soil erosion and the social erosion that accompanies them. In this one volume is outlined an enormous amount of the federal government's reclamation and conservation program. Here in 1878 is the blueprint for all the still-to-come valley authorities; for reclamation dams, flood control, forest reserves, and reforestation programs and the practice of withholding certain lands for planned social reasons.

By the middle of the twentieth century, little by little, grass could creep up the hillsides again and the dust bowls come back to relative fertility. None of the waste need have happened if Powell's program of 1878 had been applied then. He was the last of the explorers and the first of the great regional planners, and though he would have been the last to claim consideration as a literary man, it is somehow right that the book which was in many ways the most important single volume of the whole period should have been a handbook on how to settle and conserve what Manifest Destiny had tossed in our laps. Many of the writers considered earlier gave us pictures of how life was lived, or might have been lived, in the West. Powell gave us an uncannily accurate picture of how it would have to be lived. And, in writing without literary intent, he wrote more vital literature than did many a story teller or poet of the West.

# 54. REALISM DEFINED:
## WILLIAM DEAN HOWELLS

ONE answer to the literary dilemma of the seventies and eighties was thus to waive literary intent, as Franklin and Jefferson and Lincoln had done in earlier times; but the story teller and poet will not be so easily silenced. For every Franklin there is an Irving, for every Jefferson a Cooper, and for every Lincoln a Whitman. And in these later times, there appeared a William Dean Howells, a Henry James, a Mark Twain, each in his own way ready to grapple with reality and reduce it to literary terms.

Realism is as old as fiction itself. Though often considered the antithesis of romance, it was actually developed by the romancers to make their creations plausible. In the nineteenth century it received its greatest stimulus from Sir Walter Scott's descriptions of scenery and costumes, his effort to depict dialects and manners, especially in characters from humble life. Balzac began the Comédie Humaine after reading the Waverley novels, and Galdós, Merezhkovski, Tolstoy, and many others besides the English novelists acknowledge Scott's influence. As early as 1826 the word *réalisme* was used in France to describe a literary method that attempted the faithful imitation of originals found in nature; it was contrasted, not with romanticism, but with classicism, which tended toward the imitation of art rather than nature. Both romanticist and realist tried to give detailed transcripts of the world about them. The romanticist wanted a background picturesque, yet real enough to be plausible, against which to display the subjective passions that were his main interest, while the realist's aim was an accurate, objective reproduction of scene and character for its own sake. The difference lay less in their choice of material than in their intention.

This affords the best criterion for distinguishing local color writers from true realists, though the impossibility of determining intention forbids dogmatic classification. Realism must always be a relative term, varying with the author's view of reality. To Stendhal it meant the effort to state truly and precisely "what men are in the world that is." George Eliot showed a Wordsworthian influence with her emphasis on homely subjects; her principle of "the faithful representing of commonplace things," enunciated in *Adam Bede*

(1859), is identical with that of William Dean Howells. "Ah! poor Real Life, which I love," he wrote in 1872, "can I make others share the delight I find in thy foolish and insipid face?" His definition is well known—"Realism is nothing more and nothing less than the truthful treatment of material"—but the seldom quoted conclusion of the sentence, "and Jane Austen was the first and the last of the English novelists to treat material with entire truthfulness," reveals his limitation.

Many parallel definitions might be cited (Trollope's "faithful reproduction of the manners of real life," and Eggleston's "correct portrayal of life and manners," for example) to demonstrate that American realism in the nineteenth century was part of a world movement. Through mistaken patriotism, historians have too often treated our literature in isolation. One has only to open an American magazine of, say 1850, to see how much of our reading came, in the absence of a copyright law, from the pens of the most popular English authors. The English periodicals circulated in America, too, reaching Howells in Ohio and Harte in California, and played a significant part in the education of our realists. None of them was college-bred: De Forest, Howells, Eggleston, Mark Twain, even Henry James escaped the possibly stultifying effect of a conventional education. Most of them traveled widely. De Forest lived abroad six years before he began his novels, Howells for five, and James spent much of his life there. The dominant realism of the seventies and eighties was closely related to that across the Atlantic.

Certain native factors doubtless favored its development. A strain of transcendentalism is apparent. Like Whitman, the realist (as Howells remarked) "feels in every nerve the equality of things and the unity of men"; he "finds nothing insignificant," "nothing that God has made is contemptible." The growth of the democratic spirit made it easier for writers to accept the low and the common as suitable literary material, and the Civil War, mingling men from widely separated regions, stirred interest in local peculiarities and violently destroyed certain romantic misconceptions. Yet the assumption that realism was brought into American literature from the Western frontier cannot be supported by fact. While the excitement over Bret Harte's California stories stimulated genre writing everywhere, New England writers had for decades been describing curious characters in their native surroundings. Harte was brought up in New York, wrote with his eye on the East, and returned there as soon as his success permitted. De Forest, the first professed realist, and in many respects the stanchest, lived on the Atlantic seaboard. Howells and Eggleston followed the same pattern: born west of the Alleghenies, drawn toward a literary career by youthful enthusiasm for the romantic and sentimental, they became realists only after settling on the East coast. Eggleston was living in Brooklyn when Taine's *History of Art in the Netherlands* inspired him to write about the Indiana of his childhood. Howells, more fastidious in some respects than his Cambridge friends, turned from mediocre romantic verse to realistic fiction with the encouragement of Lowell, James, and others of the *Atlantic Monthly* circle. The early realists were all in one way or another innocents abroad; like Mark Twain, they found their impulse to write in the contrast between their native manners and those of a longer established, more cosmopolitan culture. They were back trailers, thrown by circumstance into an older, more sophisticated society.

2

Some of them moved only from a rural community to a great city. Elizabeth Drew Barstow Stoddard, for example, who came to New York after her marriage to Richard Henry Stoddard, drew her first novel, *The Morgesons* (1862), from memories of her childhood in Mattapoisett on Buzzards Bay. She herself was the rebellious, passionate heroine Cassandra, and many other characters in her books were recognized by their originals. Veronica Morgeson, the sensitive and eccentric young recluse, is both strange and lifelike; Colonel Higginson certainly had her in mind when he wrote his wife that she would understand what Emily Dickinson was like if she had read Mrs. Stoddard's novels. Even more remarkable are the repressed, middle-aged women, intense and yet restrained, memorably portrayed in Sarah Auster in *Two Men* (1865) and Roxalana Gates, "the passionless soul," in *Temple House* (1867). The men fall into two types: fascinating, dissipated, Byronic wanderers like Desmond Somers and George Gates ("as handsome as Romeo, as dissolute as Antony"); and stalwart, middle-aged, homespun heroes like Jason Auster and Argus Gates, who marry the young heroines at the end. Of the three novels *The Morgesons* is the best because it has fewest of the romantic obtrusions that mar Mrs. Stoddard's realism. Her emphasis on suppressed or abnormal emotion and her abrupt and obscure narrative method give her novels a curiously modern tone. Though her descriptions of everyday manners are minutely realistic, the emotional relationships are too strange to pass for truthful transcriptions of life. On the surface the characters seem exact and varied portraits; within they are no more typical of New England than the inhabitants of Wuthering Heights are of Yorkshire.

Realism is mingled with sentiment in the work of Rebecca Blaine Harding Davis, a prolific writer of novels and short stories, who consciously sought her material in "this commonplace, this vulgar American life." Born in southwestern Pennsylvania, she moved to Philadelphia after her marriage; as a child she had lived in Alabama and in Wheeling, West Virginia, where she observed the industrial conditions that comprise her most original contribution to realism. In "Life in the Iron Mills," published in the *Atlantic* in 1861, Hugh Wolfe, a consumptive iron puddler with a talent for sculpture, and his sister Deb, a hunchbacked cotton-mill worker, are favorably contrasted with the rich mill owner and his dilettante friends. In her effort to rouse pity in the manner of Dickens, Mrs. Stowe, and Kingsley, Mrs. Davis violates her own rule of the commonplace. Few mill workers are hunchbacks, and except in a reformer's tract no consumptive could long be an iron puddler. In *Margret Howth* (1862), a study of slum life, the same romantic contrasts are drawn in the struggling young manufacturer who gives up a rich heiress for the poor but earnest Margret, and the same deliberate pathos surrounds the death of the crippled Negress, Lois Yare. Sentimental propaganda for the Negro distorts *Waiting for the Verdict* (1868). The earlier stories like "John Lamar" (*Atlantic,* 1862) with its fine description of the bewildered slave Ben are closer to the truth. At the farthest extreme are tales like "Volcanic Interlude" (*Lippincott's,* 1880) in which two girls brought up with the greatest luxury in New Orleans learn as they are about to come out that their mother was a Negress. Of her numerous novels *John Andross* (1874) is the strongest; in an atmosphere of political corruption in the Pennsylvania state capital Mrs. Davis studies Anna Maddox, one of the best of those seductive and ruthless women who lead men to ruin in the novels of the period. Unfortunately, the faults of melodrama and didacticism mar even her best work.

3

The first American writer to deserve the name of realist was John William De Forest, who treated the Civil War, the freed slave, the female lobbyist, and other aspects of contemporary life with a complete objectivity he seems to have developed abroad. The son of a prosperous manufacturer at Seymour, Connecticut, he spent two years (1848–1849) traveling in the Near East and four more (1851–1854) in France, Germany, and Italy. During a nine-month stay at Divonne, where no one else spoke English, he came to know Europeans of every shade of opinion and read deeply in French literature. Wide experience of foreign life made him neither a blatant Yankee nor a sycophant. His first book, *History of the Indians of Connecticut from the Earliest Known Period to 1850* (1851), a pioneer study, manifests the realistic tendency of his mind. His first novel, *Witching Times* (*Putnam's,* 1856–1857), brings a cool rationalism to bear upon the religious delusions of Salem during the witchcraft persecutions. Though the background of common life is created with well drawn details, the sentimental plot destroys what realism had been achieved in the minor characters, and De Forest judged wisely in not reprinting the story. Realism contends more successfully with melodrama in the contemporary story *Seacliff* (1859). Again the most original characters are the minor ones, old Warner and Ma Treat, in whom De Forest catches to perfection the authentic Connecticut flavor.

After his marriage in 1856 he lived part of each year in Charleston, South Carolina. He was there when the war broke out, escaping with his wife and child on the last boat. Having organized a company of volunteers in New Haven, he served as their captain in the Louisiana campaigns and later in the Shenandoah. His rhymed accounts of certain episodes, "Under the Colors," collected with earlier verses in *Poems: Medley and Palestina* (1902), are labored and wooden. De Forest was no poet. The long, descriptive letters to his family, however, provide the most vivid picture we have of army life. From these he made seven articles such as "The First Time Under Fire" and "Forced March" which appeared during the war; and with eight new chapters he made of the whole series an absorbing narrative, *A Volunteer's Adventures,* which was not published until 1946. At the cessation of hostilities he was placed in charge of the Freedmen's Bureau at Greenville, South Carolina, where he observed at close range the difficulties of Reconstruction. Parts of his account of this experience appeared in the magazines of the day.

By the end of 1865 he had completed the ineptly named *Miss Ravenel's Conversion from Secession to Loyalty* (1867), his finest novel and quite the best story of the Civil War. War had never been depicted so truthfully. Instead of a chivalrous romance of Blue and Gray, De Forest tells of the wearisome struggle against mud, filth, sickness, stupidity, red tape, and graft. Fear and panic, the anguish with which the bravest face battle, such horrors as the field hospital are all described uncompromisingly. In the characters good and bad traits mingle as in real life. Colonel Carter, one of the most vigorous portraits in American fiction, combines great personal courage and professional skill with an unfortunate flexibility of moral principles. Tender affection for his wife continues during his affair with Mrs. Larue. The generous motive of providing for his family overcomes his deep sense of honor and tempts him to misuse army funds. When he dies during battle, declining the chaplain's ministrations, a friend justly observes, *"Il a maintenu jusqu'au bout son personnage."* Mrs. Larue is another character long without equal in our fiction. A "child of Balzac's moral philosophy," she shocks the young New Englander Colburne (whose military experience coincides with De Forest's) by declaring Don Juan "a model man." To her, love is a game, pleasant, and even necessary, but "she would not have isolated herself from society for any man." De Forest studies her unflinchingly, concealing neither her immorality nor the undeniable goodness in her nature. Left at the end of the story more prosperous than before, she is the first profligate woman to escape retribution in an American novel. Lillie Ravenel is also an innovation. Unlike the pious, submissive heroines of the age, she has a mind of her own; she disagrees openly with her father, usually getting her own way. In spite of his disapproval she married the magnetic Carter. De Forest shows how much of her attraction to him was unconsciously physical; it mastered even her prejudice against Yankees. Her feelings after discovering his infidelity and on learning of his death are subtly delineated. If the account of her widowhood and eventual marriage to Colburne is a little reminiscent of Thackeray's Amelia and Dobbin, it is done with a firm, masculine hand. At the start Colburne is almost too perfect, but in the army he grows more credible and by the time he returns to civilian life, wasted by fever and fatigue, he is a completely natural character. Like De Forest he was mustered out a captain, while the promotion went to the arrant coward Gazaway, a political boss whose hold over the Governor eventually secured him a colonelcy and a safe command of a conscript camp, where he made $2,000 a month by letting substitutes escape.

Political corruption is the theme of two other novels, *Honest John Vane* (1875) and *Playing the Mischief* (1876). John Vane, a shallow fellow in whom honesty is mere policy, finding it impossible to live in Washington on his $5,000 Congressional salary, sells his vote for the "Great Subfluvial Tunnel Road" (a satire on the Crédit Mobilier) but escapes ruin during the investigation by declaring that he had bought the stock, not knowing it was a fraud. As an exposure of lobbying the story is more effective than *The Gilded Age*. De Forest's zeal to denounce the scandals overshadows his interest in the characters; John's wife Olympia is as shallow as he, and many of the others are only flat figures in an allegory. The Vanes and Senator Ironman reappear in *Playing the Mischief,* a longer and more carefully constructed novel. The central character, Mrs. Josie Murray, a clever and beautiful female lobbyist, has come to Washington to press a $100,000 claim for her father-in-law's barn, destroyed in the War of 1812! Using her charms without scruple, she cheats Pike the lobbyist out of half his share of the spoils and is left at the end ostensibly triumphant. The bribery theme here is subordinated to the study of Washington society, in which De Forest includes such varied types as the doting senator Old Jake Hollowbread, and an amusing Bloomer girl, Nancy Appleyard, known as "the Jael of California," very feminine in spite of her trousers and pistols.

Howells considered *Kate Beaumont* (1872) De Forest's best novel. It describes a feud in South Carolina, but except for the sensational opening episode, Frank McAlister's rescue of Kate from the burning steamer, a high level of realism is maintained. Kate's father, Peyton Beaumont, a low-country planter aristocrat, scarred in many a duel, beginning each day with two cocktails, hot-tempered and profane, yet with a lofty honor that commands

the reader's respect, is easily the best character in the book. His children ar
well differentiated. Nellie, the elder daughter, is married to the handsom
drunkard Randolph Armitage, whom she can't help loving in spite of hi
abuse. He represents the seamy side of Southern chivalry; returning from
cracker ball in the cabin of the "lone women" (a picture of poor whit
degradation that anticipates Faulkner and Caldwell), he beats his wife an
threatens her with a knife for hiding his whisky. The daring of these scene
is striking when one recalls the timidity with which Howells a decade late
described Bartley Hubbard's coming home drunk. The McAlisters, less care
fully detailed, represent the more democratic, upcountry Scotch-Irish aristoc
racy that supported the common schools and the electoral system. The story
holds interest throughout; even the happy ending, in which marriag
terminates the feud, fails to destroy the reader's impression of having observe
real life.

The reading public, however, preferred not to look at real life, and De
Forest was forced to turn his hand to more popular formulas. *Overland*
(1871), written for the *Galaxy* in the lurid style of Theodore Winthrop's *John
Brent* (1862), combines De Forest's hobbies of ethnology and military tactics
and employs realism, as do his later novels, to bolster an impossible plot. The
descriptions of the crucifixion of the maid Pepita by the Apaches and the trip
down the Grand Canyon in a canvas boat are tours de force quite wasted on
the juvenile mind the story aims at; De Forest had never been in the West,
but collected all his information in the Yale Library.

In 1886 after some years abroad, he began a novel to be called *A Daughter
of Toil* which treated the problems of lodgings, wages, and cost of living in
the vein of Howells' *The Minister's Charge,* then appearing serially. Noting
that Howells' story was taking the same line, he wrote to disclaim any intention of stealing his thunder. The manuscript has disappeared, and one can
only speculate as to whether it marked any further development in De Forest's
realism. There is no sign of that in *A Lover's Revolt* (1898), a contribution to
the wave of historical romances about the Revolution, which concludes the
list of his novels. The military maneuvers of Bunker Hill interest him more
than the frail love story. He must have known that to make his heroine turn
Tory and abandon the Yankee hero would insure the book's failure with
women, who form the greatest part of the novel-reading public. Essentially a
man's novelist, he could never flatter the feminine mind. Howells' explanation of his failure to attain popularity cannot be improved:

Finer, not stronger workmen succeeded him, and a delicate realism, more
responsive to the claims and appeals of the feminine oversoul, replaced his inexorable veracity. In the fate of his fiction, whether final or provisional, it is as if

this sensitive spirit had revenged the slight it felt, and, as the habit of women is, overavenged itself. It had revealed itself to him as it does only to the masters of fiction, and he had seemed not to prize the confidence.

## 4

Astute knowledge of the feminine oversoul and his own delicate taste made William Dean Howells the most popular exponent of realism. Both as novelist and as editor of magazines he consistently advocated "poor Real Life" as the artist's material, and he came to be considered the leading spokesman of the movement in America. In the calm perspective of time it may seem that he simply gave a name to a kind of writing that others in some degree had been doing for years. Like most critical theories, his was derived from his own practice, and it suffers from his limitations. But there is no doubt that he formulated the principles of realism about which the prolonged debate raged in the eighties. He had a strong ally in Henry James; and in England other discerning critics like J. A. Symonds were advancing much the same arguments. If the champions of romance, among whom Andrew Lang and Stevenson were the most vocal, appeared to be victorious, their triumph was only temporary; for when American fiction reached the peak of its influence soon after Howells' death, the realistic strain was dominant.

The view of the realist as a back-trailer to a more sophisticated society is illustrated perfectly in the case of Howells. He was born in Ohio, the son of a Pennsylvania German mother and a Welsh father, who had been compelled to turn his hand to many trades, of which printing was the chief. After an unsuccessful attempt to found a magazine, he moved when William was three to Hamilton in southwestern Ohio, where friends lent him money to buy a newspaper. Howells describes the life of those days with humorous candor in *A Boy's Town* (1890), *My Year in a Log Cabin* (1893), *Years of My Youth* (1916), and, thinly disguised as fiction, in *New Leaf Mills* (1913). "I do not know when I could not set type," he wrote. At the age of seven he set up an essay of his own writing; at twelve he was a swift compositor, working regularly in the shop. After several business failures, his father moved to Jefferson in the Western Reserve, a Free Soil community more sympathetic with his principles, where the family found a permanent home. In "The Country Printer," the best essay in *Impressions and Experiences* (1896), Howells recalls his work on the newspaper there. "The printing office was mainly my school," he said.

He got what formal education he had during the earlier years in Hamilton. His most vivid recollection of school was the discovery at the back of his reader of the rules of prosody, which set him to writing verses modeled on

those his father read aloud from Scott and Moore. He learned most from th
books that came to his hand by chance. Goldsmith's *Greece* and Jarvis' trans
lation of *Don Quixote* were his earliest favorites. They were soon followed b
Irving's *Conquest of Granada,* which, with Longfellow's *Spanish Student*
fired his ambition to learn Spanish. A printer of some literary taste interested
him in Shakespeare and joined his self-conducted inquiries into Latin, Greek
and German. A Yankee machinist inspired a brief enthusiasm for Macaulay
and an English organ builder and house painter introduced him to Dicken
and Thackeray, deploring his preference for the latter.

Each author in turn became for a time Howells' favorite, to be read and
imitated to the exclusion of all others. His unreserved account in *My Literary
Passions* (1895), tracing the development of his mind through this eclectic
course, reveals the defect of the method in the gaps it left. Richardson, Field
ing, and Smollett, from whom the future realist might have learned so
much, he missed altogether. Though Tennyson shared his heart with Long
fellow, the "divine poet I have never ceased to read," he could never force
himself to read Wordsworth, and, despite his interest in German, he saw no
greatness in Goethe. In the Howells household the works of Swedenborg
replaced the Bible.

In the village of Jefferson, Howells passed for something of a youthful
prodigy. Both his knowledge of languages and their number were exaggerated in local report, and late in life he confessed that he had probably been
less fond of study than of the effect it created. His final judgment on his blind
struggle for an education was the rueful one, "Self-taught is half-taught."
There emerges from the autobiographical accounts the image of an undersized, oversensitive youngster, earnestly doing a man's work, shy and aloof
from boys of his own age, intolerably homesick when away from his family,
and haunted by horrible fears. In 1855 overwork and overstudy brought on a
serious nervous breakdown, of which the worst symptom was an obsession
that he had hydrophobia. An intense fear of dogs, which he never overcame,
figures in several of his novels.

In 1856 his father was appointed a legislative clerk in Columbus, and
Howells went along to write daily letters on the proceedings for several
newspapers. Offered the city editorship of the Cincinnati *Gazette,* he gave it
a brief trial before the usual homesickness and the unpalatable duty of reporting police-court cases made him abandon the lucrative post. "My longing," he
wrote, "was for the cleanly respectabilities." After a second period of nervous
prostration he returned in 1858 to Columbus to be city editor of the *Ohio
State Journal,* recently reorganized to serve the growing Republican Party.
The society into which he was now introduced made an impression that can
be felt throughout his novels. Governor Salmon P. Chase, ambitious for the

Presidency, befriended the bashful young reporter, and Howells soon found himself at home in a congenial circle, of which he gives a vivid account in *Years of My Youth*.

For him it was largely a feminine society, and with the zeal of a diffident convert he adopted its most delicate refinements of etiquette. Since early childhood he had despised the coarse crudity of frontier life; he longed to be a dandy and dressed with extreme fastidiousness. His literary taste also turned naturally toward the genteel. With the young ladies of Columbus he read the English periodicals, discussed the novels of Thackeray, George Eliot, and Trollope as they appeared, and fed on the soft praise of his own rhymes in the manner of Tennyson and Heine. "Ah! if I only could write something worthy of the *Atlantic*!" he exclaimed. His first contribution, a poem called "Andenken," was held for months while Lowell made certain that it was not a translation from Heine.

With John J. Piatt, Howells published his first volume, *Poems of Two Friends* (1860). His verses, painstakingly modeled on Tennyson, Heine, and Longfellow, have been justly forgotten. Only "The Pilot's Story," which had appeared in the *Atlantic,* achieved any popularity, and that was rather for its lurid account of a slave girl's plunge to death in the Mississippi than for the awkward hexameters in which it is written. The newspapers, to its author's chagrin, sometimes reprinted it as prose. With his first profits Howells made a literary pilgrimage to New England, described in glowing detail years later in *Literary Friends and Acquaintance* (1900). He liked Hawthorne, but could not understand Thoreau and got on badly with Emerson. His Ohio publisher next commissioned him to write the *Life of Abraham Lincoln* (1860), who had just been nominated for the presidency. Howells himself would not go to Springfield to interview the candidate, but sent a law student to gather material for him. Though his failure to sense Lincoln's greatness at that time is quite pardonable, the reader of the *Life* feels a discord between the honest, manly subject and the flashy style in which it is presented.

After the election Howells' friends suggested that he apply for a consular post abroad; and, recommended by all the prominent Ohio Republicans from the Governor down, he secured the consulship at Venice. His five years there affected him less profoundly than one might expect. For an appreciation of the *Divine Comedy*, which he studied with "an ingenious priest" (the original of Don Ippolito in *A Foregone Conclusion*), his education had hardly fitted him; and he says plainly that much of the poem bored him. The only result of his study was a long effort in *terza rima* about the Civil War, which no editor would print. His reading soon turned to more modern authors, especially Goldoni and the later dramatists. Through the Tauchnitz editions he kept up with English fiction; *Romola* in particular was a profound ethical revelation that he never forgot. In Paris in 1862 he married Elinor Mead of Brattleboro, Vermont, whom he had met in Columbus. She came of a talented family and was a second cousin of President Rutherford B. Hayes, to whose campaign in 1876 he contributed a biography.

Under the skies of Venice he toiled vainly to invoke the Muse; he should have been writing realistic stories instead of romantic idyls in hexameters. One of these poems, "No Love Lost: A Romance of Travel" (1869), a gentle satire of Americans in Italy written in 1862, is cast in what was to be the typical Howells pattern: a pair of lovers kept apart for a time by too delicate scruples are at length united. Failing to interest English or American editors in his poems, he turned to writing short prose sketches of Venice, which, after their appearance in the Boston *Advertiser,* were reprinted as *Venetian Life* (1866). While the book leans inevitably on standard works of history and travel, it is notable for the fresh, personal style of a polite but quizzical observer. The realist's aim to represent ordinary things truthfully is plain in his resolve to tell "as much as possible of the everyday life of a people whose habits are so different from our own." How well he gauged public taste is attested by the book's success. A second edition was called for the next year, when he also published *Italian Journeys,* a similar collection of sketches reprinted from the *Nation* and the *Atlantic.*

For a few months after his return to America, Howells worked as a free lance in New York. His literary ambition, however, was centered in Boston, and when Fields offered him the assistant editorship of the *Atlantic* he accepted gladly. For $50 a month he agreed to sift the manuscripts, correspond with contributors, write many of the book reviews, and read all the proofs. It was not kept from him that his experience as a practical printer was "most valued, if not the most valued, and that as proof-reader I was expected to make it avail on the side of economy." His Italian connection brought him an invitation to Longfellow's Dante Club, where among the great of Cambridge he found a heaven higher than the *Paradiso.* His literary taste had been so formed on the *Atlantic* model that when he was made editor-in-chief in 1871 he took over the wheel without perceptibly altering the course. The success of the Italian sketches prompted him to turn to similar themes at home; his colored cook, an organ grinder, a beggar, and even a stroll through the dullest outskirts of Cambridge are invested with an interest Howells rarely fails to invoke. "If the public will stand this," he told Henry James, "I shall consider my fortune made." Collected as *Suburban Sketches* (1871), they passed through many editions.

His novels grew from his travel sketches. *Their Wedding Journey* (1871), he wrote to his father, is "the story of our last summer's travels, which I am giving the form of fiction so far as the characters are concerned." Most of the book consists of descriptions of the American scene—the night boat, the sleeping car, the parlor car (which never ceased to fascinate him), the sordid New York streets, the Hudson and Mohawk rivers, "romantic Rochester," Niagara Falls (at excessive length), Montreal, and Quebec. Except for a minor steamboat collision, the book is without incident. But Howells' theory of realism is already defined; he avoids "the heroic or occasional phases," seeking man "in his habitual moods of vacancy and tiresomeness," in "his vast, natural, unaffected dulness." Apology for the rawness of America contends with his pride in its native honesty and beauty. Basil March, who reappears in seven other stories, is the scarcely disguised projection of Howells himself, commenting on the new scenes as he had on those in *Venetian Life* and *Suburban Sketches*. Isabel March, vivacious, humorous, illogical, and charming, is the first of his subtle feminine portraits.

5

With *A Chance Acquaintance* (1873) his work as a novelist properly begins. Though the "scenery" element is not yet wholly fused with the dramatic, Howells made some effort to subordinate it to the social conflict that was to serve as his major theme in nearly a score of novels: the story of a sensitive country girl or boy thrown into a more sophisticated society. It is, of course, his own experience. Kitty Ellison, like her creator the child of a Free Soil editor in the Middle West, has grown up in democratic ignorance of social differences. On an excursion to Quebec she meets a cultivated Bostonian, Miles Arbuton, the first of Howells' coolly superior and impossibly refined young men, who could hardly be expected to understand the culture of Erie Creek; indeed, he is a mere foil for its homely virtues, and Howells admitted to James that he was "a simulacrum." But Kitty really comes to life. In her homemade dress, naïve, fresh, natural, and sincere, she is the first of those girls who were to demonstrate the superiority of American simplicity to the conventions of a Europeanized society.

In the succeeding novels Howells transports his heroines to Italy to be studied with varying degrees of realism against a romantic background. Florida Vervain in *A Foregone Conclusion* (1875) is brought to Venice, where the watchful young artist-consul Ferris protects her from the hopeless love of the priest Don Ippolito, a variety of sentimental romance that Howells did not repeat. In Venice also, Lydia Blood, the charming heroine of *The Lady of the Aroostook* (1879), focuses the conflict of three cultures. Reared north of Boston in simple ignorance of such customs as chaperonage, she sails for Italy, the only woman aboard the *Aroostook*. Attracted by her beauty, two "cultivated Yankees," aware that the upcountry ideal of propriety is "very different from ours," resolve to "preserve her unconsciousness" of the anomalous position her friends have placed her in. So scrupulous is the Bostonian Staniford that he refrains from telling her he has fallen in love with her until she is properly in her aunt's charge. Such delicacy merely perplexes Lydia, though she is gravely shocked by Sunday opera and the easy immorality of Venice. She is humbler and less sophisticated than her contemporary, Daisy Miller, but more genuinely American—a quality emphasized by contrast with her aunt, who toadies to the English colony. Howells' faculty for writing dialogue as direct and natural as conversation overheard in real life reaches full pitch in this novel. Lily Mayhew, the heroine of *A Fearful Responsibility* (1881), is another country girl who comes to Venice to visit her aunt. But Howells had exhausted the theme; the only noteworthy thing about the book is the deliberate avoidance of a happy ending.

He had already begun to exploit native material. *Private Theatricals,* laid in a country boarding house, originated in the summer of 1874, which he spent at Jaffrey, New Hampshire. Published in the *Atlantic* (1875–1876), it was not reprinted until after Howells' death, when it appeared as *Mrs. Farrell* (1921). That Howells studied his originals closely is suggested by an unauthenticated legend which says that the family with whom he boarded at Mountain Farm recognized themselves in the Woodwards and "threatened him with the law" if the story were reprinted. If the charm of the flirtatious young widow is not quite convincing, some of the minor characters are drawn with Howells' maturest art. In a sentence he sketches the meeting of two old neighbors, who,

when they had hornily rattled their callous palms together, stand staring at each other, their dry, serrated lips falling apart, their jaws mutely working up and down, their pale-blue eyes vacantly winking, and their weather-beaten faces as wholly discharged of expression as the gable ends of two barns confronting each other from opposite sides of the road.

It is ungracious to remark that this superb realism is largely external. The Woodward family are revealed only through the eyes of their boarders, who observe such details as Mrs. Woodward's "large, toil-worn, kitchen-coarsened hand, with its bony knuckles and stubbed, broken nails," without penetrating far into her mind. Howells had not yet attained his deepest understanding of the silent granite of New England character.

In *The Undiscovered Country* (1880) he turns for a fresh setting to the Shakers, who, except for Hawthorne's brief glances, had not been used in fiction. The community at Vardley (a composite of Harvard and Shirley, where Howells stayed in 1875) serves merely as a picturesque background for the love story, varied with spiritualistic phenomena, of which Howells and the Shakers both take a skeptical view. Shakers are the principal characters in two thin volumes published in 1896, *A Parting and a Meeting* and *The Day of Their Wedding,* highly implausible triumphs of celibacy over young love, in which the tradition of local color is stronger than realism. Another of Howells' favorite settings is the seaside hotel, which he uses first in *Dr. Breen's Practice* (1881). No one has recorded the trivial and malicious conversation of the rocking chairs with more accurate realism. The book solicits interest from the current debate between allopath and homeopath and the problem of medicine as a suitable profession for women. Neither issue is treated more than superficially. The true issue is whom Grace Breen shall marry. A Puritan conscience had turned her to medicine as a sort of atonement for wealth and ease. By nature, however, she is completely feminine and, having refused the attractive young man who has been camping on the beach to be near her, finally proposes to him herself.

Marcia Gaylord, the heroine of Howells' only study of married life, *A Modern Instance* (1882), behaves even more passionately. Bartley Hubbard, the husband on whom she throws herself against her father's advice, is a shrewd, enterprising young journalist drawn, as Howells perceived years later, from himself. The village paper in Equity, Maine, where the story opens, could hardly hold a man of his talent; in Boston he quickly wins his way as a free-lance writer and with borrowed money secures an interest in a weekly magazine. But like George Eliot's Tito Melema, who had obviously impressed Howells deeply, Bartley was created to serve as a horrid example of moral decay. Though the progressive disintegration of his character has been praised, there is really no change in him beyond a growing stoutness, the result presumably of drinking beer. From the start he was self-seeking, self-indulgent, unscrupulous, with "no more moral nature than a baseball." In real life these qualities would not necessarily have prevented his becoming a successful journalist, and, if his destruction were not foreordained, marriage might have improved his morals. The Marcia of the opening chapters, whose "elemental" and "animalistic" qualities troubled contemporary reviewers, might well have become a mate worthy of his early ambitions. After their marriage, as Howells steadily blackens Bartley, he reveals in Marcia an unexpected strain of moral delicacy incompatible with her fundamental possessiveness. Ben, the sensitive, lame, pious, and incredibly noble hero, with more than a reminiscence of *Romola,* sends her back to Bartley: "No man can be your refuge from your husband!" Ben's love for her increases unaccountably as the reader's sympathy declines. With all her inconsistency Marcia is Howells' most notable attempt to portray a complete woman. No reader can fail to admire his skillful drawing of such minor figures as Judge Gaylord, the perfectly wrought background of the village in winter, and the Boston boarding houses.

Resigning from the *Atlantic* in 1881, Howells spent the following year in England, Switzerland, and Italy. Besides such work as *Tuscan Cities* (1885), illustrated by Joseph Pennell, his only novel was *A Woman's Reason* (1883), which suffers from fatigue and remoteness from his material. It is a transitional book, marking a change in Howells' attitude toward Boston society, to which he returned in *The Rise of Silas Lapham* (1885) with a new perspective.

The Laphams are the first *nouveaux riches* to be studied sympathetically in our fiction. A poor farm boy who has made his million in paint, Silas was (like Howells himself) building a house on the water side of Beacon Street. With complete mastery Howells notes the distinctive traits of the American; his massive physique inherited from generations of laborers, his casual dress, his love of speed, and wholehearted dedication to business are observed and recorded kindly. Persis, his plain, unpretentious wife, adapting herself to the city less easily, is helpless to guide her daughters' social life. Against the background of a preposterous drawing room or calamitous dinner party, Howells can describe their perplexities without rousing ridicule so much as pity. Through it all they keep a kind of simple dignity bred of solid worth that makes one forgive mere ignorance of manners. The Coreys, "a little beyond the salt of the earth," but studied more critically than Howells' earlier Bostonians, serve as a foil to the Laphams' homely virtues: "stalwart achievement against sterile elegance." Tom Corey, the link between the old order and the new, combines grace with an energy his father lacks; and though his behavior before he proposes to Penelope is so discreet that every one, including the young lady herself, believes him in love with her prettier sister, he is one of the most likable of Howells' heroes. For those days the business ethics that make Silas prefer poverty to a legal sale that would have saved him are perhaps somewhat idealized. But the episode was necessary to complete his "rise," and it gives the book a symmetry of form Howells seldom achieved. In contrast with *A Modern Instance,* the setting, masterfully rendered, is completely fused with the action. On the whole, popular taste has judged well in declaring this his best novel.

*Indian Summer* (1886) may be a finer technical achievement. Here Howells keeps well within his range, writing mostly about women, in this case cultivated Middle Westerners living in Florence. The germ of the story seems to come from memories of his early days in Columbus. Colville, one of our first expatriates and a curious forerunner of James' Strether, is a middle-aged hero who falls into an ambiguous intimacy with Mrs. Bowen, a widow whom he had known years before, and with her young protégée Imogene

Graham, who imagines herself romantically in love with him. Like many of Howells' men, Colville is slow to perceive his own happiness. When at last he proposes, Mrs. Bowen, out of pride and pique, refuses him with a woman's "No" that is quickly reversed. The conflicting motives in her mind are traced with great subtlety, and Colville, for all his obtuseness, is drawn sympathetically. While it lasts, the spell wrought by a rare unity of tone conquers the reader; it is only on analysis that one sees the frail structure of the book.

6

Howells' reviews in the *Atlantic* and *North American* constantly praised the merits of De Forest, James, and others who were striving to make a faithful transcription of the world about them. In "The Editor's Study," which he conducted in *Harper's* from January, 1886, to March, 1892, he waged a crusade for realism that roused violent opposition on both sides of the Atlantic. A group of these articles, too carelessly assembled, make up the little volume called *Criticism and Fiction* (1891). The critic's function, he says, is like the scientist's, "to discover principles, not to establish them; to report, not to create." He has only to ask if a novel is "true to the motives, the impulses, the principles that shape the life of actual men and women." While Howells professed to see little difference between *Literature and Life* (as he declares in a collection of articles published under that title in 1902), what he calls Life sometimes seems to the reader merely Literature. His theory omits several important phases of human experience. Tragedy is excluded because it is rare in the United States: our novelists "concern themselves with the more smiling aspects of life, which are the more American"; Romance is also barred because it is exceptional; and Sex is banished completely for the inconsistent reason that interest in it is all too common.

The genteel atmosphere of Boston has been unfairly blamed for Howells' extraordinary prudishness. His letters show that Lowell, James, and others steadily urged him toward a stronger realism and stimulated an interest in social problems, which the *Atlantic* had fostered before Howells joined it. His autobiographical books yield ample evidence that his squeamishness about sexual relations and the nude in art was fully developed in his boyhood on the Ohio frontier, which, as Mrs. Trollope observed in 1832, was ridiculously sensitive about such matters. He is not quite candid, then, in attributing the necessity for reticence to the young lady reader—the "Iron Madonna," as Boyesen called her. His own sensibility dictated it. There was also another reason. Though an *Anna Karenina* can be printed as a book and locked up from the children, no American (or, he might have added, English) magazine would publish anything that "a father may not read to his daughter, or safely leave her to read for herself. After all, it is a matter of business."

Business and prudishness combined to make Howells' practice incompatible with his theory of realism. His income came chiefly from the magazines, and, like the modern writer, he had to accept their limitations. The damage done his art by serial publication was serious, though there is no sign that he was restive under the restrictions. Despite his insistence that realism "prefers to avoid all manner of strange coincidences and dire catastrophes," his books abound in them. Three plots turn on train wrecks, three on fires; two characters are removed by brain fever, a number by sudden sickness; two commit suicide with poison; one hero is shot, another knocked down by a horsecar, and two others killed by locomotives. Yet realism is determined less by choice of material than by intention and method of treatment; if Howells seems now to have conceded too much to his public, he also sacrificed a good deal for his principles.

His reviews widened America's literary horizon, introducing such foreign authors as Galdós and Valdés, Ibsen and Björnson, Turgenev, Tolstoy, and Dostoevski. Howells' increasing concern with abnormal states of mind like the jealousy of the half-insane husband in *The Shadow of a Dream* (1890) or the remorse of the embezzler in *The Quality of Mercy* (1892) may have been quickened by the reading of Dostoevski. Tolstoy, however, whom he first read when *War and Peace* was translated in 1886, he considered the supreme influence of his life. While his literary method remained unchanged, his ethical outlook was profoundly affected; he began to regard the poor with a new sympathy.

In his next novel, *The Minister's Charge; or the Apprenticeship of Lemuel Barker* (1887), moral problems occupy him more than manners. The central theme is "complicity," the responsibility every one in society shares for the deeds of every one else. The story is written from the point of view of Mr. Sewell and the Corey family of earlier books, but the poor factory girls Statira Dudley and 'Manda Grier are depicted truly and without sentimentality; they are low because they like to be. Lem Barker, the humorless country boy who rebukes conventional insincerity by his dogged honesty, has little else to recommend him. The reader welcomes even so palpable a caricature as Miss Vane, distributing bouquets to the poor to prevent crime. *Annie Kilburn* (1888), a slightly less uncomfortable book, teaches the Tolstoyan lesson that money is useless without the sympathy that comes from suffering. Through the stern and uncompromising young minister Mr. Peck, the heroine learns that the prosperous, since they are agents of the system that causes poverty, cannot help the poor. The grim theme is lightened with some amusing satire on the vapid society ladies' futile efforts at charity. There is no such relief in *An Imperative Duty* (1892), Howells' worst violation of the commonplace, where he applies Tolstoy to the Negro problem, evading the obvious difficulties of mixed marriage as Mrs. Stowe did by shipping the couple off to live in Europe.

The influence of Tolstoy was soon reinforced by a more immediate acquaintance with socialism. In the fall of 1887 he heard Laurence Gronlund lecture in Buffalo and was led to read his book, *The Co-operative Commonwealth* (1884), Kirkup's article in the *Encyclopædia Britannica,* the *Fabian Essays,* and some of William Morris' tracts. The "civic murder" of the Chicago Anarchists, November 11, 1887, stirred him to active protest and greatly increased his discontent with the shallow Boston society he was dissecting in *April Hopes* (1888). Since his resignation from the *Atlantic* in 1881, his novels had been serialized in the *Century* and *Harper's*; the center of his interests had shifted, and in 1889 he moved to New York, where *A Hazard of New Fortunes* (1890) is laid. On a canvas of Tolstoy's panoramic dimensions he strives to include all the groups involved in the class struggle: the established aristocracy, the new plutocracy elbowing their way in, the business and professional classes, and the poor of the lower East Side. Though the point of view is necessarily Howells' own in the person of his *alter ego,* March (who has relinquished the moribund refinement of Boston to edit a New York magazine), the poor are studied realistically but compassionately. Their spokesman is the patriarchal socialist Lindau, a refugee of 1848, who lost his left hand in the Civil War and lives by choice in the slums "among my brothers"; he was drawn from the bookbinder who taught Howells German. Dryfoos, recently enriched by the discovery of natural gas on his Ohio farm, has come to New York to watch his money breed more money in speculation. Created to play the villain, greedy, an avowed enemy of labor unions, domineering over his family, Dryfoos is depicted without the sympathy that illuminates Silas Lapham; his melting after Lindau's death is improbably sentimental. His ignorant, pushing, and vulgar daughters are described with a more authentic realism than the hero, Conrad, sensitive, continually blushing, holding at the age of thirty ideals of "virginal vagueness" about women, and longing, if he dared, to join an order of Protestant celibates. Amidst philosophies ranging from Dryfoos' free enterprise to Beaton's aesthetic indifference, Howells stands close to Lindau, who proposes by orderly political action to achieve state control of resources and a program of social security. The streetcar strike of 1888 brings the plot to a melodramatic close.

New York's social contrasts are treated more mildly in *The Coast of Bohemia* (1893), which depicts the struggles of a talented Ohio girl studying art. *The World of Chance* (1893) is a better novel. The hero Shelley Ray, a "neat, slight, rather undersized" Ohio newspaperman, who is clearly autobiographical, has come to New York with the manuscript of a romantic novel, which succeeds only because a reviewer took it home by mistake. The best character in the book is the old socialist David Hughes, who had lived at Brook Farm; he probably speaks for Howells in criticizing Tolstoy's "eremitism": "Society is not to be saved by self-outlawry. . . . The way to have the golden age is to elect it by the Australian ballot."

Howells seems to have known nothing of Karl Marx except what he picked up from Gronlund and younger men like Hamlin Garland. In *A Traveller from Altruria* (1894) and its sequel *Through the Eye of the Needle* (1907), Aristides Homos disrupts an American summer hotel by helping the servants with their work and, in a lecture arranged by the rattle-brained Mrs. Makely, describes Altruria, where inequality and competition have given way to what seems a rather dull life. The utopias of Bellamy and Morris had preceded Howells', and parallels for many of his ideas have been pointed out in Gronlund's *The Co-operative Commonwealth.* Though he called himself a socialist and was troubled by inequality and poverty, Howells never actively revolted against the established order. He wrote Henry James in 1888:

After fifty years of optimistic content with "civilization" and its ability to come out all right in the end, I now abhor it, and feel that it is coming out all wrong in the end, unless it bases itself anew on a real equality. Meantime, I wear a fur-lined overcoat, and live in all the luxury my money can buy.

He was always sensitive to changes in literary fashion. As realism deepened in the nineties into naturalism and veritism, his own work took a stronger tone. In *The Landlord at Lion's Head* (1897) the tubercular Durgin family on their lonely New Hampshire farm make his bleakest picture of New England life. The country people in *Private Theatricals,* a sort of preliminary study for *The Landlord,* were subordinated to their boarders; now Howells develops them more fully. Mrs. Durgin is a thoroughly lifelike character, one of his masterpieces. Westover, the artist who comes to paint Lion's Head and suggests to her the possibility of a summer hotel, acts as a sort of Jamesian reflector throughout the story; the social problem of a hotelkeeper's son at Harvard, on a picnic with the summer boarders, or in Boston society, bothers him much more than it does Jeff Durgin. In Jeff, his only character in whom passions are not blinked, Howells comes closest to creating a real man. Before the ruthless male had been popularized by the apostles of the strenuous, Jeff is given the iron will of a Nietzschean superman, a powerful, masculine physique, and a magnetic attraction for women. He holds weakness the only sin. His flirtation with the Boston society girl is more convincing than the absurd scruples of his fiancée, a waitress at the hotel, who finds a worthier mate in the overrefined and much older Westover. The reader is repelled by her preternatural delicacy, while Jeff's imperfections, so honestly owned, evoke a sympathy Howells did not mean us to feel. In spite of its flaws, *The Landlord at Lion's Head* is one of Howells' best books; it has been undeservedly neglected.

Few novels of his last two decades demand consideration. *The Kentons* (1902) shows how a love affair affects a whole family, exiled from their comfortable home by one daughter's unhappiness. Without unkind satire Howells portrays Judge Kenton's nostalgia and the whole family's lack of interest in foreign countries, which they judge by comparison with Ohio. The fifteen-year-old Boyne is Howells' best study of adolescence. Among all his works *The Kentons* seemed to James the perfectly classic illustration of Howells' spirit and form. *The Son of Royal Langbrith* (1904), a novel of richer texture, is less true to the commonplace but more absorbing to read. The chief interest lies in the autumnal romance of Mrs. Langbrith, nineteen years a widow. There is only one obstacle to her marriage: her son Jim has never been told that his father, whose memory he idolizes, was really a drunken brute, who beat his wife and kept a mistress. Jim, an undergraduate at Harvard, has enough influence over his mother to make her delay her decision, and while she hesitates, Howells deliberately removes her fiancé by typhoid fever.

From 1900 until he died Howells conducted "The Editor's Easy Chair" in *Harper's,* though he continued to contribute to other magazines, notably the *North American Review.* His encouragement of young writers—Howe, Crane, Garland, and Norris—is well known; it is not always remembered, however, that his advice to more famous contemporaries was often important. James acknowledged his gratitude warmly:

> You held out your open editorial hand to me at the time I began to write—and I allude especially to the summer of 1866—with a frankness and sweetness of hospitality that was really the making of me. . . . You showed me the way and opened me the door.

A talk with Howells in England in 1897 revived the desire to write novels that flowered in his greatest work. More than anyone else Howells stimulated and directed Mark Twain's genius, which he recognized at the beginning. Without Howells there might have been no *Life on the Mississippi.* Antipodal in personal habits, they maintained for forty years the friendship of which *My Mark Twain* (1910) is an intimate record. Howells has been unjustly blamed for imposing a prudish gentility on Mark Twain's native genius; his advice was generally sound, and the replacement of "hell" and "damn" by milder expressions is editing no more drastic than a modern film scenario or radio script must undergo today.

As the years passed, Howells received honorary degrees from Yale, Harvard, Oxford, Columbia, and Princeton; he was elected the first president of the American Academy of Arts and Letters. In 1920, the year of his death, a realistic novel, *Main Street,* became a best seller. His long crusade was at an end. The realism for which two romantic generations had abused him was already being ridiculed as timid by new realists whose art owed more to Howells than they cared to admit. Although he embraced too narrow a segment of human experience, few of his successors surpassed his power to draw exactly what he saw.

# 55. EXPERIMENTS IN POETRY:
## SIDNEY LANIER AND EMILY DICKINSON

*by Stanley T. Williams (Yale)*

Prose was by no means the sole me-
dium for the literary exploration and exploitation of the new America. By
the year 1870 all the arts had felt the onrush of contemporary events, and
among the resultant fresh ideas poetry played its part. Poets born in the
second, third, and fourth decades of the century were destined to quicken
in the tingling currents of intellectual discovery. The new ideas varied in
dignity from grossly materialistic concepts of America to spiritualized ideologies worthy of the nineteenth century thinkers to whom so many of these
poets were in debt. How much each poet beheld of the proud growth of
America, of the ominous transition (after the industrial revolution) to the
era of the machine, of the birth and death of doctrines, depended of course
upon his length of life. William Henry Thompson, for example, the author
of the fine martial poem, "The High Tide at Gettysburg," lived on until
1918; visible to him were the changes in poetry incipient in the revolts of
Sidney Lanier and Emily Dickinson. Yet all the poets of the latter half of
the century, even Henry Timrod who died in 1867, felt the impact of the
new science, of the new industrialism, and of the shattering war between the
North and the South.

Certainly one may detect, if faintly, in the poetry of the sixties and seventies
the rumble of the approaching storm. Many poets experienced merely the
uneasiness of the times, but all sensed the moral problems posed by the new
science, and all were excited by the national spectacle which Lanier celebrated
in his "Psalm of the West." Walt Whitman, whose *Leaves of Grass* (1855)
was without imitators before the end of the century, had at any rate spoken
out. Meanwhile the fact of war had elicited the harsh truthfulness of Melville's verse and had prepared the public for Stephen Crane's grim *Black
Riders* (1895). A few poets had begun to recognize the power of fresh, realistic
material communicated by blunt, experimental methods. To this ground-
swell of realism we owe, despite their compromises with conventions, the
adventurous poetry of Sidney Lanier and Emily Dickinson.

Yet the traditionalists clung to the old subjects and forms. Antiphonally
to the rebels' bold chants they repeated the melodies of the Victorian song-

book; through their pages echoed the cadences of Byron, Shelley, Keats. T
such gods the loyalty of certain poets was intense, among them Edmund
Clarence Stedman, the banker-poet, and Thomas Bailey Aldrich, singer of
red and white roses; others, such as that rare spirit, Edward Rowland Sill
never escaped from the finely spun chains of Tennyson's verse. Sometime
the magic wand of influence was transferred to an American poet in th
same tradition, as in Poe's influence over Father John Banister Tabb. It is eas
to understand a prevailing conception of Whitman as a rowdy outlaw, if we
grasp these poets' unwavering conviction that the principles of verse had
been fixed for good and aye; that Parnassus was closed save through the
single door of the English romantic poets.

Even when the staggering episodes of the era crept into their poetry
these elegant writers divested them of life, softening the rude facts to the
proprieties of their Victorian verse. See, for example, what Stedman makes
in poetry of that same Titan industry which later became the theme of
Dreiser's bitter novels; or how Cincinnatus Heine Miller, in "Kit Carson's
Ride," tames a prairie fire to the nineteenth century anapaest. Thus Thomas
Buchanan Read, in "Sheridan's Ride," was typical of versifiers of the North
and South who abandoned pretty poems on gardens for the subject of the
war, which they somehow made, despite its heroism and suffering, quaint
and costumed. The material was fresh and stirring, but the poetry itself was
in the age-old manner.

Possibly this conflict between the new realism and the old conservatism
encouraged a limited style of experiment by a few poets, such as Lanier and
Emily Dickinson—experiment with new techniques still contained within the
old patterns and using the old materials. To embrace the new utterly, like
Whitman, was fantastic; to retire completely into the old, like Aldrich, was
irrational. Beside these two experimental poets, the subject of the present
chapter, we occasionally find a few others who think poetically ahead of their
time. In the seventies, for example, Frederick Goddard Tuckerman, recluse
and dreamer, was writing sonnets and other verses which, though a more
conventional side of his writing pleased Longfellow and Lowell, exhibited
this restless search for a new technique.

Tuckerman knew [says Witter Bynner, who brought him to light] what he
was doing when he ended a sonnet with an Alexandrine or shortened the last line
by a foot, or when he shuffled the rhyme-scheme to suit the roll and rise and fall
of his meaning.

Did Tuckerman, like Emily Dickinson, divine that his audience had not yet
appeared? One wonders, too, whether others, still unknown to us, were not

xperimenting; or even whether Lanier, Emily Dickinson, and Tuckerman
nay not in the long history of our poets have developed apprehensions more
elicate than those of their conventional contemporaries. In any case, such as
hese were the heralds of the great changes impending in the poetry of
America.

2

Of these conservatisms and of these stirrings toward a new poetry Sidney
Lanier sometimes seems a feverish epitome. For sixteen years after the Civil
War he enunciated and practiced a dynamic but tryingly inconclusive gospel
f the identity of poetry and music; and he became an almost fanatical experimenter in the techniques of verse. Yet his originalities of both content
nd form, despite his deep personal sincerity, have a japannish quality. Apart
rom his stimulating philosophy concerning the two arts, his verse is often
orrectly Tennysonian. The pupil excelled the master in filigree, but not in
precision, strength, and self-control. Not one of his adventures with irregular
ines and farfetched metaphors had the daring, inner symbolism which in-
eres in Emily Dickinson's stanzas; it is pertinent that the rude, salt spray
f Walt Whitman's poetry really shocked Lanier, although it also refreshed
im.

Likewise, though he clasps nature in strange embraces, proclaims the
acredness of art, worships the sun, and denounces "trade," he is at heart
uriously orthodox. He never, like the two contemporaries just mentioned,
trips himself of old beliefs before he builds a new universe. On the con-
rary, he clings to the familiar concepts of nineteenth century romantic
Christianity; and he tries to adjust the evil world and its subversive science
o his "crystal Christ." He is not remote from the Southern Christian-cavalier
radition to which the poets Chivers and Poe belonged. Thus his moral world
emained a narrow one; from first to last he was evangelical. In his teleologi-
al attitude, he is a John Fiske in poetry, and in his forms, he is often less
haracteristic of new principles in verse than of its reluctance to renounce old
raditions. In the emergence of the new poetry Lanier typifies its uneasiness
ather than its rebirth. Like Emily Dickinson and like Whitman, he felt
he trammels of established verse, but, unlike them, he never truly initiated
ew forms.

Yet Lanier, like some "bearded meteor trailing light," moved through the
ourse of poetry after the Civil War, persuading by the delirious intensity of
iis feeling and by the magic complexity of his melody, until we can hardly
onceive of this epoch without his enriching influence. His opulence was
eeded in an age reared upon Longfellow and Whittier. His fame, enhanced

by his gallant warfare against poverty and disease, and by his spectacula
career as a musician, began slowly and reached a climax at about the time o
his premature death; in its present revival, induced partly by his allege
anticipation, in his social ideas, of Southern agrarianism, it rests less upo
his chivalric war novel *Tiger-Lilies* (1867), upon his volumes of sophomor
literary criticism (in which, for example, he refers to Fielding as that "muc
of the classics"), or even upon the seminal *Science of English Verse* (1880
than upon a dozen poems. Unique in the story of poetry, these probably insur
him against oblivion. For they add to our literary history his Southern land
scapes, his delicate pictorial art, and his sensitivity, which was the mainsprin
of his genius. Let us always remember that throughout his periods of poeti
productivity Lanier was a sick man; this fact is more than a partial explana
tion of his ardors and ecstasies. Behind him pressed ever near time's winge
chariot; he knew the doomed mortal's craving for multiform experienc
Though we may shake our heads over his cloying extravagance and thoug
we may talk of the need for restraint or for criticism from peers wiser tha
his friends, Paul Hamilton Hayne and Bayard Taylor, this passionate
hurrying eloquence, so reminiscent of Shelley's, was Lanier's own peculia
charm.

The excitement of Lanier's poetry is matched by that of his tempestuou
life; "the hottest of all battles," he called it. Born in Macon, Georgia, o
February 3, 1842, he inherited from the Elizabethan Laniers, and, mor
directly, from his mother, his golden legacy of music; "he could not remem
ber the time when he could not play almost any musical instrument." Whil
undecided, after his graduation from Oglethorpe University, between th
careers of musician and lawyer, he was swept into the Confederate Army
the war, the deeply shaping experience of his youth, bestowed upon hin
memories of battle and prison, the companionship of his beloved flute an
of Father Tabb, and tuberculosis. This affliction was to make his remainin
years a struggle to maintain the integrities of his art and of his own soul i
the face of certain extinction.

In the confused and broken South, in the "dark raven days," as he calle
them, he essayed many trades and professions; hotel clerk and lawyer, thes
were but two of his numerous occupations. His poor lungs made him trave
as with John Sterling, of whom he sometimes reminds us, his every yea
demanded new altitudes of both body and spirit. Yet his persistent consecra
tion to his "twin-goddesses," Music and Poetry, brought fruition in the sev
enties when he became first flutist of the Peabody Orchestra of Baltimore
in this decade, also, he wrote "Corn," "The Symphony," "The Marshes o
Glynn," and his "Centennial Cantata." There followed misdirections of hi
talent, among them the lectureship on English literature at Johns Hopkins

University and his immersion in literary criticism, inconclusive except for the causative *Science of English Verse.* It is pardonable to dramatize the conclusion of his heroic effort against his "living egg of pain"; in 1881 he died, at the age of thirty-nine, shortly after completing a characteristic poem, "Sunrise," written when he had a temperature of 104 degrees.

Like Sill, Lanier was an undergraduate when the *Origin of Species* appeared. He admired Darwin intensely, and carefully annotated his copy of the book; for him, as for many young poets of the era, it was less a revelation of the organic world than a culmination, a symbol, and a harbinger of the future. At Oglethorpe the brilliant, German-trained tutor, James Woodrow (the grandfather of Woodrow Wilson), had opened to him the portals of scientific study; these Lanier never closed. His was a common nineteenth century point of view: the implications of science drove him into fresh views of nature, but not out of the old faith which haunted him to the end in a tangled congeries of paganism, amateurish learning, and Christianity.

Thus he could write of

> Th' indifferent smile that nature's grace
> On Jesus, Judas pours alike.

Yet in the next moment he was kissing the "friendly, sisterly, sweetheart leaves" or celebrating the Saviour in his "A Ballad of Trees and the Master." Like Tennyson, but with far less success, he attempted to reconcile the warring claims of science and of personal religion in some far-off event. In the same vague fashion, he was aware of the social upheavals of the age; Carlyle was an enduring influence, and he has often been called Ruskinian. Yet his apostasies from childhood beliefs were intellectual rather than moral. He took shelter under the illusive adjustments of the nineteenth century, in "progress" and in the "somehow good." For all his wailing concerning "trade," one senses his buoyant hope that all may yet be well with mankind in an America so remarkable for material prosperity.

Lanier, despite his eager curiosity, never did any hard thinking concerning the philosophic problems raised by science and the machine. His plastic mind entertained all the faith-doubt psychoses of the nineteenth century; and concerning them, in contrast to Emily Dickinson, he was voluble. That on these matters he had anything of importance to say is another question. Like Carlyle, whom he echoed even in his diction, he romanticized the conclusions of thinkers whom he could neither supplement nor contradict. What does he offer as a cure for "trade" save his misty personifications, his jargon of Love or Art? Even his finest poem, "The Symphony," ends:

And yet shall Love himself be heard,
Though long deferred, though long deferred:
O'er the modern waste a dove hath whirred:
Music is Love in search of a word.

Very pretty, but not worthy, this, of a student of *In Memoriam*. Basically, toward the thought of the time Lanier's reactions were always emotional, and if any one tone dominated his emotions, it was that of nineteenth century literary romanticism. Only in his special fields of music and the craftsmanship of verse was Lanier a constructive thinker.

3

*The Science of English Verse* is a mature recapitulation of Lanier's years of experimentation in poetry. Its origins lie not only in his passionate interest in his own craft and in the pedagogic streak in his nature, but also in the nineteenth century's inquisitiveness concerning the interrelation of the arts. Through his dual allegiance to music and poetry, Lanier's entire life had been an exploration of the laws governing each; gradually he had convinced himself that these laws were identical. It is undemonstrable that all of Lanier's faults as a poet arose from this oversimplification of an aesthetic link, but his growing belief affected deeply the quality of his verse. His climactic study remains a challenging exposition of a theory, now less definitive, in the light of modern studies in prosody, than provocative in its minor perceptions concerning a difficult subject.

Since, according to Lanier, the organic principles of music and poetry are the same, and since, therefore, sound relation is the essence of both,

it is clear that what we call "verse" is a set of specially related sounds . . . when we hear verse, we *hear* a set of relations between sounds; when we silently read verse, we *see* that which brings to us a set of relations between sounds; when we imagine verse, we *imagine* a set of relations between sounds.

We think at once, in qualification, of the gulf between the definiteness of musical sound and the unevenness of spoken English syllables, but Lanier proceeds to study scientifically (he thinks) such elements in sound relations as duration, intensity, pitch, and tone color. All this is enlivening, but who can read English verse so that the sound relations are precisely equal? Who can escape the use of *accent,* which, after all, in English, for the normal ear, is likely to remain the workable unit of measure? Lanier discusses accents, phrases, lines, and stanzas, but he regards these as subordinate elements. In the end we must feel that, however stimulating to the study of prosody, *The*

*Science of English Verse* is too forced, too artificial, to alter finally principles in either the creation or the reading of poetry.

Indeed, the weakness of Lanier's creed is connected with the fact that it was a fulfillment, a creed taking form throughout his life, rather than an initial impulse, like Whitman's, determining the full course of his poetic effort. The poetry written before "Corn" (1874) shows slight identification of the sound patterns of music and poetry; it reveals merely Lanier's ingenious use of established aural devices. It is difficult not to reason that his subtle playing with alliteration, assonance, tone color, or syzygy convinced him of the intimate union of music and poetry rather than the reverse; that is, the fully formed theory did not, until late in life, beget such experimentation. Two facts are certain: "Corn," "The Symphony," "The Psalm of the West," and other poems written during the last seven years of his life, reflect a conscious, belated attempt to make such workmanship serve his crystallized belief regarding the identity between the two arts. Also, the earlier verse is simpler, less characteristic of the Lanier best known to the world, in its conventional preoccupation with the quatrain, blank verse, or the sonnet. The later work suggests a poet armed with a thesis. In this appears all the brilliance of Lanier's technique, as well as, unfortunately—when he failed to capture this elusive dove, his favorite bird of poetic music—all his virtuosity and inanity. Apart from the elaborate theory and its relation to practice, we may perceive his instinctive mastery of his craft in his beautiful cadences, in, say, the familiar lines from "The Marshes of Glynn":

> Emerald twilights,—
>   Virginal shy lights,
> Wrought of the leaves to allure to the whisper of vows . . .
> Of the dim sweet woods, of the dim dark woods . . .
> Ye held me fast in your heart and I hold you fast in mine . . .
> As the marsh-hen secretly builds on the watery sod,
> Behold I will build me a nest on the greatness of God.

Theory or no theory, Lanier's sport with musical words and his excited pleasure in sound at the expense of ideas, helped to fix him in strange eccentricities of expression. His investigation of sound patterns (with his rationalization of his discoveries at the end of his life in *The Science of English Verse*) are really the only instances of his sustained thought; neither his literary criticism nor his articles show cerebration concerning the problems of literature or life. From the moment when we see him in his youth pluck a reed from the river bank to imitate, as on his flute, the Georgia robins, or watch him tossed along the emotional afflatus of war, Lanier's approach to life was through feeling. Hence the almost comic excesses of his poetic diction and of his imagery are less ascribable to any firm intellectual creed that "Music is Love in search of a word," than to an innate sentimentalism, of which this vague definition is an apt illustration.

The diction of Lanier's poems is hardly more fervid than that of his letters or of his conversation or his own emotional life. In long stretches, few writers in prose or poetry pall more than Sidney Lanier: the simple reason is his mistiness, created by his unrestrained use of language, his abstractions, his bookish allusions, his repetitions of favorite adjectives, such as "sweet," his grotesque hyphenated words, his disorder of ideas, his wordiness, his archaisms, and his excess light, flame, and color. His golden images, moreover, dim more than single lines or metaphors—they obscure also his meaning, his utterances concerning his epoch. He had become a student of the new science, but his prognosis of its place in the world is far from distinct. On one occasion he declares that science is a sham that "cannot prove proof is." Yet in his vision in his "Psalm of the West" of an expanding America, it is a shaping force. This same cloudiness exists in his denunciations of the "terrible towns," the "hell-colored smoke of the factories." Although appalled at the consequences of the industrial revolution, he conceded the importance of commerce, and his sectionalism altered into a semimaterialistic nationalism not unlike Whitman's.

What remains, we ask ourselves, in this overwrought, overelaborate poetry? Merely the Georgia landscapes of a local colorist? For few poets are more strongly regional than Lanier. The delicate medallion-like imagery of

> blooms and leaves
> lichens on stones and moss on eaves,

or the harmonic waves of fast-beating, ecstatic verse? What remains is his matchless pattern of sound. This fact is even more arresting than the sudden, beautiful simplicity in his dialect poems or in the "Revenge of Hamish," one of the best modern ballads. For since his natural sense of melody was superb, it was inevitable that the best products of Lanier's genius should be connected with the subtle music of verse. When we yield uncritically to his throbbing ecstasy, in the rose-leaf passage in the "Symphony," or in that on the oaks in "The Marshes of Glynn," or in that on the shimmering corn, we feel a power transcending both his theories and his practice.

Fortunately, our two poets of sound, Poe and Lanier, were never able to fulfill their own elaborate aesthetic principles; in each, the inner poet was greater than the outward theorizer. Lanier, like Poe, to whom as an experimenter he was closer than he realized, carries us along in the rush of n emotion which cannot be translated into exact meanings, fulfilling the ictum of Coleridge that poetry gives the greatest pleasure when only generally and not perfectly understood. Such power Lanier's poetry sometimes displays in spite of its opaqueness of thought or eccentricity of technique. All nature is tense at the moment of sunrise; or we are lost in the music of he soaring violins; the reality of our emotion mocks the inadequacy of intellectual meaning; momentarily at least we are rapt in his "strenuous sweet whirlwind." This was the musician Lanier's great, almost involuntary achievement in poetry; and parallels for this "indefinitiveness" of sensation, this ommunication of the excitement of music to verse, we shall find only in such oets as Poe and Swinburne.

4

Meanwhile, in the North, Emily Dickinson was writing, garnering up in ecret an immortality which is now assuredly hers. Perhaps undesired and ertainly unattained in her lifetime, her fame as a breathless, perceptive poet and as an interpreter of the soul's relations with eternity has passed far beyond the applause of a cult into established acceptance; together, she and Walt Whitman (whom she probably never read) represent the farthest pioneerings of the nineteenth century American mind in the trackless regions of spirit, in so far as they are reflected in poetry. Emily Dickinson, with a terrible, beautiful intensity, expressed the most aspiring experience of the Puritan soul, sharp-reined in her by a new realism, and released in distilled, gnomic verse; her extraordinary seizure in art of the apexes of despair and ecstasy may well endure:

> At least to pray is left, is left
> Oh Jesus! in the air
> I know not which thy chamber is,—
> I'm knocking everywhere.

Reminding us of Christina Rossetti, of whom she was, except for five days and eight years, the exact contemporary, and of Elizabeth Barrett, without the fulfillment of love in marriage, she lived for fifty-six years on the quiet Amherst street her thrilling life as an adventuress in eternity—and as eternity's witty critic, too. Outwardly there is little to chronicle. To her austere lawyer-father, Edward Dickinson, the treasurer of Amherst College, she was bound by inviolable ties of duty and inarticulate affection. "You know," she wrote of him, "he never played." In the narrow yet superior society of the New England village, and in the cultivated, orthodox home life with her brother Austin and her sister Lavinia, her character took on its distinctive traits of devotion, self-reliance, and ceaseless scrutiny of her own mind. As in Hawthorne, ordinary New England life was in her marrow, but the beginning of some strange celestial apprenticeship is early hinted in a letter of 1853, written at the age of twenty-three: "I do not," she says simply, "go from home." About 1861–1862 she was definitely committed to her retirement from the world.

Small, like a wren, with eyes whose color was like the sherry left by the guest in the wineglass, so she describes herself; soft of voice, quick in the movement of body or mind; even then, as she tended her flowers or baked bread for her father, she was forging mysterious bonds. Events, still obscure in detail or meaning, accented her isolation and projected abroad clouds of misleading legend. Despite her normal girlhood at Mount Holyoke Female Seminary and Amherst Institute, despite her gaiety and her friendliness, we see her also through the eyes of the puzzled townspeople. The winged stories flew: she refused to address her own letters; she listened to music downstairs from the "polar privacy" of her own room; or she flitted on summer evenings always in white, through her garden, like a moth. She became indeed, in vulgar speech, a village character. For her own good reasons Emily Dickinson's habits of withdrawal from society increased; thus Thomas Wentworth Higginson, editor and literary critic, who divined her greatness without understanding it or interpreting it to the world, remarked: "I saw her but twice face to face, and brought away the impression of something as unique and remote as Undine or Mignon or Thekla." So lovely, so intensely alive, what secret vows were hers, and why?

The minutiae of her story must remain conjectural; we can only speculate with fluctuating assurance on her spiritual experience, recorded in emotional moments (the "esoteric sips of sacramental wine"), often on the backs of envelopes or brown paper bags or on scraps of newspapers or discarded bills. Though neither nun nor mystic, Emily Dickinson was, in many ways, of their identity. Yet her renunciation of life was reinforced by human love and anguish; hers were authentic sufferings, worthy of one who loved truth:

> I like a look of agony
> Because I know it's true.

Practically all that we can learn of her deep draught of actual experience, we must deduce from a brief autobiographical parable, written in her second letter to Higginson on April 25, 1862:

I went to school, but in your manner of the phrase had no education. When a little girl, I had a friend who taught me Immortality; but venturing too near, imself, he never returned. Soon after, my tutor died, and for several years my exicon was my only companion. Then I found one more, but he was not contented I be his scholar, so he left the land.

Several men played influential roles in her life, but two especially strengthned her links with eternity. One, a certain Benjamin F. Newton, a young awyer who had fed her deep-seated craving for study, died early, and conerred on her the privilege of sorrow. The other, an older, married man, the Reverend Charles Wadsworth, a minister second in power only to Henry Ward Beecher, inspired in her an attachment thwarted by his and her own high standards of conduct. About these centers of reality much of her poetry evolves. Yet a close correlation in her life of persons and events in her passionate lyrics is still dangerous: Emily Dickinson was a poet as well as a woman, and we must reckon both with her artistic detachment and with her dramatization of moods. Surely, her love poetry was not, like Emily Brontë's, without factual basis. Love, frustration, and death she tasted with all the eagerness of a sensitive spirit. She lived on, in her garden, in her chamber, more and more the denizen of a metaphysical domain of her own. This world she suffused until her death in 1886 with the light of a severe exaltation, but darkened it at times by her broodings concerning what she called the "underside of [God's] divinity." Her introspection, her "latter-day transcendentalism," belong to the long story of the gradual liberation from the old Puritan orthodoxy.

So cloistered, so fugitive a life, hints at Emily Dickinson's ignorance of the subversive events of her America, such as the fissure of the Civil War, science, or the amazing emergence of our literary pantheon. On one side of her nature she seems to symbolize New England's cultural isolation, its retreat into itself. Yet her lack of particular allusion is deceptive; in some ways she was a legitimate child of her time. The full enormity of war, like other grossnesses, she did not grasp; to her its baseness seemed, she said, "oblique." Yet she knew, if only from the bullet which struck down gallant young Frazer Stearns (son of the president of Amherst College), the grief of others; and its realities she transmuted into the imagery of her verse. "Sorrow," she wrote, "seems more general than it did, and not the estate of a few persons, since the war began." The claims of science, too, though muted in comparison with Lanier's rhetoric, find echoes in her verse. Among our men of letters she was aware of Poe, and of Hawthorne who, she said, "appals and entices." Puritanism, transcendentalism, and even the burgeoning Yankee humor of the times were fertile strata in which sprang up her strong and delicate flowers of thought.

For reasons still regrettable, perhaps her horror of a "frog-like" publicity, or her fear of commercializing her writing, she would never emulate her only "literary" friends, Helen Hunt Jackson or kind, editorial Higginson; she would not soil her pure, white banner of poetry in the world of publishers. "My barefoot rank," she said, "is better." Probably she realized that her conception of poetry was ahead of her time. Yet she loved those who had written openly for humanity; besides the Bible, Shakespeare, and Sir Thomas Browne she acknowledged Keats, and she ecstatically compared George Eliot to "glory." On the walls of her room hung portraits of this novelist, of Elizabeth Barrett, and of Carlyle. Among her American contemporaries, though specific references are elusive, she was most in debt to Emerson, for staccato forms and also for the bright courage of her tense speech.

It would be helpful to know how faithfully Emily Dickinson connec Emerson's techniques; or how much of her frugal verse economy she derived from her innate distaste for what he called the "jingling serenader's art." Presumably she owes little to others, even to him. Her earliest rhymes show a robust condensation, and in every poem her mannerisms declare the instinctive independence of her craft, itself a protest against such verbosity as Lanier's. Of some eight hundred poems and of the 650 later published in *Bolts of Melody* (1945), relatively few number in length more than a dozen lines. Her favorite measure is reminiscent of the hymn meters with which she had been familiar since childhood, with beautiful variations of three-stress, two-stress, and even one-stress lines. She does not disdain conventional devices—her alliteration and her assonance are effective—but these tricks are likely to take a characteristically impish turn, as in her blithe use of liquids in the conclusion of her eight-line stanza on evening:

> Lightly stepped a yellow star
> To its lofty place,
> Loosed the Moon her silver hat
> From her lustral face.
> All of evening softly lit
> As an astral hall—
> "Father," I observed to Heaven
> "You are punctual."

For the sake of such conciseness, monosyllabic and dissyllabic words predominate, frequently those of the homespun New England life, of which she was so inseparable a part: broom and bonnet; rut, stile, and overcoat. One fancies a cause and effect between her ever more emphatic solitude, with its consequent silences, and her laconic diction in verse; nothing, *nothing* should be communicated save the kernel of the thought—no rind, no glossy surface. Therefore, like other American writers deprived of the smooth ing, standardizing influence of the "circle" or of the stings of critical friends, she preserved the stiff, rude edges of her thought; she developed a technique indisputably her own, however much it has puzzled other writers, such as Higginson, or even the determined semiscientific, modern student of poetry. She omitted conjunctions; used half- and quarter-rhymes; played with the subjunctive mood or with legal phrases; dispensed with agreements of nouns and verbs; cut and clipped her sentences. Thus she was often cryptic—"half-idiotic," says one impatient, obtuse critic—and she was always on the wing. Speed was this Atalanta's joy, nor would she stop for a golden apple. Such fleetness she attained partly by her intense, rapid methods of composition; she strove to capture the telegraphic thought. Moreover, in her half-rhymes, her irregularities of speech and rhythm, her spasmodic quality, she mirrored the incongruities and frustrations of human experience; the awkwardness in her poetry became a metaphor of life itself.

## 5

Yet the factor of conscious plan in the poetry of Emily Dickinson is almost negligible. For us a penalty of her solitude is her silence concerning the theories underlying her art. There survive, of course, no prefaces, nor any synthesis of her poetic principles, but only here and there flash illuminating implications, in a letter, in hints within the poetry itself. For to this shy, intellectual, spiritually wayward woman her craftsmanship seems to have been a natural glove for her thought. Yet principles she had; in her reflections on the analogies of poetry to life she grappled with age-old problems. A primary one was the relation of the concrete to the abstract; that is, the connection between her New England world, with its pattern of facts, and its divine prototype. Thus she had the philosopher's passion without his reconciling power for the thing seen and the thing unseen, for the biting contrast of appearance and fact.

Now of this conflict she is sternly conscious; this schism is everywhere in her poetry; the lace and surge of the wave; the mist and the Apennine; the film and the thought. She writes in this basic metaphor. Ever she sought an absolute, but rued the price of its momentary attainment:

> Perception of an
> Object costs
> Precise the Object's loss.

So Emily Dickinson's dualism, repudiating such a monism as animates the poetry of Whitman, permeated her life. She is intensely curious, on the one hand, concerning God, and on the other, concerning the daily newspaper (her character of recluse has been exaggerated). The dualism is evident, too, in her poetry, in such a metaphysical concept as

I died for beauty,

or in a realistic line on a snake:

A whip-lash
Unbraiding in the sun.

Thus, from one point of view, Emily Dickinson is a realist examining, as she says, each splinter in the groove of the brain; a witty piquant preceptress on all the common life about her, and also on its divine origins. She writes of the bee, the bobolink, the spider, the bat, the storm, noon, the sunset, or the preacher with his preposterous sermon on "breadth." In this role of commentator on things visible and invisible she aphorizes on God, human love, death, and also on mermaids and angleworms. In her poetry the sublime and the trivial jostle each other and evoke from her mingled reverence and satire, as in the response to her prayer for "content," that is, for a modest little heaven of her own:

A smile suffused Jehovah's face;
The cherubim withdrew;
Grave saints stole out to look at me,
And showed their dimples, too.

For the poem conveys her conviction, held momentarily, that a voice does not come out of silence. That God answers our prayers, is the certain "swindle."

This is, perhaps, enough; few readers demand more. To adopt her own metaphor, she does little sums of spiritual arithmetic; and her epigrammatic conclusions, sometimes somber or even Freudian as in her dream of the worm, are as memorable as Hawthorne's elaborate clinics in the moral impulse. His symbols too often wear the solemn splendor of his letter A in the heavens; hers shine with the frosty twinkle of the stars. She is a detached critic of men's hopes and fears; this is especially true of her poems on human problems. Yet, particularly in her poetry on nature, she cherishes a fairylike intimacy with plant and bird. No naturalist, still she knew them all and believed that these mute creatures expressed thoughts surpassing her own. At the same time she is enchantingly literal. The snow falls in the ruts like "alabaster wool"; the dog goes along on "feet of intermittent plush"; the bat wears his "small umbrella, quaintly halved"; the moon has a "chin of gold"; the grass "threads the dews all night, like pearls"; the bobolink is the "rowdy of the meadow." She startles with a phrase: the dead, in their alabaster chambers, rest "under rafter of satin and roof of stone." She personifies sharply, in contrast to Lanier's vague figures, Death who stops for her in his carriage; or she invents adverbs:

> Kingdoms like the orchard
> Flit russetly away.

In brief, poetry is her "playmate" with which she tries a thousand games of color, light, and sound. This Emily Dickinson should indeed suffice.

Yet, though perceptive, though alive with spiritual sustenance, this Emily Dickinson is a fragmentary, occasional poetess. The intensities of her despair and exultation suggest a wholeness of experience concealed by her reticence, by the disorder of undated poems, and by editings under such captions as "Love," "Life," "Nature," "Time and Eternity," "Our Little Kinsmen," "The Mob within the Heart," "The Single Hound." Among her tangential poems on nature, on homely incident, on the specters or fancies of her mind are lyrics which, if rearranged in the proper order, reveal her progress in a deepening spiritual life. The late poems in *Bolts of Melody* reveal the growth in Emily Dickinson of this universalizing tendency. Under the swift-running river of her poetry glides ever this deeper current of her being, rising to the surface in sparkles of light or flashes of brilliant intuition, ever submerged yet ever continuing through the recesses of her mind toward that ocean which she invokes so gaily: "Eternity, I'm coming, sir!" In brief, the real meaning of Emily Dickinson's poetry must reside in its inner record of an elevated human spirit suffering, battling, growing toward a victorious purgation. Such an integration of the poetry lifts it from the rank of brittle epigram into an organic unity. It is a kind of American *Vita Nuova*, a rival of *Sonnets from the Portuguese* or of other great verse sequences. She is more than a pretty aphorist; she is an interpreter of universal experience.

A firm exposition of Emily Dickinson's pilgrim's progress of the soul or of her modern cosmology is sadly hampered in several ways. First, the dating of many poems is dubious, the verses in the *Complete Poems* and *Bolts of Melody* demand regrouping, and, even if a chronological order could be established, we should still not be sure that the time of composition did not postdate materially the moment of emotion. This brings us again to the distressing difficulty, that of correlating specific poems with events and crises in the poet's life. For instance, the following familiar lines may—or may not—refer to the deaths of her friends Leonard Humphrey and Ben Newton:

> My life closed twice before its close;
> It yet remains to see
> If Immortality unveil
> A third event to me.

Or does a poem on domestic happiness reflect directly a period of hope prior to the frustration of her love affair? How can we be really assured concerning the identities of the "absentee" or the "dim companion"? Who will censure the poet carried away with the beauty of an idea itself? Certainly she may have magnified the little incident of love for poetry's sake, until the dream became the passionate reality in art. Wise is he who can translate the events in these lyrics into actual farewells, into particular conversations, into, for instance, a lantern held high in the garden by her father over the head of an unfavored suitor, into a parting at noon; who can here discover an individual as real as Robert Browning in the songs of Elizabeth Barrett! Finally, as part of this sublimation, there is her identification of human love with heavenly love:

> Given in marriage unto thee
> Oh, thou celestial host!
> Bride of the Father and the Son,
> Bride of the Holy Ghost!

> Other betrothal shall dissolve,
> Wedlock will decay;
> Only the keeper of the seal
> Conquers mortality.

Yet after homage has been paid to such cautions, most of us will still subscribe to the verdict of the scholar who says that the poems of Emily Dickinson

record with minute veracity the subtle changes in a woman's nature as she becomes conscious of her heart's unalterable commitment, passes through self-sustained illusion and painful disillusionment to an agony of frustration, and emerges at last, impregnably fortified on a new plane of being.

All these verses, in the end, revolve about one axis, and it is idle to speculate on which stage of Emily Dickinson's "Calvary" (a favorite word) produced particular poems. Each type of poem has its faults, from the too playful joy of her "illusion," through the gnawing neurotic agony of her "disillusionment," to the overintellectualized, somewhat jocose eternity of her "new plane of being." As the crown of her growth we must necessarily be most interested in this last phase. At this final point occurred an intense detachment and a crystallization of her memories and sorrows:

I measure every grief I meet
With analytic eyes.

On this plane of being she attains a kind of peace which, ever-simplifying, we may say atoned for her loss of earthly love. In the end she acquired a vivid sense of God, a being whose tantrums, futilities, and "duplicity" perpetually annoyed her—again her conflict between the abstract and the concrete—yet who remained a compensation for her frustration. Hers was an austere heaven, that in which the later poems center, as cold as Emerson's, less serene, too, but more lighthearted, and jocund with her wit. Here dwelt her Friend, her "burglar, banker, Father."

In this world, after her adjustments to earthly griefs, Emily Dickinson lived, finding in it—except for periods of depression, also recorded in her lyrics—a permanence lacking in her human relationships. Here she enjoyed an almost comfortable existence with the Father, the seraphim, and the stoled angels, that is, with her own high thoughts. Her sense of well-being has inspired an opinion, demanding qualification, that she was a mystic: we note her use of the word "light," and her certainty of God:

I never saw a moor,
I never saw the sea: . . .

I never spoke with God,
Nor visited Heaven;
Yet certain am I of the spot
As if the chart were given.

She had read the seventeenth century mystics; she mentions Henry Vaughan. Yet other traits of mysticism, namely the passivity, the transiency of the union with God, and the ineffability of the experience are less distinct, less discernible than the poet's own special quality of mind; in particular, her overwhelming sense of everyday fact, her levity, her resolute retention of her own individuality. The contrasts in her nature are amazing; where, in all the august company of mysticism do we find her like? Her conjunction of the cosmic and the comic? She is a saint in cap and bells. Frail and heroic spirit!

## 6

So bizarre was the current of Sidney Lanier's experimentation and so hidden was that of Emily Dickinson's, that after their deaths, in 1881 and 1886, no immediate consequences of their heresies were apparent. In fact, in 1947 we understand better that their restlessness was a symptom, not a rebellion. Few writers have specifically imitated either. They were simply our first cultivated poets to realize the incongruity between the Victorian canon for verse and the subjects of a new America and of a free spiritual life; between the orthodox technique and the crazy universe warped by war, the machine, and science. Lanier, despite his conservative doctrine of love, sensed the end of this old serene world, and Emily Dickinson privately renounced the time-worn securities. Both sought an expression which would more accurately reflect the *insecurity* which to thinking men and women was a bitter characteristic of America after the Civil War: to express this, they shared a common trait, an intense desire for experiment in verse. Lanier's culminated in his bold concept of the relations of music and poetry, a theory, despite its excess, of marked historical importance, which has exerted influence on modern scholars and probably upon modern poets. Emily Dickinson's experimentation, in debt to Emerson, and in love with the image, the word, and learning, anticipates the metaphysical strain in the verse of today. Taken together, their originality heralded afar off new themes, new forms; their verse (and Whitman's) formed the pronaos of modern poetry; as did the tales of Mark Twain the pronaos of modern prose.

# 56. MARK TWAIN

"I am persuaded," wrote Bernard Shaw to Mark Twain, "that the future historian of America will find your works as indispensable to him as a French historian finds the political tracts of Voltaire." By his own participation, no artist in our literature save Lincoln spans so broad a segment of typical American experience in the last century. Samuel Langhorne Clemens, known by the most famous pen name that an American ever bore, is a matchless annalist of his times. His life makes those of literary men in Boston and Concord and New York resemble (in Hawthorne's phrase) the flowering of talents that blossomed in too retired a shade. He knew the greatest river of the continent as Melville knew the high seas. He witnessed the epic of America, the westward tide at its full, with perception keener than the shallow appraisals of Bret Harte and Joaquin Miller. When in his *Autobiography* Mark Twain recalls after forty years the tragedy of an emigrant lad stabbed to death by a drunken comrade, and adds, "I saw the red life gush from his breast," we are reminded of Whitman's affirmation, "I was there"—with the difference that Walt's immediacy was imaginative, Mark's actual. In the activities of the external man as well as in character and temperament, Mark Twain was a representative American— from idyllic ante-bellum boyhood in a river town, to maturity enmeshed in the cross-purposes of the Gilded Age which he christened, and thence to the sunset years of mingled hope and disillusion in the Progressive Era. Despite his own avowal, "There is not a single human characteristic which can be safely labeled as 'American,'" Mark Twain is stamped unforgettably with the national brand. If he failed finally to reconcile reality and ideality, he absorbed and gave expression to both. That failure was not his; it belonged to his generation.

In old age his incurably Calvinist mind saw all the events of his life, from birth on November 30, 1835, in the village of Florida, Missouri, as a chain of causation forged by some power outside his will. Like his Connecticut Yankee he was led to reflect upon heredity, "a procession of ancestors that stretches back a billion years to the Adam-clam or grasshopper or monkey from whom our race has been so tediously and ostentatiously and unprofitably developed."

His father, an austere restless Virginian, bequeathed the family a vain hope of fortune from "the Tennessee lands," like Squire Hawkins in *The Gilded Age*; he also gave his son an object lesson in failure like the example set by the father of a genius whom Mark the Baconian once rose to challenge, Shakespeare of Stratford. The wife and mother, Jane Lampton Clemens, of Kentucky pioneer stock, sought by her strong Presbyterianism to balance her husband's village-lawyer agnosticism; their famous son inherited the self-tormenting conscience with the latter's will to disbelieve. As for derivations more remote, Twain the romantic relished his maternal tie with the Earls of Durham through "the American claimant," while Twain the democrat reserved his sole ancestral pride for a Regicide judge, who "did what he could toward reducing the list of crowned shams of his day."

In 1839 the Clemenses moved to Hannibal, on the west bank of the Mississippi, and set the conditions of boyhood and youth from which flowed the wellspring of Mark Twain's clearest inspiration. Thanks to *Tom Sawyer* and *Huckleberry Finn,* its aspect in the forties has become the property of millions: the wharf giving upon the turbid waters where rafts and broadhorns, fast packets and gay showboats passed endlessly, the plank sidewalks where Tom and Becky trudged to school, the tanyard where Huck's drunken father slept among the hogs, the steep slope of Cardiff (really Holliday's) Hill, the surrounding woods of oak and hickory and sumach, and a few miles downstream the cave where Injun Joe met death. Hannibal lay in its halcyon summer between frontier days and the convulsions of the Civil War, the latter forecast in the mobbing of an occasional abolitionist and the tracking down of runaway slaves. On the whole, happiness outweighed grief; prized in retrospect was the large freedom of a boy's life, with the swimming hole and woods full of game, jolly playmates banded against a world of adult supremacy, and dinner tables groaning with prodigal hospitality. "It was a heavenly place for a boy," Hannibal's first citizen remembered.

Sam Clemens' schooling ended early, when he was about twelve. After his father's death the lad was apprenticed to a printer's shop—"the poor boy's college," Lincoln called it. Lack of formal education doubtless gave the later Mark Twain an eagerness to have his genius certified by convention, and also led him occasionally to discover shopworn ideas with a thrill impossible to sophisticates; but it also delivered him from those cultural stereotypes into which the genius of New England, for example, for generations had been poured. Fatalist that he was, Twain liked to date his career from certain accidents. The first of them came one day on the streets of Hannibal, when the young printer picked up a stray leaf from a book about Joan of Arc, and for the first time saw magic in the printed word. Henceforth the itch of scribbling was strong upon him. His earliest known appearance in print, a crudely humorous sketch called "The Dandy Frightening the Squatter," appeared in the Boston *Carpet Bag* of May 1, 1852. He left Hannibal the next year, wandering on to New York and Philadelphia, and began to send home-town papers the first of those facetious travel pieces which he wrote sporadi-cally for the next half-century. In 1857, after tarrying awhile in Cincinnati, he set out for New Orleans with a notion of shipping for the Amazon. But, lacking funds, he became a steamboat pilot under the tutelage of Horace Bixby. That veteran gradually taught him the ever changing aspects of the Mississippi, by sun and starlight, at low water and in flood.

For two years after that Clemens turned his wheel atop the texas deck, drawing a licensed pilot's high wages, while he gained postgraduate schooling in human nature. Oft quoted is his later assertion: "When I find a well-drawn character in fiction or biography I generally take a warm personal interest in him, for the reason that I have known him before—met him on the river." A born worrier, he felt the responsibility that lay within a pilot's hands as he steered past narrows and snags and sand bars, or for the sake of prestige raced his rivals until the boiler nearly burst under its head of steam. His old master, many years later, stated that Clemens "knew the river like a book, but he lacked confidence." One may speculate whether a very human incertitude, deep in his being, did not chime with a classic type of humor in his constant self-portrayal as the man who gets slapped: the bumptious yet timid cub of *Life on the Mississippi*; the fear-bedeviled soldier of "The Campaign That Failed"; the tenderfoot of *Roughing It,* setting forest fires and just missing wealth through sheer stupidity; or the harassed traveler losing his tickets, browbeaten by porters and shopkeepers, falling foul of the authorities, who appears in a long sequence from the juvenile Snodgrass letters to *A Tramp Abroad*.

2

Clemens' career on the river ended in the spring of 1861 with the outbreak of hostilities. With brief enthusiasm he joined a Confederate militia band, savoring the boyish conspiracy of war in its early stages. In the lack of dis-cipline the band soon broke up; and Sam, with qualms about fighting for slavery, yielded to persuasion from his Unionist brother Orion, lately ap-pointed Secretary of the Territory of Nevada. In July, 1861, the two set out for the West. The outlines of the story told in *Roughing It* are true enough: the nineteen-day trip across the plains and Rockies to Carson City; an attack of mining fever that left Sam none the richer; his acceptance of a job on the Virginia City *Enterprise*; a journalist's view of San Francisco in flush times; and a newspaper-sponsored voyage to the Sandwich Islands. His dream of becoming a millionaire by a stroke of fortune never forsook him; lingering in his blood, the bonanza fever made him a lifelong victim of gold bricks, quick-profit schemes, and dazzling inventions. But his return to journalistic humor—the vein he had worked in his late teens and early twenties, imitative of such professional humorists as Seba Smith, J. J. Hooper, and B. P. Shillaber, in whose productions every newspaper office abounded—proved to be his really lucky strike. In 1863 the Missourian of twenty-eight met Artemus Ward on the latter's Western lecture tour, and watched a master storyteller in action: the adroit timing, change of pace, and deadpan obliviousness to the point of one's own wit. Twain's "How to Tell a Story" (1895) acknowledges these profitable lessons.

It was Ward who encouraged him to seek a wider audience than the red-shirted miners of Washoe and nabobs of the Golden Gate. The first fruit of this encouragement to appear in the East—a piece of jocular sadism against the small fry who made day and night hideous at resort hotels, "Those Blasted Children"—was printed early in 1864 by the New York *Mercury*. Meanwhile in 1863 Clemens had begun to imitate current funny men like Ward, Orpheus C. Kerr, and Josh Billings, by selecting a pen name, the river-boat man's cry for two fathoms, "Mark Twain." Clemens stoutly maintained he appropriated it soon after an eccentric pilot-journalist of New Orleans, Captain Isaiah Sellers, relinquished it by death. No contribution in the New Orleans press, however, has ever been found under that name; also, Sellers' death occurred a year after Clemens adopted this pseudonym. Whether original or borrowed, the name served an important purpose. It created an alter ego, a public character, which Clemens could foster through the years while doffing it in private as he pleased. It set definable limits to his role of being what the age called a "phunny phellow." A speculative critic might guess that his abiding interest in transposed identities, twins, and Siamese prodigies mirrored a dualism which self-observation would have shown running like a paradox through his nature: gullible and skeptical by turns; realistic and sentimental, a satirist who gave hostages to the established order, a frontiers-man who bowed his neck obediently to Victorian mores, and an idealist who loved the trappings of pomp and wealth. Incessantly he contradicted himself on a variety of subjects. His was not a single-track mind, but a whole switch-yard. The creation of two more or less separate identities—Clemens the sensitive and perceptive friend, Mark Twain the robust and astringent humorist—springing from the same trunk of personality, helped to make him like those ligatured twins in *Pudd'nhead Wilson,* Luigi and Angelo, "a human philopena."

Under the name of Mark Twain the wild-haired Southwesterner began to contribute to the press yarns swapped about the legislative halls of Carson

City, the bars and billiard parlors of San Francisco, and the hot stoves of miners on Jackass Hill. From these last, about February, 1865, he first heard the old folk tale of the Jumping Frog. To the anecdote he added the salt of human values which the genre usually lacked, in garrulous Simon Wheeler and simple Jim Smiley the Frog's owner. Published in the *Saturday Press* of New York, November 18, 1865, it was swiftly broadcast. The author grumbled in a letter home about the irony of riding high on "a villanous backwoods sketch," but already he was tasting that sense of popularity which soon came to be his elixir of life. In October, 1866, back from Honolulu and planted on a San Francisco lecture platform, he first encountered another powerful stimulant, the instant response. Early in 1867, at Cooper Union in New York, he won his eastern spurs, and began to be hailed as rightful heir to Artemus Ward, lately dead of tuberculosis in England. Soon, as his friend William Dean Howells phrased it, Twain learned "all the stops of that simple instrument, man." The lecturer's effect upon the writer was great. Increasingly Twain came to write by ear, testing his books by reading aloud, while making the expanded anecdote or incident the unit of his literary composition. Sometimes, of course, without benefit of his infectious personal charm, that mane of fiery red hair and hawklike nose, the gestures of an artist's hands, and the inflections of that irresistible drawl, a reader of cold print missed qualities which on the platform redeemed humor of a perishable sort.

"When I began to lecture, and in my earlier writings, my sole idea was to make comic capital out of everything I saw and heard," he told the biographer Archibald Henderson. After his first volume, of chiefly Western sketches, named *The Celebrated Jumping Frog* (1867), he reinforced this reputation by distilling a humorous travelogue out of the letters sent back to the *Alta California* from his cruise to the Mediterranean and Holy Land on the *Quaker City* in 1867. Comic capital was readily furnished by the flood of tourists, affluent merchants and their wives, war profiteers, former army officers on holiday, and clergymen for whom Jerusalem justified the junket, which swept over the Old World after Appomattox. Knowing themselves to be innocents, they faced down their provincialism by brag and cockalorum, and haggling over prices. Mark Twain gladly joined them, joking his way among the shrines and taboos of antiquity, comparing Como unfavorably with Tahoe, bathing in the Jordan, finding any foreign tongue incredibly funny, and pitying ignorance, superstition, and lack of modern conveniences. *The Innocents Abroad* (1869) helped to belittle our romantic allegiance to Europe, feeding our emergent nationalism. Instantly a best seller, it delighted those Americans in whom "the sense of Newport" (as Henry James later called it) had never been deeply engrafted. A slender minority like James

himself felt that Mark Twain amused only primitive persons, was the Philistines' laureate. Years later, in 1889, in a letter to Andrew Lang, Twain would
glory in this charge:

Indeed I have been misjudged, from the first. I have never tried in even one
single instance, to help cultivate the cultivated classes. I was not equipped for it,
either by native gifts or training. And I never had any ambition in that direction,
but always hunted for bigger game—the masses. I have seldom deliberately tried
to instruct them, but have done my best to entertain them. . . . Yes, you see, I
have always catered for the Belly and the Members.

3

Yet this is not the whole story. From an early date, Mark Twain, the
playboy of the Western world, had begun to feel the aspirations of an artist,
to crave deeper approval than had come to the cracker-box humorist like Sam
Slick and Jack Downing. In Honolulu in 1866 the diplomat Anson Burlingame gave him advice by which the aged Twain avowed he had lived "for
forty years": "Seek your comradeships among your superiors in intellect and
character; always *climb*." On the *Quaker City* voyage the Missourian fell
under the refining spell of "Mother" Fairbanks, wife of a prosperous Ohio
publisher, and tore up those travel letters which she thought crude. Always
enjoying petticoat dominion, he eagerly sought her approval of the revised
*Innocents* and was enchanted when she pronounced it "authentic." "A name
I have coveted so long—and secured at last!" he exclaimed. "*I* don't care anything about being humorous, or poetical, or eloquent, or anything of that
kind—the end and aim of my ambition is to be authentic—is to be considered
authentic." In a similar thirst for higher recognition he told Howells, reviewer
of *Innocents* in the *Atlantic*: "When I read that review of yours, I felt like the
woman who was so glad her baby had come white." Nevertheless, as Twain
found to his intermittent chagrin, his reputation throughout life kept returning to that of a "phunny phellow," turning cartwheels to captivate the ground-
lings—until at length he built up the defensive attitude expressed to Lang. At
*Atlantic* dinners, the author of "Old Times on the Mississippi" and *Tom
Sawyer* found himself seated below the salt, ranked by Longfellow and Lowell
and Whittier, as well as by such adopted sons of Boston as Howells and
Aldrich. Despite the new decorum of his life and the growing richness of his
art, the wild man from the West was expected, some time, somehow, to disgrace himself. And, by the meridian of Boston, he eventually did so, when at
the celebrated Whittier birthday dinner on December 17, 1877, he made his
speech of innocent gaiety about three drunks in the high Sierras who per-

sonated Emerson, Longfellow, and Holmes. The diners were shocked, refusing their laughter while he stood solitary (as Howells said) "with his joke dead on his hands." The next day or so, when Twain's haunting distrust of himself and his own taste had induced a penitential hangover, he sent apologies, writing characteristically: "Ah, well, I am a great and sublime fool. But then I am God's fool, and all his works must be contemplated with respect." He then begged Howells to exclude him from the *Atlantic* for a while, in the interest of readers' good will. The gravity with which both the saints and the sinner regarded this incident reveals the massiveness of the genteel tradition in New England and the probationary status upon which Mark was kept for so many years.

Between the publication of the *Innocents* and this indiscretion, Clemens had taken a wife whose remolding influence has been the subject of much debate. The story of their courtship is familiar: his first sight of her delicate face in a miniature carried by her brother on the *Quaker City* cruise; Twain's meeting with the original, Olivia Langdon, ten years his junior, a semi-invalid who had turned to faith healing; their two years' betrothal while her father, the richest businessman in Elmira, and her kin were slowly won over; and their wedding early in 1870, with Clemens the bridegroom trying unsuccessfully to establish himself as a solid newspaper editor in Buffalo, but moving to Hartford in 1871 to resume a free-lance life. His veneration of women and their purity was almost fanatical. "I wouldn't have a girl that *I* was worthy of," he wrote "Mother" Fairbanks before his engagement. "*She* wouldn't do."

About the sexual make-up of Mark Twain speculation has been indulged since the Freudian era. In that famous sophomoric sketch *1601,* written in mid-career to amuse his clerical friend Joe Twichell, he had Sir Walter Raleigh describe "a people in ye uttermost parts of America, y$^t$ copulate not until they be five-&-thirty yeeres of age." This, it happens, was the age when Clemens married a semi-invalid wife, as if some inadequacy in himself, some low sexual vitality, made such a woman his fitting mate. And yet respecting their physical love for each other and the fruitfulness of their union, with its four children, no doubt can be raised. What illicit experience might have come to a boy growing up in the accessible world of slavery, and passing his green manhood upon river boats and in bonanza towns, can only be guessed at. In later years, respecting the idealized Hannibal of his boyhood, he went so far as to deny the existence of sexual irregularities; and by confining his two great novels about Hannibal to adolescence he was able in a manner to carry his point. Obviously certain taboos about sex, personal as well as conventional, appear in his writings from beginning to end. Unlike his friend Howells, he attempted no probings of desire, no analysis of the chemical affinity between man and woman beyond the calf love of Tom and

Becky and the implausible treatment of Laura the siren of *The Gilded Age.* Only under the protective shield of miscegenation, in the person of the warm-blooded Negress Roxana in *Pudd'nhead Wilson,* does he venture even to approach passion which overleaps the bounds of society. Joan of Arc, a virgin of exquisite purity, plainly is the heroine after his inmost heart. A certain fear of sex, like the shrinking of primitive races and some adolescents from carnality as if it meant degradation of the body, seems to lie at the root of Mark Twain's nature. The exceptions of his occasional bawdry—in *1601* and a few unprinted works like his speech before the Stomach Club in Paris and his manuscript "Letters from the Earth"—but prove the rule, in ridiculing the body and its ways sufficiently to suit the most fanatic Puritan.

Yet Twain was in no sense a misogynist. He loved the company of women, of the refined women whose tastes and restraints fitted his own pre-suppositions about them. His understanding of the feminine mind has left no more delightful evidence than "Eve's Diary," written in 1905 shortly after Olivia's death, so that Adam's final bereavement becomes the epitaph of his own loss: "Wherever she was, *there* was Eden." In summary, Mark Twain's personal make-up and the conventions of gentility surrounding the kind of success he aspired to, joined to suppress the recognition of sex as a key motive in human actions—leaving woman not an object of desire but of reverential chivalry.

The effect of his wife upon Twain the artist has provoked latter-day discussion. One school of thought holds that Clemens was forced, first by his mother and then by his wife, to "make good," i.e., to make money and be respectable. Moreover, thanks to the censorship of his wife, they say, he became not the New World Rabelais but a frustrated genius incapable of calling his soul or vocabulary his own. It is clear, however, that proof of Livy's "humiliating" dominion rests largely upon Twain's letters to Howells: that pair of devoted husbands married to invalids who made a gallant little joke over being henpecked. The notion that women exercised a gentle tyranny over their menfolk, for the latter's good, always appealed to Mark Twain, schooled in Western theories that man was coarser clay and woman a rare and special being (as among the Washoe miners in *Roughing It,* who chipped in $2,500 in gold as a gift at the miraculous sight of a live woman). All his life he encouraged women to reform him, improve his taste and manners. His three little daughters who shared in the family rite known as "dusting off Papa," and the "angel-fish" of adolescent girls in his Bermudian Indian summer, were among the youngest of the sex whose devoted slave he rejoiced to be. It was a kind of game in the feudal tradition, which he adored. But to assume therefore that Twain the genius was henpecked, baffled, unmanned by women in general and Livy in particular is to convert a jest into a cry of anguish.

About the converse influence of husband upon wife something deserves to be said. For Twain's vitality rescued her from abysses of timorous living, his banter relaxed her serious disposition, and his religious skepticism destroyed her Christian faith.

As for the specific question of censorship, we know that Twain liked to read aloud *en famille* the results of his daily composition, usually meeting the approval he craved, sometimes encountering a chill disfavor to which he was equally sensitive. He was a poor self-critic and knew it. He plunged into writing without much plan or foresight. Livy's judgment in matters of simple good taste and in pruning wordiness and irrelevance was clearly superior to his own in the heat of incubation. A careful examination of his manuscripts shows that Mrs. Clemens, like that other long-standing adviser William Dean Howells, objected to certain vivid words and phrases— "wallow," "bowels," "spit," "rotten," and realistic allusions to stenches and putrefaction which always tempted Mark Twain, so that he grumbled about her "steadily weak-ening the English tongue"—but that in mild profanities (like Huck Finn's "comb me all to hell") and in rare inclinations toward the risqué (such as the farce of "The Royal Nonesuch") the author on second thought was his own most attentive censor. He was not above playing an occasional hazard with his critics to see how far he could skate on thin ice; then doubled on his own track back to safety. Just as he dreamed of the unabashed nakedness of a boy's freedom on a raft floating down the Mississippi, now and again he yearned for the lusty old ways of medieval speech, "full of unconscious coarsenesses and innocent indecencies," "good old questionable stories," as the Connecticut Yankee says. But quickly he reminded himself, as he observes in *A Tramp Abroad,* that the license of the printed word had been "sharply curtailed within the past eighty or ninety years." To this curb in the main he gave unstinting consent.

4

Up to the time of his anchorage in Hartford in 1871, the most important facts about Mark Twain are the things that happened to him, shaping his development as an artist and filling the granaries of memory. After that date the chief milestones are the books he wrote out of that accumulation. His maturity and self-assurance can be gauged, growing from book to book through the next two decades, as he lectured at home and abroad, met the captains of literature and politics and finance, read widely if desultorily, and perfected his early journalistic manner until it became one of the great styles of American letters—easy, incisive, sensitive to nuances of dialect, rich in the resources of comedy, satire, irony, and corrosive anger.

One group, of secondary importance, consists of his travel books. Between *The Innocents Abroad* (1869) and *Roughing It* (1872) he learned, under emancipation from newspaper reporting, to take greater liberties with fact for art's sake. Both books owe such structure as they have to a rough chronology. Upon this thread Mark Twain the raconteur strings one story after another. The latter volume offers us almost all the classic types which Americans in general, frontiersmen in particular, had long since favored: the tall tale, the melodramatic shocker, the yarn of pointless garrulity, malapropian humor, the canard of impossible coincidence, the chain of free association that wanders farther and farther from its announced subject; the comedy of man in his cups, the animal fable, and the delusions of a lunatic. Paradox, surprise, and understatement often heighten his effects. Anecdote continues to be the fiber of those later travel books, which show more fluency in repeating the essential pattern, but grow in world-weariness after the early gusto of the Innocents and the Argonauts. They include *A Tramp Abroad* (1880), with more travesty of European languages, guide books, and art criticism, and *Following the Equator* (1897), which reports Twain's lecture tour in Australia and India. Inevitable become his burlesques of sentimental poetry, parodies of romantic situations, yarns picked up in new places or recollected from the limbo of years. In this last book, however, flippancy at the expense of peoples and customs vanishes when the traveler reaches the threshold of Asia, as if the ancient disillusioned torpor of that continent had stricken the satirist dumb. These travelogues do not show Twain's gifts to greatest advantage. Flashes of notable writing occur, but intrinsically they are the potboilers of a master improviser.

The earliest novel he attempted was *The Gilded Age,* in collaboration with Charles Dudley Warner, published late in 1873, just as the panic was ringing down the curtain upon the worst excesses of that age. It harks back to their common knowledge of Missouri, where Warner had been a surveyor, and to Twain's passing observation of Washington in the winter of 1867–1868, when after return from the Holy Land he had served briefly and unhappily as private secretary to pompous Senator William Stewart of Nevada and more successfully had begun to write humorous commentaries on the news (anticipative of the late Will Rogers) for the *Tribune* and the *Herald* of New York. This phase left him with an abiding scorn for politicians, their intelligence and honesty. ("Fleas can be taught nearly anything that a Congressman can," is as characteristic as the remark that we have "no distinctly native American criminal class except Congress.") Beside the bungling amateurs of Carson City, these were graduates in graft, scrambling for the spoils of what a later critic termed the Great Barbecue. This same spectacle of post-bellum Washington which sickened fastidious Henry Adams and led even Whitman th optimist to pen the darker pages of *Democratic Vistas,* gave Mark Twain his first shining target for satire.

Warner supplied conventional plot elements of romance, gentility, pluck and luck, harmonized with the theme of material success, which the novel debunks at one level but praises fulsomely at another, when it is sanctioned by what passes among the majority as honesty. Twain himself was always dazzled by the romance of fortune, especially if it followed the ascent from rags to riches, as he shows in a story like "The £1,000,000 Bank Note" (1893). Yet he was aware of the ironies and unhappiness springing from the root of all evil, as revealed in "The $30,000 Bequest" (1904) and most superbly in "The Man That Corrupted Hadleyburg" (1899). In *The Gilded Age* the authors' wavering purpose resembles a mixture of Jonathan Swift and Horatio Alger. Satiric punches are pulled by the constant impulse to strike out in all directions but follow through in none. The vulgarity of a chromo civilization and the urge to keep up with the Joneses mingle with churchly hypocrisy, pork-barrel politics, high tariff, oratorical buncombe, abuse of the franking privilege, bribery, personal immorality in high places, profiteers of "shoddy," and the wider degradation of the democratic dogma.

The Gilded Age is clearly a world of optimistic illusion, proudly putting its best foot forward though the other limp behind in a shabby mud-bespattered boot. In the backwoods, stagecoaches with horns blowing enter and leave town at a furious clip, but once out of sight "drag along stupidly enough"—even as steamboats burn fat pine to make an impressive smoke when they near port. Credit is the basis of society; a typical parvenu boasts: "I wasn't worth a cent a year ago, and now I owe two millions of dollars." Most engaging specimen of this psychology is Colonel Sellers, a New World Micawber, who deals in imaginary millions while he and the family dine off turnips and cold water (man's best diet, he loftily assures them), and warm themselves at a stove through whose isinglass door flickers the illusory glow of a candle. Drawn from Twain's Uncle James Lampton, the Colonel is an epitome of the American dream that remains a mirage—impulsive, generous, hospitable, scheming to enrich not only himself but relatives and friends, and incidentally benefit all humankind, a colossal failure who basks forever in the rushlight of the success cult. Not dishonest by nature, in the heady milieu of Washington he begins to apologize for bribery ("a harsh term"), while hitching his wagon to the baleful star of Senator Dilworthy, drawn from the lineaments of Kansas' notorious Pomeroy. In certain passages Mark Twain's irony is whetted to a cutting edge, but the book's total effect is far from mordant. In many ways both authors were children of the Gilded Age, with hands too unsteady to strike a mortal blow of parricide.

Like everybody else Twain grew fond of Colonel Sellers and tried to resuscitate him. The modest laurels of a dramatic version of *The Gilded Age,* produced in 1874, led Twain and Howells to attempt in 1883 an hilarious sequel which, however, the stage Sellers of the earlier script, John T. Raymond, declined to play because that character had been exaggerated to the brink of lunacy. The plot, as embalmed in Twain's novel, *The American Claimant* (1892), justifies the actor's verdict. It is one of the humorist's most strained and least successful efforts.

### 5

Three years after *The Gilded Age* Twain published *Tom Sawyer,* the first of three great books about the Mississippi River of his youth. Beyond question, *Huckleberry Finn* (1885), *Life on the Mississippi* (1883), and *Tom Sawyer* (1876) are, in that order, his finest works. The reasons for their superiority are not far to seek. In plotting a book his structural sense was always weak; intoxicated by a hunch, he seldom saw far ahead, and too many of his stories peter out from the author's fatigue or surfeit. His wayward technique, as Howells recognized, came close to free association:

So far as I know, Mr. Clemens is the first writer to use in extended writing the fashion we all use in thinking, and to set down the thing that comes into his mind without fear or favor of the thing that went before or the thing that may be about to follow.

This method served him best after he had conjured up characters from long ago, who on coming to life wrote the narrative for him, passing from incident to incident with a grace their creator could never achieve in manipulating an artificial plot. In travel books and other autobiography written under the heat of recent experience, Mark Twain seemingly put in everything, mixing the trivial, inane, and farcical with his best-grade ore. But in the remembrance of things past, time had dissolved the alloy, leaving only gold. The nostalgia for a youth's paradise "over the hills and far away," for the fast-vanishing freedom of the West, appealed deeply to the age of boyhood sentiment enriched by Longfellow and Whittier. It also led to Mark Twain's strength; namely, the world of the senses and physical action. What he felt was always better expressed than what he had thought or speculated about. A boy's world freed him from those economic and political perplexities, adult dilemmas and introspections, where in rages and knotty casuistries he lost the sureness of touch that came to him through the report of his five senses, or through the championship of justice when the issue was as simple as the conflict between bullies and little folk.

In his heart Mark Twain must have realized that essentially he was a man of feeling, too sensitive to serve merely as a comedian, too undisciplined to be the philosopher he sometimes fancied himself. His forte was to recapture the sheer joy of living, when to be young was very heaven. A great river flowing through the wilderness set the stage for a boy's own dream of self-sufficience, of being a new Robinson Crusoe on Jackson's Island. In the background moved the pageantry of life, colored by humor, make-believe, and pure melodrama; but the complexity of the machine age and the city lay far, far away.

Mark Twain did not write his first books about this dream world, but let the haze of ideality collect about it, reserving it luckily for the high noon of his powers. Apparently the first hint of this motif comes in one of his New York letters to the *Alta California,* in the spring of 1867, in which he happens to recall the town drunkard of Hannibal, Jimmy Finn (destined to return as Huck's father), and also the Cadets of Temperance which Sam Clemens joined in order to march in funeral processions wearing their red scarf. This latter incident crops up in *Tom Sawyer.* Shortly afterward in *The Innocents,* among the pleasures and palaces of Europe, Twain interpolated other boyhood memories. In February, 1870, on receiving a letter from his "first, and oldest and dearest friend" Will Bowen, one of the flesh-and-blood components of Tom Sawyer, he sat down under the spell of the past and wrote a reply calling up some eight scenes which later appear in *Tom Sawyer* and *Huckleberry Finn.* Around this time he wrote a nameless sketch about a romantic lovesick swain who beyond question is Tom Sawyer. Designated as "Boy's Manuscript" by Twain's first editor, Albert Bigelow Paine, it was not published until 1942 in Bernard De Voto's *Mark Twain at Work.* Some four years later Twain made a fresh start, scrapping the earlier diary form in favor of third-person narrative. By midsummer, 1875, it was done, and off the press late in the next year (a few months after Clemens with his usual inconsistency had written Will Bowen a stern letter on August 31, 1876, bidding him dwell no more in the sentimental never-never land of boyhood, denying that the past holds anything "worth pickling for present or future use"). In this latter year Twain began *Huckleberry Finn* as a sequel, laid it aside during six fallow years, went back to the story after his visit to Hannibal in 1882, and published it a little over two years later.

The first reader of *Tom Sawyer,* William Dean Howells, disagreed with the author that he had written a book for adults only. He quickly persuaded Twain that it was primarily a story for boys, which grown-ups would enjoy by reading over their shoulder. Twain therefore withdrew a few gibes against Sunday schools and tamed several phrases that smacked of backwoods frankness. Nothing of importance, however, was altered, nor did Tom suffer transformation into the neat, obedient paragon which fiction for the young so long had held up to their resentful gaze. The first chapter announces that Tom "was not the Model Boy of the village. He knew the model boy very well though—and loathed him." The only resemblance Tom bears to the fictional creations of his time is in sensibility: he yields to self-pity, relishes every neighborhood tear shed over his supposed drowning, and almost faints upon hearing that even a villain like Injun Joe has been sealed in the cave. Otherwise, our hero is of very different mettle. He steals from and outwits Aunt Polly, luxuriates in idleness, misbehaves in church, huffs and brags, and like his friend Huck employs lying as protective coloration in a world of adult tyrants. Consequently, in some American homes the new book was read by grown-ups, then tucked away out of a boy's reach; its successor, *Huckleberry Finn,* soon after publication was ejected from the town library of Concord, Massachusetts (where, a generation before, John Brown had been welcomed by Thoreau and Emerson), because Huck elected to "go to Hell" rather than betray his friend, a runaway Negro.

In 1870 Thomas Bailey Aldrich had published his mild *Story of a Bad Boy*; twenty years later Twain's friend Howells would reminisce of adolescents not too bright or good for human nature's daily food in *A Boy's Town*; a little later came Stephen Crane's recollections of Whilomville and William Allen White's of Boyville. They helped maintain the tradition of realism. In extreme recoil from priggishness, a line beginning with *Peck's Bad Boy* in 1883 flaunted incorrigibility above all. It is possible to overstress the picaresque intent of *Tom Sawyer* in turning upside down the world of Peter Parley and the Rollo books, or its analogues with that still greater novel, Cervantes' *Don Quixote,* in which some critics find the model of Tom the dreamer and Huck his commonsense henchman. Mark Twain's verisimilitude should not be overlooked in this search for "purpose." He wrote about boys from having been one in the Gilded Age, in a river town before the war.

To a stranger in 1887 he described this book as "simply a hymn, put into prose form to give it a worldly air." These lads no more resemble Peck's Bad Boy than they do the model children of that improving story-teller, Jacob Abbott. Within a framework of superb dialogue and setting, of sensitive perceptions that turn now and again into poetry, against a background where flicker shadows of adult humanitarianism and irony, Tom and Huck grow visibly as we follow them. The pranks and make-believe of early chapters— whitewashing the fence, releasing a pinchbug in church, playing pirate in *Tom Sawyer,* and in its sequel the rout of a Sunday school picnic under the guise of attacking a desert caravan—are dimmed as the human values deepen and occasional moral issues appear. The Tom who takes Becky's punishment in school, and testifies for the innocent Muff Potter at risk of the murderer's

evenge, parallels the development of Huck from a happy-go-lucky gamin
o the epitome of generosity and loyalty. Mark Twain makes no account of
igid consistencies in time. His boys vary between the attitudes of nine-year-
lds and those of thirteen or fourteen, despite the fact that *Tom Sawyer*'s time
pan is one Missouri summer, and that of *Huckleberry Finn* a few more
nbroken months. Like the creator of perennial comic-strip characters, Twain
rrests or syncopates the march of time as he pleases. In the latter novel he also
gnores the fact that Nigger Jim could have escaped by swimming across to
he free soil of Illinois early in the book, and commits other sins against
iteralism which he would have ridiculed unmercifully in the pages of his
*ête noire* James Fenimore Cooper.

*Huckleberry Finn* is clearly the finer book, showing a more mature point
f view and exploring richer strata of human experience. A joy forever, it is
inquestionably one of the masterpieces of American and of world literature.
Here Twain returned to his first idea of having the chief actor tell the story,
with better results. Huck's speech is saltier than Tom's, his mind freer from
he claptrap of romance and sophistication. Huck is poised midway between
he town-bred Tom and that scion of woodlore and primitive superstition
Nigger Jim, toward whom Huck with his margin of superior worldliness
tands in somewhat the same relation that Tom stands toward Huck. When
Tom and Huck are together, our sympathy turns invariably toward the
atter. A homeless river rat, cheerful in his rags, suspicious of every attempt
o civilize him, Huck has none of the unimportant virtues and all the essen-
ial ones. The school of hard knocks has taught him skepticism, horse sense,
and a tenacious grasp on reality. But it has not toughened him into cynicism
or crime. Nature gave him a stanch and faithful heart, friendly to all underdogs and instantly hostile toward bullies and all shapes of overmastering
power. One critic has called him the type of the common folk, sample of
the run-of-the-mill democracy in America. Twain himself might have objected to the label, for he once declared "there are no common people, except
in the highest spheres of society." Huck always displays a frontier neighborli-
ness, even trying to provide a rescue for three murderers dying marooned on
a wrecked boat, because "there ain't no telling but I might come to be a
murderer myself, yet, and then how would I like it?" Money does not tempt
him to betray his friend Nigger Jim, though at times his conscience is
troubled by the voice of convention, preaching the sacredness of property—
even in the guise of flesh and blood—and he trembles on the brink of surrender. Nor can he resist sometimes the provocation offered by Jim's innocent
credulity, only to be cut to the quick when his friend bears with dignity the
discovery that his trustfulness has been made game of. Even as Huck surpasses Tom in qualities of courage and heart, so Nigger Jim excels even

Huck in fidelity and innate manliness, to emerge as the book's noblest character.

Sam Clemens himself (who in the first known letter he wrote his mother on the day he reached New York in August, 1853, had indulged the easy sarcasm, "I reckon I had better black my face, for in these Eastern States niggers are considerably better than white people") learned in time, much as Huck learns, to face down his condescension. In later years he became a warm friend of the Negro and his rights. He paid the way of a Negro student through Yale as "his part of the reparation due from every white to every black man," and savagely attacked King Leopold of Belgium for the barbarities of his agents in the Congo. Mrs. Clemens once suggested as a mollifying rule to her husband, "Consider everybody colored till he is proved white." Howells thought that as time went on Clemens the Southwesterner was prone to lose his Southern but cleave to his Western heritage, finding his real affinities with the broader democracy of the frontier. On other issues of race prejudice, Twain looked upon the Jew with unqualified admiration, defended the Chinese whom he had seen pelted through the streets of San Francisco, and confessed to only one invincible antipathy, namely, against the French—although his most rhapsodic book was written in praise of their national heroine.

The final draft of *Huckleberry Finn* was intimately bound up with the writing of Twain's third great volume about his river days, *Life on the Mississippi*. Fourteen chapters of these recollections had been published in the *Atlantic* in 1875; before expanding them into a book Twain made a memorable trip in 1882 back to the scenes of his youth. In working more or less simultaneously on both long-unfinished books, he lifted a scene intended for *Huckleberry Finn*—about Huck and the raftsmen—to flavor the other book, but the great gainer from his trip was not the memoir but the novel. The relative pallor of *Life on the Mississippi,* Part II, is due in a measure to the fact that so much lifeblood of reminiscence is drained off into the veins of *Huckleberry Finn*. The travel notes of 1882, written up soon after Twain's return home, are suffused with some of the finest situations in his novel: the Grangerford-Shepherdson feud, Colonel Sherburn and the mob, and the two seedy vagabonds who come on-stage as the Duke and the King, with a posse in their wake, who "said they hadn't been doing nothing, and was being chased for it."

Mark Twain's renewed contact with life among the river towns quickened his sense of realism. For *Huckleberry Finn,* save in its passages about the peace and freedom of Jackson's Island, is no longer "simply a hymn," and so dim has grown the dream of adolescent romancing that Becky Thatcher reappears but perfunctorily under the careless label of "Bessie" Thatcher. The odyssey of Huck's voyage through the South reveals aspects of life darker than the occasional melodrama of *Tom Sawyer*. We are shown the sloth and sadism of poor whites, backwoods loafers with their plug tobacco and Barlow knives, who sic dogs on stray sows and "laugh at the fun and look grateful for the noise," or drench a stray cur with turpentine and set him afire. We remark the cowardice of lynching parties; the chicanery of patent medicine fakers, revivalists, and exploiters of rustic ribaldry; the senseless feudings of the gentry. In the background broods fear: not only a boy's apprehension of ghosts, African superstitions, and the terrors of the night, nor the adults' dread of black insurrection, but the endless implicated strands of robbery, floggings, drowning, and murder. Death by violence lurks at every bend of road or river. Self-preservation becomes the ruling motive, squaring perfectly with the role of the principal characters, Huck the foot-loose orphan and his friend Jim the fugitive—puny in all strengths save loyalty, as they wander among the Brobdingnagian boots of white adult supremacy. The pair belong to the immortals of fiction.

Never keen at self-criticism, Mark Twain passed without soundings from these depths to the adjacent shallows of burlesque and extravaganza. The last fifth of this superb novel, *Huckleberry Finn,* brings back the romantic Tom Sawyer, with a hilarious, intricate, and needless plot for rescuing Jim from captivity. The story thus closes upon the farcical note with which the Hannibal cycle has begun, in the whitewashing episode. On the same note many years later Mark Twain tried to revive his most famous characters, in *Tom Sawyer Abroad* (1894), with Tom, Huck, and Jim as passengers of a mad balloonist and their subsequent adventures in Egypt. Though inferior to its great predecessors, this book does not lack humor, gusto, and rich characterization. *Tom Sawyer, Detective* (1896) dishes up a melodrama of stolen diamonds, double-crossing thieves, and that immortal device of Plautus and Shakespeare, identical twins, whose charm custom could not stale for Mark Twain. Here haste, artifice, and creative fatigue grow painfully apparent.

Uneven quality appears in *Life on the Mississippi,* even though it came at the high tide of his powers. Chapters IV–XVII were written for the *Atlantic* after Twain's chance reminiscences led his friend Twichell to exclaim, "What a virgin subject to hurl into a magazine!" Fresh, vivid, humorous, they recall the great days of river traffic: the problems of navigation, the races, the pilots' association, the resourcefulness and glory of the old-time pilot. The addenda, which came after Twain's return to the river for "copy," sometimes attain the former standard—the description of Pilot Brown the scold, or the account of the *Pennsylvania* disaster and Henry Clemens' death—but more often prove disappointing after the white heat of the book's inception. The first two chapters on the history of the river are merely an afterthought; the later ones too often wander among irrelevant yarns, like the revenge of Ritter the Austrian, or vignettes of picturesque New Orleans. Sam Clemens' year and a half as cub pilot are followed by almost no mention of his two years as a licensed skipper. Instead we are treated to such vagaries as Twain's famous theory about Sir Walter Scott, whose "Middle-Age sham civilization," he claimed, inspired the chivalry of the Old South, which in turn provoked the Civil War.

Yet with all its flaws of disunity and untidiness, *Life on the Mississippi* remains a masterpiece. Its communicable delight in experience, its rich picture of the human comedy and tragedy on the river (which Melville alone among great artists had tried to bring into focus in *The Confidence Man* in 1857), lend it real durability. Howells believed that the author long regarded it his greatest book—pleased with assurance to that effect from the German Kaiser and also from a hotel porter, whose praise he accepted with equal satisfaction. In other moods, toward the end of his life, Twain favored *Joan of Arc,* in part because it cost him "twelve years of preparation and two years of writing. The others needed no preparation, & got none." Thus again he displayed the blindness of self-appraisal. The book that required probably least effort of all, drawn from a brimming native reservoir, *Huckleberry Finn,* unquestionably is his finest, with *Tom Sawyer* and *Life on the Mississippi* as runners-up.

6

Mark Twain's later years show a drift toward the remote in time and place, in a fitful quest for new themes, new magic—a search that proceeded apace with a growing sense of personal dissatisfaction, frustration, and heartbreak. While the aging artist began to lose much of his creative fire, Clemens the generous, erratic, moody, and vulnerable human being remained, standing at bay against the disillusions and disasters that gathered to ring him around and mock his fame as the world humorist of the century. The development of this last phase is worth tracing.

From recollections of his Hannibal boyhood he gravitated toward a new but distinctly artificial romanticism, "the pageant and fairy-tale" of life in medieval Europe. His earliest treatment of the theme is *The Prince and the Pauper* (1881), a story mainly for children, built upon the old plot of transposed identities. Here to a degree, and still more in *A Connecticut Yankee in King Arthur's Court* (1889) and *Personal Recollections of Joan of Arc* (1896), the romantic's fascination with knights and castles is counterbalanced by the iconoclast's itch to shatter that world of sham and injustice, where crown and miter lorded it over the commons. The savage indignation which Twain so loved to unleash found hunting that gratified him: the prey bore some resemblance to the contemporary, without committing him to the consequences of a frontal attack upon modern authoritarianism, convention, and orthodoxy. *A Connecticut Yankee,* best of the cycle, shows just such an ingenious mechanic as Clemens must often have met on visits to the Hartford shops of Pratt & Whitney, a Yankee who is swept back in time to Camelot. With one hand he transforms Arthurian England into a going concern of steam and electricity; with the other, seeks to plant the seeds of equalitarianism. He remarks that in feudal society six men out of a thousand crack the whip over their fellows' backs: "It seemed to me that what the nine hundred and ninety-four dupes needed was a new deal." This passage, as the late President Roosevelt testified, furnished the most memorable phrase in modern American government. The Connecticut Yankee asserts that the mass of a nation can always produce "the material in abundance whereby to govern itself." Yet the medieval mob is shown collectively to be gullible, vicious, invincibly ignorant, like the populace of Hannibal or Hartford, so that the Yankee sets up not a true democracy but a benign dictatorship centering in himself and his mechanical skills—a kind of technocrat's utopia. Dazzled by the wonders of applied science, Mark Twain always hoped for social as well as technological miracles from the dynamo.

Twain's apotheosis of the Virgin—in terms of Henry Adams' dilemma—of spiritual forces in conflict with materialism and the stupid cruelty of organized society, appears in *Joan of Arc*. The Maid was his favorite character in history. But as Twain's imagination is better than his knowledge of medieval life, the result at best is a *tour de force*.

*Joan* was published anonymously, in hope of giving this book a head start free from a reputation which the world had come long since to regard as synonymous with comedy. Indeed, most people continued to hail with uproarious mirth Mark Twain's explosive attacks upon power politics, imperialism, malefactors of great wealth, hypocrisy in morals and religion, and other manifestations of what he increasingly came to call "the damned human race." They refused to forget "The Celebrated Jumping Frog," or his reputation for convulsing any crowd whenever his mouth was opened. Meanwhile, as the satirist gained upper hand over the humorist in his nature, and age diminished his ebullience, Mark Twain not only yearned vainly for a serious hearing but also came to flinch from the role of platform zany.

Lecturing, however, became a need more urgent than ever. For, beginning with the Panic of 1893, the tide of Mark Twain's luck suddenly changed. The famous writer, with ample cash in hand and enviable royalties rolling in, still vigorous in health and self-confidence, the adoring husband and beloved father of three charming daughters—this self-made "jour" printer and riverboatman whom the world delighted to honor—upon him fortune suddenly began to rain blow after blow. The first losses were financial. The Paige typesetting machine, brain child of an erratic inventor who came close to anticipating the fabulous success of Mergenthaler's linotype, failed after years of costly maintenance from Clemens' pocket; instead of making millions, he lost hundreds of thousands. Then the publishing firm of Charles L. Webster (named for the son-in-law of Mark's sister, but backed by the author himself through suspicion of the big commercial publishers) crashed into bankruptcy. Twain's new friend Henry H. Rogers, Standard Oil magnate and by the lights of the muckraking age a robber baron, advised him that the ethics of literature were higher than those of business, and "you must earn the cent per cent." Mark's own conscience fully acquiesced. Even though his old exuberant energy was flagging, he set out in 1895 on a world lecture tour, after giving a statement to the press:

> The law recognizes no mortgage on a man's brain, and a merchant who has given up all he has may take advantage of the laws of insolvency and start free again for himself. But I am not a business man, and honor is a harder master than the law. It cannot compromise for less than 100 cents on the dollar and its debts never outlaw.

The profits, together with royalties and the astute management of Mr. Rogers, eventually enabled him to pay the last dollar to these creditors and add an American parallel to the case of Sir Walter Scott.

Twain's last notable book about American life, *Pudd'nhead Wilson* (1894), written on the brink of financial disaster but before the onset of deeper tragedies, is about a nonconformist who is too witty and wise for the backwoods community where his days are spent; miscalled "Pudd'nhead," he at last wins recognition by solving a murder mystery through his hobby of fingerprints. In so doing he also unravels a case of transposed identities for which the Negress Roxy—a character of magnificent vigor and realism—had been responsible. The novel is a daring, though inconclusive, study of miscegenation. Significant of Mark Twain's growing pessimism are the cynical chapter mottoes ascribed to Pudd'nhead's "Calendar," such as: "If you pick up a starving dog and make him prosperous, he will not bite you. This is the principal difference between a dog and a man." Or, still more typical of the aging Twain: "Whoever has lived long enough to find out what life is, knows how deep a debt of gratitude we owe to Adam, the first great benefactor of our race. He brought death into the world."

These notes—the ingratitude and folly of man, the vanity of human wishes, the praise of death as the nepenthe for life's tragedy—echo increasingly through the later writings of Mark Twain. This drift was no new departure, but the accentuation of a lifelong trend. In youth he had been subject to fits of melancholy and disillusion. In Cincinnati at the age of twenty he had listened avidly to a homespun philosopher expound the gospel of scientific determinism; as a cub pilot he read Tom Paine "with fear and hesitation." Later, in San Francisco, Mark said he had come within a trigger's breadth of suicide, and in 1876 for obscure causes yielded to a bad season of the blues. Still later he discovered Jonathan Edwards, brooding for days over the "dominion of Motive and Necessity," and was powerfully drawn to the agnosticism of Huxley, Haeckel, and Ingersoll. As a boy he had been terrorized by the fickle and vindictive Jehovah of Sunday schools; as a youth he graduated to the God of scientific law, impersonal but just; as an old man he returned to the cruel God, now stripped of anthropomorphic whims, but no less terrible as causation and fate. As early as 1882, in an unpublished dialogue between Negroes written on his river trip, Mark Twain sketched out the logic elaborated sixteen years later in his "wicked book" *What Is Man?*—not printed until 1906, then privately and anonymously because he thought it so blastingly incontrovertible. Its argument, developed between an earnest Young Man and a cynical Old Man, is that self-interest and self-approval are the mainsprings of human conduct, however cleverly they mask themselves as honor, charity, altruism, or love. Hunger for self-esteem is the master passion; under this demon of the ego, free will is nothing but illusion.

While Mark was lecturing around the world for "honor," news reached him that back home his favorite daughter Susy had suddenly succumbed to meningitis. Would the girl have died if her parents had not deserted her? It was perhaps a foolish question, but natural to a self-accusing heart like Clemens'. Unpublished papers bear witness to his bitterness in those days, savage reflections about how God gives us breath and bodies only to undermine us with the million plagues of disease and heartbreak, to show what Twain calls His "fatherly infatuation" toward us. Meanwhile Mrs. Clemens sank deeper and deeper into a hopeless invalidism that ended only with the mercy of her death in 1904; and their daughter Jean, whose moods had long puzzled them, was discovered to be an incurable epileptic. Mark Twain's own robust health was beginning to crumble, and—as a still more tragic circumstance to the artist who had begun to use hard work as an anodyne for grief— his magnificent creative powers were now sadly on the wane. His unpublished papers are full of fragmentary stories and novels that simply would not come out right, and were endlessly reworked, rewritten, finally abandoned. Many are reminiscent, in plot and character, of his golden period; the magician fell back upon his old repertory, made the same passes, but somehow failed to pull off the trick. They are also eloquent with personal revelation. Twain in old age kept tormenting himself, in a dozen allegorical disguises, with the problem of "guilt" which (as his Calvinist conscience whispered) must somehow be antecedent to punishment, the cause of all the failures and bereavements fate had inflicted upon him. The artist keeps asking himself: Was I to blame, for something I did or left undone? The motif of a doting father with a dead or missing child is frequent, and of course transparent.

One such story concerns the dream of a man who has fallen asleep after gazing at a drop of water, swimming with animalculae, beneath the microscope. He dreams that he is on shipboard in the Antarctic seas pursuing his lost child who has been carried off by another ship, in a chase that continues like some nightmare in a fever, while terrible creatures arise to roam the deep and snatch passengers off the deck. The captain of the ship is called the Superintendent of Dreams, and it is his cunning to destroy the seafarers' sense of reality, while they circle toward the ultimate horror of the Great White Glare —actually the beam cast through the microscope's field by the reflector—a vortex of death into which all things, including the craft with the missing child, are being drawn. Seldom has determinism found a grimmer symbol.

The greatest story of Mark Twain's later period, too often neglected in the appraisal of his work, wins at last the personal answer for which he sought so desperately. In the light of those unfinished manuscripts among the Mark Twain Papers, it attains true perspective. This is *The Mysterious Stranger*, begun in the gloom of 1898 after Susy's death and Jean's hopeless prognosis, but not finished until several years later and published posthumously in 1916. Like the last act of a Greek tragedy, or *Samson Agonistes* with "all passion spent," it achieves a wintry serenity beyond despair. The story is that of some boys who are really Tom Sawyer's gang in medieval dress, in the Austrian village of Eseldorf, who strike up acquaintance with a supernatural visitor able to work miracles and juggle with lives. Calling himself "Satan," he claims relationship with the prince of fallen angels, but appears to live in a sphere beyond both good and evil. Laughter and tears, joy and torment, saintliness and sin, to him are but as the sound of lyres and flutes, and at last he grows bored with his own wonder-working caprices. He then tells the wide-eyed Theodor:

It is true, that which I have revealed to you; there is no God, no universe, no human race, no earthly life, no heaven, no hell. It is all a dream—a grotesque and foolish dream. Nothing exists but you. And you are but a *thought*—a vagrant thought, a useless thought, a homeless thought, wandering forlorn among the empty eternities!

And in his heart of hearts the boy knows this is true. Here, in the closing pages of *The Mysterious Stranger*, Mark Twain solved his riddle of grief and

f-reproach, and clothed his soul in the only invulnerable armor of despera-
n. Good and evil, like reality itself, are only illusions, such stuff as dreams
e made on, and our little life is rounded with the best gift of the Artist who
ves it to the last—extinction.

 Like Halley's comet in 1835 and 1910, whose appearance Mark Twain saw
 setting the beginning and the end of his life, the luster of his genius flashed
rth now and again against this darkened sky of fatalism. He wrote and
oke with sparkles of his old wit, and few were aware of the encircling
oom. Oxford gave him her degree of Doctor of Letters in 1907, and his
rthdays became national events. In his famous white clothes he seemed a
nd of ghost from America's buried life, recalling the nostalgia of her youth,
visiting these glimpses of the modern city and its vast industrialism. But his
eat creative genius had almost gone—that energy which he spent and
uandered so freely, when he had it, with the recklessness of the Old West.
or Mark Twain the artist had always been a kind of pocket miner, stum-
ing like fortune's darling upon native ore of incredible richness and exploit-
g it with effortless skill—but often gleefully mistaking fool's gold for the
nuine article, or lavishing his strength upon historical diggings long since
ayed out. If latterly he seemed to deny his role as America's great comic
irit, perhaps the key can be found in his last travel book: "Everything
man is pathetic. The secret source of Humor itself is not joy but sorrow.
here is no humor in heaven."

*- disillusion, reform, definition*

# 57. A WORLD TO WIN OR LOSE

THE forces that stirred within that huge, loose-jointed America of the latter half of the nineteenth century came to focus in the life of Mark Twain as in probably that of no other man of his generation. With his generation he groped his way in a world of thought made unfamiliar by ideas born of science that flowed into America from across the Atlantic. To follow the trail of Mark Twain is to traverse America in one of its decisive epochs.

It was a period of change, change that increased in tempo with each passing decade. In the nineties when Clemens, well past sixty, had already sketched the outlines of his pessimism, his fellow countrymen were pressing hopefully forward into a new world whose landscape was already becoming clear. The frontier that started at Jamestown and Plymouth made its final advance against the wilderness as wheatgrowers fenced in the eastern Dakotas, cattlemen established permanent ranches on the High Plains, and settlers laid out farms on the terraces of the Snake Valley.

Life moved fast enough on this last frontier to develop before the outbreak of the First World War a rudimentary sense of history. "Charlie" Russell, ex-cowboy, made himself a kind of folk hero of the Montana cattle country when he set down on vigorous and authentic canvases, in order that it might be preserved for posterity, the life of the old free range where as a young man he had punched longhorns. Through Russell's home town, Great Falls, ran one of the four new railway systems that, surmounting the continental divide, had united the Pacific coast with the economic life of the Middle West and East. Trade caused the cities from San Diego to Puget Sound to surge with new life. On the western slopes of the Sierras, in such communities as that of Mark Twain's Calaveras County, the mood of living for a moment in a town that might play out tomorrow gave way to a sense of responsibility as Californians took steps to preserve the groves of giant sequoias and the majestic valley of the Yosemite. Colorful seaports grew beside Pacific harbors and sleek orchards covered the interior from Oregon to the Imperial Valley. A sense of history brought in California a revaluation of the Spanish period, now seen as a picturesque prologue that gave the

943

dignity of tradition to a state escaping from a somewhat uncouth frontie chrysalis.

History also filled the thoughts of saddened and impoverished ex-Con federates for whom "the War" and Reconstruction had brought an epoch t a close. Although by the end of the century the Union had been reestablishe in spirit as well as in form, the surviving soldiers who surrendered at Appo mattox and their sons looked back to a romantic and romanticized plantation culture. At the same time, however, they busied themselves laying the founda tions of a New South in what was in fact a new nation. By 1900 even th South, wrecked by war, had begun to feel the effects of that scientific and technological advance that, starting in the late eighteenth century, was now a hundred years later, bringing about an industrial revolution in that portion of America that lay east of the Mississippi and north of the Ohio and th Potomac.

Scarcely had the Civil War ended when America, leaving behind th wooden waterwheel and sailing ship, entered upon an age of steam and stee in which the nation's bituminous coal fields powered an expanding industrial ism. In the *fin de siècle* years electricity and the internal combustion engin that drew power from the oil pools of America further transformed th material foundations of the national life. Cities located at the crossroads o commerce grew vastly. In Chicago and New York, pioneer skyscraper marked out new sky lines where before there had been only the dead leve of flat-roofed, six-storied buildings, pierced here and there by church spires Each year the new steamships that plied the oceans brought to the sidewalk of these sprawling urban centers a confusion of strange faces, as immigrant poured in from the four corners of the world. The cross, lifted above at increasing number of Catholic schools and churches, forecast a future in which Catholicism would assume a place of power and importance beside ; dominant Protestantism in American civilization. Henry Adams, whose New England family tradition ran back beyond the beginnings of the Republic declared that he and his generation were witnessing change that had accelerated to a pace without precedent. Change is the inevitable start ing point for a consideration of American civilization at the turn of the century.

Not many years before the entry of the United States into the First World War the imported word *Zeitgeist* appeared in the conversation of more thoughtful Americans. A few made a conscious effort to discover the spiri of the kaleidoscopic age in which they lived. Henry Adams, William Graham Sumner, Lester Frank Ward, and William Dean Howells were among the more important analysts of the scene contemporary to them. The middle year of the twentieth century give perspective on that yesterday when the horse

rawn carriage was about to give way to the Model T. Its *Zeitgeist* seems to
ave been a blend of three basic moods: a sense of security, a belief in progress,
nd a malaise arising out of the impact of scientific naturalism and rampant
naterialism upon traditional ideals of the good life.

2

Security is the basic aspect. It was associated with a new spirit of national-
sm emerging as the memories of Gettysburg and Cold Harbor grew less
listinct and the wounds of fratricidal conflict healed. The hundred-day war
gainst decadent Spain disturbed only for a moment the feeling that America
ad little to fear in the world. No powerful potential enemy crouched beyond
ither of the land frontiers of the Republic. The Atlantic, in spite of its cross-
ng by Cervera's fleet, seemed to hold Europe at arm's length, while the
nterminable Pacific washed on the west a continent that even after 1898
nd the acquisition of Hawaii and the Philippines remained a blurred and
ndistinct image in the American mind. So subtle and so pervasive was this
ense of security that only a few recognized its importance. Americans as a
nation looked upon themselves as free to make what they could of the con-
inent which they and their forefathers had reclaimed from the wilderness.
They were free as individuals to plan their lives without hedging their liber-
ies to meet the demands of military necessity.

Theodore Roosevelt practically alone in his day feared that this sense of
security might lead to trouble and perhaps disaster. Yet in the first decade
of the twentieth century even his thought did not run so much to the danger
of foreign war as to that of internal degeneration. Strength had enabled
Americans to conquer the continent and to accumulate wealth surpassing that
of the Indies. The enjoyment in security of this wealth, he thought, might
well cause that moral decay, that flabbiness, which would bring down American civilization to the low estate of Spain. Stirred by such apprehensions,
Roosevelt reminded his fellow countrymen that Fate had cast the United
States in the role of a great power and that they must choose whether the part
would be played well or ill. In a day when Thorstein Veblen was caustically
pointing out the phenomenon of "conspicuous consumption" among the new
lords of industry and finance, Theodore Roosevelt urged the ideal of the
"strenuous life." The former rancher and Rough Rider made himself one of
the great preachers in American history. His colorful personality and the
White House sounding board gave currency to his message in the most remote
corner of the nation. He succeeded in catching the ear of his fellow countrymen primarily because his philosophy of the strenuous life ran with, rather
than against, the main current of American life. We were an active rather

than a contemplative people. Roosevelt gave verbal expression to a firmly held
folk ideal. Americans had been on the move since the *Susan Constant* dropped
anchor before Jamestown. The pace had grown immeasurably faster by the
time that Roosevelt was elevated to the Presidency.

> Afoot and light-hearted, I take to the open road,
> Healthy, free, and the world before me,

Whitman had written many years before. The mood still held as Americans
set forth confidently into what they believed would be a glorious twentieth
century.

It is true that Americans at the turn of the century, for all their sense of
safety, were troubled by insecurities within their national life. Western
farmers, the Grangers, and the Populists, frightened by what they looked
upon as ravening corporations whelped by industrialism, organized popular
fronts of resistance. Eastern capitalists feared the crackpot economic theories
of the Populist horde that formed in 1890 in the upper Mississippi Valley.
Industrialists watched with a deepening apprehension a succession of labor
revolts—1877, 1886, 1892, 1899—whose tradition of violence culminated, in
1911, in the dynamiting of the Los Angeles *Times* building. Washington
Gladden, statesman-preacher who achieved national stature as an advocate
of unity among the Christian churches and as a conciliator in labor disputes,
feared in the nineties that centrifugal forces in American life were about to
overcome the forces tending to hold American society together. In this and
the following decade the muckrakers sounded the alarm that municipal corruption and corporate greed were threatening both the political and the
economic foundations of democracy itself.

Josiah Royce, philosopher who knew America from California to Cambridge, rejected what had become a popular thesis of European commentators
that American civilization was engulfed in a tide of materialism, and insisted
that materialism and idealism were evenly balanced in the national life. He,
the last of great nineteenth century idealists, sought to turn the energies of his
fellow countrymen toward the creation of a richer culture by his doctrine of
regionalism, by his consideration of the problems of Christianity, and by his
philosophy of loyalty. The work of Royce, of the muckrakers, and of a
growing army of urban citizens who were spurred to action by a sense of
social responsibility illustrated that malaise, arising out of the tension between
new forms of materialism and idealism and adapting itself to a new social
scene. But these domestic apprehensions were blunted by the sense of security
from foreign aggression, which made possible the comforting belief that in
due time Americans could and would set their house in order.

### 3

Never before in the history of the Republic had the idea of progress been so influential in American thought as in that period beginning in the early nineties and ending in 1917 which American historians have come to call the Progressive Era. The completion of the occupation of the continent, the overseas expansion following the defeat of Spain, the swift transformation, after Appomattox, of a civilization built on agriculture and commerce into an industrial culture, all combined in an American dream of a rosy-hued future.

Underneath this dream was the conviction that advance in the natural and biological sciences would make possible the creation of a new world. To the common man, science expressed itself most simply in the machine which each year grew more complicated and more important. Two events in particular in the first decade of the twentieth century dramatized for the average citizen the augmented role of science in the age in which the fortune of birth had placed him. Walter Reed in Cuba, making use of the new knowledge of bacteriology, discovered the secret of the dread yellow fever; and at Kittyhawk the Wright brothers began the conquest of the air. Such achievements broke ancient fetters binding the imagination.

At the same time students of the ways of man, pioneers in emerging social disciplines, began to dream of the possibility of a science of society that would become in the realm of social action the counterpart of the new technology. The prestige of the words "science" and "scientific method" and the universality of the new faith in the potentialities of the sciences were evidence that a cult had appeared and that the man of the laboratory was threatening to replace the minister as the accepted guide to human salvation. In the Progressive Era, August Comte's positivism reached its American apogee. New thinkers in the emerging social sciences substituted for the certitudes of theology what they thought to be the certitudes of science. Herbert Spencer, whose name ranked second only to that of Darwin, was their patron saint. He persuaded thousands of Americans, who thought of themselves as forward-looking, that society is an organism, that there is a law of progress leading in social as in biological development from the simple and homogeneous to the complex and heterogeneous, and that evolution ends in a state of peaceful and happy "equilibration." Spencer taught that society moves upward from the primitive hunting stage to the final triumph of the industrial stage, passing through the stage of the military society on the way. Behind the forward push is force, working through laws that science reveals. The social world of August Comte and of Herbert Spencer rested squarely on determinism. At the end of the scholar's road lay certainty. Spencer's was not the optimism of hope but of assurance.

Henry Adams dissented. Like his generation he saw the importance of
the new technology, but he stood relatively alone when he suggested, in the
face of the current optimism, that the harnessing of natural energy was putting men in chains as well as setting them free, and that malevolent as well
as beneficent forces were being loosed in the world. He spoke of the modern
man as being made to dance by the live wire he grasped, unable to let go his
hold, and suggested that in the twentieth century men were being educated
by bombs doubling each decade in number and power. Adams, historian and
philosopher, was one of the ablest among a new and small group of naturalists appearing among American men of letters.

The position of the atypical Adams suggests a basic conflict in American
thinking. His pessimism stemmed from what seemed to him the implications
for society of the new physics that was modifying the old Newtonian conception of the cosmos. The pessimism of Clemens began with Darwinian identification of man with the animal world. What seemed to many Darwin's
degradation of human nature found support in Ernst Haeckel's biological
dictum not only that man arises ultimately from the most primitive forms
of life but that the child before birth recapitulates the course of evolution. It
was a hard doctrine. Spencer with his intellectual device of the Unknowable,
the domain of religion, had compromised with long-held beliefs. But the
German Haeckel and his Darwinian contemporary Nietzsche seemed to
destroy the ancient theological canon that God had created man a little lower
than the angels and had set the beasts of the field under his feet. There were
some Americans too for whom the harvest of the new biology was frustration,
futilitarianism, and despair.

4

As the end of the nineteenth century came and passed, Americans faced
another tension in social thought. They sensed that the frontier ideal of the
self-sufficient individual must be modified to make it accord with a new
understanding of the community. Josiah Royce, protagonist of individualism,
yet insisted that men are "saved by the community." He symbolized in his
effort to combine in his philosophy individualism and collectivism a conflict
in American social thought that grew more intense with each decade. The
idea of the importance of the individual was an aspect of American tradition
too important to be quickly abandoned even as a result of the vast social
changes of the end of the century. In fact, individualism reached a new apogee
in the triumphs of those men of finance and industry who created the promi-
nences in the landscape of the new industrialism. Individualism was implied
in the sobriquet robber barons, justly applied later to some of them.

Yet economic power proved to be a sobering influence in the lives of many of the new capitalists. Andrew Carnegie, master of steel and of trade, took the lead in formulating a philosophy of stewardship which he called the Gospel of Wealth. He declared that the individual who has demonstrated his superiority to the common crowd by his skill in building new economic structures and amassing economic power must assume a compensating responsibility to extend his leadership to a broader social field and to do for the average man those things which mediocrity prevents the commoner from doing for himself. This new and revolutionary doctrine of stewardship was expressed, among other ways, in hospitals, museums, libraries, new or enlarged universities, and in that novelty in American life, the endowed foundation. Big business, whose ruthlessness and lawlessness were responsible for much human suffering between 1885 and 1917, made at the same time contributions of the first importance to the advance of the finer aspects of American culture.

Individualism in the American tradition had always expressed itself in inequality. As the nineteenth century drew to a close, the men and women of the United States became increasingly aware, particularly in the swollen cities, of the contrast between Veblen's conspicuous consumption and that conspicuous destitution for the amelioration of which Jacob Riis led a ten years' war on Manhattan Island. The sentiment and practice of humanitarianism, old in American life, manifested themselves in new institutions, and the career of Jane Addams suggested that the relief of suffering was perhaps the most important field in which the genius of American women could express itself. For a time after Appomattox, humanitarians, spurred to great efforts by the definitive victory over slavery, believed that poverty could be destroyed with a similar finality. Nor throughout the entire period to the entrance of the United States into the First World War did they completely give up their faith, although each year hundreds of thousands of the world's poor crowded as immigrants hopefully into American communities to undertake in a new life the individual's struggle to better himself. The cities of the Republic became expanding reservoirs of the defeated and the exploited and of the morally and physically diseased. Poverty also marred the countryside of the South, emerging from tragedy, and of the Western plains where men gambled with the forces of nature and lost. Beside the humanitarians appeared a group of American men of letters for whom the realities of American life were the biographies of the demoralized and the defeated.

Individualism flourished, as it had previously, partly because no serious external threat forced American nationals into sacrifices of some of their liberties in the interest of protection. Internal insecurities caused the emergence of new ideas, ideas that remained for the most part in the speculative stage before the First World War, but which were to become important in the middle years of the twentieth century. Trade unionism, after the collapse of the idealistic dreams of the Knights of Labor in the eighties, continued the fight to establish the practice of collective bargaining. Lester Frank Ward, challenging the prophet of individualism, William Graham Sumner, assumed intellectual leadership among a growing company who would abandon laissez faire and establish the social service state. Ward, scientist and government servant, foresaw the state undertaking social experimentation to provide a part of the necessary data for social planning. He believed that a lumbering and somewhat haphazard democracy could be made to evolve into an efficient and scientific "sociocracy." Simon Patten, economist, denied the traditional assumptions of an economy of scarcity and insisted that science could be made to provide for all men an abundant life.

Neither Ward nor Patten had great importance for even the liberal politicians of the age. These latter, calling themselves Populists, Insurgents, or Progressives, contented themselves for the most part with battles to achieve governmental supervision of business and the conservation of the nation's resources. The new horizons suggested by such pioneers as Ward and Patten, together with the actual achievements of the reforming statesmen, bred such hopes for the future as to make it difficult for Marxian socialism to establish itself as a significant force in American life. Equally important in creating a blockade against the influence of Marx was the tradition of individualism carrying on in an expanding economy. This tradition tended to channel in America what the author of *Das Kapital* had described as the inevitable class struggle into individual efforts on the part of the natural leaders of the proletariat to escape from the class to which they were born and to achieve the dignity and power inherent in management. It is true that Marxism appeared and that its doctrines were disseminated by a political party and by a press that, about 1912, was surprisingly large. But even in its heyday before the First World War, it remained for the vast majority of Americans a foreign thought pattern imported by immigrants and of little relevancy to American life. Suggestive of the exotic nature of Marxism were the pains taken by its protagonists to minimize or even to deny the challenge of Marxian materialism to traditional Christianity.

5

But the "old-time religion" of the frontier group camp meeting did not go unchallenged. Geology, historical criticism applied to the Bible and, above all, Darwinism brought first rage and then consternation to the theologians of Protestant orthodoxy. When Andrew D. White published in 1896 *A History of the Warfare of Science with Theology in Christendom,* the theologians were in full retreat. Out of the struggle emerged new and somewhat vague patterns that came to be known as modernism, representing efforts to reconcile religious affirmations with science and objective scholarship. By 1917 modernism seemed to have triumphed in American Protestant circles. But the victory had been won at a price that was nothing less than the loss of that old sense of religious and moral security that the common men in a previous age had gained from the doctrine of the literal inspiration of the Scriptures. After the First World War a crusading fundamentalist revolt was to attempt a recovery of the old religious certainties. But before that conflict, Protestant leadership had sought to minimize and perhaps forget the new difficulties in the field of theology by turning to a social gospel. Influenced by the growing humanitarianism in an age of tension and suffering, they proclaimed the "law of love." In harmony with the optimism of the day, they declared the possibility of the establishment of the Kingdom of God on earth. Walter Rauschenbusch, clergyman and professor of church history, became the Isaiah who held up to scorn the smugness of the well-to-do urban church members and who took the lead in bringing a new social consciousness to American Protestantism.

William James, psychologist and philosopher, was disturbed by that religious insecurity that impaired the prestige and authority of modernism. In his *Will to Believe* he gave a pragmatist's reason for faith in a beneficent, if not omnipotent, God. Belief in a Power striving for good in the universe with which man can associate himself, James argued, makes for optimism, and optimism releases human energy. Faith, therefore, is justified by its results. Protestant leadership in the Progressive Era found comfort and even inspiration in the Jamesian formula. But pragmatism, the work of Peirce, James, and Dewey, had more significance than the reduction of the anxieties of theologians. The pragmatists' concept of an open and unfinished universe, conditioned by no fixed and eternal pattern, seemed to many men of the age a liberation from old absolutisms of both religion and science and a challenge to creation. Their definition of the good as that which works not only was a rationalization of changing customs in changing culture, but helped in the process of transformation. Pragmatism launched industrial America into an age of ethical relativism, an attitude of mind that was to be of importance in the period between 1918 and 1941.

The instrumentalism of the early Dewey and his gospel that man, through the use of ideas, can create his own world became the orthodoxy of education and helped to raise the American faith in the educative process almost to the level of a national religion. Dewey's instrumentalism was, from another point of view, merely a projection into philosophical thinking of the inherent optimism of the age. Pragmatism, as a philosophy of practicality, harmonized with the American genius for getting things done. Like Theodore Roosevelt's gospel of the strenuous life, pragmatism stimulated Americans to action rather than to thought. The emphasis of the pragmatists on experimentalism put them in the cult of science. The devotees of the new philosophy, however, mistook experimentalism for the scientific method, failing to recognize that only logical and criticized theory makes possible the formulation of the questions that are answered in the laboratory.

It was no accident that pragmatism appeared in the Progressive Era. It gained immediate and widespread popularity because in it practically all the moods and the trends of the time found expression. Change, swift and confused, was the central fact of the period from 1865 to 1917; the pragmatists affirmed that flux is the ultimate cosmic reality and distilled from change a philosophy for America. Liberal political thinkers seized upon this philosophy for assurance that the transition from the old agrarian to the new industrial nation could be made without destroying the sense of security and the belief in progress of the old ways. The evils in the new ways could be corrected by reform. From the Populist movement of the nineties to the Square Deal of the first Roosevelt and the New Freedom to come, liberal political leadership held a straight course through the flux of intellectual, moral, and social change.

# 58. LITERATURE AS BUSINESS

A$_T$ the same time that traditional individualism was being challenged by the development from rural America into urban and industrial America, changes in intellectual outlook were raising doubts about many venerable assumptions that directly affected the business of writing and publishing. Once again, as in the period immediately following the Revolution, the American writer found himself permitted—and indeed required—to deal directly with the facts and ideas of American life. Not only the experience out of which literature is made, but the conditions under which authors live and write, were undergoing a revolution.

The writers who in 1910 pleaded pathetically with the editor of the *Century Magazine* for "another damn" were winning a battle which had begun in earnest only twenty years earlier. In 1890 "damns" were forbidden rather than rationed; yet in that year Richard Harding Davis' "Gallegher" was rejected by the *Century*—not for its profanity but for its slanginess. Only a few years before, the *Century* had stopped the presses because of a reference to dynamite (in relation to labor troubles) in Howells' serial *The Rise of Silas Lapham*; and the same author had been scolded by the editor of *Harper's Monthly* for reviews too friendly to Mrs. Humphry Ward's "anti-Christian" *Robert Elsmere* and to Zola's *La Terre*. Scribner rejected a novel of Hamlin Garland's (which probably deserved no better fate) on the ground that it contained slang, profanity, vulgarity, agnosticism, and radicalism; *Harper's* dropped a chapter of James' translation of Daudet's *Port Tarascon* as offensive to Christian readers, and in 1892 warned Constance Woolson against unrelieved pessimism. Yet many of the rejected works got into print in book form. In 1895 Scribner was unable to accept Harold Frederic's *The Damnation of Theron Ware* as a serial, but offered to publish it as a book. Stephen Crane's *Maggie* got nowhere with editors, but Appleton printed four thousand copies of it between 1896 and 1900. *Harper's* bowdlerized Hardy's *Jude the Obscure,* but seductive or sensual novels like *She* and *Quo Vadis* were best sellers. Howells claimed that in this last decade of the nineteenth century any slightly dirty novel, which magazine editors would not touch, could get a substantial sale as a book.

953

It would be easy to arrange such evidence as this to show, first, that in the space of two decades our wall of taboos—aesthetic, social, moral, religious, political—crumbled to the ground, leaving only scattered bricks to be hammered to bits in the Jazz Age; and second, that a major cause of this phenomenon was the transfer of critical and selective authority from the once omnipotent monthly magazines to the publishers of books. There is some truth in both suggestions, but true enlightenment in neither. The repressive forces continued in operation, but they somehow lost, as the years passed, their power to block every channel in the literary market. By 1910 there was a welcome, in the book, magazine, and newspaper world, for every shade of opinion and every grade of excellence; and if only a faint chorus greeted the writer whose method, purpose, or message appealed only to a small minority, it is demonstrable that this minority was growing larger daily. The fact that Americans were buying wood pulp by the ton should not obscure the equally significant fact that in 1900 Scribner gave Henry James an advance of $2,000 for the book rights to such caviar as *The Sacred Fount,* and that *Harper's Monthly* offered him $5,000 for the serial rights to *The Ambassadors.* The Comstockery of the period was pernicious, but Dreiser's *Sister Carrie* finally found both publisher and audience. One may well ask how the magazines' taboos against the subjects of capital punishment and anarchism could prevail in a period which began by making best sellers of *Looking Backward* and *Caesar's Column,* and ended in a wave of muckraking journalism. From the publishing point of view, the key to the period is the diversification of the American reading classes, the breaking up of once solid cultural and social groups, and the readiness of enterprising editors and publishers to feed or exploit new audiences.

2

Basic, as always in American social mutations, was the advance of education. Granted that mere literacy was and is potentially as much a threat as an aid to high culture, by 1910 there were only 5,500,000 Americans (about 8 per cent of all people over ten years of age) who were not possible buyers of print. Of the schoolgoers in 1902 more than 500,000 were moving on to public high schools which had tripled in number during the nineties. Whether the adoption, in the public schools, of educational theories which stressed preparation for "life" rather than for college led also to preparation for independent thinking and reading is a question still unsettled. Mass education on the higher levels was still in the future, for in 1900 only 11 per cent of all high-school students were preparing for college; and in 1904 not many more than 100,000 students were enrolled in higher institutions. Graduate study, begun in the seventies, was growing rapidly. In 1901 there were some 6,300 graduate students, about three-quarters of them in the humanities; and in 1903 a total of 266 doctorates were conferred. Significantly, a Western institution, the University of Chicago—rich, progressive, and only twelve years old— was second only to Yale in the number of degrees granted. The effects of expanding higher education on literary production and consumption were necessarily intangible—except in one respect: the nineties saw the first full development of university press publishing, which was eventually to contribute importantly to the diversification of the book market. During the period, presses at Harvard, Johns Hopkins, Columbia, Chicago, Princeton, and Yale began to serve as outlets for subsidized scholarly studies which were of no commercial significance except to the popularizers who soon learned to ransack them for salable facts.

In a period when the average schooling of Americans was only five years, adult education had much to offer. The Chautauqua system, at its peak at the end of the century, brought the subject matter of the liberal arts curriculum—through its publications and summer schools and the mails— to adults in every state in the Union. Under the leadership of President William Rainey Harper of the University of Chicago, it grew beyond its original connection with the Sunday school movement, and became a force for general culture. Equally successful was a movement begun by the New York City Board of Education in 1888 to provide lectures for working people, many of them immigrants, at public expense. Attendance of seven million in the first fifteen years of the New York program revealed an appetite for cultural advancement which had not been equaled, except by Chautauqua, since the great days of the town lyceum. The idea that school buildings might be of use to adults after the children had departed, quickly spread not only to other cities, but to universities as well, for extension courses were also an innovation of the period.

Equally, perhaps more, important for the encouragement of the reading habit among the population at large was the growth of the free public library. The states had been passing ineffective permissive library laws since the Civil War, but it was not until 1893 that a new departure was made by New Hampshire, when it passed the first state law requiring its townships to create libraries. By 1900 there were 1,700 free libraries which owned more than five thousand volumes. The existence of many of these was made possible by Andrew Carnegie's gifts of buildings—300 by 1904. It may have been, as Mr. Dooley remarked, that these were for the dead authors, and that live authors stood outside and wished they were dead; but there is no question that Carnegie's Gospel of Wealth was taking tangible form. Live authors like Mark Twain might complain that librarians had arbitrary powers of censorship when time after time *Huckleberry Finn* was banned from the shelves, but many were likely to feel, with Frank Norris, that the growth of the reading habit was the important thing because it must lead ultimately to more liberal views and better taste.

In a period extraordinary for philanthropy only 2 per cent of all private gifts of money were for libraries, compared to 43 per cent for education, 37 per cent for charity, and 9 per cent each for museums and religion. Much of the money for education was poured into institutions of higher learning; in fact, benefactions, the rate of which tripled in twenty years, kept step with the growth of national wealth. The Carnegie and Rockefeller foundations, which distributed money not only for general college use but for research and teachers' pensions, did much to stabilize and improve higher education and to broaden its functions. If, as Veblen and others thought, industrial wealth controlled as well as subsidized many of our universities, its influence was neutralized by the people's willingness to help themselves. During the period, total university income from city and state increased almost twenty-four times, and from tuition fees almost six times. Of a total income of eighty millions in 1910, only eighteen millions came from private benefactors.

A more immediate influence in the American writer's milieu during these years was middle-class women—as readers, as guardians of the family, and as representatives of religion. The two best paymasters in the magazine world in the nineties were *Harper's Monthly* and the *Century,* both of which often and frankly explained to contributors that they were pledged not to offend religious sensibilities and not to print anything that could not be read by the women of the family circle. But the American woman was changing, and the family in the old sense was disappearing. The employment of women (five and a third million were at work in 1900, half of them under twenty-five years old) was rendering them more independent and less willing to reduce their standard of living by early marriage and large families. College education seems to have had the same effect. Other tendencies, such as migration to the city, the popularity of apartments and boardinghouses, birth control, and divorce (except for Japan's ours was the highest divorce rate in the world) resulted in the decline of the family from an average of four in 1890 to less than three in 1910. The shrinkage took place chiefly among the urban middle classes which constituted the richest book market.

At the same time, the horizon of the women of these families was widening. By 1898, 70 per cent of the colleges of the country were coeducational, and by 1902 women made up 25 per cent of the undergraduate, 26 per cent of the graduate, and 3 per cent of the professional enrollment of all colleges. Women's colleges, 128 of which had been founded by 1901, had only 25,000 students in that year, but 37,000 more were enrolled in normal schools, and almost 400,000 in secondary schools, where they were in the majority. Small as these numbers were in a nation of 76,000,000, they were relatively large in relation to the groups which bought and read books and magazines of literary quality. Presumably, also, these women were prominent in the culture clubs, which had a membership of perhaps 1,000,000 in 1910.

Increasing education and freedom for women must have tended to relax the rigid codes of propriety and morality which men had always inflicted on them. When Edward Bok of the *Ladies' Home Journal* began his columns of advice for girls and young mothers, he was generally ridiculed; but these columns were born of his conviction that women had been kept in enforced ignorance of the facts of life, and their response helped run his circulation above the 750,000 mark by 1900. Henry Mills Alden of *Harper's* had sensed the emancipation, for in 1894 he justified his acceptance of Du Maurier's *Trilby* on the grounds of "the increasing tolerance of our moral judgments as a people." He seems to have been right, for this story of the Latin Quarter became the greatest serial success of the decade, and Saint-Gaudens is said to have remarked, "Every other woman you meet thinks she could be an artist's model." When, in 1900, the police raided Clyde Fitch's adaptation of *Sapho* because the leading man carried the heroine upstairs, many women signed a public protest against the closing, and women stormed the theater when the play reopened. It is likely that the decline of the *Century Magazine* toward the end of the period was due in part to the quiet refusal of women to agree with the editors' ideas of what was good for them.

A comparable phenomenon was the growing liberality of religious groups. The social historian finds it easy to collect a distressing amount of evidence of narrow orthodoxy, sectarianism, and bigotry in the nineties, but such reactionary thought must have been inspired by opposite tendencies. The evangelist Moody's cry that the Bible was not meant to be understood was the sign of a widespread desire to understand. The popularity of Washington Gladden's *Who Wrote the Bible?* (1891) and its use by Bible and Y.M.C.A. classes show that the Higher Criticism was no longer a merely scholarly preoccupation. The sectarianism of the time must be balanced against the vogue of such novels as Margaret Deland's *John Ward, Preacher* and Mrs. Humphry Ward's *Robert Elsmere* in 1888, and against interest in the Parliament of Religions at the Chicago World's Fair. Orthodoxy could not have been too powerful in a period when Henry Drummond, as a Chautauqua lecturer, expounded Darwinism. Blue laws were still a live issue, but the circulation of Sunday newspapers and attendance at Sunday baseball games showed that the Sabbath was no longer monopolized by the churches. Protestantism may have been primarily the faith of the comfort able middle classes, but Christian Socialism was a Protestant phenomenon and the millions of readers of the Reverend Charles M. Sheldon's *In His Steps* (1896) could not have been entirely indifferent to the problems of poverty and labor. Certainly the prolabor statements of the Federal Council of Churches in 1908 were the climax of steady change rather than a new departure.

For the writer and publisher the pertinent question was the extent of the power of religious sects and organizations to inhibit free expression and to dictate standards of propriety. Confusing as are the statistics of church membership in the period, it would seem that half the population were churchgoers. The fact that in these decades thirty-one new schools of theology were opened, as against thirty schools of medicine and twenty-four women's colleges, and that they were given two or three times as much money as these others, is evidence enough that the age of religious enthusiasm had not yet passed. But the power of sectarian groups to influence the general literary market was waning. On the publishing side, a major tendency was the shift of religious books from the general publisher to specialists like Fleming H. Revell or to the organizations set up by the Presbyterians, Methodists, Congregationalists, and Baptists. Moreover, the traditional ties between publishers and denominational sects, like that between Harper and the Methodists, were breaking because the economic motives for such connections were no longer strong; and the tendency of denominational publishers to invade the fields of general literature occasioned much bitter criticism.

There were changes in the magazine world also. Rose Terry Cooke said in 1885 that she sold a story to a religious magazine because it paid better than any other periodical except the *Youth's Companion*; by the end of the century, commercial magazines were no longer subject to such competition. General magazine editors, who had once lived in terror of attack by the sectarian press, now apparently were taking the point of view that the unreasonably prejudiced minority of religious readers and editors—always the most vocal—were too insignificant to affect seriously the great national literary market. Similar considerations were weakening the ancient prejudice against the theater. Of what avail was the Methodist Discipline against the drama-hungry crowds and the enterprising producers of the nineties?

3

The fact was that publishing had become big business, a force so great that it could no more be seriously hampered by minority groups than the growing automobile industry could be frustrated by lovers of horses. Especially in the so-called "merger prosperity" of 1898–1903, publishing boomed, along with other forms of enterprise. In the twenty years preceding 1910, the national wealth tripled, while population increased only 50 per cent. In the same period, the value of printed materials increased from less than $480,000,000 to well over $1,000,000,000. As a big business, publishing was falling into current industrial and financial patterns and sloughing off its antiquated habits and techniques in the struggle to survive. Two dips in the business cycle, the panic of 1893 and the silver campaign depression of 1896–1897, tended to put publishing, like other businesses, under the control of finance capitalism, with the result that the banks and investment trusts, which supplied it with capital, insisted on greater efficiency in the interest of surer profits. The reorganization in the nineties of great firms like Harper and Appleton reflected this tendency. The history of Harper is a case in point: a company which, as a close family partnership, had enjoyed a dominating position in the book world for almost three-quarters of a century, became at the end of the century an impersonal corporation under the temporary guidance of a bank.

Nor was the book business exempt from the movement toward consolidation and near-monopoly. As early as the eighties the American News Company had become so powerful as a distributor of reading for travelers that it was accused of dictating policy to some of the publishers from whom it bought extensively. In 1890 the American Book Company absorbed five other publishers of school texts, and for a while had a practical monopoly in its field. The cheap reprint business went through two such phases—once in 1890 when the United States Book Company came into control, and again about 1900, when Grosset & Dunlap proved that they could handle cheap editions more efficiently than regular houses. Publishing was also directly affected by combinations of manufacturers. During this period the American Typefounders Company absorbed twenty foundries; and in 1906 the Department of Justice was impelled to break up a powerful paper trust.

Technology was the basis of many profound changes. The perfection of the Mergenthaler typesetting machine in the mid-eighties, and of rounding, backing, case-making, gathering, and other machines for the manufacturing of books in the early nineties, solved so many problems that soon after the turn of the century a completely mechanized production schedule was practicable. By the nineties photoengraving was so well developed that the older illustrated magazines like *Scribner's* and the *Century* no longer had an advantage over the rising ten- and fifteen-cent periodicals which could not stand the expense of woodcut techniques.

Distribution, still the chief problem of the publisher, was modernized somewhat. The old-fashioned wholesale auction or "trade sale" was dropped in the nineties when it was obvious that it served little purpose except the getting rid of slow-moving stock. By 1900 booksellers' and publishers' organizations had succeeded to a certain extent in stabilizing retail prices and discounts, but as the department store developed into an important outlet for books, it created new problems of price control. The subscription-book business which, except in the case of Mark Twain's books, had never been very successful in the distribution of literary works, entered a new phase. Such magazines as *Collier's* began to distribute books as premiums and as low-priced sets got up for subscribers. In spite of new methods, however, books were not easily available to most of the population. W. H. Page estimated in 1905 that only 2 or 3 per cent of the people lived near bookshops. Nevertheless, by 1910, 46 per cent of all Americans lived in towns large enough (2,500) to support shops which could stock books, and the rest had been rendered more accessible to publishers by the inauguration of rural free delivery routes in 1897. For periodicals the latter was important. By 1908, 64 per cent of the total weight of mail consisted of newspapers and magazines.

That mechanization and improved distribution did not result in cheaper books was due to other business factors. As manufacturing costs went down, other costs went up. Royalty rates, for novels especially, reached an all-time high between 1900 and 1905. Outlay for traveling agents and salesmen mounted steadily. Long-term credits to booksellers made necessary increased capitalization. But the most conspicuous increase was in the cost of advertising and promotion. Competition for authors and readers led publishers to spend fortunes on publicity. Many of the big promotion campaigns for best sellers seem to have had the same object and effect as the advertising of "loss leaders" in department stores: advertising costs sometimes killed the profit on a particular book, but the publisher earned prestige with authors and booksellers. Of the "free" publicity which inheres in the news value of book-and-author gossip, there was as yet comparatively little. Edward Bok's syndicated column of literary chat had some popularity in the late eighties and nineties, but the modern weekly newspaper review did not begin until 1896 when the New York *Times* instituted its Saturday literary supplement. Even so, newspaper book reviews in general were still the province of overworked desk men who contrived to "cover" twenty to thirty volumes in an hour's time.

The centralization of publishing and printing in a few cities was another sign of the new age. In spite of the denials and protests of such enthusiastic Westerners as Hamlin Garland and Frank Norris, New York was now definitely the center of the industry. In 1905 the total value of its book and job printing was $44,000,000; that of Chicago, $26,000,000; Philadelphia,

$14,000,000; St. Louis, $8,000,000, and Boston, $7,000,000. Though New York had the lion's share of literary publishing, Boston and Philadelphia were maintaining their great tradition of book and magazine production. Chicago had an enormous printing and book wholesaling business, but though in 1894 fifty-three of its firms published 243 titles, few of these were new literary works, and by the end of the decade even the Chicago authors were taking their business to New York publishers. A few firms like Stone & Kimball did some distinguished literary publishing for a while, but they did not long survive. Nevertheless, the civic enthusiasm which created the University of Chicago in 1890 and the great World's Fair of 1893 kept that city in the front ranks as a cultural center.

4

The differences between publishing and other big business were as important as the similarities. Fundamentally the publisher neither was nor is a producer. His "goods" are "made" by the writer and the printer, and his own essential function is to publicize and distribute. The status of his goods as property is complicated. Ordinarily he does not own what he sells: he buys the right to sell from a producer who loses his property after a period of time fixed by law. Durable as his product is in one sense, he cannot ordinarily build up a permanent demand for it. Hence his advertising problems are special. These problems are inherent in his business. Certain others were solved, or moved toward solution, between 1890 and the First World War.

Up to 1891 American publishers had been forced, by the lack of an international copyright law, to sell both foreign and native goods which were in competition with each other. If the difference in the cost of the two had consisted merely of the amount of royalty paid to the American author, this competition would not have mattered; but because competition for new uncopyrighted material among publishers forced down the price of foreign books and at the same time vastly increased the number and the variety of commercially attractive titles, the American writer was at a double disadvantage. Ordinarily he could not allow his books to be sold at the prices of foreign reprints—ten to fifty cents—because, unless the sale was enormous, even high royalties brought him small returns.

Generous and idealistic as many publishers were in the long fight for an international copyright law, their real motive was self-interest. Lack of clear title to literary property gave impetus to disorderly competition which proved fatal to many publishers. Trade courtesy had served as a restraint for a time in the mid-century, but when business morality degenerated in the Gilded Age, courtesy ceased to be effective. In the final successful struggle for copyright, moral force, exerted by those who believed that our theft of foreign property was a national crime, stood in the same relation to economic force as abolitionism stood to Northern industrialism before the Civil War: moral force could prevail only when economic conditions were right and ready. The evils of competition broke down the resistance of even the reprint publishers, and the manufacturing clause requiring the printing of foreign copyright works in the United States procured the support of manufacturers and of labor. In the political dynamics of the campaign, the influence of the International Typographical Union was crucial, as was the confusion of Congress about the nature of literary property and its relation to tariff. The trick seems to have been turned by personal pressure cleverly applied to lawmakers who did not feel that copyright mattered very much one way or the other.

Although by the end of 1892, nineteen thousand copyrights had been granted to foreign authors and composers, the results of the law were obscured by the depression of 1893. Perhaps the earliest repercussion was the unmourned death of the old reprint companies, some of which had been hastily organized in the late eighties in order to strip British lists while there was still time. Among salutary effects was the decrease in the reprinting of the trashiest English fiction, the publication of the good British works in reliable texts, and a general reduction in the price of standard foreign works. The most significant result for the author was that in 1894, for the first time, more American than foreign novels were published in the United States. That British titles continued to be well represented in our best-seller lists after 1891 is evidence that lack of copyright was not the only factor in Anglo-American competition in the nineteenth century; but the fact that American titles soon won and kept a majority on these lists shows how quickly our production of commercial literature was able to develop once fair conditions were established.

Whether or not James Bryce was justified in hoping that copyright would enlarge the horizon of English and American authors by broadening their market, the new law had the effect of internationalizing the publishing business. In 1896 three great English houses incorporated in New York—the Oxford University Press, John Lane, and Macmillan (which had founded its New York House in 1869); and many large American firms which had not set up English agencies earlier, rushed to do so. The law also probably helped to bring about a revival of good printing in America. In a period ripe for reaction against the horrors of Victorian taste, publishers now had the opportunity to offer attractively printed works to a public increasingly able to afford the necessarily higher prices. Among the designers, printers, and publishers who opened new paths, the most distinguished were Daniel Updike, who established the Merrymount Press in 1893; Bruce Rogers, whose work at the

Riverside Press began in the nineties; Thomas Bird Mosher of Portland, 1891; Stone & Kimball of Cambridge and Chicago, 1893; and Copeland & Day of Boston, 1895. It was not long before the work of these pioneers was emulated by large general publishers, who found that the public was willing to pay for well bound, well printed books.

5

One of the new conditions of the period was the change in the status of the publisher as a buyer of manuscripts and interpreter of reader demands. He had always had to compete not only for readers but for authors, but he had rarely exercised more than a negative control over the kind and quality of manuscripts that he bought. Competition now forced him to develop authors as well as readers, and to persuade writers to direct their energies into profitable channels. Frank Norris, who was a reader for Doubleday, wrote:

No one not intimately associated with any one of the larger, more important "houses" can have any idea of the influence of the publisher upon latter-day fiction. More novels are written—practically—to order than the public has any notion of. The publisher again and again picks out the man . . ., suggests the theme, and exercises, in a sense, all the functions of instructor during the period of composition. . . . Time was when the publisher waited for the unknown writer to come to him with his manuscript. But of late the Unknown has so frequently developed, under exploitation and by direct solicitation of the publisher, into a "money-making proposition" of such formidable proportions that there is hardly a publishing house that does not now hunt him out with all the resources at its command.

Correspondence of the day shows that publishers begged for "b'gosh" fiction when *David Harum* (1898) proved successful, only to warn authors away from it when Irving Bacheller's *Eben Holden* (1900) soaked up the market; that when one theme of historical fiction had been overdone, they suggested new ones; and that established authors were under constant pressure to produce in quantity the kind of work which sold best. The better publishers were careful not to force their authors too much, but some of the newer magazines and syndicates were relentless. George Ade wrote Howells in 1902 that he had determined four times to write "no more of this sickening slang," but that each time his publisher had weakened him by figuring the cash return from syndication in seventy newspapers. At the turn of the century the heaviest pressure was on novelists; the proportion of novels to all titles published was 1,278 to 6,336, or 20 per cent.

In spite of the great expansion of the book market (the number of titles published in 1910 was 13,470—three times the size of the output of 1890), the book continued to be an appendage to the magazine. The magazine in America had profited by the lack of a copyright law; the postal system took care of its distribution problem; ever increasing circulations enabled it to buy the best literary and editorial talent in the country; it offered much in the way of names, variety, and pictures for very little money; and it adapted itself to a stratified reading public. When a reader bought a magazine addressed to his level of interest and opinion, he received, as Howells said in 1893, literature with "the warrant of a critical estimate"—the warrant of editors and critics far better trained than the average publisher or his "readers."

For the novelist of the period, to quote Howells again, the reward was "in the serial, and not in the book." Established writers were paid $1,500 to $10,000 for serials, which apparently helped rather than hindered the book sale. Some magazines like *Harper's* could pay especially high prices because they published large editions in England. Young publishers like Stone & Kimball, who owned no magazine, frequently had to buy and sell serial rights in order to get book contracts. Situations like this encouraged the use of literary agents, and it was evidence of the increasing impersonality of the publishing business that such agents as A. P. Watt, Paul Reynolds, and J. B. Pinker were resorted to by authors who shrank from the growing financial complexity of the business of writing. Business seemed to many authors to be dominating art. Henry James complained bitterly of being "condemned to the economy of serialisation," which subordinated the writer to "catchpenny picture-books" by putting arbitrary limits on the length and number of installments. Other writers, like Harold Frederic, cheerfully submitted serials set up in blocks of ten thousand words, much as later writers designed their novels for easy transformation into movie scenarios.

As for illustrations, though there is little evidence that magazine fiction was chosen primarily as a vehicle for expensive artists, it is clear that authors of the stature of Howells, Lafcadio Hearn, and James Branch Cabell were sometimes engaged to write the text for a projected set of pictures. Generally speaking, the literary integrity of the standard magazines was carefully protected by the admirable editors of the day—Henry Mills Alden of *Harper's,* Horace Scudder, W. H. Page, and Bliss Perry of the *Atlantic* (which was not illustrated), Richard Watson Gilder of the *Century,* and Edward Burlingame of *Scribner's.* Inasmuch as all these magazines were the property of general book publishers, who asked for book rights when they accepted serials, it is obvious that the judgment of these editors is a key to the literary tone of the period, and that the decline of the circulation of their magazines about 1910 was an omen of a cultural change.

Robert Underwood Johnson of the *Century* crystallized the problem in a letter to his publisher in 1910. His magazine was not prospering, but the new ten- and fifteen-centers, "the cheap, illustrated all-story periodicals [were] making money hand over fist." His solution was to emphasize the *Century's* old policy of appealing to women, religious people, and the West, "where the American reading public is to be found." Unfortunately for him, all three seemed to prefer the cheaper periodicals created by journalistic editors and publishers like Bok, McClure, and Norman Hapgood of *Collier's,* who were not committed to nineteenth century notions concerning women, religious people, and the West. *McClure's, Munsey's, Cosmopolitan, Everybody's, Collier's,* and the *Ladies' Home Journal* were discovering new interests and tastes in American readers; and by 1905 they were taking their pick of American authors who could no longer afford to write exclusively for the editors they revered.

The new readers were more interested in facts and diversion than in principles and art. The reform campaigns of Gilder and Alden seemed stodgy compared to the solid factualism of muckraking articles about matters that touched the common people everywhere; and the fiction of O. Henry, Jack London, and George Randolph Chester seemed less like literature than like life. The financial heart of the new magazines was advertising, and when Bok decided in 1896 to run his stories back among the advertisements, he was merely being realistic about the relation of one to the other. General literary weeklies in 1909 had a circulation of almost 6,000,000 an issue.

The syndicates were equally realistic. The Sunday supplement was the only magazine for myriads of readers, and the economy of selling the same matter to scores of newspapers was obvious to the author. Bok, Bacheller, McClure, and Dana of the New York *Sun* had discovered the possibilities of this new market in the eighties, and by 1900 it was an important outlet for fiction. Howells thought that for second-rate literature the syndicate offered the best pay, but that though it had "enlarged the field of belles-lettres," it could not foster good fiction because newspapers were read not by women but by men and boys who wanted only to beguile their leisure. By the time his statement got into print, a Chicago newspaper had found it necessary to reprint installments of his own novel *The World of Chance* (1893), and by 1900 he was thinking of starting an international syndicate which would pay authors thousand dollar advances.

As it turned out, the Sunday newspaper, as a vehicle for literature, proved ephemeral; but if Howells was right about newspaper readers, and if the success of O. Henry's stories (in the New York *World,* for example) was symptomatic, it is probable that syndicates helped to spread the reading habit by bringing good if not profound fiction to people who had been reading nothing else of literary quality. If, as many claimed, the syndicates also tended to vulgarize the talents of men like Stephen Crane, Frank Norris, Jack London, and Richard Harding Davis, they deserve credit for doubling the rates for serial matter in the nineties and for offering sometimes the security of a salary.

Security was a new element in professional authorship. Literacy, new business methods, the rising standard of living, the adjustment of reading matter to diverse levels of taste, all helped to broaden and stabilize the literary market and thus to make writing income not only large but predictable. It is not very important that eighteen books of the period sold over a million copies each, but it mattered very much that the competent professional writer was finding an increasing number of outlets for his work. Novels and some other types of prose could by 1910 be serialized in newspapers, weeklies, or monthlies at prices which were usually higher than the total of book royalties. Royalties for American cloth editions rose from an almost universal 10 per cent on the retail price in the eighties to a fairly normal 20 per cent (for established authors) after 1900, though after that date there was a definite trend toward graduated royalties. Fifty-cent paper editions, and special cheap cloth editions made up for large jobbers, brought smaller royalties but bigger sales; and an author as popular as Richard Harding Davis could expect generous rates on sets printed as magazine premiums. In 1913 new horizons opened in the reprint field when Sears Roebuck printed from Harper's plates of Lew Wallace's *Ben-Hur* an edition of one million at a royalty of twelve cents. In the foreign markets, English, Canadian, colonial, and German rights could be counted on for small sums. Dramatic rights, which had been generally ignored earlier, became important in the nineties when producers began to scramble for every successful novel. Most book contracts granted the author one-third or one-half of the dramatic proceeds, which in the case of *Ben-Hur* totaled over half a million dollars in twenty years. Still larger vistas were appearing in Hollywood; but story-telling on the screen was not common until 1908, and the application of copyright laws to the movies was not clarified until some years later when a movie producer tried to get the rights to *Ben-Hur* from a theater producer who was trying in turn to get it from the publisher in order to cash in on the movie rights.

By 1914 a writer might have sold his novel in ten or twelve forms to as many different audiences, if he knew and did not spurn the common denominator by which they were all divisible. What was the result for literary culture? Was the contemporary success of Harold Bell Wright the goal toward which writers and educators had struggled for a century? Had financial security for authors been achieved at the expense of artistic integrity? Publisher Page in 1905 took a gloomy view of rapacious authors and of public taste. "It is a hard world," he said, in which *When Knighthood Was in Flower, Graustark,* and *Alice of Old Vincennes* "make fortunes," while Howells and James "write to unresponsive markets and even Mr. Kipling cannot find so many readers for a new novel as Mr. Bacheller of 'Eben Holden.'"

6

It is not easy to compare the taste of one era with another, and it is almost impossible to compare eras which differed vastly not only in literate population but in the proportion of educated to uneducated readers. Yet the facts about the popularity of authors from decade to decade are instructive. In 1872 the Public Library in Boston, a city of comparatively high culture, reported that the authors most in demand were the now forgotten Mrs. E. D. E. N. Southworth, Mrs. Caroline Lee Hentz, and Mary Jane Holmes. Fifteen years later things were not much better: the order books of a Midwestern wholesaler showed that the equally insignificant E. P. Roe led the same group in popularity, but that Cooper and Hawthorne stood tenth and eleventh.

But in the nineties something was happening. A survey of libraries in 1893 showed that only Alcott and Roe of the old group were still high on the lists, and that Dickens was first, with Scott, Cooper, George Eliot, Hawthorne, O. W. Holmes, and Thackeray close behind. Of the novels, *David Copperfield* was first, with *Ivanhoe, The Scarlet Letter, Uncle Tom's Cabin, Ben-Hur, Adam Bede, Vanity Fair,* and *Jane Eyre* following in order. As the century wore away the best-seller lists contained more and more books that have won a permanent place in literature. Page seemed not to have noticed that in the lists of the top ten, from 1895, were works by J. M. Barrie, Stephen Crane (*The Red Badge of Courage* ranked eighth in 1896), Kipling, and Finley Peter Dunne ("Mr. Dooley" ranked eighth in 1899). In 1904 Ellen Glasgow's *The Deliverance* ranked second (two years earlier she had assured her publisher that her "big," "deep," human documents could never be popular). In 1905 Mrs. Wharton's *The House of Mirth* ranked eighth. In 1906, a banner year, Winston Churchill's *Coniston,* Upton Sinclair's *The Jungle,* and novels by Margaret Deland, Mrs. Wharton, and Ellen Glasgow were among the top ten. With Howells in twenty-sixth place (in the 1893 list), Hardy in forty-sixth, and Henry James and the Russian novelists nowhere at all, Americans had little occasion for smugness; but the fact that both James and Howells were making comfortable, sometimes handsome, incomes shows that the better magazines and their readers were willing and able to support the better writers.

All things considered, the business of literature, which Howells called an infant industry in 1893, had come of age by 1910. Certainly it had been weaned from the mother country, and was self-supporting. Still more important, in the perspective of time, the democratic patronage of literature was proving its potentialities. It was still possible for the "venal novelist," as Frank Norris said, to gull the many who "for the moment . . . have confounded the Wrong with the Right, and prefer that which is a lie to that which is true." But Norris' faith that "The People, despised of the artist, hooted, caricatured and vilified, are after all, and in the main, the real seekers after Truth," and Howells' steadfast conviction that "Democracy in literature . . . wishes to know and to tell the truth, confident that consolation and delight are there" were finding their justification in the ever-increasing popularity of good literature.

# 59. THE LITERATURE OF IDEAS

THE group of writers that most courageously dealt with the new issues—social, economic, and philosophical—of America after the Civil War were those who addressed themselves in plain prose to the philosophy of change and to the problems it raised in American life. Broadly speaking, this "literature of ideas" falls into three main categories: that which justified traditional individualism in terms of traditional ideas; that which justified the older individualism, economic and philosophical, in terms of rising ideas and conditions; and that which endeavored to provide a synthesis of the old and the new. But any such classification is, at best, rough indeed and fails to do justice to the varied nuances of thought in these writers.

The individualism that had served as a primary assumption for Emerson, Whitman, and even Melville and Poe, was undoubtedly threatened. It was becoming increasingly clear that sporadic, unplanned efforts on the part of individuals to advance knowledge could no longer meet the needs of a more complex society. Well before the year 1900 government agencies, industrial corporations, universities, and philanthropic foundations were all contributing to knowledge through specialization, planning, and cooperation. It was no longer so apparent as it once seemed that the individual alone is the only or even the chief source of knowledge and light. Knowledge, in other words, was in part at least a social product. It might, moreover, be used not merely for the well-being of the individuals possessing it or controlling it, but for society as a whole. Such was the implication of the new movements for public health, the conservation of natural resources, and the application of science to business, agriculture, and government itself. At the same time that an ever larger company of men and women questioned the idea that individual effort and genius alone explain additions to knowledge, a rising group of economists maintained that wealth is likewise a social rather than an individual product. It was consequently plain to them that society might and should assume a responsibility for the just social use of wealth.

The intellectual revolution was even more profound than these changes suggest. To many the Darwinian theory seemed to rob man of his essential

969

divinity by associating him with the lower animals, to despoil him of his freedom of will by reducing him to a mere automaton responding in a mechanistic way to the stimuli of his environment. The related philosophy of Herbert Spencer was frequently interpreted as materialistic or deterministic, as robbing man of divine impulse, of God Himself. The very method of science now seemed to many devout men far more dangerous than they had supposed: it threatened to destroy the validity of the intuitive approach to truth, an approach long regarded in some circles as the most satisfactory, if not the only adequate, justification of spiritual values, of man's universality and permanence—of all, in short, that made life worth living.

The Darwinian theory did not altogether militate against the older individualistic body of thought. In fact, it reenforced it at many points. This was particularly true in economic and social theory. Certain economists and an even more impressive group of business leaders used the doctrine of survival of the fittest to justify the process by which weak economic competitors were driven to the wall by the more competent monopolists. The free enterprise aspect of classical economic theory seemed, indeed, to gain a new scientific validity thanks to the findings of the Darwinists. Likewise individualism profited, or seemed to profit, when social theorists applied the whole concept of evolution through struggle and survival to society itself. Such applications of scientific theory to economic and social issues posed problems for the plain people and their intellectual champions who were trying to develop a new program in which cooperation, social responsibility for the individual, and sustained planning for the public good figured prominently.

**2**

The considerable body of literature which held that new conditions and problems might best be solved by the reassertion of traditional faith and ideas may be illustrated by the writings of John Lancaster Spalding. This brilliant and gifted son of well-to-do Kentuckians was, by the 1880's, a recognized leader in the Catholic Church. At the seat of his bishopric in Peoria he wrote, besides several volumes of regional and patriotic poetry, a half-dozen books widely read in Protestant and Catholic circles alike. His *Lectures and Discourses* (1882), *Means and Ends of Education* (1895), *Thoughts and Theories of Life and Education* (1897), and *Socialism and Labor* (1902) contain the essence of his thought.

Sensitive to the ways in which the new science challenged religious faith and authority, and aware that what passed for the modern temper was not to be brushed aside, Bishop Spalding argued with force and clarity for the thesis that the Catholic Church must enter into the living controversies of the time. The church must not only prove to Protestants that notwithstanding its reliance on tradition and authority and its untutored immigrant following, it was in no sense opposed to science, learning, and culture. It must actively contribute to American thought and literature, and so reflect the faith that the evils of American life could be remedied solely by Christian character, ideals, and values. The moral power of the church, its divine and mystic character, could incorporate much of modern life, could mitigate the materialism of science, could come to grips with the new age. Christian character, values, and ideals alone, insisted Spalding, could preserve the dignity and integrity of the individual, could bring him into harmony with the permanent and the universal, could direct him to his proper destiny. This it could do, not by denying modern knowledge, but by interpreting it and directing the uses to which it was put.

Among the specific evils in American society which Bishop Spalding especially deplored was the exploitation of immigrants in city slums. His valiant efforts guided many newcomers into carefully planned colonies in the Western states. The ill effects of cutthroat competition, of the power of business monopolies, and of the sacrifice of human values for property rights, disturbed the Bishop of Peoria no less than the degradation of immigrants in city slums. The press, the public school, such legislative devices as the inheritance tax, and such organizations as the trade union could do something to remedy all these evils. But at best, Spalding urged, such agencies and laws could do very little. The true remedy for the "tyrannous sway of commercialism" and for "the ignorance and misery" of urban slums lay rather in the primacy of Christian character. The social gulf between the steady, thrifty laborers and the loafers and criminals was not economic but moral, and consequently "all real amelioration in the lot of human beings depends on religious, moral, and intellectual conditions."

Although Spalding denounced socialism as a mechanical device ruinous to the liberty of men, although he preached class collaboration in the name of religion and reason, he forthrightly condemned the avarice of employers. "Only those who look above property to the peace of society, and strive in all earnestness to live in the infinite and permanent world of truth, beauty, and goodness, can hope to rise to the full height of a noble manhood." The captains of industry, mere mechanical men, mere victims of their own success, could, like the poor whom they exploited, truly live only in those "inner goods which make men wise, holy, beautiful, and strong." In preaching a gospel the effect of which was in large measure to make the lowly and poor content with their lot, a lot they could spiritually enrich by will and faith, and in calling on the rich and powerful to seek God, Bishop Spalding argued with engaging charm for the primacy of spiritual values in the here as well as the hereafter.

The respect for authority and for the past which sets the tone of Bishop

Spalding's inspirational essays is also reflected in the writings of a non-Catholic educational leader and philosopher, William T. Harris. The son of a New England textile manufacturer, Harris rose rapidly in St. Louis to the superintendency of the public schools. In this position and subsequently as United States Commissioner of Education, Harris became the leading educational philosopher of his day. At the same time he wrote voluminously on philosophy, on literary criticism, on the arts, and on political and economic questions. Coming under the influence of a picturesque German-born thinker, Brockmeyer, Harris accepted Hegelianism. In 1867 he established and edited for a quarter of a century the *Journal of Speculative Philosophy*. The first American periodical devoted exclusively to philosophy, the *Journal* familiarized Americans with philosophical writings, old and new, European and American. As a close student of Hegel's *Larger Logic* and popularizer of his philosophy, and as an essayist who took the whole range of culture as his own, Harris expounded his ideas with authority and with force. He took an active part in the Concord School of Philosophy, an informal summer group before which the lingering transcendentalists and younger philosophical minds discussed Plato, Kant, Hegel, and their disciples.

In Hegelianism Harris found a thoroughly optimistic and idealistic philosophy which infused the world with a divine purpose and which, like Christianity, endowed the individual with a noble and immortal destiny. At the same time it justified the existing order and authorities by assuming that whatever exists is an inevitable stage in the unfolding of objective reason or the world spirit and is, consequently, right. Without sacrificing the individualistic ideals of self-help and "self-activity," Hegelianism seemed to lift the individual to a higher plane of self-realization. At the same time it subordinated him to existing social institutions by maintaining that his true, spiritual self, which was constantly subjected to conflict with his natural or physical self, could be realized only by adjusting himself to the divinely appointed environment and the social institutions that actually existed. What Harris thus did was to provide cogent arguments for regarding the individual and the solidarity of society as one and the same. The individual, according to Harris, could realize himself only through the family, school, church, and state.

In the mind of Harris, no conflict existed between the values of capitalism and those of the mind and spirit. Under capitalism the mass of men were destined to enjoy, not only competence and security, but leisure time for the cultivation of "the good life." Hegelianism, in his writings, served to reconcile any dichotomy between the material and practical and the intellectual and spiritual. Harris saw no threat in monopoly, or in technological and seasonal unemployment, to the realization of individual potentialities.

In justifying the ethics and practices of capitalism, Harris explicitly attacked as fallacious and as socially subversive the single tax, the utopianism of Edward Bellamy, and the "scientific socialism" of Marx, Engels, and their American disciples. No one can say in what degree Harris strengthened bewildered individuals by his assurances that their security and destiny lay in willingly subordinating themselves to the dominant aspects of the society in which they lived. Nor can anyone measure the effects of his teachings in reenforcing the conservative tenor of much American thinking. It is reasonable to assume, however, that he was one of the most influential intellectual leaders of his time. The very fact that his ideas found expression, not in elaborate and lengthy books, but in a vast number of essays and lectures, tended to increase his influence in his own day.

The writings of another absolute idealist, Josiah Royce, were less widely known than those of Harris, but they are even more important. The distinction of Royce's work rests only in part on the literary style in which he clothed his ideas. Occasional brilliance, humor, and imagination are apparent in Royce, but there are grandiose sentences and a kind of verbose dullness. Nor was it a particularly original thing to espouse Hegelianism, already becoming popular. But Royce gave it a new turn, and his distinction rests on the answers he thus gave to some of the perplexing problems of the individual in American society.

True to the doctrines of absolute idealism, Royce held that all reality is the idea, experience, or act of the mind and that there is but one Mind to which all others are related as parts to a whole. The Absolute has, however, endowed the individual with a moral will and independence which can be realized only through the community. Each individual, being thus a necessary part of the Absolute, makes his unique, indispensable contribution to the whole.

Here was a philosophy which restored to the individual the purpose and dignity of which Darwinism and the new interdependent society of urban industrialism seemed to so many to rob him. Here, too, was a system of thought serviceable to an older individualistic democracy which was being threatened by new aggregates of mass power, whether in the form of overwhelming corporations or a national state forced to wield more and more direction over the common life in the interest of common well-being. The individual's salvation in such circumstances, Royce believed, was in loyalty to a cause—to some cause to which the community, through which he could alone realize his moral independence, professed allegiance. It was not surprising that Royce commended the cause of regionalism. For regionalism had already found expression both in political movements and in the engaging local color school of literature. In loyalty to one's section or province,

Royce held, was to be found the needed training for the larger loyalties to the nation and to humanity itself.

In *The Philosophy of Loyalty* (1908) Royce developed the thesis that inasmuch as conflict of loyalties is inevitable, the individual must escape such conflict by loyalty to loyalty. Thus the individual, in the indirect support he gave to the whole realm of causes through his loyalty to loyalty, found his needed adjustment to life. He found it by coming into a closer relation with the Absolute, whether this be regarded as God or as the Absolute Idea or as the Ideal Community. In *The World and the Individual* (1900, 1901) Royce formulated this general position in maintaining that nature is a social product necessarily resulting from stable and cooperative intercourse. In thus emphasizing the voluntary and active aspects of absolute idealism, in making room for individual purpose and choice, and in laying stress on the individual's appreciative capacities and values, Royce gave direction to those Americans who were trying to relate their lives to a society and a universe that presented on so many levels obstacles and vexing conflicts. It is not hard to see why, in an America beset with class and regional tensions and with conflicts between the authority of science and that of religion, a philosophy at once empirical and idealistic, activistic and voluntaristic, a world view which found integrity of the individual in the community without in any way weakening the individual, appealed to thoughtful men in search of support for the traditional individualism.

3

Another group of writers sought to validate traditional individual values in terms of new currents of thought. The most challenging of these currents was the theory of evolution which gradually, in the sixties and seventies, won converts among scientists, social philosophers, and ethical and religious leaders. No single figure in this group was more representative or more influential than John Fiske. As the author of delightfully written popular histories of the American colonies and the American Revolution, as the interpreter of American political ideas, as a highly successful lecturer, and as a philosophical writer, Fiske was one of the most widely known American intellectual leaders of the last quarter of the nineteenth century. In many respects he and his Harvard associate Royce stood far apart, for Fiske was a disciple of Herbert Spencer and had no traffic with absolute idealism. But like Royce he offered reassurance to men and women to whom Darwinism seemed a repudiation of the dignity of the individual and a denial of Christian faith. In his engaging interpretations of American history he developed the theme that a guiding Providence had from the very start directed America on her successful course.

In his equally popular lectures on philosophy he brought to thousands of people the essential message of his book, *Outlines of Cosmic Philosophy* (1874).

In the last chapter of the *Outlines* Fiske asserted that there is no necessary conflict between Christianity and the doctrine of evolution.

We are not the autocrats, but the servants and interpreters of Nature; and we must interpret her as she is,—not as we would like her to be. That harmony which we hope eventually to see established between our knowledge and our aspirations is not to be realized by the timidity which shrinks from logically following out either of two apparently conflicting lines of thought—as in the question of matter and spirit—but by the fearlessness which pushes each to its inevitable conclusion. Only when this is recognized will the long and mistaken warfare between Science and Religion be exchanged for an intelligent and enduring alliance. Only then will the two knights of the fable finally throw down their weapons, on discovering that the causes for which they have so long been waging battle are in reality one and the same eternal causes,—the Cause of truth, of goodness, and of beauty; "the Glory of God and the relief of man's estate."

Although other intellectual leaders, including Henry Ward Beecher, Francis Abbot, and James McCosh, reconciled religion and the theory of evolution, no one appealed to so wide an audience as the versatile John Fiske. What he did in the religious and philosophical sphere William Graham Sumner did in the social and economic. The justification of the free competition of individuals in economic life by invoking the sanctions, not of traditional orthodox ideas, but of the new evolutionary theories, gives Sumner a prominent place in the group of intellectual leaders in the last quarter of the nineteenth century. Like Fiske and Harris, he sought to provide a formula which would give order and stability to an America torn by agrarian uprisings and labor troubles. In epigrammatic language, characterized by an appealing and homely wit, Sumner popularized from his chair of political and social science at Yale his essentially Darwinian version of laissez faire, his opposition to all notions of community responsibility for individual well-being, his denunciations of what appeared to him to be the soft sentimentality of reformers and radicals. Both as a celebrated teacher and as a widely read essayist, Sumner insisted that when social abuses appeared they must be met only by scientific procedures sponsored by competent authorities.

Sumner's individualism was the stark and somewhat questionable application to social issues of Darwin's doctrine of the struggle for existence and the survival of the fittest. This is clearly evident in "What Social Classes Owe to Each Other" (1883) and "The Absurd Attempt to Make the World Over" (1894), and "Commercial Crisis," to cite three of many essays.

The "strong" and the "weak" are terms which admit of no definition unless they are made equivalent to the industrious and the idle, the frugal and the ex-travagant. . . . If we do not like the survival of the fittest, we have only one possible alternative, and that is the survival of the unfittest. The former is the law of civilization; the latter is the law of anti-civilization.

The influential *Folkways* (1907) emphasized the doctrine that human sanctions lack rational validity and are relative to time and place. In this notable contribution to social theory Sumner still further lent support to an economic conservatism that found the security of the individual in the accept-ance of his lot as both necessary and, in the larger scheme of things, good. The fact that he spoke in the name of the new evolutionary conception lent all the more weight to his justification of competitive individualism. This had resulted in great economic inequality, in widespread social insecurity, and in the preservation of a laissez faire philosophy which militated against the advance of the social legislation on which industrial societies in the Old World had already embarked.

The great limitation of Sumner's social thought was, of course, that with no understanding of the fact that government is a function of the groups able to exert power, he assumed that Jefferson's doctrine of "free men in a free society" was as valid in a highly interdependent and increasingly stratified America as it had been in the simple agrarian economy of the early nineteenth century.

In this assumption, to be sure, he was not alone. E. L. Godkin, editor of the New York *Evening Post* and of the *Nation,* a brilliant and witty Irish immigrant, represented, in the fashion of John and John Quincy Adams, the doctrine of an intellectual elite devoted to public honesty. Champion of prop-erty rights and critic of agrarianism and of organized labor, Godkin in true laissez faire spirit condemned the protective tariff as unwarranted favoritism to a special interest. His writings, largely editorials in the *Nation* and the *Evening Post,* advanced his social philosophy in pungent phrases and ironical twists of contemporary slang. His pen made even the driest subjects lively and memorable. His distinguished literary style showed no falling off as he became older; but his conception that the individual might, through exposing error and battling for decency, purge American society of its grossest faults, failed him in the end. The future came to seem to him too dark for his ideas to win their way.

In one notable respect both Sumner and Godkin differed from many writers who, like them, justified the traditional individualism in terms of evolutionary theory. Neither accepted the doctrine of the white man's burden in advancing a superior civilization among the more backward peoples of the globe. On the contrary, they stoutly opposed the growth of military and naval force and the imperial path which the country took during and after the Spanish-American War. They refused to be beguiled by the arguments of the Reverend Josiah Strong in *Our Country* (1885). They denied that Strong was justified in invoking the theory of evolution in support of a militant Protestant imperial program. Godkin and Sumner also vigorously condemned the doctrine of navalism popularized by Captain Alfred Mahan in his widely read and cogently written book, *The Influence of Sea Power upon History* (1890)

### 4

It is, of course, impossible to draw a hard and fast line between adherents of traditional doctrines and those who dealt with the new movements of thought and the new forces in American life. Yet in the last quarter of the nineteenth century and in the first decade of the twentieth a more or less clearly defined group did try to work out a synthesis between the older values and concepts of individualism and the newer concept of social responsibility for all individuals. In a general sense, this group was convinced that the root of the trouble in America, the great threat to the old-fashioned society in which individuals enjoyed relative security and freedom of opportunity, lay in the economic dislocation incident to the exhaustion of the open frontier and the startling growth of monopolies with their ruthless methods of competition and their strangle hold on government. Without giving up the conviction, cherished by Godkin, that public enlightenment is indispensable, the exponents of various types of radicalism were convinced of the ineffectiveness of the unorganized individual approach in reform, and favored some measure of collective action and the expansion of the functions of the government over private interests.

Yet the Marxist doctrines of economic determinism, class struggle, and the abolition of private property formed no part of the ideology of this group. As individualists anxious to restore waning individual autonomy they took their stand on the natural rights philosophy and insisted that they were merely extending it and giving it fresh applications which new economic conditions necessitated if the great creed of the Declaration of Independence were not to become a mere dead memory.

Among the significant writings which illustrate this general body of thought, Henry George's *Progress and Poverty* (1879) takes high rank by reason of its content, style, and influence. The central question posed in the book is: Why should increasing poverty accompany increasing civilization; in other words, how was it that more men had less of worldly goods as the country became more and more settled, and as more and more railroads, cities, and other instruments of civilization might logically be expected to ease man's lot? The central idea in the book is that every man has a natural right to apply his labor to land and to enjoy the full fruits thereof, and that this natural right had come to be greatly curtailed by the dominance of landlords. The increasing value of land in settled communities, George insisted, is created, not by the effort of the individual who had invested in it, often for mere speculative purposes, but by the contributions of the whole community. Therefore landlords in exacting economic rent—the "unearned increment" or the margin between the original outlay and the value of improvements he had made on the one hand and the market value on the other—are in effect robbing the user of the land of a part of his labor and the community of its social contribution to the increased market value.

This idea had been anticipated by the physiocrats, by Thomas Paine, by John Stuart Mill, by Herbert Spencer, and by a half-dozen less well known British and American land reformers. But George, a self-educated, poverty-stricken California journalist, had read none of their writings and had come to the idea as a result of his own observations and experiences. In relating it to American conditions he gave it an original turn. The central solution which *Progress and Poverty* proposed was to tax the unearned increment of land, to take back for the community that part of its value which the community, as it developed, had created. Such a tax, George maintained, would relieve industry and labor from all other taxes, inasmuch as it would be ample for the functions of the state: hence the term "single tax" readily became attached to his program.

The wide appeal of *Progress and Poverty* can be understood partly because of its clarity and its persuasiveness. George wrote simply but eloquently. He spoke with the conviction of a prophet. His trenchant indictment of speculation in land, of ownership by absentee landlords, and of monopoly of the earth, captured the imaginations of countless Americans. Its appeal was related to the fact that Americans were finding it increasingly hard to take up good land near channels of communication, and were feeling the pinch of high freight rates and dear prices for goods produced with less and less competition by larger and larger corporations.

The book went through a hundred editions before it was a quarter of a century old. It expressed the feeling of frustration of innumerable tenants, small businessmen, workers, indebted farmers, and struggling professional people. It cast its spell over Hamlin Garland, Brand Whitlock, and, to a certain extent, William Dean Howells. It provided a sort of corroboration for the drama depicted by Frank Norris in *The Octopus*. It inspired a few single-tax colonies, such as that in New Jersey where Upton Sinclair lived for a time.

The single-tax doctrine did not succeed in its larger purposes. Nor could it have done so in view of George's failure to implement the movement by building an organization capable of wielding political power; in view, above all, of its oversimplified economic theory, its failure to comprehend fully the nature of the new capitalism with its endless ramifications. Yet no one can deny that the book inspired, or at least accentuated, general awareness of the evils of land monopoly and the bearing of this condition on the relative autonomy so many Americans had once enjoyed. *Progress and Poverty* is of its time and place, but it is more than this. It is a great human document, a powerful statement of popular indignation and popular aspirations. It is a classic in the literature of American ideas.

Even when its greatness is fully recognized, the appeal of *Progress and Poverty* can hardly be understood without recalling that it was only one book among many which passionately protested against the encroachment of great aggregates of wealth on the ordinary individual. Two years after its publication William Dean Howells accepted for the *Atlantic Monthly* an article which had already been rejected by more conservative editors. It was entitled "The Story of a Great Monopoly." Its author was Henry Demarest Lloyd, a free-trade enthusiast and free-lance Chicago journalist. It portrayed succinctly and dramatically the methods by which the Standard Oil Company had risen to power by pushing its competitors to the wall by any methods, however unethical, so long as they "worked." It brought home to its readers the idea that business, hitherto either applauded or ignored by most men of letters, possessed antisocial characteristics: thus it heralded the essential message that Thorstein Veblen was later to develop. If any single piece of writing may be said to have inaugurated a new movement, this article did. "The Story of a Great Monopoly" introduced to America "the literature of exposure," or, as Theodore Roosevelt called it at its height, some twenty-five years later, "muckraking."

The *Atlantic* piece was followed by other writings in which Lloyd exposed the acquisitive and antisocial practices of the grain elevator magnates and manufacturers and the railroad men who trafficked in rebates. But Lloyd's writing was in no sense merely negative. He defended the interests of small businessmen, consumers, organized workers, even the Haymarket anarchists, whose belief in direct action he deplored. His impassioned plea for industrial justice in *A Strike of Millionaires Against Miners* (1890) indicated a sympathy with labor far stronger than Henry George's. *Man, the Social Creator* (1906) approached in quality the writings of the Christian Socialists. In this work Lloyd emphasized his faith in the ability of struggling, suffering humanity to achieve a common well-being through fusing economic cooperation with Christian ethics. It reflected his basic conviction that since men are sufficiently intelligent and honest to manage the business of other men for them, they are likewise intelligent and honest enough to be entrusted with the commonwealth of society—its mines, mills, and stores.

Lloyd will be remembered not so much for these later writings as for an elaborate documentation of the little article on Standard Oil which had launched his career. *Wealth Against Commonwealth* (1894) undermined much classical economic doctrine by showing the gulf between prevalent laissez faire theory and actual practice. Its facts were challenged at the time and have been challenged since; but the picture he painted of powerful men accumulating riches through an unfettered acquisitive bent and by the molding of government, churches, and education to their purpose, has, at any rate, the broad essentials of truth. Here Lloyd proved, whatever else he demonstrated or failed to show, that it was possible to present the findings of Congressional committees and court decrees with such clarity and human appeal that writing on economic issues could rise to a high level.

Lloyd's wit and skillful turning of phrases, his startling antitheses, the passionate depth of feeling revealed even in his most factual statements, gave to *Wealth Against Commonwealth* a distinguished place in the literature of ideas of the last quarter of the nineteenth century. Although Lloyd's work was continued by the muckrakers, who, during the Presidency of Theodore Roosevelt, exposed evils in the industrial and political life of the nation, *Wealth Against Commonwealth* remains the classic in "the literature of exposure."

Perhaps one reason for this is the sustained and positive conviction of its author that the individual can achieve earthly salvation only through cooperation with his fellows for economic and social well-being. The theoretical basis of this conviction was elaborately explored and systematized by Lester Frank Ward, government employee and natural scientist, who ranks with Spencer and Comte in the founding of modern sociology. Ward was profoundly influenced by the doctrine of evolution, just as were Fiske, Sumner, and others, but he drew from it more than Sumner's justifications for laissez faire and rugged individualism. To him evolution is not merely a blind, mechanistic, trial and error process, in which planned foresight and intelligence are negligible, but rather a cosmic force in which the active efforts of men's minds have played a decisive role. Ward urged that, whatever differences there may be between individuals in their innate gifts, or between the sexes or the races, every individual can realize his potentialities far more effectively than is supposed possible by people who accept the prevailing laissez faire theory. Thus Ward advocated a new type of education on a mass scale, an education in which the scientific spirit and method figured in a large way. Above all he favored the use of the government as an active, creative agency in such economic and social planning as might best achieve men's highest possibilities.

Ward invented a whole series of obscure, strange terms and these, together with his ponderous and often opaque style, kept his lengthy treatises, *Dynamic Sociology* (1883), *Outlines in Sociology* (1898), and *Pure Sociology* (1903–1918) from being widely known. The most readable of his books, *The Psychic Factors of Civilization* (1893), remains an arresting and significant statement of his beliefs. Its distinction lies in its forceful insistence that within a monistic and activistic universe the human mind has been and can be in the future in even larger degree, a creative force for the democracy and humanitarianism without which only a handful of individuals can truly live.

Among those who were particularly indebted to Ward, the most important figure is Thorstein Veblen. His skeptical and iconoclastic mind owed something to the Populist fever, which publicized the attack on "predatory" Wall Street in the Middle West where Veblen was born and reared; it owed at least as much to his revolt against the conservative Norwegian-American community he was part of and to his failure ever to feel thoroughly at home outside it. After graduating from Carleton College in Minnesota, Veblen studied at intervals at Johns Hopkins, Yale, and Cornell. Although some of his early work reveals the germ of his theories, these were not fully presented until 1899, when *The Theory of the Leisure Class* appeared. In 1904 *The Theory of Business Enterprise* carried his social theory still further.

Veblen approached the economic institutions and values of modern capitalism from evolutionary, anthropological, and psychological points of view. In his mind the production and distribution of goods had been, from the earliest times, subject to a struggle between the predatory and the industrious: the modern captain of industry was a lineal descendant of the robber baron, the hard-working laborer of the old-time artisan. Modern business, which Veblen regarded as something very different from industry, ruled through the price system—a system which, with modern machinery, frustrated the instinctive creative urge in the worker to see and enjoy the fruits of his toil. Modern business, moreover, covered its wastefulness with all sorts of rationalizations which, Veblen believed, infected religion, education, and every aspect of society. In his later life he sought to demonstrate that war and patriotism had become functional to business and equally hostile to the interests of mankind; and he was much impressed by the Russian Revolution and by the possibility of the direction of industrial life by engineers and technologists in the interest of all individuals.

Veblen's style is verbose and at times turgid. He makes use of elaborate anthropological analogies, and resorts to baffling phrases and to the twisting of conventional meanings. In its irony this writing is frequently powerful, even devastating; but it is too heavy to attract many readers.

Veblen failed to revolutionize orthodox academic theory, but he presented a sweeping and profound indictment of production for profit and of its impact on individuals. The social and economic theory of no other American writer is so original. In time a younger generation was, consciously or unconsciously, greatly influenced by his basic theories.

## 5

Yet it was not, after all, Veblen to whom, among all the writers of the literature of ideas, the future really belonged. Although it probably cannot be said to have belonged to any single one, William James presents the best synthesis of the ideas of his time and presents them in a literary style which no other, not even Henry Adams, surpasses in directness and clarity.

In the first place, James brought together and harmonized in a new working relationship the conflict between religion and science. Inheriting from his Swedenborgian and philosophical-minded father a deep and abiding interest in spiritual values and in religious ideas, James as a young man felt poignantly the conflict between these and the scientific theories he came to accept. It was, above all, the apparently deterministic implications of science, especially Darwinism, that troubled James. The result of his reflections on the conflict between the doctrines of free will and determinism was at length presented in *The Varieties of Religious Experience*. The meaning of this book cannot be understood apart from his philosophical thought, which was comprised in *The Will to Believe* (1897), *Pragmatism* (1907), *A Pluralistic Universe* (1909), and *Essays in Radical Empiricism* (1912).

Acknowledging his indebtedness to Charles S. Peirce and to the whole tradition of British empiricism, James maintained that the test of the truthfulness of ideas is to be found in the relationship between these ideas and their practical consequences in action. Ideas, even so-called supernatural ideas, are to be regarded as instruments subject to constant retesting in the hazardous experiment which all life in essence really is. If in this process, ideas provide personal and emotional satisfaction, then they are to be regarded as true in the sense only that they enable the individual for the time to deal satisfactorily with concrete problems. An idea "true" at any given time for any given person may not be true for others, or even for that person under different circumstances. This is necessarily so since the universe itself is an unfinished experiment, so rich and varied in its meanings for each individual that no final, absolute "truth" is possible.

Such a position enabled James to hold, as he did in *The Varieties of Religious Experience,* that any item of religious faith is true for any individual for whom it provides emotional satisfactions. This position could not satisfy the craving for final truth, for the Absolute, but for those who could accept it, it provided a working equilibrium of satisfactions: it harmonized faith with scientific knowledge and method by denying any necessary conflict in the never-finished open universe.

In his later philosophical thought James carried the implications of pragmatism even further. In the spirit of the experimentalist he gave the connections between sense experience a psychological status on a par with whatever was actually connected. The way was thus opened still further to the reconciliation of faith with the scientific method: the data of faith, the ideas men have about things, become true and important in themselves by virtue of the status given to relationships.

It is impossible to separate James' philosophy from his psychology. More than any other American, he pioneered in the application of the concept of evolution to the explanation of mind. In so doing he came to the conclusion that mind cannot properly be regarded as the antithesis of body: that it must rather be thought of as the function by which the human organism, like all organisms, adjusts itself to its environment. This was the basic position in his great *Principles of Psychology* (1890). James' emphasis was, it is true, on the individual as an adjusting mechanism, rather than on his environment. Thus the role of instincts and habits played a major part in his psychological thinking. Nevertheless his functional conception of mind as an instrument of adjustment enabled him to reconcile such "deterministic" forces as heredity and biology with effort, choice, and, properly defined, with "free will" itself. Toward the end of his life James argued for a functionalism which sees in the term "mind" not an entity different from the body, but a general name for certain types of symbolic adjustment. It was James' psychology that, extended by Dewey and others, influenced the great majority of American educators to adopt, in theory at least, the ideal of education as training for adjustment to life. Education became psychologically based. The school became child-centered. Individualism was reenforced; but individualism in terms of adjustment to environment. Above all, James' psychology provided ammunition against the lock step in the classroom.

What were the larger implications of James' thought for the conflict between the traditional emphasis on the autonomy of the individual and the demands of the new interdependent society for cooperative living? Hating all forms of tyranny, power, bigness, loving the infinite variability he detected in the universe, convinced that human nature could mold a better future, James celebrated the energies of men, actual and potential. In his scheme men are morally free agents determining their own destiny. He emphasized the "instincts" of competition, acquisitiveness, and freedom of action; and his social attitudes were largely those of the traditional laissez faire school of his political mentor, E. L. Godkin. "Religiously and philosophically," James wrote, "our ancient doctrine of live and let live may prove to have a far deeper meaning tnan our people now seem to imagine it to possess." Though he had not lived in any part of the country which had recently borne the impact of the frontier, James' social philosophy in a considerable measure expressed that democratic individualism which Frederick Jackson Turner in his famous essay on "The Significance of the Frontier in American History" made the key to American experience. To James there was something heroic and exhilarating in the struggles of the poor man against all sorts of material odds. The assumption was, of course, that such struggles breed character, bring out all one's potentialities, and add true zest to life.

In all this there was much that was traditionally American. The philosophy of James was optimistic, melioristic, individualistic. It postulated faith in newness, in beginnings, in youth, in the freedom to make mistakes, to pick up and start over again. There was something very American in this cosmopolitan's insistence on an open universe, on the active and voluntary nature of human behavior, and, most important of all, in his rejection of absolutes and his doctrine that hypotheses help to make the truth they declare—if they prove effective instruments in living. He spoke for the faith of the old America in disparaging system makers and systems, in taking his stand on the broad ground of experience, concrete realities, tolerance for dissidents, and the glories of choice and risk. What was more American, more democratic, indeed, than the pragmatic conviction that beliefs *become* true by *making good?* What was more American and more democratic than the insistence that philosophy must give satisfactions to the emotional, the temperamental needs, not only of the philosopher, but of the common man? Here was the reassertion of Emerson's emphasis on self-reliance and of Whitman's song of the open road.

Yet James offered more than the reassertion of the traditional values of the democratic individualism for which his fellow countrymen longed, had faith in, but knew not exactly where to find. Although he could see good in the existence of inequalities in wealth, he also on occasion declared that if the odds in the struggle were too great, the human spirit might be broken rather than tested. Although he believed that the pugnacious instinct made war "natural," he maintained that this "instinct" need not necessarily express itself in war. In his famous essay on "The Moral Equivalent for War" he advocated the channeling of man's "instinctive" love of a fight into a cooperative attack on the obstacles of physical nature in behalf of the public good; he envisaged bands of youth fighting forest fires and drought, building hazardous highways over and through mountains, reclaiming physical environment for the commonwealth. In other words, James sensed, and explicitly said in his last years, that the society of the future would become, by necessity, more socialistic. He tried to show how at the same time the traditional American values of self-help, initiative, competition, and the zest for living might also survive. This was the synthesis of the old and the new that James offered his fellow countrymen.

The ideas of William James, especially some of his social opinions, betrayed the limitations of his personal experience as a member of the advantaged class. Many Americans, even democratic and individualistic Americans, rejected his philosophy on the score that it justified an opportunism and a narrow expediency. In denying the possibility of fixed moorings, he may have opened the gate to the confusion, drift, and ineffectiveness which, according to some writers, characterized the modern man who has rejected ultimates and absolutes. James does, indeed, open himself to these and to still other charges. But he himself would have admitted as much. He would have insisted that the risks and chances so characteristic of his philosophy are necessary unless life is to be so restricted and ordered that the joy of individual living is lost altogether.

The idea of an open universe was unquestionably deeply related to American experience and faith, and time has shown that it was not to be lightly laid aside. In James it found its most brilliant and engaging champion. In demanding a world that left plenty of room for effort and that made effort the most valued of man's activities, and in relating this demand to the confident faith that the individual need not be defeated by nature or by his fellows or by himself, James was epitomizing the dominant theme in the literature of ideas that made his generation a pivotal one in American intellectual development.

# 60. FICTION AND SOCIAL DEBATE

F OR these direct traders in ideas, literary form presented no problem; but for writers of poetry, drama, or fiction, the problem was one of altering old structures so that they might contain the new views of man and his universe. It was the problem, in a new form, that had beset Brockden Brown, Cooper, and Melville in their turns.

Whatever their ideologies, the novelists of social debate generally understood the craft of fiction as it had been conventionalized in the nineteenth century. From its very beginning, the novel in England had disseminated ideas as well as stories, and had served to instruct and illumine as well as to entertain. As the industrial revolution matured in the United States, it provoked here, as previously in England, a vigorous critical movement in which men like Henry George and Edward Bellamy wrought at the same tasks that occupied such great Victorian critics as Carlyle, Dickens, and Morris; and as in them, it suggested the use of story for the illumination of ideas.

The American social and economic novelists knew and practiced the narrator's fundamental business, that of getting an interesting story under way and keeping it going. Their plots follow the old, established patterns, adapted with considerable skill to the portrayal of the American industrial scene and to the illustration of the authors' ideas. It is their scenes and characters—particularly their characters—that reveal how much they enlarged the area of awareness known to the American novel. For better or for worse, their pages throng with a miscellany of types hardly anticipated in the era of Irving and Hawthorne: the abandoned urban poor as a class, the corrupt walking delegate, the prostitute, the old-fashioned middle-class businessman, the business adventurer, the capitalist's henchman, the venal politician, the social climber, the wealthy dilettante, the reformer, idealist, and settlement worker, and, far from least, the great capitalist himself, prime mover in the whole upsurge of industrialized big business.

The problem novel of the eighties and nineties was an instrument of the still powerful middle classes whose civilization was threatened by the disruptions of the machine age and particularly by the dominance of big business. Though uneasily aware of the proletariat, the typical middle-class author fe the essential conflict of his times as a struggle, not between capital and labor, but between the plutocracy and the people; and it was in relation to this central conflict that he tried to interpret the many subsidiary debates over the currency, immigration, the slums, the idle rich, the Populist movement, and the manipulation of the government by big business. Yet the novelist could not, if he would, have sorted his ideas into watertight compartments and thereby have isolated these economic issues from others. A story of economic struggle was likely to become also a story of politics or marriage or prostitution; and if the writer were aware of Spencer and Darwin, it might easily pass on to the profounder issues of chance versus teleology, of science versus religion, of the material versus the ideal.*

Curiously enough, the novel of politics, which might well have flourished among a people so politically minded, was long in outgrowing a narrow scope of experience and a limited philosophy. The usual subject of the political novelist was the corruption of the government, whether municipal, state, or federal; or, at the least, the manipulation of the government by special interests. It matters little whether these interests derive from the Pennsylvania whisky ring, as in Rebecca Harding Davis' *John Andross* (1874); or from the traction enterprises of a great city, as in Charles K. Lush's *The Autocrats* (1901); or from the railroads, as in Winston Churchill's *Mr. Crewe's Career* (1908). In all, with a few exceptions such as Henry Adams' *Democracy* (1880), the plot arises out of the struggle between the general public on the one hand, and the corrupting forces of special interest and privilege on the other.

The novel of economics, while more various than the novel of politics, developed despite its variety a fairly clear-cut intellectual pattern. Ideologically, the majority of economic novels occupy a position just left of center; that is, they look toward the exposure and reform of the abuses of private enterprise, not to the abolition of private enterprise itself. Overwhelmingly middle-class, these novels are in effect weapons forged for use in the struggle for class survival; but they are also a great deal more. They are an expression of the middle-class economic code of productive work, prudence, thrift, and honesty. They are a product of the continuing American quest for a better life for each one among all the people; they embody the American version of that nineteenth century liberal philosophy—lingering twilight of the Enlightenment—which seeks social justice as a prelude to the limitless development of the individual. While they occasionally reveal influences and illuminations from abroad, they are chiefly a creation of American social idealism working upon American materials.

* Four novelists who explored the philosophical implications of this conflict—Garland, Crane, Norris, and London, are discussed in Chapter 62.

Within the intellectual pale of the left center, there was scope for vigor and keenness in treatment, and for abundance and variety of subject matter. The economic novelists could, and did, make fiction out of such issues as the humanitarian's effort to alleviate suffering, the corrupting influence of big business, the trust problem, widely debated issues such as the currency and Populism, and impulses toward Christian Socialism or the Social Gospel. Among the subjects most frequently and ably handled was that of the emptiness of merely financial or merely social "success." The bourgeois folly of acquiring wealth and position without values is exposed in dozens of novels, including Charles Dudley Warner's *A Little Journey in the World* (1889), H. H. Boyesen's *Social Strugglers* (1893), and Robert Grant's *Unleavened Bread* (1900).

Ideologically, the novelists of the left center are at their best in destructive criticism; their examination of the evils of laissez faire capitalism is wide-ranging, informed, and vigorous. They abound in specific illustration of the knaveries of business; they dramatize unforgettably the splitting of a relatively homogeneous, democratic people into sharply defined classes of the rich and the poor. But, representing no single self-conscious movement or literary school, they failed to agree on any single program of reform. Their constructive energies are dissipated in miscellaneous proposals for slum clearance, settlement work, profit sharing, labor organization, or the gradual Christianizing of the social order.

In the critical examination of capitalism, the few novelists of the middle-class left were in general agreement with those of the left center. In the advocacy of radical reform, they might be found either in the individualistic camp of Henry George, as was Garland in *Jason Edwards: an Average Man* (1892), or in the collectivistic camp of Edward Bellamy, as were many of the lesser utopian romancers who were drawn along in the powerful wake of *Looking Backward*. More numerous than the radicals, and on the whole an abler group of writers, were the moderate conservatives, whose position was right center rather than definitely to the right. From the conservatives proceeded a few vigorous defenses of old-fashioned "solid" individual enterprise such as Alice French's story of the economic education of John Winslow in *The Man of the Hour* (1905), and a somewhat larger number of attacks on organized labor, including John Hay's popular but superficial treatment of the labor organizer in *The Breadwinners* (1884), and F. Hopkinson Smith's ably written study of union-conducted persecution in *Tom Grogan* (1896).

But the best and most characteristic product of the right center was the romance of economic conflict, in which the author, unconcerned with social justice, satisfied with the status quo, uses as a narrative framework the conflict of business, force with force or man with man. Among others, Will Payne in

*The Money Captain* (1898) and of course Frank Norris in *The Pit* (1903) cleverly developed suspense and dramatic tension out of the incidents of business struggle. From the hesitant beginnings of J. G. Holland and others in the seventies down through the vigorous portrayal of the self-made Harrington in Robert Herrick's *Memoirs of an American Citizen* (1905), the characterization of the big businessman advanced from conventionality and moral primness toward original comprehension and adequacy; so that the studies done by Payne in *The Money Captain,* by Norris in *The Pit,* and by Herrick in the *Memoirs* are worthy forerunners of Theodore Dreiser's massive Cowperwood trilogy.

2

In the words Goethe once applied to Carlyle, Edward Bellamy was, first of all, a moral force. The matrix of his character was the moral idealism which he developed amidst the liberal Christianity of his childhood home at Chicopee Falls, Massachusetts. As a youth, he nourished a Miltonic sense of dedication to high and noble ends, along with a non-Miltonic vein of mingled gentleness and melancholy. Except for a certain dearth of robust energy, Bellamy's was the personality of a major creative artist. He had imagination; he had emotional elevation and intensity; he had, above all, the curiosity, the intellectual élan which urged on his wide-ranging inquiries into history, biography, philosophy, military science, languages, and mathematics.

The focus of Bellamy's life work, and indeed of the whole movement of latter nineteenth century liberalism in America, is the Utopian *Looking Backward, 2000–1887* (1888). Few books appear, on the surface, more deceptively simple; only the greatest represent, actually, the confluence and creative fusion of more numerous and widely disparate forces. From young manhood, almost indeed from childhood, Bellamy had been sensitively aware of social injustice, and had felt that the most fundamental of all reforms would be a more equitable distribution of wealth. During the seventies, as reviewer and columnist for the Springfield *Union,* he had vigorously criticized child labor, the "caste" system in society, and the "feudalism" of industrial organization. During the eighties he could not have avoided, even had he wished, the currents of fresh new thought that were blowing in America over the subject of social reform; but one cannot yet say with certainty just when, or from just what causes, he experienced his conversion to socialism. In all likelihood he was affected by his knowledge of the Inca civilization of old Peru, and no doubt he was deeply impressed by the possibility of using for industrial ends the principle of universal military service. Nevertheless, the decisive turn in his thinking (although the matter is still controversial) appears to have come with his reading of Laurence Gronlund's *The Cooperative Commonwealth* (1884), and from the blending of Gronlund's modified Marxism with his own previous democratic, humanitarian, and Christian philosophy.

Meanwhile, although Bellamy had written one social novel, *The Duke of Stockbridge* (serially published, 1879), his chief experience in fiction had been in the genteel romance—in the subdued but finely imagined stories, *Dr. Heidenhoff's Process* (1880) and *Miss Ludington's Sister* (1884). Although this kind of story might appear ill-suited to provide the narrative frame for a significant Utopia, the unlikely combination had already been made, successfully, by John Macnie in his futurity story, *The Diothas* (1880), some elements of which, through Bellamy's conscious or subconscious memory, reappear in the pages of *Looking Backward*. Altogether, the complexity of the sources that contributed to Bellamy's Utopia is only less remarkable than the creative effort by which his imagination fused them into harmonious and almost organic life.

As a romance, *Looking Backward* relates how its hero, Julian West, awakens from a century's mesmeric sleep in Boston of the year 2000, and, utterly alone in that alien though splendid century, finds companionship in the love of Edith Leete. As an essay in Utopian thought, it relates how Julian West is instructed both in the advantages of the new cooperative commonwealth and in the evils of the abandoned system of competitive capitalism. For the Utopian form of fiction has remained true to the patterns employed by Plato and More; it is more than a dream-vision, it is a keen-edged knife of critical attack, and as such Bellamy employs it in penetrating exposure of the weaknesses of private enterprise: the wastefulness and inefficiency in production, the creation of futility among the rich and misery among the poor, and the fatal attrition, at all levels of society, of the finer human values. How different, all this, from the felicity of the cooperative state of the twenty-first century, from which poverty and exploitation have been forever banished. There, the Machine gives man the mastery over nature and creates for him an economy of abundance; and the State, through its command of production and distribution, guarantees that all share equally in the opulence they have helped create. Nor has this socialistic state been purchased at the cost of violent revolution; it has come into being in the course of the natural evolution of middle-class democracy from the political realm into the economic.

The end of that evolution is not to be material prosperity alone; it is to be, rather, the building of a vaster spiritual home, for the habitation of a progressively finer race. Leisure and abundance find their proper fruitage not merely in universal comfort, but in universal higher education, in learning, in creative art, in the fulfillment of the loftiest spiritual aspirations. Above all, the institution of marriage, freed from its ancient economic clogs, is to foster progressively in the race the finer virtues of love and awareness, and is to improve them, by sexual selection, from generation to generation. The co-operative commonwealth is therefore to be more than just an economic system; it is to mark "the rise of the race to a new plane with an illimitable vista of progress." "Humanity has burst its chrysalis. The heavens are above it."

The artistry of *Looking Backward* is essentially that of romantic contrast —not, of course, a contrast of moods or scenes or even of personalities, but that of two great systems of living, the competitive system of the past and the cooperative system of the future. Almost from the beginning, the intellectual conflict between these two is felt. As scene follows scene, the conflict heightens, like the tightening suspense of Elizabethan drama. At the last it culminates in the hero's return, in sickening dream, to the hideous slums of a competitive metropolis, and his sudden awakening from this nightmare into the clear, free morning of the new cooperative world. And yet, carefully wrought as is the artistry of *Looking Backward,* the book as a whole is more—far more— than that. More successfully than any previous work, it carries our American democratic ideology over from politics into economics. Alongside the Marxian collectivism of class conflict and revolutionary violence, it sets up an American collectivism of orderly democracy and peaceful evolution. The huge potentialities of the Machine it assimilates, imaginatively, into the ancient aims and uses of humane culture. In its optimism, its expectation of progress, its democracy, and its spiritual pioneering, it is one of the major expressions of nineteenth century liberalism; and in its blending of these with a hundred other mental and spiritual resources, it achieves one of the great modern syntheses of humane values.

Along with certain repercussions abroad—notably William Morris' *News from Nowhere* (1890)—*Looking Backward* initiated in the United States a vogue of Utopian debate that lasted until after the turn of the century. The book became all but universally known, and its immense popularity over-shadowed and determined Bellamy's later work. With the formation of numerous Bellamy clubs, with the rise of the amorphous Nationalist "party," Bellamy felt it his duty and opportunity to lead in the reform movements directed toward the realization of his own dreams. Instead of continuing the romancer and artist, he became the publicist, the propagandist, the editor of the reform journals, the *Nationalist* and the *New Nation.* Evidently he felt it his duty, too, to make his case for the cooperative commonwealth as system-atic, as logically impregnable, as it was emotionally satisfying. Toward this objective, largely, he directed the elaborate sequel to *Looking Backward, Equality* (1897), a closely argued, informed, and ingenious treatise, but one whose elaborately buttressed arguments are, after all, no substitute for the art and the emotional power of its predecessor.

3

The middle-class novel of social debate, though it developed a discernible consensus of interest and opinion, was never a clearly defined, highly integrated genre. It is reflected in novels as widely different from Bellamy's as were those of Harold Frederic, whose writing anticipates the mingled realism, naturalism, and disillusion of the twentieth century. Frederic's first novel, *Seth's Brother's Wife* (1887) anticipates Garland's *Main-Travelled Roads* in its removal of the false glamour with which the romantic era had invested rural life, and in its curiously provocative study of passion touches deep instinctive motives which the genteel novelists of the period preferred to avoid. *The Lawton Girl* (1890) is akin to the typical middle-class social novel in its awareness of the capital-labor conflict, but differs in its unsentimental and unconventional treatment of sex.

It was in *The Damnation of Theron Ware* (1896), however, that Frederic most appealed to his contemporaries. *Theron Ware* is a strongly imagined, vigorously developed story of a Methodist minister who, while increasingly aware of the crudeness, even the coarseness and hypocrisy necessitated by his evangelical environment, is nevertheless unable to make a successful escape. In its unsympathetic study of small-town Methodism the novel anticipates Sinclair Lewis, but without Lewis' distortions and exaggerations. Quite different from *Theron Ware,* Frederic's later novels, such as *Gloria Mundi* (1898) and *The Market Place* (1899), products of his residence abroad, disclose his interest in English society and in the romance of financial intrigue.

As Frederic's atypical writing suggests, the novel of social debate was losing, even before 1900, the clearness of focus which it had possessed as an expression of nineteenth century liberalism. From 1900 on, problem novels, while increasing in numbers, had still less cohesion as a genre. Temporarily, the novel advocating liberal reform declined in favor of the amoral story of economic or political conflict. After a time, the reforming energies of the middle class once more found expression, though of limited scope, in the work of the "muckrakers" and in the "progressive" attitudes associated with Theodore Roosevelt. Class-conscious spokesmen for the proletariat were appearing, meanwhile, in the persons of Jack London and Upton Sinclair.

The muckrakers were by no means the first writers to expose the scandals of business and politics. They differed from their predecessors, however, in the specific, personal direction of their attacks, and in their intimate liaison with popular journalism. The discovery of the mass appeal of exposure was made by the publisher S. S. McClure, who assembled for *McClure's Magazine* such brilliant writers and investigators as Ida M. Tarbell, Ray Stannard Baker, and, ablest thinker of them all, Lincoln Steffens. With little of the broad general philosophy of a Bellamy or a George, the muckrakers wrote out of a simple code of individual effort and honesty, and rested their hope of reform on the power and popularity of exposure. Although their chief medium was the feature article, they affected fiction through their provision of milieu and materials for stories of a "progressive" slant, such as those of Winston Churchill and William Allen White.

Perhaps the ablest novelist associated with the muckrakers, David Graham Phillips, served his apprenticeship as a journalist with the New York *Sun* and *World* in the nineties, and emerged as free-lance writer and novelist shortly after 1900. Phillips was a talented writer—artistically serious, somewhat didactic, capable of sustained hard work, and, above all, equipped with a certain rugged integrity. His scheme of values, while not so inclusive as Bellamy's, was a substantial one, firmly held. Genuine success, genuine fulfillment, meant to him "the exaltation that comes through a sense of a life lived to the very limit of its possibilities; a life of self-development, self-expansion, self-devotion to the emancipation of man." Most of his stories deal with the quest for success, in which only a few of his people discover the genuine thing, while the majority arrive only at the specious rewards of acquisition, power, and social prestige.

In the earlier novels of Phillips, economic and political themes are primary, while the impact of social forces on sex and marriage is secondary; in the later novels, the proportion is reversed. His first novel, *The Great God Success* (1901), relates how a young journalist finally sacrifices his integrity to the winning of worldly "success"—a term which Phillips later sarcastically defined as meaning "the accumulation of riches enough to enable one to make a stir even among the very rich." Others illustrate the destructive effect of great wealth on a family, the working of the money power in politics, and the notorious insurance scandals of the times. But in *The Second Generation* (1907) Phillips' theme has deepened from mere exposure to the moral renaissance which a wealthy young brother and sister experience when subjected to hard work and responsibility; and, in the subplot of Adelaide Ranger and Dory Hargreave, he approaches those problems of marital adjustment which he examines more fully in the complementary studies *The Hungry Heart* (1909) and *The Husband's Story* (1910). The latter of these, especially, in the firmness of its handling and in the sustained objectivity with which the husband-narrator is made to reveal not only his wife's personality but his own, is a worthy creation of the same vigorous talent that elaborated the immensely detailed pages of *Susan Lenox, Her Fall and Rise* (1917).

Less the journalist, less the teacher than Phillips, his contemporary Robert Herrick was at once the humanist, devoted to the discovery and statement of values, and the artist, striving to realize imaginatively his world. Surrounded by an industrio-capitalistic society, drawing his materials almost wholly from it, he neither defended it nor tried directly to reform it, but, instead, in story after story assayed its possibilities for creative, civilized living. For, to Herrick, the civilized life was, at bottom, the creative life, whether the creative talent wrought itself out in the work of farming, or of merchandise, or of the professions, or of the fine arts. True creation, he felt, requires of the individual a firm sense of personal responsibility, an austere integrity. The ideal life would balance in supreme tension the utmost adventurousness with the utmost order. For an American, it would be lived with vigorous realism in contemporary America, but it would be illumined by an awareness of the long European experience in civilized living.

Of Herrick's characters, those with whom he is most in sympathy struggle to live themselves into some such experience of humane values. His hero or heroine strives to build, within the conditions imposed by modern American society, a fine adult personality. The antagonist is seldom an individual; it is usually the crass Philistinism of society as a whole, the coarsening and enervating influence of a vast system of competition for a wholly materialistic "success." The conflict between these two forces seldom ends "happily." Herrick's characters either sacrifice integrity for profit, or develop lives of tragic emptiness, or at best arrive at the severe calm of renunciation. His indictment of society is, then, simply that it makes fine living so tragically difficult and rare.

Herrick's earlier novels, such as *The Common Lot* (1904), illustrate this conflict between creativeness and acquisition; but the *Memoirs of an American Citizen* (1905) is a realistic story of the rise, work, and character of a self-made executive and capitalist, Edward Van Harrington. Acting on the Nietzschean principle, "the strong must rule," Harrington competes and bribes without scruple, yet remains true to his own tough-minded code of personal responsibility and productive work. Credible, finely imagined, told with a consistent detachment that almost attains objectivity, the *Memoirs* is the most impressive American picture of the great capitalist prior to Dreiser's *The Financier*.

*Clark's Field* (1914), one of Herrick's happiest efforts, is a remarkably successful blend of fantasy and realism, at once a delicately beautiful Cinderella story and a study, which would have delighted Henry George, in the social effects of unearned increment. Unlikely enough in itself, the plot of *Clark's Field* takes on, under Herrick's full, even-toned, and consistent elaboration, the texture and the credibility of fine fiction. *Clark's Field* was the last of Herrick's writings to be cast largely in the nineteenth century mold. For, between this and his next major novel, he lived through the tumultuous years of the First World War, the Versailles Conference, and America's return to "normalcy" in the early twenties. During these years, he witnessed the rise of the "new poetry," the sudden popularity of such adventurous spirits as Lewis and O'Neill, and the vogue of a social criticism concerned less with injustice than with the limitations of our total culture.

Within this fresh, invigorating milieu, Herrick returned to the theme of certain of his earlier novels—the rebellion of a sensitive professional mind against the life-destroying forces of commercialism; but now he was able to treat that theme with less reserve, upon a larger canvas, and with the assured power of practiced maturity. In *Waste* (1924), the engineer Jarvis Thornton, who has found in the Progressive Movement only disillusion, whose marriage and liaison are both wrecked because of the excessive property sense of society, comes to feel in that society "a sense of corruption working at the very roots of life, turning it into some obscene joke, a meaningless tale told in the void. . . . Waste! All waste!"

Herrick did not again achieve the richness and the tragic scope of *Waste*. In *Chimes* (1926), he disposed against an academic background, suggestive of the University of Chicago, a number of deft characterizations illustrating the interaction of the higher learning with the pressures of a moneyed society. In *The End of Desire* (1932), he exposed the decadence latent in the new cult of sexual freedom. And in his last full-length fiction, the Utopian *Sometime* (1933), he expressed his despair of present American civilization and his hope of a remote future in which men will begin the search for the good life not by accumulating possessions, but by building personalities at once governable and creative.

If fine fiction required only acute observation, significant ideas, integrity, wisdom, and craftsmanship, then it would be difficult indeed not to regard Robert Herrick as America's foremost social novelist. But these resources, however indispensable, are not, in themselves, quite enough. Within them and above them must be also the elusive tension, emotional and imaginative, which fuses and kindles the novel into an actively experienced delight. This dramatic tension was low-keyed or lacking in Herrick; and the effect of his novels is often, in consequence, not that of artful and kindling story, but that of intellectual analysis, frequently static and sometimes dull.

4

Unlike Herrick, his younger contemporary Upton Sinclair had the born story teller's knack of swiftly moving action; and as a young writer of pulpwood fiction he developed also the knack of mass appeal and of enormously prolific production. As a novelist of ideas, Sinclair is first of all the product of his family, whose aristocratic connections had their share in the forming of his generous though somewhat self-conscious culture, and whose financial insecurity was one source of his proletarian sympathies. His early Christianity survives, too, in his sturdy clinging to immaterial values in a materialistic age and in an ethical earnestness which has been inaccurately labeled as "Puritan." His own youthful temperament, first fully manifest during his college days, was one of intensity, of overpowering energy. Careless of classroom routine, he educated himself by voracious reading, during which he grew passionately devoted to the prophets and poets of rebellion and social justice—to Isaiah and Jesus, to Milton and Shelley. He sought the good life actively, in dynamic pursuit, and he continued to seek it. The inquirer, the searcher for values, was never wholly absorbed in the propagandist.

Sinclair's first novels, apart from hack-writing, grew out of a deliberately chosen struggle to express himself as a creative artist and to survive by means of his creative work. The struggle was heartrending; and the bitterness of it helped turn the potential poet into the rebel and partisan controversialist. Of these early writings the best is *Manassas* (1904), a historical novel in which much of the mature Sinclair appears in the germ. Here history is treated not romantically, after the fashion of the times, but ideologically, as seen now by Sinclair himself, now by the Southern-born hero who deserts his own class to fight in behalf of the slave. And it is also treated powerfully; the unsparing battle scenes come alive with a sense of reality equal to those in Crane's *The Red Badge of Courage*.

Meanwhile, Sinclair was finding, through his contact with Socialists such as George D. Herron and his reading in *Wilshire's Magazine,* an explanation of and sanction for his own battles with an unfriendly world. Socialism came to him as more than an intellectual conviction; it came as a magnificent discovery, as a combined religious conversion and revelation, in the light of which he saw clearly the ends for which he might live. It came also as a stimulus to action, in the form of an assignment from the Socialist *Appeal to Reason* to study the Chicago stockyards area and to use his findings in a serial. Out of his studies there, and also out of the emotions born of his own bitter struggle with poverty, came *The Jungle* (1906), the most powerful novel associated with the muckraking movement, and one of the very few actuated by forthright proletarian sympathies.

A victim-of-society story, *The Jungle* delivers a hard-hitting, ruthless indictment of the exploitation which destroys a family of Lithuanian immigrants—all except the hero, Jurgis, who belatedly finds help and instruction with a group of Socialists. Coarse, ungenteel, unsparing, heavily documented with brutal detail, *The Jungle* develops a cumulative power; its luridly melo-dramatic climaxes come alive with the grotesque conviction of nightmare. Little in Zola or Dostoevski surpasses the nightmarish strength of the scenes where the penniless Jurgis is befriended by a young drunk, or where he haggles with a reluctant midwife while his helpless Ona lies dying in child-birth. Yet for all its power, *The Jungle* is not quite "the *Uncle Tom's Cabin* of wage slavery," as Jack London called it. Too angry, too furiously imagined, it lacks the flair for racy characterization, the humor, the humanity, that enrich the older book, while its fierce partisanship estops it from being the fine naturalistic novel implied by some of its philosophical premises.

The reception of *The Jungle* caused Sinclair chagrin, for the public appeared more interested in the problem of a corrupted meat supply than in that of the exploited worker. But the book brought him fame, and the royalties relieved him of financial pressure. Nevertheless, the quality of his writing temporarily declined. He was absorbed in his Helicon Hall project for co-operative living, he was undergoing the strain of the gradual breaking down of his first marriage, and he was suffering the ill health of nervous tension. These conditions passed, in time, with his divorce, his remarriage, and his permanent settlement in southern California. Yet the weakness of his next novels was probably owing less to external disturbances than to a lack of the absorbing enthusiasm he had felt for *The Jungle*; for during the same general period of his life he was able to produce another strong novel in the autobio-graphical *Love's Pilgrimage* (1911), which contains—in its passages on the capitalistic distortion of religion and education, of the press and the arts—the germs of much of his later writing.

The full development and documentation of these ideas took form pres-ently, not as fiction, but as the series of expository, historical, and propagandist works which Floyd Dell calls "the great pamphlets": *The Profits of Religion* (1918), on the church; *The Brass Check* (1919), on the press; *The Goose-Step* (1923) and *The Goslings* (1924), on the schools; and *Mammonart* (1925) and *Money Writes* (1927), on the arts. In all six books Sinclair endeavors to show how agencies of learning and of culture are affected by economic pressures, and how, in our own time, church and press and university are made over into instrumentalities of capitalism. With dramatically told illustration, with abundant documentation, Sinclair makes an impressive case; too glaringly impressive, perhaps, for it becomes apparent that just as economic forces have often controlled the American press, so they control the controversial works of Upton Sinclair. The proletarian bias is as obvious in the one case as the capitalistic is in the other. As a consequence the author is repeatedly drawn into the fragmentary or partial statement of truth or into misleading simpli-fications, as in his tendency to transform Jesus of Nazareth into a proletarian rebel. Yet the pamphlets remain the most noteworthy essay yet made in this country toward a complete Marxian interpretation of culture, and their very partisanship contributes to their power to stimulate and to awaken.

Hardly was the series of pamphlets complete before Sinclair revealed, in *Oil!* (1927), new and larger resources as a novelist. *Oil!* is, technically, the story of the development of Bunny Ross, son of a big California oil operator, of his education in the ways of love and of business, and of his abandoning the interests of his own class in order to aid the workers; but it is much more than that. It is the story of the Harding era, with its industrial warfare, its oil scandals, its pervasive corruption, and of southern California society, from its glamorous movie stars to its lurid popular evangelists. And it is also in all ways a big, finely conceived novel, dramatically imagined, abundant in incident, rich in the lightly stated *obiter dicta* of an urbane and mellow conviction.

*Boston* (1928), based on the Sacco-Vanzetti case, is weaker; but *American Outpost* (1932) tells of the writer's first thirty-five years with the same urbanity he had displayed in *Oil!* At the time of its publication America was already struggling in the trough of the great depression, an event to which Sinclair presently responded with his unsuccessful candidacy for governor on the famous EPIC platform—End Poverty in California. That the Democratic party should have sponsored a Socialist platform and candidate is sufficiently astonishing; but already forces were stirring abroad which were to drive these and other American groups still closer together. The rise of the Nazi-Fascist coalition in Europe, equally a threat to American Left and Right, tended to force both toward rapprochement. In the midst of this new unity of resistance to Fascism, and under the shadow of the Second World War, Sinclair designed his most ambitious work of fiction.

The Lanny Budd series—so called from Sinclair's versatile hero—is a sequence of novels, or, rather, one vast novel under several titles, giving a Marxian interpretation of the course of history from the eve of the First World War into the midst of the Second. Seven volumes of the series appeared by 1946—*World's End* (1940, also the title of the series), *Between Two Worlds* (1941), *Dragon's Teeth* (1942), *Wide Is the Gate* (1943), *The Presidential Agent* (1944), *Dragon's Harvest* (1945), and *A World to Win* (1946)—and later ones, continuing the story to the downfall of Mussolini and Hitler, were then projected. The series is planned, apparently, not merely on a vast but on too vast a scale; all but the first three volumes document a familiar theme with needless iterations and with decreasing credibility, and the first of the volumes alone has an impressive unity within itself. In *World's End* as in *Oil!* the narrative proper is the story of a young man's growth into sophistication in business and in love, into self-possession and knowledge of the world. But the real subject is the "World" itself, the *grand monde* of early twentieth century aristocratic and capitalistic power. Paradoxically, yet truly, the appeal of the book lies in the author's evocation of the variety and interest, the beauties and the graces, of this very order to whose destruction he himself is committed. There is a charm reminiscent of Burke, but more various, in the portrayal of this later *ancien régime*; and there is real tragic intensity in the picture of its disintegration in its very nucleus at the Versailles Conference, for want of intelligence, moral responsibility, and realistic leadership.

*Between Two Worlds* and *Dragon's Teeth,* though they never reach the high tragedy of *World's End,* have their own rich and varied interests, carrying Lanny Budd through the intricacies of *la vie à trois* and of marriage, and carrying also the political story through the diplomatic futilities of the early twenties, the economic collapse of 1929, and the rise of the Fascists and Nazis. By no means all of even the political story, however, dwells on the level of high intellectual interpretation. In *Dragon's Teeth,* for instance, Lanny Budd's negotiations with the Nazis for the release of his friends Johannes and Freddi Robin tend rather toward the anti-Nazi melodrama of Hollywood and the popular magazines, and in that resemblance show how completely Sinclair had come to share the mass feeling of his wartime America. Thanks to the author of *Mein Kampf,* the author of *The Jungle* had achieved, at last, respectability. Faced with the threat of arbitrary power abroad, American socialist and American capitalist could be, at least temporarily, united.

Regarded as art, the social novels of the later nineteenth and early twentieth centuries appear neither better nor worse than other novels of the period. Most of them are merely run-of-the-mill fiction; the genre achieved momentary fusings of art and idea only when it was employed by some mind of superior creative power. It achieved that superiority in Mark Twain's blasts at man's inhumanity and stupidity in the *Connecticut Yankee.* It achieved it fleetingly in some of the finer stories of Hamlin Garland's *Main-Travelled Roads,* and more abundantly in Frank Norris' vigorous stories of economic conflict. It achieved it in William Dean Howells' clear-eyed analyses of the ills of free enterprise, and in the best work of Howells' strangely gifted friend and fellow socialist, Edward Bellamy. But in most of the specifically problem novels of the period, ideas were mixed rather than fused with art, with the resulting production of many good rather than a few great works.

# 61. THE EMERGENCE OF THE MODERN DRAMA

WHILE popular fiction was taking on a more realistic and a more controversial character, which at once served and flourished upon the social and philosophical issues of the day, the stage continued to thrive upon revivals of old favorites in the romantic or heroic vein. The impressive activity of the stage in Europe and the United States during the middle of the nineteenth century produced very little living art.

The Civil War was neither the beginning nor the end of an epoch in American drama. The demand for popular theatrical entertainment, which actually increased in the North during the war, produced only variations upon such established traditions as the comedy of eccentric character, domestic melodrama, and the sensational play. The stage continued to be dominated by a generation of great actors—Edwin Forrest and Edwin Booth, Charlotte Cushman, Clara Morris, Lester Wallack, E. L. Davenport, and James E. Murdoch—who kept alive the literary masterpieces of the past, especially the plays of Shakespeare, by their inspired if sometimes grandiose performances. Most of the new plays, by contrast, were ephemeral, sensational, or sentimental legerdemain evoked by the huge popular demand for entertainment or escape. Thus by contrast is emphasized the importance of James A. Herne, Bronson Howard, David Belasco, Augustus Thomas, Clyde Fitch, and William Vaughn Moody, who were the principal progenitors of the vigorous modern American drama.

Between 1860 and 1890 there had occurred certain changes in the "show business" which deeply influenced dramatic authorship. Even though in 1890 the stock company still persisted, it depended in a large measure upon visiting stars on tour who were unlikely to pay royalty for new American plays while they could pack the houses by offering Shakespearean revivals or pirated translations of foreign works. The laws of copyright were inadequate even within the nation before 1856, and afforded no international protection until 1891. Subject to constant piracy, a play had little value as literary property unless an actor took it into his repertory under terms forbidding the author to publish it. Thus *Metamora* and *The Gladiator* became identified with the reputation of Edwin Forrest, while the authors, John A. Stone and Robert

Montgomery Bird, were forgotten. A dramatist could hope for a career only if he was also a producer or actor, as were William Dunlap and John Howard Payne in the earlier period or Boucicault, Daly, Herne, and Belasco at a later time.

After the Civil War the traveling company, stimulated by the development of the railroads, tended to replace the old stock companies. Although the change produced new problems, like that of the monopolistic syndicate, its ultimate effect was to encourage dramatic authorship. While fewer plays could be performed under such conditions, they remained longer upon the stage and assured professional income for such dramatists as could overcome severe competition. The result was the establishment of a new profession of dramatic authorship attractive to talented writers, of whom Bronson Howard was the earliest.

Against the romantic traditions of the older actors and the inertia of popular taste this movement made at first but slow headway. Until the end of the century the older conventions lingered on. The plays of Robert Montgomery Bird, *The Broker of Bogota* and *The Gladiator,* introduced by Forrest in the thirties, continued after Forrest's death to be performed to enthusiastic audiences by John McCullough until 1884—indeed *The Gladiator* was persistently revived until 1893. Robert T. Conrad's *Jack Cade* was acted by Forrest, McCullough, and Edmund Collier until 1887. Boker's *Francesca da Rimini,* introduced by E. L. Davenport in 1855, became a standard repertory play of Lawrence Barrett in 1882, and was revived for a year's run by Otis Skinner in 1901.

2

The older tradition of romantic and heroic tragedy is best represented in the work of George Henry Boker who gave our literature its most original plays of the type. The earlier heroic play, as befitted the literature of a country recently born of a democratic revolution, had shown a marked preference for the theme of popular revolt against the oppression of a ruling class or a foreign despot. From Dunlap to Bird it mattered little whether the protagonist were an American patriot, Peruvian Indian, Greek slave, or British commoner, so long as he struck for freedom. Boker was the first American playwright to enlarge this concept and to deal with the tragedy of the great individual at desperate odds with society, with his own nature, or with malign destiny.

Like so many writers of his generation, Boker was in revolt against his own environment. In devoting himself to poetry in a society which measured achievement only in terms of the financier or scientist, and in reacting

earnestly against the materialism of urban society, he resembled his fellow
poets, Stoddard, Taylor, and even the younger Aldrich and Stedman. Yet
Boker's poetry retained a firmer grasp on actuality than that of most of his
associates, and his tragedies were swiftly paced portrayals of real men and
women, written in a blank verse which evoked the poetry inherent in the
speech of life.

Of Boker's eleven plays, the tragedies if not the comedies deserved a
robust life on the stage. Yet the first of them, *Calaynos* (1851*), played in the
United States only about two weeks altogether even though it ran for one
hundred performances in London without its author's knowledge, consent, or
profit. No producer could be found for *Anne Boleyn,* a good play on Henry
VIII and the tragic fate of his second Queen. *Leonor de Guzman* appeared
for ten nights during the winter of 1853–1854; and *Francesca da Rimini* was
thought by E. L. Davenport to be worth just a week's run in 1855. In the face
of such apathy Boker, like Bird, gave up the stage. In 1882 when Barrett
triumphed in *Francesca* and added the play to his permanent repertory, the
author wrote pathetically, "Why didn't I receive this encouragement years
ago? Then I might have done something." He tried to write again for the
stage but the fire that animated his earlier tragedies had waned.

This fire was the inextinguishable integrity of a great human spirit
embodied, in each play, in the protagonist. Calaynos, an austere and patrician
scholar of ancient Spanish lineage, came from his seclusion to take up arms
against the licentious court which had connived at the betrayal of his young
wife. Boker's Anne Boleyn rebelled against the cynicism of a court society
which would spare her life in return for a false confession of adultery in order
that the King might remarry as he wished; but her sacrificial stubbornness
assured the rights of succession for her child, who became England's great
Elizabeth. Leonor de Guzman, mistress of Alphonso XII of Castile, sacrificed
her life in conflict with a debased and materialistic society, in order, after the
King's death in battle, to secure the succession of her illegitimate son whom
the King had designated in preference to the weakling son of the Queen.

In *Francesca da Rimini,* the story of Dante's star-doomed lovers, Boker
found his masterpiece. Of seven plays on this theme in four languages, his is
the only one to conceive the pathos of the deformed husband, Lanciotto,
without sacrificing the enduring appeal of the young lovers, Paolo and Francesca, and to understand that callous society, not fate, was the agent of the
tragedy. As a result of this interpretation, Lanciotto hides his deformity on
the battlefield, sends Paolo to woo in his stead, and finally, because of an
inexorable code of social honor, kills the young lovers even though he "loved

---

\* The dates attached to titles of plays in this chapter refer to the year of production in each
instance.

them more than honor, more than life." With this play, romantic tragedy in America achieved the dignity of art.

3

This type of drama was not the only survival from the prewar theater. Conventional types of comic character made popular by such native comic actors as James H. Hackett, Joseph Jefferson, and J. S. Jones, who preferred to portray country bumpkins, still continued to flourish, urbanized by Edward Harrigan. Harrigan's comical and sympathetic interpretation of the plight of the immigrant in the American city made him, both as author and actor, a popular figure on Broadway until the turn of the century; and even now a reference to the "Mulligans" will recall the shanty Irish immigrant of the last century, and his colorful influence on the life of the large American cities, especially New York.

The domestic melodrama, long associated with the presentation of eccentric types of character, usually rustic, now became increasingly citified, but no less conventional and sensational. While a number of forces were stimulating a new art of the drama, the bulk of the theatrical fare, except for the revival of older masterpieces, continued until about 1885 to be composed of tear-jerkers, side-splitters, and hair-raisers. Nor was the situation improved by the vogue of adaptations from foreign plays and from novels foreign and American. Bad taste dominated the theater in France, Germany, and England, which, with popular fiction, afforded an inexhaustible reservoir of plots and stories for adaptation to the demands of a voracious American audience. Daly brought to the stage at least ninety plays, and Boucicault produced 132 or more. Yet only five or six of Daly's plays are thought to be wholly original, and even the best of Boucicault's were recent French plays transferred to Irish settings and given Irish characters and humor. As a result of the indiscriminate preference of the popular audience for sensationalism, Daly was only following an inevitable practice in turning Reade's *Griffith Gaunt* into a melodrama. If a novel happened to be sentimental in the first place, the results of adaptation were certain to be excruciating, as in the stage versions of *The Old Curiosity Shop* or *Uncle Tom's Cabin*. Even playgoers whose initiation occurred in the present century will recall the death of little Eva, and her visible ascent toward heaven on not quite invisible wires from the loft, while an inconsolable Uncle Tom prayed with her family.

Dion Boucicault, whose associations with the theater were international, could write a historical drama so substantial as *Louis XI*, which for a half-century held the stage as a favorite of Charles Kean, and later Henry Irving, who selected it for his farewell appearance in London in 1905. Yet his popular appeal for a half century was based on such plays as *The Poor of New York* (1857), in which a financial crisis and the failure of the banks provide a contrast between crafty villainy and impoverished and deserving virtue. The concern of the age with the theme of seduction led the same playwright to adapt French plays like *Mimi*; and the theme recurs in his popular *The Octoroon* (1859), in which the villain attempts to secure Zoe, the beautiful octoroon, by ruining her widowed mistress and forcing the sale of the plantation. The ending, in which Zoe drinks poison while an Indian retainer pursues the villain on a flaming steamboat, provides a curtain that is unforgettable, if nothing else.

Augustin Daly's productions of Shakespeare won him international fame but his few published plays reveal a master of theatrical technique whose works remained subliterary. *Horizon,* his best original play, gave a new realism of setting and atmosphere to the frontier drama; *Divorce* and *Pique* were early approaches to the social problem play; but even such plays made only a feeble and losing struggle against melodrama and sentiment. It was plays like *Under the Gaslight* (1867) that really packed Daly's Theater after the Civil War. This is a crook melodrama involving the kidnaping of an heiress, the mistaken identity of a changeling child, and the heroic endeavor of a one-armed newsboy to save the heroine. She, in turn, rescues him when he is overcome and bound to the railroad tracks in the path of the express, by chopping her way out of the baggage room with an ax.

4

Such examples not unfairly suggest the conditions of the popular stage when James A. Herne and Bronson Howard entered upon careers which were to prepare the way for the modern drama. The development of Herne from the domestic melodrama of *Hearts of Oak* (1879) to the domestic tragedy of *Margaret Fleming* (1890) reflects the improvement of popular taste. At that Herne was obviously ahead of his times, for those of his plays which discriminating criticism now most approves—*Drifting Apart, Margaret Fleming,* and *Griffith Davenport*—were all financial failures.

Herne was educated in the earlier theater of sentiment in eastern stock companies and on tours through the West. Such plays as *Uncle Tom's Cabin, The People's Lawyer, East Lynn,* and sentimental versions of Dickens were then preferred by the playgoers of San Francisco where Herne became a stage manager and leading character actor in the seventies. There he began to collaborate with David Belasco, a youth of barely twenty-one. The principal product of this association was *Hearts of Oak* (1879), which became one of the most famous plays of the century in the hands of the Herne family who played it over and over for a score of years. The play is remarkable among

domestic melodramas for its fidelity to character and to its rural setting, surpassed only by *Rip Van Winkle,* which entranced audiences of the twentieth
century long after all the famous Rips, like Charles Burke and Joseph
Jefferson, had taken their last curtains.

Unlike *Rip Van Winkle,* Herne's play does not stand the test of discerning criticism, even though it is vastly better than the domestic melodramas of Boucicault and Daly. Yet uncounted thousands wept as the blind
and dying father, unrecognized by his little daughter, talked to her in the
churchyard beside the shaft erected in his memory by his wife and her new
bridegroom, whose nuptials are then being celebrated with music in the
adjoining church. The domestic melodrama of eccentric character or humble
life survived also in Steele MacKaye's *Hazel Kirke,* and Denman Thompson's
*The Old Homestead,* which are inferior to Herne's play, even though they
both outlived it. *Way Down East* (1898) ran for a full year before becoming
a permanent possession of the rural stock companies. Winchell Smith's
*Lightnin'* (1918) was the most popular play in this tradition until *Abie's Irish
Rose* (1922) began a six years run.

Herne himself did not follow this path further. Instead his growing
interest in realism produced the unpopular masterpiece *Margaret Fleming,*
in 1890. This is a grim study of the effect of a husband's infidelity on a wife
who loved him deeply. It seems curious that playgoers who manifested a
high degree of tolerance for the romantic treatment of seduction should
have balked at the realistic treatment of the theme. There were objections to
Margaret's taking into her family the child of her husband's affair, and
instinctively preparing to suckle it as the curtain descends. Her repeated
request for a lamp in a room flooded with afternoon sunshine reveals the
agony of soul beneath her outward calm, for she had been warned that
blindness would result from any emotional strain. In *Shore Acres* (1892)
Herne again appealed to the popular affection for the rural setting and "the
old homestead," but without the sentimentality which usually beset this type
of play. It deals with the struggle of a successful and hardheaded father to
control his daughter's life, while his brother, the unworldly Uncle Nat,
quietly brings about her freedom, her marriage, and her ultimate reconciliation with her father. The play remains a satisfactory domestic comedy, even
if the social life which it depicts has passed from the American scene. Herne
had brought realism to the theater.

5

Bronson Howard restored the social comedy as a civilized art in the
United States, a form which had lapsed in the middle years of the century,
and it was he who chiefly prepared the way for the social comedies of Clyde

Fitch, Augustus Thomas, and the playwrights of the present century. At the same time the social comedies of Howells, for the most part one-acters though not produced, were widely read, and no doubt played their part in broadening the area of good taste.

Howard addressed himself to the social consciousness of the new audience produced by the growing urbanization and sophistication of American life. While his older contemporaries had often simply translated foreign plays for the American stage, Howard based his plot for *Wives* (1879) on two plays of Molière, but kept his characters truly American. Daly's social comedies in the same period, like the popular *Divorce* and *Pique,* broke down into melodrama. This defect Howard learned to avoid. His early plays, *Moorcroft Only a Tramp* (1874), and *Lillian's Last Love* (1873), are problem melodramas; but his revision of the last of these produced a convincing and well developed drama in *The Banker's Daughter* of 1878. In the earlier version Lillian's marriage to an older man saves her father's banking business during a panic, but the reappearance of her former fiancé causes her husband to leave her, taking their child with him; and the youthful lover is killed in a duel. This was no more than the favorite situation of continental melodramas like the famous *Frou-Frou,* which Daly had just adapted for American audiences. In the revised version of his play Howard made living people of both husband and wife, and gave their behavior an American meaning. Rejecting the male code of honor of their French friends, the husband now proclaims his faith in his wife's virtue and helps her to face the death of her former fiancé. The convincing truth of the subsequent reconciliation is attested by the number of plays, down to Barry's *Paris Bound* and Crothers' *As Husbands Go,* in which the long comradeship of shared experiences between husband and wife proves stronger than romantic infatuation.

Howard's mature social comedies reveal his knowledge of American society, and that growing awareness of international social contrasts to be found in the contemporary novels of Howells and Henry James. *Young Mrs. Winthrop* (1882) presents the mid-channel crisis in modern marriage caused by a husband's absorption in his professional interests while his wife takes refuge in social affairs. In *One of Our Girls* (1885), Kate, a forthright and independent American girl, arrives in France among her aristocratic relatives in time to save her cousin, Julie, from a marriage *de convenance* and to enable her to marry the middle-class lad whom she really loves. Unlike her prototype, Daisy Miller, whose story James had dramatized two years before, Kate survives the inevitable suspicions concerning her own character, to marry the awe-stricken English aristocrat of her choice.

Even in *Shenandoah* (1888), the elements of social comedy contribute vitally to the effect, although this, Howard's best play, is remembered chiefly as the first fully successful drama of the Civil War. Only Boucicault's *Belle Lamar* (1874) had earlier attempted to use the war as dramatic material, and it failed, both artistically and at the box office. William Gillette's *Held By the Enemy* had appeared the year before Howard's play, but it held interest primarily by its taut, hair-trigger action. The same might be said of Gillette's later and more famous *Secret Service* (1895). The action of *Shenandoah* is intense, yet Howard preserved the elements of comedy in his portrayal of four diverse sets of lovers whose lives and loyalties are curiously snarled by the war. In all of his social comedies, Howard made excellent use of broad elements of comic relief: in *Shenandoah,* Jenny Buckthorn and her ridiculous but likable suitor, Captain Heartsease; in *The Banker's Daughter,* the first American business "go-getter" on the stage, the absurd George Washington Phipps; and in the *Young Mrs. Winthrop,* the breezy Mrs. Chetwyn, who had been married so often that her several husbands became a blur in her mind. The later plays of Howard represent a decline of his powers, but he left play writing a profession and the American social comedy an art.

6

The really spectacular development of the social comedy, however, did not occur until the complexities of the present century furnished dramatic materials for such playwrights as Langdon Mitchell, Rachel Crothers, Gilbert Emery, Philip Barry, George S. Kaufman, George Kelly, Sidney Howard, and S. N. Behrman, whose work falls beyond the scope of the present chapter. While Augustus Thomas and Clyde Fitch devoted perhaps their best talents to this form, their earlier, and some of their most famous plays, were inspired by the romantic tendencies which still flourished at the end of the century, at the very time when Herne and Howard were contributing to a vital realism.

This *fin de siècle* romance influenced fiction as well as the drama, and provided a spate of romantic novels for dramatic adaptation. At the same time there appeared a new generation of romantic actors, like Lawrence Barrett, Richard Mansfield, E. H. Sothern, Julia Marlowe, and Otis Skinner, who revived the older heroic plays and especially Shakespeare, while at the same time encouraging the new tendency. Barrett's appeal as an actor was established by the success of *Pendragon* (1881), by William Young, whose *The Rajah* (1883) ran for two hundred and fifty performances, and whose dramatization of Lew Wallace's pulsating romance, *Ben-Hur* (1899), held the stage for three years before becoming a perennial of the stock companies and the films. Mansfield wrote, or sought from other playwrights, dramas which presented types of romantic character agreeable to his talents as actor and popular with his audiences. In Henry Guy Carleton's *Victor Durand* (1884) he played a quixotic lover who sacrificed himself for the woman whom he loved hopelessly. His own play, *Monsieur* (1887), portrayed a poverty-ridden music master who sacrificed his life for his art, to die of starvation amid the luxuries of a great house where he was playing for the entertainment of guests. These two situations were skillfully united by Clyde Fitch in his first play, *Beau Brummell* (1890), written to order for Mansfield. The latter meanwhile had played *Dr. Jekyll and Mr. Hyde,* and he continued to exploit the interest in the romantic "bad man" in a succession of plays like *Don Juan, Nero, Napoleon Bonaparte,* and Booth Tarkington's *Monsieur Beaucaire* (1901).

Another actor-author of the period who popularized a romantic character conception suited to his own temperament was William Gillette. His Sherlock Holmes is the most familiar example of the cool, shrewd man who steers a safe course through overwhelming complexities, perplexities, and dangers, physical or social. This character was suggested in his first play, *The Professor* (1881), and reappeared with profuse variations in such dramas as *Drum Taps* and *Secret Service,* his spy plays of the Civil War; in *Esmeralda,* in which the country suitor outwits sophistication; and in mad and merry farces like *The Private Secretary, Mr. Wilkinson's Widows,* and *Too Much Johnson.*

David Belasco is also most properly considered in connection with the romantic revival of the century's end. Belasco came to New York in 1882 after twelve years of tempestuous experience in the West, including a variety of associations with such actors and playwrights as Herne, Boucicault, and Bartley Campbell. He wrote or adapted almost every type of play that flourished after 1870. In his sensitiveness to popular taste he was chameleon, prophet, and phoenix. His collaborators were many, and all but one of his more important plays resulted from these associations. Among the seventy-five plays in which he is known to have had a hand one may find domestic melodramas, crook melodramas, farces, domestic problem plays, Civil War plays, frontier plays like *The Girl I Left Behind Me,* historical dramas, and exotic romances of spiritual revolt in semipoetic language, such as *Madame Butterfly, The Darling of the Gods,* and *Adrea.* Apparently without collaboration he wrote a fine romance on the nature of death, *The Return of Peter Grimm.* Two of Puccini's operas derived their librettos from *Madame Butterfly* and *The Girl of the Golden West.*

All of Belasco's plays are romantic in nature and his valuable contributions to stagecraft in details of setting, costume, and lighting were romantic in effect, however realistic in theory. He was a master of the theater, and it is probable that he contributed more than any other producer of his times to the mechanical perfection of the modern stage and playhouse. He continuously struggled against the monopolistic theatrical trust, supported coura-geously experiment, and promoted the talents of such actors as David Warfield, Mrs. Leslie Carter, Frances Starr, and Blanche Bates.

As a man of letters, however, his record is less impressive. His plays were "smash hits" in their own day, eminently satisfactory between the first and last curtain; but few of them are literature. Exceptions may be *The Darling of the Gods* (1902), *Adrea* (1904), and *Madame Butterfly* (1900), written in collaboration with John Luther Long, and his apparently independent play, *The Return of Peter Grimm* (1911). The first two are romantic trag-edies in each of which a beautiful high-born woman, in revolt against the outrages of society and fate, gives all for love and counts a world well lost. Both of these plays present a never-never world, while their language, though passionate and often poetic, is so highly stylized as to intensify the sense of unreality. More can be said for *Madame Butterfly,* the tragic story of the little Japanese girl who made the mistake of falling in love with the American naval officer who bought her, according to the custom of the country. Cho-Cho-San's toy world is destroyed by her lover's marriage to an American girl; her suicide is an inevitable and thoroughly moving consequence. *The Return of Peter Grimm* has remained familiar by virtue of revivals on the screen and in radio performances. Its theme, the survival of personality be-yond physical death, has retained its vitality in this century of world wars, and its characters give a sense of reality.

In its mixture of romantic and realistic impulses, the work of Belasco is typical of the American theater even beyond the end of the century. While American writers of fiction progressed from the realism of Mark Twain and Howells to the sterner naturalism of Stephen Crane and Hamlin Garland, the American dramatist was inclined to compromise. The same phenomenon may be observed in British literature. The sentimental and sensational *Saints and Sinners* of Henry Arthur Jones was typical in 1884, and Pinero's well named *Sweet Lavender* was not deemed old-fashioned in 1888. It was not until 1896 that Jones attempted a play like *Michael and His Lost Angel,* and no play of Pinero satisfies the modern sense of realism before *Iris* of 1901. Wilde's plays have the modern temper, but he was not influential in America until the late nineties, and the same must be said of Shaw. Our modern theater has responded strongly to the realism, the delicate symbolism, the analysis of psychology and social forces achieved by a number of modern continental dramatists. Various factors, but principally that of moral censor-ship, restricted Ibsen's influence on the English-speaking stage until late in the nineties. It was not until after the nineteenth century that the modern con-tinental theater made its influence felt through the work of such playwrights as Strindberg, Chekhov, Gorky, Hauptmann, Sudermann, Schnitzler, and

Maeterlinck. These considerations increase one's appreciation for the contributions to the theater made by Howard, Thomas, and Fitch, especially when one compares them with such British contemporaries as Pinero and Jones.

7

For example, Augustus Thomas, like Howells and Bronson Howard, was reared in the Midwest, yet contributed to social comedy through his hard-won understanding of American life in various localities. His picture of American life is broader than that of Howard. He had the journalist's perception of the striking local characteristics of American regions so diverse as Alabama, Missouri, Arizona, Colorado, and the cities of New York and Washington. These, among other localities, he observed during his roving youth as Congressional page, transportation agent, lawyer's clerk, box-office man, amateur producer, dramatic critic, manager for Julia Marlowe, and agent for a mind reader. His mature work began when he succeeded Dion Boucicault as adaptor and revisor at the Madison Square Theater in May, 1890, where Mansfield was then presenting Fitch's first play, *Beau Brummell.* His *Alabama,* a romance of the Reconstruction, was ready for the stage at the Madison Square Theater the next year and once more dramatic authorship, unsupported by other enterprise, furnished a career.

Thomas wrote or adapted at least sixty-four plays. They fall into two groups which illustrate the development of the American stage of his day. All his best plays are social comedies in the larger sense. His earlier plays, like the earlier work of Clyde Fitch, belong to the *fin de siècle* romance. Later Thomas' preference was for a more sophisticated metropolitan society, sometimes involving international contrasts.

His *In Mizzoura* (1893) provided the famous character actor, Nat Goodwin, with the role of an uncouth Western sheriff who wins the love of a gently bred girl, an example of the persistence on the stage of the heroic Western "bad man" or the seemingly crude character who proves his worth in the supreme test. Bret Harte's stories had popularized such characters as John Oakhurst the gambler, and "Tennessee's Partner." Their stage progeny was legion, the poor relations of the more sophisticated characters portrayed by Mansfield. Variations of the themes are found, for example, in Daly's *Horizon* (1871), Fitch's *The Cowboy and the Lady* (1899), Belasco's *The Girl of the Golden West* (1905), and even in Moody's *The Great Divide* (1906). The motif still flourishes abundantly in the movies. In Thomas' *Arizona* (1899) which vividly portrayed the life of the ranch and army post, the "bad man" whom the girl loves is really the victim of a set of suspicious circumstances which have caused him to resign in disgrace from the army.

After 1900 Thomas produced a series of light social comedies, almost farcical in situation, but so lively in wit and dialogue that the best of them, *The Earl of Pawtucket* (1903) and *Mrs. Leffingwell's Boots* (1905), suggest comparison with Wilde. In 1907 appeared the first of his realistic dramas of character, *The Witching Hour,* in which the mysteries of human personality are investigated in a tense episode involving hypnotism, thought transference, and the control of fear. *The Harvest Moon* (1909), less popular, but even better than its predecessor, again deals with the power of the individual to control his personality by the force of his will. In this case it is a father who teaches his daughter to gain control of her life and her love, by conquering the haunting doubts of her own stability implanted in her by the bitter woman who brought her up. *As a Man Thinks* (1911) involved a social problem and a broader sweep of life than Thomas had hitherto employed. It portrayed the effort of an intelligent woman to indemnify herself for an infidelity of her husband by seeking a love affair of her own, and her discovery that a man's assurance of his fatherhood, and in consequence the whole structure of his society, rests upon his confidence in the virtue of his wife. This play was probably a retort to Rachel Crothers' first important play, *A Man's World* (1909), and together they introduced a question which was to be debated on the stage for a quarter of a century. Maurice Barrymore, in *The Burglar* (1889), was the first actor to make a professional appearance in a play by Thomas; his son Lionel starred in Thomas' last important play, *The Copperhead* (1918). In this convincing Civil War play his ability to reproduce local color united with his practiced command of the character problem.

## 8

Herne and Howard foreshadowed the modern realistic theater, but four plays of Thomas and the latest plays of Fitch, in the first decade of this century, constitute the actual beginnings of what we now recognize as contemporary realism. Clyde Fitch, like Thomas, began to write under the spell of the romantic theater, but ended his short career with a number of realistic character-problem plays. He wrote about sixty plays in twenty years, most of them comedies of manners and social comedies; he became, next to Belasco, the most spectacular figure in the international theater of his day; he had six plays on the stage in New York or London in the winter of 1901. It is a wonder that a dramatist producing at that rate the popular hits of each season could contribute to the permanent advance of the drama.

Yet even the romantic social comedies, melodramas, and period plays which gave Fitch an international eminence during his first decade were decidedly in advance of their times. The appeal of a play like *Beau Brummell* (1890) is enduring. This was written for Mansfield, who made famous on the stage the character of the late Georgian fop and dandy. The portrayal of his personality involves the artificial court life during the Regency, and a love story in which the Beau sacrifices himself and his favor with the Prince in order to give the girl whom he so hopelessly loves to the man of her choice.

Fitch surpassed his mid-century predecessors in such romantic or even melodramatic situations by his wit, and by the appeal of the characters whom he has projected upon scenes so obviously idealized or exotic. *His Grace de Grammont,* for example, gave Otis Skinner a quite memorable opportunity to act the gracious cavalier, and *Mistress Betty* (later called *The Toast of the Town*) afforded Modjeska, and afterward Viola Allen, a part redolent of eighteenth century manners and the glamorous theatrical life of that period. *The Moth and the Flame* is one of the best of the many romantic melodramas on the theme suggested by its title, and its popular success gave its author his first real financial security. In *Barbara Frietchie* Fitch caught the morning freshness, if not the power, of the Romeo and Juliet situation which he so obviously imitated, and the play had sufficient vitality, twenty-eight years after its first performance, to furnish the libretto for one of the most successful of modern operettas, *My Maryland*.

The character problem plays of his last decade no doubt constitute Fitch's more lasting contribution to the literature of the stage. *The Climbers* (1901), for example, is a social satire dealing with the perfervid aspirations for the material rewards of life on the upper levels of a city like New York. His last play, *The City* (1909), dealt somewhat less successfully with the same theme, although both plays are remembered. This satire is touched at all points with compassion. *Lovers' Lane,* however, is mordant satire in its portrayal of a wise and liberal clergyman confronted by the petty intolerance of the small-town mind, especially in its female manifestations. A world removed from this scene is that of *Her Great Match*. In depicting the refusal of an American girl to accept a morganatic marriage with the young prince whom she loves, Fitch revealed the subtle national variations in gentle behavior without suggesting the necessary superiority of one to another, and especially without apologizing for the American variety.

A number of Fitch's plays demonstrate a similar mastery of the delicate art of social comedy. Their success upon the stage is evidence of the rapid advance in taste in those urban communities where, only a score of years before, the preference was decidedly for slapstick and sensationalism. Even lesser dramatists might now sometimes approach his competence in this field. One of them, Langdon Mitchell, surpassed him in lightness of touch if not in depth of meaning, in *The New York Idea* (1906), in which the kaleidoscopic divorces and remarriages among a group of well bred but bored social leaders afford the dramatist an opportunity to reveal his delight in the human comedy. In all of his plays Mitchell proved his ability to portray convincing characters amid the artificialities of social life, but his earlier *Becky Sharp* and his later *Major Pendennis* have not the vitality of the social comedies of Clyde Fitch.

Fitch's best plays are *The Girl with the Green Eyes* (1902) and *The Truth* (1907). Again with compassionate understanding, he presents in each play the problem of a girl who has been conditioned in youth to a psychopathic reaction destructive of personal and social relations—in the first case, jealousy, and in the second, falsehood. His dramatic instinct was to avoid the intense clinical examination which weakens certain European dramas on such themes. Some critics have felt that the author manifested a fatal weakness in not pursuing the logic of these situations to the tragic conclusions ordained by the conventions of modern naturalism. Perhaps, however, there is another logic in the power of love to cancel the predetermined consequences of heredity or environment. Jinny Austin and Becky Warder have each been driven to the brink of a disaster from which she is saved by her husband's discovery, in a violent climax of action, that she is suffering from a profound and early spiritual injury which only his love and sympathy can heal.

9

The early death of William Vaughn Moody cut short the career of a poet already distinguished, and probably robbed our dramatic literature of a playwright who might have contributed more than any other, save Eugene O'Neill, to the modern symbolic drama of spiritual struggle in which romantic and realistic tendencies are blended. Fine humanist and university teacher that he was, Moody retained as artist a profound understanding of everyday life, and the ability to interpret its complexities in simple and passionate symbols of action. Moody's trilogy of poetic dramas was never produced; yet his two plays in prose, which were successfully presented, can be fully understood only in the light of his poetic *Masque of Judgment*. All of his dramatic work, in prose and poetry, through a variety of human situations, relates to a central problem which has persisted as a major theme in every period of American expression.

This theme is the sense of sin and, more particularly, its destructive power upon the freedom and expression of the human soul. The distinction is intended between evil, which may be an absolute, and the sense of sin or evil, which may have no absolute sanction, and may spring, indeed, from hereditary inhibitions, or from prohibitions which bear little or no relation to truth and justice. It is a commonplace of American history, and a principal clue to American behavior, that this sense of sin which Moody attacked in all of his plays was sharpened by the persistence of the Puritan inheritance, the Calvinist conception of the original sin and total depravity of mankind. For more than a century this problem has engaged the profoundest efforts of writers so diverse as Hawthorne, Whitman, Melville, and Edwin Arlington Robinson.

Thus the philosophical significance of Moody's plays is greater than their practical merits on the stage, although the two prose plays, *The Great Divide* (1906) and *The Faith Healer* (1909), continue to hold their own for the reader and in revivals on the stage and screen. The three poetic dramas of *The Masque of Judgment* present such a sweeping Miltonic canvas that generalization must prove unsatisfactory. Yet it seems clear that the central meaning of the first play, also called *The Masque of Judgment,* lies in Raphael's belief that God blundered in allowing sin and then ordaining its punishment. In this play the God of Wrath, conceived by the ancient Hebrew and worshipped by the modern puritan, is finally defeated by the Serpent for his mistake in punishing man for following his natural impulses instead of teaching him the full use of his powers. In the second play, *The Fire Bringer,* the classical story of Prometheus is given messianic meaning, as mankind through suffering learns the religion of rebellion against all that prevents man's service to man and his full expression of himself. In the unfinished *The Death of Eve,* the last of the trilogy, Eve was to bring back Cain and Adam to Eden, the place of original sin, and to find the sense of sin vanquished by the love of her descendants.

This brief analysis cannot show the wide range of these poems, their richness in secondary motivations, the interest of their action, and the nobility of their language, but their meaning is consistent with that of the two prose plays. *The Great Divide* presents a modern girl of New England, stunted in her expression of life by puritanical inhibitions. On a Western trip, alone in the wilds, she submits, in order to save herself from the others, to the best of three men who attempt to attack her. Ghent falls in love with her and she with him, but while he rises strengthened and purified to a successful life as mining prospector, Ruth tortures herself with his statement that he was brought to her by "whiskey, the sun, and the Devil." Impelled by her conviction that they must cleanse themselves by abnegation, she flees to her home where Ghent follows her to wage a difficult but finally successful battle against her lantern-jowled Puritan ancestors whose portraits line the walls.

*The Faith Healer,* a better play, presents an accurate study of a Midwest farming community, and a large number of convincing characters. The central story deals with Michaelis, a mystic who has come up on a mysterious mission from a hermitage in the grazing country of the Southwest. He has healed Mary Beeler, invalid aunt of Rhoda, a young girl, and news of this has brought a host of seekers to his door. In the midst of his work of healing he discovers his love for Rhoda, to whom sex has meant only sin, in her former experience of seduction. Their mutual sense of guilt causes Michaelis to lose his power of healing with almost tragic results for those whom he is helping until their great discovery, in this crisis, of the unity of the flesh and the spirit.

10

The story of the development of American drama from Boker to Moody is that of the formative stage of an art. The subliterary theatricality of the period, by illustrating the popular and prevailing taste, particularly in urban America, emphasizes the importance of those playwrights who gradually created, in spite of overwhelming handicaps, a native drama which gave deeper meaning to the theater, portrayed modern character and life with fidelity, and pointed the way toward imaginative maturity.

In the older period of romantic drama, Boker had rejected the prevailing heroic themes of national idealism, and had devoted his art to great tragic crises of the personality. This impulse has always afforded the themes for the noblest tragedy. The modern drama has drawn its strength from the ability of dramatists to find such subjects in the stuff of everyday life. Possibly this characteristic finds its point of origin, historically, in that series of Ibsen's dramas which began with A Doll's House in 1879. In American drama, Herne's Margaret Fleming, in 1890, marks an epoch. In the first years of the new century, the dramas which best stand the test of time are concerned with the mysteries of the human mind and spirit, or with some struggle of the will of the individual to overcome a fate that seems ordained in destiny or human frailty. That the important dramatists of the period were still entranced by the human miracle which Moody called a "mystical hanker after something higher" is demonstrated by such plays as Fitch's The Truth, and The Girl with the Green Eyes; Thomas' The Witching Hour, and The Harvest Moon; Belasco's The Return of Peter Grimm; and Moody's entire work.

Theatrical and melodramatic plays persisted until the end of the century, yet a new vitality was discernible after 1880. Stimulated in part by native forces and later by the experimental European theater, American drama gradually acquired social responsibility and seriousness, a surer grasp of psychological and spiritual realities. Enriched by the complexities of life in the twentieth century, these same convictions later found a more masterful statement in the dramatic symbolism of Eugene O'Neill.

# 62. TOWARD NATURALISM IN FICTION

Even at the close of the nineteenth century the realistic tendency in the American drama had thus failed to respond to the European discoveries and theories of science which, by demanding a new definition of nature and its part in human destiny, had given philosophic depth to the plays of Ibsen, Strindberg, and Hauptmann. But in American fiction there was evidence of an increasing effort to find new techniques with which to reinterpret the unchanging central issues of human experience in terms of naturalism.

In France, Emile Zola had carried the realism of Flaubert and De Maupassant to depths of sordidness and bitter criticism that defied even a tragic solution. In Russia, Dostoevski, Tolstoy, and Turgenev, each in his fashion, had proposed views of life which at least made the catharsis of tragedy possible. In England, Hardy was discovering a new tragic intensity in the simple lives of the Wessex folk. Although Howells and others report that all of these foreign writers, as well as the popularizers of science who gave them their view of man, were being read in the United States soon after they appeared in Europe, the full force of the movement in this hemisphere was dulled by a traditional optimism reinforced by prudery. Naturalism—an old word for these new ways of thinking—could not take root here as quickly or as firmly as it could in the richer soil of Europe. Zola had demanded in 1880 that "a novelist must be only a scientist, an analyst, an anatomist, and his work must have the certainty, the solidity, and the practical application of a work of science," but until Dreiser's *Sister Carrie* (suppressed in 1900), no American novelist took this prescription seriously and produced a wholly original work of pure naturalism. In the closing years of the nineteenth century the influences of Darwin and Spencer, of Zola and Turgenev, took no single form. One can discover many phases of naturalism in American fiction—in the moral confusion and dismay of Mark Twain and Harold Frederic, in the harsher forms of realism of E. W. Howe and Hamlin Garland, in the robustious action tales of Frank Norris and Jack London, or in the bold miniatures of Ambrose Bierce and Stephen Crane. But there was no single writer who could be described as a naturalist, no one wholly devoted, before Dreiser, to the philosophy, the material, and the method of Zola.

The writers who came nearest to practicing the formula of naturalism at the turn of the century are four: Hamlin Garland, Stephen Crane, Frank Norris, and Jack London. Each of these in his way made a significant break with the literal realism of Howells or the unthinking romance of F. Marion Crawford; each attempted to apply to art some part of the method or the meaning of the physical and biological sciences. Mainly in the work of these four the technique and the philosophy of serious modern American fiction took shape.

2

As Howells had defined the literal form of realism in his essays gathered together as *Criticism and Fiction* in 1891, so Hamlin Garland expounded the next step in the movement in his *Crumbling Idols* (1894). Howells was concerned only that the novelist be faithful in his work of representing reality as he knew it, and he limited the range of permissible material by conventional standards of taste. He failed to raise the question of the metaphysical nature of the reality which he thought should be described, and he formulated no theory of art beyond its function as record.

Although Garland in later life became narrower in his sympathies while the mind of his mentor opened, in the nineties the poor boy from the Iowa prairies was the spokesman for the young radicals gathering in Chicago and New York. His new theory, which he called "veritism," raised many of the issues which Howells had avoided. His wide but superficial reading in popular science, his personal bitterness at the harshness of his own boyhood, and his casual knowledge of the French impressionists in both writing and painting carried him beyond some of the limitations of literal realism. He asked that American fiction divorce itself from tradition and imitation, that it explore truth to its underlying meaning, that it deal with the unpleasant as well as the pleasant aspects of life, and that it develop a form based on the moment of experience, acutely felt and immediately expressed. A sensitive observer and chronicler rather than a great artist, he failed to realize in his own stories the possibilities of his theory. But in *Crumbling Idols* he made himself the public apologist for such younger writers as E. W. Howe, Henry Blake Fuller, Harold Frederic, and Stephen Crane, who were not afraid to discuss poverty, hardships, and the problems of society and religion, and who were working toward an instrument of expression which would interpret as well as record.

Garland's early life was a bitter struggle to extort the promised plenty from a rich but plague-ridden soil. The conflict between his soldier-father's consecration to frontier hopes and the wasting poverty and toil of his mother gave him his one great theme. Even in his first published writing, *Boy Life on the Prairie* (1885, 1899), he exploited the poverty and hardships of his boyhood at West Salem, Wisconsin, and in Iowa, as well as the zest of rolling hills and open prairies.

This was to be the material of all his best writing, but at twenty-four he thought he had left it behind him. In youthful rebellion he rejected his father's move to Dakota when the cinch bugs drove the family on, and with his brother Frank worked his way to Boston. There he sought out alone a rented room, and blindly struggled on toward his goal of becoming a writer and orator. Soon he was teaching at the Boston School of Oratory and reading Taine's *History*, Véron's *Aesthetics*, Henry George's tracts on the single tax, and the exciting new ideas of Spencer and Darwin. He had renounced the frontier except as literary material, and had taken to the back trail as Irving and Cooper had before him, and as Mark Twain and Howells were doing in his own day.

The turn left a sense of guilt at his heart, and his lifelong nostalgia was to be concentrated on the lot of his mother. His new life was dedicated to expiation for the old. There must be a Garland homestead somewhere, and where better than West Salem, his mother's childhood home? A peaceful old age could be found for her there, if his father would admit defeat. The Oedipus complex was here no deep source of buried tragedy; it shaped the life of a family and created a chronicler.

*Main-Travelled Roads* (1891) and the volumes of poems, plays, tales, and essays which clustered about it in the next few years are simple, honest, and sharp impressions of life as he had lived it. Howells urged him to tell his story straight; a Kansas editor, E. W. Howe, had set an example of how to treat the narrowness of a small community in *The Story of a Country Town* (1883); Joseph Kirkland had written two novels of the Middle West, *Zury* (1887) and *The McVeys* (1888), and encouraged Garland to exploit the same material. From Taine he had learned to blame environment rather than the dark soul for the hardships of the human lot; from Henry George he had learned that those hardships were attributable to the mishandling of resources in land; from Spencer he had concluded that all life is a part of a single physical and biological process working upward and outward from simple to complex forms, from homogeneity to variety, from the mass to the individual. His life confirmed these teachings.

The tales in *Main-Travelled Roads* and in its first sequel, *Prairie Folks* (1893), tell of the unadorned hardships, lightened by occasional small pleasures and made meaningful by the power of nature, that fill the lives of the people of the coolly country and the prairie. Predominantly bitter like "Lucretia Burns" or pathetic like "Mrs. Ripley's Trip," there is courtship and family loyalty to ease the burdens, prairie spaces and sunsets to give joy and hope, minor follies of men to add a touch of grim humor. Throughout all, the exploitation of the farmer by the social system and the tragic lot of the pioneer woman bind the stories to central themes. Several of these tales were expanded into short novels, the best of which, *Rose of Dutcher's Coolly* (1895), conjectures the life of Garland's older sister as it might have been had she not died after her first move toward a larger life. But by 1899, in spite of the encouragement of B. O. Flower and the receptive pages of the radical *Arena,* his vein was nearly exhausted.

After his marriage to Zulime Taft, sister of the sculptor, and his mother's death in 1900, New York became the Garland headquarters and his writing changed in subject, purpose, and style. He now published with the successful firm of Harper and the romances of the next decade bear little superficial resemblance to the early work. In their genre, however, they stand reasonably high, even though they have suffered by contrast with the Middle Border books, as well as with the more vigorous action tales of Harding Davis and Jack London. Based on trips to the peaks and high plateaus of Colorado, Wyoming, and Montana and to the Klondike, each has serious purpose, swift action, and balanced though often conventional plot. When adventure and prosperity came into his experience, his emotions changed color and he celebrated the admirable. Biology acclaimed the independent man of vigorous action, and Garland followed the path of Roosevelt, Frank Norris, and Jack London toward the brute-man as he had previously followed that of Eggleston, Howe, and Howells toward the influence of environment. It was the other half of the same equation.

The third and last phase of his work was ushered in by *A Son of the Middle Border* (1917). Nostalgia had crept upon him again and as his daughters grew older he turned back, but in a softened mood, to his boyhood memories. Life was different for them from what it had been for him—and he intended that it should be so, but they and their contemporaries should know their cultural inheritance. In four books he told the whole story: in *Trail-Makers of the Middle Border* (1926) he followed his father from Maine to Wisconsin; in *A Son of the Middle Border* (1917) he continued the migration to Iowa and Dakota, and back to the purchase of the homestead in West Salem, again proving that this was the richest and most fruitful period of his life; in *A Daughter of the Middle Border* (1921) he told of the dividing claims of his middle years to the death of his parents and through the early years of his marriage; and in *Back-Trailers from the Middle Border* (1928) he carried his story to New York and London and told of his literary compromises and successes and of the careers of his daughters. Here was the story of an American family through three generations, a domestic chronicle of the frontier, a cycle in biological sociology, a chapter from an American Taine.

There only remained in the later years the narrowing stream of his literary reminiscences which filled several large volumes but which are now of interest mainly to his biographer. One other book of this period, *Forty Years of Psychic Research* (1936) was a by-product of his pseudoscientific romanticism. In an early novel, *The Shadow World* (1908), based on notes he made immediately after sittings and on his reports to the American Psychical Society, he states his position in the character of a young chemist:

I am a scientist in my sympathies. I believe in the methods of the chemist and the electrician. I prefer the experimenter to the theorist. . . . I am ready to go wherever science leads, and I should be very glad to *know* that our life here is but a link in the chain of existence.

In forty years it failed to lead him past the great divide.

Thus Garland turned to nature to solve and harmonize all the problems of man. He shared the hope of his contemporaries that science, especially chemistry and biology, would answer the riddle of an increasingly complex civilization of which the old idols had crumbled. Not a profound thinker nor a wide reader, he accepted the current dogma of the evolutionists and attempted, like Zola, even though he rejected and resented Zola's preoccupation with sex, to use his art as a means of illustrating the theses of the most radical scientists of his day. The result was a new movement in art which was to go far beyond these beginnings as they in turn had moved beyond the literary recordings of De Forest, Howe, Eggleston, and Howells. That movement was to leave Garland behind because he failed to accept his own challenge to an open mind.

### 3

Garland's instant recognition of Stephen Crane is tribute to his literary theory, for the boy practiced instinctively and with ease the impressionistic veritism of *Crumbling Idols*. As Emerson had defined the man of nature and the poet only to discover the actualities later in Thoreau and Whitman, so Garland found in Crane the artist he could describe but could not himself become. When the younger man tramped the four miles from the Bowery out to Garland's flat in Harlem in 1893, the "nice Jesus Christ" fed him, introduced him to Howells, helped him sell a story to B. O. Flower, and lent him money to have *The Red Badge of Courage* typed. It was the beginning of Crane's short and colorful career.

"Let it be stated," wrote his biographer Thomas Beer with acute understanding, "that the mistress of this boy's mind was fear." Poverty, innate cruelty, war, and death are the themes of all his best work as they were in Ambrose Bierce, yet there is little in his life or reading to account for the pessimism and the sensibility of his tales and poems. The poverty, illness, and early death of this member of one of the oldest and most respected families in Newark, New Jersey, seem to have resulted from the pressure of nervous energy rather than circumstance. He lived intensely a life of his own choice.

The record of that life is confused and shrouded in myth, for, like Poe, he threw himself into his fiction and was not unwilling to become a part of it. His own reticence and the jealousy of lesser "Bohemians" conspired to distort into a legend of drink, drugs, and petty social crimes the simple facts of a small-town boyhood as the Methodist minister's youngest son, a few years of slumming in New York City's nascent artist colony, another few of reporting the color of the West and South as far as Mexico for a newspaper syndicate, involvement as correspondent in the Cuban and Greek comic-opera wars of independence, and a final attempt to find in English manor-house life the haven that his country was too busy to supply. It is the familiar story of romantic youth seeking escape from life into art and achieving a fleeting mastery before the overtaxed body gives way. The term of twenty-nine years, the late marriage to an older woman, and the death by consumption at a health resort follow an almost classic formula. Mastery was achieved in a half-dozen short stories and novelettes, near mastery in three short novels and in innumerable sketches, but two more ambitious novels failed. His slim volumes of epigrammatic and symbolic verse give him a minor but significant place in American poetry.

The appearance of an original artist, springing without antecedent into life, is always illusion, but the sources of Crane's philosophy and art are as yet undeciphered. Neither the cold-blooded determinism of his belief nor the sensuous awareness of his writing can be without source, but nowhere in the scant record he has left is there evidence that he, like Garland, read widely in the current books on biological science. A direct influence of Darwin, Spencer, Haeckel, or their American popularizers cannot be established. Rather he seems to have absorbed these influences at second hand through Russian and French writers. For Tolstoy's *Sebastopol* and *War and Peace* he confesses an early enthusiasm, but probably because of his interest in war rather than for deeper reasons. Of Dostoevski and Turgenev he admits no knowledge, yet internal evidence makes such knowledge possible. His tales, in theme and form, bear a striking resemblance to those of De Maupassant and he knew

Flaubert early in *Salammbô*, even though he resented its length. There is no doubt that he took direct inspiration from these French realists, and even more certainly from Zola, for *L'Assommoir* probably provided the plot for *Maggie*, and *La Débâcle* bears a close resemblance to *The Red Badge of Courage*, though he denied ever having read it. His work shows the stamp of European naturalism and contributed to the break of American literary history with the English tradition. With Zola he shared the philosophy of the *roman expérimental*, with De Maupassant and Turgenev the sensory acuteness, the brevity, and the repressed intensity of impressionistic art.

This can be said even though the superficiality of his acquaintance with these writers be acknowledged. It is probable that discussions with fellow artists—mostly painters—who shared the makeshift lodgings at the "Art Students League" on East Twenty-third Street in 1891–1892 had more direct effect on him than had any reading. Such sources can never be traced with accuracy, but the selection of an impressionist painter as hero of his semi-autobiographical novel, *The Third Violet* (1897), is revealing. The adolescent love story is Crane's own in essential respects and he tells it as a painter in prose. Monet's paintings he knew.

*Maggie* (1893) and *The Red Badge of Courage* (1895) came directly from these associations, the first a Bowery story based on observation, the other a wholly imaginative analysis of a boy's first battle experience in the Civil War. Yet the difference between them is not as significant as some critics have averred. Both are impressionistic studies of elemental fear, the one as shame, the other as failure of courage in action. Each takes as central character a youth, impersonal and typical (their names were assigned later), facing life at its crisis, and each analyzes the profound emotional forces bearing upon a point in time by presenting the color and movement of circumstances governing events from the outside and the strong psychological drives from within. To Crane, Maggie Johnson and Henry Fleming are elemental woman and man in the first moment of meeting with death.

In *Maggie* the mind is not entered; the crisis is presented only by swift and ironic reconstruction of environment and surrounding characters. By sheer sincerity the story rises to a conviction in which Howells could detect the "fatal necessity which dominates Greek tragedy" and the simplicity of effect of true art. Naïve and overwritten, it flung Crane's challenge to his times by its unprecedented candor of theme, its sense of fate, and its directness in dealing with sordid material. Its lack of sensuality makes it seem almost pale today, but the fire in its unsold paper-backed copies smoldered until the acclaim accorded to his next work made a new edition possible. With that republication (1896), modern American fiction was born.

In *The Red Badge of Courage* Crane marks his artistic advance by moving easily from the description of the countryside, the advance and retreat of armies, the din of battle, and the color of the sky to the alternating hopes and fears of his boy soldier. Because he can now reveal both inward and outward forces, his determinism carries its own conviction, and Henry Fleming's realization that, "He had been to touch the great death, and found that, after all, it was but the great death," strikes to deeper levels of reality than does Maggie's suicide. From books, from the tactical lore of his brother William, and from conversations with veterans like his teacher at Claverack Academy, General Van Petten, he could now transcend the realism of Howells and Garland because the fear that Henry Fleming felt was in his own heart.

Even in these early stories Crane was far in advance of the psychological knowledge of his contemporaries. His understanding of the effects of environment and instinct on the individual anticipates the theories of the behaviorists, the social psychologists, and the psychoanalysis of a decade or more later. Henry James, the leading current exponent of the psychological novel, had accepted the theory of association, depicting an almost molecular movement of ideas, without defined motivation, on the clear plate of the mind. Crane probed deeper into the problem and, especially in his analysis of Henry Fleming, gives us the anatomy of fear.

Here is a naturalistic view of heroism unknown to the war romances of the time, with the possible exception of those of Bierce, but its bitterness was lost on most of its readers because the hero seemed to be following the usual formula and discovering his manhood by violent action. The story was a success, but it transcends itself by its dismaying revelation. With less plot than *Maggie* it avoids the pitfall of melodrama, but its mood is so intense and its imagery so overwrought that it is led to the brink of another. The reader who can, like Joseph Hergesheimer, feel a sudden revelation in the image, "The sun was pasted in the sky like a wafer," is prepared for its repressed violence of conception and style. True restraint was to come later.

Crane was already familiar with newspaper work when he sold his Civil War novel to the Bacheller syndicate. As a boy he had worked for his brother's press bureau in Asbury Park and he had been the local correspondent of the New York *Tribune* during his year at Syracuse University. He had even held a job on the *Herald* for a short time when he went to New York at the age of twenty, only to lose it and become a free-lance reporter for the rest of his life. His best stories are reports, more successful as illustration than as news, because he could not, like his popular contemporary Richard Harding Davis, stop short at the action and the event. Life came to him in its primary colors, blue, red, and yellow, and he asked its meaning. The newspaper is not interested in such notions.

His reportorial art achieves its maturity in "The Blue Hotel," the scene

of which is laid in a Nebraska town in midwinter. Crane, as "the correspondent," is gathered in by the cheerful Irish host as he steps from the train
with a cowboy, a quiet Easterner, and a Swede. The tone of the action is set
by the light blue of the hotel "always screaming and howling in a way that
made the dazzling winter landscape of Nebraska seem only a grey swampish
hush." The premonition of the Swede that he will be murdered is but the
inner reflection of this screaming blue, the manifestation of Crane's own
tense fear. His murder by the professional gambler is an act of necessity; the
force which makes it inevitable is beyond any single person in the action.
"This poor gambler isn't even a noun," comments the Easterner afterwards.
"He is a kind of an adverb. Every sin is the result of a collaboration . . . the
apex of a human movement." Crane has now grasped, in a minor incident, the
meaning of fear and death, which had eluded him in his earlier and more
fully written stories.

The "correspondent" again appears with three companions in "The Open
Boat," this time the captain, the cook, and the oiler. A simple record of the
actual wreck of a filibustering vessel off the coast of Florida, this story, Crane's
masterpiece, achieves its effect by understatement. Its opening sentence, "None
of them knew the color of the sky," exactly describes the negative mood of
the men in the dinghy. The blue of the sea is slaty, canton-flannel gulls fly
overhead, brown mats of seaweed float by to measure movement and distance, the black and white of trees and sand mark the near but unobtainable
shore line, and when at last the carmine and gold of morning is painted on
the waters, it seems that the impending fate of drowning within sight of help
must come to them all. The lone death of the oiler, strongest of the group,
is the culminating irony. "When it occurs to a man that nature does not
regard him as important . . . he at first wishes to throw bricks at the temple,
and he hates deeply the fact that there are no bricks and no temples." This is
the meaning of life, in so far as it has a meaning. In no other story does
Crane understand his fear so clearly and state it so effectively. Yet here he is
apparently recording merely an event which happened to him, without altering a fact or a sequence.

In these and other Western, Mexican, and Cuban tales and sketches where
he is recording his mature observations on life in moments of crisis, Crane
achieves that instantaneous balance between reality and imagination which
makes for great art. Tales in lighter mood like "The Bride Comes to Yellow
Sky," "His Majestic Lie," or "The Lone Charge of William B. Perkins" prove
that he is capable of comic as well as tragic treatment of his theme. His irony
runs the entire gamut from sentimental melodrama, through tragedy and
comedy, to travesty like "The Second Generation." Lewisohn feels that "An
Experiment in Misery," the bleak account of a night in a flophouse, is his

best work because here his "impassiveness" is most extreme, and he himself preferred the drunken shooting spree of "The Bride Comes to Yellow Sky," but both these tales are too slight to give him full scope. In neither his purely imaginary Civil War stories like "A Mystery of Heroism," a distillation of the theme of futile bravery, nor in the more literal accounts of London and the Irish countryside in "The Reporter Errant" does he strike the necessary balance as effectively. Critical consensus returns to "The Open Boat."

In his memories of childhood the mood is less intense, but the tone is still bitter, the meaning dark. The earlier story, "An Ominous Baby," had made a direct statement of his belief in the essential and dispassionate cruelty of childhood, on the theory that the cycle of the individual is the cycle of the race and that the truth of experience is most stark in the infancy of either. But the *Whilomville Stories* (1900), based on his adventures in Port Jervis, New York, as a small boy, are somewhat more mellow. Jimmie Trescott relives the shame and adventures of childhood with a starkness and a sincerity lacking even in much of Mark Twain.

His two longer tales based on early memory, *George's Mother* (1896) and *The Monster* (1899), are less incisive but explore psychological problems even more deeply. The first is only remotely autobiographical, but it suggests, in its analysis of the degenerating effects of too solicitous a mother for the last of her many sons, a possible clue to the emotional complex at the core of Crane's fears. The second is the most horrible of his tales. Though it has been erroneously linked to the school of Poe and Bierce, horror is not its primary purpose. The reaction of a small town to the imbecile Negro who has saved Jimmie Trescott from fire, only to have his face burned away and his mind destroyed, is Crane's major experiment in social satire. The sin is communal, but it appears inevitable as convention conspires with natural law to reject its own morality.

As the *Whilomville Stories* were Crane's last work, it cannot be said that declining health and the social demands of life in his old manor house at Brede, England, where his wife's "biscuits" lured innumerable uninvited guests, killed the art of which he was still capable. In spite of an encroaching consumption, aggravated probably by the fever which he had contracted in Cuba and which haunted him in his last journalistic filibuster to Greece, he could still write sharply and vividly of the fears within the human soul and their reflections in the primary colors of life. But he could not successfully stretch his art into a popular novel, as he attempted to do in *Active Service* (1899), nor into the swashbuckling Irish romance of *The O'Ruddy,* left unfinished at his death. He was still best at the vignette, the finely studied record of a moment, the swift thrust to the meaningless meaning of experience. His vivid impressions of life, with their linking of instinct and circumstance to chain the individual will to its own tragic issue, had provided a pattern for the writing of the next generation. He gave to the naturalistic short story its characteristic form, later to be exploited by Hemingway, Steinbeck, and a host of others.

4

Among the few to join Howells and Garland in critical appreciation of *Maggie* was a young man in San Francisco, Frank Norris of the *Wave*. "Stephen Crane has written a story something on the plan of the episode of Nana in *L'Assommoir*. . . . I think that the charm of his style lies chiefly in his habit and aptitude for making phrases—sparks that cast a momentary gleam of light on whole phases of life." Yet he finds that, "The author is writing . . . from the outside. Mr. Crane does not seem to *know* his people." The kinship and the contrast in the work of these two pioneers of American naturalism are both revealed in this comment. Norris instantly recognized the common debt to Zola, but he objected to Crane's aesthetic objectivity, his feeling for style rather than for "life."

Other critics were not slow in linking the names of the two men when Norris' *McTeague* finally appeared in 1899, three years after *Maggie* became known. In spite of temperamental differences and the span of a continent, they were working toward the same goal, experimenting with the same methods; and they were almost of an age—Norris was born in 1870 and Crane in 1871. Yet they met only once—as fellow correspondents on the tug *Three Friends* off Santiago when they were doing their part to avenge the sinking of the *Maine* by reporting, the one to McClure, the other to the *World*. To Norris, Crane then seemed a seasoned correspondent, the equal almost of his fellow correspondent Harding Davis, for he had "been in peril of his life on a filibustering expedition, was tanned to the color of a well-worn saddle." But natural reserve on both sides prevented a friendship between the "Bohemian" and the tall, serious, well dressed young college man from California, Harvard, and the Julian atelier. Norris was made of different stuff. Actually less deeply immersed in life than Crane, he had thrown himself into college high jinks whereas Crane had retreated, hurt, from his hazing; he had gone to Paris to study painting whereas Crane had merely associated with painters in New York's east side; he had rejoiced, on a grand tour of Africa, to be caught in the Boer uprising whereas Crane snarled and scoffed at the Greeks and Turks; he had never seriously lacked money—his father was a wealthy jewelry merchant—whereas Crane had early known poverty. These two could not talk of their art, their failures and successes.

The most striking fact about Norris and his work is that by temperament, education, and written statement of his philosophy of art, he denies kinship with the realists and allies himself with "Romance." Such easy generalizations as that of Irvin Cobb, "He was a pioneer of the modern school of native realists," can be true only if reconciled with his own statement: "Realism stultifies itself. It notes only the surface of things." In the year before his death, 1901, he proclaimed his creed to be derived from Zola and Kipling, denying the fiction of Howells as "respectable as a church and proper as a deacon." Accepting Howells as spokesman for the method, he rejected his limitations in so far as he could. In thus aligning himself with the romantics, according to some critics, he read himself out of the society of naturalists entirely.

But the conflict is largely a matter of definition. "Romance," he says, "is the kind of fiction that takes cognizance of variations from the type of normal life. . . . [It] may even treat of the sordid, the unlovely." To find her, you need not take her "a weary journey across the water—ages and the flood of years"; rather you should take her "across the street to your neighbour's front parlour," or to Fifth Avenue or Wall Street. She would note details to be sure, on the way, but she would find the heartache or the memory beneath the surface facts. Such searching for truth rather than for reality is quite respectable and may even resort to the ugly and the violent when safely removed to "the castles of the Middle Ages and the Renaissance châteaux." May it not also be used as "an instrument with which we may go straight through the clothes and tissues and wrappings of flesh down deep into the red, living heart of things?" This is the veritism of Garland in the hands of a man who plunged directly from feeling into action and then paused briefly afterward to think out his reasons. His critical terms may not be carefully weighed and his logic not always perfect, but he gave American fiction another dimension. When he said, "Life is not always true to life. . . . In the fine arts we do not care one little bit about what life actually is, but what it looks like to an interesting, impressionable man," he was speaking, like Crane, as the painter, but also as the dramatist. He was a novelist because of his passionate conviction that the novel "expresses modern life better than architecture, better than painting, better than poetry, better than music." The novel can speak directly to the people, as all art should, because the people will read and reread it. At her best, "the muse is a teacher, not a trickster." The realist who stops short at the surface fact, or the "Bohemian" who loses himself and his sincerity in the intricacies of style, tone, and effect, are equally at fault. To Norris, fiction was a vital, two-fisted art, the art of the future.

He did not reach this position at once, nor did he hold to it consistently. His work does not show a steady advance; in some ways, he came nearer his purpose at the start than at the close of his short career. He never achieved the discipline of the school to which he was instinctively allied, that of scientific naturalism, because his love of the story for itself was too likely to run away with his ideas about it. Although he tried to reject the conventions and the sentimentality of popular romance, his critical distinctions were not sufficiently clear to keep him out of the traps against which he warned others. Furthermore, as he did not publish his work in the order in which it was written, the progress which some critics have attributed to him is an illusion.

Nevertheless it is possible to trace his development with a fair degree of accuracy. It falls into four stages: his youth when he was completely immersed in the far away and the long ago; his college years when, under the spell of Zola, he did his best work; his years as a newspaper man and social dillettante when, in trying to find his own métier and at the same time to gain a hearing, he wrote his romances; and the last years of his life when, as publisher's reader and free-lance novelist, he undertook his trilogy of wheat. A further confusion arises from the fact that most of his short stories and sketches were potboilers, and many of them were gleaned from novels already written. Few are useful to the critic either as sources or as representative art. Unlike Crane, Garland, and London, Norris was a novelist, and he cared for no other prose form.

His first published work, *Yvernelle* (1891), a long narrative poem on a medieval theme, is the enthusiastic effort of a boy of nineteen who had spent long childhood hours playing lead soldiers with his younger brother and who had later immersed himself in Froissart and the *Chanson de Roland*. His interest was in medieval armor during his art-student days in Paris—the days of Zola, the Goncourts, and De Maupassant—and there is no evidence that he even then knew of the existence of these later masters. For the time, the Musée de Cluny held more life for him and his artist friend Ernest Peixotto than did the streets of Paris. Let it not be forgotten that when Norris made his final plea for romance, he was offering a justification for his own deepest nature.

Why then his sudden discovery of the first and greatest of the naturalists when he was a student at the University of California? Sensitive, acute, energetic, he instinctively turned to life rather than to books for his learning, but Zola gave his love of romance a present anchorage in the world he saw and felt and smelled, and about which he speculated with eager interest. "Naturalism, as understood by Zola," he wrote later in the *Wave,* "is but a form of romanticism. . . . Everything is extraordinary, imaginative, grotesque even, with a vague note of terror quivering throughout like the vibrations of an ominous and low-pitched diapason." To his early enthusiasm for Scott, Dickens, and Stevenson, instilled by his mother, Kipling was added. The British teller of tales had easily blended science with adventure, and his American disciple was off on a South African exploration when a return of "the attack of Harding Davis" seized him. It would be hard for him to disentangle the threads of science and popular romance, but a way would be found if sincere effort could find it.

*McTeague* (1899) was his first sustained experiment in fiction. This novel and *Vandover and the Brute* (1914), written during his year at Harvard when in Lewis E. Gates he found his first real teacher, follow the Zola formula strictly but, in spirit if not always in execution, are sincere explorations of his own experience rather than imitations. The one a story of a Polk Street dentist, the other of a privileged youth of his own class, they are both studies of slow degeneration through an overwhelming of the finer instincts and aspirations by the suppressed brute nature. McTeague has all the physical and mental characteristics of the brute, but he is harmless—almost admirable —in his childish acceptance of life. But he and Trina, his "mate-woman" as Jack London would have called her, relapse atavistically into avarice, as Norris notes step by step the slow inroads of poverty, the creeping degeneration of all his principal characters. The inherent ugliness of life, the gold symbols of aspiration—false because merely material—the dual nature of man, are examined with ruthless power. Up to the magnificently restrained scene of the murder the novel is a unified masterpiece of naturalism, superior in execution to *Maggie,* unequaled for a generation in American literature. Even Dreiser is less successful in fundamental grasp of motivation and in sensuous description of significant details.

There are romantic flaws: The love story of Old Grannis and Miss Baker, introduced into Norris' original plan with the valid intention of providing contrast but sentimentalized in the conventional fashion, and the melodramatic conclusion of pursuit and death in the desert—added later after the manuscript had long lain fallow—are the most striking. Both, however, are so well presented that they do not offend, and the total effect of the story is unified and powerful.

*Vandover* takes its theme as well as its method from science. It is autobiographic in the sense that it studies the form of atavism to which a young man of wealth, pliable disposition, and sensitivity like Norris would be subject. In Vandover the typical naturalistic weakness of will and consequent dissipation take the form of a recognized ailment, lycanthropy, a type of insanity in which the patient imagines himself a wolf or other animal and imitates its actions. Norris had experimented with the theme of reversion to primitive type in "Lauth," a short story in which a scholarly youth is awakened to his savage nature by the sight of blood of his own taking. But in *Vandover,* by following Zola into clinical realms, he violates his own warning that actuality is sometimes not artistically convincing. In the early part of the story, when the suppressed brute is merely an idea, a horrible fear, there are brilliant passages of narrative description and psychological subtlety; but when Vandover actually goes down naked on all fours the result, however sound medically, verges on the grotesque. Norris doubtless recognized this weakness, for he failed to complete his story and it was not published until long after his death; but it must now take its place beside *McTeague* as an early and daring example of naturalistic fiction, far more authentic than any of London's later and more acceptable treatments of the same theme.

If there is a mystery as to why the boisterous romance, *Moran of the Lady Letty* (1898), rather than either *McTeague* or *Vandover,* was Norris' first published novel, it is dispelled merely by taking his cheery little love story *Blix* (1899) as autobiography. The same mild vices of party-going and card-playing that led Vandover into degeneration are in Condy Rivers, the hero of *Blix,* diverted into success as a popular novelist and virtuous husband by the "thoroughbred" Travis Bessemer. "Blix," as Condy calls her, is the "new woman" on the Charles Dana Gibson pattern. She has an independence of mind that makes her all the more feminine, even though the reviewers objected when Norris described her as tall and solidly built as a man, radiating health, with small, twinkling, brown eyes. In a civilized way, she is the Viking type that Norris so much admired rather than the conventional heroine—an accurate portrait of his wife Jeannette Black, and the summer idyl of comradeship was his own love story. For the stories of Norris and of Condy are one. The suggestion for *Moran* is to be found in a letter, probably authentic, that Condy received from a New York publisher with the return of a manuscript of collected short stories. "The best-selling book just now is the short novel—say thirty thousand words—of action and adventure." Condy took the suggestion and pulled himself out of the inertia of Sunday supplement editing and the debilitating association of the Bohemian Club in which he was caught. Norris wrote *Moran.*

The story of Condy's novel was suggested by Captain Jack, an old sea dog that he and Blix had discovered in their harmless adventuring. Ross Wilbur of *Moran* is again Norris, now to be shanghaied from a season of "afternoon teas, pink, lavender, and otherwise," and carried by the schooner *Petrel* on a shark-hunting expedition with a crew of Chinamen and a beach-combing captain to Magdalena Bay. The education of Ross into manhood is started by the Captain's fist and continued by the Viking maiden Moran when a series of accidents with a derelict leave the two young people in command of the ship and its coolie crew. Here is the theme which London later developed more fully in *The Sea Wolf,* but Norris turns attention rather to "action and adventure." The naturalistic theme of Moran's awakening to womanhood and the sensuous wealth of descriptive detail aroused the enthusiasm of even the vigilant Howells, and Norris' career was assured.

He was summoned to New York, the "literary center" which he was soon to deny, and put a winter of effort into reading for Doubleday and expanding a story of Arctic adventure into another naturalistic romance of primitive love, *A Man's Woman* (1900), "grinding out the tale, as it were by main strength." But the bread had no yeast and his powers were being wasted on the secondhand adventures of Captain Jack. The one significant event of the winter was his discovery of Theodore Dreiser, his instant appreciation of the manuscript of *Sister Carrie*.

Suddenly there came to him "an idea that's as big as all outdoors," and McClure agreed with him that "the big American novel is going to come out of the West." The trilogy of wheat which he was never to finish had been conceived, and he hastened back to San Francisco and the San Joaquin Valley for local color. "It involves a very long, a very serious, and perhaps a very terrible novel," he wrote a friend.

*The Octopus* (1901) is usually studied as our first great economic thesis-novel, but to Norris it was "the big, epic, dramatic thing." His literary problem is written into the poet Presley who goes to live on the Los Muertos ranch in Tulare County in preparation for his epic of the West.

Just what he wanted, Presley hardly knew. On the one hand, it was his ambition to portray life as he saw it—directly, frankly, and through no medium of personality or temperament. But on the other hand as well, he wished to see everything through a rose-coloured mist—a mist that dulled all harsh outlines, all crude and violent colours. . . . He searched for the True Romance, and, in the end, found grain rates and unjust freight tariffs.

Presley accomplished no more than his poem "The Toilers," an idea modeled on Markham's "The Man With the Hoe," but Norris, putting his vast idea into more versatile prose, wrote *The Octopus* and very nearly achieved the masterpiece he visioned. Since *Moby Dick,* by then virtually forgotten, there had been nothing like it in American literature.

In sheer spread of canvas *The Octopus* achieved all that Norris hoped for it, but as a work of art it has obvious faults. With romantic fogginess of mind, Norris resolved none of his major issues, artistic, economic, or philosophic. His main story of the decline of Magnus Derrick, the master of Los Muertos, follows the course of those of McTeague and Vandover, although outside circumstance as well as moral weakness undermines the structure of character. This in itself is an advance in naturalistic understanding, a recognition of the force of environment as well as that of biological defect, a movement away from the merely psychological to the sociological novel. But the story of Magnus is intertwined with the primitive and tragic love of the rancher Annixter for his milkmaid Hilma Tree (again the mating of Moran but now on a more civilized and restrained level), and with the mystical romance of the shepherd Vanamee with the spirit of his dead Angèle, reminiscent of *Trilby,* a book which Norris scorned. These three strands, together with lesser ones, are woven by an epic theme and a common philosophy into an intricate pattern—or at least it was Norris' intention so to weave them. Presley abandoned his Milton and Homer for Mill, Malthus, Henry George, and Schopenhauer.

He trembled with excitement as the relations between the [Railroad] Trust and the [Ranchers'] League became more and more strained. He saw the matter in its true light. It was typical. It was the world-old war between Freedom and Tyranny.

All these personal stories became merged in one impersonal conflict between the Life Force, as symbolized by the Wheat, and the Machine, as symbolized by the Railroad. Magnus, as leader of the wheat growers, and the potbellied S. Behrman, as spokesman for the railroad, became primary antagonists in the struggle. The vigorous California story teller saw the tragic issue of the time and place as the New England recluse Henry Adams saw it: the Wheat and the Railroad were the Virgin and the Dynamo, less subtly and profoundly understood.

The climactic scene where the ranchers meet the representatives of the railroad at the irrigation ditch more than satisfies Norris' requirement that a novel build up to a "pivotal event" and explode in a "rush of action," but the somewhat fortuitous conclusion—S. Behrman buried by his own wheat in the hold of his own vessel—fails to achieve the effect of naturalistic determinism which it was obviously designed to produce. "Men were naught," Presley had finally decided, "death was naught, life was naught; FORCE only existed." But the traditional idealist in Norris would not down so easily and he pushes past this force to the "primordial energy flung out from the hand of the Lord himself, immortal, calm, infinitely strong." Hence the fecundity of earth may find its expression equally in the warmth of Hilma Tree or the unreality of Angèle; the shepherd Vanamee may conquer death while the impersonal Force is crushing out the lives of his friends; and the demon behind it all, Shelgrim, the president of the Pacific and Southwestern Railroad, may plead that he, too, is a puppet in the impersonal drama of natural law. Dramatic it all is on a grand scale, both epic and tragic in its power, but logical it is not. The book finally fails as tragic drama because Norris has no consistent position on the vast economic and metaphysical problems he raises. Fiction need not provide answers to such problems, but its angle of view must be consistent. Norris shifts with his poet Presley from sympathy with the capitalistic ranchers to support of the "reds" and back to excuses even for the railroad, from mechanistic determinism to mystical theism and back. The principles at the foundation of the book were never thought through.

A great failure is akin to a success. *The Octopus* is the most ambitious novel of its generation. Though planned as the first of a trilogy which was to follow the Wheat through the three stages of growth, marketing, and export to famine-ridden Europe or Asia, it must stand alone, for its sequel *The Pit* (1903) is a relapse into the conventional novel form, and the third work, *The Wolf,* was never written. In *The Octopus,* the wheat itself could be the central character, for it was ever present. "There it was. The Wheat! The Wheat! In the night it had come up. It was there, everywhere from margin to margin of the horizon." But in the Chicago grain pit, it is off stage, a column of figures in a ledger, a few miles of ticker tape, an object of man-made speculation rather than of elemental force. Nevertheless, Norris' contemporary reviewers were not far wrong in greeting the story of the rise and fall of Curtis Jadwin as his most mature novel. Its theme is of profound social significance; the characters of Jadwin and his wife Laura Dearborn, like those of McTeague and Trina, studies of degeneration through greed, achieve sympathy through understanding and powerful treatment; and the plot, in spite of its unfortunately happy ending, has originality within its conventional frame. Anticipating Dreiser's *The Financier* (1912) and *The Titan* (1914), it is a sincere and impartial study of the meaning of American capitalism, of the degenerating influence of greed in high places. In this last novel Norris finally blended what he understood of naturalistic fiction with the romance of contemporary life. The result is not his most impressive work, but it is sound, and it was acceptable to his readers. He had proved, at least to his own satisfaction, that romance could find the truth in contemporary life as well as could realism.

## 5

Many of the abortive pseudoscientific trends in Frank Norris found their popular apologist in Jack London, author of forty-nine volumes of fiction, drama, and essay, who published his first book two years before Norris died. The illegitimate son of an itinerant astrologer and of a spiritualist, London preached the more obvious radicalism of his day in romantic fiction that, during sixteen years (1900–1916), raised him from obscurity and poverty to fame and wealth, brought him all the rewards of adventure, love, learning, and worldly possessions that his insatiable body and mind craved, and led him to egocentric despair and probable suicide. The personification of the romantic impulses of the new century, vigorous, naïve, and prolific, he provided his magazine readers with unstinted fare, and left a small body of writing which, for sincerity and vitality, deserves to be rescued from the oblivion to which his artistic faults threaten to condemn it. Primarily a skillful teller of tales, he achieved originality and significance by enthusiastic acceptance of the new doctrines of society and science that made a ferment of the popular mind.

"There is an ecstasy that marks the summit of life," he wrote, "and beyond which life cannot rise. . . . This ecstasy comes when one is most alive, and it comes as a complete forgetfulness that one is alive." It was this spirit, here ascribed to the dog Buck of *The Call of the Wild,* that drove him relentlessly through his forty years, as it drove his elder contemporary Theodore Roosevelt. Before reaching the age of nineteen, according to his own account, he had lived a life "raw and naked, wild and free" as an oyster pirate in San Francisco Bay, he had shipped as an able-bodied seaman on the schooner *Sophie Sutherland* for Japan, he had worked sixteen hours a day at a cannery and in a jute mill, he had hoboed his way across the United States with Kelly's "industrial army" in its march on Washington, and he had spent thirty days in the Niagara Falls jail for vagrancy. In spite of confessed abhorrence for alcohol he had proved his manhood by meeting the sociable John Barleycorn on his own terms.

Always a haunter of libraries as well as of saloons, he had as a boy devoured popular fiction, and, suddenly in 1895, he decided that he would sell brains rather than brawn. He would climb the class barrier with the aid of "the books." Like the hero of his semiautobiographical novel *Martin Eden* (1909), he identified the upper class and the university with all that was noble, and he diverted his burning zeal into a program of reading and writing which covered high-school studies and a term at the University of California in two years; then dropped it all and was off to the Klondike. Returning after a year to Oakland as poor as when he left, he began selling stories, jokes, light verse, and essays to the struggling *Overland Monthly,* to many a lesser journal, and even to the remote *Atlantic,* pawning his overcoat and his bicycle between checks to pay for his rented typewriter and boasting that he worked nineteen hours out of every twenty-four. In 1899 the unaccountable whirlwind of success that he describes in *Martin Eden* brought him fifteen checks from magazines and the acceptance of his first collection of tales, *The Son of the Wolf* (1900). His hero Martin brushed success from him and sought morbid peace by drowning; London, like Melville and many another, sublimated his restlessness in writing.

Eight years had to pass before he could understand this crisis well enough to record it. Those years saw his best work but none is so revealing nor so powerful as *Martin Eden.* The chronicle of a sick ego, this thinly screened confession, with its fidelity, its misunderstanding of naked tragic forces, and its failure of resolution, is the central document of his career. Martin's defeat was the tragedy of his times because in him the emotional and intellectual conflicts of the new science were brought to a focus.

Jack London was a confessed Spencerian evolutionist and Marxian socialist. He had familiarized himself with evolution and socialism by undisciplined and voracious reading, and by constant talks with men more learned than he was or ever cared to be, but he knew both movements as the ultimate consumer, the people, rather than as the scholar or critic. From Spencer and his popularizers he accepted the thesis that man evolved from lower forms of life, differing from them in degree rather than in kind, and he followed the doctrine of the "synthetic philosophy" through to a positive faith in progress and a benevolent anarchy of Anglo-Saxon supremacy that would allow both social harmony and complete individualism. His mind rejected the Nietzschean doctrine of the superman, but his temperament accepted it with a deeper logic. From the *Communist Manifesto,* which he had read while on the road, and from the writings of American socialists rather than from *Das Kapital,* he drew the doctrines of class warfare, revolution, and the ultimate triumph of the working class over the capitalists. He resented the socialists' demand for political action as a threat to individual prerogative, but he fell in with their program and became an active worker in their cause. Such inconsistencies were enough to tear him apart, but the real source of his sickness, an intense and inhibited egocentricity, he revealed with complete candor and total incomprehension.

These three issues, biological evolution, socialism, and psychological inhibition, became one in Martin Eden's attempt to win fame, fortune, and love by determination. The original of Ruth Morse of the novel was Mabel Applegarth, a college friend who at once symbolized for him the ideals of upper-class culture and the dream woman of the male animal. When he discovered the bourgeois conventionality, dishonesty, and materialism that he had mistaken for ideality in her and her set, he rejected both illusions, and with them the dying literary code of ideality. In his own life, London turned without love to the "companion" and "mother-woman" Bess Maddern, but he allowed Martin no such escape from his crisis. His divorce, after two years of marriage and two daughters, had taught him the fallacy of this solution, an argument that he worked out with the help of another "companion," Anna Strunsky, in *The Kempton-Wace Letters* (1903). His second marriage in 1905 to his "mate-woman" Charmian Kittredge had seemingly solved his own problem and had provided him with sufficient perspective to tell Martin's story; but he gave Martin suicide rather than a mate. His own crisis was deferred in his "Valley of the Moon," a pretentious but never completed ranch in Sonoma County, California, where success, wealth, and love brought with them recurrent alcoholism and a deep despair that belied his healthful buoyancy of spirit. The unwritten chapters of *Martin Eden* are added by his most sincere book *John Barleycorn* (1913), a personal analysis of the power of drink, where he confesses to "roaming with the White Logic through the dusk of my soul," and by *The Little Lady of the Big House* (1916), a "design for living" in which jealousy defeats the supreme experiment of free mating and brings the old and inconclusive answer, suicide.

In *The Sea Wolf* (1904) the failure of the amoral superman is illustrated with even more clarity. Wolf Larsen is London's most fully conceived character. Captain of a sealing schooner, he knows only the primitive law of survival through predatory ruthlessness. He is a wolf in fact as well as in name, with the shrewd intelligence as well as the brute power of the wolf. But he, like London, has grappled with "the books" and become conscious of his motives and deliberate in his actions. His awakening of the dilettante Humphrey Van Weyden provides a magnificent theme for a great novel, and the first half almost realizes the possibilities by showing in a parallel situation what Norris might have done with the opening chapters of *Moran of the Lady Letty*. But the sudden appearance of the "mate-woman" Maud Brewster, afloat in mid-ocean, throws the whole plot off balance and turns a study in naturalism into a desert island romance. Larsen's fall is caused by the accident of blindness rather than by a tragic flaw in his character or philosophy, and the island sequences, with their absurd mixture of Victorian prudery and primitive law, their painful stretching of probability, leave the novel a worse wreck than the vessel the *Ghost* or its master.

The two dog stories, *The Call of the Wild* (1903) and *White Fang* (1906) are more successful because they are uncomplicated by the problem of sex in society. The love of dog and man may be studied in primitive terms more readily than may that of man and woman. In the one book a dog breaks with the codes of civilization and reverts, step by step, to its wolf origins in the other a part-wolf is gradually weaned from the wild and takes his place in the world of his man-god. *The Call of the Wild* is London's most satisfying work. The theme and action are in tune, the character of Buck is fully realized, the story proceeds with the economy and sure strokes of a writer in full command of his material. But never again, except in occasional short stories where the task is easier because less ambitious, did he so sharpen his focus and so completely realize his biological thesis in fictional form.

There is of course an underlying social significance in the rejection or acceptance of civilization by the primitive individual in all studies of atavism and its contrary, but the message of social revolution is expressed better in essay and tract than in any of his fiction. His contribution to the muckraking movement, *The People of the Abyss* (1903), is a study of English rather than American, economic rather than political, degradation. It is the narrative of his own experiences when he donned old clothes and lived in London's East End in order to study poverty and crime at its worst. A patronizing tone is not sufficient to injure the graphic realism of his account. In the essays of *The War of the Classes* (1905), *Revolution* (1910), and *The Human Drift* (1917) he states with passion but without philosophic depth the position of the American social revolutionist and his faith in the rise of the working class. Only once did he attempt to garb his thesis in fiction, in *The Iron Heel* (1908), a terrifying forecast of Fascism and its evils.

In the title essay of *The Human Drift* London comes to grips with his problem and realizes that social revolution is only an incident in the process of evolution. Returning to Spencer with the intellectual comprehension of a Garland and the emotional acceptance of a Norris, he declares that "man, the latest of the ephemera, is pitifully a creature of temperature, strutting his brief day on the thermometer," driven onward by his need for food—a thought that once occurred to Benjamin Franklin. All the red-blooded eagerness and purity of the open life, which had been honestly his own at the start but which had by now become merely his marketable product, had faded into a cynical negation. He had felt and thought deeply enough to be able to cry with Richard Hovey, "Behold! I have lived!" but he had come finally, in spite of his buoyant temperament, to the pessimistic conclusions of the philosophy of biological and mechanistic determinism. It remained for Henry Adams to define and for later naturalists like Dreiser, Hemingway, Farrell, and Steinbeck to grapple more significantly with the problems which he, Norris, and others had raised. Jack London had become story teller extraordinary to William Randolph Hearst.

With London's failure to realize its possibilities, naturalism as a movement in American fiction reached the end of its first and experimental phase. When Dreiser published *Jennie Gerhardt* in 1911 and republished *Sister Carrie* in 1912, it entered its second.

Thus the demand of science that human life be reconsidered as the manifestation of natural laws had led these experimental story tellers in two quite contrary directions. The method of science suggested a further development of realism toward analysis of data, and the frank discussion of all—and especially the abnormal, the sordid, and the socially unjust—aspects of experience. On the other hand its attendant philosophy of dispassionate force stimulated new generalizations and created new symbols to represent the basic drives in man and in nature—thereby developing a new form of romance. Neither impressionistic realism in Garland and Crane nor the romance of power in Norris and London proved adequate to its demand.

The movement succeeded, however, not only in this country but abroad, in forcing the artist to confront once more the fundamental issues of human destiny, and because it chose the novel and the short story rather than the drama or poetry as its principal forms of expression, it gave them a depth and a sincerity which they had seldom before achieved. The faith in the possibilities of naturalistic fiction, which Garland and Norris preached with the zeal of fanatics, was not yet justified in their day, at least in the United States. Only once before had an adequate philosophy been put into the hands of the American teller of tales, when Poe, Hawthorne, and Melville wrote of sin, free will, and fate. When the new view of the universe proposed by science could develop a metaphysic and an ethic in harmony with it, the way would again be open to these fundamental issues. What the twentieth century held for the American writer of fiction, no one in 1910 could even guess.

# 63. HENRY JAMES

$O_N$ the level of the ideal—on the level of art—American fiction achieved in the novels and short stories of Henry James a kind of reality different from both the literal record of a Howells and the philosophical naturalism of a Zola. This reality was his response to the human predicament of his generation, which James felt with unusual acuteness because of the virtual formlessness of his education—the predicament of the sensitive mind during what may be called the interregnum between the effective dominance of the old Christian-classical ideal through old European institutions and the rise to rule of the succeeding ideal, whatever history comes to call it. To express that predicament in fiction no education could have been more fitting than his, for it excluded him from assenting to the energies of social expansion, of technology, of the deterministic sciences, and of modern finance and business. Unconscious assent to these forces, over and above any rebellion against their moral values, caused most active minds in his day to conceal the fact of interregnum. James' mind reacted only to the shadows of those forces as revealed in human emotion and in social behavior and convention. With his abiding sense of the indestructible life, he expressed the decay and sterility of a society pretending to live on conventions and institutions but lacking the force of underlying convictions. He described what he saw, and he created what lay under what he saw.

They tell a story of Henry James which cannot be verified as to fact, but one which is so true and just in spirit that we may take it as the scriptural text for this chapter. Once, in the nineties, while James was staying in an English country house, the only child of a neighbor died of a sudden illness; and although James had quarreled with the neighbor and they had not been on speaking terms he announced to his host that he would attend the funeral of the little boy. His host argued that, in the small church in the small village, it would be conspicuously unseemly for him to go—the bereaved parents could only take it as an affront; but James was obstinate. When he returned, his host asked him how on earth he could have brought himself to go, and to sit, as he had, in the pew directly behind the mourners. James brushed all argument aside and, with that intensity in his eyes which made his face seem naked, stated firmly: "Where emotion is, there am I!"

All his life long, and in all but his slightest work, James struggled to use the conventions of society, and to abuse them when necessary, to bring himself directly upon the emotion that lay under the conventions, coiling and recoiling, ready to break through. So to bring himself, and so to see, was for him action in life and creation in art. "Where emotion is, there am I!" If he could find the emotion he could for himself realize life, and if he could create the reality of the emotion in his art, in terms of actual characters and situations, he could make his art—in James Joyce's phrase at the end of *The Portrait of the Artist As a Young Man*—the uncreated conscience of his race. The story of that struggle to realize life as emotion and to create it as art is the abiding story of Henry James, as near as we can come to the Figure in his Carpet.

With the events of his life we have here little to do except see how their conditions, both those imposed upon him and those which he imposed upon himself, led him to an increasing devotion to that struggle, and to the final decision at full maturity that in the very passion of pleading for full life in others, for him life had to be sacrificed to art. As he sometimes put it, his own life had to disappear into his art just to the degree that he was a successful artist. The conditions imposed upon him were freedom of sensibility and conscience and the emotional insecurity that is apt to accompany that freedom. His was a minimum financial security and the curious need to prove one's own value that in responsive natures sometimes goes with that security. His also was so wide a variety of social and educational exposures, which had in common only their informality, that he was left the most social man in the world but without a society or an institution that could exact his allegiance. His, further, was an accidental injury by a slip or a fall in early manhood which seems to have left him with the sense of a physical uprootedness and isolation that only aggravated, as it fed upon, his emotional isolation. Like Abélard who, after his injury, raised the first chapel to the Holy Ghost, James made a sacred rage of his art as the only spirit he could fully serve.

2

Henry James was born in New York City, April 15, 1843, the second son of Henry James, Sr.—a peripatetic philosopher and dissenting theologian of considerable means, a friend of Emerson and Carlyle, and a great believer in a universal but wholly informal society. It was he who on his deathbed directed that the only words spoken at his funeral should be: "Here lies a man, who has thought all his life that the ceremonies attending both marriage and death were all damned nonsense." To his sons William and Henry he gave a kind of infant baptism after his own heart by taking them abroad before they could speak and dipping them generously in the font of Europe: a rite which was to mark them both with particular strength and weakness for life. After Europe in 1843 and 1844, the family alternated between Albany and New York. The children were sent to at least three schools before 1855, when in June they went to Europe for a three-year educational experiment at Geneva, London, Paris, and Boulogne. The year 1858–1859 was passed at Newport, Rhode Island; 1859–1860, at Geneva and Bonn. Thus the boys learned languages and manners and fragments of many systems of formal education; but more important were the incalculable effects of years of exposure to the sights and sounds and tones of "other" worlds than that in which by birth they might have been expected to grow up. Part of their father's intention was to give them, by keeping them safe from any particular soil, the richest and most varied human soil to grow in. When he had given them as much of Europe as possible, he removed them to what was at that time the least American of all towns, and for two years they lived again at Newport. There they came under the influence of a young man who was to become the least American of all American painters, John La Farge. Then, in 1862, Henry James made his one attempt at formal education, in the Harvard Law School, a venture which seems to have had no effect on him at all. It was at this time that he sustained his injury and was kept out of the Civil War, the great historical action of his time.

The young James then turned to literature, at first uncertainly and as a "possible" occupation but within four or five years firmly and fully as a profession. His earliest story appeared in the *Atlantic Monthly* in 1865, when he was twenty-two, and he published stories, sketches, and critical reviews frequently thereafter in that magazine, in the *Nation,* and elsewhere. In the fiction and sketches the writing was easy to the point of facility, romantic in tone except where it was humorous, and distinguished chiefly by its competence; in the criticism, it was high-toned and even captious. It showed the influences of Dickens and Hawthorne, Washington Irving and perhaps a little Balzac, in short the dominant literary influences of his time. The American scene, as characterized by Boston and New York, kept him alive but did not provoke reaction or experiment in his writing.

In 1869 he went abroad again, this time to literary as well as social Europe, and for ten or twelve years paid visits to America rather than to Europe. Abroad he alternated between London and Paris, London and Italy. London was to live in, Paris was to learn in, Italy to love; America had become chiefly something for his literary and social sensibility to react on. London gave him the support of an institutionalized society which made for security and position. Italy gave him color and form and warmth, and the ideal satisfaction of all his romantic nostalgia for those qualities. But Paris gave him his profession; for there he met Turgenev, whom he called the "beautiful genius," and Flaubert, whom he found vulgar in person but perfect in writing. It was in Paris that he learned that the novel was an art and that art was the mastering, all-exacting profession that alone made life tolerable by making it intelligible. He learned also that the art of literature, like the art of painting or of music, was an international art, however locally rooted it might have to be in inspiration, and for himself he made the decision that his inspiration might well be as international as the art. It was a decision for which his education had prepared him, just as was his decision to live in London but to keep up his American and French connections. Perhaps it was the very informality of his education that made him grasp for safety at the formalism of English society and the form of the French novel of Flaubert and the Russian novel of Turgenev who was himself a result of the French influence. Formalism and form were for him the means of understanding the formlessness which was life itself; but he never confused the two, though he sometimes made the mistake of refusing to see the life, either in America or in the novels of "disorderly" writers like Dostoevski and Zola, if the form was not within the habit of his perception.

The effect of these years of discipleship and decision was triple. They transformed James from one more American writer working at his trade to an addicted artist working to perfect the form of his chosen art. They gave him his three themes: the international theme, the theme of the artist in conflict with society, and the theme of the pilgrim in search of society. And through his work, the form of the novel in England and America was developed to a new maturity and variety and responsibility. In 1881, with the publication of *The Portrait of a Lady,* the European novel as a form became part of the resources of the English language, and James himself a great novelist, for in that novel his three major themes were for the first time combined in a single objective form.

These years ended the first long period in James' literary life with a high climax, at the same time that they ended the actually international aspect of his personal life. Perhaps his father's death in 1882 helped diminish his sense of personal American connection. Perhaps his loss of popularity after *The Portrait of a Lady,* which was the last book to sell really well in his own lifetime, forced him into the more private reality of his English connection. Perhaps he had merely finally made up his mind. At any rate, he remained in England without visiting America until 1904 (when he made the tour which is recorded in part in *The American Scene*), and in the nineties he established himself in the nearest he ever had to a real home, at Lamb House, Rye, in Sussex.

The "middle period," from 1882 to 1897, when he published *The Spoils of*

*Poynton,* was one of experimentation, refinement of medium, exacerbation of sensibility, and extreme sophistication of perception. Nothing written during that period reached the stature of *The Portrait of a Lady;* much of it was water in sand that only rearranged the grains, though much of it was exquisitely molded. It was then that he earned his reputation for finickiness, difficulty beyond the necessities, unreality, and remoteness. His disappointment was so great that, during the latter part of this period, he succumbed to the temptation to write deliberately "popular," deliberately "well made" plays, none of which did well, and one of which, at its London performance, brought him the humiliation of personal hisses when he appeared on the stage at the call for author. Yet he had finally mastered the art that was to make it possible for him to write, in the third period, from 1897 to 1904, first-rate novels and tales, among them the series of three great novels, *The Ambassadors, The Wings of the Dove,* and *The Golden Bowl.* Perhaps his failure in his one effort at treason to his high calling when he turned to drama, and the personal humiliation of that failure, jolted him back with new strength by reaction to his old conception of the novel; perhaps he had merely needed the long time of experiment for secret incubation; in any case, preparation was necessary for maturity of technique and, more important, for maturity of sensibility.

The fourth period began with a visit to America in 1904 and 1905 and might well have prepared him, had he lived longer or had the First World War not intervened, for the still greater art of which we can see the signs in the volume of stories called *The Finer Grain,* collected in 1910. These years were spent in the revision of his novels and tales for the New York Edition, in the volume on *The American Scene* (1907), and in the writing of several volumes of memoirs. After 1910 two experimental novels were begun but never finished, *The Ivory Tower* and *The Sense of the Past.* War and sickness prevented their completion and they were published as he left them after his death in the winter of 1916. At his life's end he had a number of friends but none close, many acquaintances but none important to him, and considerable influence on the younger writers of his time, though nothing commensurate to the influence he was later to exert when the luxury of his sensibility and the rigors of his form became increasingly necessary to a larger number of readers and writers. Howells, Bennett, Wells, Ford Madox Ford, Conrad, and Edith Wharton gained by his example, and the last three avowedly made use of his method—Conrad notably in *Chance* and *Under Western Eyes,* Ford in *The Good Soldier* and his remarkable tetralogy about the war, of which the first volume was *Some Do Not,* and Mrs. Wharton in all but her early work. Of the later generation, Virginia Woolf and Dorothy Richardson would have been impossible without him, as less directly

Faulkner and Hemingway and Graham Greene would also have been impossible without the maturity to which he had brought their craft. But essentially he died, as he had lived, lonely both in art and in life, a very special case indeed.

3

Yet he is no more special than Swift or Donne or Proust. He is merely one of those writers in whom succeeding ages find differing values and to whom each age assigns a different rank; nor is it likely that within a particular age he will ever escape violently opposed opinions as to the character of what he wrote. He is thus a perpetual anomaly. How he came to be so, why he must remain so and for what literary good and ill, it is the purpose of this chapter to inquire. For in the stresses and oppositions and active conflicts that make him anomalous, we see what he stood for and we measure the varying stature of what he did.

He stood for that universal human society which is held to underlie any and all existing forms of society; and what he did was to attempt to express the supremacy of universal society over the very narrow existing society he fed on for material. What he stood for was deep in him, a shaping part of his nature; but for what he did he was ill equipped with the conventional kind of sensibility, though excellently equipped with the passion—the suffering readiness and tenacity—of extraordinary sensibility. He was therefore driven to excesses of substitution and renunciation and refinement (in experience and morals and style) beyond warrant of any other successful author's use. Yet in these very excesses lay the virtue of his fundamental insight. Given the broad poverty and intense riches of his known world, it was his insight that forced upon him his excesses. He had to go out of the world to judge the world.

That necessity, the privations which caused it, and its consequent excesses were almost family traits. They show in William as well as in Henry, and pretty much combine in their father. Each of the three suffered in youth a central damage from an experience of the immanence of overwhelming evil and its menace to the self, a damage which was never repaired and never forgotten, so that life always remained perilous. But each was able to balance his experience of evil by an experience of something like religious conversion. None of these conversions except that of the father were on Christian terms; none left its subject attached permanently to any particular form of religion or to any particular form of society. Each of them was left rather with the sense of access to the very center of society itself. William James gives an account of his own conversion anonymously in *The Varieties of Religious*

*Experience*; Henry gives his, in adumbration, in the story called "The Jolly Corner," and in a manuscript note of a New Year's visitation of his Genius which Lubbock prints in his edition of James' *Letters*. But the version which the elder Henry James gives will do for all three. The last book he himself published, *Society the Redeemed Form of Man,* suggests the works of his two sons as well. There the old man, thirty years after the event, said that in his own religious conversion he had been "lifted by a sudden miracle into felt harmony with universal man, and filled to the brim with the sentiment of indestructible life." Such experiences left all three with what the younger Henry was to call in his old age that "obstinate finality" which had made him an artist in spite of all privations.

If the nature of those privations remained always vague, like an obscure and spreading hurt, and if the experience of conversion was always vague, a force from outside that compelled him to go on beyond and in spite of the hurt, nevertheless the result in Henry James' written works is as clear as need be. There is everywhere in it the presence of a deep, almost instinctive, incentive to create the indestructible life which, to his vision, must lie at the heart of the actual life that has been hurt. He began at once to cultivate what his father had planted in him, the habit of response across any barrier—the more barrier the more response. His peculiar education had given him the straight look, acute ear, keen touch, and receptive mind. In his writing life, that mind received so much and reacted so constantly that it became itself a primary and trustworthy sense. This is the hallmark of the homemade mind, and it serves pretty well for home affairs, but in the affairs of the wide world it drives its victims partly to makeshift and partly to reliance upon naked humanity. To the elder James, such a mind was enough, because he never had any real intent to do more than goad and gad the society he lived in. To William James it was not enough, but he was partly able to make up his losses by the systematic study of physiology and philosophy. To Henry James it was not enough either, and he was driven all his life long, without ever acknowledging it, to make substitutes pass for the real thing. It was perhaps that necessity that made him an artist. At any rate the eloquence and passion with which he made the substitutes, rather than the act of substitution, pass for the actual, were what gave his writing stature a kind of contingent or inner reality. Not until war came in 1914 did he see that the true forces of society had all the time been leading to a final treachery to the values its conventions could no longer defend. He had seen it in his art, but not in his life. His immediate response was to throw himself into the war and to become a British subject. The British gave him the Order of Merit; but his response had been lifelong and was already recorded time after time in book after book.

There, in his "International" books, he set the two kinds of society he knew against each other for balance and contrast and mutual criticism. There are two kinds of society which demand writing like this of James: the society of Europe where the vital impulse has so far run out that all its meanings are expressed by the deliberate play of conventions and their refinements; and, second, the society of America where the original convictions and driving impulse have not yet matured in conventions adequate to express them on high levels. James belonged by birth and primary exposure to the second (New York and New England so far as he could deal with them by instinct), and he had a vision—alternately ideal and critical, alternately discouraged and disillusioned—of the first in the Europe of France and Italy and particularly England. Each gave him the means of dealing with the other; each kept the other from seeming the only society on earth; and together they gave him, at his best, great formality and passionate substance.

The International Theme, in short, was what his education had led to. It was the machinery at hand, and in the lack of anything else it had to provide momentum for everything else. Unlike most writers of his time, but a precursor of many who came to maturity after the First World War, he was barred from the help of religion and history, and a perverse critic might say barred even from the help of literature. He could not use religion because he knew nothing of the Christian Church, hardly even so much of its language as remains alive in the speech of those outside it. He did not know what had happened either to the institutions or the practice of religion; he had only the core of religion within him, and it got into his work only by indirection. He could not have written, like his brother, *The Varieties of Religious Experience*, because he was so obstinately a central form, beneath all varieties, of the religious experience itself. He was an example of what happens to a religious man when institutional religion is taken away. What happens to Maggie Verver in *The Golden Bowl*, to Milly Theale in *The Wings of the Dove*, to Isabel Archer in *The Portrait of a Lady*, to George Stransom in "The Altar of the Dead," are examples of religious experience outside a creed, just as what happens to John Marcher in "The Beast in the Jungle" is an example of the privation of religious experience, and just, too, as what happens to the governess in "The Turn of the Screw" is an example of what happens when positive evil inverts religious experience. James would have been wholly unable to relate any of these affairs in formal Christian terms; where for once, in "The Altar of the Dead," he tried to invoke the experience of the Catholic Church, he saved his story to actuality only by the eloquence of his hero's emotion.

As with religion, so with history, only the other way around. If religion was in James an inner primal piety, history was a felt objective residue. He took his history in a single jump from the living man to the ancestral Adam. He was contemporary to an extreme. He took his tradition almost entirely on its face value; yet because he knew so much must have been behind that face, he actually felt more continuity, more unity, than had ever been really there. In that feeling lay the intensity of his sense of history. He lacked historical imagination because his mind lacked historical content; he had never been inside any history but his own; but he had the sense of history because he saw all around him in Europe how he himself came at its end, and all around him in America how he came at its beginning. He felt in himself, so far as history went, the power to represent the flash between the two eternities.

The strangest privation in James, and one that troubled him even less than the others—though it has caused much trouble for many readers—was the privation of his relation to the whole body of literature. He was, as Santayana ironically said of himself, "an ignorant man, almost a poet." It was because he knew so little great literature in quantity that to many he seemed excessively literary in manner; there were not enough professional barriers between himself and the printed page to prevent his mere unredeemed idiosyncrasy from now and then taking over. He knew well enough the things read around the house as a boy—Dickens and Scott and Hawthorne; he knew even better his chosen masters, Balzac and Turgenev and Flaubert; but it is not an exaggeration to say that he had no organized command of any of the possible general traditions of literature a writer living in his time might have taken up. There is very little evidence of reading in his letters, except for the books of his friends; and when his brother complained that he ought to read more, he answered that he had no time. His critical writing, even when it was not frank book reviewing, was almost entirely contemporary, of narrow range and narrower sympathies; it is worth reading chiefly as an illumination of his own mind and writing. Only when he tackled the technical problems—by the very narrowness of his solutions of which, in his own work, he so greatly stretched the scope and responsibilities of the novel as a form—was he critically at home and master in his house.

He was indeed virtually an ignorant man, actually a poet; but he had, besides that sense of the human which he shared with his father and brother, only the two natural weapons of a direct eye and an expert knowledge of surfaces. He had thus everywhere to depend more on his method than—in Plato's sense—on his madness. Only by resources of method which he had often to develop and sometimes to invent could he get his poetry into the objective form of novel or tale; for example, put another way, his use of dialogue is an example of development from illustration to substance; his use of an active consciousness interposed between the story and the reader, as in *The Ambassadors,* is almost an invention. He had to find means to get around the problems which trouble most novelists—as war and lust, love and God, troubled Tolstoy—in order to get at the problems that troubled him. Between him and the world he knew he had to interpose the story of the story, the passion of the passion, the problem of the problem; otherwise he could not aesthetically possess the story, the passion, the problem.

So central were morals to James, even though he was a dissenter to the forms in which morals are abused, that there was not ever quite enough for him in any part of the world either to fall back on or to go forward with. It was so in his own mind; his convictions never matured as ideas, but as images or metaphors, as aesthetic creations, always to be created afresh. As he never went backward into the full Christian tradition, but tapped his sense of what underlay it, so he never went back into the whole force of love, only into so much of it as could be conceived morally. It is for reasons such as these that, though he aimed always at the full picture, the full drama, James had to resort successively to the lesser forms of the allegory, the fable, the ghost story, and at the end, where he was nearest his target, to a kind of cross between the drama and the fairy story; for this is the journey James made between "A Passionate Pilgrim" and "The Madonna of the Future," through "The Turn of the Screw" and *The Sacred Fount,* to *The Golden Bowl* and "The Bench of Desolation," where the last two are almost pure Cinderella and Ugly Duckling dramatized and made haunting for every reader who can see himself in their terms. This is the reverse of what happens in novels wholly dramatized. Whereas great drama seems to rest on the driving power of myth, the thing deeply believed and subject to change and criticism only in externals, the fairy tale seems to rest on an insight anxious to prove itself ideal and therefore dependent on externals for access to essentials. In the fairy tale the skeleton is on the outside, sometimes so much so that there is nothing else, while in the drama the skeleton is always fleshed. This is what Edith Wharton meant when she asked James why he left out of his novels all the fringes of what really happened to his people; to which James answered that he didn't know that he had. James leaves the reader relatively everything to put in; all his density and richness develop in the details of his chosen skeleton. The big things are all fairy tale, with that threat of sudden dark illumination at the edge of which the fairy tale, even more than the fable or the ghost story, so often hovers. The bones that articulate the skeleton can be named. Candor, innocence, aloneness, the pure intelligence on one side, and mendacity, unspecified corruption, crowdedness, and a kind of cunning rapacity on the other are given at equally high value; but are given always at a point where each is about to break down, in the contest with actual life, either into renunciation (which to James as to Emily Dickinson was a "piercing" virtue) or into some deep and ambiguous kind of capitulation of good to evil and evil to good—as in the end of *The Wings of the Dove* or of *The Golden Bowl,* where the capitulations are mutual, affirmative, abysmal, shifting. At that point of capitulation, the dramatized fairy tale becomes the instrument and substance—form united with content—of revelation and judgment. This was the prodigy James made of the novel.

4

If this account of privations and defects is any way correct, James' accomplishment in the art of fiction was certainly a prodigy. No writer in the England or America of his time surpassed him, whether with or relatively without his defects, and his peers—Stevenson and Hardy and Moore and Meredith, Mark Twain and Melville and Howells—played in different fields. He had the extraordinary luck to come on a whole baggage of themes and conventions and situations in the same process by which he himself lived, and the luck, too, that made them suited to replenish each other in his chosen forms of the fable and the fairy story; he had had the luck to find a garden which he could cultivate, and did. He deliberately undertook, and invoked for himself, the profession, the role, the vocation of what he called "that obstinate finality" of the artist. As a profession, art gave occupation to his habit of omnivorous curiosity and to his knowledge of surfaces, and it made the sacrifice of other forms of life acceptable for the sake of good practice. As a role, it gave him both an inner independence and the protection of an outer identity no matter what sacrifices and failures might come his way. As a vocation, it overrode or made negative all sacrifices and failures whatever with the conviction of purpose, and so put him in unassailable relation with that universal man and that indestructible life which he felt under any society, no matter what any society in existence might think of his feelings about it. Art was his pride of energy. So much so that the profession and role of artist—both for themselves and as foils and ideal contrasts to other professions and roles—provided the major obsession for his fictions, as did the obsession of the International Theme, of which it was only another, and equivalent, version.

Where the International Theme showed the American against the European, whether as pilgrim or victim, the theme of the artist showed the writer or painter or actress against the world. The underlying theme which he used perhaps first in *Daisy Miller* (1879), but first clearly in *Washington Square* (1881), and at the last made his chief overt theme, was that of the innocent, loyal, candid spirit at the mercy of the world but reacting to it with high intelligence and spiritual strength, precisely with the artist's perception of what for good and ill it actually was. These stories of young

American girls smirched or driven out of society by the cruel stupidity of its conventions alternated with stories of artists who were also smirched or driven out. In James' imagination the two themes became identical. Perhaps this is again a sign of the interregnum in the thinking of modern man: that the artist should suddenly come to have exorbitant value as subject matter—should seem a hero or a traitor to his proper heroic role—and should seem so to the artist himself and not merely to his biographer. In this James is not alone; he is followed by Mann and Proust and Gide and Pirandello and Joyce, to all of whom the artist became the type of hero most precious; but James was first and most copious and most intransigent in moralizing the desperate straits through which the artist pursued his role—sometimes as if he had chosen it, as in "The Figure in the Carpet" (1896), sometimes as if he had been condemned to it, as in "The Lesson of the Master" (1892), and sometimes, as in "The Middle Years" (1893) as if he had accepted it.

In all these stories the fate of the artist is somehow the test of society. As a consequence he finds his own value so high that he cannot assent to society as it is, but has a great craving to assent to it as it ought to have been, for he knows that his very being declares, or is prevented from declaring, its possibilities. The degree of self-consciousness in these tales is equal to this conscious sense of self-value, and it is hard to say which overcomes the other. In "The Figure in the Carpet," the author Hugh Vereker has a secret pattern to his work that, when he dies, no amount of fanatic frenetic work can reveal. In "The Middle Years," on the contrary, the dying author leaves such a sure consciousness of his essential value that his disciple, a young doctor, gives up the certainty of a fortune to remain in the presence of the master to whom in his disciple's "young voice" is "the ring of a marriage bell." To them both, without "the madness of art," which both share, life is frustration. In "The Lesson of the Master," the Master urges the disciple to give up everything, marriage, money, children, social position—all the things to which the Master has himself succumbed—for the sake of his art. The artist is not a man, declares the Master, but a disfranchised monk, and the rarity of his art must be his only passion. To this teaching the disciple is true; he makes his retreat, and writes; but when he returns he finds that the Master, having become a widower, has married his girl, "partly" to make sure that the disciple sticks to his art, and has himself given up writing. James ends his fable with the remark that the disciple felt himself dedicated by nature to intellectual, not personal, passion. One hardly knows whether society or the artist is worse flayed in this brilliant story; but one knows certainly that the moral of the fable, and of that final remark, lies in the representation of the artist's life as the fullest possible human profession.

James thus raised his profession to a vocation—a calling from beyond himself by a familiar within himself—which, as he followed it, was a virtually continuous conversion, for strength, for identity, for piety to life, of his whole being. Who will say that it was not an invoked obsessive device, a ruse to transform life otherwise intolerable? But who will say, in the conditions of his life, that he had an alternative? To him the sense of his vocation was a predominant part of his sense of the animating truth, as anyone can see who reads his own invocation to his own genius, quoted by Lubbock in his edition of James' *Letters*. Unlike his friend Henry Adams, who thought that if anything he sat too much in the center of the whole world, James knew himself actually at the periphery, and had therefore to make himself a center in invoked reality. As an individual he felt himself to be so many *disjecta membra poetae*. But by raising his profession to a vocation, he celebrated, like priest and prophet at once, a rite in his own chapel of the true church. He became thus the individual who knew best how little individual he truly was, and was therefore able to overcome the dead weight of all those who merely thought themselves individuals because they wielded power and direction and routine to society by the accident of rank or privilege or money. The difference lay in the presence of the sense of vocation; and the only profession James could by nature see as vocation was that of artist; and he saw the artist as alternately cheated and blest in his vocation regardless of his immense task.

But he went further; the sense of vocation is primary in most of his fiction. He made a dramatic transposition of the artist's sense of vocation and he saw it as motivating rare and precious conduct everywhere. James habitually envisaged people as either with vocation in an extreme devoted sense—Isabel Archer in *The Portrait of a Lady* no less than Miriam Rooth in *The Tragic Muse* or Fleda Vetch in *The Spoils of Poynton* or Lambert Strether in *The Ambassadors*—or as without vocation, as in the foils to the characters just named, and more or less brutally against those who had it. He did not deal with the much greater numbers of people who are merely occupied as confused human animals. That is the difference between a writer like James and writers like his masters, Balzac and Flaubert. Hence perhaps his failure to understand the degree of remove at which the conventions of society actually work out (at some distance from where any of us are sitting) and how much of human energy other than the animal is merely manipulated rather than absorbed by the conventions. His novels have no ordinary people, except as barriers to the extraordinary; his people feel either the passion of the passion, or they feel nothing.

As an instance of the extremity to which James carried his transposition, one might take that great and beautiful tale "The Altar of the Dead" in which the hero devotes his life to the cultivation of the memory of his loved dead and is led finally, at the moment of his own death, to celebrate also the memory of the one dead man he hated, who seems suddenly to have been equal in need and just obligation to all the rest. But perhaps an example more sharply drawn may be exhibited in the bare bones of "Maud-Evelyn." Here a young man named Marmaduke, after being as he mistakenly thinks half jilted, goes off to Switzerland where he falls in with an elderly American couple named Dedrick. The Dedricks had some years since lost their daughter Maud-Evelyn, and now, to salvage their loss, take up the new young man in the role of imaginary son-in-law. The young man so far falls in with the fantasy that the role becomes as good as the thing itself, and he proceeds to realize it, stage by stage, for all it is worth: that is, as a vocation. Thus he passes through courtship, wedding, married life, into widowerhood and mourning till finally the Dedricks—whose fantasy he had authorized in the transformation of his own nature—die at peace. Shortly afterwards he himself dies, leaving, as his one gesture toward his erstwhile life, all his money to the girl to whom he had been originally engaged. Perhaps the theme is like Proust's, that the past, brooded on, grows and grows. What the old couple wanted was to get from the past what they would have wanted of the future. They made a temple of death in order to profane it, to stretch its precincts to cover the living world. To the young man—otherwise, by James' assertion, empty of clear intent—it was a chance to seize on the offered backward pattern with the intensity of vocation, in full belief that he might make out of it a true self. Thus, in this story, obsession with the dead reaches hallucination and hallucination reaches the new reality of art.

5

Further than this James never went, though in "The Friends of the Friends" he went as far, for he was eager to perfect his mastery of substance as well as of form. In that story an ordinary ghost is made into something monstrously human, and presides over one of those deep abortions of the human spirit which are yet, in their catastrophe, but "a response to an irresistible call": that is, are acts performed in the assumption of vocation. Had he gone further James would not have been so much unreadable—as this last example nearly is—as silly. He was content with his handful of dark fables of unassayable devotion, because they complemented and hinted at the filling out of such clear dramatic fables as *Washington Square* (1881) and *The Tragic Muse* (1890). The first of these is a light piece, done on the side, to show the opposite case to that of *The Portrait of a Lady*, which was published the same year. Catherine Sloper is the only one of James' heroines who is all round dull and plain, the only one whose intelligence is not equal to her innocence. Without intelligence, she is unable either to reject or to assent to her gradual exile from society at the hands of an egocentric father and a casually mercenary lover; she merely sticks it out. Her story is not there, and neither are the stories of her father and her lover. If anything carries the book along it is the atmosphere suggested in the title, neither of which— atmosphere nor title—have anything except accidentally to do with the theme of the book: which is that human decency, even when unaware of its grounds and its ends, can, if it is taken as a vocation, come cleanly through any soiling assault. It would have taken the passion of a Flaubert for working the riches of ordinary and inarticulate things to have made excellence out of this Madame Bovary in reverse; and perhaps James was trying to do so; but he did not have that skill, and his book remained in the deep sense only an intention.

Miriam Rooth in *The Tragic Muse,* on the other hand, has at least a real struggle because she has the weapons of beauty and intelligence and a vocation as artist to fight with. She makes the center (together with the bright figure of the aesthete Gabriel Nash a little off center for fun) of a brilliant account, in large scale, of the perpetual struggle between the artist of any sort and society of any sort. But there is more gaiety, more business of the great world and the studio without the concrete representation of the underlying perception of and reaction to it, than a novel can stand and still ring true. James himself thought it moved too fast, and certainly the values asserted are far ahead of the values rendered. As a result, the validity, whether for triumph or assault, of Miriam Rooth's or Nick Dormer's vocation is not so much proved as it is by its own self-insistence impugned. In short, it is very much the same sort of relative failure, but at the opposite extreme, as *Washington Square.* But it is often in his relative failures that an artist's drive is most clearly defined; if only because in his purest successes there is the sense of the self-born, self-driven, and self-complete and these qualities escape definition.

What we can see in these novels which relatively fail, and indeed in a full ten of the nineteen novels which he published in his lifetime (as in perhaps a greater proportion of his hundred-odd shorter pieces), is that James' work constitutes a great single anarchic rebellion against society—against the laws of society—in the combined names of decency, innocence, candor, good will, and the passionate heroism of true vocation. His work as a body is the dramatized or pictured exhibition, at those chosen points most familiar to him in his own society, of the revolt implied in the title of his father's book, *Society the Redeemed Form of Man.* Both Jameses were basic dissenters to all except the society that was not yet; and in both cases the rebellion or dissent was merely eccentric or extravagant in life and manners, but central and poetic in work and insight. That is why in these tales of people who renounce or ignore so much of life which to other eyes would have been precious and even necessary to living, the last legitimate cry is still: Live, live all you can! James was compelled to accomplish his rebellion of the ideal through the very conventions he meant to re-create; they were the given medium in which the underlying reality and the invoked ideal could meet and, in dramatic actuality, merge; conventions were what he knew.

The importance of this is worth any amount of reemphasis; for James is only an exaggerated instance of the normal author, and his works are only a special case of what always goes on in the relations between an artist and a society whose values have become chiefly secular without having quite lost the need or the memory of values divinely ordered. His case is representative of literature in America, whenever it has been ambitious, to a degree greater than we care to say; in their necessary addiction to external conventions, Hemingway and Dos Passos, for example, are no less representative than James. But, granting the addiction, we are here concerned with what the conventions were and what happened to them in James' imagination.

With the *haut monde* and the *beau monde,* somewhat of Italy and France, and particularly of England, together with their high Bohemias—to none of which did he actually belong—James had the expert familiarity of the observer. He knew the dinner table and drawing room, the country house and tea table, the library and smoking room, the city square and the estate park, the spas and hotels and promenades, and all the means and times and ceremonies for moving from one to another. They were the straps the people he knew swung on, and with which they held against the lurches which proved that their society was a going concern. Similarly, he knew how they got married, or jilted, or cheated; and he knew beautifully how they made cads and swindlers and lackeys of themselves almost as often as they made berths for themselves. To all this he turned first as to the form of a living society. Then he saw, rather, that this was but the mechanical arrangement of a society, that it was but the reflected tradition of values which the society might not otherwise possess and which indeed it often possessed only to soil and sully— though it could not destroy them. Those who ought to have embodied the truth of tradition in living conventions were in fact those who most demeaned it. He saw through the people, but what he saw was still the convention: the ultimate decency between human beings that could be created or ruined, equally, only by convention.

Thus James knew expertly what people's superficial obsessions were. If he did not know what their ordinary day-to-day preoccupations were, nor what, in consequence, they were likely to do, he did know the basic preoccupations of all people without regard to country or manners: he knew at what point of value men or women wanted, regardless, to live or die and what barriers they could put between themselves and affirmation. Hence he had, as a writer, to combine his two knowledges and jump the ignorance that lay between. Like a child, also a moralist, he had to use fables as the means of the jump.

Sometimes, of course, James tried to make his fables carry more than they could bear. We have touched on two examples in "The Figure in the Carpet" and "Maud-Evelyn." "The Great Good Place" is another, in which the heavenly world is seen as resembling an unusually comfortable club. But *What Maisie Knew* (1897) and *The Awkward Age* (1899) are better and fuller examples still, for in each a major use of social convention was attempted, and in each the failure was virtually, but not actually, saved by the bounty of the author's sensibility and the fertility of his technical invention. In the first the question is asked, what will happen to a little girl exposed to the breakdown of marriage in a succession of increasingly shabby divorces and liaisons? James was able to give so much through the innocence of his beautiful little girl's exposed consciousness that his story constantly both winces and cries out because the conventions through which Maisie is compelled to see her situation prevent the rest of the story, the whole story, the true story, from being told. In *The Awkward Age* the primary question is, what will happen to the publicly exposed relations of a set of people when the daughter of the house comes of social age and first takes part in those public relations? It is sometimes said that the relative failure of this book comes about because James restricted his presentation of his answer to a masterly use of scene and dialogue. But that argument would reduce Congreve to the stature of Wilde. The true cause of failure would seem to lie in the inability of all the characters in the book, including its presumably fresh and plastic young heroine, to bring into the conventions to which they restrict themselves the actual emotions and stresses that the conventions are meant to control, but of which they were never, in a living society, meant to be the equivalent.

In short, neither the domestic economy of social conventions nor the vocation of the artist was ever enough to bring out in James a mastery of substance equal to his mastery of form. What he seems to have needed was either an enlargement of the theme of the artist into terms of ordinary life, an enlargement of the social conventions into the International Theme, or a combination, in the press of one composition, of the artist and the international and the ordinary. At any rate, within these three fields lie his great successes, in which are to be included some fifteen or twenty tales as well as six or seven novels. The International Theme in its simplest form is the felt contrast of Europe and America. But it is a very different thing from the internal American contrast between New England and Virginia, and it resembles the contrast between the Old East and the New West only to the limited degree that, during James' lifetime, the Old East had digested and reversed its contrast with Europe. For the prime purpose of the contrast to James was that it furnished him with a reversible dualism which created as well as adjudicated values. It was not just a question of American girls marrying European men and of European women never, or seldom, marrying American men, though that question suggested many others having to do with the relative values of the maternal and the paternal in the conventional great world. Nor was it only the question of why American men went to Europe for culture, except in the secondary question of whether or not they could apply what they got in Europe to the American scene. It was these and much more. It was a dualism of right and wrong, of white and black, home or exile; and like any true dualism, before it becomes lost in an institution, its terms were reversible, without impairment of their reality. Reversed, right and wrong became fresh and stale, white and black became decent and corrupt, home or exile became integrity or destruction. With these reversals in mind, the questions at the heart of the International Theme can be put afresh. What happens to Americans in Europe? What does Europe do to them? bring out of them? give them, by threatening its loss, to struggle for? And, on the contrary, what happens to Europeans under impact of Americans? What new source do they find to make up for the loss which the exposure has laid bare? And so on.

In the beginning the American is conceived as having in him a dead or unborn place, and is, in moral perception if not in moral nature, gray or black; the European, in contrast, is conceived as alive with inherited life as well as his own and is all gold and pearls in moral perception, however black he may be in moral nature. Thus the gain of the European adventure ought, for the American, to be greater than the loss risked: James never quite rid himself of this speculative frame of mind and could supply, at the peak of his writing life, in the novel he cared most for, *The Ambassadors* (1903), an example in which one American gains every possible strength for his own moral nature through immersion in European moral perception. But he became increasingly forced to draw from his chosen examples the opposite conclusion, and in so doing he was only carrying one great step further the conclusion drawn in his best early work. In *The American* (1877) and in *The Portrait of a Lady* (1881) Newman and Isabel Archer are victimized by Europe; Europe is the disillusion for Newman, and for Isabel the evil and treachery, which overcame them; if they are left intact they are also left shrunk; their strength was in the strength to renounce. But in *The Wings of the Dove* (1902) and in *The Golden Bowl* (1904), the two American girls, Milly Theale and Maggie Verver, although victimized by Europe, triumph over it, and convert the Europeans who victimized them, by the positive strength of character and perceptive ability which their experience of treachery only brings out. Neither Milly's death nor Maggie's re-creation of her adulterous marriage is an act of renunciation or disillusion; they are deliberate acts of life fully realized and fully consented to, done because it is necessary to keep intact the conviction that life has values greater than any renunciation can give up or any treachery soil. By these means, in the figure of the American girl, candor, innocence, and loyalty become characteristic though not exclusive American virtues which redress the deep damage done by a blackened Europe. Thus James dramatized a reversal of the values in his International Theme so full as to make of the American's necessary journey to Europe a pilgrimage reversed. It was as if in his writing life he had made a series of withdrawals into a waste in which he assumed there must be an oasis, only to find himself strengthened, on each return, to meet the high values which had all along flourished at home.

It might be said that James had taken for his text the verse from the Sermon on the Mount, "For where your treasure is, there will your heart be also," and used it alternately, first just as it is and then with a reversal of the two nouns, so that a man might expect to find his treasure where and when he had discovered his heart. If we ask by what means he had come to be able to do this, an answer which is at least possible suggests itself: by merging the dynamic dualism of his International Theme with the static, if tragic, insight of the theme of the artist in stories of people extraordinary only for their unusual awareness of life and their unusual liberty to maintain their awareness. Putting it more strongly, if less certainly, James by combining his obsessive themes managed to equip his central insight into the indestructible life of man with a genuinely contingent body of morals and living tradition, regardless of the privation of his life, his education, and his times; and further, in so far as he was able to do this, he found released for use the inexhaustible wealth of felt life in quantities and qualities capable of receiving, and filling out durably, the stamp of form.

The stamp of form was itself a prodigy of accomplishment—and we shall come to it directly—but first it ought to be reemphasized how difficult it was for a writer like James to get hold of life in a way amenable to that stamp. Having no adequate tradition to fall back on for morals (values) or ethics (decision or judgment), James had to make the intelligence do for both, had to make it do as the equivalent of order and law in operation; and, not finding enough of intelligence in the world, he had to create it, and in creating it, had to put it in conflict with facts and stupidities it could not face without choice. For to James the height of intelligence was choice; intelligence was taste in action, and the utmost choice taste could make was the choice to live or die. It was by taste that James got hold of, valued, and judged the life to which his intelligence reacted. If this is so, it explains why his readers divide into such hostile camps of repulsion and attraction. Those who are repelled think the result, in the face of actual life, drivel; those who are attracted seem to find that taste and intelligence operate through his various themes and combinations of themes to drag into being a kind of ultimate human decency which expresses all the values a given soul can stand.

To those who recognize that decency in his work, James was full of the terrible basic ambition—but stripped of its ordinary ordeals—to create characters who meet the conditions of society so as to choose to live or choose to die. Thus his characters take on the heroism and the abnegation, as alternative and equivalent roles, of the artist and of the man or woman who ought to have been an artist in life itself. Isabel Archer in *The Portrait of a Lady,* Milly Theale in *The Wings of the Dove,* Maggie Verver in *The Golden Bowl,* and Lambert Strether in *The Ambassadors* are all clear examples of human decency operating through taste and intelligence to confront life heroically and with success. One is divided between thinking that the force of this decency is a transformation of the force of sex, and that it is a new kind of vocation in morals; in either case specially designed for the novelist to represent in the figures of ideally normal human beings; for such, in the four great novels named, he has created his three American girls and his one American man.

6

But the explanation of how James harmonized his substance and his art had better be put on a little lower plane. Just twice in his life was James able to lift his work to major stature, once at the age of thirty-eight in *The Portrait of a Lady* and once again for a five-year period beginning at the age of fifty-eight, when he produced beside the other three great novels just spoken of, two characteristic projections of the artist's faith, *The Sacred Fount* (1901) and *The American Scene* (1907). The first set up the conscience of the artist to act as the conscience of people who did not have enough for themselves; the second demonstrated the record of that conscience in action during his American visit—the first in over twenty years—of 1904. The period before the *Portrait* was no doubt the normal period of the growth and formation of his own character as a writer; the novels of that time could almost as well have been written by someone else, for they were carried forward by a combination of the existing institution of literature and the élan of first impressions. Then, suddenly, in his seventh novel, James added to the institution a momentum or élan which was his own; the character and fate of Isabel Archer were greater than both the social and the novelistic conventions through which she was exhibited. James had combined his themes for the first time, and for the first time told a story that demanded of him his full powers. Not until he again combined his themes, in *The Ambassadors* (1903), did he again reach full power. It is further notable that the best of the novels that came in between, *The Spoils of Poynton* (1897), is really only an elongated tale or *nouvelle,* like "The Turn of the Screw" or "The Altar of the Dead," and that it lacked the American or International Theme. Its story remains a melo-dramatic fable and never reaches the state of dramatized fairy tale in which the novels of full power are so strangely happy. Otherwise, aside from *The Awkward Age, What Maisie Knew,* and *The Tragic Muse,* which have already been discussed, there are two experiments in a genre of which James never became a master, *The Bostonians* and *The Princess Casamassima* (both dated 1886).

On their faces both Balzacian novels as modified by the general current of French naturalism, they were actually inhibited from becoming naturalistic by certain elements in James' own character as a writer, and so were partially transformed into something else. Each of these novels plunged him into centers of human conduct and motivation and obsession—into conditions of behavior—of which he was only superficially aware. In *The Bostonians* he made his center the infatuation of a grown woman for a young girl, with its havoc in each of them, and its final destruction by a violently conventional "rescue." In *The Princess Casamassima,* the center is the equally disastrous infatuation of the Princess for the little bookbinder's clerk, Hyacinth Robin-son, against a general background of conspiratorial, underground, bomb-throwing revolution, ending in the violence of Hyacinth's suicide in the shabbiest, blackest room in London. Being fascinated by such subjects, James tried to make what he could see stand for what he could not; and if his attempt had been on a lesser scale—on something not the scale of a naturalistic novel—he might well have succeeded.

What did happen to his attempt in these two books suggests a general conclusion about all his work: his repeated argument that the artist should be released from the burden of things as they were ordinarily understood to happen, probably came from his ignorance of ordinary things in general. It also suggests a rudimentary principle for the art of fiction; that if you want the surface to stand for the whole you must put in enough specifications to make sure it is the surface of the thing wanted and not merely the surface of the writer's mind. In shorter forms this certainty may be provided by inten-sity of form or perception, but the full-length novel requires extensiveness of form and perception, and extensiveness requires knowledge and specification all around. Then James' argument against naturalistic detail would be sound; economy of strong specification would persuade the reader to put in, out of his own stock of perception, all else that was required. Then, too, the further argument would have been sounder still, that most of what we know deeply comes to us without ever fitting the specifications we had prepared for it. If we deliberately free ourselves of all specifications except those that lay us open to experience, who knows what of the vast unspecified actual will not press in?

It is this last question that must have lurked under James' practice, and this inviting risk he must often have felt he was taking. In *The Bostonians* and *The Princess Casamassima* he made a misjudgment of what detail he could do without and of what he needed, as a carpenter says of his tools, to do with. It is not that he left out the details that clutter but that he omitted to put in those that would lay his readers, and in effect the novels themselves, open to respond to the pressure of the actual—the special shabby underground menacing actual that presses inchoate at the threshold of the stories without ever getting in; so that the novels have a strangely transformed air of protecting themselves from what they are really about.

In the four great novels this is not so. There the unspecified actual does press in as the general menace of folly, inadequacy, or sheer immanent evil. Whatever it is, it ruins loyalty, prevents love, sullies innocence. It is the morass in which some part of every human being is in a nameless mortal combat, and which is felt as the dumb part of despair, the horror at the nether end of boredom, or the futility no bigger than a man's hand in any perspective of effort looked at; it is the menace of life itself. To measure, to represent, to reenact the force of that menace is one extreme of the moral feat of art; as the other extreme is to reenact the equally nameless good that combats it. To reenact both in full measure required of James his combined sense of the reversible dualism of Europe and America, the heroism of the artist's vocation, and the two focused in an otherwise ordinary set of characters. In the shorter pieces, intensity of form and relatively limited perception are enough to give the sense of the menacing, altering force without need of any further articulation. It is its intensity that gives the sense of the jungle to "The Beast in the Jungle," of the corner to "The Jolly Corner," of the screw to "The Turn of the Screw," of the dead to "The Altar of the Dead," and of desolation to "The Bench of Desolation." Each of these tales, if you asked for articulation, would fall flat, but when inarticulated, each shows an indestructible habit of growth into at least the hallucination of actual experience.

The one occasion on which James at all successfully tried for full articulation by direct means was in that testamentary novel *The Sacred Fount*. There the nameless narrator records the passage of the force of life through half a dozen people, with himself as the medium whereby they become conscious of the exchange, and, gradually, conscious of the nature of the force exchanged. He is their conscience and their creator because he is their intelligence; he makes them see what they are. In the end they reject his intelligence, and the reader is left with the ambiguous sense either that the author is crazy and had merely invented his perceptions or that he was right but his creations had now taken over the life with which he had endowed them, with a quite human insistence on mutilating and battening on each other as they themselves chose. The halves of the ambiguity shade into each other interminably in that indestructible association of the moral life in which evil is ignorance but actual, and good is knowledge created real.

Such success as *The Sacred Fount* has is by tour de force; but it is the essential tour de force of James' sensibility; it is the represented hallucination of what, as artist and as man, he wanted to do for life; it is the poetic equivalent, the symbol and example, of what, on his own shaking ground, he wanted to stand for. If he could not say what it was, that is because it was so deeply himself that he could only show it in action, like a man in love or deadly fear. But read with good will and with a sense of the title kept turning in the mind, *The Sacred Fount* becomes the clue to the nature of the intent and to the quality of the achieved substance of the novels and tales, and then in turn becomes clear itself. If there is a secret in Henry James and if there is a way in which we can assent to that secret, both may be found in *The Sacred Fount*. It is the secret of why he was obsessed with the story of the story, the sense of the sense, the passion of the passion. He wanted, in all the areas of life he could reach, to be the story, the sense, the passion not just of the life itself but of the conscience he could create for it. So deep and hidden were the springs of conviction within him, and at the same time so sure the credit he gave to his actual perception, that he could not help believing what he created to be the conscience of truth as well as the reality of art. The being was one with the seeming.

## 7

In such a life work, making so little call on the ordinary means whereby we symbolize the struggle for our relations with God, society, and ourselves, it was necessary for James to make extraordinary demands upon the formal resources of the institution of literature. His essential subject matter compelled him to transform not only the English novel but also the French and Russian novel from something relatively loose and miraculous to something relatively tight and predictable. Neither *The Sacred Fount* nor *The Golden Bowl* could have been written within anything resembling the form of *Madame Bovary* or *Vanity Fair*. His own view of what magnificence his transformation amounted to may be found in the critical prefaces he wrote for the collected edition of his novels and tales. Perhaps the best sense of it is contained in the single phrase: "the coercive charm of form," and perhaps its best aspiration is found at the end of the preface to *The Ambassadors*: "The Novel remains still, under the right persuasion, the most independent, most elastic, most prodigious of literary forms." For, in James' argument, form coerced true freedom upon the novel; form freed the novel for independent prodigies which, without the force of that form, it could not undertake. For his own work, that is what his rules of form did. He developed out of the resources of the old novel, and by invention of new resources, what we now call the James novel.

Since other novelists have used and misused the James novel and since by contagion it has modified the actual practice of many novelists who never read James at all, we had better try to say what the James novel is. It is consistent to its established variety of skeleton forms; it is faithful to its established method of reporting; and it insists on its chosen center of attraction. To do these things it first of all gets rid of the omniscient author; the author is never allowed to intrude directly or in his own person; the story is always some created person's sense of it, or that of some group of persons, so that we see or feel the coercive restriction of someone's conscious experience of the story as the medium through which we ourselves feel it. Secondly, the James novel uses device after device, not merely to invite the reader's ordinary attention, but to command his extraordinary attention. For example, the dialogue in all the later work is as close in structure and in mutual relationships, and as magnetic upon the reader's mind, as an essay in mathematical logic. The scenes between persons are dramatized as substance, not as ornament; true action is in speech and gesture; and thus the dialogue creates a new form of attention, in which we always sail close-hauled or trembling on the tack. As the command to attend is obeyed, the reader learns a new game which, as it seems to partake of actual experience, he can take for truth; and which, as it shows a texture of sustained awareness never experienced in life, he knows to be art. To gain that effect, to make art truth, is the whole object of James' addiction to the forms of fiction; it was the only avenue to truth he could recognize.

Hence he was compelled to be tight, close, firm, restrictive, and extraordinarily conscious in the process of his art; and had to pretend to be so, like any believer, when he was not, because to an unexampled degree he was unconscious of all the other machineries of the mind and of many of the forces to which the mind reacts. He could not think otherwise, as he grew older and lonelier, than that only the most restrictive possible form could stamp his vision of life as recognizable truth and transform the fine conscience of his imagination into recognizable art. That he wrote both novels and tales only less than the very greatest, and that he added permanently to the scope and resources of his art in the process of doing so, was for him only the achieved act of his nature, the "obstinate finality," as he called it, of what he was—an artist. For us, the finality is equally obstinate, but it is also, as he thought the novel was, independent, elastic, prodigious; a version, not the vision, of life; a language, which, as we learn its beauty for his purposes, we can adapt and develop for our own—especially when we are in those moods he has himself created in us—those moods when taste is intelligence, intelligence is conscience, and the eloquence of conscience is heroic truth. Then he is the special case of our own point of view: he is one version of the story of our story, the sense of our sense, the passion of our passion—to be satisfied nowhere else.

James seems to inspire intoxication either of taste or disgust. But these opposite reactions come to the same thing. Born in 1843, designed by his father to be a perceptive luxury in a society whose chief claims to luxury lay along singularly imperceptive lines and whose institutions during his lifetime grew predominantly deterministic, he took to himself the further luxury of expression as a profession. So long as he expressed chiefly, or at any rate superficially, what was taken for granted, he had a fair share of popularity: he was taken as a smart if somewhat overrefined young man. As his expression came under control and exhibited deeper perceptions, he lost most of his small audience. As the quality of his work not only enriched but became characteristic and informed with passionate taste, his work was positively disliked and regarded as a luxury no one could afford.

This was about 1890. Exiled and alienated as well as dispatriated, he was stung to a new and powerful reaction by his failure with the well made play. He became again a novelist, and in this second life, beginning in 1896, more than any other writer, he was ever consciously himself; it was his self that had grown, and was more fully and formally a luxury of expression than ever, so that fewer and fewer could afford to read him. At the same time, he had become an institution, by no means ignored but not in much resort. There were always those who read him, some as a cult and as a means of escape, others because he added to the stature of their own perception. He visited America, after twenty years, not as a triumph but as a venture in discovery. Then he revised and collected his work, deepening his tone and making a cumulus of his weight, and began a new career, partly in the form of memoirs, partly in what promised to be a new form of fiction of which the only finished examples are the stories in *The Finer Grain* (1910) where he began to show a remote intimacy, through the poetry of his language, with the preoccupations of ordinary men and women. That same year—1910—his brother William, then in England, fell ill and he went with him to help him die in America. On his return to England, his own health weakened and he finished nothing but memoirs and short essays in the remaining five years of his life.

But he was more an institution than ever. On his seventieth birthday he was presented by three hundred friends with his portrait by Sargent. In July, 1915, he became a British subject; in the following New Year Honours, he was awarded the Order of Merit; and in February, 1916, he died, still a luxury of perception and expression. Gradually that luxury has become an institution of increasing resort for those who require to find upon what assumptions, in a society like ours, unconscious of any unity and uncertain even of direction, the basic human convictions can yet grow—whether for life or for the judgment of life in art.

# 64. THE DISCOVERY OF BOHEMIA

Out of the *beau monde* of Europe and the "good society" of New York and Boston and Newport, Henry James had fashioned his novels and tales on the International Theme. This had been his way of responding to the predicament of a society which did not yet know that it had to be redeemed. A further phase of the disenchantment of the late nineteenth century was a turning aside from the materialism of the modern industrial world, the conflict of science and religion, in the quest for a happier land of carefree life and impressionistic art of a mythical Bohemia.

A dominant movement in the literature of Western Europe, a minor but clearly distinguishable trend in the English Pre-Raphaelites and the contributors to the *Yellow Book*, this quest for Bohemia never achieved the form and focus of a literary mode in America. Writers here and there, in this respect or that, reflected one or another of its characteristics. A few like Saltus and Hearn succeeded in living its life of detachment without making notable contributions to literature; others like Garland or Henry Adams caught up its spirit for a moment, only to relapse into more sober methods of dealing with life and its problems. But our literary history would not be fully recounted without a sketch of its more striking manifestations, even though the method must be that of holding up a mirror to catch only the more obvious reflections. Sporadic as its direct influence was on our literature, it helped to reform our naïve criticism of the arts.

Notoriously vague are the boundaries of Bohemia. "Is it a state, not of soul, but of the purse?" asked Huneker. As a way of life it is evidently both; it involves both social and psychological consequences; it offers both the vicissitudes of a precarious career and the adventures of an enlivened sensibility. Its earlier devotee, in both respects, was Poe. But, though his work met affinities among the Pre-Raphaelites in England and even became the object of a cult among the Symbolists in France, he founded no aesthetic school among his countrymen. His campaigns against didacticism and his experiments with technique were continued in the United States, not in organized movements, but by isolated figures. Whitman may seem, when we view the fifties in retrospect, to have dominated the writers that forgathered at Pfaff's beer

cellar under Broadway; but the official record of those forgatherings is Bayard
Taylor's "Diversions of the Echo Club" (1872), a faint echo of mild diver
sions. A heartier atmosphere of literary conviviality was exhaled by San Fran
cisco during the sixties, but within another decade its Bohemians had become
lions: Mark Twain, Bret Harte, and Joaquin Miller had drifted eastward
Oscar Wilde, carrying the gospel of Ruskin and Morris to the American
lecture platform in 1882, merely created advance publicity for the Gilber
and Sullivan *Patience*. For Howells, under the spell of Cambridge Brahmin
ism, Bohemianism was "a sickly colony, transplanted from the mother asphal
of Paris, and never really striking root in the pavements of New York."

The *vie de Bohéme* was deeply rooted in the interstices of European
society, in the rift between artists and Philistines, between a radical intelli
gentsia and a predominant bourgeoisie. In America where expansion lef
further room for individualism, the tensions were less explicit and the protest
more superficial. When artistic flowering required intensive cultivation, how
ever, Americans still sought training and encouragement on the other side o
the Atlantic. What the Latin Quarter was to Parisians or Soho to Londoners
the whole of Europe was to them: a seacoast of Bohemia. Some of them, like
Whistler, were destined for fabulous exploits within that international
domain. Henry Harland, having tried unsuccessfully to catch the local color o
Manhattan in his earlier stories, later emerged as editor of the *Yellow Book*
and one of the arbiters of English aestheticism. Francis Vielé-Griffin and
Stuart Merrill were naturalized into the innermost circles of French poetry
and Merrill completed the cycle by translating a selection of Symbolist prose
into his native language. But the contributions of the expatriates—unless, like
Henry James, they were still preoccupied with American themes—belong to
the foreign cultures they embraced. We are more concerned with repatriates
with the new ideas and attitudes they brought home from the Old World
with the enrichment—or, at any rate, the sophistication—they brought to th
nineties, which transcended the range of more genteel criticism by looking
beyond England to the continent and beyond the art of literature to musi
and the plastic arts.

Thomas Beer has suggested that mauve, which Whistler defined as "pink
trying to be purple," is the shade that characterizes this decade. It is an ap
characterization of the popular blends that a domesticated Bohemianism pro
duced. With the success of *Trilby* (1892), the Franco-English Du Maurier
reinforced that picturesque and sentimental conception of the artist's life
which the German-French Murger had popularized a generation before. The
quizzical hedonism of Omar Khayyám, bound in crushed leather, made it
appearance on many a parlor table. The Boston Irishman, John Boyle
O'Reilly, tossed off a maudlin lyric, "In Bohemia" (1885), which was endlessly

reprinted and parodied. Richard Hovey, after some translation from Mallarmé, collaborated with the Canadian poet, Bliss Carman, in the breezy series of *Songs from Vagabondia* (1894-1901). A vagabond pose, congenially flouting the lesser conventions, was becoming respectable and even profitable. Elbert Hubbard, reversing the process of William Morris, converted art into industry; his personal literary organ, with conscious and unconscious irony, was called the *Philistine*. Up-and-coming cities now boasted of their Bohemian clubs; the oldest, established at San Francisco in 1872, has outlasted the rest; its businessmen, to be sure, have long outnumbered its more professionally Bohemian members. It was in this club that the poet George Sterling committed suicide in 1926. Though he was a disciple of Ambrose Bierce, he was in his own right the leader of Bohemia in California. Sterling lived into the age of imagism and naturalism, still faithful to the kind of poetry which conveys a "sense of the remote, the mysterious, the sadly beautiful." A year before he took his life he mourned the solemnity of the new era in which there was no more "make-believe, no more masks and garlands." Of all these symptoms the most significant was the eruption of "little magazines" throughout the country. Many of these were hardly more than manifestoes, but a few survived long enough to introduce lively talents and open exciting horizons—notably the San Francisco *Lark,* the Chicago *Chap-Book,* and the cosmopolitan *M'lle New York.*

To distinguish a clear-cut direction or a guiding coterie behind these fads and trends would be to oversimplify. Yet they point to the growth of a class of self-educated intellectuals, whose characteristic form of expression might be described as aesthetic journalism. As a cultural influence it differed from its European counterpart, by striving rather to educate than to shock the middle-class reader. As a means of education it was not addressed to a privileged few or concentrated upon the past, but eager to spread a wide awareness of contemporary developments in taste and thought. Despite this world of difference between the academic and the journalistic, the lines were occasionally crossed. Charles Warren Stoddard, whose South Sea vagabondage terminated in religious conversion, assumed the first professorship of English at the Catholic University of America. Harry Thurston Peck, sometime professor of Latin at Columbia, subsequently edited the *Bookman* and championed the moderns. Henry Adams, abandoning both a professorial and an editorial chair, could look down from the lonely eminence of his leisure; whereas the aesthetic journalists, enunciating views which often paralleled his, had to write for a living. Though their American market—to judge from George Gissing's account—was not quite so discouraging as Grub Street, they inevitably wasted a good deal of talent in boiling the pot. Free lances for better or worse, they accepted the conditions of their profession. Much of their writing was bound to prove ephemeral; some of it remains worthy of reconsideration.

2

The militant independence of the free lance is personified in Ambrose Bierce, the earliest American author after Poe to reflect the recognizable qualities of the movement. Resisting all other affiliations and categories, his restlessness finds its appropriate haven in Bohemia, which—according to his definition—was the "taproom of a wayside inn on the road from Bœotia to Philistia." A youthful veteran of the Civil War, a belated Argonaut to the west coast, he relived his affrays and disillusionments in the rough-and-tumble of the San Francisco press. Joining the American invasion of London during the seventies, he mingled with the cockney wits, published some grimly facetious books under the pseudonym of Dod Grile, and even broke a lance in defense of the exiled Empress Eugénie. Failing to capture the British public that lionized Clemens and Harte, he retreated to California where his later career linked the bygone frontier generation with younger writers like Jack London and George Sterling. His principal employer was the up-and-coming William Randolph Hearst, who was wise enough to give him free rein. His most effective journalistic coup was to prevent Collis P. Huntington from lobbying a railway-refunding bill through Congress. Bierce's separation from his wife, and the tragic deaths of their two sons, embittered his private life. After the turn of the century he made his home—in so far as he had one—in Washington, which afforded increasing scope to his misanthropy. At the age of seventy, after supervising the publication of his collected works and revisiting the battlefields of his youth, he disappeared across the Mexican border, leaving biography to trail off into legend.

No reader, thumbing through those twelve volumes of *Collected Works,* can avoid being struck by their monumental disproportion. As if in a last effort to compensate for the good books he might have written, Bierce padded the set with outdated editorials and stale hoaxes and forgotten polemics, disregarding his habitual distinction between journalism and literature. Frequently the degree of animus seems disproportionate to the issue, and usually the style is disproportionately superior to the subject. *Black Beetles in Amber* (1892) aims at the kind of elegant preservation that Pope accorded his enemies in *The Dunciad,* but Bierce's fluent verse seldom rises very high above its occasion. His prose, on the other hand, has a crisp precision which is almost unparalleled among his contemporaries; his puristic standards of usage, which he may have brought back from England, are set forth in his little handbook *Write It Right* (1909). America needed, but did not want, a Swift. It needed

ae sharp reservations of the satirist, armed like Bierce with the weapon of wit.
: wanted only the blunt affirmations of the humorist. "Nearly all Americans
re humorous; if any are born witty, heaven help them to emigrate!" ex-
aimed Bierce. Though many of his satirical sketches suggest that Gulliver
aight have discovered another Brobdingnag in California, one of his serious
ssays laments "The Passing of Satire." His points were too fine, his targets
ao ubiquitous. His phobias included millionaires, labor leaders, women, and
ogs. His values were ultimately the negative values of war.

Though *The Monk and the Hangman's Daughter* (1892) is still readable,
aough it skillfully handles the ironic situation of Anatole France's *Thaïs,* it is
aerely Bierce's revision of G. A. Danziger's translation of a German romance
y Richard Voss. And, though *The Devil's Dictionary* (1906) is still quotable,
 is no more than an alphabetical compendium of Bierce's deadliest witticisms
ad most philosophical epigrams. His securest achievement is concentrated in
vo volumes of short stories. "Denied existence by the chief publishing
ouses of the country," he informs us, *In the Midst of Life* was published
rivately in San Francisco under the original title of *Tales of Soldiers and
'ivilians* (1891). The second collection, *Can Such Things Be?* attained a New
ork publisher two years later. There is no padding here. Defining the novel
s "a short story padded," Bierce preferred the abbreviated form for its
otality of effect. His technique of directing suspense toward a dramatic crisis
 modeled on Poe, but Bierce's horrors are more realistically motivated: thus
remature burial, in "One of the Missing," becomes a war casualty. Sometimes
is settings encroach upon Bret Harte's territory, but Bierce's miners are far
om sentimental, and even his "Baby Tramp" comes to a macabre end. Most
f his denouements take place at graves. Editors, comprehensibly, were fright-
ned away from these tales. Their violent obsession with sudden death cuts
arough the conventional twists of fiction to a mordant sense of reality.
Dreams, flashbacks, hallucinations, as in "The Mocking Bird," provide irony
ut no escape.

Bierce's heroic theme, which Stephen Crane undertook a few years later,
*as not the Civil War in its strange grandeur, but its impact upon the
adividual consciousness. Every story is a single episode of conflict: son against
ather, lover against rival, a house—one's own—destroyed, a spy—one's
rother—shot. Underlying them all, evoked in vivid imagery, is the contrast
ormulated in "An Affair of Outposts" between the civilian's preconceptions
f military glory and the soldier's experience of ugliness and brutality. In
Chickamauga," an excruciating study in point of view, a child's idyl turns
ato a battle and the child turns out to be a deaf-mute. Further tales seek a
aoral equivalent for war in claim jumping and psychic experiment, ghoulish
ractical jokes and pseudoscientific fantasies. Naturalism did not exclude the

story teller's concern with the supernatural, and Bierce's rationalism operate
to lend credibility to his ghost stories. Peculiarly haunting is "The Death o
Halpin Frayser," with its interpolation of Bierce's own recurrent dream, it
Kafkaesque nightmare of the poet lost in the wood, its Freudian realization o
"the dominance of the sexual element in all the relations of life." But his mos
nostalgic reminiscences are reserved for Chickamauga and Shiloh and Kenne
saw Mountain. He himself is the lone survivor of "A Resumed Identity,"
Rip Van Winkle of the Civil War to whom everything afterward is an anti
climax. Even when he describes the Sierras, in "The Night-Doings at Dead
man's," it is with the eye of a former topographical officer in the Union Army

Snow pursued by the wind is not wholly unlike a retreating army. In the ope
field it ranges itself in ranks and battalions; where it can get a foothold it make
a stand; where it can take cover it does so. You may see whole platoons of sno
cowering behind a bit of broken wall. The devious old road, hewn out of th
mountain side, was full of it. Squadron upon squadron had struggled to escap
by this line, when suddenly pursuit had ceased. A more desolate and dreary spc
than Deadman's Gulch in a winter midnight it is impossible to imagine.

## 3

Lafcadio Hearn is not less completely the Bohemian for having remained
a foreigner, a transient contributor to American literature. On his devious pil
grimage from the Old World toward the Orient, he spent more than twent
years in this country, and nearly all of his work encountered its audience here
Born in 1850 on an Ionian island to a Greek mother and an Anglo-Irish father
he had been educated sporadically in Ireland, England, and France. Emigrat
ing in 1869, he was appalled by the grinding mechanisms of New York; h
sought out connections in Cincinnati, and there obtained his earliest news
paper assignments. He was estranged from his friends, however, when the
opposed his marriage to a mulatto. By 1877 he was glad to move on to th
Latinized environment of New Orleans, where his journalistic and literar
activities exfoliated. Always drawn toward the tropical and the primitive, h
served for the better part of two years as correspondent in Martinique and th
neighboring islands. Travel sketches in various periodicals and two or thre
miscellanies of exotic lore established his reputation, and he went to Japan i
1890 under the auspices of *Harper's Magazine*. When the customary misun
derstandings arose, he was forced to seek other employment: he taugh
English in government schools, wrote editorials for the Kobe *Chronicle,* an
lectured for a while in the Imperial University at Tokyo. Meanwhile he ha
fallen in love with the country, married a Japanese woman, and been adopte
into her Samurai family under the name of Yakumo Koizumi.

The striking paradox of Hearn's career is that so deracinated a personality should ultimately sink his roots into so conventionalized a civilization. In one of his innumerable essays on "Ghosts" he refers to himself as

the civilized nomad whose wanderings are not prompted by hope of gain, not determined by pleasure, but simply compelled by certain necessities of his being,— the man whose inner secret nature is totally at variance with the stable conditions of a society to which he belongs only by accident.

Was it his hyphenated origin, his diminutive stature, or his disfigured eye that compelled him toward the Tennysonian vision of a summer isle, a savage woman, and a dusky race? Certainly, as his letters reveal, he was ill at ease among the so-called improvements of the Occident, and out of sympathy with "the Whitmanesque ideal of democracy." Murger's Bohemianism counter-poised the ideal of art for art's sake, and Wilde's derided lecture tour—which Hearn defended in the New Orleans *Item*—was an "acute provocative to the consideration of estheticism in the United States." From first to last he professed himself a romanticist; his boyish solace from the commonplace realism of city life had been the public library; afterward, when he gathered together a small collection of his own, he boasted that every volume was quaint or curious. Valuable by-products of this wayward bookishness were his graceful translations from Gautier, Flaubert, and Anatole France. Loti's *Madame Chrysanthème* was his prospectus for Japan.

Knowing that I have nothing resembling genius, and that any ordinary talent must be supplemented with some sort of curious study in order to place it above the mediocre line, I am striving to woo the Muse of the Odd, and hope to succeed in thus attracting some little attention,

he had frankly resolved. Because he was never at home in America, he retained a traveler's perception of its strange corners and colorful survivals. As a reporter he specialized in the romance of reality; lurid murders and artist's models, madhouses and carnivals, voodoo rites and Creole cookery. His Louisiana friend, Père Rouquette, had lived among the Choctaws and written a *Nouvelle Atala*; the most charming memento of Hearn's sojourn in the West Indies was *Chita: A Memory of Last Island* (1889), which also embodies localized memories of *Paul et Virginie*. Local color, heightened by his imaginative strokes, blends into exoticism. The intense expressiveness of his own style is attributable to the quality he admired in Poe: "the color-power of words." American cities made him yearn for "a violet sky among green peaks and an eternally lilac and lukewarm sea." The Japanese tones of his later writing are more subdued. The suggestiveness of the word "ghostly" was for him an incantation; for him, as for many agnostics, fantasy replaced belief. Believing that ghosts represented ancestral experience, now banished by steam and electricity, he tried to recapture them in books like *Kwaidan* (1904).

"The dominant impression made by his personality," Huneker remarked of Hearn, ". . . is itself impressionistic." A posthumous title, *Diary of an Impressionist* (1911), subsumes his entire work, which—fragile and casual though it be—has extended since his death into a seemingly endless sequence of volumes. The books by which he is most likely to be remembered are the twelve that deal with his adopted country, from *Glimpses of Unfamiliar Japan* (1894) to *Japan: An Attempt at Interpretation* (1904). Their naïve charm has tended to fade in the light of more recent years. Hearn was anything but a shrewd observer of mores or politics, and his ignorance of the language disqualified him from interpreting the literature. His most memorable episodes are descriptions of shrines, gardens, fans, insects, and bric-a-brac. "A land where lotus is a common article of diet," where everything is marshaled in aesthetic order, where egotistical individualism is conspicuous by its absence— as *Kokoro* (1896) reminds us—does not lack attraction. But Japan was already becoming aggressively and mechanically Westernized; while Hearn, who continually warned his students against this unholy synthesis, was swept from his university post in a rising wave of hostility toward Westerners. Tired of lotus-eating, he might have gone back to America if ill health had not finally overtaken him. He never escaped from what he had never found himself. "Ironically," as Katherine Anne Porter points out, "he became the interpreter between two civilizations equally alien to him."

4

Since Hearn had departed from the United States at the very outset of the nineties, he could only help from a distance to set the scene. And Bierce, though he heard "the note of desperation" sounded in the final decade of the century, had been shaped by a more rugged period. It was left for Edgar Saltus to play the sophisticate, to dramatize the cut-glass brilliance of the *fin de siècle*. Where the others were intellectually sequestered, he belonged to society in the exclusive sense of the term. Scion of a New York family, brother of a minor poet, he responded more fully to literary and philosophical studies in France and Germany than to the Columbia Law School from which he was graduated in 1880. His fellow student, Stuart Merrill, was enabled to function in an artistic milieu by remaining abroad; by returning home, where art was hardly more than an ornamental plaything, Saltus cast himself in the part of a dilettante and a dandy. His sobriquet, "the pocket Apollo," implies a varied endowment, and his legend is seasoned by three marriages and two divorces. His career on various newspapers was less sensational than his career in them. He traveled widely, gravitating in later years to southern California. Toward 1900, under the pressure of hack writing, his work begins to repeat itself; his earlier books best preserve the leisurely skepticism and nonchalant preciosity of his once fashionable manner. By the time of his death in 1921 it was thoroughly outmoded.

When Saltus is recollected, he is sometimes regarded as an American disciple of Oscar Wilde, to whom he devoted a succinct memoir. Actually he parallels, rather than emulates, the English aesthete, who was his junior by a year. In *Love and Lore* (1890), a year before the preface to *The Picture of Dorian Gray,* Saltus defended fiction against the prudishness of Anthony Comstock by recognizing only two kinds: "stories which are well written and stories which are not." Two years before *Salomé* he had touched upon the same subject, which was common property since Flaubert's *Hérodias*. Saltus, like Wilde, derived his critical outlook from France, as he duly acknowledged in one of his poems:

> I chat in paradox with Baudelaire,
> And talk with Gautier of the obsolete.

His first book, an anecdotal monograph, shows that he was also on speaking terms with Balzac. From these and other French writers, including Mérimée and Barbey d'Aurevilly, he translated extensively. German metaphysics, in its realistic and pessimistic phase, was a further influence. *The Philosophy of Disenchantment* (1885), a pocket exposition of the doctrines of Schopenhauer and von Hartmann, jauntily concluded that life was an affliction. *The Anatomy of Negation* (1886) followed logically as well as chronologically; it proceeded down the ages with the iconoclasts, pausing here and there to admire a shattered idol; Jesus, to cite the crucial instance, was "the most entrancing of nihilists but no innovator." Long afterward, reenchanted by theosophy, Saltus strolled through the museum of the world's religions in *The Lords of the Ghostland* (1907).

But philosophic doubt and religious denial were the starting point for epicurean pastimes. The next stage was history, and the ideal theme was Rome, not in its grandeur so much as its decadence. *Imperial Purple* (1892), a scandalous chronicle of the Caesars, luxuriated in passages that matched its title. Saltus, considering it his most sumptuous triumph, subjected the Tsars to a similar treatment in *The Imperial Orgy* (1920). Among his potboilers loomed a three-volume survey of great lovers, and *Historia Amoris* (1906) gave full indulgence to his rather prurient sense of the past. Under the guise of historical documentation it was possible to discuss matters still too delicate for fictional handling, and Saltus was well versed in those authorities that book-

sellers classify as erotica and curiosa. An unexpurgated library of such works
"everything, in fact, from Aristophanes to Zola," is catalogued in *Mr. Incoul's
Misadventure* (1887). This piquant novel, the first of sixteen, observes an
amoral code whereby murder and adultery are far less heinous than cheating
at cards. A typical intermingling of pornography and hagiography, which
reads like a collaboration between Flaubert and General Lew Wallace, is
*Mary Magdalen* (1891). How it was received by Henry James, to whom it is
dedicated, tempts speculation. Other novels, set against modern backgrounds
are spun out increasingly thin. Their mounting reliance on artifice and sensation, on perfumes and poisons, on bejewelled luxury and operatic vice, point
directly to the detective story.

Not content, as a stylist, to contrive epigrammatic phrases, Saltus coined
experimental words: grammatical audacities like "longly" or "parallely,"
imported novelties like "fatidic" or "lascive," along with other pedantries and
Gallicisms. This brief specimen, from *Daughters of the Rich* (1909), is suggestive of the general effect:

An agony made of a thousand wounds, each distinct, each more lancinant than
the other, caught and enveloped him. The torture of it thrust into being memories
long ablated.

Diction like this can only be justified by an ironic tone. If some university
had been endowed with a chair of irony, Huneker declared, Saltus might have
found his niche. A latter-day Bohemian, Carl Van Vechten, has credited
him with giving New York a mythology: "harpies and vampires take tea at
Sherry's, succubi and incubi are observed buying opal rings at Tiffany's." But
these fantastic shapes could not linger in that worldly climate without partak-
ing of its corruptions. Saltus' preoccupation with the imperial theme was an
oblique commentary on the private scandals of contemporary empire-builders
he compared the Vanderbilts to Caligula, sketched Delmonico's as if it were
situated on the Via Sacra, and underlined the analogy between Newport and
Nero's Golden House. The "Gold Book" compiled by Bradstreet's, the
"Gilded Gang" frequenting the society columns, the alliterative collusion of
"Manners, Money, and Morals" were the stuff of his essays and tales. These
if taken seriously, illustrate Pater's refined epicureanism; otherwise, we can
take them as a comic supplement to Veblen's *Theory of the Leisure Class*.

5

In contradistinction to those that cut dashing figures or enact poignant
roles against the aesthetic backdrop, James Gibbons Huneker is less of an actor
than a spectator. Whether before a stage or a table, whether at a piano or

desk, we think of him as comfortably seated. Owing perhaps to the advantages of this position, he was able to work out the implications of Bohemianism, both as a critical approach and as an attitude toward life, more explicitly than any other American writer. It was more than the warmth of a disciple that led H. L. Mencken to designate him "the chief man in the movement of the nineties on this side of the ocean." More precisely, Huneker protracted this momentum into the twentieth century; for his first book, *Mezzotints in Modern Music,* did not appear until 1899. But his long apprenticeship went back to the days when, as a Philadelphia schoolboy, he had escorted Whitman to concerts; when, as a musical student in Paris, Villiers de L'Isle-Adam had bought him a drink; when, as a pupil of Joseffy, he had taught piano for ten years at the National Conservatory in New York. His career as a critic, starting on the *Musical Courier* in 1887, continued through the *Sun,* the *Times,* the *World,* and other New York papers, interrupted only by occasional travels in Europe. Most of his twenty volumes were pasted together from magazine articles and newspaper reviews. He disliked being called a journalist, and styled himself with genial modesty "a newspaper man in a hell of a hurry writing journalese."

His rambling autobiography, *Steeplejack* (1920), introduces Huneker as jack of seven arts and master of none. Undoubtedly his interests ranged beyond his accomplishments, and he approached other fields with varying degrees of amateurishness; but he had qualified as a professional musician, and his criticism stays closest to the object when confronting the keyboard of his instrument. His most substantial book, *Chopin, the Man and His Music* (1900), for once subordinates biographical details to technical comments; while *Old Fogy: His Musical Opinions and Grotesques* (1913) playfully exposes romantic enthusiasms to classical prejudices. The Symbolist doctrine that conferred upon music the primacy of the arts was reinforced by Pater's dictum that all arts aspire to the condition of music. Thus encouraged to venture afield, Huneker recalls, he wrote of painting in terms of tone, of literature as form and color, and of life as a promenade of flavors. "I muddled the Seven Arts in a grand old stew. I saw music, heard color, tasted architecture, smelt sculpture, and fingered perfumes." In this pleasant state of synesthesia, the concertgoer became a gallery visitor, working "in the key of impressionism." His hurried critiques became, if not adventures of a soul among masterpieces, then *Promenades of an Impressionist* (1910). Taste, to so practiced an epicure, was no mere figure of speech; gusto was his canon, and degustation his critical function. His impressions of cities, in *The New Cosmopolis* (1915), were documented with menus. He would savor a painter, sip a composer, recommend an author, and announce, in *Variations* (1921): "There is no disputing tastes—with the tasteless."

To his axiom that the critic was primarily a human being, the corollary, expressed in *Unicorns* (1917), was: "All human beings are critics." And, when the critical medium was a part of the daily news, timeliness was as important as human interest. Paul Elmer More, in asking where Huneker dug up "all those eccentrics and maniacs," indicated the cultural lag between journalistic and academic criticism. *Iconoclasts: A Book of Dramatists* (1905) and *Egoists: A Book of Supermen* (1909) were pioneering achievements which did much to direct the swirling currents of European modernism toward these shores. Huneker's pantheon was eclectic, if not eccentric; he exalted the individual above the type, the artist above the school; the dominating personalities were "Anarchs of Art" like Shaw and Nietzsche. If it seems incongruous that these image breakers should themselves receive hero worship, the incongruity is explained by a Nietzschean phrase which Huneker borrowed for one of his books, *The Pathos of Distance* (1913). Slyly he wondered whether the sordid circumstances of Gorki's *Night-Lodging* would be understood "in our own happy, sun-smitten land, where poverty and vice abound not, where the tramp is only a creation of the comic journals." But Europe had also a greater abundance of genius than his musical studies had trained him to expect from his compatriots. Poe, his father's acquaintance, was among his rare American admirations; but Poe, he thought, was no more American than English; and Poe, furthermore, would have been wiser if he had lived in Paris like Chopin.

The appropriate reward for Huneker's labors was that Rémy de Gourmont and Georg Brandes respected him as a colleague. Though he could not vie with the acumen of the one or the erudition of the other, he acted as a well informed and sympathetic American spokesman for the impressionism and the cosmopolitanism that they respectively exemplify. His style added a "personal note," an air of improvisation which now sustains the excitement of discovery and again diffuses into beery rhapsody and polygot exclamation. Names invite epithets, which bristle with additional names: Huysmans, for example, is "the Jules Verne of esthetics." Allusions are multiplied into virtual litanies: a single page on Flaubert contains references to nineteen other artists. Titles reflect the paraphernalia of symbolism: *Ivory Apes and Peacocks* (1915). Two volumes of short stories about art and its problems, *Melomaniacs* (1902) and *Visionaries* (1905), fall somewhere between Henry James and O. Henry. Huneker's novel, *Painted Veils,* written at the age of sixty, ushered in the twenties. "In it," he confided, "the suppressed 'complexes' come to the surface." Sex, heavily orchestrated in the manner of Richard Strauss, comes to the surface of the old Bohemian fable; the Seven Arts are symbolized by seven veils, which ambiguously drape the Seven Sins. The prima donna heroine is an up-to-date incarnation of the goddess Istar, and the critic-hero—an Irish-American steeplejack of the arts—resembles Huneker

It is Rémy de Gourmont who advises him to return to America, and it is Edgar Saltus who tells him he should have remained in Paris.

6

To return was no mistake; for the age of innocence abroad was expiring, and the time was ripe for sophistication at home. The Exhibition of 1893 made Chicago an international point of distribution for the latest artistic fashions. Concurrently, in many large cities, art museums and symphony orchestras were acquiring a public which needed guidance. Men like H. E. Krehbiel, Henry T. Finck, and W. J. Henderson did helpful work, but seldom strayed from the field of musical reviewing. The theater and the fine arts had exponents, but they lacked Huneker's breadth. His collaborator on *M'lle New York*, Vance Thompson, could report literary gossip and editorialize against philistinism; but Thompson's *French Portraits* (1900) owed its ideas, as well as its illustrations, to Gourmont's *Livre des Masques*. Percival Pollard would chat about central European literature in *Masks and Minstrels of the New Germany* (1911); earlier, with *Their Day in Court* (1909), he had driven home an invidious comparison. "The case of American letters," as Pollard had stated it, stood less in need of judicial inquiry than of medical diagnosis. The feminine bias, the commercial motive, the other symptoms were analyzed to show how quantity had superseded quality. Yet a neglected Boston critic, Walter Blackburn Harte, was Pollard's example and authority for the statement that the United States scarcely contained half a dozen writers who pursued literature as a serious profession. Bierce was his culminating instance of neglect, Huneker the exception that proved his rule: "A cosmopolitan, who happened to live in America. But who was not, primarily, interested in American art."

But if the trouble could be traced—as Pollard argued—to "our lack of proper criticism," the establishment of criteria depended upon a groundwork of importation and translation. The opinions Huneker imported, the books Hearn and Saltus translated, did much to eradicate the taint of provinciality that Henry James had detected in Poe. Though traditionalists had kept in touch with England, the current stimulus came largely from France. And, though the importers and translators were equally versatile as creative writers, their accomplishment was largely critical. Its results may be counted in educated audiences, rather than achieved masterpieces. Where literature had been traditionally connected with oratory and theology, it could now be envisaged through its relation to purely artistic disciplines; hence the old-fashioned didactic presuppositions gave way to aestheticism. Art for art's sake was never a very positive credo, but it aided in releasing the artist from ulterior con-

straints—particularly the taboos of sexual reticence. Sometimes, it may seem
to us, the prudery of the moralists was outmatched by the prurience of the
aesthetes; the struggle between them, at all events, would be prolonged and
embittered before the subject could be faced in frank simplicity. To turn from
subject matter to technique is to note the paradoxical devotion of a group of
journalists to the cult of style. Affectation and mannerism did not obscure
their genuine feeling for the cadence and the nuance. If they no longer
excite us, it is because their successors reaped the benefits of their imitation
and experiments.

What these isolated stylists had in common was the endeavor to reproduce
experience at the level of consciousness, to relay sensations in unimpeded
immediacy, which is connoted by the term impressionism. It is this method
which Stephen Crane applied to naturalistic fiction in *The Red Badge of
Courage* (1895), and which Lewis E. Gates reconciled with academic criticism
in his essay on "Impressionism and Appreciation" (1900). Since impressionists
are by nature individualists, they cannot be herded very closely together
within a concerted movement; their lasting achievements, such as Bierce's
tales, are likely to be the fruits of solitude. A negative program, however, may
be discerned in their consistent antagonism toward middle-class standards,
toward everything that the popular lady novelists stood for, toward the distin
guished—albeit inhibited—man of letters whom Bierce dubbed "Miss Nancy
Howells." That the two men, born within a few years and a few miles of each
other, should have ended so far apart emphasizes the divergence between the
genteel tradition and the Bohemian protest. The latter developed, with the
twentieth century, into a recognized opposition; it found a local habitation in
Greenwich Village, and vociferous organs in *The Smart Set, Reedy's Mirror*
and *The Masses*. The Philistines were reduced by Gelett Burgess to Bromides,
by Sinclair Lewis to Babbitts, and by Mencken to the *Booboisie*. The seacoast
of Bohemia became the comic opera kingdom of James Branch Cabell's
novels, and romantic bookishness was pushed to its illogical conclusion in his
*Beyond Life* (1919).

Whether we glance ahead to Cabell and Mencken, or backward to Poe
and Whitman, it is clear that Bohemianism has continuously oscillated
between the poles of escape and revolt; between an imaginative retreat from
and an iconoclastic attack upon, the restrictions of the commonplace. That our
means of cultural expression have gradually broadened to comprehend both
extremes is due, in large measure, to the work of the aesthetic journalists.
Edmund Wilson, paying his respects to Huneker and Mencken, has recently
asserted that the heyday of the literary free lance is past; that such potential
ities will hereafter be absorbed by staff-written periodicals, by educational
institutions, or by Hollywood. If true, this terminates an epoch which goes

back to the Civil War and reaches its height in the last years of the nineteenth century. The *fin de siècle* was confused by many contemporaries with the end of the world; Max Nordau's *Degeneration* (1895), which advanced pseudo-scientific reasons for disliking modern literature, was widely circulated and approvingly underscored in America. But Americans could not wreathe themselves in the laurels of decadence, as self-conscious Europeans were doing; for, regarding the new century as peculiarly theirs, they welcomed its innovations. They did not always realize that their own nineties harked back to the European sixties, to the ferment over impressionism, symbolism, naturalism, and nihilism. They chose instead to look forward to the American twenties, to a generation which would win the struggles they had initiated. In short, they were not victims of the romantic agony, but the couriers of critical realism.

# 65. HENRY ADAMS

Even an age of disillusionment must have, if not its prophet, at least its interpreter. Whitman and Emerson gave full expression to the regenerative hope of democratic man in a new world. Mark Twain recorded the first shock of discovery that human nature could not be so suddenly changed, and the confusion and despair of his latter years was reflected in all our serious writers as the nineteenth century came to a close. No one of them confronted the problem as a whole, however clearly an Emily Dickinson, a Henry James, a Stephen Crane, or a James G. Huneker might see a part of it. Henry Adams asked the central question of the age, and explored it with inexhaustible energy. Why had man once more failed? What new conditions made the hope for perfection again seem vain?

Just as the First World War was drawing to a close, a little old man died quietly in Washington, leaving a privately printed book which he had called *The Education of Henry Adams*. For it he wrote a preface which his friend and former student Henry Cabot Lodge obligingly signed, when the book was given to the public a few months later.

Here was the story of an eighty year search for the meaning of life in a modern world of machines, a story which professed to be a mere record of failure ending with a prophecy of universal dissolution. The tone was almost bantering, the mood dark. The public was slightly shocked, not immediately impressed, not at all amused.

In using the third person for his revelation, Adams had covered his inherent shyness but, whether deliberately or not, he had also created an impersonal voice. In the years that followed, a generation, younger but no less disillusioned than his, gradually discovered that voice to be its own. Like the age in which he lived, this man offered a new paradox at every turn. He spoke its contradictions and its dilemmas, its thoughts and its feelings; he arranged neat and balanced equations to expound its insoluble riddles; he set up contrary images that could nod to each other across the chaos. With its companion, *Mont-Saint-Michel and Chartres*, the *Education* became a testament of faith urgently needed rather than of faith achieved.

But was the strange power that these books came to exert tragic or merely norbid? Would they survive, would they grow in stature, as the particular problems with which they dealt became history, the dilemmas which they so clearly formulated resolved or forgotten? Had they, like *Paradise Lost,* the *Divine Comedy,* or *Faust,* bored to the subterranean rivers? At least once before this had happened in American literature when the flying turn of the harpooner's line caught Ahab about the throat and snatched him after Moby Dick into the sea. Had it happened again? If so, the little old man, sitting in his low chair alone among the exotic trophies in his big Washington home, would be the most surprised of them all.

## 2

As autobiography the *Education* is not altogether satisfactory. Like Walt Whitman, Adams sought to explore himself in order to discover the cosmos. He did not spare himself when he thought confession relevant to his theme, but when it suited his purposes to do so he completely suppressed important facts except by inference. Much must be read between the lines and between the chapters. Even with the aid of his many letters, subsequently published, the life story of Henry Adams is not easily told.

Like Whitman's also is the romantic pose assumed for dramatic intensification—here a pose of reticence and failure rather than one of vigor and success. Unlike the *Autobiography* of his brother Charles, this book is more than a memoir; it is a portrait thrown on a screen for analysis and study. Here, in effect Adams says, is a life—my life. What does it mean?

The reticence was real enough if not the failure. It was a trait common to all members of the Adams clan. Late in life, when rejecting the Buddhist retreat for the more active code of Brahma, he wrote:

But we, who cannot fly the world, must seek
To live two separate lives; one, in the world
Which we must ever seem to treat as real;
The other in ourselves, behind a veil
Not to be raised without disturbing both.*

This inwardness was Adams' chief source of strength as an imaginative writer, and it made the *Education* "a book deep enough and strong enough to be a bible to some natures"; but it also makes it, as a more recent critic has noted, "a grand-scale study of maladjustment, of the failure of an exceptional individual to mesh with a prodigious civilization." The biographical critic could find no nicer problem. Strength repressed must burst forth somewhere

* *Yale Review,* n.s. V, 88 (Oct., 1915).

and somehow. In the repression, the maladjustment, must lie the clue to the power of the resultant expression. As Adams himself apparently hoped, the failure of the individual must stand for the failure of man. In recounting the impact of events, facts, and people he reveals the growth of an imaginative mind, an artistic consciousness searching through a long life for an adequate form of expression, and not recognizing it himself when at last he had found it. The account of the search is itself the end of the long trail, the achievement of his destiny.

To be an Adams was by definition to make history rather than to record it. The hand of the fathers lay heavily upon the young boy growing up in the old Adams homestead at Quincy, studying at Harvard and in Germany, accompanying his father to London to help guide the policy of a distraught country through a civil war. Doubtless the progenitors of many a man have shaped his course as much, but the shadow of two Presidents and almost a third in their line made the children of Charles Francis Adams more than usually conscious of their blood. With the Adams and Brooks, admixtures of Boylston, Bass, Quincy, and even Alden had assured a firm planting in Massachusetts soil. The White House was a family homestead like that at Quincy, and the Presidency a family habit. The pattern for Henry Adams was already set when he was born, February 16, 1838, on Boston's Beacon Hill, the third son of Charles Francis, third son of John Quincy, eldest son of John Adams—of the eighth generation of the name in Massachusetts. The Adamses were born to rule.

With so imposing an inheritance, life in Quincy and Boston could be upright and rewarding, but not joyous. Sprung from farmers rather than divines, the Puritan strain nonetheless ran strong in the blood. The father, coming home from fishing on Mr. Greenleaf's wharf on a summer day, records in his diary: "Perhaps this consumption of time is scarcely justifiable; but why not take some of life for simple enjoyments, provided that they interfere with no known duty?" Such comment was the product of "the only perfectly balanced mind that ever existed in the name," as the boy later records. The mother was a silent partner in this somber household, making no deep impression on his memory. Like Ruskin's, such parents provided much to admire, but little to love. Natural affection, with the exception of family loyalty, was turned inward. There it dwelt for the time with the souls of grandparents, living and dead.

Adams liked to think that he was a variant from the family norm and attributed this divergence to scarlet fever which left him even shorter and lighter in frame than was usual in the family, reticent, and sensitive in nerves although sound in health and vigor. But the "habit of doubt" was common to his brothers, if not "love of line, form, quality." Charles, in his *Auto-*

*biography,* confirms most of Henry's early memories, but he recalls most accurately from these days the gloom of the Boston house; Henry, the sunlight on the yellow kitchen floor at Quincy, the taste of a baked apple when he turned from sickness to convalescence, the smell of rotting peaches and pears on his grandfather's closet shelf, selected carefully for seed. More than any other Adams, Henry developed acute senses.

His habit of miscellaneous reading for enjoyment was also formed in these years when he lay on his stomach on a pile of Congressional documents and read Dickens, Thackeray, and Scott. Later he laid the novels aside and helped in the proofreading of his great-grandfather's *Works* or did his Latin in an alcove in his father's library. Such experiences, rather than his schooling, educated him both as the formal writer of history and as the informal seeker for truth, beauty, and goodness which he was to become.

Perhaps most important discovery of all, the contrast of the seasons, the severe and sharp winters of Boston Common against the warm indolence of the Quincy summer, suggested the habit of balancing of idea against idea, impression against impression. In thought and emotion, this pattern was to provide Adams with his substitute for singleness of drive, for logic leading to the inescapable conclusion. In its balance, life remained for him open to the end.

This trait was at once responsible for his lifelong sense of failure and for the distinguishing quality of his achievement. He became more aware of it during his Harvard years, acutely so during his years in Europe. Unable to reconcile his natural inclination to literature with the family directive toward action, he developed many of the characteristics of the dilettante unable to plan his path. The choice of a career was difficult. Even at college he had known that he must write. The essays which he contributed to the *Harvard Magazine* were carefully clipped and bound. They show a feeling for form suggestive of the classroom; their models are Macaulay and Irving. As index to his reading, they tell much. The interest in novels persisted, but to them he added the "literary" historians: Carlyle, Gibbon, Niebuhr, Grote. There is no evidence of concern for politics or contemporary problems; this was to come later when he went to Germany to study law and language. Gradually a single objective seemed to form: law would provide a living and at the same time a core for his study and his writing. "But how of greater literary works?" he wrote his brother in 1859. "Could I write a history, do you think, or a novel, or anything that would be likely to make it worth while for me to try?" And he adds later: "If I write at all in my life out of the professional line, it will probably be when I have something to say, and when I feel that my subject has got me as well as I the subject."

His brother replied by urging journalism as a more immediate occupation, and when he returned in 1860 he went willingly with his father to Washington, then to London. Although he had thus early formulated exactly what he was to make of his life, the path was not clear. He could not bring himself to enlistment in the actual fighting as could Charles—besides, his father needed him—yet in the thick of events, even he responded as an Adams and put his pen in the service of family and country. "Our Washington Correspondent" of the Boston *Daily Advertiser* became "Our London Correspondent" of the Boston *Courier* and the New York *Times*. The letters are lively and well written, with flashes of description interspersed with sharply reasoned argument. Irony plays lightly over them. The boy was earnest, and his moods of gaiety and despair alternate with the course of events. Primarily he hoped to support his father's efforts to keep England out of the war by giving out accurate information for consumption at home. In this task, he showed energy, fearlessness and skill, but little diplomacy. He did not always succeed in doing "good by sustaining papa at home."

3

But the role of "Special Correspondent" was too limited and too shallow to satisfy him for long. He was soon back on his main track with an article in the *Atlantic* and others in the *North American Review*. He wrote to his brother in 1862:

> The more I see, the more I am convinced that a man whose mind is balanced like mine [the second of the name!] . . . cannot be steadily successful in action, which requires quietness and perseverance. . . . What we want is a *school*. We want a national set of young men like ourselves or better, to start new influences not only in politics, but in literature, in law, in society, and throughout the whole social organism of the country—a national school of our own generation.

In short, the Adams brothers and their friends henceforth would guide the country through the press rather than from the White House.

Chance and the audacity of a young college president, Charles W. Eliot, further opened the way for the writer in public life by offering respectively the editorship of the *North American Review* and an assistant professorship of history at Harvard. With hesitation as to his fitness and grave fear that he might be wasting his time, Adams accepted both in 1870. That these were steps along his chosen way was not as clear at the time as it appears from the vantage point of the finished career.

One of his students describes him at this time as "a small man, blue eyes, brown hair, pointed beard auburn verging to red, perfectly but inconspicuously dressed in brownish gray tweeds (as I remember), of easy and quiet movement and distinct but quiet speech." Another thought of him as "a man of pure intellect." Laughlin recalled that "his nature was positive, not negative. His smile had in it fellowship, welcome, and heartiness; but his laugh was infectious, preceded by a sibilant intake of the breath, with a gay twinkle of humor in his eyes and in the wrinkles at their corners."

To prepare for his courses, he read assiduously, but his scholarship in the Middle Ages was not yet profound. The syllabus of his course is a mere digest of facts. From medieval, he moved into general European history, and then into American; and his better students followed him. The climax of these seven years was his seminar at his home, 91 Marlboro Street, the product of which was *Essays in Anglo-Saxon Law,* four Ph.D. degrees for his students, and the real beginning of his original historical work.

The same independence of spirit marked his conduct of the *North American Review,* first alone, then with the help of Lodge. He wrote to David A. Wells upon accepting the post that he planned to make it "a regular organ of our opinions . . . which should serve as a declaration of principles for our party." This party was composed of the independents who were discontented with the conduct of both the regular parties and who were called together by Carl Schurz in 1875, shortly after Grant's reelection, when it became apparent that civil service reform was not in the offing. Here was Adams' "national school of our own generation."

The best of the essays from this period are closely reasoned and highly technical arguments in the economics of politics. Confronted by the anarchy of the Reconstruction period, with its rapid economic expansion, its wildcat finance, its government by deals and dickering, Adams made a valiant effort to apply to the situation the traditional family principles of conservative fiscal policy, stable currency, centralization of authority, civil service reform, and planned economic development. The task was hopeless, but he put acid and dynamite in his pen. Two of his essays, "Civil Service Reform" and his second essay on "The Session," were reprinted in pamphlet form from the *North American* as campaign documents even though, like his progenitors, he stood on principles rather than platforms and changed his party affiliations as leaders changed their policies. Other essays in the same and other journals studied the course of nineteenth century British finance by way of analogy and warning or exposed and attacked the breakdown of the American political and fiscal structures. Of them all, the most readable today is his account of the Erie Railroad grab, "The New York Gold Conspiracy," where ideas become actions and exposition becomes dramatic narrative.

During all of this discussion of contemporary problems, Adams was gradually forming his working philosophy of history. His reviews in the *North American* reflect his impatience with the narrative method of the English and

American schools, his growing admiration for the pioneer research of the German legal and institutional historians. History, he decided, should be both a science and an art. As science, it must examine the laws and institutions of the Middle Ages for in them rather than in the overworked theme of the "Discovery" are to be found the germs of modern American society. His medievalism was a fresh discovery rather than an inheritance from that of Keats or that of Longfellow. History must also be exact. "The Germans have these qualities beyond all other races," he wrote to Lodge. "Learn to appreciate and to use the German historical method, and your style can be elaborated at leisure." He would lead the younger historians away from the easy but unsound narrative method of a Bancroft.

From De Tocqueville and Michelet he learned the art of constructing his story about dominant ideas. Once, Thwing recalls, he boasted to his class that he never tried to remember dates; rather he remembered events, not in relation to time, but in relation to each other, as cause and effect. Laughlin reports that "his disposition to try out all possible points of view led him to say extravagant and fantastic things." This was a tendency which grew upon him and provided the framework for his more imaginative writing of later years.

Following his own precept, he moved from the study of Anglo-Saxon law to the documents of New England Federalism, a volume of evidence in the cases of Pickering, Otis, and others who had tried to separate Massachusetts from the Union in 1814–1815. From the Pickering manuscripts in the Massachusetts Historical Society, he was led to the papers of Albert Gallatin, Secretary of the Treasury under both Jefferson and Madison. Gallatin, though of Swiss origin and a Republican, had hewn close to the Adams line in his fiscal policy and had demonstrated that one could be a scholar as well as a man of affairs.

Here was man, theme, and exhaustive documentation for the kind of history which Adams had been preparing himself to write. The result, four heavy volumes, is the most thorough and Germanic work he ever did. He never again wrote with such sureness, such calm, such repression of personal bias. But only about one third of one volume is original work; the rest is a printing of the letters and essays of Gallatin.

As Adams himself might have put it, lines of force were bearing upon a single point—his *History of the United States of America During the Administrations of Thomas Jefferson and James Madison,* a task which required nine volumes and more than as many years. The work on Gallatin led directly to Washington and into the Jefferson and Madison papers, then in the State Department. From there, the trail took the historian to the archives of London and Paris where he spent the summer of 1879 attacking these new sources. Gradually the massive work took form. For the first time, Adams adopted a procedure which became habitual with him of printing his more important work privately in six copies only, interleaved for the corrections and comments of his friends.

To adapt the scientific method of the Germans to the problem of American democracy required first the definition of the problem, then the fixing of a segment of material to be examined.

The scientific interest in American history [writes Adams in his final volume] centered in national character, and in the workings of a society destined to become vast, in which individuals were important chiefly as types. . . . Should history ever become a science, it must expect to establish its laws, not from the complicated story of rival European nationalities, but from the economic evolution of a great democracy.

The point of focus alone remained to be chosen, not in terms of an individual like Gallatin, or even like John or John Quincy Adams, but rather as a segment of social and economic evolution. About such a trend, the art of history could construct a unified whole.

For this purpose, what period could be more suitable than that which lay between the Presidencies of the two Adamses when the new-formed democracy was undergoing its first major test? Here he could use all the material on which he had cut his eyeteeth as well as the vast store of manuscript which had recently come to hand. If one wished to understand the complex of the present, as well as the principles of relationship between the individual and society in the modern world, these sixteen years of Old World convulsion and New World expansion offered the best possible laboratory material.

Economic determinism had not yet been invented in the sense in which more recent historians have defined and applied the term, but the philosophical base of Adams' theory rests as firmly on its premises as does that of F. J. Turner. The central theme of his history is the incapacity of the individual to control his own destiny or to shape the course of events outside himself. The focus of the opening and closing chapters is upon the American character and the American environment. Individuals and events, whether in Congress, court, or battlefield, are given the fullest treatment in detail of fact and analysis. Leaders, silhouetted against this background, are followed with painstaking care through every step of their progress. But everything happens because it must. Jefferson, the dynamic and determined, left the country in near ruin; Madison, lacking in the gift of leadership, restored it by drifting with the current of events. The point of view is as naturalistic as is Dreiser's in *An American Tragedy,* and the two central figures of the story are as helpless in directing the world over which they preside as is Clyde Griffiths in controlling his minor destiny.

Intellectual exhaustion would be the natural result of so great an effort, and the other three historical works which followed were mere by-products. The *History* as a whole had been a study in the capacity of man to survive in spite of the stupidity and helplessness of individuals. The careers of the tempestuous John Randolph and the unprincipled Aaron Burr stood out as extreme cases of the whimsy of fate. Some perverse force within Adams urged him on to separate studies of these two men whom he thought despicable. The *Randolph* (1882) appeared during the course of writing of the *History*; the *Burr*, if ever completed, was never published and the manuscript is either lost, hidden, or destroyed. Basically unsympathetic, the former is nevertheless a vivid portrait and a unified miniature of the method used in the larger work; of the latter we have no real knowledge.

The final volumes of the *History* were yet to appear when Adams fled with his artist friend, John La Farge, to the South Seas in 1890. But he was not to escape so easily. Adopted into the family of Tati Salmon, a Tahitian chief of mixed Polynesian and English stock, his curiosity was aroused by the history of the island as recounted by its last Queen, Tati's sister Marau, and by her mother, "the Old Chiefess." Here was a third and an unexpected by-product of his investigations, for the competition of England, France, and Spain, which formed the backdrop for his drama of American struggle, had served the same function in this remote island. Here was the great theme of modern history in capsule form. The Queen herself became interested in the problem and long hours were spent in helping her mother to recall the family history. The written record Adams took home with him and fitted into the accounts of explorers and missionaries. From these sources he was able to reconstruct the story in outline from 1690 to 1846, when the memories of the Old Chiefess are edited from her own words. With this, Adams' work as an historian came to an end. His work as artist and philosopher had scarcely begun.

4

"The other in ourselves, behind a veil"—Adams was so eager to suppress the story of his inner life that he revealed its emotional power even more effectively than would an explicit statement. From the facts of his marriage and of his friendships, at least the outer form of that life can be distinguished, the inner significance conjectured.

The thirteen years of his married life and the seven years following the suicide of his wife are omitted from the *Education*. Adams claims that his education ceased in 1871 and that he began then to put it to practical uses. In 1892 his experiment was finished and his account with society settled. He was not impressed with the result.

But there were more personal reasons for this silence. Wordsworth omitted the French romance which determined the course of his emotional life from his account of the "growth of a poet's mind." Adams omitted the years when his emotional life was both most fulfilling and most dismaying from his account of his "education." The cases are closely paralleled: in both, the events struck too close for public discussion. They would throw emphasis upon the individual actor rather than upon the general principles of organic growth.

Such reasons for suppression, however sincere, are unsound, and the historical critic must supply the deficiency from letters and other available sources. Adams met Marian Hooper (of Boston) in London in 1866 and married her on June 27, 1872, shortly after he had begun teaching. During the preparation of the greater part of the History, she was with him in Washington where she made of their home on H Street a haven of Boston hospitality in a sea of national politics.

His facetious account of her to his friend Gaskell at the time of his engagement cannot be taken as evidence of coldness. He describes her as possessed of "a very active and quick mind . . . fond of society and amusement," accustomed to look after herself, and a Boston "blue" in spite of her protests to the contrary. Certainly the pair was well matched in family and personality, in common interests and tastes. He professes himself "absurdly in love," and her niece Mabel La Farge recalled from summer days at Beverly Farms "an impression of oneness of life and mind, of perfect companionship." Mrs. Adams' weekly letters to her father are filled with accounts of casual teas and formal dinners, of horseback rides and the adventures of the dog Boojum, of the repartee of men but not of women. There were no children. The strain of nursing her father through his last illness threw her into a nervous depression from which loving family care could not rescue her.

At her death by her own hand on December 6, 1885, Adams was plunged into a mood of despair which made him turn to friends, to books, to travel, and to introspection as sources of relief. Once before, when his sister died of tetanus in Rome in the summer of 1870, he had resorted to blasphemy rather than stoicism. The God who indulged in such cruelty could not be a person.

Flung suddenly in his face, with the harsh brutality of chance, the terror of the blow stayed by him thenceforth for life, until repetition made it more than the will could struggle with; more than he could call on himself to bear.

When tragedy next struck even closer home, it was greeted by stoicism.

These are the few given facts and one is left with the dangerous task of reading biography from fiction. Two novels, *Democracy* (1880) and *Esther* (1884), were the anonymous by-products of his married years. The work of an inspired amateur rather than a finished artist, they deal respectively with the two most pressing problems of the day, the corruption which resulted from the grasp of business upon government and the religious doubt which resulted from the attack of science upon established dogma. They thus help to fill the twenty years of silence in Adams' account of his life and give us at least some of the links of thought and feeling between his early and his late work. The one leads to the *Education,* the other to the *Chartres,* as he himself liked to call it.

In both, the central theme is the unwillingness of a woman of intelligence and feeling to seek fulfillment in marriage, the one with a senator who has sacrificed his moral integrity for political advantage, the other with a clergyman who has lost his right to faith by clinging to dogma and refusing to deal honestly with the questions which science proposed. In a political context, the trend toward disintegration in ideals and values had led to the corruption of the second Grant administration and called out the stinging satire of *Democracy.* In the context of the church, the same trend made it imperative that man reject traditional securities and accept as the working basis of a new quest for truth the provisional and morally discouraging terms of the new concept of nature. Both novels have many defects as art, but they stand comparison with the work of Eggleston, De Forest, and Frederic or even the early Howells or Henry James. In the handling of plot, incident, and character except for the principals, Adams is an inferior craftsman, but for psychological insight and for wit in expression he is superior to most of his contemporaries.

To draw a close analogy between these novels and the lives of Marian and Henry Adams, as some critics have done, is to oversimplify. Although *Esther* has many traits in common with Mrs. Adams, Madeleine of *Democracy* is more masculine, more nearly like Adams himself. The latter's motives for coming to Washington were his:

To see with her own eyes the action of primary forces; to touch with her own hand the massive machinery of society; to measure with her own mind the capacity of the motive power.

And there is nothing in the characters of Senator Ratcliffe or Stephen Hazard, physically, mentally, or emotionally, to suggest the self-effacing scholar that Adams had become. To push identification is to strain the evidence too far. If these novels are records of their author's emotional failure, they are evidence only of a failure of the ideal. Because the union was so great, it taught the inadequacy of all such meetings.

As studies in emotional failure they have nevertheless profound significance for their author. Adams has drawn on his own sensitive and suppressed inner life to depict the conflicts which these two women suffer, and he has applied his discoveries to human nature at large. Marian Hooper taught him to know himself, to admit that the riddle of life cannot be solved by the mind alone. In both novels, the theme is the conflict of the inner demands of the individual for unity and integrity with the requirements of a world which, in its materialism and its confusion, had substituted conformity for values. Whether the framework be politics or the church, modern man must accept doubt rather than faith in order to preserve his two remaining values, self-respect and the right to speculation. This is the final stage in the progress from an authoritarian to a pragmatic morality which might be followed down from Jonathan Edwards, through Channing, Emerson, and Whitman, to the passionate skepticism of Henry Adams. But the Puritan core is still there.

Whether viewed as a personal or an objective problem, the dilemma in which Adams found himself, when in 1892 he once more took up his "education" upon completion of the *History*, is not hard to define. "It belongs to the *me* of 1870," he wrote to Elizabeth Cameron from Tahiti; "a strangely different being from the *me* of 1890. . . . I care more for one chapter, or any dozen pages of *Esther* than for the whole history, including maps and indexes." *Esther* was suppressed even though the reason given was that he wished to experiment with the public—to see whether or not an unadvertised book would sell. He had written into it too much of himself, and he had not yet achieved the larger perspective which was necessary to an expression of his discoveries. The historian and commentator who could use his scholarship and skill to investigate and to influence the course of American democratic thought had died with his wife although he had still much unfinished business to complete; the poet who must use symbols to express the deeper meanings of the inner life had still much to learn.

His first experiment in symbolism was made by proxy in an art other than that of writing: the hooded figure which he commissioned Augustus Saint-Gaudens to place over the grave of his wife—and later of himself—in Rock Creek Cemetery, Washington. It is somewhat difficult to separate that which is Saint-Gaudens from that which is Adams in this profoundly mystical conception, as the specifications were purposely indefinite. Many of Saint-Gaudens' statues have a vague poetic quality; the figure of "Silence," for example, made for the Masonic Temple in New York, has the heavily draped anonymous head and figure of the Adams monument, but lacks its massive impassivity, its sexlessness, its timelessness, its power. The stark simplicity and the deeper meanings of the statue can safely be attributed to Adams.

From the moment of giving Saint-Gaudens the commission, Adams refused for five years to approve or disapprove the progress of the work. He spent the summer of 1886 with the artist La Farge in Japan. There he met the Americans, Ernest Fenollosa and his cousin Sturgis Bigelow, both of whom had renounced their native heritage for Oriental faith. No hint of Brahman or Buddist mysticism creeps through the skeptical and worldly tone of his letters, but the seed was planted. An early note in the artist's scrapbook reads: "Adams—Buddha—mental repose—calm reflection in contrast with the violence or force in nature." Photographs of Michelangelo's Sistine frescoes and other such objects were advised as inspiration, as were talks with La Farge, but no books. Hints were to be drawn from Chinese Buddhas; an early sketch shows the figure of Socrates.

Gradually the conception was transferred from the spirit of one man to that of the other. When this act had transpired, Adams left once more with La Farge for a year and a half in Honolulu, Tahiti, Sydney, and Singapore, and home via Paris and London, bearing with him the sorrow of the loss of both father and mother. When he returned to Washington in February, 1892, the statue was cast and in its place. He was being drawn to the East by the lure of the reopening Orient, as were Lafcadio Hearn and Sturgis Bigelow.

Meanwhile, Adams had journeyed to Anuradhapura in Ceylon to meditate under the sacred bo tree of Buddha on the mysteries of two thousand years and the ruined temple of a living faith:

> Life, Time, Space, Thought, the World, the Universe
> End where they first begin, in one sole Thought
> Of Purity in Silence.

From his now deeper knowledge of Asiatic religion, he was satisfied with the work he had inspired. "He supposed its meaning to be the one commonplace about it—the oldest idea known to human thought." Later he discovered that it was "a sealed mystery to the American mind." For him it was no more than a mirror to reflect what one brought to it, and the habit of returning to learn what it had to tell him became a ritual. That his contemplation, however abstract, was not impersonal is revealed in a letter to Gilder in 1896:

> The whole meaning and feeling of the figure is in its universality and anonymity. My own name for it is "the Peace of God." La Farge would call it "Kwannon" [the Japanese Goddess of Mercy], Petrarch would say: "Siccome eterna vita è veder Dio."

This is the opening line, "As to see God is eternal life," of the sonnet which, in his novel, had brought Hazard into his first rapport with Esther, and had made him feel "that to repeat to his Laura the next two verses of the sonnet had become the destiny of his life:

> So to see you, lady, is happiness
> In this short and frail life of mine—"

He was not alone on these pilgrimages to Rock Creek Cemetery, nor did he go merely to brood over a personal sorrow. His tragedy had become his secret index to the mystery of life and death. The burden of meaning which neither history nor fiction was strong enough to bear was beginning to find expression in symbol; but adequate symbols were yet to be discovered.

## 5

But first, the meaning itself must be explored, and the mind alone was insufficient instrument. Forced back into himself by the death of his wife, Adams turned once more to his friends and to his books.

The capacity for making and holding close friends was one of the most pronounced traits of this presumably cold and intellectual man. No idea, feeling, or experience was complete until it had been thrown back to him from the sounding board of another's consciousness. Because no thought or emotion ever settled into a fixed pattern for him, he awakened in others something of the questing spirit which was always his. Every important facet of his versatile personality is directly reflected in at least one other person. Such friends virtually lived in his home or he in theirs; they traveled with him to every corner of the earth; they suggested books which might satisfy his cravings and then had to submit to a complete experience with him in what such books offered. There were women as well as men in the group, artists as well as statesmen and historians. The only prerequisite was that they should share with him some part of the never-answered riddle of experience.

In his English friend Charles Milnes Gaskell, Adams found the connoisseur of life who, between 1863 and 1908, shared with him an ironic perspective on its strivings and its follies. His letters to Gaskell are his best, but he depended more for the closer intimacies of friendship on the American statesman John Hay and the geologist Clarence King. These two, with Mrs. Adams and Mrs. Hay, made up the "Five of Hearts" during the Washington years, the nucleus of a larger circle. Hay understood Adams thoroughly and confesses that he depended on him "to keep me in the straight path by showing me the crooked." It was he who commissioned Saint-Gaudens to make a caricature medallion with the wings of an angel and the body of a porcupine: "Henricus Adams Porcupinus Angelicus." Doubtless the mutual friendship with the leading geologist of his day, Clarence King, was the bond which held them most firmly, but in many respects, Hay accomplished where Adams failed: he met the nineteenth century world and put it to his own uses. His private life was a model of domestic happiness; his public, a triumph of international policy. The *Education* ends with his death, leaving the last of the trio in the "depths of Hamlet's Shakespearean silence."

For King had gone before, in some ways the closest of all Adams' friends. Adams wrote:

His only ultimate truth was the action, not the thought. To him all science and all life were in that law, which, after all, is the only result of his generation—the law of Energy. Those of us who gladly and carelessly gave ourselves up to his influence and let him swing us as he liked—those he loved.

It was largely under King's influence that Adams embarked upon his most profound exploration of human experience. While in London in the sixties, he had talked with Sir Charles Lyell and the door of scientific speculation had been opened to him. Later he reviewed the *Principles of Geology* in the *North American*. When, with this common interest already deeply rooted, he met King in Estes Park and, sharing room and bed, "talked till far towards dawn," it was "never a matter of growth or doubt." The friendship was sealed. King's pioneer work in geology was a mere starting point for a philosophy of energetic skepticism. Once more, in another's success, Adams had recognized his own failure. His mind and feeling went with his friend into the High Sierras and into the depths of emotional abandon with the defiance of personal danger, which his body could not summon. King expressed in action what Adams could experience only vicariously. But King did not stop to reason, to analyze, to explain. Adams was the historian of the adventure in books which contain scant if any reference to King by name. It was not Langley, but the spirit of inquiry awakened by King which sent him exploring the speculations of Stallo, of Karl Pearson, of William James, even though Willard Gibbs and Raphael Pumpelly helped. It was King who stood behind his shoulder when he wrote *A Letter to American Teachers of History* and who first prompted the final pages of the *Education*.

As King led Adams into the profundities of scientific speculation, so John La Farge, without benefit of passion, led him into the world of color and form and idealization which is art. Twice the historian sought the artist when the only answer to his sorrows and perplexities seemed to lie in travel. Both times they turned to the East, first to Japan, then to the South Seas and India

The diary letters which he wrote to Elizabeth Cameron from these trips merely skim the surfaces of color and form of the sea and the islands; the naïveté and spirit of the native girls dancing their native dances; the hospitality of the queens and princes of a dying race of primitives. But such experiences led Adams out from his sorrow and spread a surface gaiety over his numbness. Under La Farge's tutelage he tried painting, but only learned to see color, not to reproduce it. Through borrowed artist eyes he awoke to the beauties of the physical world at their most brilliant, the gaiety and warmth of primitive people who knew how to live in the sun even when their European oppressors were closing in upon them. Vague stirrings of response to Asiatic religions sent Adams to books on Buddha, as earlier he had read Dante in a garden at Nikko, the sacred heart of Japan, while La Farge painted the fountain below his veranda. Here were the first tentative explorations of those depths which he had sighted in *Esther* and which he was to fathom with the aid of the Virgin of Chartres. But La Farge could not accompany him on these later journeys.

With La Farge, the story of Adams' formative friendships loses its sharper outlines except for his brothers Charles and Brooks. The first early helped him shape his career, the second debated with him during the summer of 1893 the collapse of the Exchange and the theory of history which made all civilization ultimately follow the exchanges into disintegration. Like Henry in many ways, Brooks was even more a solitary, even more a concocter of historical if not cosmic theories. "The two brothers could talk to each other without atmosphere" and together they worked out the theory of history which in the one became a law of decay, in the other a dynamic entropy.

But the deeper levels of experience were still to be explored. Perhaps Adams went on these journeys alone, perhaps his reticence kept him from acknowledging his companions. "Adams owed more to the American woman," he once wrote, "than to all the American men he ever heard of," and, especially in his later years, he formed the habit of turning to women for guidance. The book upon which he expended most of himself, the *Chartres,* was written for his "nieces." In these later years Elizabeth Cameron, niece of Senator Sherman, as well as Mrs. Lodge and visiting nieces, helped with the hospitality at 1603 H Street. To Mrs. Cameron he wrote the record of his travels for the broken circle of friends in Washington; with her and her husband he traveled to London and on the continent.

The other "nieces" were actual nieces of Mrs. Adams. One of them, Mabel Hooper, later Mrs. Bancel La Farge, has spoken for them all and has given his letters to print.

To them all [she writes], he was the *generic Uncle,* the best friend—to whom they not only could confide their innermost secrets, their perplexities, hopes and aspirations, but also at whose feet they could sit endlessly, listening to the most thrilling talk they had ever heard, or were likely to hear again.

It was to them and to such foster nephews, or "nieces in wishes," as Cecil Spring-Rice that the childless and lonely old man opened his home and his heart; and it was under the tutelage and care of Aileen Tone, an adopted "niece" and a Catholic, that he discovered, after his paralytic stroke in 1912, his last great enthusiasm, the music of the old French songs of which he had known the words for so long. Mabel La Farge and Mrs. Winthrop Chanler, who knew him well in these days, have expressed the belief that he was himself virtually a member of the church in faith, but most other Catholics do not agree with them. The Virgin of his *Chartres* was at heart a pagan.

6

On the assumption that Adams was primarily, if not wholly, a man of intellect, the majority of his critics have attempted to evaluate his final accomplishment as a logical statement of the philosophy of mechanism applied to history. With comparative ease they have pointed out fallacies in his premises, faults in his logic, and exaggeration in his conclusions and predictions. Some have argued convincingly that Brooks Adams, in his *The Law of Civilization and Decay* (1895), has made out a better case for the application of the thought of Newton, Comte, Darwin, and Marx to the history of Western civilization than did Henry. The result has been a tendency to discount the achievement of the latter almost as effectively as he did himself.

Throughout his life Adams thought of himself as a man of letters rather than primarily as a historian, scientist, or philosopher. He never lost his eager interest in the central and tragic conflict of man and nature; but he was thwarted, as all American writers have been until very recently, by the absence of a matured and autogenous literary culture. He instinctively knew, as Cooper and Melville and Mark Twain had each discovered in his own way, that American literature must be a reinterpretation of the eternal issues in human experience in terms of life in contemporary America. Politics, economic history, science, philosophy, and art itself were means and materials only. To the man of letters, no truth is new, its expression never done.

The discovery of an authentic and adequate medium of expression was his life's quest, and the recognition that form cannot be imposed, that it must result from understanding, made "education" for him the primary good. His confession of failure is merely, in its larger implications, his version of the failure which underlies tragedy from Æschylus to Eugene O'Neill.

For Adams was primarily a man of feeling, and his ultimate strength lay in his long delayed but overwhelming discovery of that fact. Before he could justify his choice of a career of writing in his own eyes or in ours, he had to rid himself of two assumptions that inhibited his development: that thought without action is void, and that thought without emotion is valid. He had to learn that living thought may be in itself a kind of action and that thought cannot live when divorced from emotion. His career as publicist and historian proved to him that writing could be a form of action; his personal tragedy and the release of his emotional life into friendships taught that no scientific truth could be final without imagination, no writing could be intrinsic action if it relied upon reason alone.

His transition from the man of thought to the man of feeling was, however, so gradual that the stages in the progress can readily be lost and the issue confused. In its last and crucial phase it centers on the application of the findings of science to history. But before science could produce original art, it had to become an instrument of the imagination rather than merely a method for the discovery and analysis of facts; history a record of man's whole development rather than merely a narrative of his past adventures and vicissitudes.

In the decade between the publication of the first volume of the *History* and his address to the American Historical Association in 1894, his view of the possible relationship between science and history had progressed far beyond the mere use of the inductive method and the assignment of historical evidence to man-made law. "The situation," he told his fellow historians, "seems to call for no opinion, unless we have some scientific theory to offer." From this day forward his energies were devoted to the search for that formula rather than to the writing of history itself according to established premises and rules. Although he does not seem fully to have appreciated the fact, such a quest was as romantic as those of Ahab for Moby Dick or Parsifal for the Holy Grail. As in those cases, it became a search for the symbol of the life force, an effort to wrest the meaning of man from a reluctant nature by sheer violence. The discovery of a new and scientific basis for history would mean the creation of a new religion.

The task of Adams' generation was not the completion of that creation. Rather they were to break down old structures by techniques which science had given them, to define issues, to set up working hypotheses for the new synthesis. Adams took as his particular task the discovery of an organic aesthetic form which could give expression to the significance of his age as he saw it. He proceeded direct from the experience to the expression because he had rejected all models. The result was the single gigantic but incompleted act of the imagination which resulted in the *Chartres* and the *Education*.

The final chapters of the *Education* state briefly the "dynamic" theory of history which Adams had adopted as his tentative instrument, a theory which is more fully expounded in *A Letter to American Teachers of History* (1910), his last important book, which his brother Brooks edited posthumously, adding the unpublished essay on "The Rule of Phase" and giving the whole his own unfair but provocative title, *The Degradation of the Democratic Dogma*.

The choice of the second law of thermodynamics, the law of dissipation of energy, as the needed formula was dictated by the stage to which physical science had developed by 1910. If the attempt were made today, Adams might equally well have adopted the law of relativity and developed a science of history in quite other terms. To him the important factor was the relation of the two components, science and history, to each other, not the final truth of the findings of either one. In the later and even more daring essay on the law of phase, he allows his imagination such range as to venture by computation to fix a date for the moment of dissolution. Impatience with the rapid progress of science and the stodgy conservatism of historians provoked heroic measures.

Adams' version of the more fully developed theory of entropy which he adopted for his two major literary works may, for convenience, be stated as two related hypotheses:

(1) Accepting force as ultimate fact, two kinds of force are recognizable in experience: an inner force which makes for unity and which man has traditionally known as religion or God, and an outer force which makes for multiplicity and which has come to be known as science or nature. Absolutely considered, both these forces may be traced to a common center in a mechanistic view of the universe, as in the past both were traced to a theistic center, but in human experience they have always been and probably always will be differentiated and in opposition to each other. This is no more than a restatement in modern terms of the classic theory of metaphysical dualism.

(2) Historically considered, experience shows that man reached the peak of his development in the era of medieval Christianity because he then succeeded through the instrument of the church in attaining the highest degree of unity; but the discovery of the inductive method of reasoning and its application to physical science in modern times introduced a new "phase" of evolution in which nature supplants man as dynamic center of the universe. Unity was then mortally challenged and the universe began to move toward disintegration by a law of accelerated entropy which should by now be reaching its culmination and which should be followed by complete dissolution or by new and unpredictable forms of life. Thus the historical framework is provided for the application of the theory of dualism.

These two hypotheses are complementary when treated in purely intellectual terms, but they present a fundamental inconsistency when viewed in the light of emotion. Adams thus also creates, perhaps unwittingly, a dichotomy between intellect and emotion which supplies the pattern for his art form, but which destroys the validity of his theory as an instrument for the logical explanation of the universe. Art alone could resolve this inconsistency because art records and evaluates rather than accounts for the evidences of experience.

Adams' creation of an arbitrary cosmology for his purposes suggests Milton's similar acceptance of the Ptolemaic system at a time when his own reason might have dictated the Copernican. Adams' acceptance of a modified Newtonian mechanism is a necessary premise to his artistic construction, and its degree of logical soundness has no bearing on its aesthetic validity. It was many years before Miltonic criticism could free itself from this difficulty and accept *Paradise Lost* as a great epic poem in spite of the fallacious cosmology upon which it is based. The criticism of Henry Adams has not yet reached that stage.

Only in the aesthetic expression of his position did he reach any degree of finality. To him the two major works of this period, the *Chartres* and the *Education*, formed a unified, albeit an imperfect, whole. The importance of their interrelationship is stressed by his quoting in his preface the key passage from Chapter XXIX of the *Education* when he finally decided that his time was up and he could bring his work no nearer to completion:

Any schoolboy could see that man as a force must be measured by motion, from a fixed point. Psychology helped here by suggesting a unit—the point of history when man held the highest idea of himself as a unit in a unified universe. Eight or ten years of study had led Adams to think he might use the century 1150–1250 expressed in Amiens Cathedral and the Works of Thomas Aquinas, as the unit from which he might measure motion down to his own time, without assuming anything as true or untrue, except relation. The movement might be studied at once in philosophy and mechanics. Setting himself to the task, he began a volume which he mentally knew as "Mont-Saint-Michel and Chartres: A Study in Thirteenth-Century Unity." From that point he proposed to fix a position for himself, which he could label: "The Education of Henry Adams: A Study in Twentieth-Century Multiplicity." With the help of these two points of relation, he hoped to project his lines forward and backward indefinitely, subject to correction from anyone who should know better.

The student who reads this passage ten times should need no further elucidation of these two books. He will not make the mistake that many critics have committed of assuming a finality in Adams' logical position; he will know that the two books in concept are one, a planned work of the imagination rather than an historical, autobiographical, or scientific record or argument; he will evaluate their timeless quality rather than their circumstantial reference.

As art, these books should therefore be approached only as companion studies in unity and multiplicity. As contributions to the philosophy of history, they may be accepted or discredited at will without invalidating this approach. Man's inner need for discovering a system of unity in his experience and his constant difficulty in reconciling this need to the multiple influences of the world outside of himself is the most persistent theme of all literature. It is the problem of Oedipus, Hamlet, and Faust, of Tom Jones, Ahab, and Ma Joad. Emerson discussed it for his age; Henry Adams did the same for an age when the conflict was infinitely more acute and the solution less apparently obvious.

We have seen at least some evidence that Adams at one time hoped to find his center of unity in Oriental art and religion and his symbol of that unity probably in Buddha. His poem "Buddha and Brahma," not published until 1915 but written earlier, reveals the failure of Buddhist quietism to make unity dynamic, of Brahmanism to achieve unity beyond action. When he turned from travels in the East to travels in France, he discovered in the arches and spires of Mont-Saint-Michel, Amiens, Coutances, Paris, and Chartres the symbol of unity which he sought, and communicated it in his only other known poem, "Prayer to the Virgin of Chartres." Not much more than adequate in technical skill, these two poems have an intensity of blended feeling and thought which gives them the dignity of art.

In exploring the nature of unity, Adams was led back to his study of medieval history, and he added to it a wide reading in chivalric poetry, works on medieval architecture, and the writings of Christian philosophers from Abélard to Thomas Aquinas. Again he was the inspired amateur rather than the documentary scholar or the conventional man of letters. He read books only when they "helped." Slowly he formed his pattern about the symbol of the Virgin—not Mary as person or as divinity, but the Lady of Chartres as creation of the medieval imagination. The selection of the century 1150–1250 was dictated by the facts because then the conception of the Virgin had become, for one moment in history, an effective symbol of man's eternal desire for inner and outer harmony, expressed both in art and philosophy. Just how this image evolved and what significance it might have not only for medieval but for universal man became one half of his life's concern. The result has served as a study of the medieval mind; it is only now coming to be recognized for its insight into the universal mind.

The structure of the book is apparent only when this central purpose is kept in mind. Adams' facetious statement that it is merely a tour de force for the entertainment of his nieces and "nieces in wishes" is obvious screening of its profound value to him. His light bantering tone persists throughout, but the careful unfolding of his plan is not hampered by it.

The book falls into three somewhat unequal parts: the preparation of the medieval mind for its gigantic effort of synthesis just before its collapse; its achievement of emotional unity in the first half of the thirteenth century as represented in the Cathedral of Chartres; and the translation of this process into the rational terms of medieval philosophy. For the first the Archangel Michael serves as personal focus, for the second the Virgin, for the third St. Thomas. Above them all, the Virgin becomes the symbol of unity achieved. The transition from worship of a masculine to that of a feminine deity is hinted at in the *Roman de la Rose* and acknowledged in the religious chivalry of Thibaut. Poetry, history, and architecture combine, with all their intricate details, in an aesthetic synthesis which makes manifest the sovereignty of the Virgin. Abélard, Bernard de Clairvaux, St. Francis, and St. Thomas add each his philosophy to emphasize the result and to translate it back from emotion to scholastic logic, from the supreme feminine intuition to the masculine approximation of truth through reason. For once, man's inner need for harmony seemed, at least in the perspective of later centuries, to have been partially supplied.

The truth which Adams here tacitly recognizes is that unity may be achieved through emotion even when denied by reason. His Virgin is completely irrational, her power nonetheless centripetal. Mary filled her church without being disturbed by quarrels because she "concentrated in herself the whole rebellion of man against fate. . . . She was above law; she took feminine pleasure in turning hell into an ornament; she delighted in trampling on every social distinction in this world and the next." Yet she answered the prayers of her suppliants because she judged by love alone. She could put in terms of positive symbolism what the hooded figure in Rock Creek could only permit by reflection. This is what Adams had learned from the American woman, but he had to trace it back to twelfth century France to find it unembarrassed and whole. Intuition is above reason; love may triumph over logic; art can speak deeper truths than science.

With the same detachment Adams then turned immediately to the other half of his problem: the study of multiplicity. Here the age of obvious choice was the present, the person of obvious focus himself. Even at the risk of being accused of merely writing his autobiography, he undertook *The Education of Henry Adams: A Study in Twentieth-Century Multiplicity*. The detachment of the third-person pronoun is not an affectation; it is an integral part of his scheme. He might have written of someone else had he known any other experience as well as his own. As the forces which he wished to examine are universal, as well as peculiar to the age, he would do as well as another for their point of impact. For the impersonality of the Ego, he turns again to Oriental thought. In a biographical testament of friendship to George Cabot Lodge, published in 1911, he states that the poet seeks unity in "some one great tragic motive." Lodge's

was that of Schopenhauer, of Buddhism, of Oriental thought everywhere,—the idea of Will, making the universe, but existing only as subject. The Will is God; it is nature; it is all that is; but it is knowable only as ourself. Thus the sole tragic action of humanity is the Ego,—the Me,—always maddened by the necessity of self-sacrifice. . . . In order to raise the universe in oneself to its highest power, its negative powers must be paralyzed or destroyed. In reality, nothing was destroyed; only the Will—or what we now call Energy—was freed and perfected.

Thus perhaps from the analysis of his own experience, Adams might witness the action of this tragic movement in the modern world and in harmony with the new concept of Energy which science had supplied. This he attempts in the *Education*.

This book also falls roughly into three parts: the inadequate and misleading preparation of a generation which reached maturity at the moment in history when the challenge of modern science became generally felt; the effort of one individual to adjust to this new and centrifugal world of multiplicity; and the translation of the result into a rational formula. The problem was more baffling because the perspective of time was lacking. On the other hand, the material was more familiar. Nor was a central symbol as easy to find. Frank Norris, at the same time on the same quest, adopted the railroad as symbol in *The Octopus*. Adams, in the high excitement of discovery, chose the dynamo which he saw first at the Chicago Exposition in 1893, later in Paris in 1901. Here was the outward image of his second kind of force, almost specific enough to excite worship if worship were due.

It would be dangerous to press the symbolic parallelism of these two books too far, but the temptation to explore it is great. As the power of the Virgin is humanity on the level of divinity, so that of the dynamo is mechanism raised to the infinite. In the one case, the power operated on an impassive and nonhuman object, the Cathedral of Chartres, which in a sense becomes a subordinate or reflective symbol; in the other, the object of the mechanistic force is human, is Henry Adams made impersonal and passive. From this perfectly balanced equation, the symbolism is developed on the one hand in terms of architecture, art, philosophy, persons and events (stained-glass windows, figures of saints, the rebellion of Pierre de Dreux, the poetry of Thibaut, the philosophy of Abélard); on the other in terms of politics science, philosophy, and again persons and events (Anglo-American diplomacy, the geology of Sir Charles Lyell, two World's Fairs, William Henry Seward, and Lord John Russell).

Intricate and balanced as these imaginative elements are, it would be a mistake to hold that Adams had perfected a new sort of epic or symbolic form. The result gives the impression of work still in progress as Adams felt that it was. The over-all form is massive and sprawling as are those of Melville or Whitman, rather than balanced and finished as one knowing the man Adams might expect. He was never satisfied with it, published the books privately, allowed them reluctantly to be offered to the public. But they are thoroughly American in that whatever order and discipline they achieve is organic. The refined inheritor of Adams' energy had allowed his feelings and his understanding to mold their own form about them.

> The pen works for itself [he confesses] and acts like a hand, modelling the plastic material over and over again to a form that suits it best. The form is never arbitrary, but is a sort of growth like crystallization, as any artist knows too well.

In his style, Adams came nearer to a classic restraint, but here too he indulged in extravagance when the pen became willful. His revisions of his historical essays when he collected them show a peeling off of the superfluous phrase, a stripping down to clear and explicit statement. When he turned from direct to imaginative writing, he deliberately created an *alter ego* and from an oblique angle surveyed himself together with other phenomena, past and present. The direct style would no longer do and he deliberately cultivated, even in his personal letters, the irony which had always been his. A careful reading of Pascal, Montaigne, and Voltaire helped in this study. In his final testament of futility and affirmation, his vein was comic in spite of the tragic intensity of his feelings. Wit alone could bear the burden.

# THE UNITED STATES

*--- confidence and criticism*

# 66. THE HOPE OF REFORM

$B$Y 1912 Eastern liberalism was swerving to the left. That year Walter Weyl championed the New Democracy—what with the New Nationalism and the New Freedom and even the New Republic, everything was new then—and his opening chapter furnished a mordant analysis of the "disenchantment of America." The revelations of the Pujo Committee furnished abundant support to the theory of disenchantment, and those who boggled at government reports could read the same story, with no perceptible improvement in style, in Dreiser's *The Financier*. The undismayed Roosevelt, always radical during election years, led his shouting followers out of the Grand Old Party to some Armageddon where they prepared to battle for the Lord, and for T. R. At Baltimore Woodrow Wilson, with the aid of the veteran Bryan, nosed out the noncommittal Champ Clark for the Democratic nomination, and that November the New Freedom officially supplanted the New Nationalism and the promise of American life seemed not hopelessly beyond fulfillment. The Eastern intellectuals—older men like Wilson and Brandeis and Villard, and younger men like Croly and Weyl and Lippmann—prepared to catch up with the homespun Western radicals after a lapse of only twenty years.

There was, to be sure, little that was new about the stirrings and strivings of the second decade of the new century, except the stage on which they were presented and the accent in which they were expressed. Even here the change was but relative. Jacob Riis, after all, had told how the other half lived, and Henry George had campaigned for the mayoralty of New York, and De Leon had taught socialism at Columbia University back in the eighties and nineties. Nor was there much the Pujo Committee could uncover that had not been known to Henry Demarest Lloyd, or much the *New Republic* could say that had not been anticipated by Flower's *Arena*, while men like Altgeld and Weaver and "Sockless" Jerry Simpson had known the realities of disenchantment long before Croly learned the meaning of the word. Indeed it is difficult to discover anything in the New Nationalism or the New Freedom that was not explicit or implicit in the Populism and the socialism of the nineties, except respectability. Otherwise, the distinction was quantitative rather than qualitative: whereas Bryan had persuaded but six and one-half million voters, Wilson, Roosevelt, and Debs, together, attracted more than eleven million. These figures dramatized the fact that public opinion had at last become aware of the problems that had confronted America ever since the decade of the nineties.

For in the second decade of the twentieth century the nation faced a crisis in the conflict of forces within itself that had first declared themselves in the nineties, and creative energies were released, with their doubts as well as their confidence, into literature and criticism. The outlines of that conflict had by then emerged clearly and even boldly. On the one side lay an America predominantly agrarian, concerned with domestic problems, conforming—intellectually at least—to the political, economic, and moral principles inherited from the eighteenth century: an America still in the making, physically and politically, an America on the whole self-confident, self-contained, and conscious of its unique character and of a unique destiny. On the other side lay the modern America, predominantly urban and industrial, inextricably involved in world economy and politics, troubled with the social and economic problems that had long been thought peculiarly the burden of the Old World, desperately trying to accommodate its traditional institutions and habits of thought to conditions new and in part alien.

2

The era of the New Freedom (1913-1921) and its subsequent disenchantment was the climax of the age of reform. That age (1890-1912) had been experimental rather than dogmatic, given to exploration rather than to the establishment of sovereign claims. It was a time of protest and reform, of the rejection of what was old and the championship of what was new, of speculation and experiment. There was boundless enthusiasm for good causes and endless tinkering with the political machinery. Armies of reformers advanced upon the battlements of vested interests, bands of humanitarians waged guerrilla warfare upon every form of social injustice, visionaries imagined felicitous Utopias and some even indulged in them, less felicitously. There was a youthful ardor to weed out abuses, democratize government, redistribute property, humanize industry, improve the lot of the workingman and the farmer, rescue the victims of social injustice, elevate the moral tone of society. It was the day of the music makers and dreamers of dreams, of world seekers—though rarely of world forsakers. The great figures in politics were all reformers, the great movements all reform movements. Bryan, La Follette, Roosevelt, Wilson, and Debs bestrode the national political scene; Altgeld, Tom Johnson, "Golden Rule" Jones, Hazen Pingree, Charles Aycock, Ignatius Donnelly, "Bloody Bridles" Waite, Tom Watson, Joseph U'Ren, gave color to state and local politics.

The era was ushered in by the Populist Revolt in the nineties, bowed out by the New Freedom and the crusade to make a democratic world. Agrarian reformers captured the Democratic party, and urban progressives the Republican; socialism became respectable and was taken up by the churches, and settlement houses blossomed in every slum. New England liberals emerged to take up the battle for the Negro and the Indian and, after Manila Bay, a crusade against imperialism enlisted the intellectual elite of the whole country. There were countless other crusades: for temperance, for conservation, for peace, for woman suffrage, for children's rights, for civil service reform. The conscience of the nation was troubled, and each exposure of sin or neglect brought contrition and penance. In those years Americans learned *How the Other Half Lives,* heard *The Bitter Cry of the Children,* were shocked by *The Shame of the Cities,* outraged by the *Treason of the Senate,* revolted by the fate of *The Daughters of the Poor,* initiated into the iniquities of *Frenzied Finance,* alarmed by *The Greatest Trust in the World,* came at last to understand the dichotomy of *Wealth Against Commonwealth.* As a result laws to clear slums, protect women and children, curb monopolies, supervise insurance companies, free the public lands, save the forests, frustrate corruption, and safeguard the ballot box crowded the statute books.

All this was eloquent of optimism. Despair leads to apathy or revolution, it is the incorrigibly hopeful who spend their energies in reform. Though the bright promise of American life seemed to be fading, there was no inclination to despair of the Republic, to abandon democracy, or even to challenge a capitalist economy. There was, on the contrary, an all but universal confidence in the beneficent workings of democracy and of the profit system—if only they could be operated honestly and by virtuous men. Carnegie's lyrical description of American material prosperity was, after all, entitled *Triumphant Democracy.* There was nothing fundamentally wrong with American institutions; it was merely that abuses had crept into them, that they had been exploited by shortsighted men to selfish purposes. What was needed was not the abandonment of democracy, but more democracy, not the abolition of private property, but the wider and more equitable distribution of property. "The evil," said Woodrow Wilson in his first inaugural address, "has come with the good, and much fine gold has been corroded." The task was to get rid of the evil and hold fast to what was good.

This is what explains the crusade for Social Justice, for the Square Deal, for the New Freedom, for all those catchwords and phrases which confessed a reassuring—and perhaps a naïve—optimism. Was democracy failing? The answer was to double the electorate by giving votes to women. Was there corruption at the ballot box? The Australian ballot, or formidable corrupt practices acts, would eliminate that. Were legislatures deaf to the voice of the people? The initiative and the referendum would once more give expression to that voice. Was the Senate a stronghold of privilege? Elect senators by direct vote, and that body would become a stronghold of democracy. Was Congress caught in its own cumbersome machinery? A revival of the Jacksonian·doctrine of presidential leadership would make the cumbersome machinery of government work. Did bosses manipulate political parties? Direct primaries would circumvent them. Were wealth and privilege entrenched in the judiciary, as Jefferson had warned? The recall of judicial decisions, or even of judges, would assure a democratic interpretation of the Constitution.

In the economic arena, too, there was confidence in the soundness of institutions and the virtue of the majority of men. Roosevelt could talk of "malefactors of great wealth," but he distinguished sharply between "good" and "bad" trusts, and the moral distinction was carried over into the judicial realm as "reasonable" or "unreasonable" restraint of trade. The Grangers had denounced the railroads as the Great Monopoly, and the Populists had demanded that they be publicly owned; but these demands were easily watered down to regulation and supervision, and Roosevelt—who better than any other figure typified the optimism and opportunism of the reform movement —compromised even here. There was much ado about the maldistribution of wealth, but no attack upon wealth itself, and if the reformers were not quieted by Carnegie's confession that it was a disgrace to die rich they were willing enough to settle for income and inheritance taxes. Communism was not unknown, but it completely lacked the native roots of the earlier Utopian movements; and it was the Debs wing of the Socialist Party, not the radical De Leon wing, that won.

All this suggests that the reform movement was thoroughgoing in criticism, but opportunistic in its tactics. It formulated no logical system, subscribed to no universal principles. It accepted in practice Justice Holmes' dictum, "Legislation may begin where an evil begins," and put a touching faith in the efficacy of legislation. It was romantic in its philosophical implications, but realistic in its recognition of the economic basis of politics. It was, above all, secular—even the Christian Socialists seemed more socialist than Christian, more concerned, that is, with the material than with the spiritual welfare of men. It lacked, or rejected, the basic philosophy that had animated the reformers of the 1840's—the passionate religious conviction of the identity of man with God, of the infinite worth of every human soul. It was more concerned, indeed, with equality of income than with equality of soul, and demanded justice in the name of the Declaration of Independence and the Populist platform rather than of the New Testament.

There was disintegration, but no reintegration. Pragmatism, for all its merits, offered not stability but an open universe and the chance to make ideals truth; and most of the reformers were pragmatists even when they used the vocabulary of mechanistic determinism. Fiske, to be sure, illuminated history with Cosmic Philosophy, but Fiske's day was past, and Henry Adams had already traced the explosion of unity into multiplicity. Veblen was profound but scarcely constructive, and Lester Ward, who was constructive, was largely neglected. Holmes, greatest of American jurists, had no confidence in abstract notions of Law or Justice and no faith in reform, but merely an unassailable conviction that he was not God, and that in a democracy people had a right to make fools of themselves. Even criticism in the grand manner had lost its earlier assurance; it was significant that when Bryce came to portray America he was descriptive and tentative where Tocqueville had been analytical and magisterial, and that even Bryce seemed profound by comparison with native American interpreters.

By 1912 the reform movement began to seem curiously opportunistic and fragmentary. The agrarian reformers were not, on the whole, concerned with the welfare of the workers. Labor, especially after the demise of the Knights and the advent of the Federation, seemed completely self-centered and even boasted its opportunism; its leaders rejected Marxist philosophers and asserted: "We have no ultimate ends. We are going on from day to day." Many of the muckrakers were reformers only fortuitously, and few of them were inspired by ideals or sustained by convictions. It was not surprising that Ida Tarbell, who had laid bare the malpractices of Standard Oil, should later write a laudatory biography of Elbridge Gary; that John Spargo, who had first heard the bitter cry of the children, should end as an implacable opponent of the New Deal; that Burton Hendrick, who exposed the iniquities of life insurance, should celebrate the virtues of Andrew Carnegie. It was characteristic enough that Moorfield Storey should champion the cause of the Negro but bitterly oppose the elevation of Brandeis to the Supreme Court and the admission of Jews to Harvard University; that Tom Watson should fight for the tenant farmer and the mill hand, but inflame his followers against Negroes, Jews, and Catholics; that William Allen White should expose the corruption of politics and of wealth, but oppose Bryan, Wilson, and F. D. Roosevelt. Bryan was radical enough when it came to banks and railroads, but reactionary in matters of religion and education; Theodore Roosevelt enunciated reform principles, but exhibited distaste at their practical application; even Wilson, who spoke eloquently of the New Freedom, acquiesced in the suppression of freedom of speech and of the press during the war.

Because the reform movement lacked a pervasive and sustaining philosophy there is about it a depressing inconclusiveness. Many of the reformers lacked staying power; few of them were concerned with the whole scene.

They dissipated their strength, they wandered off on strange bypaths, they compromised. Their followers were even more unreliable. For most of them a touch of prosperity was all but fatal. With an increase in the price of wheat the agrarian revolt collapsed. Gold in the Klondike ended the free-silver crusade. Labor was persuaded by the argument of the full dinner pail. Southern deserters came trooping back to the ranks of the Bourbon democracy when the bogy of race equality was dangled before their horrified eyes. The succession of Roosevelt by Taft in 1908, the readiness to jettison La Follette for Roosevelt in 1911, the disintegration of the Progressive Party after 1913, all cast a curious light on the sincerity or the intelligence of the reform movement as it entered the new century.

3

Even before the opening of the new century the geographical center of reform had shifted from the Middle Border to the urban East. If, as Denis Brogan has observed, farmers confessed to few ills that dollar wheat wouldn't cure, the Eastern reformers recognized few that would not yield to Honesty and Philanthropy. These end-of-the-century reformers—men like Norton and Atkinson and Storey in Boston, like Gilder and Low and Roosevelt in New York—constituted a distinguished group. Their radicalism, however, was tempered by good manners and by a total inability to understand violence. They were the heirs of Godkin and Curtis rather than of Horace Greeley or Wendell Phillips. They had gone to the best schools—one sometimes feels that a degree from Harvard was a prerequisite to admission to their club—associated with the best people, read the *Nation* and the *Independent,* and knew poverty only at second hand. Their intentions were laudable, but their vision was limited and their interests narrow. They thought of reform almost exclusively in terms of politics, and they were inclined to think that honesty in politics was the sum of political science. Good government, they thought, would follow inevitably from the civil service system and gentlemen in politics. They had the same abiding faith in the efficacy of noble moral sentiments that Wells ascribes to the English liberals of the same period in *The New Machiavelli.* When they thought of the civil service they thought of England. When they thought of gentlemen they thought of one another, and though animated by no vulgar ambition for office, they were not unwilling, from time to time, to sacrifice themselves to the public good.

They had no interest in the agrarian crusade, little sympathy for organized labor, and they thought panaceas like the Single Tax or Bellamy's Nationalism as eccentric as Mormonism. Free silver they held to be simple dishonesty, and outbreaks like the Haymarket riot and the Pullman strike filled them with horror. They were equally fearful of socialism, communism, and anarchism, and inclined to place any economic heresy indiscriminately in one of these categories. For men like Bryan and Weaver they had only contempt; Altgeld and Debs, they damned as un-American.

Yet they had both sympathy for the poor and the underprivileged and a strong feeling of social responsibility. They were ready enough to remedy injustice or alleviate misery, when made aware of them by a Jacob Riis or a Jane Addams. Like the Western agrarians they opposed trusts and protective tariffs, approved government regulation of railways, urged the conservation of natural resources, and worked to wipe out slums, protect women and children, ameliorate race relations, humanize industry, and "socialize" Christianity. It was the humanitarian strain that was most pronounced in them. Because most of them were economically immature, had been raised in a Christian tradition of charity, and were heirs to the social tradition of *noblesse oblige,* they turned instinctively to good works rather than to the state. They engaged in earnest efforts to organize charity, help newsboys, maintain lodging houses, save delinquent girls, rescue homeless waifs, enforce Sunday closing hours, eliminate the sweatshop, mitigate the rigors of the penal code.

The best representative of this Eastern group is its most prominent member—the ebullient Theodore Roosevelt. He was, like most of the good-government enthusiasts, primarily a moral crusader. His earliest venture into politics had been on behalf of tenement house reform—reform nullified by the courts. Under the tutelage of Jacob Riis he had seen Mulberry Bend and Poverty Lane, the sweatshops, the vice and crime of the lower East Side. He had fought the machine, and been rewarded with an appointment as civil service commissioner. His enthusiasm for reform was temporarily dampened by the radicalism of Bryan and then deflected into navalism and nationalism. Later, as governor of the Empire State, he renewed his attack upon the bosses and consolidated his reputation as a liberal.

In Roosevelt, even before he came to the Presidency, we see harmoniously blended the qualities characteristic of the Eastern reformers: optimism and opportunism; distrust of economic, and confidence in political, panaceas; sentimentality and superficiality. Alert, zealous, and upright, he no sooner saw an evil or an infirmity than he exposed and excoriated it. He was against corruption, bosses, those who betrayed the public trust or looted the public domain, he opposed trusts and monopolies, impure foods and drugs, the exploitation of women and children; he was for honesty in politics and the Square Deal and conservation and red-blooded Americanism. Elihu Root once chid him for thinking that he had written the Ten Commandments. Sensitive as he was to wrongdoing, he could never see that particular injustices were the natural product of an inequitable economy or believe that any evil was so deep-seated that it could not be cured by tinkering with the political machinery.

Because Roosevelt compromised on every important issue and evaded every dangerous issue, the transition to Taft seemed natural enough. Yet it was the Taft administration that brought home to the nation the failure of the reform movement. For while Roosevelt sounded like a progressive even when he acted like a conservative, it was Taft's misfortune to sound like a conservative even when he acted like a progressive. By the end of the first decade of the century it was clear that the Roosevelt-Taft brand of progressivism was inadequate to the needs of the day. With all the frenzy of trust busting, the trusts were stronger in 1910 than they had been in 1890 or 1900. With all the fever of railroad regulation, the railroads still managed to evade effective regulation of rates. With all the denunciation of malefactors of great wealth, the distribution of wealth was more inequitable at the end than at the beginning of the period. The protective tariff was untouched; centralized control of banking, unaffected; even conservation—the most sincere of all Roosevelt's reforms—proved woefully inadequate; the forests and soil of the nation disappeared with terrifying rapidity.

With the election of Wilson in 1913 the Progressive Movement reached such maturity as it ever attained. Both the country and Wilson had caught up with the radicalism of the nineties and were prepared to do, now, what should have been done twenty years earlier, as well as to make clear what had to be done twenty years later. Wilson, for all his academic antecedents, his passion for Mill and Bagehot, his curious reluctance to include Jefferson in his calendar of great Americans, his hostility to socialism and Populism, proved a far more realistic, thoroughgoing, and idealistic reformer than Theodore Roosevelt—and a far more effective one.

Like Roosevelt, Wilson was a moralist in politics, though his morality was more personal than that of his great rival, more a matter of principles than of good or bad men, more of the New Testament than of the Old. He was a Southern gentleman, brought up on the tenets of Manchester liberalism, Godkin respectability, and Virginian *noblesse oblige*. He had achieved a national reputation by playing the role of St. George with the dragon of corruption in New Jersey; and, except among those dazzled by the brilliance of T. R., the support of liberals and radicals throughout the country came to him almost by default. His mind was logical and consistent, and when he found himself cast in a democratic role he embraced the whole reform program much as he might have embraced the conclusion of a mathematical theorem. To a profound, almost a religious, conviction of the rightness of such causes as he espoused, he added an astonishing capacity for learning, genius in the manipulation of public opinion, and an iron determination to have his way. No wonder that he succeeded where Roosevelt had failed, and no wonder that his success, and the methods whereby he achieved it, outraged his critics and alienated his friends.

It is legitimate to personify the New Freedom in Woodrow Wilson, but a capital error to suppose that it was all Wilson's achievement. Without Wilson the New Freedom might have been inconclusive; without the support of public opinion it would have been impossible. Wilson had behind him not only the Bryan wing of the Democratic Party, but a substantial part of the Progressive Party. The nation, as a whole, was impatient for reform and ardent for leadership. As Wilson said, with characteristic eloquence:

The Nation has been deeply stirred, stirred by a solemn passion, stirred by the knowledge of wrong, of ideals lost, of government too often debauched and made an instrument of evil. The feelings with which we face this new age of right and opportunity sweep across our heartstrings like some air out of God's own presence, where justice and mercy are reconciled and the judge and the brother are one.

The country was ready, too, for a positive program which would translate these noble sentiments into constructive legislation.

That legislation came, the most comprehensive and effective program since the days of Polk, and under Wilson's driving leadership the progressive forces came closer to realizing their objectives than at any other time in our history. The Underwood Tariff, the Federal Reserve System, the Clayton Anti-Trust Act, the Federal Trade Commission Act, the Adamson eight-hour law, the income tax, farm relief, child-labor laws, the good-neighbor policy, all brought to a logical and impressive climax the agitation of a generation of reformers.

Yet even in its years of triumph it was clear that something had gone out of the reform movement. It had lost something of that elemental strength, that emotional fervor, that economic realism, which had characterized it in the days of Henry George and Peter Altgeld and Tom Johnson. Most of the leaders who had inspired it and molded its character had passed from the scene, or diverted their energies into different channels. Bryan, to be sure, retained his simple idealism; but he seemed to have lost touch with his old associates, and concerned himself increasingly with temperance and peace. Roosevelt, embittered by the spectacle of Wilson playing the role he felt rightly his, abandoned himself to vindictiveness and chauvinism. La Follette lingered on, harsh and irascible, flouted except in his own state. With the transfer of power from state to federal government, local reform movements diminished in importance. The shift was fateful. When the reactionaries moved in and took over, there were no local or regional groups powerful enough to counteract them or to maintain laboratories of liberalism in the states.

4

The First World War marked the end of the great reform movement which had set in about 1890. That the war, and the peace which followed, brought disillusionment is clear; what is not clear is why they should have done so. No historian has yet analyzed the anatomy of reaction after 1918, and the manifestations of that reaction are more obvious than its pathology. Just as the Civil War had canalized all the reform movements of the forties and fifties into the crusade against slavery and disunion, so the First World War canalized the reform movements of the previous decades into an all-embracing crusade for world democracy. After 1917 the interests and energies of the nation were deflected into new channels; prosperity, war, and the post-war problems of international order made most of the issues which had agitated the previous generation seem remote and unreal. Then, too, the inevitable idealization of the crusade for democracy brought an almost equally inevitable reaction into cynicism, while the identification of reform with Wilson himself involved it in the general repudiation of Wilson and Wilsonism. His collapse at Wichita undermined domestic liberalism as well as internationalism. Finally the wartime emphasis on national unity made it easy to distort even constructive criticism into obstructionism and disloyalty and seemed to justify not only the deportation hysteria and the Red scares but state and federal laws destructive of free thought and speech.

The details of the reaction are too familiar to justify rehearsal. President Harding in 1920 dedicated his administration to the return to "normalcy"; Coolidge in 1924, to the proposition that the "business of America is business"; Hoover in 1928 to the Spencerian concept of "rugged individualism." There was widespread hostility to foreigners and to foreign ideas: indeed, ideas themselves were suspect as somehow contrary to genuine Americanism. Aliens suspected of radical notions were rounded up and deported by the thousand; legislatures were purged; teachers were required to take loyalty oaths, and textbooks revised to conform to the concepts of Americanism entertained by the American Legion and the Daughters of the American Revolution. The Ku Klux Klan, which boasted a membership running into the millions, anticipated Nazi doctrines of Aryan supremacy, and its hooded Klansmen intimidated Catholics, Negroes, Jews, and radicals. Religious fundamentalists sponsored laws against the teaching of evolution in the public schools or the dissemination of information about birth control, and censorship laws emasculated moving pictures, plays, and books. In two notorious cases—those of Sacco and Vanzetti in Massachusetts and of Mooney and Billings in California —the victims were punished more for their radicalism than for any crimes proved against them. The Supreme Court, by its genial reinterpretation of the antitrust laws and its nullification of child labor and minimum wage laws, revealed its sympathy with the reactionary tendencies of the time.

There is no more representative figure in this whole period than William Allen White, of Emporia, Kansas. He tells us, in his charming *Autobiography*, how, in the 1920 convention, he led the Kansas delegation onto the Harding bandwagon.

I was too heartsick [he wrote] to rise and fight. . . . The whole liberal movement which had risen so proudly under Bryan, Theodore Roosevelt and La Follette, was tired. The spirits of the liberals who called themselves Progressives were bewildered. The fainthearted turned cynics. The faithful were sad and weary.

Not all of them, to be sure; there were some who fought on. Eugene Debs kept socialism afloat, and even from his cell in the Federal Penitentiary at Atlanta commanded almost a million votes. New parties arose in the Northwest, only to be paralyzed by the hostility of bankers and shippers. That sturdy oak, La Follette, refused to bend to the new winds howling out of the caves of Mammon and, in 1924, organized a party that won five million votes —and disappeared. The *Nation* and the *New Republic* kept up their shrill clamor for social justice; but only the faithful read them, and there were few converts. The liberal movement persisted—without it there could have been no New Deal—but it was a thin and shallow stream running beside the mighty torrent of reaction.

The whole intellectual atmosphere changed, too—more sharply perhaps than in any previous decade in our history. It was not that the artists and writers acquiesced in the new dispensation, but that their rejection of it was so desperate. The novelists and scholars and artists of the Bryan-Roosevelt era had been in revolt, but their revolt was not an expression of their alienation from or contempt for their society, but of indignation and pity. Their protests were designed not to display their own superiority, but to improve the common lot. No one could doubt their sincerity or integrity. When they spoke the language of the farm or the street it was because that language was rightly theirs, not because they wanted to deride it. They were not afraid of passion or indignation, and they directed these toward the oppressors, not toward the victims of oppression. Though they were often troubled by the contemplation of the helplessness of man, it never occurred to them that the only significant thing about man was his insignificance.

The intellectuals of the twenties revealed the same talent for exposure, the same revolt against the farm and the village, the same distaste for Mammon and for Mrs. Grundy, that had animated their predecessors. But they were more concerned with dissociating themselves from these things than with improving or changing them. They did not suffer, like Garland, with the farmers and villagers but, like Lewis, from them. They were not really rebels, but iconoclasts, which is a very different thing. They were too sure of their own superiority to be greatly troubled by the lot of the average man and woman, and their hatred of injustice was not nearly so lively as their hatred of vulgarity and spiritual decline. Others, like Willa Cather and Ellen Glasgow, turned to the past and celebrated the ideals, the achievements, and the failures of earlier Americans rather than attempting to reform their own times. They served art better than most of their predecessors, but lost force as propagandists for a new order. Where the writers of the nineties found it intolerable that a virtuous people should suffer, the literary rebels of the twenties found it intolerable that virtue should be so dull, and financial success so devoid of spirituality.

For all their rage and frustration, the writers of the twenties, with few exceptions, showed little concern for reform. They were not conspicuous in the fight for the League of Nations or the cleansing of politics or the improvement of the lot of the workingman and the farmer. There were no farm novels like Garland's *A Spoil of Office,* no labor novels like Sinclair's *The Jungle,* no political novels like Churchill's *Mr. Crewe's Career.* One might almost say that, even with the celebration of Freud, there were no sex novels like Crane's *Maggie* or Phillips' *Susan Lennox,* for the interest in sex, as in almost everything else, had become psychoanalytical rather than sociological. It was somehow appropriate that the 1890's should be ushered in with *How the Other Half Lives,* and the 1920's with *Main Street* and *This Side of Paradise.*

# 67. CREATING AN AUDIENCE

A NEW and vigorous nationalism, self-critical and analytic, was the underlying trait of both literature and journalism in the years immediately following the end of the First World War. It offset the lack of a reforming spirit of the times. Since the beginning of the twentieth century, new types of readers of books, and particularly of periodicals and great metropolitan newspapers, had been maturing; and the society thus formed now became self-conscious and avid for news of itself, its problems, its responsibilities, its humors, and its emotional needs. In the great cities, still rapidly increasing in population although the growth of the country as a whole was slowing down, Whitman's race of races had become a fact. The war had accelerated what the great depression of the 1930's was to complete, a breakdown of the formerly dominant social (and to a lesser degree intellectual) groups. The absorption of second and third generations of immigrants from all the North European races had also accelerated, and these no longer felt themselves less American than the so-called Anglo-Saxon stock. It was a mobile society, with a mobility very different from the westward streaming of the pioneers, a society urban rather than rural, national rather than sectional; a society ready—or almost ready—to support and encourage authorship.

Serious writers worked under greater financial handicaps in the period before 1910 than after it. It is true that authorship had already become a profession by which men lived; by which they even prospered like successful merchants. Book prices were low after 1900, at the most not more than $1.50 for a popular novel, but royalties were high by later standards; and very successful novelists expected to receive 20 per cent of the list price of every copy sold in the trade edition. Kipling was paid 30 per cent, which may be the highest royalty on record. Even at 20 per cent, authors could earn large sums from single novels; for example, Mary Johnston received more than $60,000 from the publishers of *To Have and to Hold,* not counting her income from other sources, such as magazine publication, second serial rights, and foreign rights. Gene Stratton Porter must have earned three times as much from *Freckles,* with its sale in the trade and reprint editions of nearly two million copies. Jack London had a yearly income of more than $75,000, most of it from magazines, which paid him $3,000 each for his more popular short stories.

With these rewards on the horizon, there had come to be a recognized path to preferment for younger writers. Those who followed the path attended an Eastern university, preferably Harvard, where they took Professor Baker's course in the drama; they came to New York with letters of recommendation; they worked as cub reporters for one of the metropolitan newspapers; and each of them, in his leisure time, wrote a novel, a play, or a book of short stories. If the book or play was successful, the author was launched on his career. But many of the young writers who appeared after 1910 had other aims than making a hit on Broadway or breaking into the list of best sellers; they were rebels and realists who could never be popular, so it seemed, and could scarcely even hope to be commercially published.

Two or three of the lucky ones had private incomes, like Amy Lowell; the rest supported themselves in fifty different ways. A few worked on the fringes of literature, either as newspaper reporters, in what had become the orthodox fashion, or else as hack writers or publishers' readers. Dreiser and Willa Cather were successful magazine editors. Others who would afterward have wide reputations earned their living outside the literary world; they included a farmer (Robert Frost), a struggling lawyer (Edgar Lee Masters), a suburban doctor (William Carlos Williams), a bank clerk (T. S. Eliot), an insurance executive (Wallace Stevens), a professional chess player (Alfred Kreymborg), a wanderer who read poems for bread (Vachel Lindsay), a paint manufac- turer turned advertising agent (Sherwood Anderson), two secretaries to Socialist mayors (Carl Sandburg and Walter Lippmann), and a customhouse clerk. The last was Edwin Arlington Robinson, who was appointed to his post in 1905 after Theodore Roosevelt had read his early poems. Before that time Robinson had been an inspector in the New York subways, then under con- struction. The new literature in his time was also something under construc- tion, and underground. As his fellow authors were doing symbolically, Robinson carried a real lantern, a prickle of light in what seemed to be an endless tunnel.

But the tunnel had exits, and the authors of his generation, even the poets, finally emerged into day. It was sooner than most of them had expected, but dangerously late in what should have been their literary careers. Robinson himself was forty-one years old before he felt able to resign from his clerkship in the Customhouse and fifty-eight before his poetry wholly supported him. Dreiser was almost forty when he resigned from the editorship of the Butterick Publications and devoted all his time to writing novels; Willa Cather was thirty-six when she resigned from *McClure's*. Frost was thirty- nine when he published *North of Boston*; Anderson, forty-three when he published *Winesburg, Ohio*; Masters, forty-six when he wrote *Spoon River Anthology* and abandoned the law for literature. In a sense all these men had gained by their apprenticeship to other crafts, for they brought something new into American letters, a sense of the world outside the Eastern universities and the polite magazines; a sense of bigness, rawness, loneliness. But they also lost by not having had time enough to practice writing or a chance for early contact with a cultivated audience. Of many of them it could be said that they were deficient in general knowledge, that their taste was uncertain, and that either they lacked technical skill or else—if they had begun by writing for the slick-paper magazines, like Hergesheimer and Lewis—they had too much skill of the wrong sort.

2

The new audience had been in the making since the opening years of the century, but in its earlier stages of development it was more notable for increase in size than for improvement in taste.

By 1910 there was in fact a larger public for books than would exist for many years after the First World War, provided that the books were of the sort this earlier public liked and could understand. It liked novels chiefly; it liked them if they were full of sentiment or swordplay, adventures in far places or local color; and if, at the same time, they moved by resolute steps toward an ending that satisfied the Protestant conventions. It liked Gene Stratton Porter, who by 1915 had written *Freckles* and four other novels with a total sale of eight million copies. It liked John Fox, Jr. (*The Trail of the Lonesome Pine*), Jack London (*The Call of the Wild*), Kate Douglas Wiggin (*Rebecca of Sunnybrook Farm*), and Harold Bell Wright (*The Shepherd of the Hills*). In all, between 1901 and 1915, it liked nineteen books well enough to buy more than a million copies of each, whereas there were only eight books, three of them nonfiction, with a sale of more than a million copies between 1916 and 1930.*

The early years of the century were an exciting time for publishers who could gauge the public taste. Men like Colonel Harvey of Harper & Brothers, George H. Doran, and Walter Hines Page had reached an eminence from which they looked down on literary critics and treated authors like children to be spoiled or birched. The same years, however, were a dull period for American literature. The public that adored Pollyanna and her sisters would have nothing to do with novels that denied its belief that virtue was rewarded in this world as well as the next. It would not attend serious plays; it would not read verse written in manners other than those of Ella Wheeler Wilcox

* *An Outline of History, The Story of Philosophy, The Sheik,* and five others.

and James Whitcomb Riley. It would not even read most of the authors whose reputations had been established late in the nineteenth century: the collected edition of Henry James had few buyers, and by 1915 even Howells described himself without much exaggeration as being "a comparatively dead cult with my statues cut down and grass growing over them in the pale moonlight." Younger men who hoped to write like James or Howells were advised by their publishers to choose a safer model, like one of Winston Churchill's historical epics—at any rate something big, colorful, and optimistic, with a plot that was easy to follow. During those flush years of popular fiction, there was an almost complete break in the literary tradition that had been founded in New England before the Civil War. If serious literature was to flourish again, a new beginning had to be made. Besides new writers, there had to be new magazines and publishing houses to present their work; and there had to be a new audience to support the authors and the publishers together.

The audience was at least partly created in the simplest manner, by formal schooling. Education above the secondary-school level developed rapidly in both quantity and quality after 1910, particularly in the prosperous twenties. Although the growth in population was being checked by a declining birth rate, and further checked after 1924 by restrictions on immigration, high schools and colleges attracted more students year by year. From 1910 to 1940, enrollment in high schools increased by 540 per cent, and that in institutions of higher learning by 321 per cent. During the twenties alone, enrollment at both levels doubled, and education, faced with crowded classrooms and inadequate equipment, sought new endowments, new buildings, and new methods. Public and private expenditure kept pace with expanding numbers of students by increasing 559 per cent, while colleges and universities pushed their endowments upward and built new buildings. A great deal of the increase was concentrated in special fields: notably in Southern universities, in city colleges, in Catholic colleges, and in graduate schools; also in junior colleges, of which more than four hundred were founded during the twenty years after the First World War.

Efforts to recapture some of the intimate quality of the earlier colleges led Harvard and Yale to institute "house" or "college" plans by which student bodies were broken up into complete residence and study units—a movement followed by a few other institutions where the necessary funds were available. Two major trends in educational method are noticeable. The Progressive Education Association, founded in 1918, and reflecting the influence of experimental and naturalistic thinking, began its reforms on the nursery and elementary-school levels and gradually advanced upward until it could challenge the traditional college entrance requirements and demand a more flexible and "child-centered" curriculum throughout the entire educational process.

On the other hand, colleges and universities, under the leadership of Woodrow Wilson, Frank Aydelotte, A. Lawrence Lowell, and John Erskine, began experiments with "Preceptorials" and "Honors" courses for small groups of selected students, tutorial systems, and "colloquia," in an effort to regularize once more the content of higher education and to individualize its methods. Although apparently similar in many respects to the Progressive Movement, such experiments reflected rather a tendency to develop humanistic and neo-scholastic influences. They allowed greater freedom of intellectual inquiry to the student, but at the same time they sought to raise standards and to liberate the mind through the newly developed disciplines of modern natural science, social science, and the humanities. Thus, while the educated reading public was rapidly increasing, intellectual leadership was stimulated by selective and intensive programs of higher education.

The growth of secondary and higher education not only created a potential audience for books larger than had existed before in any single country, or in all Western Europe, but also furnished new training grounds for writers. Until 1910 Harvard had graduated a disproportionate share of American literary men; after 1910 writers came in large numbers from other universities: first Princeton and Yale (with its brilliant class of 1919); then Chicago, Vanderbilt, Stanford, the Western and Southern state universities, and the new city colleges. Student writers who in the past had found little recognition in the academic system were once more given the stimulus and sympathetic atmosphere of the coterie. As during the literary revival of the early nineteenth century undergraduate clubs appeared, like the Elizabethan Club at Yale, devoted to good talk about books and writing.

About 1915, adult education began to be preached with enthusiasm and even practiced, if more tepidly; it was the new name for cultural activities that had continued in one form or another since colonial times. Some of the activities were now being institutionalized, while others were beginning to decline—among them the Chautauqua reading circles, which gradually disappeared from the two or three hundred cities where they had flourished. Their place was partly taken by university summer schools and extension courses, both of which were popular with grade-school teachers seeking academic credits. Most of the public lyceums dwindled away; indeed there was a temporary decline in the whole art and business of public speaking. The educational programs formerly offered by labor unions to their members were neglected or abandoned after the First World War, except by the two powerful unions in the garment trades; much later they would be adopted by the new unions of the post-depression years. Women's clubs all over the country increased rapidly in number and maintained a certain level of cultural effort; the level fell during the Wall Street boom, when Browning gave way to bridge; then it rose again in the depression and the early days of the New Deal, which was a period of self-education and general cultural activity.

The little-theater movement, beginning in this country about 1912 and reaching its height about 1924, was in one aspect a form of adult education. It created an audience for serious plays. Most of those plays, in the early years, were German or English or Irish or Scandinavian, so that the audiences became familiar with the ideas of the new European dramatists. Later, when there were more than a thousand little-theater groups, the audience learned to applaud American dramatists like O'Neill, themselves trained in the little theaters, whose work belonged to what had formerly been called the European current of thought. Pessimism, naturalism, lyricism, fantasy, expressionism, all these moods and methods were presented on the stage before they were embodied in any American novels that reached a wide public.

Motion pictures and radio, on the other hand, did little toward creating a literate audience; they might have been described in the beginning as forms of miseducation. The silent movies were, with few exceptions, written and directed to reach the twelve-year-old mind that was taken as the average of the population. Possibly they resulted in a leveling down of intellectual interests, while consuming time that had formerly been devoted to other cultural activities. It was not until after 1930 that the movies, transformed into talkies, began to have a positive effect on American reading habits. Radio at first was simply an electrical gadget; then it became a popular art that competed with wood-pulp fiction and, for a time, reduced the sales of confessional magazines like *True Stories*. Literary programs to which people willingly listened, like "Invitation to Learning" and "Author Meets Critic," were a comparatively late development.

With all the new claims on their time, of which the automobile was the most insistent, it is a wonder that Americans had time to read at all. Yet public libraries continued to be built and patronized; merely from the gifts of Andrew Carnegie, 1,677 library buildings were erected between 1896 and 1923, not to mention all those erected by states and municipalities. By 1935 there were in all 6,235 public libraries, serving 63 per cent of the population; they had more than 100,000,000 books on their shelves and a circulation for the year of 450,000,000. In general there was a steady increase in the number of books they lent, though most of the new readers belonged to special groups in the population: young people rather than adults, women rather than men, and—a point of interest—the working class as opposed to the business class. During the depression, when most public libraries were forced to operate on smaller budgets, the circulation of books grew larger year by year; in Muncie, Indiana (which the Lynds called "Middletown"), it more than doubled during the five years beginning with 1929. It reached a peak in

1933 and declined afterwards, although it remained far above the 1929 level. There was, in other words, a vast new audience that was ready to read good books as well as bad ones if it heard about them; that was ready to buy them, too, as soon as the publishers presented them in cheap editions.

### 3

After 1910 there was a great upheaval in the magazine world. Periodicals that seemed as fixed and predictable in their appearance as the days of the week were suddenly discarded like last year's calendars. The greatest mortality was among the muckraking monthlies. These had achieved great circulations for the time by exposing the sins of American business, government, churches, and social life, sometimes in merely sensational attacks, but sometimes, too, in sound and well documented articles written by the ablest journalists the country had so far known; a few of them, including Lincoln Steffens and Ray Stannard Baker, reached a higher literary level than the contemporary novelists. As for the magazines that published their work, *Everybody's, McClure's,* the *Cosmopolitan,* and *Hampton's,* all had circulations close to half a million copies a month in 1910. Two years later they all changed their editorial policies, and *Hampton's* had ceased publication— as had also the *Arena,* the *Twentieth Century, Success,* and *Human Life.* It was said at the time that the public had lost interest in muckraking; but later revelations by publishers and editors made it appear that the muckraking magazines had been ruined by their own success. They had frightened the business community, while at the same time they had become dependent on advertising and bank credit. When the advertising was withdrawn, page after page, and the loans were called, as if on a concerted signal, they had to stop their investigations or go out of business.

The great literary monthlies also changed or disappeared, but in a more leisurely fashion. *Harper's, Scribner's,* and the *Century,* with their elderly and, at the time, impoverished cousins the *Atlantic* and the *North American Review,* had exercised a long dictatorship over American taste; they were the guardians of the tradition of ideality, which, with the fabric worn shabby and more starch to conceal it, had become the genteel tradition. In 1910 the first three still had a combined circulation of more than half a million. All except the *Atlantic* lost readers during the next ten years, although *Harper's* would also revive after 1920 under new editors. The *Century* lived on until 1930, but only as a quarterly. *Scribner's* and the *North American Review* had a melancholy fate; both changed hands several times and ended (like *Littell's Living Age*) after coming under control of propagandists for Axis governments.

Other famous magazines disappeared during or after the First World War. *Harper's Weekly* was among the first to go, in 1916; brilliantly written in its last years under Norman Hapgood, but deserted by advertisers, it was merged with the *Independent,* which in turn was merged with the *Outlook,* which ceased publication in 1935. *Current Literature,* renamed *Current Opinion,* had been the best popular record of cultural life during the immediate prewar years; but it died from loss of circulation. The *Youth's Companion,* once the most successful American magazine, followed from week to week by adults as well as children, was defeated more by slipshod accounting methods than by lack of readers; it lived until 1929. The three humorous weeklies, *Puck, Judge,* and *Life,* starved to death on a diet of their own jokes. The *World's Work* was taken over by the *Review of Reviews,* which was taken over by the *Literary Digest,* which was laughed out of existence after its famous poll of presidential voters had revealed that Landon would sweep the country in 1936. The *Bookman* (like *Book Chat* and the *Book Buyer), St. Nicholas* (like the other established children's monthlies), the *Forum* (with all the periodicals intended to serve as open platforms for debates)—it was not only single magazines that perished, but whole families and groups. One after another they dwindled away, they vanished with their dignified names, leaving the field to new magazines less hampered by their own traditions.

These new periodicals were of many types. The *Yale Review,* founded in 1911, was the first of the university quarterlies to achieve a general reputation; it became the precursor of many others which provided a small but influential audience with a mixture of information, interpretation, and creative writing. The *New Republic,* founded in 1914, was the first of the new weeklies. With a brilliant editorial board, it tried to set a standard of intelligent discussion and good writing. The older *Nation,* founded in 1865, was transformed into a vigorous political organ after Oswald Garrison Villard became the editor in 1918; but it remained a literary organ, too, and its new critics supported the new generation of novelists. The immediate postwar years were the heyday of the "liberal weeklies," not all of which were either weekly or liberal; besides the *Nation* and the *New Republic,* there were also, for a time, the *Freeman,* which believed in good prose and the single tax, the radical fortnightly *Dial* (in the years 1916–1920), and the conservative *Weekly Review.*

Reviewing and criticism were the chief purpose of the *Saturday Review of Literature* (1924), which succeeded, under the same editorship, the *Literary Review* (1920) of the old New York *Evening Post.* Here a determined effort was made to bridge the gap between university scholarship and the interests of the educated public. In the years between 1915 and 1925, a group of teachers and scholars that included John Erskine and Carl Van Doren from Columbia, Henry Seidel Canby from Yale, and Stuart P. Sherman from the University of Illinois, migrated into the increasingly hospitable areas of literary journalism. Book reviewing in the Sunday supplements of the New York *Times* and the New York *Herald Tribune,* as well as in the *Saturday Review of Literature,* reflected this new vitality.

By an easy transition, the most skillful and powerful commentators on the political and literary weeklies slipped into the newspapers, where, over their own names, and often at variance with the editorial policy of the paper, they widened their audience and satisfied the demand of a society craving intellectual guidance. The career of Walter Lippmann is characteristic of the whole movement. Beginning on the staff of the *New Republic,* he became a writer of books (*Public Opinion,* 1922, *A Preface to Morals,* 1929), and finally the author of syndicated commentaries on national and world affairs which, thanks to his expert knowledge and the clarity of his exposition, gave him a national reputation and influence. Other commentators, when equipped with a good voice and the right background of experience, were able to flourish in the illimitable field of radio. During the thirties and forties they interpreted for the millions the complexities of politics, war, and international affairs.

As older periodicals lost their readers after the First World War, new ones were appearing year by year. In 1922 it was the *Reader's Digest,* modest in its beginnings but destined to have the largest circulation in the world. The next year it was *Time,* first of the news weeklies; in 1924 it was the *American Mercury,* edited by H. L. Mencken and George Jean Nathan; in 1925, the *New Yorker,* which tried not to be serious but didn't always succeed. Later there would be other magazines that helped to change the character of American journalism: *Esquire,* appearing toward the end of the decade with its luscious ladies reproduced in several colors; *Fortune,* in 1930, with its careful studies of American business and its beautifully drawn graphs which, for the first three years, showed only business declines; and the new *Life,* in 1936, first and most successful of the big picture magazines.

*Time, Fortune,* and *Newsweek* (1933) were, in one respect at least, a radical departure in American journalism. They proposed, at least, not so much to influence opinion as to supply facts for opinion. They were cooperative, collective efforts to cover the news, extending into science, literature, business, and the arts. Backed by staffs of researchers, they were not so much written as rewritten by a staff of subeditors. This procedure was the exact opposite of the personal journalism which elsewhere determined both the magazine and the newspaper worlds.

Some of the new periodicals had a level of technical competence never achieved before. Their reporters gathered more facts and better pictures; their editors had a better eye for lively stories and a surer judgment of the treatment they deserved; and yet—except sometimes among the staff of the *New Yorker*—there was not the same passion for discovering new writers or the intellectual curiosity often to be found in the stodgier magazines of half a century before; and magazine contributors were seldom given the freedom of opinion that the muckraking journalists had taken for granted. The new periodicals depended for much of their circulation on the public that also read serious books, but they had done less than their share toward creating that public.

### 4

When Harriet Monroe published the first issue of *Poetry: A Magazine of Verse* in October, 1912, she put a quotation from Whitman on the back cover: "To have great poets there must be great audiences too." Miss Monroe during the next few years was able to find a few great and many distinguished poets of all schools to print in her magazine. She was less successful in creating a great or at least a wide audience, for *Poetry* never had many more than 3,000 readers. This, however, was a much larger public than most of the poets it printed could have reached without its help.

Little magazines like *Poetry* become important in any era when there is a gulf between the tastes of the broad public and the aims of serious writers. They were especially important in the years after 1910 because they gave a first hearing to a whole rebel generation of poets and novelists. One after another they struggled through their usually brief span of life; but they printed more new authors, and sometimes better authors, than many magazines that lived for a financially profitable half-century. *Others,* the little magazine edited by Alfred Kreymborg, had three hundred subscribers and a life span of four years; but it printed William Carlos Williams, Alfred Kreymborg, Marianne Moore, Conrad Aiken, Wallace Stevens, and T. S. Eliot, when much of their work was being rejected even by *Poetry*. The *Little Review* had a longer history. Founded in Chicago in 1914, it moved first to New York and then to Paris, while moving intellectually from anarchism and feminism through a whole series of enthusiasms to cubism, surrealism, and tired cynicism, so that its files are an intellectual history of the period in which it flourished.

The *Masses,* founded in 1911, had its great period from 1914 to 1917; it was the organ of all the story-tellers, reporters, poets, and cartoonists who were criticizing the old society and trying to build a new one. *Reedy's Mirror,* in St. Louis, gave their first hearing to many of the new Midwestern poets, including Edgar Lee Masters; it printed most of his *Spoon River Anthology*. The *Smart Set* for the year 1913 was a little magazine in spirit, and almost in circulation. Willard Huntington Wright was its editor that year, and he had signed a contract giving him complete control of editorial policy. He celebrated his freedom by printing Joyce, Lawrence, Beerbohm, Wedekind, Schnitzler, and other authors unknown to most of his subscribers. Until his contract expired, to the owner's relief, after twelve monthly numbers, the *Smart Set* was the most interesting magazine in the English-speaking world. The *Seven Arts* was another successful experiment that lasted only a year. It assembled the best of the new American essayists, poets, and story-tellers; and it presented them in an impressive fashion, as if to say, "It is now time for these men to be publicly recognized." The recognition came, but not enough of it was pecuniary; and when the editors opposed our entrance into the war and their financial backer withdrew her support, publication had to be suspended. That was in the fall of 1917, when the *Masses* had been suppressed and its editors were standing trial for sedition.

After the war, most of the little magazines represented another generation of writers, more interested than their American predecessors in literary form and experiment. Some of them were founded by groups of critics or poets; the most interesting was the group at Vanderbilt University that published the *Fugitive*. In New York the principal spokesman for the generation as a whole was the monthly *Dial,* which was founded—or, better, re-created from the fortnightly *Dial*—in January, 1920. It was a well printed, dignified, but adventurous magazine that printed the best work it could find anywhere in the world; perhaps its most frequent contributors, among younger Americans, were E. E. Cummings, Marianne Moore, and Kenneth Burke. It started a tradition of technical as opposed to moral or social criticism that would be continued later by the *Hound and Horn,* and by at least three of the university quarterlies: the *Southern Review,* the *Sewanee Review,* and the *Kenyon Review.* But most little magazines of the twenties were printed in Europe, where costs were lower and many of the younger writers found it more convenient to live. *Broom, Gargoyle, Secession,* the *Transatlantic Review, This Quarter, Exile, Tambour*—there was a long succession of these magazines; but *transition,* which lived from 1927 to 1938, was the biggest and most influential.

## 5

In the early years after the First World War, newspapers rather more successfully than magazines adapted themselves to the new literate and sophisticated society of the great cities. It was an unsettled, uncertain, but

in general a prosperous society, cheerful, good-humored, and seeking ur
banity and information. It was a liberal society, even in the midst of the
postwar political reaction. It was opposed to the genteel, the snobbish, the
dogmatic, and the heavy materialism of business which dominated American
politics and economics. Yet it was speculative and inquiring rather than
radical, repelled by revolutionary action—since it liked its own world well
enough—and was marked by none of the vindictiveness that accompanies a
violent clash in ideologies. The intellectuals among this reading class culti
vated tolerance for everything except the closed mind.

As a whole, this new society craved much more than ideas and information. It was a society in which loneliness was prevalent, the loneliness of the
individual lost in great crowds of men and women in a city to which he had
usually come from somewhere else. What he lacked was a sense of personality, of warmth, of the familiar if not the intimate. His desire for personal
experience was frustrated in the standardized life that seemed to be the price
of success. From the resulting loneliness, since there is no such thing as
standardized friendship, from nostalgia for the intimate contacts of a small
community, from the drabness of anonymity, the more intelligent sought
escape in the highly personal journalism of commentators and columnists,
where they could find kinship, at least on paper, among the like-minded.
An analogy with eighteenth century London in the days of the coffee-houses
and the periodic essays of the *Tatler* and the *Spectator* is not too remote.

The modern variety of highly personal journalism had, of course, begun
long before these decades in the so-called yellow press, a creation of Joseph
Pulitzer in his New York *World* of the 1890's. Pulitzer, an immigrant who
had worked his way up, knew that the masses were hungry for news of
human nature, and that a murder or a scandal or a sensation in public affairs
warmed them into lively attention, where a narrative of colder events, no
matter how important, passed over their areas of interest. The more sophisticated readers of books and magazines in the 1920's, particularly in the
massed and lonely great cities, were equally hungry for more personality
and more human interest in their journalism, but they had no taste for
crude sensationalism. As the narrower group of intellectuals began to take
their leadership less and less from the editorial columns and more and more
from the signed commentary, so this urbane audience, college-bred most of
them, asked for wits and satirists (on the stage and in books as well as in the
press) to give them a sense of belonging to what they felt was a sophisticated
civilization that was escaping from the stuffiness and tight morality of the
Genteel Age.

What Artemus Ward and Petroleum V. Nasby and Mark Twain had
done upon the lecture platform to release the lighter emotions of an earlier

period now, in these 1920's of vast populations not yet accessible by radio, was paralleled by writers for the great newspapers, and institutionalized in what soon came to be called the column, with a columnist in charge. The column, satiric, lightly literary, pleasantly personal, and definitely sophisticated, became, with the comic strip, the recreational feature of the paper.

These columns, of which the earliest were written in the Middle West by Eugene Field and Bert Leston Taylor, were no longer mere collections of burlesque, smart anecdote, and horseplay, such as were common in the nineteenth century. Typical of the genre at the time of its greatest popularity among good readers was the "Conning Tower" of Franklin P. Adams, a transplanted Midwesterner who made his reputation on the New York *Tribune* and *World*. More of a true humorist, less of a wit, was Don Marquis, also from the Middle West, whose reputation was made on the New York *Sun*. He was an ironist, a creator of humorous characters, a keen observer of folly, who, at heart, was a romantic tragedian. The plays and the many sonnets he wrote from his inner being were more competent than distinguished, but this inner seriousness gave his humor an emotional coloring and often an ironic edge. His column also was a commentary on the news of the town, but he enriched it with creatures of his own fancy who spoke for his moods and for his philosophy.

Both these men, like Ring Lardner, could hear and reproduce the rhythms and vocabulary of the new American language, and their columns will be source books for the students of the city speech of their age. And, indeed, B. L. T., F. P. A., and Don Marquis and their columns were the taste-makers for the satire of such stories as Lardner's and F. Scott Fitzgerald's, and the ironic plays so popular on the stage in the twenties and thirties. They were essentially critics and observers rather than creators of life, and their success was to make the minds of their numerous readers more receptive to the new wave lengths over which American literature was being transmitted. Both mood and appeal were different from the writer-audience relationship of such earlier newspaper columns as, say, Eugene Field's "Sharps and Flats" in the Chicago *News*.

Another columnist of the later period, Christopher Morley, came from a different American environment, the academic-literary soil of the East, refertilized in his case by the ancient earth of Oxford. His column, "The Bowling Green," published first in the New York *Evening Post*, and afterwards in the *Saturday Review of Literature,* might have been called Adventures Among Books, and he was instrumental in giving a wide audience to many an author, like Joseph Conrad, who had been regarded as caviar for the public. He wrote many books, some very successful in the difficult field of fantasy, but his mark on his generation was made in a columnist's mood of the twenties. Alexander Woollcott succeeded him as what might be called a caresser of books, choosing the radio as his means of access to the public.

The column as a feature of the daily paper soon began to lose its literary qualities and its illusion of wits, artists, critics, and satirists in the heart of a materialist society. With each merger of newspapers some columnist lost his job and had to seek a new environment; and as journalism became big business, standardization and the rapid increase of syndicating cramped the finer talents. The good columnist needed to feel a well known community about him in order to do his best work.

## 6

New publishers likewise helped to create the new audience. In the years from before 1920 there were several of these, and, as a rule, they proved hospitable to the new poets and novelists whose work had not interested the long established firms. Mitchell Kennerley was the first of the new enterprisers; his business was founded in 1905. It was discontinued after 1916, but not without leaving behind it a record of literary as opposed to purely commercial publishing. B. W. Huebsch, another of the new men, paid special attention to European authors; he published Joyce, Hauptmann, Sudermann, Strindberg, Chekhov, and Gorky. In 1925 he carried many of his authors to the newly founded Viking Press. Alfred A. Knopf, after working for Doubleday, Page and for Kennerley, started his own business in 1915. He too specialized in European authors, including an amazing number of those who would later win the Nobel Prize; among the younger Americans, he published Cather, Hergesheimer, and Mencken.

There was beginning to be a conflict in the book world between the "old-line" publishers, who were accused of stodginess and commercialism, and the new publishers, who were accused of recklessness, bad taste, and financial instability. The new firm of Boni & Liveright, founded in 1917, sharpened the conflict by being the most reckless of all; it became famous for its advances to unconventional authors (including Dreiser, Anderson, Jeffers, O'Neill) and for the Roman banquets of its president, Horace Liveright. His cofounder Albert Boni retired in 1918 and his other associates were always leaving to start new firms of their own; so that Boni & Liveright became, in a sense, the parent of Albert & Charles Boni, Thomas Seltzer, Simon & Schuster, Random House, Julian Messner, and Covici-Friede—not to mention its relation to the Liveright Publishing Corporation, which acquired the copyrights of the parent house after the death of the founder. Another new firm, founded in 1919, managed to build a bridge between the old and the new: Harcourt, Brace began by publishing John Maynard

Keynes' *Economic Consequences of the Peace* and went on, in 1920, to publish *Main Street,* the first book by any of the new novelists to reach a sale of half a million copies. That same year Eugene O'Neill's first full-length play, *Beyond the Horizon,* was a success on Broadway. The rebel authors of the wartime years, having found their audience, were becoming the dominant authors of a new era.

One after another the established publishing houses began changing their policies. The chasm between new and old-line publishers disappeared after 1925; the fact was that some of the older houses, including Scribner and Houghton Mifflin, were showing more hospitality toward experimental writing than several of their younger competitors. The older houses, if not too strictly bound by their own traditions, had a better chance for survival in a highly competitive field. Some of them declined and a few went out of business, but most of them held their own or entered a fresh period of expansion. Of the fourteen large publishing houses each of which issued more than a hundred books in 1942—to carry our story ahead—only three had been founded after 1910, and the others included some of the oldest firms in the trade. Macmillan still published more new books than any other house; and Harper, founded in 1817, came second. Counting reprints as well as new books, however, the lead was held by Doubleday, Doran.

More and more the publishing trade was concentrated in New York City. There were two large trade-book publishers in Boston, one in Philadelphia, one in Indianapolis; but even these four maintained New York offices for contact with authors and agents. Most of the other publishers outside New York had special fields of activity; for example there were textbook publishers in Boston, medical-book publishers in Philadelphia and Baltimore, and reprint publishers in Cleveland and Chicago. Scholarly books —a few of which appeared as if by accident on the best-seller lists—were issued by the presses founded at more than a score of American universities. Either the Harvard University or the Johns Hopkins Press was the oldest of these—depending on how one interprets the records; while those issuing the largest numbers of books were at Columbia, Harvard, Chicago, Yale, and Princeton.

In New York the publishing trade had become more than ever a mixture of business, art, and profession. Perhaps its purely professional standards were lower than in the years before 1910, but its literary standards had risen. Many publishers tried to keep ahead of the public taste and were willing, at times, to spend money on books that would have no sale except in a problematical future. They listened to serious reviewers, where earlier publishers would have brushed them aside; they even read the little magazines; and they found scope to exercise their individual tastes and talents. The history of most of the newer publishing houses, and some of the older ones, during the interwar years, should be a study of individuals rather than institutions. To mention only a few names, it was individuals like Alfred Knopf, with his passion for well designed books that other publishers would copy; like Horace Liveright, with his disregard for finances and his arbitrary kindness to rebel authors; like Alfred Harcourt, with his intelligent interest in public questions; like Maxwell Perkins, of Scribner, with his support of Fitzgerald and Hemingway and his inspired editing of Thomas Wolfe; like Warder Norton, with his faith that the public would read scholarly books if they were well written—it was these and others like them who were directly responsible for changes in the publishing world.

Individuals, too, carried on the fight against censorship that reached a climax between 1915 and 1925. In the preceding years there had been comparatively few censorship cases involving reputable publishers; and one reason was that the publishers acted as their own censors. They refused to publish books that might have offended the public taste, including many books that deserved to be published; they omitted realistic passages from others—sometimes after publication, on the complaint of one or two newspaper reviewers—and if any conflict was threatened with the Society for the Suppression of Vice, they simply withdrew a book from circulation. As late as 1914, a chapter was omitted from the posthumous first edition of Frank Norris' *Vandover and the Brute* at the request of the publishers, who thought that readers might be offended.

Yet authors had begun to fight against censorship after the suppression of Dreiser's *The "Genius"* in 1916; and soon the new publishers were supporting them. Horace Liveright, Thomas Seltzer, and later James Henle of the Vanguard Press played important parts in the struggle. The authors whose books aroused the most violent objections were Dreiser, Cabell, Schnitzler, and James Joyce. Dreiser's experience with censorship, from the quiet semi-suppression of *Sister Carrie* in 1900 to the triumphant reception in 1925 of *An American Tragedy,* might stand as an epitome of the whole struggle. There was also, however, a great battle over Joyce's *Ulysses,* parts of which were published serially in the *Little Review.* Four numbers of the magazine were burned by the Post Office Department; and in 1920 the editors were fined $100 by the New York Court of Special Sessions. In 1933, however, Judge John M. Woolsey of the United States District Court ruled that *Ulysses* was a serious work of art, that it was not obscene, and that it could therefore be admitted to the United States. Judge Woolsey's decision was interpreted at the time as a permanent victory for rebel authors, American as well as foreign; but it proved to be only a truce in a long struggle that would be renewed in the 1940's.

# 68. THE BATTLE OF THE BOOKS

Oₙₑ of the earliest signs of a maturing literature is the appearance of literary critics in force. Exploratory literatures like those of colonial times or of the frontier have little use for definitions, rules, and directions. But when a civilization becomes mature and its culture relatively settled it requires of its artists that they formulate their working principles. It asks: What is literature? What are the relationships between literature as expression and the life that it expresses? Upon what traditions is this literature based? What is the relationship between the literary artist and his art?

These are the questions which Poe attempted to raise early in our literary history; but he was too early, and there were no other critics to join with him. They are the questions raised with more success by Emerson, Thoreau, Whitman, Lowell, and others of the fifties and sixties, when American culture reached a temporary fulfillment. With the unsettled state of the modern mind and the expanding forces of American development at the end of the century, the efforts of Henry James, Howells, Norris, Huneker, and others to raise these questions again resulted in much critical activity without great results in systematic literary criticism or understanding of its own original artists like Emily Dickinson, Crane, Robinson, and Norris. Not until about 1910 did the intellectual and social ferment of these years take shape as a critical movement concerned with literary theory in and for itself. Not until then did the age become, in Emerson's sense, "introspective"—in the phrase of Van Wyck Brooks, "self-critical." Not until then was there a concerted effort on the part of a large number of literary critics to reformulate the basic problems of art.

The sense of newness in the critical movement of the years 1910–1925 is of course illusory. Nothing then said was really new, because all of it had roots deep in the American soil and all of it partook of the general ferment of the modern mind. It was new only in its sense of sudden recognition, in its concerted effort at clarification. But in American literary history the battle of the books waged during those years is a phenomenon of major importance and assignable dates.

In essence, it was but one engagement in the perennial war between age and youth, between the ancients and the moderns, between conservatives and radicals. Efforts to classify these critics into schools—as naturalists, humanists, impressionists, idealists, etc.—usually fail because the critics themselves refuse to conform. They were inconsistent in their basic aesthetic positions; they could not answer the fundamental questions of literary criticism because the questions themselves had not been clearly reformulated in a modern American idiom.

The chronology of the movement is as hard to follow as are its schools to classify. The only developed school of literary criticism in the United States in 1910, the academic "defenders of ideality" (see Chapter 50), was united merely in its effort to avoid disturbing issues, to preserve a tradition from the great days, and to adapt it to modern usage. Alarmed at the inroads of materialism into American life and of skepticism into American thought, these critics clung to the old certainties with waning assurance. Conviction was less vigorous in Woodberry than it had been in Stedman, less confident in Stedman than it had been in Emerson and Lowell. The ground of American literary theory needed replowing.

The first critics to start this work were drawn from the ranks of the conservatives themselves. They were W. C. Brownell, Irving Babbitt, and Paul Elmer More. These men broke with the idealists as early as 1892 by refusing to accept without careful reconsideration the traditional moral assumptions underlying the popular literature of the day. Inspired mainly by Matthew Arnold and Sainte-Beuve, they demanded a restudy of the relationship between art and life, a revaluation of values. But they joined with the idealists in protesting the current breakdown of standards and of tradition. Too individualistic to form a school and too intellectual to gain much of a public hearing, their influence was limited to a narrow circle of devoted disciples until, in the thirties, their principles had become dogmatic and their methods combative under attack. Not until then did "neo-humanism," as a reactionary movement of power, declare itself.

In the meantime the self-styled "literary radicals" had issued their challenge to conservatism in all its forms. Young men like Van Wyck Brooks, H. L. Mencken, Lewis Mumford, Waldo Frank, and Randolph Bourne were drawn together in common protest against their elders rather than by a common aesthetic philosophy. To these young men the differences between the idealists and the humanists were not so significant as the similarities in their traditionalism and in their refusal to accept the inductive methods of thinking developed by modern science. The literary radicals demanded a complete and open-minded restudy of the whole relationship between literature and American life, past and present. In the excitement of the attack, they did not take time to formulate their underlying principles or to assure the accuracy of their statements. They merely threw in their lot with the swelling current of naturalism in fiction, poetry, and drama; and they denounced all of the accepted American tradition as false because they found parts of it stultifying.

By 1915, when Brooks sounded the tocsin in *America's Coming-of-Age,* the battle was on. Its issues and its outcome have not been clearly understood, because of the distracting brilliance of forensic skill displayed on both sides. Oversimplified, the main issue may stand thus: the literary radicals demanded a closer bond between literature and "life," in the sense of vital experience; the conservatives agreed, but they defined "life" as moral values established by tradition. There were also a few critics, like Joel Spingarn, who denied the importance of immediate connection between literature and life in any sense. These three groups, but mainly the first two, defined the complex pattern of modern American literature between 1910 and 1925 by their very antagonisms.

2

The demand for a new link between literary and social criticism was signalized by John Macy's *The Spirit of American Literature* (1913), but it was Randolph Bourne who became to rebellious youth the clear-minded leader and critic, then after his death the canonized saint. "I shall never forget my first meeting with him," wrote his closest friend Van Wyck Brooks, "that odd little apparition with his vibrant eyes, his quick, birdlike steps and the long black student's cape he had brought back with him from Paris." Successful in his struggle against both the middle-class complacency of his birthplace, Bloomfield, New Jersey, and his own physical deformity—his curved back was only one of his bodily distortions—he gained a serenity which allowed him to understand and to explain their bright new world without the inhibitions and fears that beset others.

While still a student at Columbia, Bourne lashed out against an elder generation whose values served only "to buttress a social situation." They could no longer think or feel or generalize. His essays, collected as *Youth and Life* (1913), suffered, as his friend Paul Rosenfeld pointed out, from "the gingerly *Atlantic Monthly* style, with its mincingness of persons perpetually afeared of stepping on eggs"; but they contained his central challenge. Radicalism for its own sake was to be his calling; irony—as he put it, the entering of the soul into iron—his method.

When war came to his country, and the liberal leaders to whom he had looked for inspiration—notably John Dewey and Woodrow Wilson—joined the vested interests with what seemed to him a false rationalization of the American cause, he turned from literature to oppose all those who would twist values to serve ends, and became a social critic. His essays for the short-lived *Seven Arts* magazine, collected later by James Oppenheim as *Untimely Papers* (1919), were timely enough. The energies of his last years were devoted to exposing the fallacy of service to the state rather than to the self. In a blind search for values in a distorted world, he died.

Van Wyck Brooks collected Bourne's papers as the *History of a Literary Radical* in 1920, the most important of which is a fragment of a novel. Here the young man Miro—Bourne himself—finds his escape from the "sweetness and light" which tainted the American tradition by the aid of the "abounding vitality and moral freedom" of Thoreau, Whitman, and Mark Twain. And Bourne, like Miro, turned to writers who were not afraid: to Dostoevski, because of his success in closing up the gap between the normal and the abnormal; to Cardinal Newman, because of his acceptance of skepticism; to Dreiser, because of his "revelation of a certain broad level of American life." Bourne's criticism had the negative virtue of exposing hypocrisy and cant rather than the positive virtue of formulating a doctrine and a program. But even in the few papers that he left he demonstrated his fearlessness, his irony, and his dialectical skill.

At Bourne's death Van Wyck Brooks more than anyone else took over the leadership of the radical cause and formulated its program. He had long been working closely with Bourne, for in *The Wine of the Puritans* (1909) he had diagnosed the causes of America's blindness and stupidity. Bourne had similarly warped the term in "The Puritan's Will to Power" to make it convey all the traits and none but the traits that these two young men disliked. Mencken and others accepted the thesis of the Puritan bogy as basic. The enemy was defined, and the battle could proceed. The issue was the fate of the American artist.

In order to create his straw man, Brooks used both psychological and historical criticism with acute insight but little regard for historical facts. The rational intensity of the Puritan ideal, he found, was a valuable trait for the starting of a new civilization; but as that civilization became extensive rather than intensive the social dominance of the New England mind fettered the growth of a new culture. By the fixity of his ideal for the inner life, the Puritan cut off the possibility of moral development and forced the "lofty and inspired sophist" Emerson and others into a formless transcendentalism. On the other hand, the Puritan settlement of all conflicts of the inner life made it possible to turn attention to the problem of subduing a wilderness and developed a practical materialism which tended to absorb vital energies. Moral inhibitions thus conspired with business success to divorce the American tradition from life.

The half-truth of this analysis was true enough to hurt, and it seemed to Brooks and his friends to be a kind of revelation. The weaknesses that Brooks found in contemporary American culture were real, even though his explanation of their causes was oversimplified. His own career as a critic is involved at all stages in this hypothesis: its statement (1908–1913), its application to specific cases (1913–1932), and its defense by a historical re-creation of the cultural past (after 1936).

In *America's Coming-of-Age* (1915) Brooks is on firmer ground because he is speaking of the present and the immediate past, and his historical distortion plays a smaller part in his analysis. In this book he sees the Puritan duality of view become a mere distinction between "Highbrow" and "Lowbrow." Literature had cast its lot with the thin moral earnestness of the "Highbrow" and had entered a sphere where life was rejected. There were two kinds of writing, and there were two publics. Each was only half human because of the rejection of the other. Only such a synthesis as Walt Whitman had attempted could bring them together and form a socialized individualism. America had a tradition if she would but recognize it.

The next step was to apply the thesis in detail to specific cases. After several lesser experiments, Brooks settled upon Mark Twain as the perfect American example of this dilemma; for he, more than any other, presented the case of the artist in the new, modern, and floating universe, a keen intelligence in a sturdy body, dragged down into the past by a moral tradition that his mind rejected, lured into the future by a chaos of forces in which he could discover no moral synthesis. *The Ordeal of Mark Twain* (1920) is the culmination of Brooks' thought on this problem, for Mark Twain faced the dilemma and succumbed to it, a noble but pathetic failure. To make his thesis tight, the critic deliberately dug out and then over-stressed the buried psychological forces which had warped Twain's aesthetic career: the comparative cultural naïveté of the Mississippi Valley in which he was born, the Calvinistic inheritance from his mother, his bondage through his wife and his friend Howells to a false code of respectability in letters. His original genius, so the reader must infer from the evidence of his imperfect but powerful work, had been blighted in turn by each of the three factors against which the literary radicals were directing their attack: provincialism, Puritanism, and the "professors." With the defeat of the individual within him, he could only revert to his pioneer heritage and speak for the race character rather than for himself. "Has the American writer today," asks Brooks, "the same excuse for missing his vocation?"

Overdrawn as is this portrait, it is the most vigorous account to date of the curious and typical phenomenon presented in Mark Twain: the high-spirited humorist with the heavy heart, the bitter satirist who could not resist the temptation to torture himself with barbs meant for others, the sensitive artist who never developed a mature and formal art. In spite of the tirade of protest which the book immediately aroused, no critic of Twain has since been able to ignore this analysis. It has provoked others into an honest exploration and reevaluation of the American cultural inheritance.

Brooks survived the hubbub and brought out in a few years a "revision" in which he took back nothing. Doggedly he turned to Henry James as typical of a second possible reaction to the dilemma of the American artist. Mark Twain had surrendered; James tried the outward avenue of escape to Europe, in common with Howells, Henry Adams, and a whole company of lesser but no less sensitive spirits. *The Pilgrimage of Henry James* (1925) uses the same thesis of the blighted genius and the same method of psychological analysis to illustrate a second type of aesthetic failure. For James achieved his "high passivity" early in life when he was unable to participate in the Civil War. He would be the spectator rather than the manager of life. He would analyze, in innumerable expatriate Americans like himself, the division in his own soul. But the excesses of morbid psychology which had made his study of Mark Twain so unacceptable to many were now become pathological in Brooks himself. The dilemma was in command of the critic as well as of his subject, and a nervous breakdown resulted. The mirror was clouded beyond the possibility of a clear image.

It was this mirror which was next held up to the "lofty and inspired sophist," for Emerson's centrality in American cultural history must be explained if the thesis were to hold. The writing of this, Brooks' crucial book, was interrupted by its author's own breakdown, 1927–1932, when other American authors were migrating to Europe. *Emerson and Others,* containing six episodes, appeared in 1927. When its revision, *Emerson,* appeared as a completed study in 1932, a new note was struck in the final paragraph: "At last there was left only a sense of presence . . . the universe had become his house in which to live." Emerson alone of the prototypes of failure failed to fail. He had a narrow escape, but he emerged from the ordeal as a guide toward a possible solution rather than as the obviously planned example of defeat. Lofty sophistry had become dynamic idealism.

With the publication of the vigorous *Freeman* essays of earlier years as *Sketches in Criticism* (1932), the first phase of Brooks' work came to a close. His work as radical critic for the attack was completed. He believed that he had succeeded in presenting the case against aesthetic and spiritual sterility by exposing the falsity of the tradition of ideality and had opened the way for a reconstructed idealism. From now on he would devote his energies to the constructive spadework of supplying America with her "usable past." Lewis Mumford in *Sticks and Stones* (1924), *The Golden Day* (1926), and *The Brown Decades* (1931) had already demonstrated how this might be done by the application of a dominant thesis to the history of the arts and letters. In 1927 this would have been Brooks' method also, but in 1936, when *The Flowering of New England, 1815–1865* appeared, he was ready to take a more objective view—to let the past tell its own story. No nearer than he ever was to a systematic moral philosophy, he gives us in the person of his alter ego, in *The Opinions of Oliver Allston* (1941), his matured position as an idealist turning from the attack to the defense.

Because he was fresh from Emerson, the mid-century period was the obvious one with which to open his series of studies in cultural history. But his plan was chronological, extending from *The World of Washington Irving* (1944), through *The Times of Melville and Whitman* (1947) and *New England: Indian Summer, 1865–1915* (1940), to a projected volume on his own era to 1914. The Colonial period, with its Puritans, was omitted because nationalism rather than Puritanism now seemed to be the key to the American tradition; and the psychological method was abandoned in favor of an invented method of aesthetic sociology. These later books move swiftly and vividly across the surface of the cultural past, applying the techniques of critical biography to society, painting the moving picture of a composite national personality in its evolving configurations. By deliberately limiting his range and defining a single achievable task, Brooks has converted, for himself at least, the malaise of the twenties into a single original work of aesthetic and historical criticism. More literature than literary history—they even suggest the method of historical fiction—these books give full scope to his sense of personality, his love of the picturesque, and his delight in "the literary life."

### 3

The careers of Bourne and Brooks demonstrate that literary radicalism without a philosophic base or a constructive program is inadequate to form a movement. In the early stages of their attack they drew to themselves a substantial following; but their demand that literary criticism come to terms with modern American man and his society posited the need for a moral and social philosophy which they were not prepared to supply. Theirs was the hopeful but always inconclusive voice of liberalism *per se*. Even in the early twenties, when Brooks, like Ludwig Lewisohn and later Matthew Josephson—in his *Portrait of the Artist as American* (1930)—was concentrating on psychological criticism, strongly influenced by Freud, others in the group of literary radicals, like Waldo Frank, Max Eastman, and John

Reed, were moving toward the dialectical materialism of Marx and making it a social cause. All were being drawn away from traditional aesthetic and ethical bases of literary criticism to the study of man and society with the aid of the techniques of social science. In spite of Brooks' later assertion that he had always been an idealist, the method indicated by him and the other literary radicals was that of empirical criticism. If a new morality were needed, and if experience rather than tradition were to supply it, the new social sciences rather than the old philosophies must provide the dogma and the method. Brooks' rediscovery of idealism in Emerson, and Stuart Sherman's final and reluctant acceptance of Dreiser were but two sides of the same coin, both reversals of earlier positions. The root issue was philosophic; the choice between idealism and naturalism. Brooks, like Emerson, would rediscover the ideal by fresh and fearless analysis of living man and nature.

Meanwhile Theodore Dreiser was fumbling his way toward a naturalistic moral basis for art, and H. L. Mencken was his prophet. Like many another artist, Dreiser was himself very nearly inarticulate in his attempts at critical analysis. His one volume of criticism, *Hey Rub-a-dub-dub* (1920), does little more than echo the complaints of his fellows without their sustaining idealism. His chapter on "The Essential Tragedy of Life" echoes Mark Twain's despair in the helpless, hopeless state of arrogant man, protesting against the "truth" that he, like all other phenomena of the universal machine, is nothing more than a cog himself. That on "Life, Art, and America" is a bitter protest against the division in American life, so much more clearly defined by Brooks' terms, Highbrow and Lowbrow. Dreiser's work lay in the development of the new art of fiction initiated by Norris and Crane, not in criticism. His indignation sought and found a creative idiom.

But without adequate criticism it might well have remained unappreciated for at least his lifetime. Largely because of Mencken's essay (1917), the acceptance or rejection of Dreiser became the test of a literary critic's contact with his times. Mencken could perform this service only because he had long before worked out for himself a naturalistic philosophy which could serve as the tool of critical analysis. His book on *The Philosophy of Friedrich Nietzsche* (1908) is the key to his subsequent career. The German philosopher had given him a formula for dealing with metaphysical and ethical questions for which Dreiser had only an instinctive and unrationalized feeling. It also supplied him with a political and social philosophy which divided him sharply from those critics who found in the Marxian dialectic a similarly useful ideology with which to describe and evaluate the material universe. Although a literary radical like Bourne and Brooks, his social and political philosophy was more akin to the reactionary views of Brownell, More, and Babbitt than to those of Eastman and Frank.

In a deliberately naïve and charming series of reminiscences, *Happy Days* (1940), *Newspaper Days* (1941), and *Heathen Days* (1943), Mencken has given us an intimate picture of his boyhood and early manhood in Baltimore. His attack on the provincialism of his contemporaries was firmly rooted in his own attachment to the "immemorial lares and penates." He could never be long separated from Baltimore—was, in fact, Baltimore incarnate. The child of a German cigar maker, he knew creature comfort if not luxury, from his early years—a shoddy but none the less private school, summers in the near-by country, a home library of modest scope if not over-refined taste, a hand printing press of his own in the comfortable house on Hollins Street which was always his home to his later years. His years on the Baltimore *Evening Herald* merely intensified his sense of values in immediate experience and made it forever impossible for him to admit even the slightest divorce between life and books.

He soon knew that he was one of those people that are born to write, and he did fairly well around 1900–1902 with short stories in the *Criterion,* "the only solvent survivor of the literary movement of the nineties." Although he thus took his place in that movement, its lapse of vitality between 1900 and 1910 caught him in his third decade when his career as a writer would normally have taken shape. Instead of continuing with fiction, he tells us, he became interested in Shaw, and through him in Nietzsche. "After that I was a critic of ideas, and I have remained one ever since."

Most of Nietzsche's dominant concepts sank into his mind and remained his substitute for the decalogue. The issue, as he came to see it, lay between Dionysus and Apollo, between doubt and dogma. His own choice, both for himself and for his age, was clear: "The civilized world has disposed of supernaturalism and is engaged in a destructive criticism of the old faith's residuum—morality." A Puritan had arisen to challenge Puritans, a scholar to call the professors to account.

With the technique of doubt went other of Nietzsche's dominant ideas— the aristocracy of the Superman in a class-divided society, the antipathy for the proletariat, the deterministic biological approach to birth and love and death in a world in which man and woman have distinctive functions, and, most important of all, the fluent morality of power as a substitute for the codified morality of the Christian tradition. Thus Mencken had what most of his contemporaries lacked, a feeling that he stood on firm intellectual ground. His enemies too were sharply defined: the Marxists would hate him in spite of a common materialistic basis, and the Puritans, whether moralists who clung sincerely to the Christian code or "professors" who based an aesthetic ideality on that code, would be his sworn enemies for life.

Mencken's style changed from lucid exposition to shock and bombast when he had thus taken his stand. As the philosopher of doubt he joined the forces of the literary radicals and added to theirs a much louder and firmer voice than had yet been heard. Even his titles reflect his irony and his defiance: *A Book of Burlesques* (1916); *A Little Book in C Major* (1916); *A Book of Prefaces* (1917); *In Defense of Women* (1917); and *Damn! A Book of Calumny* (1917). Then came the first edition of *The American Language* (1919), with the first collection of the *Prejudices* (1919), and Mencken had found the two principal outlets for his message.

The *Prejudices* are the howls of a lone wolf in the wilderness of hypocrisy, a character equaled in historical picturesqueness in our literature only by the lone eagle of Whitman, and one adopted almost as calculatingly. It howled its way through six series, 1919–1927, and a supplementary one of *Selected Prejudices* in the latter year. It was heard from the pages of the *Smart Set,* which Mencken edited with George Jean Nathan from 1914 to 1923, and from those of the *American Mercury,* which he founded with Nathan in 1924 but carried on alone throughout most of its career to 1933. It even agitates the scholarly pages of *The American Language.*

This is the forensic voice of H. L. Mencken, especially in the middle years when he was taking an aggressive part in the battle of books and ideas. Those who heard it laughed, and he laughed with them, but it was the laughter of a Swift or a Voltaire. Rebellious youth in the postwar years took the *Prejudices* as its gospel of revolt, but unfortunately their very timeliness dates them. Mencken diagnosed the political, social, and cultural ills of his day, swiftly and with precision. His techniques are surgical, and his operations both sudden and major; but his patients usually survive unless they are deliberately murdered as indistinguishable from the diseases from which they suffer. Starting off bravely with a series of literary appraisals, the first volume of essays exposes the pretensions and the achievements of both small and great. But with the second series the *Prejudices* hit their stride. They are primarily political and sociological; only incidentally literary and aesthetic.

Mencken's major quarrels are two: with the Christian moral code whether in its pure state or in a diluted state, and with government by the people, whether under a democratic or a communistic form. These two themes are developed with every conceivable variation through the pages, and they finally emerge into books of their own. Nowhere in our literature is there so thoroughly damning an analysis of our political and social assumptions as in *Notes on Democracy* (1926). Is there any record that Hitler knew of it? When he turns to "The National Letters" with his two measures, the morality of power and the government by aristocracy, he describes both the disease and his remedy for it with flamboyant challenge; the lack of "a distinguished and singular excellence, a signal national quality, a ripe and stimulating flavor," in our national letters; the lack of a "civilized aristocracy" in our society. In spite of the easy assumption of his critics, Mencken was never in his own eyes, or in truth, a clown. He was always in dead earnest, and his whiplashes are all from a single whip.

Mencken's essays may fade with time except for his occasional flashes of insight into the work of his contemporaries, but *The American Language* (1919), with its four revisions and its two supplements, will stand. Fortunately the partial suspension of free speech when the United States entered the First World War in 1917 turned his attention from his column on contemporary issues in the Baltimore *Evening Sun* and allowed him time to work on his long absorbing interest in American speech. For this work he combined the instinct of the scholar with the quick wit and shrewd insight of the journalist. The result was a book that, like the *Leaves of Grass,* grew by accretion and revision more in the manner of a living organism than of a card index. In itself a gigantic work of literature, it has given the American people their language as Emerson and Whitman gave them their literature by cutting the umbilical cord. Mencken does not deny the English, and behind that the Indo-Teutonic, origins of that language. He merely denies the authority of the historical scholar to legislate for the present as well as the past. By that simple device he has given new life to scholarship in one field of major importance. This is his final reconciliation with the "professors," some of whom like T. R. Lounsbury had been themselves working for the same ends by less sensational methods, but they came to him with the white flag. They found him at the old address on Hollins Street.

## 4

Literary radicalism could go no further in protest than Mencken took it. It was at this point that the conservatives, the followers of Apollo rather than of Dionysus, came back into the fray with armor refurbished. The death of Sherman in 1926 and of Brownell in 1928 seemed to signal the launching of the neo-humanist movement as a movement. Norman Foerster called the survivors together in *Humanism and America* (1930), and the defense took the offensive. The brief and belligerent course of the movement is subject for a later chapter, but its roots go back into the early part of the century.

These men were not "defenders of ideality"; they admitted the necessity for a new deal. With Brooks and Mencken they drew no sharp line between ethics and aesthetics, between conduct and beauty, and set to work on a critical analysis of the American tradition, rejecting, also, more than they accepted. But with the idealists they rejected the concept of an open universe, the inductive method. The twentieth century world, they agreed, with its scientific advances, its industrial and political upheavals, its confusion of directions and standards, must be freshly explored; but the guiding principles of that adventure must come from within, from what used to be called the conscience rather than from the impact of natural and social forces.

William Crary Brownell was their first articulate spokesman. As Brooks had given leadership to the radicals, so Brownell, as early as 1901, had formulated the principles which were to guide his own work and that of the conservatives. Although never connected with a university, he was, in the terminology of the young radicals, a "professor" of the deepest dye. He was academic in the sense of the founders of the American Academy of Arts and Letters in 1904, with membership limited to fifty. He believed that great literature is born of great rules, and great rules are born of trained minds. He was aristocratic and antiromantic by instinct, but he believed that literature is integral with life. No aesthetic could in his judgment be complete which did not stand on the Christian ethic of character, the Platonic doctrine of form, and the Aristotelian reliance upon reason.

Brownell's short period of training on the old New York *World* and the Godkin *Nation,* and his forty years as literary adviser to the Scribner firm, 1888–1928, were in a worldly sense almost completely uneventful. Living in the geographical and economic heart of American life, his temperament remained calm but not remote; he was his own university.

Brownell began his career as a critic with two books in praise of modern realistic art, *French Traits* (1889) and *French Art* (1892), and it is on this evidence that Stuart Sherman later assigned him to the "Party of Nature." But in spite of his apparently sociological and scientific premises, derived from his study of Taine and his admiration for the French, the germ of the later neo-humanist movement is present in his corollaries. He saw a renewed emphasis upon personality as humanity's natural response to the leveling effects of the modern impersonal view of nature. Even though he used the terms "temperament" and "personality" in a sense quite contrary to that of Babbitt and More, as descriptive of fundamental man rather than of individual eccentricities, he heralds rather than contradicts the later distinction between "humanism" and "humanitarianism" which became the battle cry of the movement.

It was in this emphasis upon personality that his humanism emerged. In two books, *Victorian Prose Masters* (1901) and *American Prose Masters* (1909), he attempted evaluations of British and American culture of the nineteenth century through analyses of outstanding writers. The idea of doing these studies of prose masters was doubtless suggested, as the parallel titles would imply, by Stedman's studies of Victorian and American poets; but Brownell's position is more judicial, his analyses more probing, his method much more objective than Stedman's. He took Arnold rather than the American for his guide.

The essay on Arnold is the core of the two volumes, for in evaluating the British man and critic he presents his own apology. The distinguishing quality of Arnold was that "he developed his nature as well as directed his work in accordance with the definite ideal of reason." The man and the writing were one, a carefully wrought work of art. Culture was identified thus with personality, and personality with an impersonal ideal that sought "first of all completeness of harmonious development" in the Greek and Christian inspirations. An apostle rather than an artist, Arnold stood alone among English critics for "his candor, his measure of disinterestedness, his faculty of extracting their application from the precedents indicated by culture." Brownell's prose masters are judged by the degree to which they achieved this standard, and the fact that they all fell so far short of it makes the reading of the essays depressing as well as illuminating.

In his last four books Brownell subordinated his judgments of individuals and developed his critical theory in general terms. *Criticism* (1914) and *Standards* (1917) state his case. Criticism is an art in itself, to be carefully distinguished from the techniques of creative art and of reviewing alike, both of which are particular and specialized. "It is its function to discern and characterize the abstract qualities informing the concrete expression of the artist." The critic should know history, aesthetics, and philosophy, but rely on no one of them to the exclusion of the others. With Sainte-Beuve, Brownell feels "that our liking anything is not enough, that it is necessary to know further whether we are right in liking it." As there is no universal taste, critical impressionism is inadequate, reason alone provides sound basis for judgment. The weakness in this exposition is the vagueness of Brownell's definition of his standards. In the two essays he merely asserts that standards are needed, that they exist always in impersonal personality—but he does not himself say what they are.

*The Genius of Style* (1924) and *Democratic Distinction in America* (1927) elaborate his position without further defining or developing it. They are a call to a "general spirit of order that is organic and of movement that is rhythm." Our democracy must cease to associate distinction with reserve, as did the Romans, and learn to associate it with development, as did the Greeks and the French. The "vice of sensation," as illustrated in Dreiser and the modern school, must give way to the style which is the expression of the inner and universal personality, thereby "supplying its helter-skelter of idioms and episodes with organic order, regularizing the eccentricities of its rhythms, rationalizing its artificial intensities, and elevating its grosser naturalisms."

## 5

Although Paul Elmer More and Irving Babbitt have been credited (or blamed) with founding the neo-humanist movement in American criticism, they did little more than develop and formalize Brownell's later position. Their thought, like his, stemmed from an enthusiasm for French culture; took inspiration from Greek and Christian ideals; linked literature with the graphic arts and music; battled both with academic classicism and with romanticism; called for decorum, harmony, and standards referable to the inner and moral man; combated the current naturalism in letters; like his, failed of finally reducing to a moral basis the judgment of art.

Against the literary radicalism of Mencken and the trend of thought reflected in the work of Dreiser, Lewis, O'Neill, Sandburg, Dos Passos, and the majority of the creative writers of the twenties and thirties, Babbitt waged relentless war. He could even descend from his professorial chair at Harvard and put on the gloves offered by Mencken, his leading adversary: "To reduce criticism indeed," he flung at him, "to the satisfaction of a temperamental urge, to the uttering of one's gustos and disgustos (in Mr. Mencken's case chiefly the latter) is to run counter to the very etymology of the word which implies discrimination and judgment."

The young men who, in the twenties, were delighted by the broadsides fired monthly from the pages of the *American Mercury* were equally delighted by this counterblast from so worthy an opponent on the side of the "professors." Secretly, no doubt, many of them distrusted the Mencken wit and resented the Mencken iconoclasm. They flocked to Babbitt's Harvard courses in French literature and the history of criticism as boys run to a good fist fight, for here they found wit and timeliness reinforced by the assurance of tradition. Here was a Brahmin—more truly than the now pale ghosts of Longfellow, Lowell, and Holmes—a worthy Brahmin come to battle with the confusion of the times.

Babbitt was a philosopher of literature, a student of its theory rather than an analyst of its product. His aim was to provide others with the means of judgment; he criticized criticism rather than creative art. His six major works, from *Literature and the American College* (1908) to his final collection of essays *On Being Creative* (1932)—the miscellany *Spanish Character* was posthumous (1940)—are elaborations and applications of a single thesis: that contemporary currents of aesthetic thinking must be corrected by a return to the classical concept of humanity as distinct from both God and nature.

*The New Laokoon* (1910) applies this thesis to the graphic arts and music, challenging the confusion of poetry with the other arts and the consequent breakdown of standards. *The Masters of Modern French Criticism* (1912), his nearest approach to a study of literary men in themselves and his best work as a critic in his own right, traces the anarchy of French romantic criticism from Chateaubriand to Renan, with Sainte-Beuve's development into judicial traditionalism as its solution. In *Rousseau and Romanticism* (1919) he came to grips with his dragon, naturalism (both sentimental and scientific), in an exhaustive analysis of the romantic fallacy as he saw it, and in *Democracy and Leadership* (1924) he extended his thesis, as did Brownell, to its political implications in the false theory of natural rights as opposed to the just theory of humanistic and aristocratic democracy.

Babbitt himself conceived these books as a single work and repeated his central dogma in each of his prefaces before proceeding to its special application. As readily as Van Wyck Brooks, he bent the past to his purposes. His theory of cultural history, in brief, is that the humanism of the Renaissance in its break with the authority of the church, attempting to give man his integrity as man by distinguishing him from God, had fallen into a counter error. The experimental method of Bacon, whom Babbitt took as a symbol of the fallacy of the whole scientific fraternity, had identified man with nature and had fallen into the error of naturalistic monism in trying to escape from theological monism. Specialization and technology were the results, and man was no longer man. Instead of mastering nature with the power and progress thus released, man had become a mere cog in the inhuman machine.

From the error of specialization and technology, the second error followed as an inevitable consequence—the error symbolized in Rousseau. In his effort to regain his place in the universe, man had developed his feelings rather than his mind. Sentiment was added to scientific naturalism, and the anarchy of the romantic movement resulted. Pity for humanity took the place of respect for self; humanitarianism was substituted for genuine humanism.

The terms romanticism, naturalism, humanitarianism, humanism—each defined clearly and used consistently—provide the basic structure of Babbitt's position, and were accepted in these meanings by his peers and his followers. The first three describe the progressive disintegration of modern man; the fourth describes the corrective. Only by reasserting the balanced belief of the Greeks in a dualistic universe could man stand free once more from his world and the error be corrected. But in one of his last attempts at definition contributed to *Humanism in America* (1930), even he admits that ethical self-control might be applied on the level of religion and, by a union of all faiths, might create a new faith. He died soon enough to avoid the necessity of conversion and so saved himself from becoming, at least in the technical sense, a saint.

Babbitt's earliest disciple was his contemporary Paul Elmer More—disciple only because the meeting with Babbitt, when they were both students of Hindu literature at Harvard, marked the major turning point in More's intellectual development, and his friendship with Babbitt held him throughout life to a strict acceptance of humanistic principles much less suited to his temperament than they were to that of his more vigorous friend. For More, if not a saint, was something more than a philosopher in the logical and dialectic senses; he was a secular monk. The cloister—whether his rural retreat at Shelburne, New Hampshire, where he formed his personality and his doctrine, or his final home at Princeton, New Jersey, where he exerted his greatest influence—was much more his natural habitat than the editorial offices of the *Independent,* the New York *Evening Post,* and the *Nation,* of which he was successively an editor from 1901 until 1914. Like Brownell, More made a hermitage of the metropolis.

But his mind had been cast at Shelburne even though his residence in that mountain retreat spanned only a little over two years (1897–1899). Like Walden, it became the symbol of an attitude rather than of a place, and it gave its name to a long series of critical essays, more than half of which are specific studies of authors, only a minority essays in critical theory. For, unlike Babbitt, More was a reader of books for the books' sake. He was a literary philosopher only because he felt the need of principles for judgment, a contender in the forum only when he felt that he had been attacked.

Appropriately the first volume of the first series of Shelburne Essays (eleven volumes, 1904–1921) opens with "A Hermit's Notes on Thoreau," for *Walden* was one of the earliest discoveries of More's retirement. Reading it on the banks of the Androscoggin, this "hermit after a mild Epicurean fashion of my own" learned the value of contemplation rather than of nature herself, for at the start of his serious thought about literature and life he was deeply immersed in the romantic doctrines that he and Babbitt were so violently to attack. Here are judgments of a mystic rather than of a humanist; More, at this time, was deeply engrossed in the translations which became *A Century of Indian Epigrams* (1898), and he was searching, like Emerson before him, in the Hindu rather than in the Greek or Christian tradition for confirmation of his romantic insights into the mystery of life.

The mood did not endure for long. Before the first volume of the Essays was complete, the lawgiver was crowding the poet. In Buddhism More found, not confirmation for the life of the soul alone, but the necessity for dualism.

Religion must not be confused with the ways of the world, the things of God with the things of Caesar; but it is not necessary to renounce either one. Reading into Christ's advice to the rich young man a relative rather than an absolute injunction (*If you would,* renounce . . .), he arrived at a position in which both levels of experience might be accepted and their interactions become the subject of a life's study. The long series of critical essays, many of which were first published in magazines that he edited, was thus launched in the terms which Babbitt later shaped into dogma.

More's method was his own. Each of the literary essays takes a single proposition in this relationship between the law for man and the law for thing, as discoverable in the work of a single author, and develops it into at once an insight and a proof. Often warped to their respective theses, these essays nevertheless are the most ambitious and often the most penetrating body of judicial literary criticism in our literature.

"We think," More quoted from Halifax in the ninth volume of the series, *Aristocracy and Justice* (1915), "that a wise Mean, between these barbarous Extreams, is that which self-Preservation ought to dictate to our Wishes." Even in these excursions into political and social theory, More retained his ideal of moderation and balance. Although in forensic combat he could deliver blow for blow with the best of his adversaries, his own temperament seems to reflect this moderation. His most dogmatic assertions seem mild because they are couched in the quiet tones of persuasion, irony, and sweet reason. The main thesis of an essay is insinuated rather than forced into the reader's consciousness, its supporting evidences and arguments are assembled with the casual ease of a limpid current, the style flows and bends to a conclusion at or near the point of starting. The proposition is round and apparently whole; it can be attacked only by exposing the premise.

More's semiretirement on the fringe of the Princeton campus—where he gave graduate courses and built up a devoted following—was spent mainly in the creation of a twentieth century neo-Platonism which would embrace the best of the Christian tradition but skirt the depths of religion itself. His series The Greek Tradition opened in 1917 with *Platonism,* closed in 1931 with *Christ the Word.* Yet in *Pages from an Oxford Diary* (1924) he tells us that, as a pretended don and philosopher, he sought God in "the universe as a manifestation of one comprehensive design," and learned "to walk humbly with God, never doubting, whatever befall, that His will is good, and that His law is right."

The New Shelburne Essays, which were initiated with *The Demon of the Absolute* (1928), bear evidence of More's development from inquiring sympathy for the individual writer to an organized attack on the naturalistic movement in modern literature, particularly American and French. Any creed which rests on the "absolute," he believed was false for that reason alone, and the effort of modern writers to identify man with nature invalidated their work as art. Thus Joyce's psychology was "nothing more than a theory of objective reality which will correspond to the inner stream of consciousness"; his literary work was therefore "in English a more or less exotic offshoot of a literary movement whose regular and logical development [occurred] in France"; and "the acknowledged fathers of the whole movement were the three Americans: Poe and Whitman and Henry James." To Babbitt's battle cry of denunciation of the dominant trend in modern literature, More thus brought the evidence of his wide and careful reading, but the result is no happier. The role of Jeremiah is not one to inspire affection even though it may create followers; and Paul Elmer More, by nature a man of quiet ways and sympathetic interest in books, men, and ideas, did not wear it any too comfortably.

On an impressionable young graduate student at Harvard in 1904, Stuart P. Sherman, the impact of Babbitt in person and of More in his essays came as a light and a way. No one of the younger disciples so wholeheartedly accepted the doctrine of the masters or echoed their ideas with more vehemence. But his loyalty sprang from enthusiasm rather than from mature conviction. In spite of Sherman's intense devotion for a time to the distinction between the law for man and the law for thing—reflected in his study of Matthew Arnold and in his first collection of essays, *On Contemporary Literature* (1917)—his career as a whole is that of an impressionist in temperamen' and in mind; hence his inconsistencies and the intellectual dilemmas which pursued him to the end of his comparatively short life. Let it be remembered that, before his confession of humanistic faith, he had espoused positivism and had soaked himself in the English romantic poets at Williams College; and at Harvard he had turned from the dry scholarship of Kittredge, which he later attacked openly, not at first to the criticism of Babbitt, but to the living drama of George Pierce Baker. Let it also be remembered that, long before he resigned from his professorship at the University of Illinois in 1924 to take the editorship of the New York *Herald Tribune* "Books," he had come out strongly (though with qualifications) for both Sinclair Lewis and W. C. Brownell. Too much has been made of his apostasy to the humanistic movement. What the situation called for, he wrote early in 1923 ("W. C. Brownell"), was a mediator who understood and valued that which both the "Party of Culture" and the "Party of Nature" desired, and who could "unite their complementary virtues in a common purpose." By temperament both an aristocrat and a literary radical (he became during the First World War almost what would later have been called fascist), he was drawn into extreme statements on both sides of the critical issues of the day. He attacked

Mencken, in *Americans* (1922), for his denial of an American tradition and pictured himself in the same book as remarking to More, "I am obliged to lean a bit forward to counterbalance the stubbornness of your Toryism."

Sherman, the natural aristocrat, the man of sensibility and taste, was as much as Bourne or Brooks or Mencken a literary radical throughout his life. His acceptance of the Babbitt-More role of Jeremiah was a passing phase; at the end he returned to his belief in vitality as a higher value than moderation. After having denounced Dreiser's "barbaric naturalism" in 1915, he had the courge in 1925 to accept *An American Tragedy* as "the worst written great novel in the world"—but none the less great for its moral integrity and its final mastery of the novel form. In those ten years, the critic had not changed —nor had the novelist. In spite of apparent difference in philosophy and art, they had been working, each in his way, for the "emotional discovery of America" which Sherman proclaimed in one of his last public utterances.

6

Between 1925 and 1930, the neo-humanist movement lapsed in the excitement of a growing creative literature and a giddy stock market; the battle of the books appeared to have been fought to a stalemate. The radicals gave evidence of rout; they had produced no philosophy upon which a critical movement could be based, and no method by which it could proceed. The conservatives had proved equally ineffective. Their warning had apparently not been heard, and their voices were becoming shrill—or silent. Yet it can readily be seen in the perspective of another literary generation that the critical ferment of these years marked a genuine renaissance of cultural interest and understanding. Old assumptions had been painfully dislodged, new forces had been submitted to scrutiny, the orientation of the American tradition to the twentieth century world had been undertaken. The stalemate was apparent rather than real.

The critical controversies of the thirties and forties were to turn on sharper issues and to form more clearly defined schools than were possible earlier. But the fact that literature and the theories about it seemed, by 1930, to be of public consequence was due in large part to the crusading years of Henry Seidel Canby, a professor who early broke from New England cloisters and entered the literary market place. Like Carl Van Doren of the *Nation,* and later Stuart Sherman of the New York *Herald Tribune* Books, Canby refused to share either the esoteric zeal of fact-finding literary scholars or the careless promotionism of much current magazine and newspaper reviewing. In the Literary Review of the New York *Evening Post,* and after 1924 in the *Saturday Review of Literature,* as well as in his own critical and autobiographical writing, he did more than anyone else to bring the scholarly standards of the university into working relationship with the productive energies of writers, publishers, reviewers, and critics.

In the universities themselves, the new lines of thought were already becoming manifest before 1930. The academic antecedents of the neo-humanist controversy of that year have already been traced, but those of socio-literary and purely aesthetic criticism, the dominant trends of the later decades, had been indicated mainly in the work, respectively, of two "professors," Vernon L. Parrington and Joel Spingarn.

Parrington's *Main Currents in American Thought* (1927–1930) was, he thought, a history of American literature even though his publishers assigned a more descriptive title when finally the exhaustive work came to press. The product of long years of reading and teaching on the West Coast, it ruffled academic waters—not so much by its author's somewhat forced effort to relate all that is good in the American present to the ideas and accomplishments of Jefferson, as by his success in reevaluating the entire American tradition in political, social, and economic rather than in aesthetic and moral terms. It demonstrated one effective way to relate literature to life in a historical context. The work of the new school of historians, from F. J. Turner to Beard and Schlesinger, seemed now brought to a focus on the problems of American literary history. The reconstruction of our "usable past" that Brooks had called for, and that Calverton, Mumford, and others had attempted, seemed here to have been accomplished by an obscure professor. There was mingled protest and acclaim as reviewers and scholars vied with one another in expressing astonishment. Meanwhile the author, now ready for the honor and the condemnation that were to be showered upon him, died with his third volume unfinished. It was left for later critics and historians to carry forward, in his idiom and by his method, the new synthesis of art and life, the past and the present—and either carefully to avoid the pitfalls of too narrow a social ideology or to accept and develop a criticism based squarely on the Marxian dialectic.

As socio-literary criticism was prepared by 1925 for an overhauling, so the "pure" criticism of art as art was revived and refurbished. To Joel Spingarn, Mencken gave a not too hearty welcome in his "Criticism of Criticism of Criticism" (1919). "Major Spingarn lately served notice upon me that he had abandoned the life of the academic grove for that of the armed array . . . his notions, whatever one may say in opposition to them, are at least magnificently unprofessorial."

Spingarn had been schooled by Lewis E. Gates of Harvard and by Benedetto Croce of Italy. His separation from the academic world in 1911 was complete in fact, but his notions were not so unacademic as Mencken thought.

Possessing a knowledge of critical tradition and method which none of the literary radicals could boast (he had written *A History of Literary Criticism in the Renaissance,* 1899), he did more than anyone else of his generation to supply rationale and method for the analytical criticism of Eliot and the critics of the thirties and forties.

His own work was slight in volume as he, like Babbitt, theorized about criticism rather than practiced it. An experimental poet and anthologist, he produced only two volumes of his own essays, *Creative Criticism* (1917) and *Poetry and Religion* (1924). In the latter year he performed his greatest service to the critical movement in America by gathering the most significant critiques of his time into a volume *Criticism in America: Its Function and Status.* These essays span the period since his own "The New Criticism" (1910), and sum up the achievement of a generation. Brooks and Mencken speak for the literary radicals, Woodberry, Brownell, Babbitt, and Sherman for the reactionaries, and he, Eliot, and Ernest Boyd for the third, and as yet undefined, group.

The roots of Spingarn's theory in America must be sought in the philosophy of Santayana or in the aestheticism of Huneker and the "Bohemians," discussed elsewhere in this work, even though he denied kinship with any specific school. He differs from the Bohemians in denying their effort to validate aesthetic experience in biological science, and in so far allying himself with the humanists. But more truly he reverts to an earlier form of romantic aestheticism represented by Goethe and by Carlyle's essay on Goethe, both of which he approvingly quotes as his text: "The critic's first and foremost duty is to make plain to himself 'what the poet's aim really and truly was, how the task he had to do stood before his eye, and how far, with such materials as were afforded him, he has fulfilled it.'"

"This," says Spingarn, "has been the central problem, the guiding star, of all modern criticism"; but, he adds later, it has not been possible in America because we have had no critics sufficiently disciplined in aesthetics to achieve the exacting demands of close concentration upon the work of art itself. The disease of the age, materialism, has made critics "conceive of philosophy not as a self-creative and independent science, but as merely one, and a very subordinate one, among empirical sciences."

Spingarn's was the academic fault of spinning fine abstractions without engaging himself in the exacting task of doing what he advises. But he prepared the way for Eliot, Ransom, Tate, Blackmur, and a host of others, by objectifying the work of art for the analytical examination of the critic, by cutting away historical and circumstantial factors on the one hand and the critic's own emotional sensibilities on the other, and by stressing the intellectual and dispassionate sensibility to structure which Eliot in "The Perfect

Critic" (1920) defined as the essence of the critical function. But Spingarn's final position was one long step short of Eliot's. He developed no method of procedure. His break with the historical and judicial methods was complete, but he also denied the connection of art with life implicit in impressionism. He wrote despairingly in 1921:

> Critics are constantly carrying on a guerilla warfare of their own, and discovering anew the virtues of individuality, modernity, Puritanism, the romantic spirit or the spirit of the Middle West, the tradition of the pioneers and so on ad infinitum. This holds true of every school of American criticism, "conservative" or "radical"; for all of them a disconnected body of literary theories takes the place of a real philosophy of art.

Our criticism, he concluded, needs education in aesthetic thinking and a wider scholarship, "for taste is after all both the point of departure and the goal."

Spingarn's attempt to isolate literature from the moral and the natural experience of both its creator and its critic succeeded in avoiding, if not in solving, the problems of both the radicals and the conservatives, because for him, and in his judgment for literature, problems of conduct and of value, as well as problems of cause and effect, have no relevance to the analysis and judgment of expression. The work of art makes its own rules and must be judged by them alone. But Spingarn's Crocean formula, as Eliot was to discover, was a needed emphasis on a part rather than a definition of the whole of the critical function. Neither the waste land nor the cathedral could be so readily avoided. The battle of the books had been fought to a conclusion in which much had been revealed, nothing concluded. Before 1930 the renaissance in American criticism thus did little more than keep step with the forces at work in poetry, fiction, and drama which were giving new directions to American literature. The two great tasks of redefining the American cultural tradition and of developing a systematic literary criticism had scarcely begun.

# 69. EDWIN ARLINGTON ROBINSON

T̲HE quiet, straightforward speech in Edwin Arlington Robinson's keynote book, *The Children of the Night* (1897), was first heard amid a babel of other poetic tongues both old and new. Here were the simple words of a great poet, inaudible among bold voices: those of the humanitarian singers, like Edwin Markham in *The Man with the Hoe, and Other Poems* (1899); those of the new naturalists in poetry, like Stephen Crane in *War Is Kind* (1899); or those of the intellectual nationalists in verse, like William Vaughn Moody in "An Ode in Time of Hesitation" (1900). Insistent, too, reverberated the many special accents, the songs of the Western farms (Hamlin Garland and James Whitcomb Riley); songs born of learning in the seventeenth century (Louise Imogen Guiney and Lizette Reese); and, still influential, the Victorian melodies of Gilder, Aldrich, and Stedman, all of whom published collections of their poetry not long after the stillborn *Children of the Night*.

That Robinson approved or disapproved of these "movements," no evidence exists. Nor had he convictions concerning the other cults whose creeds until his death beat against his independent mind, sometimes repudiating his techniques and themes, sometimes claiming both as their very own. He remained quiet, he went his lonely way. Denounce him the innovators could, for he never sloughed off the time-honored forms of the past; claim him they could, for though indifferent to group ideas he had discovered for himself principles dear to imagist or expressionist. To a few individuals he was in debt (as to a few great writers of the past): to Ridgely Torrence, dramatist and poet; perhaps to Richard Hovey, for his American pioneering in Arthurian legend; and to Moody for confirming in him his passion for poetic drama. But in his aloof dedication to poetry he was singularly unaffected by the tides of contemporary criticism discussed in the last chapter. Unlike Babbitt and most of the other controversialists who wrote about criticism without much practicing it, or about literature as an illustration of theory, he was solely interested in the creation of literature itself as an expression of his own soul.

Among the poets whose influence he seems to have felt, William Vaughn

Moody, many-sided, was indeed more than a poetizer of national problems. Born in the same year as Robinson (1869) he had, by 1900, won through his timely ode and by "Gloucester Moors" a public denied his obscure friend. Robinson revered him for his learning, his fine Puritan intelligence, and characteristically for his actual success. Acclaimed as a practical dramatist in *The Great Divide* (1906) and in *The Faith Healer* (1909), Moody still explored a dark transcendental world (Robinson called it "The Valley of the Shadow") in his incomplete metaphysical trilogy of poetic plays (*The Masque of Judgment,* 1900; *The Fire-Bringer,* 1904; *The Death of Eve,* 1912).

It may be said that two kinds of poets bordered the narrow path of Robinson and interested him, adversely and favorably: the "little sonnet men," as he called the faddist craftsmen of his day; and poets like himself under the spell of the enlightenment in reverse, of the melancholy of man's doom. That Robinson owed much to Crane or Moody or to later poets of despair or nihilism is doubtful. By 1897 he had acquired a naturalistic outlook then in its infancy in America, and to this by temperament and experience he remained in bondage all his life. Thus his apparent kinship with movements suggests not plan but accident. Robinson's poetic traits arose from the basic texture of his mind. *The Children of the Night* merely demanded bare and simple words; and no "renaissance" of 1915 can claim his poetry written between the years 1890 and 1896. For the same reasons his adherence to the sonnet, the dramatic monologue, or the narrative was a personal and inevitable choice suited to his psychological purposes. The "new poetry" eventually aided him by enlarging his circle of readers, but at heart he was an adroit adapter of the traditional. "Robinson," says Robert Frost, looking back in the year of his friend's death, "stayed content with the old way to be new."

Shunning, then, the tumult of the critics and the more worldly poets, Robinson wound his solitary horn before his dark tower, an intellectual Childe Roland in our twentieth century literature. Somber, introspective, he reminds us in temperament of his Puritan ancestress Anne Bradstreet and of other New England searchers in the ways of God. Hawthorne, to whose *Scarlet Letter* he was devoted, he resembled not only in his scrutiny of the delicate moral impulses and in his sensitivity to spiritual tragedy, but even in the reticence of his art. Akin to Emerson and Emily Dickinson in their individualism, their sensitivity to fact and thrift of expression, he was at the same time a landmark of the passing of the transcendental faith. Emerson's disregard of evil became in Emily Dickinson a qualified acknowledgment of its power ("the underside of God's divinity"), and now in Robinson a controlled despair at its mastery of life. Emerson's "dawn" faded to Emily Dickinson's light of winter afternoons to Robinson's faint gleam against a blackening sky. He is closer to these than to Crabbe and Browning, of whom he reminds us in his alternate bareness and explicitness, but all such debts, American and European, Robinson seems to cancel in the singular intensity of his art and inner life, which from his earliest to his last days were consecrated to poetry.

A man without a skin, as he admitted, he suffered acutely under poverty, obscurity, and misunderstanding. Finding no positive answer for himself, he still explored the enigmas in other lives, recording these in his verse stencils of souls warped by spiritual conflicts. Endowed with such a temperament, he led during his boyhood at Gardiner, Maine (he was born at Head Tide), and during his two years at Harvard (1891–1893) a life troubled by sensitivity to spiritual unknowns and also by the criteria of worldly success, to which he could never conform. Illness in his family, economic instability, and the tragedies of "Tilbury Town's" unfortunates, unveiled more bitterly through his own capacity for pain than to these individuals themselves, confirmed him in his misgivings concerning himself and human life. From the time when he sat on the kitchen floor of the Maine farmhouse reciting verse to his mother, his course was set. He would write. His compensations were his discovery of the release in creating poetry; the friendships of understanding spirits in Gardiner and Cambridge; and his dream, not without emulation as he watched Moody, that he would be, that he *was*, a poet.

Robinson needed courage. His "darkening hill" lay steep before him. The severe musing of *The Children of the Night* on the "faith within the fear" or the stern elevation of *Captain Craig*, the tale of a New England ne'er-do-well, would hardly convert readers who preferred, he said,

> Songs without souls, that flicker for a day
> To vanish in the irrevocable night.

Acceptance was slow, even after the advocacy of Theodore Roosevelt, who secured for him a position in the New York Customhouse where he struggled unhappily for five years. To keep body and soul together he had already checked loads of stone in the subway. New York, with its infinite drama of human lives, was essential to his art. Amid these and later, happier experiences such as a stay in England and many sojourns in the MacDowell Colony, he patiently stuck to his craft until he outstripped "the little sonnet-men." His unity with himself was complete; life now meant the creation of poetry.

Although his two plays, *Van Zorn* (1914) and *The Porcupine* (1915), were unsuccessful in establishing a poetical theater, *The Town Down the River* (1910) and *The Man Against the Sky* (1916) consolidated his fame. He now struck out boldly in longer poems, complex, psychological narratives, expansions of his research into the paradoxes in human character, into the "small, satanic sort of kinks" which betray us all. Some of these poems, like the later narratives, explored the twisted minds of men and women in the trap of modern life; others—*Merlin, Lancelot,* and *Tristram*—while grappling with similar problems, vivified intellectually the Arthurian legends. The precise quality of Robinson's eminence was, at the time of his death in 1935, still controversial, but no one challenged the nobility of his contribution, in both form and content. He had fulfilled himself and had asked in ways unlike those of any other poet the old unanswerable questions.

Attempts to connect Robinson, as a symbolist, with war, with the problems of society, or with the decay of our civilization have been generally unsuccessful, except in his very last poems. He absorbed much of our science and economics as well as our lore concerning the subconscious mind; yet his concern was with the individual in his relations to one or two other individuals, or, in one human personality, with the baffling connection with an inscrutable darkness in which, hardly visible, glimmered a crystal of light, a refraction of "The Word." All the dynamic forces of society's evolution are in his poetry, but they are concentrated in particular moral problems. His assimilative power was enormous; he was the thoughtful modern man, excessively sensitized, contemplating through the screen of a constitutional melancholy the twentieth century world.

Robinson offered no synthesis, no philosophy, but to formulate his teasing, repetitious questions he employed a genius which was more dramatic than lyrical or narrative. The reader may generalize, if he wishes, on his opinions concerning death, fate, time, "success in failure," love, marriage, frustration, and these he may transmute for Robinson into terms of society; but the poet himself merely poses endless interrogations on special cases. Hence he was never humanitarian, never proletarian, never national; and he was Puritan, like the most distinguished poetical descendants of the Puritans such as Emily Dickinson and Emerson (whom he deeply admired), as he faced moral riddles with the conviction that of all themes these were the ones most worthy of the poet.

2

In *The Children of the Night* (1897) first appeared the type of poem destined to be associated with Robinson's genius: the laconic, dramatic exposition of an individual's life history. The seemingly successful Richard Cory, who "glittered when he walked," in despair put a bullet through his head; the miser, Aaron Stark, with "eyes like little dollars in the dark," laughs at those who pity his avarice; Cliff Klingenhagen tosses off the draught of wormwood and, in renunciation of life, is happy; and Reuben Bright the butcher, in his excess of anguish at the death of his wife, tears down his slaughterhouse. Such are the observations of a mind which, like his own Merlin's, "saw too much" into human suffering and frustration. These hard little poems are specimens of human experience in a world in which agony is real and happiness but a wish. To this particular form of expression Robinson turned repeatedly: in all, he made up a vast file of spiritual dossiers. These are novelettes, cryptic one-act dramas of single persons: they reveal Robinson's dual powers as novelist and dramatist, fused in intense concentration, reticence, and implication. They are microfilms, needing only the illumination of the reader's experience to be projected as reality.

Their subjects vary; often these men and women are the apostates of society. Annandale is a derelict killed in mercy by his physician friend; Miniver Cheevy longs for the romantic past but cannot act in the present. Sometimes the characters are of bygone days or are the famous underdogs of literature: Crabbe, Hood, Zola, or Verlaine. The index moments on which the poet seizes with such skill are manifold. On his deathbed we see the wreck of Annandale, but we follow Miniver Cheevy into later life—he "kept on drinking." Sometimes the sardonic point is communicated in quaint invocation in the ballad form, as in the haunting reiteration of love's futility in the dialogue between John Gorham and his mistress; sometimes the narrator participates in the victim's disillusionment: puzzled, he drinks with Cliff Klingenhagen. Occasionally the medium is autobiographical, as in the mother's fond description of her worthless son in "The Gift of God." Irony, contempt, pity, questioning kindle these sketches till we forget their prosaic language and the detachment of the poet's narration.

The implement for these subacid portraits is primarily the dramatic monologue, though their ancestry includes the sonnet, with which Robinson often experimented, the ballad, and the orthodox quatrain. In any case, the final product is triumphantly his own. The closely packed, subtle reflections of the disillusioned wife of "Eros Turannos" are an excellent illustration of his complex condensation. "Why," the poet once exclaimed in answer to the charge of obscurity, "can't they read one word after another?" It is not the words or the syntax which lack simplicity but the intimations stirring in the poet's mind, which he conveys so indirectly. Sentences are clipped; dialogue hangs in mid-air; precise explanation is wanting. The "slight kind of engine," with which the doctor ends Annandale's agony, is a hypodermic needle, but the reader is often less fortunate in his divination. Robinson puzzles not merely by ellipsis but by periphrasis. Yet in their avoidance of the explicit lies the power of these short poems. They rejoice in the strength which in moments of emotion is exhaled from silence and the unspoken word. In "The Mill," a comparatively lucid poem, the explanatory word is not set down.

The miller's wife waits long for her husband until she is "sick with a fear that had no form." His suicide and hers we deduce from "what was hanging from a beam" and

> Black water, smooth above the weir
> Like starry velvet in the night,
> Though ruffled once, would soon appear
> The same as ever to the sight.

The beauty of the first two lines of this quatrain should caution us against the notion that Robinson as a poet was insensitive to nature, to color, or to light. The latter word is everywhere in his poetry. Even the grayness of these character portraits is pierced by lambent metaphors such as the familiar one in "The Gift of God" when the doting mother dreams of her son,

> Half clouded with a crimson fall
> Of roses thrown on marble stairs.

Robinson was not insensitive to nature, though his conclusions concerning life receive little aid from her sustaining counsel; and his early work, like the later epics, is enriched by such imagery as

> Dark hills at evening in the west,
> Where sunset hovers like a sound
> Of golden horns that sang to rest
> Old bones of warriors under ground.

This facet of his art should, by way of balance, be kept in mind. The terse sentences in Mr. Flood's dilemma or Luke Havergal's tragedy would mean less without the "silver loneliness" of the moon or the "crimson leaves upon the wall."

Early in these vignettes of character, Robinson committed himself to psychological subjects and to a technique of implication. His mind, though not insensible to the "poetry of earth," was primarily analytical and, for the time being, curbed by an iron reticence. That for such a mind the brief dramatic monologue would be inadequate was certain. He was not to be at his best, even in the Arthurian poems, when more than two or three characters were together; this fact he himself may have learned from the vignettes or from the failure of his *Captain Craig* (1902), tied, in spite of revisions, to the actual character of Alfred Hyman Louis. Yet he had to talk more; he could still play with riddles but there must be more words, amplifications of his introspection. Thus the volume contained, besides the verbose title poem, the long, refreshingly clear narrative of "Isaac and Archibald" (suggestive of Robert Frost) and the sixteen-page "Book of Annandale." Eight years later, in *The Town Down the River,* he was to enlarge his gallery of inarticulate "bewildered children," but he had now embarked upon an exhaustive consideration of the tragic problems merely adumbrated in a "Richard Cory" or a "John Gorham." This was well; it was, in fact, inevitable. In 1916 appeared, side by side with brief character portraits, the two noble poetic studies of man in an indifferent universe: "Ben Jonson Entertains a Man from Stratford" and "The Man Against the Sky."

Had Robinson adhered to his original method, he might have compressed the tragedy of Captain Craig into the usual quatrains or into the fourteen lines of the sonnet form. We might instead have lived through one important day in the life of the old man, the distinguished beggar, whose hands touched sleeves so significantly in Tilbury Town's streets; we might have read between frugal lines of his wise insight into life, his humor, and his sweetness, all travestied at his funeral by the blaring band's Dead March from *Saul.* Thus Robinson could have spared us many a tedious page of moralizing and some of the Captain's complicated relations with his six half derisive, half compassionate benefactors; the poet's preference for fifty-six pages and three long parts of some six hundred blank verse lines each was not wholly wise.

For even the later recognition of Robinson's talent for involuted intellectual patterns has never made *Captain Craig* popular; Robinson reproduced too accurately the garrulity as well as the wisdom of old age. Although the Captain's "inner peace" mocks "every smug-faced failure on God's earth," his death is an escape not only for himself but for the reader of the poem. Something in the character of the aged parasite is unattractive; despite the length of the poem, the hypothesis of anterior years is less persuasively conveyed than in the shorter portraits. What we derive from *Captain Craig* is incidental: the hard, brilliant photograph of the shallow, beautiful woman; or Robinson's provocative meditations, almost a defense of his own low tone of mind, on the perils of the "demon of the sunlight." As for Melville, the "light" for Robinson is fraught with a menace more terrible than darkness.

### 3

Yet *Captain Craig* is illuminating as Robinson's first extended homily on the searcher for light in an uncomprehending world. Fourteen years later the poet's language is more trenchant and the framework for sustained meditation happier in "Ben Jonson Entertains a Man from Stratford." Again the vein is reminiscent. To a friend of "our man Shakespeare" the clever dramatist Jonson pours out his memories, half irritated, half adoring, of the incomparably wise one, Shakespeare. Certainly Jonson's shadowy audience of Shakespeare's Stratford neighbor is a restful contrast to the sextet who gabble with Captain Craig. Two skillfully drawn portraits emerge, of which that of Ben Jonson is the less vital. Is this other really the best existent imaginative re-creation in verse of the mind and personality of Shakespeare, who

> Fills Ilion, Rome, or any town you like
> Of olden time with timeless Englishmen?

Is it not rather a conventional picture, echoing too carefully the familiar facts exhumed by scholarship and repeating the worn traditions concerning Shakespeare the Man, at once convivial and inscrutable? What interests us more is Robinson's expansion of his principle: instead of a sonnet on Erasmus (1902) we may now expect the carefully wrought "Rembrandt to Rembrandt" (1921). In addition, we encounter in this concept of the dramatist, the characteristic Robinsonian twist, now more detailed, toward darkness: Shakespeare's nature is clouded by despair:

> "No, Ben," he mused; "it's Nothing. It's all Nothing.
> We come, we go; and when we're done, we're done."

In the title poem of this same volume, "The Man Against the Sky," the dramatic setting has shrunk to a mere outline: the sunset-flooded hill crowned momentarily with its lonely demigod. The flame-lit slope darkens, and the figure vanishes; then follow the measured speculations of the poet on the destiny of Man, of whom in this golden instant the heroic figure seemed the incarnation. Like "Dover Beach" or other nineteenth century poems, "The Man Against the Sky" exemplifies an age-old poetic method, the prolonged tranquil reflection born of the moment of emotion. Such old-fashioned technique was to engage Robinson often, especially in the Arthurian studies; and it promised a more downright, a more elaborate expression of his judgments concerning "the life we curse."

After the magnificent opening stanza of the poem we follow our relentless searcher for answers to the riddle:

> Where was he going, this man against the sky?

To mystical experience of God? To a comfortable prosperity? To disillusionment? To become a world conqueror? Each section· of the poem considers possible answers to the question. "Where was he going . . . You know.not, nor do I." And now, as the metaphor fades, Robinson submerges us in waves of argument against the existence of any meaning whatever. All is darkness—save in the fact that we do *not* destroy ourselves! We live on; we cling to life. By 1916 all the strands in his thought were firmly interwoven. In the next year he wrote *Merlin*, which offers in profusion his psychological insight, his dramatic crises, his indirectness and directness of speech, his receptivity to the somber aspects of nature, his understanding of the complex characters of women, his flexible use of the symbol, and his deserts of prosaic introspection.

Before we invade this continent, of which the poems already studied seem to be the preliminary peninsulas, let us examine more precisely Robinson's definition of man's dilemma. Varied in countless individuals, one theme recurs endlessly, the tragedy of each human being; namely, that not to think is to be less than Man, while to think is to be far less than God. To covet dollars like Aaron Stark, or self-indulgence like Miniver Cheevy, or vice like Annandale, means a return to the beast; yet to be wise like Captain Craig, or to love unselfishly like the mother in "The Gift of God," means suffering. Most of all, to perceive and to understand the depths of anguish in our fellows is the supreme unhappiness. Robinson's pages are filled with men like Shakespeare, Merlin, Lancelot, and Tristram, who "see too much."

Here is a universe in which elevation of spirit entails agony and frustration, vision becomes a heavy burden. Each life, if it moves upward, mounts a "darkening hill." Some, like Miniver Cheevy or Mr. Flood, are defeated and no longer challenge the ascent. Others who "climb," like Flammonde, still fail. Why, Robinson cannot say; the reasons are obscure. Only one cause seems common to us all: a crinkle of temperament, a tiny cancer in the texture of the mind which came with us into the world. Flammonde breathed upon all whom he met his subtle influence; yet he missed fulfillment:

> What small satanic sort of kink
> Was in his brain? What broken link
> Withheld him from the destinies
> That came so near to being his?

The tragedy of life is its mystery; the power of Flammonde is mysterious; the reasons causing worldly success and spiritual failure or their opposites are forever mysterious; selfless love ("The Gift of God") and trivial, sensual vanity ("Veteran Sirens") are mysterious. Most of all, man's ultimate destination remains inexplicable. Is it also meaningless? Is the "light" an illusion? Robinson does not say. Certainly the connotations of his sense of mystery are not the wonder and joy found in other poets; he is neither optimist nor meliorist. Yet he never accepts utter Night as certitude, and to tag him pessimist is also inexact. Despite his talk of "nothing" and "nothingness," he is not convinced that, "after all that we have lived and thought," the sequel is a blank. His hope, if hope it may be called, is but a tiny flower in a dark forest but this hope subdues his despair to mere doubt.

In this inscrutable world, in which no answer may be had, Robinson found at last his role, like that of his noblest characters, the role of Questioner. However fitful the light, he would essay to find it. Though Eternity hides too vast an answer for our time-born words, still he would seek that answer. Nor was this basically a moral quest, though it involved moral values. Robinson's search sprang from a kind of high intellectual curiosity; it was a fulfillment of his own "satanic kink." It was the realization of his function as a poet, a function deserving a definition better than that in his rather self-conscious verses:

> Dear friends, reproach me not for what I do,
> Nor counsel me, nor pity me; nor say
> That I am wearing half my life away
> For bubble-work that only fools pursue.

Robinson's attitude has been called transcendental in that he pursues a meaning unrevealed by empirical laws and based on the doubtful deduction that so much darkness predicates an underlying significance. Complementary to the poetry, hear his colloquial phrases concerning the world:

> I have always told you it's a hell of a place.
> That's why it must mean something.

That most men do not take their own lives, that the will to live persists, that the man against the sunset-tinted hill appears sublime, that a Shakespeare creates his timeless heroes, hint, though faintly, that we should cherish the "faith within the fear" that somehow "The Word" *may* exist.

## 4

This last idea, the true pivot of Robinson's poetry, animates his Arthurian poems, in which all his enigmas reappear in musings as calm and protracted as a summer day in immortal Camelot. Can the wise man, like this Merlin who shaves off his beard to be young again with Vivian, flee from the life of the intellect into that of the senses? Is the struggle of Lancelot between earthly passion for Guinevere and his impulse toward the Light a microcosm of the story of mankind? Is there a meaning in the love of this modern Tristram and Isolt, who are the creatures of no imperious potion on the bark from Tintagel, but who honestly realize a love transcending life and death? Nor is love the only problem analyzed; human qualities of character examined in the short poems, such as loyalty, hypocrisy, hatred, or cruelty, he now develops in a grand complexity. The "small satanic sort of kink" becomes in each of these human figures a moral labyrinth, and each problem is posed against a background of "Time" and against the insoluble mystery of the universe.

Since from his earliest days Robinson had been less interested in outward circumstances than in inward flaws impairing happiness, it was natural that, among the passions, the love of man and woman should win a central place in his poetry. In his three interpretations of Arthurian legends he invested this theme of love with a grace and majesty which rendered his trilogy more than comparable with other modern versions of these deathless tales. Here in the ease of his conversational blank verse we feel his irony, his pity, and—most surprising—the intensity of his emotion, in for example, his depiction of the sensuous black-and-red Vivian or the white-and-gold Guinevere. The *Tristram* (1927) in particular makes us view with critical eyes the analogous achievements of Tennyson, Arnold, Swinburne, and Hardy. Perhaps the ancient stories will offer new meanings to each succeeding century; perhaps our admiration is enhanced by our intimacy with the modern problems confronting these three pairs of lovers; at any rate the lovers are ourselves, the bewilderments are our own. For the unity of these poems resides not in Camelot, but in the poet's theme, his disillusioned study of the dilemmas of romantic love.

In these acres of blank verse are dusty corners, especially in *Merlin*. For our psychiatrist's thoroughness we pay heavily, his clinics are prolonged. *Merlin* is a tedious poem. With this story of the love of Merlin and Vivian, Matthew Arnold's Iseult of the Snow-White Hand beguiled her children; its moral—that even the wisest are deceived by passion—is not quite worthy of our subtle poet. Even if Merlin's meetings with the green-clad, amorous Vivian in her exquisite garden haunt the memory, the episodes of passion and satiety hardly justify Robinson's intellectualized elaboration. Only in the inner struggle of Merlin between his life of the senses and his consecration to wisdom is the poet entirely at ease. Presumably he already had in mind the higher levels in his problem of love; certainly *Merlin* takes on new meaning in its relation to *Lancelot* and *Tristram*. The three form one poem of which *Merlin* is the prelude.

Unlike Merlin, at best a shadowy figure, Lancelot is alive, a modern man, fevered, introspective, bewildered, doubtful of his way. At the end darkness covers Merlin, but Lancelot remains the searcher, and like his creator never renounces his quest for "the Light." The poem's analysis is mitigated, and its vigorous action reminds us of Robinson's petulant remark that he was "a disappointed dramatist." Readers who flag under his sustained introversion may find relief in the brutal episode of Lancelot's rescue of Guinevere from the pyre, an incident recalling Malory's primitive adventures. In the rage of Gawaine, in the plottings of Modred, in the battle scenes, in the anguish of Arthur, in the quarrels of the lovers, is good, if uneven, story-telling. What dignifies the poem is the character of Lancelot, harassed by high love, loyalty despair, and ceaseless questioning. Through him we hear again the authentic voice of the poet, as in *The Children of the Night* or *The Man Against the Sky*. In *Lancelot* recurs a moving exposition of "the faith within the fear":

> He rode on into the dark, under the stars,
> And there were no more faces. There was nothing.
> But always in the darkness he rode on,
> Alone; and in the darkness came the Light.

*Tristram,* also, is in simplest terms another study of two persons in love Again we are engulfed in a vortex of lovers' thoughts and feelings, again the framework of the Arthurian court is nobly appropriate, and again we live amid profound darkness and faint light. Yet *Tristram* is different; Robinson (and better critics than the poet) regarded it as his masterpiece. Written with "precipitancy," it pulses with an energy wanting in *Merlin* and with an unfal tering ecstasy denied *Lancelot*. The self-abandonment of the poet to passion contrasts strongly with the silver grayness of his early work. All is feeling,

> Till terror born of passion became passion
> Reborn of terror while his lips and hers
> Put speech out like a flame put out by fire.
> The music poured unheard, Brangwaine had vanished
> And there were these two in the world alone,
> Under the cloudy light of a cold moon
> That glimmered now as cold on Brittany
> As on Cornwall.

Yet the essence of *Tristram* lies rather in the adjacent lines:

> Time was aware of them,
> And would beat soon upon his empty bell
> Release from such a fettered ecstasy
> As fate would not endure.

Robinson is not so much stressing experience itself, as if echoing Browning, as the relation of such "experience" to "Time," a word forever present in his poetry, but repeated relentlessly in *Tristram*. Can complete and intense spiritual experience defeat "Time"? Though no mystic, Robinson wonders whether such triumphant, elevated human experience as that of Tristram and Isolt links itself with the eternal. Is this the "Light"? He does not finally say.

## 5

During the decade (1917–1927) which produced the Arthurian trilogy Robinson issued half a dozen other books, among them *The Three Taverns* (1920); *Avon's Harvest* (1921), a penetrative study of fear and hatred; *Roman Bartholow* (1923), an analysis of a disturbed soul; *The Man Who Died Twice* (1924), the story of the waste of an artist's powers; and *Dionysus in Doubt* (1925), an examination of the relations of a materialistic society to the poet's office. Seven other poems, besides new collected editions of his works, appeared before his final, arresting *King Jasper* (1935), printed in the year of his death. In none of these volumes, nearly a score since *Merlin,* is evidence of a decline, though many of the long narratives, such as *Cavender's House* (1929) or *Nicodemus* (1932) hardly came to life. Over them rests the haze of oft repeated questions. King Jasper cries to himself (or, perhaps to Robinson):

> You were afraid of time, and you still fear it.
> Is it worth fearing, when so little is left?

In this later work such difference as exists is twofold, a deeper consciousness (as in *Dionysus in Doubt*) of social issues, and an experimentation with symbolism. Both of these variations should be studied in *King Jasper,* a poem built upon several levels of allegory. Not only do the disillusioned king and queen face the familiar Robinsonian problems of "success" and "time," but Hebron, standing for "Labor" as "Zoe" represents "Life," reflects the poet's attempt to rise above the personal into the philosophic contemplation of his enigmas.

What do we experience as we leaf again Robinson's fourteen hundred pages of poetry? Not sadness for all that he failed to see clearly, such as nature alive with meaning or men and women happy, but a stern invigoration from his uncompromising loyalty to his own "satanic kink." So he saw life: much darkness and a little light. Man is betrayed less by circumstances than by his own character. He is, like Robinson's character Clavering, one

> who for scant wages played
> And faintly, a flawed instrument.

So Robinson saw art: the communication of thought concerning the mysterious mind, in form austere, without the traditional poetic vocabulary.

From these concepts of life and art, though their possession caused him personal distress, he never deviated. His outlook, his unique "tone," his interests, his modes of expression were, from his boyhood, innate, predestinate; in no American poet more so, save perhaps Poe. He tried few experiments, yielded to no criticisms, followed no will-o'-the-wisps, remained tenacious of one aim. "I can't," he once said, "do anything but write poetry," and he was really our first professional poet. He might have added that he could write only poetry of one kind, for it is probable that the verse which he threw away when his schoolboy friends did not understand it was akin in quality to that of his last poem, *King Jasper*. From his simple honesty we have inherited a complete brief of his case against life. Knowing him through the worst, stated without mercy, we may trust the light which he still discovered in the predicament of man.

So we may see Robinson: the solitary poet who absorbed into his thought and art the best of the old in American poetry and became the first of his generation to understand, however darkly, the new. With the death of Moody in 1910, his voice alone was heard; five years later it was but one in a chorus. And not he, but rather his younger contemporary Robert Frost, who had perforce been silent all these years, seemed destined to compose the chorale of the new age.

# 70. THE "NEW" POETRY

$A$s it turned out, 1912 was the *annus mirabilis* of American poetry. In the first place an enterprising publisher, Mitchell Kennerley, did an unusual thing. Genuinely interested in poetry, he issued late in 1912 *The Lyric Year,* an anthology of one hundred poems by one hundred poets, which the editor described as a kind of "Annual Exhibition or Salon of American Poetry." The three prizes offered in this poetry show totaled $1,000. In selecting his hundred best the editor had examined ten thousand poems by nearly two thousand writers. That so many versifiers existed whose work was worth considering proved that there was a public for poetry even among its makers.

As the editor read, he was sure he could perceive the Time Spirit at work among all these poets and poetasters. Its effect he detected in a more masculine quality than had been evident hitherto, a trend due to the ascendancy of the virile art of Norseman, Slav, and Anglo-Saxon over the decaying classical heritage. Twentieth century poetry was destined to be democratic, scientific, humane. It already showed the liberating touch of Whitman, "sweet with robust optimism." It reflected the exhilarating trend that was sweeping over Continental music, painting, and poetry.

Reading through *The Lyric Year* now, one notes that editor and publisher had not found more than a score of poets whose verse completely measured up to these new requirements. They had been compelled to depend in the main on the elder singers whose brief lyrics, usually on nature, love, and the goodness of life, were familiar to the devoted readers of the *Atlantic* and the *Century*. In the early 1900's every editor kept a handy drawerful of two- to ten-stanza poems of this kind. He used them to fill out a short page and to raise the tone of his magazine.

Eighty of the hundred poets who found a place in the anthology were "magazine poets." Typical of them was the Canadian-born Bliss Carman who, with Richard Hovey, had broken out of the dream world of the Idealist poets into a Bohemianism of the open road. Their *Songs from Vagabondia* (1894) had created a vogue. Among other contributors of the older school, Madison Cawein, Kentucky poet, still invited readers out of doors. Percy

MacKaye was still addicted to the ode, and Josephine Peabody could not forget Swinburne. Edwin Markham, whose anthology piece, "The Man with the Hoe" was a *lapsus naturae,* continued to write in the tradition of Tennyson and the "cosmic" poets. Clinton Scollard, more valiantly than any other contributor, carried on for the Idealists. In spite of its seeming serenity, the poetry of this elder generation of poets shows that they could maintain this mood only by ignoring the life around them. When they attempted to deal with it, their method was to knit up images borrowed from classical mythology into a poetical robe to drape over the sordidness of modern America. They felt no need for inventing forms which would adequately express the rhythms of the age of ragtime and the horseless carriage.

Some twenty of the contributors to *The Lyric Year* did give evidence of the working of the new Time Spirit which the editor asserted was a characteristic of the whole volume. The cleavage between these poets and their elders was noticeable enough to be commented upon by the reviewers of the anthology. Among these twenty were several whose names would be identified with the "new" poetry: Nicholas Vachel Lindsay, Sara Teasdale, Witter Bynner, Arthur Davison Ficke, William Rose Benét. The poem which most completely broke with the older order, "Renascence," was the work of a Vassar undergraduate, Edna St. Vincent Millay.

Those who recognized new cadences and themes in *The Lyric Year* had already been encouraged by the literary radicalism of a recently founded little magazine, edited in Chicago, which bore the plain title *Poetry: A Magazine of Verse.* This venture was destined to have a remarkable future. *Poetry* survives today, and it has "discovered" more good poets than any other magazine published in English.

The driving force of the enterprise came from Harriet Monroe, shy but determined, widely traveled, well read, and, as an entrepreneur, something of a genius. She had early decided to be a poet, and she worked hard at being one. When she learned that all the arts save poetry were to be lavishly honored at the World's Columbian Exposition, she resolved that the exposition should have a laureate, and she proposed to wear the laurel herself. The directors yielded. On the day the still scaffolded buildings were dedicated, 125,000 witnesses heard an actress with a powerful voice and statuesque presence recite Miss Monroe's "Columbian Ode."

She never forgot this moment. She was determined that poetry in America should no longer be the Cinderella of the arts. Architects were necessary to our civilization. Painters had their one-man shows, and more prizes went to them each year than the quality of the prize-winning works deserved. Poets must be permitted to feel that they also performed a function in our national life.

The means to this end would be a magazine of poetry. Chicago prided itself on the fact that it was taking the leadership in the arts. Chicago businessmen should therefore extend their patronage to poetry. Using her social connections and her local fame, Miss Monroe went from office to office, begging and upbraiding, until she found a hundred patrons who would guarantee $50 a year over a five-year period for the support of her magazine.

The first issue was ready in October, 1912. Miss Monroe's inaugural statement, "The Motive of the Magazine," spoke of the shameful neglect of poetry, asserted that there was a public for it in America, and assured readers that quality alone was to be the test for admission to *Poetry*. She concluded with characteristic grandiloquence: "We hope to offer our subscribers a place of refuge, a green isle in the sea, where Beauty may plant her gardens, and Truth, austere revealer of joy and sorrow, of hidden delights and despairs, may follow her brave quest unafraid." Her program was not defined beyond the desire to do good in the cause, but it was not long before she found coadjutors who were eager to provide her with a policy—with several policies in fact.

Miss Monroe possessed the essential quality required of an editor of a magazine of this kind—a willingness to be educated by her contributors. Though she was certain that the older order in poetry was passing, she but vaguely understood in 1912 what might take its place. She thought Americans should write about contemporary life, even if that meant poems about the slums of Chicago. She believed the traditional forms were played out, and she wanted poets to try freer rhythms. But it was no time at all before Ezra Pound, a young American who had expatriated himself in England, informed her that the new poetry would be far more revolutionary than she imagined. As a result of her solicitation of contributions from younger poets whose ability she had noted, two poems of Pound's appeared in her first issue. He assured her that *Poetry* would be the only magazine in America to receive his verse. In the second issue he had moved in as "foreign correspondent." Thereafter he wrote about as much of the editorial comment in each number as Miss Monroe herself.

Pound with others from abroad saved the magazine from parochialism and uplift. He brought Yeats and the "Imagistes" of London into its pages. His knowledge of verse technique, of Provençal and early Italian poetry, and of the French moderns enlarged the scope of *Poetry* and tied it to the new international movement in literature. During its first five years, the magazine published or reviewed translations from Belgian, Japanese, Chinese, Armenian, Peruvian, Hawaiian, and American Indian verse. It made much of the Bengali poet Rabindranath Tagore, who was the literary sensation of the day. Pound, Ford Madox [Hueffer] Ford, and F. S. Flint kept its readers up to the minute with developments in Continental poetry.

The pages of the early numbers of *Poetry* crackle with controversy: Chicago against Boston; the traditionalists (e.g., W. S. Braithwaite, Conrad

Aiken, Max Eastman) against the experimentalists. Pound takes command in the battle for the rights of Imagistes. Amy Lowell, with assistance, carries the day for *vers libre*. Echoes of these battles rolled into the newspaper offices of the country, and it was not long before the issues fought out on the pages of *Poetry* were the subject of newspaper editorials and of indignant letters from conservative readers. Poetry was news.

But the best proof of the magazine's usefulness was its ability to recognize promise and its readiness to support certain older poets who needed wider recognition than they had known. In its first year it published work by Pound, Richard Aldington, W. B. Yeats, Hilda Doolittle, Vachel Lindsay, Amy Lowell, and William Carlos Williams. During the second, John Gould Fletcher, D. H. Lawrence, Robert Frost, and Carl Sandburg were added to the roster. In 1914–1915 Wallace Stevens, Edgar Lee Masters, T. S. Eliot, and Marianne Moore made appearances. Young poets whose work would set the tone of the poetry of the twenties and thirties were cradled in Miss Monroe's little magazine. In still another way *Poetry* anticipated the future. Its reviewers frequently foreshadowed the critical attitudes of the next generation. Joyce was spoken of in *Poetry* as a significant modern. Rilke, Emily Dickinson, Hopkins, Hardy as poet, were given their measures of recognition.

Though Miss Monroe was in sympathy with this internationalism and gave the rein to her transatlantic assistants, she saw to it that the American poets whose careers she was nurturing had a place above the salt—quite literally so on one occasion. The issue was neatly pointed up when Yeats was given a congratulatory dinner during his visit to Chicago in March, 1914. He praised the new American poetry in his speech, but he warned the poets, critics, and editors present that they were too far from Paris: "It is from Paris that nearly all the great influences in art and literature have come . . . In France is the great critical mind." In the June issue of *Poetry* Alice Corbin Henderson, assistant editor, answered Yeats, asserting that Vachel Lindsay, who had read his "The Congo" at the banquet, did not have to go to France for it or for "General William Booth Enters into Heaven." He did not even have to cross to the eastern side of the Alleghenies. The traditions of the past are as open to the poet of Springfield as to the poet of Paris; the "tradition of the present is yet to make." Miss Monroe and Mrs. Henderson were certain that the poets of the "Chicago school," Lindsay, Masters, and Sandburg, would be the makers of the new tradition.

2

Even the receptive readers of the fourth issue of *Poetry* (January, 1913) must have got something of a shock when they found themselves swept along with the Salvation Army band rhythms of Vachel Lindsay's "General William Booth Enters into Heaven," which they were told to sing to the tune of "The Blood of the Lamb" with indicated instruments—bass drum, banjo, flute, and tambourine. Here was the "new" poetry with a vengeance, ecstatic with the responding shouts of the crowds at the street corner.

Who was this poet of thirty-four who soon had a following greater than that of any other of the Chicago group, the protégé of whom Miss Monroe was most proud? He certainly had a future: did he have a past? Actually he had been writing poems since his college days in the late nineties at Hiram in Ohio; but no publisher had issued them, and he was still hoping to make his way as an artist. His poems had only been attached to his spidery line drawings to help explain their "hieroglyphic" significance.

Born in Springfield, Illinois, a Southern boy in a Republican city, he was still tied to the strings of his energetic mother. The daughter of a Campbellite minister, she was hungry for Beauty and God and full of a thousand schemes for the religious and cultural regeneration of Sangamon County and its city, Springfield, the capital of Illinois. The indiscipline which always marked Lindsay can be traced to his parents' indulgence of his whims. They did not know what to make of their son; but they were themselves in love with beauty, and skeptically but hopefully they let him go his way. At college he schematized his future. Feeding his imagination on Poe, Blake, Swinburne, and Ruskin, he planned to roam and observe the world for twenty years; to be the great singer of the Y.M.C.A. Army; to reconcile culture and manliness; to be by 1905 the biggest man in Chicago. Whatever he might do, he would do in the service of Christ. "Curb your imagination; simplify your aim," he wrote in one of his voluminous notebooks. He paid no attention to his own advice.

In 1901 he went up to Chicago to study at the Art Institute. With a cream puff for breakfast, a lemon and a Uneeda biscuit for lunch, he dreamed in his classes and never learned to draw a face or figure. But by 1905 he was in New York, still asking for encouragement, this time from Robert Henri. The master painter was so farsighted as to praise his poems. Lindsay was now offering a few to the magazines. In a time of dire poverty, for the editors would not have them, he tried peddling his picture-poems up and down Third Avenue. The shopkeepers, annoyed or amused, sometimes paid him the asking price of two cents. At last Lindsay had begun to preach his gospel of beauty to a few startled hearers. The moment was significant. With a pack of poems he was off, the next year, on a vagabonding trip through the South.

When he could find an audience he lectured on art or recited poems. Otherwise he "traded rhymes for bread," sleeping in the hay, on the floor before the fireplace, or under the stars. He seldom worked with his hands.

If people would not give him life in return for the beauty in his poems, then he would starve. He was in dead earnest when he wrote in his diary: "If I cannot beat the system I can die protesting."

The poems for which his startled hosts gave him—sometimes—peach cider and corn pone were not in the least like the Booth poem and others of its kind which subsequently brought him fame. His principal stock in trade was "The Tree of Laughing Bells, or the Wings of the Morning." It is worth looking at, for hundreds of his poems, all but a few dozen in fact, are vision-poems resembling it.

On the Wings of the Morning (made by an Indian Maiden, from pansy buds and many morning-glories), the poet escapes to Chaos-night to find the Tree of Laughing Bells which

> Grew from a bleeding seed
> Planted mid enchantment
> Played on a harp and reed:
> Darkness was the harp—
> Chaos-wind the reed.

As he nears the Chaos-shore the red bells on the great tree sing beneath his wings "like rivers sweet and steep." He returns to the Indian Maid, bringing two bells which quench all memory in his breast. He gives the bells to her; she gives back one to him. She takes off the Wings of the Morning, and that is the end.

The reader would like to know what it means, just as he would like to know what Lindsay's Moon-Poems meant to him, and "The Comet of Prophecy," "The Spider and the Ghost of the Fly," "The Spice-Tree," and a hundred other poems. Almost any object, person, or passage in a book could set Lindsay dreaming, but his dreams were merely phantasms, lacking depth and congruity. He detached symbols encountered in his desultory reading in Egyptian, Chinese, and Christian lore and set them adrift through the aether of his fancy. As a worshiper of Swedenborg he no doubt believed, since all material objects have their spiritual correspondences, that his readers needed no guide to his visions except the "hieroglyphic" he provided. This word he constantly employed in speaking of his verse and of his pictures. What it meant to him is impossible to say. In practicing Egyptian picture writing and speculating on the "American hieroglyphic" which he proposed to evolve, he was struggling with symbols of some sort. But he never understood that poets who invent private symbols or adapt traditional symbols for their particular purposes must make their readers feel that the symbols are related and carry congruent meaning from poem to poem. Behind the mask there must be an order of a kind. Poe's "misty mid region of Weir" or Blake's Jerusalem or Yeats' Byzantium accumulates meaning from the other symbols which surround it and are related to it. There is no system behind Lindsay's hieroglyphics. His vision-poems do not even stir the irrational excitement generated by surrealist poetry. Because of his asceticism and his refusal to be a responsible man, Lindsay's unconscious was always as shallow as that of a child. Unlike the imagination of the mature poet who has loved and suffered, no dark and mysterious deeps opened into it.

Yet in his years of wandering and vacillation Lindsay was preparing himself to become the poet of a significant part of American life. He had soon tramped over most of the country, covering the South in 1906, the Middle States in 1908, the West in 1912. Though he talked with hundreds of Americans of all kinds, he returned from his adventures while preaching the gospel of beauty with no sociological statistics, nor even with memories of individuals and of individual tragedies from which the vagabonding Sandburg made poems. The people he understood were, like himself, the vision-haunted ones, the followers of his own heroes. And those heroes, one notices, are all champions and martyrs and leaders who were able to intoxicate the plain people with the hope of an America transformed and spiritualized: Alexander Campbell, who founded the middle-American sect, the Disciples of Christ; Johnny Appleseed carrying in his pack tomorrow's orchards; Old Andrew Jackson; the "eagle that is forgotten," Altgeld, who freed the Chicago anarchists; Booth leading boldly with his big bass drum, kneeling a-weeping before Jesus' face; and Bryan, Bryan, Bryan, Bryan, whose voice made the earth rock like the ocean until

> The angels in the flags, peered out to see us pass.
> And the sidewalk was our chariot, and the flowers bloomed higher,
> And the street turned to silver and the grass turned to fire.

Lindsay's first published volume, *General William Booth Enters into Heaven and Other Poems* (1913), introduced to America the Lindsay of his apocalyptic verses. Audiences soon demanded to hear him read them, and he was off on transcontinental tours which for years would be his chief source of income. With eyes closed, head thrown back, left hand on hip, right hand raised in ecstasy, he chanted and whispered "The Congo" from so many platforms that he came to loathe the sound of it. Yet, for all his protestations that he was debasing himself in these exhibitions of the "Higher Vaudeville," he exulted in his evangelical sway over his audiences. To one of his professorial admirers he wrote in 1922: "We have practically every University now in the U.S. for the asking, and we need worry about them no more. What we want now is the *whole public."* The capture of one editorial brain in each town would mean that converts would come down the aisle in droves. What they were to be converted to, Lindsay could never say, though half his poems and such books of prose as *The Art of the Moving Picture* (1915) and *The Golden Book of Springfield* (1920) were written to point the way to his Utopia. Perhaps it was enough that his proselytes were on their way.

> O nowhere, golden nowhere!
> Sages and fools go on
> To your chaotic ocean,
> To your tremendous dawn.
> Far in your fair dream-haven,
> Is nothing or is all . . .
> They press on, singing, sowing
> Wild deeds without recall!

The twenty or so poems which Lindsay's audiences demanded to hear again and again, the poems conveying the "camp meeting racket and trance," are as exciting as when they were first declaimed. Within them is the tumult of the Salvation Army rally and the Negro revival. They are tense with the joy of crowds enraptured by football games, Chautauqua lectures, and sky-painting political orations.

Each of them rises with wave on wave of rhythm until the Pentecostal moment arrives. For this kind of poem Lindsay used, beginning with "General William Booth," a four-stress line with dominant paeons. Deeply moved by the story of Booth's life, as it was told in the death notices in 1912, Lindsay brooded on the old General's heroism while the poem formed itself in the rhythms of the Salvation Army hymn:

> Have you been to Jesus for the cleansing power?
> Are you washed in the blood of the Lamb?

Within this measure, which became a unique instrument in Lindsay's hands, he could catch the cakewalk strut and revival shouts of "The Congo" and the toots of the autos whizzing by on the "Santa Fé Trail." He could also use his four-stress line with dignity and solemnity. Its effect on his readers has been so compulsive that it still echoes unexpectedly in modern sophisticated poets.

One must agree with the critic who said of Lindsay, three years before his suicide in 1931: "No other writer will have done so little with so much ability." Beside this potent handful of twenty poems possessing the "village apocalypse quality," there is not much left. In "A Rhyme for All Zionists" and "I Heard Immanuel Singing" he transfigured the gospel hymn. In *The Candle in the Cabin* (1926) one discovers a few fine poems which manifest normal human emotion. They were inspired by Lindsay's honeymoon in the Rockies. He had married at the age of forty-six.

## 3

The second of the Chicago poets to appear with a volume which gave him a national name was Edgar Lee Masters, a lawyer by profession—by avocation a poet. Before his *Spoon River Anthology* was issued in 1915, he had published eleven little noticed volumes of verse and prose, the first as far back as 1898. A friend and, later, the biographer of Lindsay, Masters was as different in temperament as one can imagine. Lindsay's Springfield is not far from Masters' boyhood homes in Petersburg and Lewistown, the villages from which he compounded his fictional village of Spoon River. While Lindsay saw visions of heavenly censers swinging above the old Courthouse dome in Springfield, Masters was turning over in his mind the life stories of the drunkards, skinflints, secret saints and private lechers, the dreamers, atheists, and idealists he had known as a boy and young man growing up beside two rivers in central Illinois, the Sangamon and the Spoon.

Several impulses generated the writing of Masters' collection of epitaphs spoken in self-justification, from the grave, by those who lie on the Hill above Spoon River. As early as 1906 he had told his father that he intended some day to write a novel based on his conclusion that the city lawyer and the country lawyer, the city banker and the country banker, have the same natures, "and so on down through the list of tradespeople, preachers, sensualists, and all kinds of human beings." In 1909 his friend William Marion Reedy of St. Louis, editor of *Reedy's Mirror* and an early champion of Masters' verse, had pressed on him a copy of *The Greek Anthology*. Under the spell of this tenth century compilation of epigrams and epitaphs reflecting on love, life, and death, Masters found that his hand "unconsciously strayed" to "Hod Putt" and "Serepta the Scold" and other sketches which would later become epitaphs in his *Spoon River Anthology*. Meanwhile he had taken note of Sandburg's success in using a new free-verse form for his poems of people. A visit from his mother in May, 1914, supplied the final impulse. As they gossiped about Petersburg and Lewistown, he determined to make a book out of the stories they knew of "Spoon River" people, "characters interlocked by fate," misjudged souls who should be given a chance to be justly weighed.

Masters was never a poet to dawdle over his verse, and by the end of the month he was turning in his epitaphs to his friend Reedy, whose Henry

George weekly was hospitable to unconventional literature. Masters often had as many as ten poems in a single issue of the *Mirror*. When the *Spoon River Anthology* appeared in book form in April, 1915, the poems numbered two hundred and fourteen. In the second edition, the next year, thirty-two new poems were added. The new epitaphs correct the overloading of sensationalism in the first form of the chronicle. Most of these speakers have kept the faith; some of them welcome "freedom from the earth sphere" after a lifetime of battle to be strong and true.

Several planets conjoined to make the book in its completed form one of the most momentous in American literature. As his autobiography *Across Spoon River* shows, Masters was, in retrospect at least, repelled by the meanness and hypocrisy of village life in southern Illinois as he had known it. But he could not forget what he had seen. His training as a lawyer helped him to look sharply into the lives of these village folk he half remembered, half invented. The epitaph form which he used in disclosing their secrets permitted the dead man or woman to give the lie to words or symbols carved on the gravestone. His fortunate choice of the epitaph form also required him to be brief and pointed. His device of contrasting characters who have exploited or hated or guiltily loved each other sets up ironic partials to the fundamental tones of sudden death, suicide, and isolated spirituality. The villagers who escape, pursuing or pursued, to the great world beyond Spoon River widen the scope of the chronicle. Some of the heroic dead have slept on the Hill since pioneering days. They cannot comprehend their degenerate descendants, and their reveries add the perspective of time.

Because he was himself a member of the generation of Dreiser and of Anderson, Masters is heard speaking through such characters as Jefferson Howard—

> Foe of the church with its charnel dankness,
> Friend of the human touch of the tavern.

He was most in sympathy with his libertarians in love, his freethinkers, and the idealists whom the money-perverted villains have defeated. Most successful as poems are the epitaphs spoken by craftsmen like Griffy the Cooper or Sexsmith the Dentist, each of whom reveals his important secret through the metaphor which encloses his life.

Thus it was that St. Louis scored on Chicago—"the one big hole in our record," as the editors of *Poetry* dolefully admitted. But Masters was soon an enthusiastic member of the "Little Room" which brought together Hamlin Garland, H. B. Fuller, the littérateurs at the University of Chicago, and the contributors to *Poetry*. After his astonishing popular success with his Spoon

River epitaphs Masters poured out verse, biography, novels, autobiography at the rate of more than one book a year; but he never again approached his achievement of 1915.

The stir caused by the *Spoon River Anthology* is in part explained by its timeliness. Americans had been made to see by the muckraking journalists and the novelists who labored beside them that Megalopolis had fouled and corrupted the part of America over which it sprawled. Writers like Sherwood Anderson and Sinclair Lewis were now ready to report that the infection had spread to the village where, so their countrymen wanted to believe, the democratic virtues still lingered. Masters' Spoon River was the first village to have its shroud of decency violently removed. Anderson's Winesburg and Lewis' Gopher Prairie were not spared for long.

4

Of the many poets whose careers *Poetry* helped to shape, none went so far on his own road as Carl Sandburg. He believed always that the best hope of the people is to be found in the men with "free imaginations, bringing changes into a world resenting change." Such a man he was himself, his ear laid to the heart of America. In his six volumes of poetry and in the six volumes of his great life of Lincoln (*The Prairie Years,* 1926; *The War Years,* 1939) he was a reporter of the dreams of the people, stronger than death; a champion of man the shaper and maker, man the answerer. Not even Whitman, with whom he is habitually compared, knew America as he knew it.

Whitman knew America, in part at first hand, in part intuitively, projecting what he experienced of it, through his imagination, into the vast spaces he had not crossed. Sandburg knew it along his senses. One is reminded as one reads his poems, from which pour all the occupations, classes, regions, types, races of America, of Lincoln shaking hands with the crowd which flowed ceaselessly through the White House, learning from each face some new thing about the people, and of how Lincoln believed, as Sandburg believed, that the collective wisdom of the people will see us through.

The struggle upward of his Swedish immigrant father taught the boy how death and despair are stood off by the foreign-born and poor in America. Galesburg, Illinois, a small prairie city filled with memories of Lincoln, was the right growing-up place for the kind of reporter and poet Sandburg was to be. He moved on from one job to another, driving a milk wagon, helping in a barber shop, a one-horse lunch counter, along the railroad, in the wheat fields. He liked to rove, listening to men talk, learning the songs the people sing. He paused to pick up a little education at Lombard College in his home town. By this time he had also been a soldier, briefly, in the Spanish-American War. From Puerto Rico he sent back to the Galesburg *Evening Mail* his first newspaper stories. He saw the inside of politics as an organizer for the Social Democratic Party. In 1913 he was in Chicago, making his way in journalism. By 1919 he had arrived as a feature writer for the *Daily News*.

His first poems were written, reporter-fashion, on rough copy paper and carried around in his pocket to be worked on when he could find a spare moment. Poetry, as he defined it in a series of thirty-eight definitions prefaced to *Good Morning, America* (1928), is "the report of a nuance between two moments, when people say 'Listen!' and 'Did you see it?' 'Did you hear it?' 'What was it?'"

His first volume, *Chicago Poems* (1916), hit genteel readers the way the butcher's maul hits the steer. Chicagoans were proud of their city's new poetical notoriety, but they did not at all like the opening lines of Sandburg's title-poem, "Chicago":

> Hog Butcher for the World,
> Tool Maker, Stacker of Wheat,
> Player with Railroads and the Nation's Freight Handler;
> Stormy, husky, brawling,
> City of the Big Shoulders.

What they had got was a completely American book and a new voice. The critics would see that he had been listening to the arguments in *Poetry* over Imagism; but there was not a poetical cliché in his book, and the style was his own.

Nor would his style change in subsequent books. There are no "periods" in Sandburg's career as a poet. His free verse is not far from prose. When one feels definite rhythmical recurrences in his lines, they are found to be of three or of four stresses, seldom longer. When they are longer, the rhythms tend to break down into prose, and Sandburg prints them as a cluster of images in a short, indented prose paragraph. His measure is seldom continuously iambic. To an ear trained to the predominant three-time of English poetry, the characteristic four-time movement gives his poems a slow pace. When Sandburg read his poetry aloud, unexpected rhythmical nuances emerged, a fact which proves that he had not constructed a form which communicates all he wished to say. Because his poems lack organic or traditional rhythmical form, the longer ones in particular do not linger in the memory. Yet for thousands of Americans the "new" poetry soon meant Sandburg. Even school children in the twenties possessed "Village in Late Summer," "Cool Tombs," "The Hangman at Home," "The Lawyers Know

Too Much." In such brief and remarkable poems the form adequately carries the vision; and the anger, tenderness, and irony.

The next three books—*Cornhuskers* (1918), *Smoke and Steel* (1920), and *Slabs of the Sunburnt West* (1922)—show no marked development. They revealed more and more of the life of the plain people, and, with hindsight, the critic can see that Sandburg was relying increasingly on the wisdom of the people, their metaphors and proverbs, for his materials. With *Good Morning, America* (1928) there comes a change. Significantly, fewer of these poems are about persons than about places. There is an undertone of brooding and pessimism, an evident indecisiveness. Symbols of mist, ashes, fog abound. Like the Methusaleh of one of these poems, Sandburg, the looker-on (even as we all are lookers-on), had seen too many "who died hungry and crying for their babies, many who died hungry and no babies at all to cry for." Having experienced so much of America, he seemed incapable of finding hope in what he had seen.

If Sandburg was full of doubt in 1928, when the rest of America was off on a wild joy-ride of financial speculation, he spoke in the midst of the depression years of his faith in the people. This testament, *The People, Yes* (1936), is a strange and powerful book which defies classification.

The poet hears someone say, "The people is a myth, an abstraction." He answers, "What myth would you put in place of the people?" The people will eat crow, but they don't hanker after it. They will suffer from the big owners, the lawyers, panderers, and cheaters who trade on their hopes.

> They will be tricked and sold and again sold
> And go back to the nourishing earth for rootholds.

But those who betray them,

> The tycoons, big shots and dictators,
> Flicker in the mirrors a few moments
> And fade through the glass of death
> For discussion in an autocracy of worms.

The people, only, are the builders. There are heroes among them, whose wise words become, as Lincoln's did, their folksay. By this wisdom they live—wary, resilient, discounting hope yet never losing it. Their dream of equity will win.

*The People, Yes* is one of the great American books. But, as so often happened in the history of our literature, its new matter required a new form, and the form is hard to name. Some of the one hundred and seven sections of the book are poems in the usual Sandburg manner, on such

themes as the death of those who die for the people, or the common man as
builder, wrecker, and builder again. Some sections merely assemble the collective wisdom of the people, on property, war, justice, and the law. One
section puts together the best words of Lincoln, and it reads, as Sandburg
knew it would, like the sections in which the people speak. Whatever may
be the name you put to it, a foreigner will find more of America in *The
People, Yes* than in any other book we can give him. But he will have to
spell it out slowly.

5

From 1908 to 1912 a diverse company of English and American poets
gathered in London were working out together a new verse-style and an
aesthetic to justify it. Representing England were Richard Aldington (who
years later became an American citizen) and F. S. Flint, master of ten languages and especially learned in French poetry. Among the Americans was
the mercurial Ezra Pound who had fled from academic philology at home.
Hilda Doolittle, daughter of an American astronomer and a graduate of
Bryn Mawr, brought to the discussions of their company more than an amateur's knowledge of Greek verse. It was this group of writers, soon to be
contributors to *Poetry,* who saved Miss Monroe's Chicago magazine from
provincialism by bringing into it the current of new ideas and new work
generated by the revolution in the arts created by Debussy and Stravinski,
Chekhov, the Post-Impressionists, the performances of the Russian Ballet,
and the philosophy of Bergson.

The dynamic force at the center of this group of London poets was
T. E. Hulme, a young philosopher whose *Speculations,* as they were called
when finally collected in 1924, were gospel to his friends. (A further compilation, *Notes on Language and Style,* appeared in 1929). Hulme was an
antiromantic. Romanticism he considered as the final decadent stage of the
humanism which had dominated Western thought for three centuries and
had produced the vicious concepts of progress and human perfectibility. He
reacted violently against the Victorian poetry which had contrived to fit the
dogmas of evolution and the new faith in English imperialism into the
master-idea of a gradual perfectionism stretching out to infinity.

To the cosmic poetry of the nineteenth century Hulme was determined
to oppose a new style. "The particular verse we are going to get," he wrote,.
"will be cheerful, dry, and sophisticated." There must be no words which
fail to contribute to the desired impression. Asking that poets consider their
work as art and not vaticination, he said, "Poetry is no more nor less than
a mosaic of words, so great exactness is required for each one." Style is simply

a means for subduing the reader; hence it is the poet's business to subdue him with economic effectiveness.

Hulme's ideas owe something to Rémy de Gourmont's *Problème du Style,* but the movement he initiated was not to be narrowly imitative. Having begun to meet as a group in March, 1909, he and his friends set themselves the task of working out, in a series of exercises, a style which would present impressions precisely. Wherever they found a poetic style or form which confirmed their purpose, as in the severe and brief Japanese *tanka* (thirty-one syllables in five lines) and *hokku* (seventeen syllables in three lines), they advertised their discoveries. But their main interest, before Pound took over, was creation, not propaganda. Even Hulme himself produced five poems as copybook models. These Pound, half in jest and half in earnest, printed as a supplement to his own *Ripostes* (1915) as "The Complete Poetical Works of T. E. Hulme." The "Autumn" which heads these five pages, is said to be the first Imagist poem.

The first article in the Imagist creed asserted the dogma of the "pure" image. None of the impressions caught in the image should be allowed to escape through weak adjectives and needless connectives. All extraneous emotion or intellectual comment should be purged. To their detractors who said that Imagism was nothing new, that all poets are imagists by the nature of their medium, Hulme's followers replied, sensibly enough, that imagism had never been fully exploited as a technique.

The dogma of the "pure image" proved to be only a mild heresy. What alarmed the traditionalists and provoked a critical war was the abandonment by the Imagists of the song forms used by English poets since the Middle Ages. The issue was joined: Was free verse, the new medium of the Imagists, verse at all? Was it not merely prose cut up into varying line-lengths?

The Imagists demanded that poets should be freed from the requirement of subduing a unique impression to a traditional metrical pattern associated through long use with particular emotional states and attitudes. To do so was to impose an alien form on an experience which had already emerged in a form of its own. In the polemical writing of the Imagists the phrase "organic rhythm" began to appear. Although the new poets were only vaguely aware of the fact, they were working in a critical tradition which begins with certain poetic dicta of Coleridge and numbers among its adherents Emerson and Whitman.

But even if one granted that the free-verse poem written by an Imagist had found its appropriate form, how could one be certain that it was still poetry and not prose? F. S. Flint tried to lift his associates from the horns of this dilemma. He admitted that there is no way to draw a fast line between free verse and prose since both are rhythmical. The difference is no-

ticeable at the extremes. The cadences which flow under impassioned utterance are of one sort and may be poetry; those which follow the pattern of
the syllogism and are useful in setting forth facts or arguments, by general
assent are prose.

Flint's argument gave the Imagists a new and precious technical term
which they could use with effect—"unrhymed cadence." Their line of defense was now that the ear of the skilled writer of free verse instructs him
how to vary the length and rhythm of his lines with precision to create
cadences suited to his theme and total image. They talked of "rhythmic
return" and of the inevitableness of the free-verse poem; of "thematic invention" in the rhythms of *vers libre,* of "concentrated stress" and the right
use of "the poetic interval—the pause."

The most sapient observations on the quarrel over free verse were made
by T. S. Eliot in an article in the *New Statesman* for March 3, 1917. The
defenders of the new form could not admit the justice of his view because
the pith of his argument is that free verse can be defended only in negative
terms. *"Vers libre* does not exist," he declared bluntly, "and it is time that this
preposterous fiction followed the *élan vital . . .* into oblivion." Its limit of
effectiveness is attained when it reaches the farthest point to which it can
depart from known patterns and still not slip into formlessness. Its strength
comes from nothing within itself but from the pattern to which, to a greater
or lesser degree, it approximates. In his own early verse Eliot proved the
soundness of his remarks by using free rhythms when they suited his needs,
but most often in ironic or emotional contrast to conventional metrical
patterns revitalized by the new content with which he filled them.

In the history of English and American poetry there have been many
battles, but none can compare in hilarity with the Imagist skirmish. At first
all was harmony in the camp of the invaders; but after Ezra Pound irrupted
among them in London peace departed. England and America were to be
conquered at once. In England he captured two magazines. In America,
as soon as he became foreign correspondent for Miss Monroe's venture,
Pound could use *Poetry* pretty much as he wished. Every issue now discussed
*Imagisme*—as it was first spelled.

The raising of the Imagist flag in *Poetry* had not escaped the notice of
an American woman with poetic aspirations who was at that moment groping for a style. When Amy Lowell of Brookline, Massachusetts, saw in
*Poetry* some verses signed "H. D. *Imagiste,"* she knew where she belonged,
and she hastened to London to seek her kind. Miss Lowell's personality was
as imposing as her physical bulk, her wealth, and the prestige of her name.
She possessed the American talent for organization, and she would spend the
rest of her life in organizing a great poetical offensive, conducted by means

of reviews which she browbeat editors to let her write, by her own books of
poetry announced by such a fanfare as only she could command, by lectures,
statements, interviews, dinners, always carried through with a storm of
hisses, applause, tears, violent exits, demonstrations, and eulogies. When she
collided with Pound in the summer of 1914, either the irresistible force or
the immovable object had to give way. Pound moved. He was ready to move
anyway, on to the company of Wyndham Lewis and Epstein and Gaudier-
Brzeska and T. S. Eliot, and to his newest discovery, "Vorticism."

He left one legacy of his generalship behind him, *Des Imagistes,* published in the spring of 1914. Pound threw into his anthology any poems of
his friends which could be called, by courtesy, imagistic. The one imagistic
poem Amy Lowell had thus far turned out, "In a Garden," went in too.

Such haphazard management would not do for a daughter of the Lowell
mills, who at the age of thirteen sold copies of her *Dream Drops, or Stories
from Fairy Land, by a Dreamer* at a bazaar for the Perkins Institution for
the Blind and netted $56.60 for the cause. Managing poets, living and dead,
was her business. On July 17, 1914, she entertained the battalion at an
Imagist Dinner at the Dieu-Donné restaurant in London. Through eleven
courses, from Norwegian hors d'œuvres to Bombe Moka, the issues of the
movement were fought over. But the rift appeared as soon as the dinner
was digested. Miss Lowell was determined that a new anthology should be
issued, to be the first of an annual series. The poets in it really must be
Imagists and not just friends of Pound's, and they must share equally in the
space. There should be a proper preface to serve as a program of action and
a declaration of independence. The poets lined up like participants in a
spelling bee. Aldington and his wife "H. D." stood with Miss Lowell. So
did F. S. Flint, D. H. Lawrence, and John Gould Fletcher, an Arkansan
who had been following the Imagist path at a distance from the rest of the
company.

Imagism became finally what Miss Lowell insisted that it was, and the
terms under which any poet who would call himself an Imagist must write
were emphatically set forth in a preface to the first of three annuals, *Some
Imagist Poets* (1915), written by Aldington and revised by Miss Lowell:

1. To use the language of common speech, but to employ always the *exact*
word, not the nearly-exact, nor the merely decorative word.

2. To create new rhythms—as the expression of new moods—and not to copy
old rhythms, which merely echo old moods. We do not insist upon "free-verse" as
the only method of writing poetry. We fight for it as for a principle of liberty. . . .

3. To allow absolute freedom in the choice of subject. It is not good art to write
badly about aeroplanes and automobiles; nor is it necessarily bad art to write well

about the past. We believe passionately in the artistic value of modern life, but we wish to point out that there is nothing so uninspiring or so old-fashioned as an aeroplane of the year 1911.

4. To present an image (hence the name: "Imagist"). We are not a school of painters, but we believe that poetry should render particulars exactly and not deal in vague generalities, however magnificent and sonorous. . . .

5. To produce poetry that is hard and clear, never blurred nor indefinite.

6. Finally, most of us believe that concentration is of the very essence of poetry.

One notices at once how much there is here which has been reiterated in every new poetic movement. Wordsworth desired in poetry to return to common speech. Kipling and Masefield and the Georgians again returned to it a hundred years after him. The Imagists, as a matter of fact, were less faithful to this principle than the Georgians. One has small chance of learning the sounds of common speech if one is born in Brookline and learns about the world from books. As to the Imagists' passionate belief in the artistic value of modern life, they actually showed a tendency to retreat from it—"H. D." and Aldington to ancient Greece, Pound to his troubadours, Miss Lowell to the newest historical curio on which her roving eye happened to rest.

When we come to the last three articles of the Imagists' program—the essentially imagistic articles—we recognize that we have come to the heart of the whole matter. We are back with Hulme and his original group in 1909. The real contribution of the Imagists was the exploration of a special technique which could be used to achieve certain ends but should not be expected to bear the weight of profound emotion or involved thought. By the determined evangelism of Miss Lowell other causes were dragged under the standard of Imagism.

After the smoke and tumult of the Imagist war cleared, it was possible to estimate how much new territory had been gained. Miss Lowell, the fugleman of the offensive, could not claim, finally, very much in her own name. With the alertness of a magpie she had fixed her attention now on the poets of the T'ang Dynasty, now on her cousin James' *Fable for Critics* which she brought up to date, now on Frost's New England tragedies which her *Legends* complimented by imitation. There is not much left of all this brave experimenting except a handful of anthology pieces. Similarly her most faithful disciple, John Gould Fletcher, expended his talent in "color symphonies" which compel poetry to drudge at tasks painting and music can more easily perform. With Hilda Doolittle the case is different, for she is the one poet of the Imagist faith who by her strict devotion to it brought forth good works. The second of the two poems entitled "The Garden," for instance, communicates perfectly in thirteen lines the oppressiveness of fructifying summer heat. The poem penetrates to essence much as Cézanne's painting of still life does. One can feel the solidity of the heat as one might expect to hear one of Cézanne's apples bump on the floor if it rolled off the table. It is not unfair to say that the chief service of the Imagists was to develop a technique which could be put to excellent use by the poets who followed them.

### 6

In the year *Poetry* was founded there arrived in England an American poet of thirty-seven who had tried with little success to persuade American magazines to take his verse. Between 1894 when the *Independent* printed "My Butterfly" and 1912, Robert Frost had disposed of fourteen poems. But he was still determined to be a poet, and he had gone to England in order that he might "write and be poor without further scandal in the family."

Born in San Francisco in 1875, he came to the New England with which he is now identified after his father's death in 1885. Twice he tried to make a go of college—at Dartmouth for a few months in 1892, at Harvard from 1897 to 1899. He farmed at Derry, New Hampshire, from 1900 to 1905. Twice he was a schoolteacher; but he had also worked as a bobbin boy in the mills of Lawrence, Massachusetts, as a cobbler, and as the editor of a weekly paper.

If he had lingered another year in America, the tidal wave of the "New" Poetry movement might have carried him to fame and perhaps to security. As it was, he found in England the companionship in craft and the appreciation for which he had waited so long. In his three years there he walked in the West Country, talking poetry with two of the Georgians whose aims were much like his own, Lascelles Abercrombie and Wilfrid Gibson. Among the new friends who admired and understood him was the critic Edward Thomas, destined shortly to die at Arras, whom Frost encouraged to turn to poetry.

In Gloucestershire Frost wrote poems about New England. There were soon enough of them for two books which David Nutt published: *A Boy's Will* in 1913, *North of Boston* in 1914. When Frost returned to America the next year, he brought with him a substantial English reputation. Norman Douglas had found in his first book "an image of things really heard and seen." Edward Garnett, in praising the second volume as containing poetry of a rare order, chid Frost's fellow Americans for their long neglect of him. "It would be quaint indeed," he warned, "if Americans who . . . are opening their hospitable bosoms to Mr. Rabindranath Tagore's spiritual poems of Bengal life, should rest oblivious of their own countryman."

The hint was acted on. Frost stepped off the boat into the hands of a reception committee. Though Miss Lowell had failed in her efforts to find a publisher for *North of Boston,* Holt issued it in the year of Frost's return. *Poetry* already knew his work, having published "The Code" in its issue of February, 1914. But Frost needed no impresario. The magazines which had once turned him down were now cap in hand asking for poems. He was known as one of the "new" poets, but he did little to identify himself with either the Boston or the Chicago branch of the movement. Always a lone striker, he still had need of being versed in country things. He found himself a farmhouse near Franconia in New Hampshire where he continued to meditate on the mysteries of birches and wild grapes, the sound of trees, and the dust of snow.

Frost was always, as any textbook will declare, a regional poet; and his region was New England, more particularly New Hampshire, "one of the two best states in the Union," the other being Vermont. Though he lived outside New England at intervals and moved in the larger world, he never had the slightest inclination to take all America for his province. However much he pitied his characters bound to the down-swing of a declining economy, he did not wish to alter their lives, never dreamed of Utopia as Lindsay did when he saw visions of his Springfield redeemed and spiritualized. Unlike Masters and Faulkner, Frost never sought to bring his characters into a regional unity. The men and women of his poems are isolated, like their farms and wood lots, or they are caught in a net which tragically or ironically encloses at most the fate of only two or three. His regionalism, in short, resembles that of Emily Dickinson and Sarah Orne Jewett. It gave him a place to stand where he could see what was close by in field or cellar hole, and, as well, a clear view above his hills to the "further range" beyond.

Politics he shunned, except to have his fun with the political poets of the thirties who reproached him for retreating from the problems of the day. He is not a religious poet, not even a nature mystic, in spite of all that nature meant to him. His verse is in the great tradition of pastoral poetry from Theocritus to Wordsworth, though his pastoralism is never, like Virgil's or Milton's, decorative or political. He is a learned poet but, as in Housman's poetry, his learning is muted to an echoic beauty. He was not the partisan of his plowmen, mowers, hired men, gatherers of huckleberries and tree gum, for all his sympathy with them and his gift of psychological penetration into their lives. He looked on them with a detachment which was ironic, humorous, or ruthful. He made of their toil and defeat what they would never have imagined for themselves.

Frost is a metaphysical poet in the tradition of Emerson and Emily Dickinson, with all that term implies of the poet's desire to go beyond the seen to the unseen, but his imagery is less involved than that of the older metaphysicals. Most of his poems fix on the mysterious moment when the two planes cross. Hasty readers, noting only the quiet beginning in what appears to be a simple anecdote about a person, event, or object commonly enough observed, fail to see how the commonness gradually disappears or, better, how it becomes transfigured. As in all great metaphysical poetry, the tension increases between the simple fact and the mystery which surrounds it, until the total meaning flashes in the final words. As one critic has observed, Frost's art consists in "his careful and deliberate laying of the material for a poetic bonfire." It has been noted often enough, and Frost commented on the fact, that poetry was to him essentially dramatic. Whatever his theme may be, he works to dramatize it for the reader, whether it is the tragedy of the hired man or the relation of the boy "too far from town to learn baseball" to the heaven-flung birches which he, one by one, subdues. The most dramatic moment in a Frost poem is the kind of anagnorisis or dénouement when the mundane fact achieves its full metaphysical significance.

Though Frost seldom strayed to alien country beyond the sight of his New England upland pastures and back meadows, his poetry widened in content and technique from book to book. Each volume disclosed a particular facet of his genius, some new attitude or tone or approach. Few modern poets have shown such a capacity for growth, on into old age.

Perhaps because Frost had long practiced poetry in silence, *A Boy's Will* (1913) was surprisingly free from the echoes of older verse which one expects to hear in a poet's first book. Three or four poems, "Storm Fear" for example, are authentic and memorable Frost. In his subsequent work there would be less dactyllic and trochaic movement (Frost's gait is usually a slow three-time); but the tone and content of the book were indubitably his and no other poet's. In *North of Boston* (1914), all the poems of which are on New England themes, there appeared for the first time his long dramatic monologues or dialogues, carefully set and lighted, and usually given, as in "The Mountain," a pervasive symbolic meaning. The marvel is that Frost could have so quickly mastered a genre which only E. A. Robinson had excelled in since Browning invented and perfected it.

Though three of the poems in *Mountain Interval* (1916) use this form, Frost had turned his attention to another kind of poem for which he became equally noted. This is a brief meditation prompted by an object or a person or an episode that seized his attention and compelled his wonder. As in the longer poems of the previous book, there is great drama in the elaborated situation, though there is no speaker and the play is done before the turning of a page. In "The Oven Bird" the starting point is an object, this mid-wood bird whose question, in all but words, is "what to make of a diminished thing." (Frost knew the answer.) In "An Old Man's Winter Night" thought moves out from a person, one aged man—one man, trying to keep a house, a farm, a countryside against ghosts, the moon, and the cold. The well known "Birches" turns on an episode: what it means, in several modes, to be a small-boy swinger of birches. But before the poem is finished it has become a meditation on the best way to leave earth for heaven.

With *New Hampshire* (1923) several new qualities emerged. The long, satirical title poem announced Frost's determination to prefer this state which has "one each of everything as in a show-case," to all others, except perhaps Vermont which lies beside it, the two of them wedged end to end. There is a new self-consciousness in the volume. The poet is willing to talk about himself and his art, somewhat defiantly. A sententiousness has crept into the longer dramatic poems, and some of the shorter ones, "An Empty Threat" for example, and "I Will Sing You One-O," are in a riddling manner which Frost sometimes carried to excess. These and the epigrams which appear in this volume for the first time anticipate the crypticism in which he would increasingly indulge. On the other hand, "Stopping by Woods on a Snowy Evening" and "The Need of Being Versed in Country Things" are as lucid and magical as anything he had written in his simpler style.

The title of his next book *West-Running Brook* (1928) has a special significance. (All the titles of his books should be pondered by those who would understand him.) Like the brook which runs west while all the other brooks flow east to reach the ocean, the speaker of the poem trusts himself to go by contraries. The black stream, striking a barrier, flings back one white wave. As it throws backward on itself, while it falls, so most of it is always raising a little, sending up a little. In this backward motion toward the source, against the stream, man most shows what he is. This stoic theme of resistance and self-realization is found in other poems in this book, in some of which there is even a suggestion of malaise. The tension between man and nature, hitherto always exciting and often harmoniously resolved, has loosened. Nature has grown more hostile, man more heroic. This increasing undertone of humanism is beautifully eloquent in the sonnet "A Soldier," one of Frost's greatest poems:

> But this we know, the obstacle that checked
> And tripped the body, shot the spirit on
> Further than target ever showed or shone.

In *A Further Range* (1936), published when Frost was sixty-one, there are two groups of poems which bear the significant captions "Taken Doubly" and "Taken Singly." The desire to sermonize had grown on him, and in the poems "taken doubly" he required the reader to keep his eye on the theme and the moral. "A Lone Striker" is a homily on individual freedom; "The Gold Hesperidee," a parable on pride. "Two Tramps in Mud Time" preaches the necessity of uniting avocation and vocation—

> Only where love and need are one,
> And the work is play for mortal stakes,
> Is the deed ever really done
> For Heaven and the future's sakes.

The poems in this group are delightful, full of an unobjectionable didacticism. Beside them the poems "taken singly" seem somewhat wan. The natural world, once a bringer of great joy to Frost, suggests to him now the closing in of age and winter.

> Petals I may have once pursued.
> Leaves are all my darker mood.

In his subsequent work he slipped the ties which had so long kept him earthbound. He grew fonder of searching among abstractions. It was not surprising that on his seventieth birthday he should try, with only a moderate success, in *A Masque of Reason* (1945), to get a forthright answer out of God for his bewildering treatment of Job and the rest of the human race.

Before the desire to escape into pure thought overcame him Frost was above all a poet of nature. But, as has been said, for all that nature meant to him he was never a nature mystic. In his early verse one feels the joy in the sensuous pleasure which nature has given most modern poets; but Frost always knew where to find the line which separates nature from man. When tired of trees he sought again mankind; but if by noon he had too much of men, he could turn on his arm and smell the earth and look into the crater of the ant. In the earlier poems nature and man confront each other across the wall, as the buck and the doe in "Two Look at Two" face the wondering man and woman, each pair in its own pasture.

Though nature watches man, she takes no account of him. On the slope where a dozen boys and girls once played, the trees are again in the mountain's lap. Deep in the frozen swamp nature is taking back to herself, "with the slow smokeless burning of decay," the cordwood meant for a useful fireplace. This is nature's way: moving at a slower pace than man, destroying man's puny work for her own ends—to provide the manure for new growth.

Man has need of nature, though he should never make the mistake of crossing the wall into her pasture. The woods are lovely, dark and deep against the snowfall, a place to linger and forget duty; but to linger only, and not to stay. Man is most himself when he measures himself against nature's pace and the barriers she places before him:

> Well, there's—the storm. That says I must go on.
> That wants me as a war might if it came.
> Ask any man.

But in the end the bond between man and nature loosened, as Frost looked on. What had been strength and indifference in nature became for him brute force and hostility; what once was balance was now seen as struggle. Man rides bareback on the earth, but he knows some further tricks to try on his wild mount, his headless horse. Or, in the metaphor of "Sand Dunes," let the sea know that even though she rises into the town to bury in sand the living who have escaped her, she is ignorant of man—

> If by any change of shape,
> She hopes to cut off mind.

As C. Day Lewis wrote in the preface to the English edition of the *Selected Poems* (1936), the simplicity of Frost's verse "is the simplicity—not of nature —but of a serious and profoundly critical spirit." Frost was early aware that he wished to take the middle ground as a thinker, that he was a skeptic, a relativist, a "sensibilist" who would refuse to adapt himself a mite

> To any change from hot to cold, from wet
> To dry, from poor to rich, or back again.

As regards his art, he likewise knew very soon where he stood. Though he wrote little about the nature of poetry, he enjoyed talking about his art. From the considerable record kept by other participants in the night-long conversations which he delighted in, and from the poems themselves, one can outline Frost's theory of poetry.

An early well-wisher told Frost to give his days and nights to the study of Lanier's mellifluous verse. The young poet presently discovered what it was he so much disliked in Lanier's poetry: "All the tones of the human voice in natural speech are entirely eliminated, leaving the sound of sense without root in experience." Another friend had told Frost that the tone of his verse was too much like talk. With characteristic stubbornness, fortunately, the poet refused to change his style. He began to realize indeed that it was just this tone that he had been striving to get into his verse. When he returned from England in 1915, he was ready to formulate, in an interview given at the time, what he had learned about "sentence-sound" and "vocal gesture." Emerson, he remarked, had set forth in "Monadnock" the theory he was trying to put into practice:

> Now in sordid weeds they sleep,
> In dullness now their secret keep;
> Yet, will you learn our ancient speech,
> These the masters who can teach.
> Fourscore or a hundred words
> All their vocal muse affords;
> But they turn them in a fashion
> Past clerks' or statesmen's art or passion.

It was Frost's contention that what we get in life and miss so often in literature is the "sentence sounds that underlie the words." Whether the individual words carry to our ears or not, every meaning has a particular "sound-posture." The listener whose ear is attuned to the spoken language is "instinctively familiar" with the particular sound which goes with the "sense of every meaning." Since language only really exists in the mouths of men, the poet must write with his ear to the voice.

Though he was trying out his idea in the midst of the excitement over free verse, Frost did not abandon conventional metrical forms. He complicated his problem (and enriched his verse) by setting the traditional meters against the natural rhythms of his speaker's sentences. The spoken word and the verse pattern must fight out the issue between them. But the struggle when supervised by a skillful poet will end in reconciliation. As Frost said: "Meter has to do with beat, and sound posture has a definite relation as an alternate tone between the beats. The two are one in creation but separate in analysis."

As will be readily seen, the kind of poetry which would result from Frost's aim would be far from a simple imitation of New England farmer speech. At its best it would be extremely complex, though always seeming to be simple, and capable of carrying a variety of tones, ironies, and emotional gradations.

Unlike many modern poets who hold that a poem is an artifact, a thing deliberately constructed, Frost declares that a poem is "never a put-up job. . . . It begins as a lump in the throat, a sense of wrong, a homesickness, a loneliness. It is never a thought to begin with. It is at its best when it is a tantalizing vagueness." Yet the poem makes itself as it grows. It finds its thought; or fails to do so, and so there is no poem. What Frost stated as a generalization is borne out in his own poems. The reader's excitement is aroused by the slow unveiling, the inevitable approach of the moment of complete disclosure. He soon finds his comprehension advancing on more than one level as he recognizes that physical objects are changing into symbols, and that these are clues to the deeper meaning of the poem. Though Frost held with the romantics that a poem is an expression of an experience, his best poems are marvels of construction, the more exciting to the reader because their form seems to evolve before his eyes and ears.

The conversational tone and the dramatic manner of Frost's poetry strike one first. More than a second glance is needed to appreciate his expertness as a prosodist. He handles, as few modern poets except Yeats and Auden have done, a great number of English meters. More remarkable still is what he makes of the "strict iambic" and "loose iambic" in which most of his verse is written. One would not have supposed there was so much blood-pulse left in this ancient meter in which English rhythms most characteristically flow.

Though he was one of the "new" poets, Frost worked his revolution in the surest way. "It's knowing what to do with things that counts." For a poet the only things he has to do with are rhythm, sound, and sense.

# 71. THEODORE DREISER

W<small>HEN</small> Frank Norris read the manu-
script of Theodore Dreiser's *Sister Carrie* in 1900 and urged Doubleday
to publish this story of a poor girl who sought love and security in the city, the
American novel faced a crisis in its development. Here was a painstaking and
exhaustive study of what it meant to be alive in growing, grasping, exuberant
Chicago, a story as free of moral inhibition as Zola, as detailed and literal as
William Dean Howells. What he, Garland, Crane, Fuller, London, and many
another had been urging the American novel to do, was here done with
assurance and naïve crudity. Would the publisher publish and the readers
read and accept? The answer for eleven years was, No. *Sister Carrie* was published without enthusiasm and then virtually suppressed. It remained largely
unread until its third and first really public edition in 1912, a year after the
appearance of the more carefully wrought study of the same theme, *Jennie
Gerhardt*.

The author of these two forthright stories apparently was not disturbed
by his rejection for a dozen years. He turned to other pursuits almost as
though he knew he could afford to wait. He wrote for the newspapers, he
edited a woman's magazine, he lived as he could. But he did not offer to
pander to the public taste in romantic fiction, even in minor respects. After
*McTeague,* Norris had largely forsaken the grim method of the realist who
saw only the ugly things; after *Main-Travelled Roads,* Garland had preached
"veritism" but had written romances of Colorado and the Yukon; after
*Maggie,* Crane had gone off to real and re-created wars; even London's *Sea
Wolf* had broken in the middle and become a romance on a Pacific isle. The
American public in 1900 was not ready to see itself wholly and literally in
fiction. The ugly things could not be revealed; the forbidden questions, asked.
Edith Wharton's genteel satire and Ellen Glasgow's moral searchings were
the strongest fare that it could take.

By waiting, Dreiser preserved his artistic integrity. Because he refused to
compromise his materials or his purposes, he became the one novelist of what
Mencken called "the literary movement of the nineties" who was fully prepared to take part in and to help shape the literary renaissance of the 1910's

and 1920's. In him the two movements become one. Why he succeeded where others failed can only be conjectured. Certainly it was not because of confidence in himself or his art, for he paints his own portrait as a blind and stumbling seeker. Probably it was because he knew the one thing that he could do if he were to write novels at all; and he persisted in doing that thing because it was all he could do. His productivity between *Jennie* in 1911 and *The "Genius"* in 1915 is proof that failure of publication had no effect on his creative energy. All his major novels were apparently either conceived or written in those years of silence, even the two, *The Bulwark* and *The Stoic*, which were prepared for publication just before his death in 1945. With *The "Genius"* he bucked the censorship of the press and public opinion for a second time and again held back his novels except for *An American Tragedy* (1925), the story of a boy who, like Carrie and Jennie, failed to come to workable terms with American society.

These years were studded with collections of shorter works and with non-fiction. There were four collections of short stories in the years between 1918 and 1929, which in theme and treatment add little to an analysis of the novels and may be compared to a painter's sketches. There were also two volumes of poems (1926 and 1935), numerous essays in philosophic and social criticism (*Hey Rub-a-Dub-Dub*, 1920; *Dreiser Looks at Russia*, 1928), and his many volumes of autobiography; but his more ambitious stories often remained for long periods unfinished in manuscript. Was he oversensitive, or did he know, as master writers sometimes do, that he could afford to wait?

2

Of all American novelists, Dreiser limited himself most sternly to what he knew of life through his own experience, mainly in his youth. He was born in Terre Haute, Indiana, in 1871; he died in California on December 29, 1945. Many of the intervening years were spent in the three cities: Chicago, New York, and Philadelphia. He knew the United States because he had lived in it.

His father was an immigrant German workman, his mother the daughter of German parents who belonged to a small religious sect in a farming region of Pennsylvania. Dreiser has described his father as a fanatically religious man, honest, hard-working, plodding. He might have been an American success on a small scale but was devoid of will and too persistently concerned with trying to avoid the fires of a theological hell. In Dreiser's writing he emerges as a strangely appealing and rather pathetic figure.

For his mother, Dreiser felt a lifelong devotion. His description of her in *Dawn* reveals her as a deeply emotional woman who gave to her large family maternal affection, warmth, and security. But for her, his life might have been as ineffectual as that of some of his own characters. In boyhood he was shy, eager, timid, brooding, bewildered, slow to develop. He has himself confessed how important his mother's love and some measure of security were to him as well as to his brothers and sisters.

His childhood and youth were not happy. His father was almost continually poor, and this family moved constantly from house to house, from one Indiana community to another; they spent one period on the crowded West Side of Chicago. Besides poverty, they usually faced social ostracism. With each move, their hopes of economic and of social betterment reawakened, only to be disappointed, and again the Dreiser children were rejected by their fellows. Theodore's suffering was further aggravated, when he passed the age of puberty, by severe fears of castration and impotence, which intensified his shyness and caused sexual panic in the presence of girls. These difficulties, with the rigid conceptions of hell taught in the Catholic parochial school and reinforced by his father, played their part in his relative slowness of mental development. He was an inconsistent pupil, responding well only when his teachers took a sympathetic interest in him—a brooding, groping boy and youth who had to learn everything for himself.

The brooding and groping style which he often used in his novels was a reflection of these inner struggles, and they provided him with one of the chief motifs of his fiction: the conflict between what was then loosely termed "instinct" by the psychologists, and convention. The biological needs of his characters lead them to actions, particularly in love affairs, which result in infringements on the social code. His autobiographical writings tell us that he experienced this conflict constantly and poignantly in his own early life. The bewilderments of his teen-age period of drifting from job to job—he worked in a Chicago restaurant, drove for a laundry, collected for an easy-payment furniture company, helped in a real estate office, in the stockroom of a wholesale hardware company, and so on—suggest the later fictional wanderings of Clyde Griffiths in *An American Tragedy*. His characters usually receive their education in life itself, in a real and savage struggle for place, money, and social prestige, rather than in schools.

Dreiser was educated, like his characters, not so much by his schooling as by his repeated moves with their resulting contrasts of urban and rural life. From the farm lands and the many towns of Indiana, he came to know the vigorous young city of Chicago in the seventies and eighties. The moral and social consequences of the triumph of town over country were impressed upon him. In his early stories his characters, whenever they move to the city, find it an exciting adventure. The growth of cities is an integral motif of all his studies of youth. The decade of the nineties, when Dreiser was a youth in

Chicago, was a crucial period in its history. By the time of the World's Fair it was beginning to play an increasingly important role in national life, especially in finance and politics. No wonder he wrote, in *Newspaper Days*:

To me Chicago at this time seethed with a peculiarly human or realistic atmosphere. It is given to some cities, as to some lands, to suggest romance, and to me Chicago did that hourly. It sang, I thought, and . . . I was singing with it.

There he saw the contrasts of grandeur and misery which he was later to describe so movingly; there his dreams and hopes of love, success, knowledge, prestige were born. It seemed to be a world city in the making, a center of gravity for the American Success Dream.

Dreiser as a boy absorbed this dream of social power and easy money as if by osmosis, at the same time that he saw poverty, failure, ignorance, and defeat all about him, even in his own family. Attending popular lectures and reading Eugene Field, he determined to understand it and to report it faithfully; to become a newspaperman. He inescapably was what Norris, Crane, and Garland envisioned the modern American to be.

3

There has been much debate among the critics as to whether Dreiser was a "naturalist" after the manner of Zola. If by this term is meant merely a franker acceptance of the ugly in life or a more faithful recording of personal experience, it can be accepted as a description of his art. If further it means a turning to the current findings of science for a philosophy with which to ask the fundamental questions about man in himself and in society, it can still be accepted. Only when it serves to confine creative genius within a formula must it be rejected, for Dreiser belonged to no school, studied no sources with intent to obey, knew little of literary movements at home or abroad.

He was an objective realist who gathered his facts impersonally, but he was more. He lived in his dreams, his hopes, his broodings. For this reason, he absorbed both the realistic method and the new conceptions of the universe from science into his thought and his writing. His views are loose in formulation, and inconsistent. For example, his theory of the relativity of morals is as inconsistent as it is challenging. But such views of man and nature as he had, however ill formed, are essential parts of his writing; without them, his works would be entirely different. They helped to deepen his imagination; they contributed toward the feeling of awe he creates concerning the condition of man; they served him in his very construction of theme, of story, of character. He was an artist, not a philosopher.

Dreiser's first two major novels, *Sister Carrie* (1900) and *Jennie Gerhardt* (1911), are stories of sensitive young girls who escape from poverty by forming liaisons with men of superior financial and social position. The salesman Drouet is but a step for Carrie toward the more attractive Hurstwood, and Hurstwood himself becomes important only as a means toward success on the stage. Jennie is similarly rescued from poverty, first by Senator Brander and then by Lester Kane. Superficially, both stories seem to be studies of struggle for the comforts and social position that money alone would bring, by thoroughly unconventional social means. But the plot in both cases is for Dreiser little more than the means for studying a more profound struggle: the struggle of an uneducated and unprivileged young girl for full realization of her own personality. Carrie's final rejection of Hurstwood because she could not love him and Jennie's final acceptance of Lester on any terms are but the two sides of the same coin. In the end and in spite of tragic circumstances, both girls achieve a degree of fulfillment that only their experiences could have brought them.

Dreiser remarks that Jennie's experience helped her to gain a "theory of existence." Perhaps the best way of describing Dreiser's total literary work is to state that he too was engaged on a lifelong search for a theory of existence. Like many another major American writer, he read to assimilate what were considered to be the best ideas of his time, to verify his own observations and brooding reflections. If there is a purpose which gives order and coherence to this spectacle, it is a secret and mysterious one. How to live in and to describe this spectacle? How to find some ideas, some values, some aims and purposes which might give more dignity, more sense, more pleasure, more human gratification to those who are a part of it?

Dreiser began his literary career when Social Darwinism was a main current of American thought, and he had, from his early years, absorbed it mainly, it seems, from Spencer, Huxley, and Loeb. Its central concept—which generally served as a means for justification of the practices of capitalism—was the equation of nature with society. It conceived the natural and the social worlds as continuous, subsumable to the same laws; in consequence, it attempted to give the status of social generalization to the conclusions of biological evolution. Dreiser, accepting this concept, developed from it an attitude of both personal and social determinism.

One of the major emphases in his work is therefore biological. Man is for him a creature with imperious biological needs. The "instincts" drive him to actions whose motivations he does not understand. Frequently, as in *The Financier* and *The Titan,* he characterizes these impulses as "chemisms," which in man are also expressions of some unapprehended force, or energy, purpose, or "God" in the universe. The universe, including the social world of man, is all of one piece, a product of unknown force, creative by nature, and resident in human organisms. Thus does man act in accordance with natural impulse. Sex, beauty, and a will to power or to dominancy are interrelated. Man seeks to satisfy himself. He seeks his mate or mates; he seeks beauty; he seeks power. The stronger personalities are best equipped to satisfy themselves; they crush the weaker, and themselves survive.

In Carrie and Jennie, Dreiser had studied the operation of these "instincts" in young women of almost no place in the social scheme. Their method of attaining a fuller life was the feminine one of exploiting the male animal to satisfy their deepest needs. In Eugene Witla of *The "Genius,"* and more thoroughly in Frank Cowperwood of the trilogy *The Financier* (1912, revised 1927), *The Titan* (1914), and the long delayed *Stoic,* he turned to the masculine version of the problem, already indirectly presented in Hurstwood and Kane.

On the character of Cowperwood, Dreiser exerted his greatest powers of observation and analysis. In this prototype of worldly success, modeled on the career of the street-railway baron, C. T. Yerkes, the primary instinct that drives the human animal forward and upward is the hunger for power. Wealth and sex are but means used by the individual to achieve mastery over the circumstances of his life and control of his own destiny. Cowperwood is a Social-Darwinian superman rather than a Nietzschean Zarathustra, for he is a victim rather than a leader. The author often mentions his personal magnetism, suggested in the look in his eyes, his manner of walking, his general appearance. It is as if universal force were planted in his very being. In paintings and in women he finds the most complete expression of beauty; he is a genius in financial manipulations; hence he is an artist, and his other satisfactions are related to his creativity.

Eugene Witla of *The "Genius"* is like Cowperwood in that he takes what he needs for his own satisfaction, but he is more emotional, more moody, less magnetic and forceful. He finds in sex the beauty which, as an artist, he seeks to recapture in his work; he feeds on women for inspiration. In the course of the novel, he has a near-breakdown and sinks into a dangerous condition of involutional melancholia. Cowperwood is an artist of power, Witla of beauty. The man of power is the stronger; and the novel of power is the greater.

The biological premise of Dreiser's writing is one side of a contradiction found in the conflict between instincts and the dictates of social convention. Man cannot harmonize the life of the body with the life of reason. He is not, therefore, fully civilized, and it becomes increasingly difficult for him to attain harmony when society is organized on the basis of Puritanical mores and a rigid moral code. "America," Dreiser writes in *Dawn,* "and especially the

Middle West, was at that time miasmatically puritanic as well as patriotic, twin states bred of ignorance and what mental or economic lacks I am not able to discern." The dictates of conventional society tend to force man to repress his nature; the need to express and to satisfy his nature pushes him toward violating social codes and conventions. Life as a search for beauty, a quest for power, an effort to express creativity, becomes a struggle, on the plane of society, for money and position, and for sexual satisfaction. In this quest and rivalry, the strongest win out; the weak are crushed.

Thus to biological is added social determinism. As the stronger man has an advantage over the weaker, so organized groups are stronger than the individual. They punish those who oppose their dictations or seem to threaten their organization. Only those individuals who are strong enough to gain control over the levers of power have a good chance of resisting social pressure. In capitalistic society the struggle for power, for gratification, is expressed in the struggle for money. Woman, as the illustration of beauty, is bought. Carrie and Jennie are "kept women"; Cowperwood "buys" the women he wants. The absence of money means defeat; it means the lack of education, of beauty; it means that one is a victim, like Clyde Griffiths, of the rich, of one's relationships with others. Dreiser directly described the pitiless-ness and the hierarchical character of capitalistic society by showing that just as the poor are the victims of the rich, the weak of the strong, so are women, inferior to men, usually victims. American tragedy, like all tragedy, is the consequence of weakness. The impulses, the passions of man pitilessly drive him to satisfy himself; the force of social circumstance, the fierce nature of the social struggle, thwart him and produce both social and biological tragedy.

In *An American Tragedy* (1925), Dreiser provides a third approach to this all-absorbing social-biological problem. Clyde Griffiths is totally lacking in either the artistic gifts of Witla or the strong personality of Cowperwood. He is more like Carrie and Jennie in that his attitude toward life is passive; but he lacks their inner poise. From start to finish of his short career he is a victim of the social and biological forces which operate upon him. His instinct for fulfillment is not only thwarted by the forces without himself; his inner weakness makes even the development of a Carrie or a Jennie impossible. Thus, by choosing for his central character a boy who had practically no strength within himself through which mastery could be achieved, Dreiser in this novel throws all his emphasis on those forces of biological and social necessity which had shaped the careers of his stronger characters in spite of their protests. But by removing the only opposition that the individual can supply, the force of his own will for mastery, Dreiser here descends to the lowest possible plane of pure mechanistic determinism. The scene of the drowning of Roberta Alden is carefully planned in order to remove the factor of will as an instrument. Clyde plots his act with the greatest care and carries it to its climax with apparently self-directed intention. But his hesitancy at the final moment transforms the murder into an accident, and his swimming away makes his act passive. The description of this story as a "tragedy" is almost ironic, even though Dreiser probably intended no irony. For the Fate of classical tragedy there were now substituted the necessities of social and biological mechanisms. But the result is less tragic, in the classical sense, than are almost any other of Dreiser's novels because the opposition of man to his destiny, in whatever terms, is not even provisional. To raise necessity to the level of tragedy there must be at least the illusion of possible mastery. In Carrie and Jennie and Cowperwood this illusion is present; in Witla and Clyde it is not.

Dreiser portrays the social-biological struggle with a certain evenness or balance, an unflagging objectivity in which he is restrained from didactic condemnation. His works say that life as he has seen it is like this: it is a condition of joy and sorrow, of beauty, wonder, terror, and above all of mystery. Human destiny is a mystery. In his poems he offers a concentrated expression of this mystical feeling for life, and in his stories he frequently turns to the occult or to religion. Telepathy occurs often; Witla and his wife, at one period, are interested in Christian Science; and *The Bulwark* is a story of Quakers. The reliance of Solon Barnes upon the "inner light" throws him, as he grows rich, into a conflict of conscience. His children drift from him and from the ideals of Quaker simplicity. In the end, a sick, a dying old man, he finds consolation in mysticism. When a poisonous snake threatens him in his garden, he looks at it with the eyes of love. The danger is averted, and he is at one with the universe. The unknown creative force in life, the force that drove Cowperwood to the heights of power, that tore the soul of Eugene Witla, that sent Clyde to the electric chair, is now revealed as universal love. Like Solon, Dreiser died a mystic. Was it his intention to say at last that Solon Barnes was a giver of laws? If so, he had denied the purely mechanistic view of life in order to admit the further necessity of religion, a necessity which had always been implicit in his thought.

4

Equipped with a "theory of existence," however unsystematic, Dreiser was in a position to ask questions about American life more searching and profound than those of earlier realists like Howells, Garland, or even James. He dramatized in fiction the American success story; his world is one of growing cities where new careers, new fortunes, are made day after day. His characters, in their search for something better for themselves, take on the color of their milieu; they gain their ideals from experience. Occupation has much to do with their destinies. Usually they find their careers as the result of accident or circumstance. Carrie and Jennie drift into their fates; Jennie's lover inherits his career with his family position. Choice is allowed only to Cowperwood and Witla, the men of power and creative ability.

In these, and in minor characters, Dreiser reveals the plight of the individual in American society; but that society itself is not static. The span of years encompassed in his novels and short stories coincides with a period of tremendous social change in America. *The Financier* opens before the Civil War. In it, as in *Sister Carrie, The "Genius,"* and other novels dealing with an older form of American society, success comes early to those who use what abilities they have. There is no contradiction between their careers and their inner natures, because society itself is plastic. But Clyde and the younger generation in *The Bulwark* are their dialectic opposites. Clyde is the most pathetic failure in Dreiser—even more so than Hurstwood, Carrie's second lover. In order to get ahead, he has to pretend, to tell social lies, and to act deceitfully. In his time the path of opportunity is no longer open, there have been alterations in the American Dream. In the early works, this dream operates as a motivation to rise on the basis of one's talents, energies, and capacities; in the later, the dream becomes one of success by marriage in order to have a life of leisure and enjoyment. Clyde is an ambitious youth in an America more stratified than that of Cowperwood and Witla. Thus Dreiser not only reveals the meaning of American social ideals in his own lifetime and during the period immediately preceding his birth; his works also mirror the changes in those ideals, and the change in the social structure of American life.

Dreiser's methods of characterization are consistent with these attitudes and social revelations. Just as he does not conceive the individual as individual, so his characterizations are not mere representations of atomized men and women struggling in the American society of their time. They appear in their social roles, and their natures as well as their actions are involved in the functions which they perform in society. Carrie's first lover, Drouet, is one of the most successful and attractive of Dreiser's minor characters. He is jolly, genial, superficial, yet he is strikingly different from the salesmen of, for example, Sinclair Lewis. Drouet does not subordinate himself to the "fetish of commodities"; a successful salesman, he is concerned with a life of pleasure, he feels secure in his world. He appears in a social role which is an integral feature of his "individuality." Similarly, Hurstwood has the charm, the savoir-faire, the sophistication of the professional major-domo in a high-class saloon, concerned with meeting important personages. When he loses this position, he loses also the personality that goes with it. His character is social rather than individual, and his defeat is that of a man who has lost his function and place in society. The tragedy in Dreiser's novels is social tragedy. His characters do not merely represent themselves; they speak for their classes and their occupations. *An American Tragedy* would remain a tragic work even if Clyde and Roberta had not died; but it is tragic in a new sense. In Dreiser, the old terms of art are reset by the social thinking of his day.

Such characterizations as his are not mere types. Their traits are linked to occupation only as growth or decay occurs in relationship with occupation or sex experience. In the instances where sex is the dominant functional aspect of a life, we can observe his method of characterization from a primarily biological angle. Carrie, when she is a "kept woman," grows, expands in desire. She begins to realize her nature; she becomes more sociable, more sure of herself; the road is opened to her so that she can utilize her potentialities. Jennie as a mistress reveals a steady deepening of emotions and sympathies. But even biological impulses are social in their expression and development. The Social Darwinism of Dreiser's basic attitudes toward human nature is distilled into a social philosophy of determinism and change. Again, without formulation of a system (ironically, he became a communist only just before he died), he supplies the means by which basic questions about twentieth century American society may be asked.

## 5

Forgetful of the integrity and power of Dreiser's whole work, many critics have been distracted into a condemnation of his style. He was, like Twain and Whitman, an organic artist; he wrote what he knew—what he was. His many colloquialisms were part of the coinage of his time, and his sentimental and romantic passages were written in the language of the educational system and the popular literature of his formative years. In his style, as in his material, he was a child of his time, of his class. Self-educated, a type or model of the artist of plebeian origin in America, his language, like his subject matter, is not marked by internal inconsistencies. As a style, in the formal sense, it never developed at all, and he frequently permitted his novels to be revised by others before publication.

Dreiser has also been upbraided because of his auctorial comments. The newness of his material and method seemed to him to need explanation, and the censorship and rejection of certain of his novels did little to convince him that such explanation was not necessary. He had no model upon which to shape his attack on the formal middle-class conventions of the times. He needed to be extensive in his realism, rather than concentrated and intensive like Flaubert or Balzac or Zola, who wrote from a richer and deeper literary tradition, and for a more sophisticated and culturally sensitive public than America could supply.

There are many passages in these novels that rise to high levels of passionate writing. In Dreiser the subject matter is always more important than the expression. Because he reveals the very nerves of American society he has exerted a more profound, a more lasting influence than any other novelist on twentieth century realistic fiction in America. Several generations of writers are already his debtors. His influence is discoverable in a seriousness of approach to the material of American life, in a greater freedom of theme, in the parallelism of ideas and phenomena. Dreiser described the broad patterns of modern American experience; his successors have been more intensive in their treatment. Because he was faithful to his art and made no compromises with the censors and the prudes, his work gives a sense of totality and finality.

## 72. FICTION SUMS UP A CENTURY

THE other major writers of fiction of this period—even those whose first important books were published in the twenties—were not innovators of a new era, but belonged to the nineteenth century in which were their roots. They were prewar in inspiration or in their sense of fundamental values, and were summary, not iconoclastic, in their artistic purposes. The women were deeply concerned with the preservation of character, and especially with virtue—*virtus* in the Roman sense, but implying more emotion and less sheer virility than the Romans gave to the word. It was the decay or survival of ideals of living resulting from the great American experiment in nation making which most stirred their imagination.

With the exception of Edith Wharton, these novelists functioned as guardians of the race, and especially of its emotional life. The men drew equally from reservoirs of confidence stored up in the American nineteenth century, but their emphasis seems to be different. They saw, angrily, a machine-made materialism sheltering behind and perverting the Protestant-Christian code, turning it into a religion of success; and they satirized the victims of low objectives, and a generation which seemed to be losing the spiritual force and the virility of its ancestors. Both men and women, when the end of the war released energy for literature, were prepared to capture the imagination of a public much more ready to become self-conscious than in the confident years before the war. It was a classic moment, the end and summation of an era, a moment also when criticism and creation were equal in power. It was a brief pause to define and distill American values before new and sharper changes in our mores and our philosophy began.

### 2

Inevitably the confusion, not to say chaos, of values which followed the wide demoralization of the Civil War had been reflected in literature. But, unlike many postwar eras, our seventies, eighties, and nineties were decades of unprecedented expansion and multiplication of wealth. Writers—and they were numerous—who felt as Henry James said in the sixties, that America needed most of all refinement, found, it is true, dramatic themes ready-made for their not always competent pens. The great theme of crude human energy developing a continent of unequaled potentiality, which Whitman had proclaimed, did not appeal to them, because this energy was too rough for refinement, and, indeed, not perfect democrats, as Whitman hoped, but powerful millionaires were its most conspicuous by-product. Yet this impact of new wealth upon old, and of a new and aggressive materialism upon the different ideals of pioneers and old aristocratic societies alike, supplied conflicts in ways of life, and hence fascinating subjects for the novelist of manners.

New wealth, for example, in this land of opportunity did not manifest itself so much in the increasing riches of the possessing classes as in new candidates for what Veblen called the conspicuous waste of the socially prominent. It was not so much oil or iron or lumber money that appeared in the ballrooms of New York as new families whose unlimited spending power was more advertised than its sources. The crudeness of the newcomers and the limitations of the settled way of life of the old dictators of society and custodians of what they called culture, were equally exposed to the imagination in search of a story.

The "outsider" to all this rush for wealth and power, such as a Theodore Dreiser, interpreting the excesses of freedom as one of the masses, could see the whole in perspective, but made the protagonists seem like figures of melodrama. An intellectual aristocrat, an "insider," not committed to any vital part of the social drama of the secure and the ambitious—such an "insider" as Henry James—recoiled from the grossness of unrefinement, yet found in the new types and new situations rich materials for his consummate art, especially when transferred to the revealing light of a European background. But his so-called disciple, Edith Wharton, was an insider in another sense. She belonged, she was committed to, the idea of society in its narrowest sense, a wealthy and secure society, the plutocratic aristocracy of New York and its affiliated capitals of American social life.

Edith Wharton was born into this society, she married in it. She accepted its self-claimed necessity; she doubted the need of secure wealth no more than did Jane Austen. It was not the attacks of barbarian millionaires and monopolists upon such economic democracy as we had been able to achieve which disturbed her. It was the narrow culture, the rigid codes, and the lack of all but defensive vitality of this American aristocracy which stung her imagination. Her first important novel, *The House of Mirth* (1905), reveals nothing in the history of Lily Bart which wealth could not cure. This novel is the tragedy of a lovely woman without money, in a society where that is the only guarantee of security. The feeble hero of the story is unable to help her with his love because he too is poor. In Mrs. Wharton's greatest novel, *The Age* of Innocence (1920), written in her maturity and the new maturity of the country, the rebellious heroine, the charming Countess Olenska, is provided with money in order to enable her to escape Lily Bart's tragedy, and she does escape, but only to a more enlightened aristocracy abroad where good talk was possible, as it was not in New York. But her lover, even when he and she are both free, is too emasculated by his traditions of hothouse security to take even an easy step toward emotional reality.

Yet in spite of the stale air, the limited visibility of this society of more or less than four hundred which Mrs. Wharton chose for her studies of American life, there was an opportunity here for the kind of fiction which Stendhal had written in France—studies of significant manners in a group where worth as human beings had little relevance to the importance of their behavior as individuals observably conditioned by a uniform environment, the thing that Cooper longed for in an earlier age when he said Americans could not have a literature until they had manners. All that was needed was sufficient skill on the part of the novelist, an intimate knowledge, and some purpose deeper than the merely descriptive.

With Mrs. Wharton the last was supplied by the sharpening social conscience of the first decades of the twentieth century. Her stories are evidently preliminary to the obsession with the values of American experience which is so characteristic of the fiction of the summary period of the twenties and the work of the somewhat younger novelists discussed later in this chapter. She had the intimate knowledge, and she had the skill. It was she and another insider, Ellen Glasgow, who began the attack upon the idols of the social temples, North and South. Hers, in wealthy New York, still dominated society; but they were clay, and, what she did not see with any conviction, they were quite unimportant in the history of the great American experiment, since this aristocracy had nothing to recommend it except its security, and was even more irresponsible than the new millionaires who crashed its gates. But she belonged—as Sinclair Lewis belonged in Main Street—and this gave her satire authenticity.

As for her skill, it is part of the extraordinary advance in the craft of construction and emphasis which developed so rapidly in the American nineties, especially in the short story of which she was a master. It is not true, as has often been said, that she learned her technique from Henry James. That great craftsman is at the same time more subtle and more natural in the handling of situations. What she learned from him was what had been rare in America before his day, the infinite care of the artist who regards perfect expression as the hardest, if not the most important, part of his task. She was his apprentice, but she does not belong to his school. His influence, which undoubtedly formed her artistic conscience, was so strong because his favorite characters spoke her language, and belonged to an environment where no lack of refinement in the art of mere living prevented the free play of the subtler emotions or suppressed the adventures and obscured the rebuffs of the intellect.

The briefest consideration of Mrs. Wharton's other books will show how much she is at her best when, like a court painter, she accepts her characters' assumption of their own importance, and gives them her finest because her most intimate work. If, as in *The Old Maid* (1924), she works sympathetically instead of satirically within her little New York world, she is superb. When, as in that piece of perfect craftsmanship, *Ethan Frome* (1911), she gets her theme in the harsh stoicism of the New England hills, it is not Ethan, or his unhappy lover or still more unfortunate wife, who gives the story its final direction, so much as the horror of the final scene of sordid misery for an observer coming from a world where the spiritual effects of crude poverty are unknown. When, as in *Hudson River Bracketed* (1929), she chooses for her subject what her social New Yorkers called "writing people," her skill is manifest, but her book is unreal and out of focus, even in its satire, for she does not seem sufficiently to care.

Mrs. Wharton, indeed, if one of the first of the new critics of American society, was one of the last of the old regionalists. America as a nation was still unreal to her. She was closer to the great regionalists of an earlier New England than to the writers of the twenties who would consciously make their stories microcosms of what was most significant to them in a culture where North, South, East, and West were blending. Historically, she is likely to survive as the memorialist of a dying aristocracy. Yet the effect of her success upon the technical standards of popular fiction must have been great.

In the other novelists of manners who either began or came into full powers and appreciation in these earliest twenties, the same discontent with a lack of emotional vitality in American society is evident. Indeed, it gives to their novels an edge and a fire usually lacking in mere stories of romantic or eccentric behavior. With the exception of Ellen Glasgow, these novelists were unmoved by the spectacle of an aristocracy slowly fossilizing. It was in bourgeois or industrial or pioneer communities that they found their themes. For them, New York was only a center of amusement, easy morals, and high finance, although it is true that for the next decades the society columns and fashion commentators were to shed a cheap glamour on a "smart set" now rapidly shifting toward the promiscuousness of café society." The best of them saw America in a national perspective as Edith Wharton could not. They were writing the fiction of that race of races, that total democracy which Whitman idealized and romanticized. An example is the brilliant analyst Zona Gale, author of *Miss Lulu Bett* (1920), who wrote too little. In her books the conventionalism of the Middle West is defeated by impulse and passion. The most high-spirited moralist among women writers of the period, Dorothy Canfield Fisher, pleads always for emotional integrity anywhere and against any odds. While Mrs. Wharton deplores the corrosions of security, Ellen Glasgow fears only that the nobler aristocratic values will die out of America with her dying Virginians. And passion, nobly interpreted, is Willa Cather's chief theme. Indeed, it is Ellen Glasgow and Willa Cather, the two finest craftsmen and artists in this movement toward a summary literature of the secure and confident nineteenth century, who best illustrate the woman's contribution to American fiction at the end of an era.

## 3

Willa Sibert Cather, born in 1876 in mountain Virginia, was transplanted to the rolling grasslands of Nebraska in time to know a frontier. Sensitive to beauty, and quick to detect significance, she saw the great land make and break its people. She saw the full-blooded European immigrants, Czechs and Swedes, plowing the unbroken land, on the way up from peasants to proprietors. She saw their puzzled admiration of American culture, which was also immigrant in these wild plains, but grown successful and a little stiff and stale. She saw the break between the generations when the children of the foreign pioneers came to town, to become more smug, more conventional than their American neighbors. Yet the fresh blood she describes was still vigorous. What reader will forget the Czech and Danish servants and working girls in *My Ántonia,* rash in love, warm in heart and body, still seeking passion in the small-town respectability of the settled Middle West!

Miss Cather was educated at the University of Nebraska. She taught, found her way back East, and became an editorial assistant on Samuel McClure's magazine, the periodical which torpedoed the great monthlies of the genteel age, then growing safe and dull. Raids against the corruption and decay of politics at the end of the nineteenth century were its specialty, but McClure opened his columns to the new literature appearing on both sides of the Atlantic. Either then or later, Miss Cather's creative mind ranged widely through literature, and she chose her tradition in craftsmanship, which was French, and her subject matter, which was the heroic but neglected *virtus* of the last pioneers of the unconquered West. In 1912 she left *McClure's*; in 1913 she published *O Pioneers!*; in 1915, *The Song of the Lark*; in 1918, *My Ántonia*; in 1920, her brilliant short stories, *Youth and the Bright Medusa*; in 1923, *A Lost Lady,* her most skillful though not her most powerful work; in 1927, *Death Comes for the Archbishop,* her masterpiece; in 1931, *Shadows on the Rock*. These are her most important books.

Willa Cather, like the greatest of her predecessors among women in English fiction, Jane Austen, was extraordinarily consistent in her art from beginning to end. She did not experiment except within the limits of her purpose; she knew exactly what she wanted to do. And this can be described in her own words from a book *Not Under Forty* (1936), in which she recorded her admiration for her master in the art of fiction, Gustave Flaubert, and for her older contemporary, Sarah Orne Jewett. After learning to write the novelist must unlearn it, she wrote, for his material must go

through a process very different from that by which he makes merely a good story. No one can define this process exactly; but certainly persistence, survival, recurrence in the writer's mind, are highly characteristic of it. The shapes and scenes that have "teased" the mind for years, when they do at last get themselves rightly put down, make a much higher order of writing, and a much more costly, than the most vivid and vigorous transfer of immediate impressions.

Every fine story must leave in the mind of the sensitive reader an intangible residuum of pleasure; a cadence, a quality of voice that is exclusively the writer's own, individual, unique. . . . It is a common fallacy that a writer . . . can achieve this poignant quality by improving upon his subject-matter, by using his "imagination" upon it and twisting it to suit his purpose. The truth is that by such a process (which is not imagination at all!) he can at best present only a brilliant sham. . . . If he achieves anything noble, anything enduring, it must be by giving himself absolutely to his material. And this gift of sympathy is his great gift; is the fine thing in him that alone can make his work fine.

This is what Willa Cather proposed to do in her novels; she succeeded, thanks to a discipline in the absolute justice of the word, which she may have learned from Flaubert, and to an art of suspense, acquired probably from her own experience with the American short story, in which she was both critic and creator. Jane Austen let what "teased" her imagination flow along the framework of a conventional plot. She twisted neither plot nor subject matter to suit her purpose, and when her sympathy was discharged and her plot unrolled, was content to end with the handiest convention. Willa Cather discarded plot from the beginning. She yielded to her subject matter, content to evoke its cadences, its qualities, its stream of significant experience. Even the poignant death of the lovers in *O Pioneers!*, surely one of the notable scenes in English literature, is known only by its preliminaries and its evidences, as if to have made it a climax of a plot would have detracted from its perfect place in a chronicle of a land so immature, so hard that passion could find only a thwarted release.

Therefore, from beginning to end, the Cather novels are not stories of plot, but chronicles, given a depth and significance lacking in the merely historical chronicle by that "sympathy" which leads to a perfect interplay of environment and character.

Her art was essentially a representation of this reaction between the soul of man and its environment. That is why the best of her stories are told against the land—the sweep of red grass on the rolling plains of Nebraska, the hard warm mesas of the Southwest tempering the unconquerable spirit of the archbishop, shadows of the wilderness and the winter crowding in upon the tiny culture of France on the rock of Quebec. Her best characters are least at home in the fabricated cities which so stirred the naïve heart of Sinclair Lewis' Babbitt. Chicago as a city, to Thea when she is learning to sing in *The Song of the Lark*, means only trivial discomfort and an irrelevant confusion.

With *Death Comes for the Archbishop*, Willa Cather left even the semblance of fiction for pure chronicle. This novel is the *vitae* of two saints, a Paul and a Peter of the desert, and its story is a record of their minds and hearts and souls. So was *O Pioneers!* the story of a group of immigrants humanizing the land, so was *My Ántonia* the story of a great woman ennobling common things and a common struggle by elemental passion. But in the two obvious chronicles, of the archbishop and of the rock of Quebec, the narrative is distilled into biography. Here were lives working upon and wrought upon by a new land and its people. And the same was true of her late book, *Sapphira and the Slave Girl* (1940), with its unsatisfactory ending, where the teller of the tale does what Flaubert (so she says) never would do, enters herself upon the scene and "encourages familiarity."

If one asks how these chronicles are made evocative, comprehensive, and interest-holding, the answer is as easy to define as it is difficult to explain in detail. There is a selection of incident and appearance, and an inevitability of language (as with Flaubert and Turgenev) so careful that the result is a candid, if delusive, simplicity. It is candid because the author so evidently has given herself to the theme and found words for her experience; it is delusive because this simplicity is, of course, not easy but a fine art. And her own absorption in her people and her land creates the suspense that she herself has felt.

She was consistent in her craft, and also in her choice of character and theme. Like all the important novelists of this end of an era, she sought an emotional vitality great enough to break through stiffening conventions and repel the ideas of materialistic success. Her stories present the old case of the artist versus the people, the heart versus what the public calls success, the life of the spirit versus materialism, a case under trial for a century in prosperous America. But she offered an interesting variant in organizing her stories about the life of a good man or woman—that is, a human being intensely, often rapturously, devoted to the experiences of deep living itself. Alexandra in *O Pioneers!* is such a person with the emphasis upon a will to tame the American land for the needs of the future. Marie, the Bohemian girl, in the same book, is the essence of being alive, the very pulse of the blood personified, doomed to be the victim somehow of what we so justly call ill nature. Ántonia is such a character, not too fine, not too nice in her ethics, determined upon happiness and getting it because she never counts the costs. Mrs. Forrester in *A Lost Lady* is not lost because of her adulteries. She is lost because her incomparable gift of charm cannot sustain itself by its own worth, but must feed on the gross sensualities of gross men. Her husband is the good man of this story, good because he understands that his wife is a precious jewel worth all the tribe about her, even though fibered with clay.

As Willa Cather grew older, she seemed to have exhausted her own best memories, and sought in history for subject matter less personal and more difficult. And so (influenced perhaps again by Flaubert) she left the present, left her own Middle West, and absorbed herself in the austere, ascetic, intractable beauty of New Mexico, and the Catholic culture of Quebec. Yet her characters have the same significance. The archbishop again is the good man endeavoring to make life and himself not more or less prosperous, but richer in spiritual passion, though he had no prejudices against the earthly variety. His good is *virtus*—character, love of experience, including emphatically the vitality of sensuous experience. He is a good man whose energy is challenged by the opportunities in a new land to create new and better experience for his followers. Thus, when he comes in the wake of American conquest to New Mexico he pioneers for his church with an almost sensual satisfaction. He is aware of the value of every genuine emotion, whether the gusto of the half-pagan priests of the old regime, or the Castilian decorum of his Spanish patrons, or the dark and true part-souls of his Indians. Only the cheap and the predatory rouse him to anger. With him is Father Joseph, a good animal irradiated by religion, a medieval saint saved from fanatical disaster by the finer intellect of the man he loves. The novel itself is the projection of these two lives against a compelling environment. It is good history, but it transcends history because its theme is the vitality of holiness. There is little to add in this respect of her later *Shadows on the Rock* which, with less power but equal purity, portrays the good life in conflict with worldly ambition and the wilderness in seventeenth century Quebec.

Thus Willa Cather usefully filled her niche in American literary history. Her youthful background in the unmade West, and her sensitiveness to the pervasive influence of new land upon European man, made her the summer-up of our long tradition of local color, now felt to be part of the history of the imagination of a great country. And her feeling for vital passion in any of its forms (passion, she says, is what she seeks in all her stories), gave her power over a theme unique in the nineteenth century, the overflow of vigorous men and women from the Old World into new country, after a thousand years of stability. She made personal history of Whitman's "race of races" in its formative century. Her art is not a big art. It does not respond to the troubled sense of American might and magnitude realized but undirected, and felt so strongly by such men as Sinclair Lewis in the same decades. It is national in significance, but not in scope. Her colleagues among the men "sweated sore" over that job, whereas her books rise free and are far more creative than critical. She is preservative, almost antiquarian, content with much space in little room—feminine in this, and in her passionate revelation of the values which conserve the life of the emotions. She knew evil, and suffered from the grossnesses of materialism and the smugness of cheap success, but preferred to celebrate the vitality of the good.

### 4

Ellen Glasgow was also from Virginia, and her ancestry is in the western mountain regions which were the first frontier of the tidewater aristocracy. But she remained in Virginia, and her impressive list of novels deals throughout with Virginians at home, or seeking new fortunes among the Virginia emigrants to New York. She spent a lifetime on deeply sympathetic studies of the end of an aristocratic culture, and the defeat of an agrarian people by their own misuse of the land. Both women were idealists, but Willa Cather was drawn to the dawn and Ellen Glasgow to the sunset. Both were concerned with values which should be conserved for the country. In Willa Cather's most characteristic novels the land is just beginning to yield its wealth to the settler, in Ellen Glasgow's it is worn out; yet in both mankind is in a state of becoming. Nor was either deflected in purpose by the current materialism which made satirists of the best of the men among their contemporaries. Ellen Glasgow's heroes and heroines triumph spiritually, Sinclair Lewis' do not.

Ellen Glasgow herself divided her novels into three groups, and discussed them in *A Certain Measure* (1943), which contains some of the best personal criticism written by an American novelist. Novels of the Commonwealth, novels of the Country, novels of the City, she calls them, the Commonwealth being Virginia, the Country being the rural and the mountain region west of tidewater, the City being Richmond. The grouping does not conform strictly to the chronology of her work. She began with Virginia history in the decades before, and in, and just succeeding the Civil War, so disastrous to Virginia. Then she moved upward to her own times, where two themes chiefly interested her: the endeavor to survive in and renew an exhausted land; and the struggle to preserve spiritual ideals of life and char-acter in a prosperous and materialistic city. She is most colorful in her early historic novels, where, with an impassioned realism, she handles the story of the Lost Cause which the sentimentalists had made into a rosy legend. She is most profound and greatest in her stories of the land. She is most subtle, most ironic, and most critical in her novels of city life. Typical examples are *The Battle-Ground* (1902), *Barren Ground* (1925), and *The Romantic Comedians* (1926).

Ellen Glasgow chose for her motto, "What the South needs is blood and irony"; but there is less irony in her collected works than one expects, and more of the blood of a discriminating idealism. When she began to write at the turn of the nineteenth century, at the very climax of a confident age, the novelists of the South were capitalizing glamour and sentiment. Their favor-ite characters came from a never-never land of imagination, and they were compensating for the defeat of one way of life by another with whitewash tinted in rose, and success stories where, on such lines, there could be no success. Their realities were the memories of childhood, and their novels had a wide sentimental appeal but not much particular truth. Ellen Glasgow, even as a girl, determined to begin a "solitary revolt" against the formal, the false, the affected, the sentimental, and the pretentious in Southern writing.

The importance of this solitary revolt seems less now that the Thomas Nelson Pages and the other Southern novelists of glamour have faded almost out of memory. Yet a familiar and sympathetic culture which has not been made truly articulate is a challenge to the best powers of a novelist. "I had no guide," she says, and so, not desiring to imitate the "regimented realism" of William Dean Howells, then dominant in the North, she went, like Willa Cather, to the old masters of fiction, Balzac, Flaubert, De Maupassant, and the great English novelists. There she learned to define the art of fiction as the "assembling of material and the arrangement of masses," which has more of construction and perhaps less of art than Willa Cather's resolve to give herself utterly to her subject matter; and also to believe that fiction itself was "experience illuminated," with which Willa Cather would certainly agree.

Thus, and as might be expected, Ellen Glasgow's novels have the effect as well as the scope of social history. She is close to Dreiser and Howells and Sinclair Lewis here, though so different in her sympathies and her interests. And yet she was utterly uninfluenced by Dreiser, the most powerful of her contemporaries. In his massive, plodding defense of the unfortunate he was oblivious to the stoic ideals of character, the aristocratic virtues which, even in her stories of poverty, irradiate sordid experience. Where Lewis attacked with savage scorn, she used irony; and her leading characters, even her happiness seekers, as she calls them, are the morally successful, not the spiritually dead. "The spirit of fortitude has triumphed over the sense of futility" in her Dorinda in *Barren Ground,* and elsewhere in her lengthy gallery of portraits. Her women especially conserve, and were chosen to conserve, true values, not to destroy false ones. And she was like Howells only in this, that her purpose was not only to create life (the chief duty, as she says, of a novelist) but to reflect, as no Southern novelist had done before, the true movement and tone of a society and an age.

In describing Ellen Glasgow as essentially a novelist of social history, there is no intent to confuse her particular art with the historian's, or with the romancer's whose leading figures are only shadowy types. Ellen Glasgow, like Sherwood Anderson, begins always with the personality manifesting itself, and stirring the imagination with its hint of a story. The black-haired girl beside a whitewashed wall, seen in a fleeting glimpse, steps out into the sunlight, puts on identity, and is the cause, if not the purpose, of *Barren Ground,* perhaps her finest novel. Judge Honeywell in *The Romantic Comedians* "had endured the double-edged bliss of a perfect marriage" for thirty-six years, when his wife's death opened the gates of folly.

And yet the ultimate significance of all these novels is social, and we remember the struggle and its background and the form and pressure of the society better than the names of the characters. These books tell the story of the conflict of generations in Richmond. They show the vein of iron in the character of a strong stock which rusts but never softens at the core. They reveal, as in *The Battle Ground,* the moral destruction of war. So morally significant are these old aristocrats, lovely ladies, determined girls, that they illustrate the types to which they belong. They are rich in what she calls "the individual graces" of the past, "the perpetually escaping spirit of the thing we call life." History in its deepest sense always flows around them. Something they lose of unique personality by comparison with Willa Cather's figures, whom one always thinks of by name.

Like her fellow Virginian James Branch Cabell, Ellen Glasgow was young in the nineties when style as an achievement in itself was most in favor among the literary. Her careful workmanship, her "single artistic endeavor," saved her, as it did not save Cabell, from the rhetoric of that period; yet as a stylist she belongs with this literary period of time. The "old guard," as she called them, of her youthful day, although genteel and complacent, at least wrote with a professional care for beauty as they understood it. She had no sympathy, though she recognized the limitations of the old patterns, for the "amateurs," the experimentalists in force, vulgarity, and brutishness, practitioners of the unlovely, disdainers of form, who in the mid-twenties took over leadership in American fiction.

Her own style is classic in a good sense, but it is not the classicism of Willa Cather. It is a style of evident rhythms, a garment of flowing words, that describes rather than evokes, though in her descriptions of Virginia backgrounds she evokes also. It is a style which, like Thomas Hardy's, moves in masses rather than word by word, reflecting "the vision of the artist in the direct light of imagination" and playing upon life with "absolute fidelity of treatment." As with Hardy, it is an all-embracing garment that sometimes diverts or strains the attention of the reader. Her simpler, less stylistic books, dealing with the unsophisticated, like *Vein of Iron* and *Barren Ground* were most popular. But in her consciousness of style as such she summarized an era of American fiction soon to end.

5

The work of James Branch Cabell, another Virginian, born in 1879 at Richmond, Virginia, was once a cult for the literary, and is still significant in American letters. Aside from some newspaper experience in New York, his life was essentially that of a Virginia scholar and gentleman, such a life as Poe aspired to live. In his fruitful period, Cabell created a saga, a mythology, and a satire of a country of phantasy called Poictesme, which was medieval in appearance, chivalric in action, and satiric and cynical in spirit. His theme was ironic, romantic disillusion. Therefore it is biographically noteworthy that he sprang from one of the distinguished families of the old Virginian aristocracy which had been supplying myth and romance to sentimental novelists. Also, that in 1896–1897 he was instructor in French and Greek at William and Mary College, the two literatures from which he drew most of his materials for symbolism, both sexual and moralistic.

In the years when Cabell achieved fame, and when his style was the admiration of younger writers, he was engaged upon variants of one general idea. Beginning very early in his career, and continuing through *Figures of Earth* (1921) and *Something About Eve* (1927), the same females, prankishly disguised as nature myths, demons, or heroines of fable, and the same hero, whose *virtus* comes from a collaboration of moral skepticism with sexual might, appear and reappear in different blends and emphases. Many parts of these books are repetitive, confusing, mannered, and gross in their symbolism. But at least once Cabell's great power over expression, his talent for phantasy, and his carefully planned satire were combined in a moving and brilliant story which sums up his literary endeavor. This book is *Jurgen,* which was published in 1919, and got much useful publicity by its encounters with Philistia and the law. *Jurgen* did much to crack the taboo on sex in American fiction.

Jurgen himself was a nihilistic epicurean, better educated in philosophy and the art of living than Walt Whitman, but further away from the true ideals of epicureanism. He was endowed with what he calls cleverness, the only trait of which he is never skeptical. Anthropologists would call it that gift of curiosity which accounts for the intellectual progress of the human race. Jurgen is a paunchy pawnbroker of Poictesme married to a nagging wife who nevertheless keeps him comfortable; but his youth has been spent in amorous and romantic adventures, and his ideas of how to live are entirely aristocratic. By a shrewd bargain with the mythical mistress of disillusion, he gets back his youth stripped of its illusions, and begins a fantastic seeking through the imagination of the past for the kind of justice which will satisfy a sensual egotist who is too clever to be taken in by shams, too gross to be attracted by nobility, too skeptical to be content with anything short of an ultimate purpose revealed in things as they are. He finds none, although in his journey he visits all the famous seductive females, the engaging myths, and interesting heroes of history, and even enters hell and heaven.

He does discover two motives for existence which seem to have validity. There is love (not the amorous variety) which is to be esteemed, but is evidently impracticable for an aristocratic poet, so much of whose time is inevitably engaged by love of a more earthy kind. And there is pride which, if impossible for whoever created this sorry world, can be attained by a clever human whose curiosity is undaunted by disillusion. Yet, except for the satisfactions of curiosity, Jurgen views all revelations and all experience with skepticism.

Cabell's philosophy, as indicated by his choice of characters, and his conception of *virtus*, was fundamentally irresponsible, as has indeed been the philosophy of many ironists of the past. Life may be an idle dream, says Jurgen, shrugging his shoulders, but "what could I be expected to do about it?" This is not the irresponsibility of a later generation of writers assailed by Archibald MacLeish (in *The Irresponsibles*) and others, who were so obsessed with their diagnosis of the ills of their country that they failed to detect and encourage the idealism and the fortitude of American youth. Yet if one considers that Cabell's novels of Poictesme are one long attack upon the stale chivalry and the perfunctory religion of Virginia, and upon a bourgeois morality and an insensitiveness to beauty and to emotional truth in the American bourgeoisie in general—why, then it is fair to say that Cabell was irresponsible. For he belonged with Bernard Shaw in his prankish moods and Anatole France in his destructive ironies, and, following them, took more pleasure in putting a symbolic Galahad to bed with a symbolic Guinevere than in any attributes useful for the progress or the survival of the race. This, of course, is a description, not a condemnation. The satirist does not have to play ball with the future. But Cabell's local animosities often limited his truth.

In another aspect, Cabell was unquestionably a link between past and future in the transition of American literature. He was a romanticist, close in his subject matter and his incidents to the cloak-and-sword best sellers of the decades before *Jurgen*. But he was a romanticist with claws and teeth. He satirized his own aristocratic Main Street while sharing its tastes and habits of life. He was unread, and was perhaps unreadable, by a later generation which was forced into entire realism by a volcanic explosion of moral evil and efficient force, and was somewhat too doubtful of any craftsman in words. The stoic energy, the passion for life, the courage of Willa Cather's best characters seem now to have been truly valuable elements in American culture, over which Jurgen's contemporary swordplay (both sexual and skeptical) flashes like a comedian's trick. Yet Cabell's irony and his skepticism were clearly a first and necessary step toward the sarcastic realism of a Sinclair Lewis, and the escape from the prejudices, religious, philosophical, and sexual, of the dying nineteenth century. It would be too much to say that later writers acquired a necessary disillusion from him; but certainly he was the most adroit psychoanalyst of American complacency, and subtlest gadfly of American hypocrisy, among the intellectuals of our early 1900's.

His style is brilliantly allusive, ornate, pointed, yet flowing. Like much of the romantic style of the turn of the century (and its architecture also), it is a pastiche, yet it is conscious pastiche, in which Cabell, like Joyce a little later, uses imitation and pseudoromanticism for his own purposes. It is, to go back to Ellen Glasgow's remark, a professional style, and unlike the experiments of Thomas Wolfe and of Ernest Hemingway in that it fits life into a literary tradition instead of the opposite. Very seldom does it escape from preciosity.

As a symbolist in the American line, he was more self-conscious than Hawthorne or Melville, and less passionate than Whitman. Cabell's symbolism translated his disillusioned observations upon things as they are into a biographical dictionary of literary history. His figures and the regions he created for them are often exceedingly beautiful, but they melt conveniently one into another, and have to be retranslated by the reader before they persist in his memory. And when they are translated, which is not always easy, the result is often scandalous.

The charge of excessive sexuality made against Cabell was based on these figures of fancy, all of whom, except Jurgen and his variants, represent attributes rather than personality and unanalyzable life. The narrative about them is two-thirds made up of episodes of the approach to or the escape from fornication. But if Cabell's sexuality is extreme, it is also sophisticated beyond danger to the innocent, and indeed more truly a reaction against the South's sentimental deification of "pure womanhood" than a call to passionate experience. The excess, for it is sometimes a tiresome excess, is part of Cabell's self-appointed mission as a devil sent to torment the genteel age and especially genteel literature. He came too soon to write, like the novelists of the thirties, naturally of natural things. Yet he passionately wished to pull off the veils of convention and announce the native amorousness of women, even when they were Virginians, and to portray man with sexual experience as his most exciting occupation. All this his symbolism permitted, and when the law penetrated some of his disguises, his rage against prudery increased to the detriment of his art. He was best when suppressed—which may be true of all fiction writers who are abler in the criticism of mores than in the creation of character and personality.

## 6

Sinclair Lewis was born in 1885 in Sauk Center, Minnesota, in the farther Middle West, a region in which, as he often asserted, were the roots of his inspiration. His mind was as sensitive to the lakes, the land, and more particularly to the small towns and energetic cities of this region as Thomas Hardy's to Wessex, or Jane Austen's to south England and to Bath—but not so affectionate!

Educated at Yale, in the class of 1907, he was a brilliant misfit in an orthodox university. Nevertheless, he sucked much from men and books in an environment easy for conformists, yet tolerant of cranks, wild men, and geniuses. His early years as publisher's assistant and writer showed no more promise than a gift for clever journalism. But in 1920 his *Main Street* astonished, where it did not outrage, reading America. In 1922 his *Babbitt* gave a name and a local habitation to an American type, which, despite frantic denials, was recognized, both here and abroad, as having as much truth as satire requires. In 1925 he published *Arrowsmith,* the best, if not the first novel of science, where materialism versus idealism supplies the theme. It is also satiric, frequently unfair, but packed, like the best social history, with authentic information. In 1930, having refused domestic honors, he was chosen as the first American to receive the Nobel Prize for distinction in literature. Already he was the most publicized American novelist of the decade.

The Middle West of Sinclair Lewis is the Middle West of Willa Cather, but with the often heroic period of pioneering on the land further in the background. His characters have come to town. The land is conquered, and no longer concerns them except as income or profit. They are bourgeois, not agrarian. Complacency, meanness, and boasting have cheapened their way of life, which was true of the small-town folk who provide the irritant in Miss Cather's stories. Main Street in Gopher Prairie and the city, Zenith, are both confident that they represent the best of the new world to come.

And yet Sinclair Lewis, no more than Ellen Glasgow or Willa Cather, was a rebel against the advertised ideals of the nineteenth century, whose deplorable end in crassness he was to depict. The morals of Protestantism, the ideals of progress, the scruples of a Christian, and the manners of a liberal gentleman, are all implicit in his reforms. It was a decadence of spirit and a hypocrisy of morals in the midst of abounding energy which provoked him to distress and anger. The energy itself and the things, the gadgets, which it had created, fascinated him, and he was furious because they had been captured by a predatory materialism, where money and size were the only standards of success. He was not, as was thought when *Main Street* was first published, the herald of a new literature, but the satirist who felt himself to be part of a matured society, which he castigated with no more intent to destroy than if he had been criticizing himself. The shock of the war had aroused desire for society's self-improvement. That Greek-Christian culture was beginning to struggle for survival had naturally not occurred to him. He was still confident.

Thanks to the First World War, there had been a sharpening of American nationalism, and also a renewed consciousness of the European tradition whose values we had begun to forget in our energetic isolationism. Thanks to the same war, the United States was building economic supremacy. Thanks to the spread of American literacy, it was possible to write for, as well as of, a wide middle class which was both sensitive and vulnerable because its economic success had made it representative of America. Discarding the historical, the romantic, the sentimental, the symbolic, and the analytic approach, adopting that very familiarity which Flaubert condemned, choosing the new journalism which dealt with behavior as his guide (though not his master), Lewis took aspects of himself, a representative man, rather than a saint or artist or great lover, as the subject of his story, and so began his series of novels.

There, as always with these writers of the end of the age of security, the values of American living provided the theme. But it was not the ideal values (which he did not question) upon which his fiery spirit turned its pity and scorn, but the actual values which determined the careers of these overconfident men and women, whose lives, outwardly successful, rang hollow, or were wrecked in emotional crises or personal disasters. The crassly materialistic "villains" who are in the background of a Cather or a Glasgow novel, take the center of the stage in his work, and are more significant than his idealists who try to escape from them. For the rough task of faithfully representing the kind of society which his Middle West was making, irony was too delicate a weapon. He chose satire and sarcasm, for which he had more talent, and carried them to the edge of caricature. He was a novelist not writing *of* a situation, as Miss Cather had recommended, but *from* the inside of a situation of which he himself was part, and thus more eager to point than to prophesy, and more concerned with behavior, with which he was intimate, than with final interpretation.

Therefore, even as the dominant social class of nineteenth century England is most truly seen in the keen observation of the novels of Anthony Trollope, so the best social history of the "white collar" class of the United States at the high tide of its success is provided by these novels of Sinclair Lewis because of their almost naïve honesty and their accurate focus upon typical experience. That all of Lewis' important books deal directly or indirectly with the Mississippi Valley does not lessen their scope, for that is the heart of America, and his satire of Zenith needed only qualifications to be true for Los Angeles or New York.

*Main Street,* for example, begins like a novel by one of the women of the period, with a talented girl caught in a cramping environment, the small and ugly town of Gopher Prairie. Yet this is to be no story of a saint or a stoic or a creative artist. Carol Kennicott is a product of genteel education, and brings with her to Gopher Prairie a thin culture, vague in its objectives, and trivial in its requirements which seldom go beyond a pretty room to sit in and good talk. She proposes, nevertheless, to reform the town, socially, aesthetically, politically, and is broken, like the butterfly she is, because her intellectual and aesthetic frippery, sterile even in herself, cannot possibly function among men and women whose vulgar grossness (and kind hearts) require a new set of values, not new manners, in order to make a culture of their own. There is no reality in Carol, not even an emotional reality, though it is questionable whether Lewis in 1920 understood how artificial were her standards. She is cold, even in her sexual relations, and the best she can do toward adjustment to life is to escape for a year or so to Washington where she can talk, if not practice, intellectual improvement, and then to come back with enough tolerance to settle down as just another Gopher Prairie woman.

The town is the real subject and the triumph of *Main Street*—not Carol, who is, after all, an example of Lewis' somewhat naïve admiration in 1920 for the "intelligentsia." Lewis must have been well aware that a thousand communities in France and England were duller, meaner, less literate than this home of the second generation of westward-moving frontiersmen, where there was at least the belief that here civilization was on its way up. But his fierce idealism for America, and perhaps some defects in wisdom and perspective, make *Main Street* not only a picture but also a crusade against the cheapness of American ambitions. His men think in stereotypes. They profess the liberalism of their forefathers (as also in *Babbitt*), but practice economic domination of the poor farmers who are too dumb to live by their wits. Their conversation seldom gets beyond the twelve-year age level. The women live by gossip, and culture is a tepid circulating of stale and harmless ideas. Yet Lewis likes them as much as he hates their current values. Dr. Kennicott loves his furnace better than the Parthenon, but he does represent science heroically at work upon one of its frontiers. And if this friendly little society is almost elemental in the pleasures which it really enjoys, at least Main Street life has more gusto than the proposed activities of Carol's "city beautiful." Lewis is a distressed and disgusted idealist, not a cynic. His anger is worth while.

As a novel of character *Main Street* does not reach the highest rank, and as satire its edge is dulled because the author keeps changing sides. The book stirred America from coast to coast, not by its philosophy, but by the inescapable truth and remarkable intimacy of his picture of American behavior.

Lewis could not get his heart into Carol. He was too much a part of Main Street himself to think that she knew the answers. The significant American there was not the second-rate intellectual, but the back-slapping, boosting good fellow who had so much energy and good will, and only a secondhand morality and third-rate objectives toward which to steer his life. Lewis needed a man for his hero, an idealist like himself even if stunted and warped by a bad education and a set of false values. George F. Babbitt was his first great character creation, because Babbitt was as human as his author. He was a far more deadly instrument of satire than the somewhat sociological figures of *Main Street*.

And the book, *Babbitt,* branded the go-getting American, and burnt through his thick hide. George F. Babbitt could not be written off as a caricature, for he was a tragic figure. The man was kind; he was pathetic in his efforts to be both happy and successful; he was as sincere as he was ludicrous in his conviction that he served the community; he was completely devoid of self-knowledge except in brief, devastating gleams of the truth that he had never done what he really wanted; he was completely inconsistent in his morals, he could be both a strutting rooster and a runaway dog trying to sneak home. In fact, he was entirely male, completely bourgeois, and as much of a personality in his way as Falstaff, who was also created for satire.

To tell this man's story with scrupulous realism was inevitably to be satiric. Babbitt is living in the speed-up of the industrial revolution. Zenith is his wonder city, whose misty towers in the morning light provide his one concept of pure beauty—Zenith where automobiles breed faster and better than men. In Zenith everything except respectability is sold or bought for a price, and buying and selling are ends in themselves. In Zenith all boasts come true, because the Babbitts boast only of size and number, both of which science has made possible to very mediocre men. No souls are necessary in Zenith, for a lack of spiritual dignity is compensated by a pride in gadgets, which anyone who works hard enough where the money is, can possess. A new cigar lighter is a baptism into a faith, a new automobile a conversion. And to control and give objectives to all this activity is a code of individualism stereotyped from the heroic age of the frontier, when the pioneer's ability to produce made or broke him.

No one had to think about ultimates, for no one could doubt the religion of success which made a Zenith possible. Yet the society of Zenith was so efficient in its production of wealth and comfort that it had to be explained by something nobler than the ethics of profit on which its practice was based. Hence the accepted morality of "Root, hog, or die" was twisted to cover anything that made money. Profit was morality, for profit was clearly service, and service justified itself. Thus it became necessary for Babbitt and his kind to conform, verbally at least, to ideals of service, because, once you denied that the go-getter served the community and was himself truly successful, the whole show became immoral.

*Babbitt,* which begins with an ironical description of a perfect bathroom and the morning ritual of a gadget-minded man, soon passes into satire. The really vigorous faith of Babbitt himself in his Rotary clubs, his deals, his capacities for leadership, soon begins to threaten wreck on the reefs of personal experience not provided for by his philosophy. His world was like a river steamer, all flimsy top, built for quick profits, sailing down broad but treacherous currents, with the rudder set on the shortest course to wealth, and no pilot on the bridge.

Like so many characters of the novels of the era, Babbitt himself is a good man with tremendous vitality. But he is abysmally ignorant of everything but salesmanship. Like Lewis himself, he really cares for the success of his country, and for its ideals as he understands them. Lewis' immediate successors in a more irresponsible decade were not to care. Babbitt does not represent Babbittry, which, as is now evident, was an endemic disease, epidemic only in his generation. He is its victim, a victim of class pressure and his own mentality, a human being with close relationship to every American of his period, even though he has become a symbol of the false motives that got him down. And he is prophetic of nothing. All that he had learned from his experience was that you should do what you really like—and so he tells his son in the last chapter. But the next generation did not know what they wanted, and were swept into the war, which recognized at least the true values of necessity.

Sinclair Lewis was never to write a more memorable book than *Babbitt*. However, in *Arrowsmith* (1925) he not only took a different grip upon the same American problem, but also brought in new sets of values, true and false. Babbitt seemed pathetic to Lewis. He was a man blown up till he burst spiritually by subservient and erroneous ideas of how to be happy and successful. Martin Arrowsmith is much closer than Babbitt to Lewis himself. His early environment is shoddy and materialistic, but he gets some real education and has more self-knowledge at the beginning of his career than Babbitt ever acquired. He chooses the hard way of science, and in his muddled and inconsistent course, fights through the shams and compromises, the temptations and false values, and finally the commercialized idealism of the vested interests of the medical profession. Babbitt intended to be a lawyer and to defend the rights of the poor. Martin does become the scientist he wished to be, learning on the way what real service to the community means, and the price that has to be paid by a searcher for the truth.

In *Arrowsmith* appears the first really likable woman in Lewis' novels. His women are usually mischief makers, or are possessive, like Martin's second wife from whom he escapes into the happiness of pure research, or negligible, like Mrs. Babbitt. Leora, Martin's first wife, never wavers in faith in her husband and the protection of his personality. Her values as a wife are sound and genuine. She plays her man's game—is indifferent to anything else. For Sinclair Lewis was no feminist. Indeed, a much later book, *Cass Timberlane* (1945), contains some of the most violent attacks on women ever written in America, and the thesis that American men are afraid of their wives. Yet it is also a setting for Jinny Timberlane, one of his most engaging characters.

*Arrowsmith* is Lewis' most informative book, and in it he again showed that his scope was broader, if his searching less deep, than that of his contemporaries. He was so fascinated with America that he could not stop with its values but rushed on to get the whole vast panorama, as he saw it, down on paper. He gorged his reader on dramatic fact. The problem of Arrowsmith was how to stay on the side of the angels. But Lewis did no cheek-turning. He could not endure what he regarded as moral cowardice or hypocrisy. This made him, sometimes, unjust and unfair.

He was the most powerful novelist of the decade when American fiction in general matured in scope and in art. He was not so powerful as the pioneer Dreiser, but was more accomplished in craftsmanship. He was not so mellow as Ellen Glasgow, nor had he the evocative quality of perfected art in which Willa Cather was a master. He had no trace of the passion of beauty as such of the nineties. Yet the genteel critics of the twenties who called him a super-journalist invading the fields of literature were quite wrong. Like his elder contemporary, the great journalist H. G. Wells, he was a reporter of new problems and types emerging in a society rapidly transforming under the influences of science and industrialism. But for Lewis—a true man of letters—the qualities of that society were more interesting than its possibilities. He pledged himself to create in words a living America, and for that he saw, as Dreiser did not, that a style was essential. It is not a beautiful style, though it is capable of great beauty. It is a style of sharp-pointed description of the gadgets of the new materialism, and of most skillful dialogue and monologue which often carry the story and reveal the characters with only a push now and then by the author. *The Man Who Knew Coolidge* (1928) is a tour de force of this monologue, here used without the frame of a story. His ear was extraordinary. That this is the way Americans of his kind talk, no one has denied. But it was not at first realized that this revelation of a people by the rhythm and emphasis of their conversation is a style of a high order, such as Petronius Arbiter and Stendhal and Mark Twain, at his best, achieved for their times.

It is interesting, therefore, to note that *Main Street* was dedicated to two contemporary stylists of different schools, Cabell and Joseph Hergesheimer. Lewis was a rebel against the rhetoric of the nineties, and owed nothing to Cabell's style. But the Virginian's attack on the hypocritical Puritanism of the nineteenth century may have first suggested to him the discrepancy between fully sexed men and women as they appeared in life, and in American books about them. He was not much interested in sexuality as such, and so the frankness of his novels irritated rather than aroused the genteel. Here again he represented the balanced end of a period rather than the defiant emphasis upon sexual intercourse for its own sake which was to be a theme for the next literary generation. In *Cass Timberlane* he used for the first time, and to its furthest reaches, the frankness permitted by modern taste, but without a trace of pornography.

All of Lewis's later books can be described in terms of the analysis above, for they are variants and extensions of his first theme. The best is probably *Dodsworth* (1929), in which a far more sensitive and intelligent Babbitt escapes from a more sophisticated and ruthless Carol Kennicott who is determined to subdue man's soul to what she thinks is culture. The most abusive is *Elmer Gantry* (1927), which fluttered parsonages all over the United States. Here the go-getting clergyman, Elmer, carries Zenith's religion of success into the church itself. Gantry makes his deal with Mammon instead of the traction company, and exploits his God. In *Cass Timberlane* Lewis learned to strip his narrative to essentials and to substitute, without loss of unity, vignettes of parallel experiences for the digressive fullness of earlier stories. In *Kingsblood Royal* (1947) he chose the most sensational theme in America, the Negro question, and made a story which avoids all subtlety, though the violence of his treatment does not exceed the tragic drama of his plot.

7

Sherwood Anderson was born in 1876 in Camden, Ohio, his mother of Italian descent, his father an unsuccessful sign painter with a genius for self-dramatization. Anderson was self-educated after the elementary schools, a sensitive boy seeking answers which might explain human nature, more at home with Negroes, laborers, and hangers-on at livery stables and the race track than with the respectable and the ambitious. His best biography would not be the account of his career as manager of a paint factory, then as advertising writer, and afterward as short-story writer, novelist, and editor, but is to be found in *A Story Teller's Story* (1924), in which he wrote of his own life with precisely the impressionistic, introspective technique—psychoanalytic in character—which he applied to the personalities of fiction. "Having made a few bicycles in factories, having written some thousands of rather senseless advertisements, having rubbed affectionately the legs of a few race horses, having tried blunderingly to love a few women and having written a few novels that did not satisfy," he settled down at last in Marion, Virginia, where he edited two weekly newspapers, one Republican and one Democratic!

Sherwood Anderson's method of story-telling was even more consistent than Willa Cather's. He had one objective, and one technique, which is often loose, sprawling, and repetitive, though sometimes tightened, and particularly in his short stories, with very great art. His purpose was to get under the surface of everyday life in the America he knew best—the Ohio country and its small towns just below Lake Erie, with excursions to Chicago and New York. But his interests were very different from Miss Cather's or Sinclair Lewis'. It would be oversimplification to say that he worked in the subconscious of men and women whose conscious thoughts and feelings were commonplace, since the violent emotional lesions he reveals in his characters have often become conscious before the story begins. It would be more accurate to compare him with the students of abnormal psychology who were his contemporaries, although they did not influence him. His characters, however, are not pathological, but show what Anderson believes to be the normal results of emotional wounds in a sensitive mind. A disciple of either Freud or Jung would say that they are all subjects for psychoanalysis, yet Anderson was in no sense a scientific psychoanalyst. On the contrary, the spiritual lesions of his characters are precisely what make them important and valuable as human beings. His object was not to adjust the individual to a society which he regarded as dull, sterile, and insensitive, but to show how love in all its variants, and especially sexual love, will resist suppression by a mechanical and materialistic society, with such dynamic energy that it may crush or cripple the passionate woman or man.

It was Anderson's idea—and he wrote out of a rich experience—that something in the life of the Middle West he knew so well (though not only the Middle West) was inimical to love. "Suppose, I suggested to myself, that the giving of itself by an entire generation to mechanical things were really making all men impotent. There was a passion for size among all the men I had known. Almost every man I had known had a bigger house, a bigger factory, a faster automobile than his fellows." Were the factory workers who boasted of their sexual effectiveness doing so because year by year they felt themselves less effectual as men? "Were modern women going more and more toward man's life and man's attitude toward life because they were becoming all the time less and less able to be women?"

Sinclair Lewis felt all this, too (as did D. H. Lawrence in England). But Anderson, though his scope and his skill are less, is more intuitive, much more mystical, and far more concerned in his stories with the hurt girl or the warped man than with the apparatus and the traits of this mechanical civilization. His best stories, indeed, go back often to the horse-and-buggy age of his youth, and smugness, commercialism, respectability—anything that cramps emotion—will serve for his narrative as well as the industrial revolution.

All of Anderson's short stories and novels begin with a gesture, a look, or an episode, however trivial, suggesting emotional tension and asking to be explained. Like the young reporter in *Winesburg, Ohio,* he was constantly being told stories, and in them one sentence would set his imagination going:

I was lying on my back on the porch, and the street lamp shone on my mother's face. What was the use? I could not say to her what was in my mind. She would not have understood. There was a man lived next door who kept going by the house and smiling at me. I got it into my head that he knew all that I could not tell mother.

This suggestive sentence is the germ of his long short story, "Out of Nowhere into Nothing," in *The Triumph of the Egg.* Such sentences (and scenes) were the "seeds" of stories. "How could one make them grow?"

And so, as Whitman rebelled against the conventions of meter and diction as not expressing his themes, Anderson rebelled against the current fashions of plot. "The plot notion did seem to me to poison all story-telling. What was wanted, I thought, was form, not plot. . . . Plots were frameworks about which the stories were to be constructed. . . . A new trick had been thought out." Willa Cather had meant the same thing when she urged the writer to give himself utterly to the situation. Both writers, as was natural at the end of a period when life seemed ripe for the imagination, spurned the half-gods of rhetoric and sought their own way of telling the truth. But a situation for Anderson contained no full-blooded woman conquering environment, or priest giving spiritual significance to a pagan landscape. Like his contemporary John Masefield, he preferred to write "of the maimed, of the halt and the blind in the rain and the cold," although for Negroes and race horses he had many a cheery word.

Confession stories, most of Anderson's tales might be called—a kind of story which, when cheapened and vulgarized, had great popular appeal. His novels are only expanded tales. As is true of so many American writers of fiction, the short story was his best medium, and there, in such stories as "I Want to Know Why" and "I'm a Fool," he did his finest work. Sometimes, as in the first of these two, it is a boy escaping from a restricted environment into the rich, easy life of the stables and track, where the Negroes take human nature and its pleasures as it comes, with no Protestant compulsions to bother them. And with the Negroes live the noble thoroughbreds, clean and courageous. How, admiring them, can human beings be so gross in comparison? (Whitman felt about animals much as he does.) Often the inspiration is neurotic but noble, as in the novel *Many Marriages* (1923), where a symbolic (and faintly absurd) nudity represents the ruthless stripping of convention necessary in order to begin a new emotional life. Sometimes the story explains the fluttering hands of a man in hiding, who had been a teacher with a gift for affection until his caresses had been misunderstood and his life broken. Nowhere is satire, everywhere sympathy, sometimes heated to anger. And if every story is a study of behavior, explained by a confession, the behavior is not for the sake of realism, though realistic enough, but is an index of thwarted or suppressed emotion.

Many of his narratives—notably *Many Marriages*—shocked readers by their sexual frankness. But it should be clear now that Anderson explored the sexual only because it is one of the chief paths to the secrets of the inner life. His courage in that still reticent time gave him a fictitious reputation as a breaker of taboos, which he did not really deserve. His true innovation was his sympathetic analysis of the inner emotional life of the victims of success in his Middle West.

He often fumbled in his narrative, which is always honest but sometimes truly artless. The style, however, is effective, and deceptively ingenuous and impromptu. Although, like Lewis, he dealt with familiar people in a familiar way, his prose is stylized. It has little of the colloquial, few differentiations between this man's speech and another's. What he did was to listen to his home-town folk with affectionate intentness, and then make out of their vocabulary and rhythms a style to express them. This is the precise opposite of sitting up nights with Addison. He resolved, as he says, to escape from the patterns of British prose as taught to his generation, and this is the way he did it. It is, nevertheless, a mannered style, supple, familiar, a little monotonous, but an excellent medium for the homely incidents he chose as revealing the inner life of seemingly commonplace people. Perhaps no American has more consciously made a personal style for his own needs.

Anderson's first book of importance was *Winesburg, Ohio* (1919), a collection of sketches of life in a small Ohio town. *Winesburg, Ohio* made a stir among the critics and pleased such writers as Dreiser and Carl Sandburg. It was rather widely attacked by the prudish, the general opinion being that the author was a pessimist whose morbidity was in sharp contrast to the healthy cheerfulness and good humor of Booth Tarkington's novels of much the same region. Actually, the difference was in selection. Tarkington was writing well for cheerful people, and, so far as they went, his portraits of the Middle West were true and excellent. He had been in Princeton, or lived far away from the railroad tracks of his home town, while Anderson was listening to the sordid tales of the village gossips at the livery stable. Born outside both Puritan and genteel traditions, Anderson felt no compulsion to make success stories of what he wrote. The somewhat stereotyped lives of the successful he took for granted as by-products of the American code of progress. Importance lay in what this emotionally sterile life of the small town and the impersonality of the big city had done to the individual. He found failures the most revealing.

His succeeding books were all built upon this theme, with no notable advance except in his growing power over the short story, which ceased to be a sketch and became organic and dynamic. *Poor White* (1920) is semi-autobiographic; *Dark Laughter* (1925) is another story of his own people with the dark laughter of the Negroes as a sardonic background and commentary. These indicate a widening of social observation. But *The Triumph of the Egg* (1921) and *Horses and Men* (1923), books of short stories, are most characteristic of his resources, his skill, and his quality—also of his faults, for each book contains narratives that do not "jell." "The Triumph of the Egg" itself, the story of an unsuccessful chicken farmer whose life is dominated by eggs until, in its grotesque, half-mad conclusion, one egg broken lifts the tale into significant tragedy, is a perfect example of Anderson's way of interpreting life.

Like the other novelists in this chapter, Sherwood Anderson did not belong with the postwar generation of writers who felt themselves to be pioneers in a new social structure and a new (but unformed) philosophy. He is to be placed, rather, in a Hegelian antithesis with Glasgow or Cabell. As part of the summary period of nineteenth century America, he wrote of its culture with the personal detachment of one who neither defends nor prophesies. His task was to explain a neglected aspect of an era of easy success. Without him and his people, the Middle West would have gone uninterpreted in an important area of emotional experience. He could not really create characters, except for boys'—perhaps one boy's—character. He lacked the power to synthesize a region as a society. He was less of a realist, more of a mystic than Dreiser; indeed, his realism was confined to the honesty with which he confessed personal experience, and to his descriptions. In these qualities he anticipated Saroyan and Steinbeck; and he explained, as Sinclair Lewis did not, why so many of the Babbitts became increasingly unsatisfied and hollow within.

His place in American literary history should be given further distinction by his very great influence in liberating the American short story from a petrifying technique. His own tales, appearing first in experimental magazines like the *Dial* and the *Little Review*, gradually acquired fame and were eagerly read by younger men and women trying to escape from the technical tradition of Poe, Aldrich, and O. Henry, which cramped expression even though it seemed to guarantee financial success. That the best and the most successful American short stories of the next decades—whether by Stephen Vincent Benét or Katherine Anne Porter or Eudora Welty—are in free forms where plot is subordinated to theme and form springs from the situation, must be credited in no small degree to the example set by Sherwood Anderson.

8

Ring Lardner was one of the least pretentious in a literary sense, and most interesting of the writers of this period. He was definitely transitional, carrying over into a more realistic age the surface good nature of the American humorists of the nineteenth century, their banter, and their evident affection for American types. And, like O. Henry, he had the nineteenth century American fondness for carefully constructed plots, ending usually with a reversal or a surprise, and as neatly made as a watch. Yet in content and in philosophy of character his writing forecast the irony and impatient disillusions of the later twenties, and a dislike for the current values of magazine-reading, bridge-playing, get-rich-and-spend-it American society as strong as the sarcasm of Sinclair Lewis, if far more skeptical and ironic. The smoldering hatred for possessive and dominating women as the enemy of the male, which was to be so characteristic of novels, stories, drama, and even comics of later American decades, is only half concealed beneath his surface good humor. The most influential magazine of the period among sophisticated intellectuals, the *New Yorker* (founded in 1925) had for its spiritual ancestor the ironical, realistic humor of Ring Lardner, with its notes of pity and its ruthless satire of dangerous human types.

Lardner was graduated into literature from the sports column of the American press, a department of journalism more influential, perhaps, than any other upon the growth of the American language. His work, like Sherwood Anderson's, was always close to reporting, and any one of his stories could have been printed as a human-interest feature containing news of life on the baseball field or in the home town, or in the suburbs of New York. Indeed, both men, regarded as journalists, were by-products of the shift from news of fact to "heart" interest, which transformed the American press in these decades, and swung its influence from ideas to emotions.

Ring Lardner and Anderson were both bored by normalcy and the respectable, and both were stirred to attack by the pressure of standardized thinking and feeling. But Anderson, an idealist of the emotions, was shocked and troubled, while the far more objective Lardner was, like his successors, uninterested in reform, and content to give his humor a cutting edge. He was at his best, not when his characters were most significant, but when they were most novel and alive. The dreadfully dull husband of "Anniversary," whom thrift and devotion to the ideals of business have reduced to the personality of a typewriter, is not so memorable as Alibi Ike, the greatest and most naïve liar of baseball. The horrifying effect of the brutality of Midge Kelly in "Champion" owes some of its effect to its satire on commercialized pugilism, but more to the carefully objective description of the man himself.

Indeed, it is probable that Ring Lardner's place as an American classic will be as a reporter of new phases of the American character, best seen through the satiric realist's eyes. In sports, particularly, there had come to be a new cohesion of American society, powerful over the imagination of millions. It had its own code, its own language, its own comedies and tragedies, its own heroes and buffoons. It was, indeed, the bourgeois equivalent of the fields of Troy, with many an uncertain Hector and boasting Thersites and sulky Achilles and wily Odysseus. Yet a corrupting commercialism, an inevitable accompaniment as elsewhere in American life, gave an opportunity to the realist that such a romantic of a previous generation as Richard Harding Davis would have been unable to take.

From sports Lardner turned to the gilded absurdities of the motion picture world, and to the deceit and cruelty which passed for humor in small-town life, as in "Haircut." His touch was light, and his victims might have read his stories without knowing that they were being damned out of their own mouths. Yet no intelligent reader could miss his ruthless summary of false values in the life he knew best. The best books are collections of short stories, *How to Write Short Stories* (1924) and *The Love Nest* (1926).

His stories are of major importance in their transcription of new American rhythms in speech, and phrases and words new at least to literature. Anderson stylized this language, Lewis used it to define his types, Lardner had no ulterior purpose except realism. It has been said that his own style is thin and often flat, and that the color and true style is taken from the mouths of his characters. This is at least relatively true. His baseball heroes talk a racy dialect which thousands of players, fans, and sports writers had shaped to fit the high excitements of the game. And he could make articulate without falsifying the shallow semiliteracy of his silly or predatory women.

Thus Ring Lardner, even if he had no obvious roots in the age of security and confidence, belonged in the summary group which firmly established the end-products of the nineteenth century in a satisfactory and expressive literature. If he also prepared for an era that liked to call itself more "realistic," meaning more concerned with the "is" and less with the "ought," his most praiseworthy quality is to have realized emerging character types of his own times.

## 9

This chapter makes no attempt to be inclusive of all the vigorous fiction of this rich period of American writing, which began to lose its summary character and give way to a new transition about 1925. It omits, in the interest of brevity, such brilliant achievements in the organization of American experience as Ernest Poole's *The Harbor* (1915), such new local color of the Negro South as Du Bose Heyward's *Porgy* (1925), such able records of increasing sophistication as Carl Van Vechten's novels. It leaves, for later treatment, the pioneers of a fiction with a changed philosophy of life behind it, such as Scott Fitzgerald in his pioneer study of postwar youth, *This Side of Paradise* (1920), a book more influential than excellent—his mature power was to be shown later; or the explorations in the changing mores of sex by Floyd Dell (*Moon Calf*, 1920), or the massive social studies of Waldo Frank (*City Block*, 1922). Some mention, however, must be made of Joseph Hergesheimer, to whom many novelists of the period, including Sinclair Lewis, owed new standards of descriptive accuracy. Hergesheimer was as much of an antiquarian as a novelist, and his books were rightly regarded as protests against the slovenly generalizations of popular romance. He was a naturalist writing of the past, who in later years applied the same scrupulous realism of detail to stories of the demoralized behavior of the Prohibition era. The research behind his novel of Pennsylvania ironmasters (*The Three Black Pennys*, 1917) or his story of Salem and the China trade (*Java Head*, 1919) was paralleled by the careful and laborious preparation made by Sinclair Lewis before each one of his novels of Middle America, who in *Arrowsmith* went as far as to use a research collaborator.

For it is clear that the most important fiction of the belated *fin de siècle*, which began in the early 1900's and ended in the late 1920's, when the young who had known no stability took over, was a study of the values which had already been established, for good or for ill, in American life. This study in Ellen Glasgow was ironic of the false, defensive of the true, historical in its point of view. In the stories of Willa Cather it was explanatory of the deep concordances between land and people, intensely creative in characters, an offering from a passing age to a new one. It was entirely ironic, egoistic, and almost wholly destructive in Cabell, an aristocrat's purge of a petrified moral-ity. It was a seeking and a rescue of the life of the emotions in the tales of Sher-wood Anderson. In Sinclair Lewis, it was a mirror held up to a whole society. He was the greatest social historian, though not the greatest artist or prophet of them all, and he was determined that his fellow countrymen should see in the light of his own fierce idealism what was happening in a country where body was out of mesh with soul. In Ring Lardner, it was the irony of the hard-boiled reporter who suffers fools gladly when they supply him with good copy but never forgets that they are fools. He, with Sinclair Lewis, has left us the best transcription of the colloquial American speech of our time.

Edith Wharton gave to the local color cult of the regionalists, who were so successful from the seventies to the nineties, an edge and a social signifi-cance which that literature lacked. Ellen Glasgow and Cabell were also regionalist, but their books took the offensive against the decaying chivalry of the South, and prepared for the later work of Paul Green, Stark Young, and William Faulkner. Anderson's mood of confession was shared by his predecessor Dreiser and his contemporary Edgar Lee Masters, but with a transference of emotion stranger than in either of the other two writers.

Indeed, it is not too much to say that the air of the twenties was electric. It inspired the older writers, such as Glasgow, Cather, Wharton, Cabell, to their best work, and created new imaginations. Even Dreiser, who belongs in style and outlook upon life to the relatively barren first two decades of the new century, published his masterpiece, *An American Tragedy,* in 1925. And one reason, at least, is the summary character of all the best of this work. With these writers, the second great era of the Republic, from the Civil War to the Long Armistice, may be said to have got adequate interpreters in novelists who were conscious of their duty to give a final reality and a diagnosis of the results of a span of human experience. And they were fortunate, as their predecessors had seldom been, in finding an aware and receptive audience.

# 73. EUGENE O'NEILL

Aт no time during the eighteenth or nineteenth century was the drama a major department of American literature; and not until just before the First World War did it show any real promise of becoming one. It is true that the early years of our century had produced Clyde Fitch and Langdon Mitchell, popular playwrights whose works exhibited some increase in literary sophistication, and also more serious writers—notably Edward Sheldon, William Vaughn Moody, and Augustus Thomas—who made a cautious effort to treat themes which had some relation to contemporary life. But none of these men was permanently important, and the works of none achieved conspicuous excellence when judged in accordance with the standards set by the contemporary efforts of novelists and essayists, philosophers and historians. They pretty consistently consented to work within the limitations of a very narrow theatrical tradition, and that tradition tolerated no bold departure from long-established stereotypes both artistic and moral.

Eugene O'Neill is, on the other hand, held by many critics to be a major figure in American literature, and it is unquestionable that he was the first American to write a number of plays which still seem possible candidates for inclusion in any future list of native classics. He is, therefore, the inevitable central figure in any discussion of the new school of American dramatists. Moreover, there are reasons why he is a very convenient as well as an inevitable central figure. His work reveals both strong originality and the effect of forces in the world outside himself which sometimes help mold and sometimes actually distort the expression of his own talents. In him, therefore, may be observed both an individual creative writer and the effect of an intellectual milieu common to him and his fellows.

At least three factors determining that milieu are of major importance: the native, non-dramatic, literary revolution which produced Theodore Dreiser, Sherwood Anderson, Sinclair Lewis, and H. L. Mencken; the somewhat belated influence of Ibsen and the post-Ibsen playwrights of Europe; and the revolutionary "little theater" movement with which O'Neill was in the beginning identified.

The first of these factors is, of course, itself complex since it includes such superficially contradictory tendencies as that toward native realism and that toward an imitation of continental sophistication. It has already been discussed in previous sections of the present work and will be merely alluded to here. In this chapter O'Neill will be discussed chiefly in terms of his individual tendencies as they were modified by the European dramatic tradition and given opportunity to develop in an experimental theater.

2

Eugene [Gladstone] O'Neill was born in a Broadway hotel on October 16, 1888. He was the son of James O'Neill, a popular actor of romantic melodrama, and he spent his boyhood partly with his father on tour and partly in various boarding schools. As the result of a prank, he was suspended from Princeton at the end of his freshman year. He worked briefly in a mail-order house, and then, possibly influenced by Jack London, Conrad, and Kipling, as well as by his own restless rebellious spirit, he left in 1909 for a gold-prospecting voyage in Honduras. Another voyage took him as ordinary seaman to Buenos Aires, where he worked at odd jobs for a time before returning to play a small part in one of his father's productions in New York and work for about a year as reporter and columnist on a New London newspaper. In 1912 an attack of tuberculosis sent him for five months to a sanitarium, and it seems reasonable to suppose that the enforced idleness there brought him face to face with the self from which he had been trying to run away. He read Marx and Kropotkin as well as Wedekind, Strindberg, and Ibsen, and during the year of convalescence following his release from the sanitarium, he wrote his first one-act plays. In 1914 he attended for a time Professor George Pierce Baker's famous class in play writing at Harvard.

Next year, during the summer of 1915, a group of Greenwich Villagers vacationing at Provincetown, Massachusetts, unknowingly prepared the way for his introduction to the public by staging for their amusement four one-act plays in an improvised theater in a deserted fish house. By the next summer, some members of the group had heard somehow that the young O'Neill, also now living in Provincetown, had a trunkful of unproduced plays. He was invited to submit something, and the result was that the one-act romantic melodrama *Bound East for Cardiff* became the first of his works to be publicly performed. That same autumn the Provincetown group remodeled a stable on Macdougal Street in New York City, named the tiny theater Provincetown Playhouse, and opened in November with a bill of three one-act plays, one of which was again *Bound East for Cardiff*. The results were so pleasing to all concerned that between then and 1924 most of O'Neill's plays—including, besides a number of one-acters, *The Emperor Jones, The Hairy Ape,* and *All God's Chillun Got Wings*—had their premières on Macdougal Street.

These facts are of the utmost importance for understanding the atmosphere in which the new American drama began. The Provincetown group was one of two most directly responsible for creating a conscious conviction that such a new drama was possible, and the attitude of its members is highly significant. Not one of them was professionally connected with the theater. The two leading original movers were George Cram Cook, a Bohemian enthusiast, and John Reed, later to become a hero martyr of the Soviet Union. Others included Mary Heaton Vorse, labor journalist, Wilbur Daniel Steele, short-story writer, and Marguerite Zorach, a modernistic painter. One, Susan Glaspell, later became a professional playwright, and one, Robert Edmond Jones, a professional stage designer; but most of the members of the group, as well as most of the authors who wrote their plays, became famous, if they became famous at all, in some other field of activity. Thus, during 1917 and 1918, plays were produced by Floyd Dell, later a successful novelist; by Michael Gold, later a prominent radical journalist; and by Alfred Kreymborg, Harry Kemp, Maxwell Bodenheim, and Edna St. Vincent Millay, all to achieve in varying degrees reputations as poets rather than as playwrights. In other words, the prime movers in the enterprise were interested in art, literature, and politics rather than in the theater as such, and they were in revolt against the long prevailing assumption that play writing was a highly specialized, artificial, and essentially inartistic trade.

Beyond this, however, the Provincetown group, unlike the German Freie Bühne or the French Théâtre Libre, had no program. Various ferments including political radicalism, aesthetic experimentalism, and timeless Bohemianism were at work in differing proportions in most if not all of the members. But there was no unifying doctrine, and the group as a whole knew rather better what it did not want—namely, respectable, conventional, and commercialized entertainment—than what it did. Freud was a prophet hardly less important than Marx. A good playwright, they obviously felt, might be a prophet of social revolution, a romantic poet, or even merely an adept at the ancient Bohemian sport of shocking the middle classes. The one thing he could not be was one who complacently accepted the statement recently made by Eugene Walter, author of the sensational play *The Easiest Way* (1908 *), and one of the admired of Broadway: "In essence, play writing is a trade."

The Provincetown Playhouse did for O'Neill one thing which no commercial theater would at the beginning have done: it gave him an audience, though this audience was, and for some time remained, a small and very

* Dates in this chapter are of first performance rather than of first publication.

special one. Perhaps it is just as well that his sponsors had no definite program, for O'Neill was very susceptible to influence; he had not by any means
found himself, and he might under different circumstances have been forced
into a pattern alien to his own genius. As it was, his sponsors took gladly
whatever he gave them; and even during these earliest years he gave them a
number of seemingly quite different things. Among his early works only
*Bound East for Cardiff* and the series of other one-act plays of the sea which
followed form a unified group. Obviously to some extent products of his own
experience as a sailor, they are poetic in tone, somewhat melodramatic in
substance, and essentially romantic despite the fact that an avoidance of the
more familiar romantic clichés and an insistence upon tragic implications
led them to be called, as unfamiliar forms of romanticism so often are,
"realistic." Their brevity and their relative simplicity enabled the author to
achieve his intentions more completely than he was to do for a long time in
more ambitious attempts, and for that reason some have always tended to give
them a higher place in the hierarchy of his works than they really deserve.

O'Neill was, however, by no means content with either poetic or tragic
melodrama. Passionately dissatisfied and restlessly seeking, he at times gave
way to a sort of Strindbergian nihilism and at others sought answers to his
questions in the doctrines of the political revolutionists or in those of the
newly fashionable Freudians. It is easy to see in successive plays the predominant influence of one doctrine or another. *Diff'rent* (1920), though
theatrically very effective, is unmistakably a fable for Freudians; *All God's
Chillun Got Wings* (1924) was, on the surface at least, a sociological problem
play. On the other hand, *The Emperor Jones* (1920) was mystical rather than
sociological or scientific, and two others, *Beyond the Horizon* (1920) and
*Anna Christie* (1921), were given their first production in commercial theaters
rather than at the Provincetown only because their method was that of a
straightforward realism far less baffling to the general public than the poetry,
the mysticism, and the preaching to some extent characteristic of his other
work.

During this period O'Neill may be said to have had styles rather than a
style, and philosophies rather than a philosophy. He was endeavoring with
only partial success to adapt to his own uses available formulas provided by
current intellectual movements, and he probably did not himself know how
unsatisfactory for him each of them was. *The Hairy Ape*, produced in 1922,
and the next to the last of his plays to have its première at the Provincetown
Playhouse, is, in some respects, the most interesting because it is the one
which most succeeds in fusing discordant elements into a new whole.

The story of *The Hairy Ape* is concerned with one of the stokers of an
ocean liner whose previous contentment with his own primitive strength and

humble indispensability is shaken by accidental contact with a female passenger representing a world of which he is totally ignorant. Arrived in port, he sets out to investigate this new world, discovers that he is not recognized as human by the more elegant of its denizens, gets thrown out of the hall where a group of self-conscious proletarians is meeting, and finally is crushed to death in the arms of a caged ape whom he has tried to hail as brother. The method of the piece obviously derives ultimately from that of Strindberg's *The Dream Play* and involves what the Germans had begun to call "expressionism"—one element of which is the effort to represent events, not as they would appear to a normal, detached spectator, but as seen through the distorted vision of a participant. The meaning of the fable (and this was to become a frequent characteristic of O'Neill's plays) was ambiguous in the sense that it lent itself readily to different interpretations. By the social revolutionist it was accepted as a protest against the brutalization of the proletariat. Yet in the text itself there is no suggestion that the hairy apes of this world could be humanized by any social system, and probably only the sociological preoccupations of an audience could suggest the conclusion that the author had affinity with the prophets of political or economic revolution. The nihilistic pessimism of the tortured playwright is the obvious source of its dramatic method.

When, however, we look back at *The Hairy Ape* and consider it in relation to O'Neill's subsequent development, we perceive that the real crux of the problem presented by the predicament of the central figure is not sociological, and we see also that the author is struggling with, rather than merely acquiescing in, the pessimism which has all but enveloped him. While the Hairy Ape was still content with his lot, he was content because he had faith that he was essential to his ship and that the ship had meaning. When he lost that faith, when he came to realize that the world which he served was unaware of his existence, and when he hence came to doubt that he had any function in a world he could not understand, he ceased to think of himself as a man and despised himself as an ape. "I belong" had been the recurrent phrase with which he justified himself. When he could no longer say that, he was lost; and the theme here for the first time clearly enunciated is the theme repeated with many variations in most of O'Neill's major works. Sometimes these works involve what appears to be a criticism of society. Sometimes they make use of a Freudian pattern. But at their most successful they are tragic rather than either sociological or psychological because at bottom the problem is, always, not what O'Neill himself has called the problem of man's relations with man, but the problem of man's relation to something outside himself, to that something to which he must "belong" if he is to feel himself more than the cleverest of the apes.

3

O'Neill's development long continued to be in zigzag or spiral rather than in a straight line, but *The Hairy Ape* marks a stage at which it is convenient to pause to consider the extent to which there was, by this time, a "new American theater," of which he can be considered a part. Certain of his contemporaries will be treated in a subsequent chapter. Here it is necessary to say only that the Provincetown group had failed completely, during the eight years which had passed since the production of *Bound East for Cardiff,* to discover any other American dramatist of importance. It had produced a long succession of pieces, usually in one act, by a considerable number of Americans. But not one of the latter was destined to become known as an important writer for the stage. Moreover, neither of the Provincetown's two rival "little theaters" had succeeded any better so far as the cultivation of significant native dramatists was concerned.

One, the Neighborhood Playhouse, which was operated in connection with a settlement house on Grand Street, was beginning to achieve a deserved reputation for its imaginative staging of poetic and fanciful productions, but had discovered no native playwright of importance. The other, the Washington Square Players—a semiamateur group founded in February, 1915, and at first not very markedly different in aims from its Provincetown rival—had achieved a somewhat more spectacular theatrical success, for under the changed name Theater Guild it had taken a full-sized uptown theater in 1919, and was soon (in 1925) to open its own newly constructed Guild Theater. It had progressed from bills of one-act plays to the increasingly elaborate and professional presentations of the major works of such established European dramatists as Benevente, St. John Ervine, Tolstoy, Strindberg, Molnár, and especially Shaw. By 1922 it had ceased to be a little theater and become instead almost a "commercial theater," specializing in the production of plays of a sort which had previously been considered impossible in commercial theaters. But it had not introduced a single American playwright destined either to conspicuous success or to enduring reputation.

What the three "little theaters" had accomplished was the discovery of an audience for a kind of play which was supposed to have none. The result was both to encourage a still unknown group to hope that it might write plays of similar quality and also to encourage the commercial managers to look with increasing favor upon works which tended more or less boldly to break with the timid conventions hitherto regarded as inviolable. Thus, while O'Neill still remained the only native dramatist of importance fostered by the little theater, certain plays either somewhat bolder or somewhat more sophisticated than had previously found a hearing on Broadway began to appear there—notably, Clare Kummer's series of "smart," "brittle" comedies beginning with *Good Gracious, Annabelle!* (1916); Zona Gale's realistic drama of small-time life, *Miss Lulu Bett* (1920); *Wake Up, Jonathan* (1921), a folk play dealing with the Southern mountaineers, by Hatcher Hughes and Elmer Rice; and *Dulcy* (1921), a comedy by George Kaufman and Marc Connelly, which pointed satire in a direction more familiar to readers of "sophisticated" writing than to frequenters of Broadway.

Almost precisely one year after the production of *The Hairy Ape,* the Theater Guild was to break new ground by presenting *The Adding Machine,* the first arresting independent work of Elmer Rice, who thus became the first "coming" playwright since O'Neill to find introduction as a "new" American dramatist through one of the "advanced" theaters. Within the next two or three years he had been joined on Broadway by several others, and the new school of play writing had been definitely launched with the production of *What Price Glory* (1924) by Laurence Stallings and Maxwell Anderson; *They Knew What They Wanted* (1924) by Sidney Howard; *The Show-Off* (1924) by George Kelly; and *Processional* (1925) by John Howard Lawson. No one of these plays could possibly have found acceptance on Broadway a decade before, and though the changed atmosphere created by the First World War no doubt had much to do with the fact that several of them were outstanding commercial successes, the spadework done by the Provincetown and the Guild counted for much.

Nevertheless it should be borne in mind that when *The Hairy Ape* was produced O'Neill was almost our only "advanced" playwright, and that the major part of the careers of most of the other important newcomers lie beyond 1925. On him, the chief immediate effect of the new developments in the theater was an expanding audience for work of a sort which had, up to then, been usually played on a tiny stage and before a few hundred spectators at most. His next two important plays were to be produced at the somewhat larger Greenwich Village Theater, which had been taken over by the management of the Provincetown; and then, in 1928, he gave *Marco Millions* to the Theater Guild, which produced the play at its own theater and has since sponsored all his New York productions, both at home and on tour.

These last facts must be mentioned because they indicate that his long struggle for a hearing outside the restricted group of consciously advanced intellectuals was by this time over; but, since O'Neill is conspicuously a writer more aware of himself than of his audience, they are probably far less important in his development than the steady growth within. To that growth we shall now again turn.

4

It would no doubt be generally agreed that since about 1915 the most conspicuous tendencies in the American novel, as well as in the American drama, have been toward realism, social satire, social protest, and what was commonly called "continental" sophistication. We have already noted that the influence of all these tendencies is observable in O'Neill's plays, but that they are essentially alien or at least peripheral, since O'Neill's chief concern had always been with the eternally tragic predicament of man struggling for some understanding and some justification of himself in a universe always mysterious and often seemingly inimical. For that reason, his work is actually less closely related to the work of most of his fellows than, superficially, it appears to be. While they have, for the most part, either adopted some form of satire or the problem play, or have, at least, taken one or the other as their point of departure, he has struggled persistently, if not quite consistently, toward the creation or re-creation of tragedy in the classic sense—toward a concern, as he put it, less with the relation of man to man than with that of man to God. Perhaps the most fruitful way to evaluate, as well as to understand the general character of his mature work, will be to consider his best plays in connection with their diverse ways of attempting to state in currently valid terms his conception of the human tragedy.

During the eleven years immediately following *The Hairy Ape,* thirteen of his dramatic pieces (two of them really trilogies and the others of normal length) were acted. He is thus a very prolific dramatist; but he is also an uneven one, and though there is considerable disagreement concerning the relative merits of certain of his works, few would deny that the most ambitious of his plays since 1922 are *Desire Under the Elms* (1924), *The Great God Brown* (1926), *Strange Interlude* (1928), and *Mourning Becomes Electra* (1931). *Ah Wilderness!* (1933) is interesting because it enjoyed considerable commercial success, and because it is a nostalgic comedy of youth, quite unlike anything else O'Neill ever wrote. Two others, *Dynamo* (1929) and *Days Without End* (1934), are also interesting, though failures commercially and perhaps artistically. Both deal more directly than any of O'Neill's other plays with the religious aspect of his problem, the first concerning itself with a man who thinks that he has found God in Force as it is symbolized by an electric generator, and the second with one who actually finds peace in an acceptance of the Roman Catholic Church. But to analyze successfully the four plays first mentioned would be by itself to gain a reasonably complete understanding of the whole sweep of their author's aims and methods.

Superficially no one of the four is like any other in respect to either the material dealt with or the dramatic method employed. Perhaps the best way to indicate their diversity, as well as the fundamental relationship among them, will be, first, to state briefly what each is, in the most obvious sense, "about," and then to point out how all are really concerned with the same theme.

The scene of *Desire Under the Elms* is rural New England in the nineteenth century. The method is strictly realistic, and the story revolves around a struggle for dominance between a son and his father—the father being a patriarch convinced that he is under the special protection of a "hard" Old Testament God, and the son competing with him for both his young wife and the ancestral farm. *The Great God Brown,* on the other hand, is contemporary in setting, fantastically "expressionistic" in method, and as completely subjective as the previous play was objective in its treatment of characters and fable. Dion Anthony, a genius, is dogged through life by Brown, a mediocrity, who marries the girl with whom Dion is in love, appropriates the plans which he has drawn for a great public building, and all but usurps his identity. All the characters wear masks which they sometimes remove in soliloquies when they reveal their private, as opposed to their public, personalities. The symbolism becomes extremely confused; O'Neill's own explanation of his intentions is rather more obscure than the play itself; and one is left in doubt whether Anthony and Brown are not actually the two aspects of a single individual.

*Strange Interlude* (almost three times normal play length) has as its central character a beautiful woman who blames her emotional sterility on the death of a lover killed in the war, but nevertheless manages to dominate the lives of three men—her husband, a lover, and her feebly genteel bachelor uncle. The method is realistic except for the fact that long soliloquies are employed to reveal the unspoken thoughts of the characters. In *Mourning Becomes Electra* even this device, used in its two immediate predecessors, is abandoned in favor of a method which is, outwardly at least, essentially realism of the most familiar sort. The story, told in what is really three plays intended for performance on three different evenings, follows very closely the Greek story of Electra, Orestes, and Clytemnestra; but the scene is shifted to the time of the American Civil War, and the motives as well as the names of the central characters are so completely modernized that a naïve spectator might never suspect that the fable was not newly invented.

Each of these four plays enjoyed a considerable commercial success, and together they brought a large financial reward to an author who, before the first was produced, had spent almost a decade developing his talents with what appeared to be a contemptuous disregard for the tastes of his contemporaries. None of the four was, however, popular in the full sense that many other contemporary plays were popular, and it is difficult not to suspect that they owed some considerable part of the favor they enjoyed among intellectuals to a fact already insisted upon—the fact, that is to say, that each was to some extent interpretable in terms of a current intellectual fashion. To many, *Desire Under the Elms* was a contribution to the fashionable effort to "debunk" the nation's Puritan forefathers whom this play was supposed to present as tyrannical and lustful. Similarly, *The Great God Brown,* incomprehensible as much of it was, seemed, after its own fashion, to constitute a satire on the American ideal of "success" and thus to have some sort of relation to the novels of Sinclair Lewis and his imitators. *Strange Interlude* could be interpreted as the study of a Freudian complex, and even *Mourning Becomes Electra,* though more than any of the others it seemed to depend for its effectiveness upon the sheer power of the fable, also presented unmistakably Freudian motifs.

If, however, one has in mind when one approaches these plays not the intellectual patterns fashionable at the moment when the plays were written, but some hint of O'Neill's own preoccupations, it becomes evident that they represent four approaches to the same aesthetic and moral problem rather than four diverse attempts to exploit current interests or prejudices. Sometime during the years when they were being written, their author seems to have become for the first time clearly aware not only that what he wanted to write was tragedy, but that the stature necessary for a tragic hero was difficult to achieve unless that hero "belonged" to something—unless, that is to say, he had a relation to something felt to be larger than himself. But contemporary man has tended to lose the sense that there is anything in the universe with which he can establish a relation, and the realistic problem may accepts the fact when it consents to deal exclusively with the relation of man to man rather than concern itself with the relation of man to God. O'Neill, therefore, seemed to be faced with a dilemma. Either he must deal with the past when man still felt that something outside himself was of supreme importance, or he must be content with the only half-tragic frustrations which arise when a Hairy Ape or a Dion Anthony cries out for the gods he has lost.

"The playwright of today," O'Neill once wrote to George Jean Nathan, "must dig at the roots of the sickness of today as he feels it—the death of the old God and the failure of science and materialism to give any satisfactory new one for the surviving primitive, religious instinct to find a meaning for life in, and to comfort its fears of death with." *The Great God Brown* states that theme explicitly and deals with it in quite contemporary terms; *Desire Under the Elms* implies the theme and achieves artistic success only because in it O'Neill chooses to write of the past. Here the struggle between father and son can reach tragic proportions, can indeed achieve a quality which

immediately challenges comparison with classic treatments of this fundamental conflict: because the father never wavers in his conviction that
Jehovah is one of the protagonists, and because even the son has not lost all
sense of living in a universe more grandiose than any which can be known
to those who acknowledge only man-made laws. Moreover, the distinction is
clearly drawn in the last scene between these protagonists to whom the
possession of the soil can be the occasion of great passions, and the typical
modern, represented by the sheriff, to whom the farm is desirable merely
as a piece of salable real estate. *The Great God Brown* is, on the other hand,
concerned with moderns who have lost their faith, and the key is furnished
by the early scene in which Dion longs first for an earthly father and then
for a heavenly one, though he can find only a sensible parent and the now
trivial legend of an "old grey beard" in the sky. As art *Desire Under the
Elms* is strikingly successful, *The Great God Brown* conspicuously unsatisfactory, in part because one has a tragic hero, the other has only a hero who
is aware of his inability to give his failures tragic significance.

If these two plays represent the two horns of the dilemma between which
O'Neill felt himself caught, the two remaining represent efforts to escape
from it by two different routes. *Strange Interlude* is the demitragedy of a
group which neither believes in God, like Old Ephraim in *Desire Under
the Elms,* nor even, like Dion Anthony, wants to believe in God. In so far
as the individual members believe in anything larger than themselves, that
thing is the Freudian subconscious, some awareness of which seems to haunt
them, very much as others have been vaguely haunted by an awareness of
God. In so far as they "belong" to anything, they belong to the "complexes"
which force them into actions of which their reason would not approve.
And, whatever else may be said for or against Freudianism, *Strange Interlude*
does demonstrate that it is capable of adding a dimension to drama. Plays
which deal only with the relation of rational man to rational man are usually
thin. One in which the passionately irrational aspects of life are recognized
to the extent which Freudianism makes possible in *Strange Interlude* has
already recovered something of the psychological truth which, in some very
real sense, makes *Hamlet* more convincing than *Man and Superman.*

*Strange Interlude* is indeed completely absorbing. In many respects its
effect resembles that of a good psychological novel. But it ends "not with a
bang but a whimper." There is no satisfactory catastrophe, only a diminuendo,
as the characters, who have neither solved their personal problems nor made
defeat heroic, subside into the quiescence of age. They do not seem very
important; they have failed to achieve tragic stature because neither intellectually nor emotionally are they convinced of their own importance either to
themselves or to anything else. They are more interesting and complex than

the characters in even the best problem plays, but they are nevertheless interesting rather than tragically important.

O'Neill has already been quoted for the purpose of showing that he was consciously aware of at least the main outlines of the project which, as a dramatist, he had set himself. He is nevertheless a dramatist rather than a philosopher and owes his significance less to any absolute intellectual originality than to the forcefulness with which he has explored in dramatic terms "the sickness of today." Since he is, in the broadest sense of the word, a poet rather than a philosopher it cannot safely be assumed that he was himself always clearly aware of the pattern into which his successive efforts, now in one direction and now in another, seem to the critic to fall. Yet, whether or not he is fully aware of the fact, *Mourning Becomes Electra* does constitute another experiment which seems logically demanded by the pattern of experimentation already laid down. *Strange Interlude* served to demonstrate that modern characters can play out a richly interesting drama even though Freudian psychology furnishes the only spiritual universe, the only large thing outside their rational consciousness with which they are willing to admit relation. Only one question remains to be answered. Can such characters satisfactorily fill the roles, not in a psychological study, but in a tragedy? Can they be made to take on the necessary stature, can they work their way through to a catastrophe of tragic proportions?

Unwilling to accept finally the negative answer which his own previous work seemed to furnish, O'Neill posed the question again in *Mourning Becomes Electra*. Here is a series of events which become great tragedy when Æschylus represents them. So far as the incidents are concerned, they might have occurred as easily during the American Civil War as during the Trojan War. Suppose, then, we give them the local habitation and the names of our civilization. Suppose we avoid all the implications which depend upon the ancient ethos, and assume that whatever appears irrational has its source, not in the will of the gods, but in that layer of the human mind which lies below its consciousness. How close can we then come to achieving a tragedy, modern in the sense that it asks no suspension of disbelief in the gods, classic in the sense that its figures will seem large enough, and its catastrophe thrilling enough to stir real terror and pity? To what extent can we judge how much of any disproportion between Æschylus and O'Neill is due to the disproportion between their respective poetic gifts, how much to the possible fact that tragedy cannot happen in a world in which there is no supernatural moral order to be disturbed and then reestablished?

In so far as the play achieves a genuinely tragic effect, it not only vindicates the claim of O'Neill to importance as a writer, but at the same time tends to dispose of what has seemed to be his own conviction—namely, that contemporary man's failure to "belong" puts an insurmountable difficulty in the way of the dramatist who would make a tragic hero out of him. And without suggesting any weighing of the balance between Æschylus and O'Neill, it must at least be said that *Mourning Becomes Electra* was astonishingly powerful in the theater, to which it held large audiences through a second and a third part. By virtue of nothing except the passion with which he was able to endow them, the characters assume great stature. They come to seem important because those passions somehow make them important to themselves. And the catastrophe achieves something of the finality as well as the magnitude which genuine tragedy requires.

5

Since 1933 Mr. O'Neill has completed two tragedies and is said to be far advanced in the composition of a cycle of seven plays. By his own desire no productions were undertaken and none of the texts were published until the autumn of 1946 when *The Iceman Cometh* was presented by the Theater Guild. This long and somewhat grotesque tragedy has as its theme the attempt of a dipsomaniac to free himself from his last hopes and last illusions. It is less appealing than either *Strange Interlude* or *Mourning Becomes Electra,* but it exhibits much of the same tragic power.

From what has already been said it is evident that, if O'Neill is probably the most important playwright ever to arise in the United States, his development has been such as to make it difficult to consider him as a member—even as the leading member—of an American school of dramatists. That school doubtless owed a good deal to his pioneer efforts, which did so much to reveal an audience for unconventional plays. Moreover, as a subsequent chapter of this work will indicate, many members of the school have themselves shown a tendency to cultivate a style of play writing in which the didactic emphasis of the European problem play, so extensively cultivated during the late nineteenth and early twentieth centuries, disappears, and either comedy or drama, rather than demonstration or argument, becomes the chief effect aimed at. But O'Neill, nevertheless, remains all but unique in his persistent and increasingly more nearly exclusive attempt to deal with modern life in such a way as to achieve the effect of classic tragedy. In pursuit of that aim he has more and more completely avoided, as though he considered them trivial and irrelevant, the criticism of current social or political conditions or the characteristic features of contemporary manners. Certainly no other significant playwright has so persisted in the conviction that, if a drama is to achieve great excellence, it must deal with man's relation to God—or, if one prefers, with his relation to forces outside himself.

However he is classified, Eugene O'Neill is one more instance of the power and the maturity of American literature, which reached in the twenties a peak from which there was no dropping back. But unlike the majority of the important novelists and at least two of the most important poets of these twenties, his plays are not so much summary of an era as a new mode and a new theme for the American stage.

# A WORLD LITERATURE

# 74. BETWEEN WARS

No period in American history is more eventful than that between the Coolidge-Hoover bull market of the twenties and the tragically sudden death of Franklin D. Roosevelt in 1945; and none furnishes greater contrasts and ironies.

From the boastful complacency of a boom era in which Americans thought that their wealth, technological power, and improved economic theories had lifted them to a plateau of absolute security, they were abruptly hurled into a whirlpool of perils, domestic and foreign. Two previous generations had endured similar periods of prolonged crisis. In the years 1775–1789 Americans had undergone a direful war, an uprooting of old traditions and loyalties, a severe depression, and all the quarrels that inevitably accompanied constitution making, state and national. In the years 1857–1873 they had experienced a panic, one of the most lethal wars of history, the bitter animosities of Southern Reconstruction, and the onset of a new depression. These were roller coaster generations—lifted high, flung far down, swallowing dizzy curves, rushing across sudden gaps. But the vicissitudes of this third period of crisis were even sharper. The panic was more savage, the war peril was deadlier, the internal discords were as harsh; while even Nature lent a hand in tormenting large sections with droughts, dust storms, and floods. The irony of the abrupt change from prosperity to poverty was grim. But it was another ironic fact that a nation which had finally adjusted itself to a chastened mood and a restricted economy suddenly in 1941 found war again spurring it to prodigies of effort, with a production that eclipsed its wildest dreams.

The political framework of the time was somewhat less simple than it seemed. The writers who speak of a Harding-Coolidge-Hoover epoch followed by a very different Roosevelt era hardly do justice to Hoover as a transitional figure. Both before and after his tardy adjustments to the Great Depression which began late in 1929, Hoover unlatched several doors which his successor simply flung wide. His principle of industrial self-government and his stimulation of the trade associations helped to usher in Roosevelt's grander experiment under the National Recovery Administration. He par-

tially accepted Federal responsibility for relief. He was the first President
to use a powerful government agency (the Reconstruction Finance Corporation) in a compensatory and balancing role in the national economy, thus
setting a far-reaching precedent. In short, great innovations of government
policy were beginning to take shape even before Franklin D. Roosevelt
assumed control. And yet an old era did die, and a new era did open, in 1933.

The inauguration of Roosevelt, relieving the national tension at a moment of terrible crisis, seemed like the rolling up of a curtain on a brighter,
more active scene. New forces, new doctrines, new characters all seized the
public attention. The vibrant personality of the new President, sanguine,
energetic, imaginative, and full of a zest for bold experiment which was
encouraged by the legal philosophy of Justice Holmes and by the advice of the
band of young men who gathered about the White House, did not cease for
twelve years to dominate American affairs. For the same length of time a
virtual farmer-labor coalition, reinforced by some small businessmen and
many intellectuals, furnished the support which Roosevelt needed. A distinct
and exhilarating atmosphere pervaded the period.

And yet the Roosevelt era, like that which preceded it, must be divided
into distinct periods. It is more correct to speak of two New Deals, for example, than of one. At the outset the administration placed its emphasis on
recovery combined with regulation, the National Recovery Administration
and the first Agricultural Adjustment Agency (which was avowedly temporary) furnishing the cornerstone of the edifice. In the second phase the
emphasis fell upon reform combined with regulation—the Labor Relations
Act of 1935, the Social Security Act of the same year, and the second or
permanent Agricultural Adjustment Agency (which provided for soil conservation) being the most important measures. Then came a third period.
The progress of the second New Deal was being steadily braked down by
conservative opposition when in the fall of 1937 Roosevelt's "quarantine
speech" at Chicago heralded an increasing preoccupation with foreign
affairs. Within two years the nation was almost entirely engrossed with the
menacing situation overseas and the demands of national defense.

As in other crowded national eras, nearly every possible mood and trend
of thought was discoverable somewhere and at some time. Fright, pessimism,
fortitude, exaltation, selfishness, altruism, corruption, idealism—all these
could easily be found. But a few elements of which there had been an unhappy superabundance in the days of Coolidge vanished completely. Placid-
ity, complacency, and irresponsibility disappeared as the charwomen swept
up the last ticker tape in bucket shops which closed in the fall of 1930, as
Iowa farmers gathered with pitchforks to stop the sheriffs' foreclosures, and
as hungry men peered into garbage cans in the streets of San Francisco and

Philadelphia. Our first impression of the fifteen years following the stock-market crash is that thought and emotion were highly chaotic: the psychology of unlimited opportunity swiftly giving way to the psychology of closed opportunity; the fascism of the pro-Nazi Bund clashing with the collectivism of Earl Browder's Communist party; the escapism of movies and radio balanced against the social earnestness of the Federal Council of Churches and the League of Women Voters; the static outlook of the Liberty League and the dynamic program of the National Resources Planning Board—where can we find a dominant trend?

Yet beneath all the surface crosscurrents and eddies a powerful trend did exist: a trend which psychologically brought together a great movement in home affairs and an irresistible reorientation in world relations. Americans learned in these stormy years that no type of security was attainable on the easy terms which they had taken for granted in the nineteenth century or in the 1920's. Security in the domestic sphere could be had only on a new social basis, through a broad governmental program of interference, regulation, and planning. It was no longer reconcilable with the stark individualism once regarded as an American birthright. Similarly, security in the world sphere could be had only on a collective basis, through courageous measures of world organization. It was no longer reconcilable with unfettered nationalism and unimpaired sovereignty. The new paths seemed strange and bewildering. Throughout nearly their whole history Americans had belonged to the go-it-alone school, which meant laissez faire in economics and isolation in diplomacy, and which seemed a natural expression of their history and genius.

Yet the change which so swiftly overtook the nation, and which came to millions as such a shock, had long been foreshadowed. For two generations progressive political leaders like La Follette, Altgeld, the first Roosevelt, and Wilson, with humanitarians like Jacob Riis, Jane Addams, Brand Whitlock, and John Spargo, had been preaching state intervention for social reform. For one generation a strong school of believers in international union—Root, Taft, Wilson, Cordell Hull—had been trying to draw the United States out of its old timidity and self-sufficiency. Now the irresistible pressure of events brought a decision. In both domestic and foreign affairs what we may call the social ideal triumphed.

What the American masses most wanted when the storms burst and the firmament trembled was security; but they had to find new paths to its attainment. The old economic formula of rugged individualism, which Hoover praised as if men still lived in Hebert Spencer's world, had proved to be not an immovable pillar, but the frailest of reeds. Other nations, caught in the Great Depression, were groping too. The fact that three great powers took refuge in Fascism or its like, which ultimately meant aggression, complicated the situation. For half a dozen years, 1930–1936, the country hoped that it need bother itself only with radical new solutions on the home front, and that foreign policy could be left unchanged. If the United States were to accept the crowding problems of modern industrialism and become a social service state like Britain and Scandinavia, that should be sufficient! In the middle thirties the spirit of nationalism and isolationism distinctly increased. But as the neglect of foreign dangers only heightened them, it was necessary to turn first toward foreign alliances, and then to flat and permanent acceptance of a world organization. By 1942 the social and collective paths toward security had been fairly adopted. It had been settled that the twentieth century road for America was not a continuation of the nineteenth, but a sharp divergence.

2

So much for the dominant trend of the fifteen years: a trend away from individualism and isolationism and toward cooperative solutions of both domestic and foreign problems. But the whole process had a rich complexity which cannot be grasped without some topical analysis.

The first impact of the Great Depression had its most obvious effect in a wave of exposure. In the wake of the Congressional investigating committees that were busy between 1930 and 1935, the press, drama, novel, pulpit, and pamphlet united to analyze and excoriate all the obvious abuses. When the mass of the population during the boom era had smugly worshiped false gods, the satirist had been more effective than the muckraker. Sinclair Lewis and H. L. Mencken had dealt with types, not individuals. But now the nation's mood was direct and grim, and the target was clearly identified. The erring bankers and brokers, the public utility magnates like Insull, the groups who wrecked such railroads as the Chicago, Milwaukee & St. Paul, the promoters of realty and stock-market speculation, came under heavy attack. Competent journalistic exposures of Southern illiteracy, poverty, and physical and intellectual anemia (the nation's Number One problem, said Roosevelt) found a literary reflection in Erskine Caldwell's *Tobacco Road*. The scope of the migratory labor problem, and the obduracy of economic royalists in the face of appalling misery, were laid bare in a monumental report by a California state commission, an impassioned sociological treatise by Carey McWilliams, and that memorable novel, John Steinbeck's *Grapes of Wrath*. From such works as these, dealing with whole sections and large populations, the literatuture of exposure ran down to attacks on labor baiters, on state and city bosses (for example, Huey Long of Louisiana and Frank

Hague of Jersey City), on racketeers, and on tax evaders. Even the chain gang had its official inquiry, its sociological reports, its motion picture, and its literary treatment in Paul Green's play *Hymn to the Rising Sun.*

An equally significant product of the depression was a new movement of economic and sociological analysis, definitely scientific in quality. In their bewilderment, the harassed population turned to the experts. Studies of industrial waste, like those of Stuart Chase; studies of labor, like Benjamin Stolberg's various books; studies of class and caste, like John Dollard's in his work on "Southerntown"; studies of the race problem in the light of anthropology, like Hortense Powdermaker's *After Freedom*; studies of agrarianism, like Arthur Raper's of the tenant farmer; studies of urbanization, like Lewis Mumford's *Culture of Cities*; cross sections of great typical communities, like J. C. Furnas' *How America Lives,* and the Lynds' *Middletown in Transition*—all these were evidence of a deeply felt impulse. Americans, long skeptical of the expert, now felt that their problems had attained a complexity which made it essential to mobilize the whole array of principles, facts, and ideas possessed by the social sciences. Much of the economic analysis was contradictory, for the old "orthodox economics" had been largely succeeded by a wildly confusing clamor. Much of the sociology was vague. But these new studies enriched American thought, banished much naïveté, broke down conventional assumptions, threw light on many hidden relationships, and defined such concepts as well-being, freedom, equality, and democracy with sharp realism.

That this more realistic and scientific approach to the problems of society would ultimately give a distinct coloration to literature could hardly be questioned. Southerners, for example, would have said in 1920 that they "understood the Negro"; but Howard W. Odum, Rupert B. Vance (*Human Geography of the South*), Gunnar Myrdal in his two volumes on the race problem, Spero and Harris in their book on the black worker, and many more proved that they did not. A still larger body of writers, like W. J. Cash in his *Mind of the South* and Clarence Cason in his gently corrosive 90° *in the Shade,* showed that they did not even know themselves. Similar examples could be cited in the field of labor relations, of the urban and rural slum, and very conspicuously of the immigrant and his children. By such scientific approaches, greater depth of understanding and a fuller sense of complexity were ultimately conferred upon all letters. Already the impact of the new sociology was not difficult to trace in James T. Farrell's studies of the Chicago Irish, Albert Halper's labor novels, and even Marjorie Kinnan Rawlings' picture of the Florida cracker.

Meanwhile, the formulation of social security as a cardinal national ideal reached below political controversy to the very foundations of American thought. The discussion shook the country for half a dozen years as men who agreed that some recovery measures were essential and that some reforms were urgent, but who disagreed on basic principles, debated the question whether a philosophy of governmental provision could safely be substituted for the old philosophy of stern self-reliance. The ghost of William Graham Sumner struggled with the spirit of Supreme Court Justice Brandeis. The grim necessities of life in a crowded, highly industrialized, and overcompetitive society triumphed; by 1936 the revolutionary social ideal was victorious, for Landon no less than Roosevelt ran for President that year on a social security platform.

But the poignancy of the issue to tens of millions of people cannot be exaggerated. On one side stood a host of men who believed that true liberty was inseparably bound up with individualism, and true progress with unfettered initiative. They passionately desired to preserve the republic of Hamilton, Jackson, and Grover Cleveland: a republic of personal independence, courageous self-sufficiency, and automatic balances. On the other side stood a host of men who believed with equal passion that this old social and political framework was outworn, inhumane, and incalculably dangerous.

The deeper implications of the inevitable decisions were destined to be more slowly grasped in America than they had been in Great Britain when Lloyd George directed a similar plunge. The new social security state was a world removed in outlook, ideas, and spirit from our individualistic nineteenth century state, and its advent seemed appallingly abrupt. After all, many men still active in the thirties remembered when our industrial revolution had been brashly new in the seventies, and multitudes recalled the days when homesteading had remained a brisk reality in the eighties. The spirit of Davy Crockett's and Kit Carson's geographical frontier, and of Rockefeller's and Carnegie's manufacturing frontier, still exercised its spell over most Americans. Even as farmers took the benefits of the Agricultural Adjustment Agency they kicked at the attendant controls, while John L. Lewis' Congress of Industrial Organizations (not to mention some gangster-led unions) accepted government benefits with a fierce repudiation of government disciplines. The novel social ideals would naturally extend their sway but gradually, and they might well be slower still in affecting fiction, poetry, and criticism. Yet the new social security order was as firmly established after 1936 as the new independence had been after 1783, and the new race and labor relationships after 1865. The country had definitely committed itself to a transformed philosophy, which demanded not only a fresh relationship between government and society but a reshaping of society itself.

A new society: for the specifications of the social security state came to nothing less. They called for a drastic curtailment of wealth at one extreme, and a systematic attrition of poverty at the other. Henceforth nobody would be so poor, and nobody so rich; Fifth Avenue and Third Avenue would swing closer together. The specifications called for a society which would save less and spend more. By increasing both the income and the security of the masses, their "propensity to consume"—that is, their standard of living—would be healthfully raised. The millionaire would not needlessly save just to have the government take his money in surtaxes and death duties, while the poor man would not needlessly save to meet exigencies with which the state now dealt. And thus, while thrift lost something of its old standing as a Calvinist virtue, a greater taste for rational enjoyments should give a brighter hue to life. The new specifications implied that less planning would be done for society by the Rockefellers, Carnegies, and Morgans, and more by federal, state, and city governments. They involved, that is, a greater reliance upon that expert bureaucracy which Jacksonian democrats had distrusted, but which, first making its full debut under Theodore Roosevelt, had expanded with irresistible and beneficial rapidity. The specifications closed a good many of the old frontiers of effort, but they opened new ones. If we relied upon science and technology to furnish the foundations of an economy of plenty, as we now meant to do, individual talent would have ample scope in promoting the activities of both. Roosevelt gave one of his campaign speeches of 1936 the significant title, "The Period of Social Pioneering Is Only at Its Beginning."

The New Deal never succeeded in bringing back full prosperity or in banishing unemployment. At one time, in 1936–1937, it seemed about to do so; but a sharp recession during 1937–1938 called back the grimmest specters of the crisis. What the New Deal did accomplish was to plant in the nation a hopeful, aspiring spirit, and to conjure up before men's eyes a vision of national renascence. The rather artificial drives of the first Roosevelt administration to raise national morale did not achieve much; the feverish propagandist activities of various departments, the futile tail chasing of the National Recovery Administration, even the President's fireside talks, had but a transient effect. But as time passed the nation did feel a freer and far more bracing atmosphere. Nor were the principal elements of this atmosphere, by the date of Roosevelt's third election in 1940, difficult to define.

The components of the new spirit were half a dozen: (1) America felt once more that it was a dynamic, not a static, nation; that, in Roosevelt's phrase, it was "on its way" even if it did not always know just to what. Progress in the war against poverty made millions happier than they had been when, under Coolidge, they were told the nation had "arrived" and could now stand still. (2) Once they accepted the idea of the interventionist state, men took pleasure in learning how many objects of a desirable kind imaginative leaders could make the state promote. It conserved resources; it apportioned crops not hit-or-miss but by plan; it developed great valleys; not least of all, through the National Youth Administration it aided education, and through the Work Projects Administration it supported stimulating projects in writing, drama, painting, architecture, and sculpture. (3) A new humanitarianism, less sentimental and paternal, but more effective, had appeared. It recognized that government "economy" was stupid when it cut taxes but neglected human erosion, wasteful when it saved cash but did not save people from degradation. (4) The instinctive craving for national solidarity, the liberal idealism of the New Deal leaders, and advanced sociological and ethnological thinking, all united in a long overdue crusade against the intolerances which had defaced the Harding-Coolidge period, intolerances of which the Ku Klux Klan had been the special symbol. A new impatience of distinctions based upon class, creed, and national stocks took firm root, and the effort to erase them all was for the first time in American history vigorously sustained. (5) Roosevelt's own buoyancy visibly affected the people, as presidential leadership always affects them. (6) A conviction arose that the country was emerging from a careless, wasteful adolescence into a maturity that demanded prudence and planning, but that offered its appropriate rewards in confidence and vigor.

3

All this would have been enough to give intellectual interest to the period. But athwart the preoccupation with domestic affairs cut a sharp current of world perplexities. In 1933 the elevation of Hitler to power struck reflective men with apprehension. Year by year, the brutal drama of the Old World moved from scene to scene—Manchuria, Ethiopia, Spain, Shanghai, Austria, Czechoslovakia—its import to America grew plainer. The attitude of the country at large down to 1939 was far from creditable. The forces which would finally compel a new internationalism could hardly be ignored. But of genuine cosmopolitanism, a feeling for world culture, Americans showed all too little. Of regard for order and justice outside their own borders, and willingness to make sacrifices to promote it, they showed hardly more. Their main concern was simply for national safety. This might be given the dubious dignity of Charles Beard's special pleading in *The Open Door at Home,* or the franker selfishness of the America Firsters; in either event it was unworthy and unhappy.

The years of especially acute crisis, between Mussolini's attack on Ethiopia and the blow at Pearl Harbor, therefore constituted a remarkably dramatic period of education and conversion. In 1935 most Americans still rejected the international ideal. "Entanglements" meant war and all its accompaniments—propaganda, profiteers, repudiated debts, internal conflict, loss of civil liberties, general confusion. Americans had learned this lesson all too well, taught by the "exposures" which followed the First World War. Pacifists, reformers engrossed in home problems, liberals of the *New Republic* stripe, Russophiles (Russia herself being isolated), and Fascist groups all joined with the un-thinking head-in-the-sand majority who wanted simply to play safe. But by 1941 the national attitude had completely changed. National safety was seen to lie in international union. It was one of the most dramatic and drastic *volte-face* in all American history. The fundamental reason for it again lay in stark necessity: playing safe had proved to be playing the aggressors' game. Twice in adult memory it had been demonstrated that the way to escape a prairie fire was not to retreat behind a few hasty furrows, but to join the neighbors in beating out the first sparks. Watching the house burn for the second time, Americans took a mighty resolve. They registered it at the Atlantic Meetings, Dumbarton Oaks, Yalta, and San Francisco.

This process of conversion, far from being confined to the political sphere, affected every department of American thought. From the beginning an unprecedented array of books by foreign correspondents and international experts had flooded the country. The newsreel and radio had made Americans feel that they were sitting on the very fringe of world events. Meanwhile, the nation's interest in world culture, the cosmopolitan tradition of Jefferson, Longfellow, and Ticknor, was being strengthened by a ceaseless irruption of refugee writers and artists. The Republic had gained much from refugees of the French Revolution, the German Forty-eighters, and the survivors of the Russian pogroms. But it obviously stood to gain far more from the tens of thousands of writers, scholars, painters, physicians, and composers who were cast on our shores by the Fascist terror. Some came temporarily, like Maeterlinck; most came permanently, like Einstein and Thomas Mann. A certain friction was visible in such professional fields as medicine. But in general the national welcome was warm; it became possible to staff an entire "university in exile"; and scientific journals, general magazines, and book lists soon showed the power of the new element in American life. Henceforth it would be a little easier for educated Americans to be at home in world culture.

An ideological emphasis upon democracy as a world force was an inevitable and notable accompaniment of the external crisis 1935–1945. Totalitarian and democratic ideals obviously stood in implacable opposition. As the United States finally moved toward guaranteeing its safety by membership in the United Nations, so it moved also toward the exaltation of democracy as an international gospel. Many diverse motives were bound up in the virtual Anglo-American alliance, in the Pan-American and Good Neighbor movements, and in Clarence Streit's Union Now program; but one of the most prominent objects was the protection and propagation of democratic ideas. In the nineteenth century America had consciously regarded herself as the exemplar of democracy; in 1917–1918 Woodrow Wilson had made her the crusading apostle. But after 1935 democracy became the basis for a grand world alliance. It was eventually made a veritable communion as against the hostile fellowship of Hitler, Mussolini, and Franco. A huge array of novels, plays, histories, and expository treatises, under the slogan "Books are weapons," was marshaled to the defense of democracy as a world force. The English-speaking peoples had long been close to one another; but now Ernest Hemingway discovered a brotherhood between the American and the Spanish rebel, and Pearl Buck a link between the Yankee and the Chinese—the brotherhood of democracy.

December of 1941 and January of 1942 were in some respects two of the darkest months in all American history. Half the battleship fleet had just been knocked out at Pearl Harbor; Japan was overrunning the Philippines; German submarines were littering the Atlantic coast with wrecks; the gravest danger existed that the Nazis would yet capture Moscow and break the spinal column of the British Empire at Suez. But out of defeat and distress, out of ten years of travail, a radiant dawn was beginning to light the national scene. America had fairly chosen its two new paths. Primarily under Roosevelt's leadership, but with the aid of Hull and Wallace, Willkie and Stimson, and many another leader in both parties, it had decided to seek domestic security in social measures, and world security in collective policies. National individualism and isolationism were seemingly forever dead.

It was dawn, moreover, in another sense. Just ahead lay such a display of power in the mass production of ships, airplanes, tanks, ordnance, and all the lesser paraphernalia of war, of skill in the mobilization and deployment of forces double those ever before put into the field, and of resolution in committing the country to colossal expenditures of money, effort, and if necessary blood, as would add fresh luster to the history of the nation. The early thirties had found the country half paralyzed; the early forties saw it exerting a giant's might. With this exercise of power in the war came a new mood of robust exhilaration—tempered, happily, at the war's end, by the sense of perplexity over still unsolved domestic problems and of the necessitated responsibility of sharing in world leadership.

# 75. HOW WRITERS LIVED

THE society of the period between wars was curious about what Americans were, could do, might do, were doing. American literature and American journalism had grown up by the 1920's. By the 1940's, a host of serious writers, with the aid of publishers, foundations, universities, and the government, had learned how to make writing a profession, how to make a living at it, and how to get themselves read.

The best of these writers were able to work on a higher technical level than had their predecessors. They had fewer financial handicaps to overcome. They appeared at a time when magazine editors and book publishers were curious about the new generation, and also when its members, with their wartime adventures, their travels and their moral revolt, had something fresh to say. While waiting for literary recognition, they were able to support themselves without going far from their own field. Newspaper work had ceased to be a taken-for-granted step in the literary career, but a few of the younger writers became foreign correspondents, notably Ernest Hemingway and Vincent Sheean. Others were advertising copy writers (Scott Fitzgerald and Hart Crane); still others were teachers (Thomas Wolfe and Thornton Wilder); but more were book reviewers, free-lance journalists, junior editors of magazines, or book publishers' assistants. Literature was becoming a specialized field, almost like medicine, in which a man could spend his life from college to the grave.

All the younger writers of the twenties planned to go abroad, and either saved money for the trip or hopefully searched the woods for windfalls. In those days windfalls were fairly numerous: in addition to the Rhodes Scholarships to Oxford, there were the American Field Service Fellowships to French universities; after 1925 there were the Guggenheim Fellowships, which provided for a year and sometimes two years in Europe; and there were private benefactors, of whom the most widely known was Otto Kahn. Best of all, since they combined financial help with the prospect of publication, were publishers' advances against future royalties. Many publishers, including some of the oldest houses and more of the newest, were willing at the time to risk a few hundred dollars on any promising young writer who needed time to finish his first novel. The money could be used for a trip to France, where living was cheap and the writer could work, so he hoped, in ideal circumstances.

Sometimes the novel was written and published and was even a success. A distinguishing feature of the writers belonging to the interwar generation is the early age at which they became established in their profession. Scott Fitzgerald at twenty-three was already selling stories to the magazines. At twenty-four he published his first novel and earned $18,000 during the year. Fitzgerald was luckier in the beginning than his contemporaries; but his friend Ernest Hemingway had an international reputation after he published his second book at the age of twenty-eight. John Dos Passos, Thornton Wilder, Glenway Wescott, Louis Bromfield, and Thomas Wolfe—to mention only a few names—were all established writers before they were thirty. As men who could devote all their time to literary work and who, moreover, were fascinated by the problems of their craft, most of them became expert technicians.

2

Financially these writers suffered less than might have been expected from the depression. The sale of books decreased sharply in 1930 and continued low until after 1935. A large publishing house and four or five smaller ones went bankrupt, with a loss to their authors of accrued and future royalties. Several magazines suspended publication, while others stopped buying articles or stories and began printing the old manuscripts that had accumulated in their files; they were like bears in winter living on their fat. But new magazines were appearing even in the depression years; the Book-of-the-Month Club prospered; Hollywood was showing an interest in serious, even high-brow novelists, especially if they could write good dialogue; and in general the authors already known to the public found it not too hard to survive.

It was a different problem for the still younger writers, those born after 1905, who in 1930 still had their reputations to make. They had the bad luck to come forward at a time when there was no demand for college graduates with literary ambitions. The magazines, shrunk to half their former size, had no room for new writers; the publishers had no money to risk on first novels that might never be finished, nor had they jobs to offer on their now smaller staffs. "Wait a while," they said to the more promising applicants. "Perhaps next season . . ." But the young writers had to live while waiting; and their general difficulties were increased by the fact that many of them came from working-class families, without the financial resources or wide acquaintanceships or merely the air of assurance that helped the middle classes to keep afloat during the worst years. Once at a meeting of young writers an older writer asked from the platform, "How do you manage to keep going?" There was giggling in one corner of the hall, where half a dozen poets sat with their wives; then one of them rose to say, "We marry schoolteachers." That was in New York, where teachers received their full salaries even in the winter of 1932, and hence were regarded as persons of economic consequence. Young writers in general had no salaries; they lived on their wives or parents, brooded in cafeterias, found odd jobs; at one time there were hundreds of them on home relief—including some who later owned Hollywood villas with swimming pools.

In the early years of the depression, it was natural for young writers to believe that the best hope for American literature lay in a complete reorganization of society. They flocked by hundreds into the radical movement; and soon there were John Reed clubs—named for the author who died of typhus in Russia after helping to found the American Communist party—flourishing in all the larger cities. At least six of the clubs published their own little magazines devoted to the theory and practice of proletarian literature. In 1935 all the John Reed clubs were dissolved on instructions from the Communist Party, which condemned them as being too "leftist" and doctrinaire.

The organization that replaced them was the League of American Writers, which had no direct political affiliations, although there were some Communists on its executive board. The League was typical of the united front during the period when liberals and radicals were collaborating in all countries from Chile northeastward round the globe to China. It recruited more than eight hundred members, most of whom were professional authors, unlike the younger membership of the John Reed clubs. It held four writers' congresses in New York, all interesting affairs; it conducted a writers' school; it issued political statements, especially in favor of the Spanish Loyalists; and then it declined after 1940, in the midst of the political quarrels that followed the Moscow trials and the Russo-German Pact. By that time many of the younger writers had turned anti-Communist or had withdrawn from politics into a revived religion of art.

By that time, too, the Federal Writers' Project was dwindling away, although it would not be formally abolished until a year after Pearl Harbor. Founded in 1935, it employed at its peak more than six thousand writers and researchers, including some who would afterward be famous, like John Steinbeck, and even some who were famous already; a poet who had won the Pulitzer prize for his selected works was glad to receive a government check of about $25 a week for his researches into local history. One desirable effect of the Writers' Project—in addition to keeping writers employed through the later years of the depression—was that it encouraged them to stay at home. Since it was organized on a state basis, writers could be more easily certified to the Project if they lived in West Virginia or Idaho than if they moved to New York; thus, it favored the growth of regional centers. Its principal work was also regional, being the compilation of guides to the forty-eight states and Alaska, as well as to the principal cities, automobile highways, and national monuments.

Hollywood during those same years had served as a sort of auxiliary writers' project with chromium plate. There was a revolution in the studios when talking pictures replaced silent pictures after 1929. The producers had to recruit a staff of specialists in the written and spoken word. For a time they would hire almost any published novelist for twelve weeks at $300 a week, with a contract that could be renewed at a higher salary if his work proved satisfactory. Famous novelists received much more, sometimes as much as $1,500 a week for their first assignments. In the thirties scores and even hundreds of writers went to Hollywood and disappeared, like travelers in a rocket to the moon. Many of them joined the Hollywood proletariat that works for a few weeks a season at a splendid salary, then haunts the agencies looking for another job. A few of them made their way into the little circle of highly skilled motion-picture artisans whose names are familiar to income-tax collectors, but almost forgotten by the reading public.

In 1938 a Hollywood producer, talking with a visitor from the East, happened to mention Scott Fitzgerald. "Why, I thought he was dead," the visitor exclaimed. "If that's so," the producer said, "I've been paying $1,500 a week to his ghost."

## 3

At the end of the thirties, there was a boom in what was coming to be known as the literature business; and the boom continued until after the Second World War. Book and magazine publishing began to be organized as a mass-production industry. Most of the 11,806 professional authors—to borrow a figure from the 1940 census reports—were still insecure and underpaid; but those who had achieved or blundered into prosperity were living like speculators in a bull market.

The new era of best sellers had begun as early as 1931, when the sale of most books was hardly enough to pay the printer's bill. In that year Pearl Buck published her first novel, *The Good Earth,* which stood at the top of the bookstore lists for two years. It was reprinted many times at various prices, was translated into many languages, and had an American sale in all editions of probably more than a million copies, although its publisher has never released the exact figures. In 1933 and 1934, the best seller was *Anthony Adverse,* the first of the oversize historical romances. It had so wide a popular appeal that it became a sort of St. Christopher for the booksellers, lifting them on its back and carrying them through the slough of the depression; its sale during the next twelve years would be more than 1,200,000 copies. In 1936 and 1937, the book was *Gone With the Wind,* with a sale in its first ten years of over 3,500,000 copies in English; both at home and abroad it was the greatest publishing success of the century. All three of these novels had been issued to its subscribers by the Book-of-the-Month Club, which, with its competitors, was changing the history of the book trade in America.

Essentially the book clubs were companies engaged in the business of selling books by mail to various types of readers. By 1946 there were twenty-six clubs, with 3,600,000 subscribers, many of whom were buying books for the first time, and some of whom lived in villages more than fifty miles from the nearest bookstore. There were special clubs for Protestants, Catholics, radicals, children, executives, students of science, lovers of the classics, Sears Roebuck customers, and mystery fans; but two of the clubs that appealed to a general audience—the Book-of-the-Month Club and the Literary Guild—were the oldest and by far the most successful.

The Book-of-the-Month Club issued its first selection in April, 1926; at the end of the first year it had 40,000 members. Its growth was steady even during the depression, and phenomenal in the early wartime years; by 1943 it was setting a limit of 600,000 on its membership because of the paper shortage. In spite of difficulties with production, it was distributing nearly 300,000 copies, on the average, of the books it recommended, besides many other volumes ordered by the members from its monthly magazine; and it was then the third largest private customer of the Post Office Department, the first two being Sears Roebuck and Montgomery Ward. Obviously the members had learned to rely on the taste of the five judges who made its monthly selections. The judges never succeeded in choosing the twelve best books of the year in point of literary merit, but they almost always chose something of general interest, and they often took chances—that is, they voted for some out-of-the-way book which, without their approval, would have had no chance for success. The growing popularity of nonfiction books was a phenomenon of the years after 1930 when even the philosopher George Santayana became a best seller. Partly it was explained by the support that many of them received from the Book-of-the-Month Club.

The Literary Guild, which began to distribute books in 1927 after several years of discussion and promotion, had a more uneven history. At first it grew as fast as its rival; then for some years it fell behind, as a result of choosing books that were either too difficult or, in some cases, simply too dull for its audience; there were times when it teetered on the edge of bankruptcy. After 1937 it began a period of rapid growth under a new editor, John Beecroft, who also made the monthly selections for two other large book clubs owned by the same publishing house: the Doubleday One Dollar Book Club and the Book League of America. But the Guild received his special attention; it overtook and passed the Book-of-the-Month Club during the war, when it had a larger supply of paper; and by 1946 it had 1,250,000 members, as against 1,000,000 for its rival.

Paper stocks, however, were only part of the story. The more rapid growth of the Guild after 1937 was also the result of its having adopted an older, safer, and somewhat more cynical policy. Its selections were chiefly novels with a well constructed plot that was easy to follow: books that Beecroft was sure its members would like. The bookstore audience liked them too; and it was largely owing to the influence of the Guild that sales of more than a million copies for historical romances and local color novels once more became commonplace, as in the years before the First World War. Indeed, the best-selling novels of the new era—like *Captain from Castile* and *The Black Rose*—were almost on the same literary level as those of the period from 1900 to 1915; on the average, they were a little better than *Freckles,* a little worse than Winston Churchill's *The Crisis*; neither better nor worse, but only franker in sexual matters, than *The Trail of the Lonesome Pine.*

The publishing industry as a whole was growing in the wartime years; after 1942 the production of books was limited, not by public demand, which seemed to have no end, but only by the supply of paper and binding cloth and the time available on the printing presses. Some publishers, looking ahead, were taking steps to reach the wider market that had been created partly by the book clubs. Books had to be cheaper if they were to be distributed to a mass audience, but that was only part of the problem; they also had to be the sort of books the public would buy, and they had to be sold through stores that the public patronized. There were still only five hundred real bookstores in the country, and most of them were concentrated in the twelve largest cities. Some other machinery had to be found for mass distribution.

The answer that slowly developed was to issue reprints of best-selling novels and nonfiction, at prices ranging downward from $1.98 for illustrated biographies and travel books to 49 cents for clothbound popular novels; and to sell them through thousands of new outlets, including drugstores, stationery stores, and chain department stores. Pocket Books, Inc., founded in 1939, carried the process even further by finding a convenient, reasonably attractive, and highly salable format for books that could be offered for 25 cents at the corner news stand. It printed ten million copies of its books in 1941, twenty million in 1942; and it continued to expand until rivals crowded the field and there were more pocket-size books to sell than even the largest news stands had room to display.

Magazines also enjoyed a period of wartime prosperity when they could sell as many copies as their paper quota made possible. The market for literary products kept expanding; and yet there were whole categories and age groups of writers who gained nothing from the boom in the book and magazine trades. Most of the younger men were in the army; many of the women and the older men were in war work that took all their energies. Poets and scholarly critics, if they had time for writing, learned that it had become harder than ever to find a publisher for books that wouldn't sell. Even the great majority of novelists and general essayists had very little share in wartime profits. Lacking the art of salesmanship, or regarding its use as a dangerous temptation, they lived very much as before, on crumbs of income from a dozen different tables: now an advance from a publisher (who was likely to be more generous in wartime), now a story sold to a magazine, now a literary prize or fellowship (there were more of these than in the past), now a lecture or a summer of teaching at a writers' conference, now a book review or a manuscript to be reported on, now a few dollars for permission to reprint something of theirs in a textbook or anthology, now an invitation to spend a month or two writing at such endowed centers for creative work as Yaddo or the MacDowell colony—in general an irregular series of little windfalls that somehow kept them going while they waited to see whether the next book would pay for the publisher's advance on it and even yield them—for perhaps the first time—an actual royalty check.

Meanwhile a few scores or perhaps as many as two hundred of the most popular writers were earning money almost at the rate of war contractors. If they were lucky enough to have a book taken as its sole monthly choice by one of the two largest book clubs, they each received, in 1946, an advance payment of $50,000; and there was the prospect of further payments from the club if its members liked their work—not to mention the royalties from bookstore sales, certain to be larger for club selections than for other books. Magazines as a class had not raised their top rates for thirty years, and the successful magazine writers of 1940 were being paid rather less than Jack London had received in 1910; but this was another situation that changed during the war. All money was "hot" in those days because of income and excess-profits taxes; and magazines that were making profits subject to high taxation often shared part of the wealth with their collaborators by giving them bonuses or higher fees, at a cost to themselves of about 10 per cent of the sums advanced. The *Reader's Digest,* which was said to be printing eleven million copies a month, paid close to a dollar a word for most of the articles it published, and more than that to some favored writers.

The growth of reprint publishing had involved very little increase in the economic rewards of authorship. The various pocket books, for example, paid royalties of only one cent a copy, equally divided between the author and his original publisher; so that the author's share for an edition of 150,000 was only $750. On the other hand, the sale of foreign rights had begun to yield respectable sums; and the digest magazines gave high prices, in a few cases $10,000 or more, for permission to make a condensed version of a popular novel.

Two young ladies, overheard by a reporter for the *New Yorker,* were discussing the latest number of *Omnibook,* a monthly devoted to book digests. "It takes five or six books and boils them down," said one of the ladies. "That way you can read them all in one evening." The other said, "I wouldn't like it. Seems to me it would just spoil the movie for you."

The movie was not only more important for these young ladies; it was also the largest source of income for many writers. As much as $250,000 was paid for the motion picture rights to successful books; as much as $300,000 for plays that had run only three weeks on Broadway. There is one case on record of a Hollywood producer who paid $150,000 for a then unpublished first novel that the critics did not like when it finally appeared.

4

Besides commercialism, two other tendencies were transforming the literary world after 1930. To name each of them in a long word, they were institutionalization and collectivization.

Literary activities were coming more and more to be centered in the institutions that were powerful enough to support them. The government itself was the largest of these and, in the days of the Federal Writers' Project, it had also shown signs of becoming the most influential. There was at one time talk of establishing a bureau of fine arts with authority to undertake cultural projects and award prizes and fellowships. A conference held under official auspices in the spring of 1941 resolved that the government had an interest in supporting the fine arts, including literature, that went beyond the measures it had already taken to keep artists and writers employed during the depression. But our entrance into the war, and later the hostility of Congress and the change in government personnel, put an end to these plans. The only government support for literature after 1945 was through the State Department in the foreign field, and through numerous research programs maintained by the Library of Congress.

Many of the functions that might have been performed by a bureau of fine arts were gradually taken over by the American universities. With their vast endowments and, in many cases, their support by state governments (in addition to help from the Carnegie and Rockefeller foundations), they became the local centers of cultural activity. They maintained, generally speaking, the best American libraries for scholarly work. They offered extension courses and free lectures that took the place of the old-time chautauquas and lyceums. They were a refuge for the little-theater movement, which was declining in most of the American cities and continued to flourish only in summer resorts. To their student bodies they gave courses in creative writing, sometimes with the help of well known authors. Teaching and creative writing, in the early 1900's, had been two separate worlds; after 1940, however, it was no longer surprising to hear that a critic, an experimental poet, a successful biographer, or even a widely praised novelist was on the faculty at Harvard, Minnesota, California, Princeton or any one of a dozen other universities.

More and more writers in all fields had ceased to be independent craftsmen and instead had become officials in public or private institutions. Besides those who worked for the government or taught in universities, there were others who wrote on yearly salaries for magazine corporations, on three months' contracts for motion picture producers, or were hired by radio advertising agencies. They were sometimes very well paid; on the largest magazines they might earn salaries of as much as $25,000 a year (or even more, if they were among the top favorites of *Reader's Digest*); and there were a very few writers for the movies who earned $5,000 a week on short-term contracts. At the other end of the scale, salaried writers for wood-pulp magazines might be given less than the rate for cub reporters under a Newspaper Guild contract. Lavishly paid or miserably paid, salaried writers as a class did honest work, the best that was possible in the circumstances; but the work was not their own. It had become collective to a degree never achieved in Russia, where collectivization is set forward as an ideal. The Russians sometimes sent "shock brigades" of writers to report on a particular situation; at one time it was the industrial and agricultural progress of Tajikistan. The writers all made the same conducted tour; then afterwards each submitted his individual report. But American writers employed by a corporation might not only be assigned to the same collective task; each of them might be expected to perform only part of it, like a single worker on the production line. In Hollywood, for example, it was a practice of some companies first to buy a story, then to set three writers to work independently preparing it for the screen. Their three versions would be combined, usually by a fourth writer, and the completed script would then be subject to further changes by the producer, the director on the set, and the editor in the cutting room, not to mention changes in the course of production by virtually all those concerned, till at last the film emerged as a vast collective enterprise.

Writing for some magazines had become almost as purely a collective process. An idea might be suggested by one of the editors, adopted after a conference of executives, assigned to one or more researchers to gather the facts, then to a salaried writer (or sometimes two or three writers in succession) to put the facts together, then again to one or more editors to whip it into final shape. In the Luce magazines, most of the articles were unsigned, for one good reason, among others, that it would have been as difficult in some cases to assign them to any single authorship as it would have been to identify the man chiefly responsible for the ten-millionth Chevrolet to move down the production line.

Even in fields where the process was less advanced, much of current American writing had come to represent not a personal vision, but rather a trend, an imprint, or a decision taken at a board of directors' meeting. The literary world had undergone vast changes since the moral and aesthetic revolt that began after 1910. There was now a much wider audience for all writing, including some of the best, and a much larger body of writers trained to meet its demands. There had been a great elaboration in technique, so that American fiction in the forties was the most skillful produced anywhere in the world. Yet there was also a greater timidity among writers, of the sort that develops in any bureaucratic situation; and there was a tendency to forget that, although a great book expresses a whole culture and hence has millions of collaborators, including persons long since dead, in another sense it must finally be written by one man alone in his room with his conscience and a stock of blank paper.

# 76. SPECULATIVE THINKERS

I<small>N</small> the twenty-five years that followed the death of William James in 1910, American speculative thought described a spiral movement. It began in idealism, swung rapidly to an opposite extreme, and then moved slowly back toward a philosophy which curiously resembled idealism but which had absorbed the results of the immense intervening progress made by science.

At the turn of the century the camp of idealism was thronged; nearly every philosopher of any standing in the country belonged to it. James began a revolt. Soon insurgents were springing up from behind every bush. Some of them were materialists, who were fortunate enough to have in Santayana perhaps the most eloquent spokesman that their ancient creed had ever found. Others gathered around John Dewey, who had picked up the weapons of James. The spread of his pragmatic revolt into the regions of educational, legal, and historical thought must form an important part of this chapter. A third rebellion came from the realists, though this ended in some confusion because of dissensions within the ranks. Another form of discontent broke out among the theologians, many of whom were repelled by the austere aridities of the appeal to reason. After all these alarms and excursions, it was curious, at the end of twenty-five years, to see thinkers from all points of the compass converging again, under the leadership of A. N. Whitehead, toward a philosophy strangely like the old and deserted idealism. The period begins with the emigration of Santayana from metaphysics and from America. It ends with a return to metaphysics led by an emigrant from Europe.

2

Santayana, Royce, and James belonged to the same department at Harvard, a department described by President Tucker of Dartmouth as not only the strongest department the country had known in philosophy, but the strongest in any field. Royce and James were Santayana's teachers; he knew them well; but almost from the beginning something within him rose in rebellion against them both. Indeed he reacted against nearly everything American. Born of

Spanish parents with New England connections, coming to this country an alien when he was eight years old, he remained throughout his life here an exotic and ill acclimated plant. It was as if there were something in his Latin blood that was determined to resist assimilation. He disliked American Protestantism and Puritanism and democracy and drive; he was always impatient to escape to Europe; and when, in 1912, it became financially practicable to give up his Harvard professorship, he abandoned it with a sigh of relief, boarded a ship almost immediately, and never set foot on American soil again.

Yet in a sense he never escaped America. "It is as an American writer that I must be counted," he says, "if I am counted at all." He adopted English as his exclusive medium; he avowed that he knew no other language well. For forty formative years New England was his home. Even his revolt against America was curiously American; it was almost as much the revolt of a sensitive American individualist like Henry James or T. S. Eliot as it was of an alien. Only by remembering how deep were his roots in American soil will one understand the animus of his criticisms. It has been pointed out that, though he regarded all religious belief as mythology, he reserved his sharpest strictures for "the genteel tradition of the Calvinists and the musty smell of duty over New England," and always treated Catholicism with gentleness and sympathy. For Santayana the thought of his past years was far indeed from a benediction; he sat singularly loose to his environment, wherever he was; and since New England was a peculiarly imperious environment, he hated it. At the same time it must be added that he was too genuine an individualist to be explained in terms of social or economic pressures, even by way of reaction against them. There are few figures in the history of American thought who, in their detachment from the scene around them, would offer to a historian of Marxist leanings a more awkward set of problems.

In some absorbing essays in autobiography (*Persons and Places*, 1944, *The Middle Span*, 1945), and still more perhaps in his single novel *The Last Puritan* (1935), Santayana revealed the source of his imperfect sympathies with New England. He believed that the Puritan character was "at enmity with joy." He therefore reacted against it with all the force of his Latin temperament and his Epicurean ethics. He appreciated the nobility of his Puritan hero, Oliver; but Oliver is a perfectionist ridden by conscience; he does everything—his work, his play, even his love-making—from an all-pervading sense of duty; and in the end it breaks him. Mario, his Latin-Catholic foil, can throw ultimate responsibilities on God and get on with his mundane hedonism. Puritanism, Santayana thought, served well enough for coarse, bluff minds who conceived of duty in the manner of good soldiers or good farmers. But when inherited by sensitive spirits, it is more than flesh can bear. It diffuses the sense of duty through all the capillaries of one's being, breeds a chronic feeling of failure, and spreads a creeping paralysis over the will. Man is not made for such self-torment. If he tries to live with his head continually in the clouds, he will only lose his footing on earth.

Santayana described himself as "a decided materialist—apparently the only one living." His materialism was not at all of the kind so often charged against Americans, that specifically moral materialism which consists in a preoccupation with the grosser goods. It was a philosophical doctrine; its "great axiom," he tells us, is "the dominance of matter in every existing being, even when that being is spiritual." This philosophy he expounded in two impressive and massive series, the five volumes of *The Life of Reason*, which formed the great achievement of his youth, and the four of *The Realms of Being*, which appeared at intervals from his sixty-fourth to his seventy-seventh year. In his own view these works expound a single coherent position. In the view of some of his critics, his early materialism underwent in the later volumes a transmutation into something richly and strangely Platonic.

According to *The Life of Reason* (1906), matter is all that exists. What then of thought and feeling? The answer is that they are by-products of the body, "a lyric cry in the midst of business," "a wanton music" babbled by the brain and wholly without efficacy in turning the wheels of the bodily machine. The life of reason is not, as it has been for so many philosophers, a life of free and speculative reflection; it consists rather in such judicious control and harmonization of our animal impulses as will secure for us most peace and satisfaction. To such mundane peace and satisfaction we shall devote ourselves if we are wise, for there is no other. The suggestion of free moral choice, uncontrolled by "the dark engine" of the body, or of a survival of the spirit beyond bodily disintegration, or of a God who presides over the course of nature and history, seemed to Santayana not so much a belief to be critically examined as the vestige of a primitive and pathetic mythology; he would say of religious creeds, as John Morley did, that they were less to be refuted than to be explained. Religion is not philosophy but poetry. If we would make the most of a brief and precarious life, let us rid ourselves of transcendentalisms, take stock of our little capital of impulses and powers, and make of it what we can. "Everything ideal has a natural basis and everything natural an ideal development." *The Life of Reason* is a leisurely and elaborate musing on that text as it applies to all the major branches of man's activity.

In the Santayana of later years there is a singular shift of interest. His preoccupation in *The Realms of Being* (1927–1940) is with the world of essences. And what are essences? We all know that when we say two and two are four, we are not saying something true at the moment merely, but something that is true always and everywhere. It never began to be true: it will never cease to be true; for twos and fours and the relations between them are not like apples that can decay or snowballs that melt; they are entities that are timeless and therefore beyond the reach of change. It is Santayana's doctrine of essence that everything we sense or imagine is in this position. We say that the odor of the violet is transitory. That, he insists, is false. To be sure, our sensing of it is transitory; we become aware of it and then cease to be aware; but that is another matter. The quality itself is as timeless as the twos and fours of our equations. So of all the colors and sounds, tastes and temperatures of actual or possible experience; all without exception are essences. Do they exist in the physical world? "No," he answers; "nothing given exists"; they are quite literally such stuff as dreams are made of. It is absurd to say that when we see or touch a chair, the shape and the hardness that we sense belong to the boiling mass of protons and electrons that is presumably out there; we may take them to belong there, and in favorable cases something like them may be there actually; but even of that we cannot be sure. In the end, philosophers, like everyone else, must rest their belief in the world around them on animal faith.

It might appear that Santayana in his age had come around to a point very close to the idealism he began by repudiating, and indeed the resemblance between his essences and the Platonic ideas is often remarked. But the resemblance is not in fact very close. Plato's ideas were also ideals; they descended into the stream of thought and action and made a dynamic difference there. Santayana's essences are "vestal virgins," beautiful perhaps to contemplate, but without issue in the world of events. All that we think, feel, or do is determined inflexibly by the distribution within our brains of a matter that even science cannot certainly know. All moral preferences, all scientific beliefs, all the dreams of the saints and the philosophers are at the beck and call of the material dynamics of nature.

The elaboration of this magnificent and melancholy philosophy was done in a prose that assures its writer of a permanent place in literature, whatever may be the fortunes of his theories at the hands of professional critics. It is a singularly quiet style, with a slow and meditative rhythm, exquisitely sensitive to the sounds and connotations of words as well as to their explicit meanings. Santayana is the conscious artist always. The words never tumble out as in informal talk; all is premeditated; dip into any page of his long row of volumes and you will find the same even flow of urbane and polished writing. It is as if a wise and traveled man of the world, released from entanglements with affairs, and free to contemplate the spectacle of life at somewhat elegant leisure, were discoursing over his tea in a world where it is always afternoon. For such a person to raise his voice or engage in logic chopping would not be seemly, and Santayana never does either. He will have it known that he is a gentleman and an amateur; he will have none of professors or their pedantic ways.

The not altogether happy result is that the professors have tended to take him at his own valuation. They have felt in him a certain lack of intellectual strenuousness, a reluctance to carry that agreeable flow of discourse into regions where the dialectical rocks in its bed might make it turbulent or turbid. It must be admitted that in his scorn of pedantry Santayana was content at times to forgo clearness and precision also. Sometimes, indeed not seldom, the reader bent on instruction feels a doubleness of purpose in his author, who, intent on catching all the fugitive lights and shadows as he strolls along, forgets that it is the philosopher's business to follow the straightest available path. Great philosophical prose is distressingly near to impossibility, for those very qualities of feeling that might give it a place in the literature of power may, by muddying its logic, exclude it from the literature of knowledge; and then it satisfies nobody. Philosophers are trained under an increasingly Spartan regime; and to persons in whom this training has produced a taste for spare and athletic writing, Santayana's prose seems lush and Oriental. Certainly he cannot be said to have solved the perhaps insoluble problem of the ideal philosophic manner. Still, there must be numberless persons who would ordinarily find a discussion of essence and existence the darkest sort of morass who have gladly pitched their tents in it because it was lighted, however dimly, by the glow of that iridescent prose.

3

Between Santayana and the next distinguished leader in the revolt against idealism there could hardly be a greater contrast. Santayana was an aristocrat, an artist, an alien among his own countrymen, a man who deliberately held aloof from the political and social movements of his time. John Dewey was a plebeian, both in his temperament—or absence of it—and in his writing. And he was an American through and through, as much at home in the Middle West, where he spent his early maturity, as in New England, where he was born into a society where homecrafts and manual skills still flourished. His philosophy was a philosophy of action rather than of contemplation, and it carried him into such crusading chairmanships as those of the League for Industrial Democracy and the committee that sought to vindicate Trotsky. Without the metaphysical gift of Royce, or the romantic and engaging personality of James, or the superb art of Santayana, he achieved a standing in American thought and an influence in the world that were probably unequalled by any of them. His life is an American success story. How is one to account for it?

Partly, no doubt, by the sheer volume of his output. Dewey sat thoughtfully and indefatigably before a typewriter for a considerable fraction of his life, and in mere years this life was extraordinary. His grandfather was born before the American Revolution. He himself was born when Washington Irving was still writing at Sunnyside, and while Lincoln still had his shingle out in Springfield. He appeared in that *annus mirabilis* 1859, which produced, among much else that was notable, Bergson, Husserl, and Havelock Ellis, Mill's essay on *Liberty* and Darwin's *Origin of Species*. In his appearing in the world simultaneously with Darwin's great book, there proved to be a special propriety. One of his own books was entitled *The Influence of Darwin on Philosophy,* and some wag has pointed out that this is a good description of Dewey himself.

There are more solid reasons for Dewey's remarkable influence, three of which should be noted. First, in a time when the theory of evolution was still engaging the general thought, he used that theory as the basis for a reform of logic and ethics. Secondly, to a people distrustful of speculation and preoccupied with practical results, he offered a philosophy that seemed to justify both the distrust and the preoccupation. Thirdly, from this new philosophy he developed a set of corollaries about education that again suited in a singularly happy way the temper of the time. All these achievements were branches that sprang from the common trunk of his "instrumentalism."

The term "instrumentalism," which Dewey preferred to "pragmatism" as a name for his philosophy, is itself suggestive of the debt he owed to Darwin. He holds that in the course of evolution thought was generated as an *instrument,* an instrument of adjustment and survival, like running, flying, and climbing. It originated in practical necessity; it maintained itself because it was practically useful; and—here is the new departure—its right employment now as in the beginning is as a means of practical adjustment. The situation in which thought first arose is typified by that of primitive man when, chased by a bear, he came to the bank of a river. In such a pass, instinct has nothing to offer; habit also is helpless because the occasion is new; it is a case of think or die. If the violent impact of necessity could strike from the man's mind the spark of an idea—say the idea of pushing out into the stream on a log—then, and only then, he might save himself. Eventually he, or someone else, did. What sort of thing was this new and potent tool which we now describe as an idea? Essentially, says Dewey, it was a plan of action, a proposal to do this or that. If it worked, it was true, in the sense of fulfilling the purpose for which it was brought into being. If it failed to work, it was false. Now the essence of Dewey's instrumentalism lay in maintaining that this first purpose of thought has remained its permanent purpose, and indeed its only purpose. The nature and end of thought marked out by biological evolution, namely the survival, growth, and better adjustment of the organism, are its true nature and end.

This theory at first glance seems innocent enough. But as Dewey gradually unfolded it, it was seen to imply nothing less than a philosophical revolution. He first applied the theory to logic. Traditional logic had assumed that the world had the changeless structure of a pyramid, with a layer of concrete things at the bottom, fixed general classes in the middle, and a set of pure eternal abstractions at the top. Since it was the business of thought to understand this world, its own apparatus of genus, species, and so on, must correspond to these outer arrangements. Dewey brushed aside this whole conception of thought and its purpose. If thought was really a tool, produced to serve the needs of the organism, then it too was in course of change, with all its methods, laws, and concepts; there was nothing static about them. It followed that the very test and nature of truth must be reconceived. The test of a theory can no longer be self-evidence, or consistency with other facts or theories, for what seems self-evident or consistent today may no longer seem so tomorrow; the test lies in whether our theories, now seen to be plans of action, achieve their practical ends. Indeed, this is all that truth *means*. For if the aim of thinking is not to get a copy of the world but to get results in practice, then in achieving those results we are also achieving truth in the only sense that is open to us. Dewey went on to take a similar view in ethics. In conduct as in thought there can no longer be any fixed standards or absolutes. That is good which conduces to human growth. What is growth? Advance toward maturity. What is maturity? It is better not to define it; for any exact definition would set before us a fixed end, and that must at all costs be avoided. Growth is that which conduces to further growth in a world without end. We must be content with that.

In Europe this philosophy gained almost no adherents; its one important representative in England, F. C. S. Schiller, finally retreated in discouragement to America. But in this country it found a congenial atmosphere and throve. It was a philosophy of results. It looked at the elaborate metaphysical and theological systems of the past and put to them one sweeping question: "How much difference do you make in terms of practical human betterment? If you mean little or none, out you go." To persons engaged in the life of action, to students of philosophy who were weary of metaphysical subtleties, or not quite equal to them, and to theologians more interested in communal improvement than in ultimates and absolutes, the announcement of such a program by a philosopher of standing flung open a door of release. When Dewey went on, in his *Reconstruction in Philosophy* (1920), to indict metaphysics as the product of an aristocratic and leisure class, the expression of a desire to escape into another world instead of facing the responsibilities of the here and now, many persons felt that they were hearing for the first time the authentic voice of democratic philosophy.

They felt this even more strongly if they turned to Dewey's *Democracy and Education* (1916). This book contains the fullest statement of an educational theory that has had its influence in almost every schoolroom of America, and in many besides in Mexico, Russia, and China. The theory is based on the instrumentalist philosophy. According to this philosophy, intelligence is not a faculty like memory, to be trained through exercise, nor is it a pursuit of the vision of truth for its own sake; it is a process of making over one's environment into something more satisfactory to one's needs and desires. It involves action in its very essence. Hence in the ideal Deweyan school, rote learning would be banished, and pupils would confine themselves to problems whose solution made a difference in practice. Their interest would be maintained by dealing with those problems in the order in which they arose in the course of their own growth; prescription from outside would be reduced to a minimum and free experimentation encouraged; subject matter would be adjusted to the child rather than the child to the subject matter; the old distinction between cultural and vocational training would be abolished, for culture that is not a means to better activity is feudal and effete; and since that part of the environment consisting of other persons is in many ways the most important part, much of the child's education would consist of experiments in cooperating with his kind.

In these theses of Dewey the  progressive education" movement found its inspiration. Schools sprang up throughout the country in which children did their learning through play, mastering their arithmetic through keeping store, their biology through keeping pets and making gardens, literature through producing plays and stories of their own. Whatever else may have been the effects of such education, there is no doubt that it made the little red schoolhouse a more cheerful and inviting center for myriads of school children.

Dewey's break with tradition was so sharp and his influence in education became so dominating that a reaction was sure to occur. Its leader, when it came, was the young Robert Maynard Hutchins, president of the University of Chicago, who in a series of trenchantly written books (*The Higher Learning in America*, 1936, *No Friendly Voice*, 1936, *Education for Freedom*, 1943), challenged the whole Deweyan conception of education. His own opposing conception received the moral support of Alexander Meiklejohn (*Education Between Two Worlds*, 1942) and of Mark Van Doren (*Liberal Education*, 1943); and it was put to a sort of laboratory test at St. John's College, Maryland, whose leaders, Stringfellow Barr and Scott Buchanan, sought to embody Hutchins' ideals in practice. According to those ideals, intelligence is not, as it was for Dewey, merely a tool for nonintellectual needs; it has an end of its own in the understanding of its world; and education, at least in its higher ranges, should devote itself to this end exclusively. Such understanding means the grasp of the permanent principles governing nature, man, and society.

How far this revolt against the Deweyan program of education will go, it is still too early to say. But in one respect the reaction against Deweyan tendencies did clearly win out. In his later years the drift in higher education was definitely away from the elective system, with its freedom of experiment, toward a considered regimentation in which studies regarded as essential were required of all.

Dewey's influence in education was so extraordinary as to raise the question recurrently how it is to be explained. One explanation is merely that the man and the occasion happily met; but it should be added that, when we speak of the man, we mean rather the thought than the personality. Seldom has a great popular success owed so little to anything picturesque or dramatic in its author, or to any of the arts of advocacy. Dewey was unostentatious almost to self-effacement; when he appeared in public, his slow, abstracted, and somewhat sleepy delivery left his audiences respectful but unaroused; he lacked the impulse to self-advertisement, and he lacked artistic temperament.

He wrote as he spoke. The writing is invariably charged with thought; it always comes at first hand out of his experience; it is downright, unpretentious, transparently honest. There is a fair supply of illustration, usually homely and helpful, but the ratio of generality to particular fact is high. And the often-repeated charge that the style is dull and pedestrian must on the whole be sustained. It is not only that Dewey had no dexterity with the minor devices which the practiced writer could hardly dispense with for an hour— variation of sentence structure, smoothness of transition, climax, balance, relief through figure, humor, or quotation. The trouble lay deeper. Dewey had none of that feeling for the magic of words which saved the most difficult pages of Santayana. He had no ear. He lacked that sense, partly logical, partly aesthetic, of economy of word to thought, which hits an idea off precisely and memorably; there is strangely little that is quotable in all the vast volume of his writing. The literary censor was lax, so lax as to pass innumerable paragraphs and pages that are awkward, verbose, and shuffling.

Of course when one is opening up new country—and the great philosophers have all been pioneers—grace of utterance is not the prime matter, and for the good of his soul the literary man may well recall occasionally that the Aristotles, the Kants, and the Hegels have perpetuated themselves without benefit of form. But the old saying that it is style that preserves is probably still true of all minds except these mountainous ones. And if so, perhaps the representative of the pragmatic philosophy who will be most read fifty years from now will not be its most competent and thorough exponent, who is undoubtedly John Dewey, but the man who invested it with his own inimitable style and charm, William James.

4

Pragmatic ideas have crept into many fields outside philosophy proper. We have seen something of their influence in education. They also infiltrated into the law. Here their effect was most notable at the top, through the work of a friend of James who was also a justice of the Supreme Court, Oliver Wendell Holmes. Judges are not as a rule heroes of the people, but it is reported that when Holmes retired from the Court, he received an acclaim from liberals and conservatives alike that had not been accorded to a member of that Court since the days of John Marshall. His life became the theme both of a successful Broadway play and of a popular biography which, under the title *Yankee from Olympus,* was a best seller. The "Olympus" refers of course to his "Brahmin" background and his sonship to the famous Autocrat, a relation that embarrassed him in curious fashion during most of his ninety-four years.

From his Boston moorings Holmes drifted far in two important directions. For one thing he became a skeptic. In his youth he and James had tried their hands together at stripping some of the obscuring garments from "our dilapidated old friend the Kosmos," but he came to think that "certainty generally is an illusion," and that we must be content with working hypotheses. "The best test of truth," he said, echoing James, "is the power of thought to get itself accepted in the competition of the market." The implications of such a view for religious belief are disintegrative.

But Holmes also moved far from the social conservatism of his forebears. Together with Louis D. Brandeis, he became a precursor of that group of justices in the Supreme Court who, in the recurring conflicts of Franklin Roosevelt's administration between property rights and human rights, stood stanchly for the latter. Though he disliked dissent in the court as weakening its authority, he became known as "the great dissenter," and his tenderness for social experimenters made him a popular hero. The question arose repeatedly whether or not some new venture in legislation or practice regarding a minimum wage or the restriction of child labor or the toleration of soap-box radicalism in public places was in accord with the Constitution. It would have been easy enough to interpret the new venture as conflicting with the rights of property and to crush it beneath the enormous weight of the Constitution. Some of his colleagues, not without an impressive show of logic, favored this. Holmes would have none of it.

The true grounds of decision are considerations of policy and of social advantage, and it is vain to suppose that solutions can be attained merely by logic. . . . There is nothing I more deprecate than the use of the Fourteenth amendment . . . to prevent the making of social experiments that an important part of the community desires . . . though the experiments may seem futile or even noxious.

Such words from the Supreme bench put new heart into faltering liberals.

Though his words were weighty, Holmes had none of his father's gift for making them sing and scintillate. The style of his decisions and of his best known book, *The Common Law*—the Lowell Institute Lectures for 1880—is precise, as befits a jurist, but it is also involved and heavy. The first Oliver Wendell Holmes won a public by his manner rather than his matter. The second won it by his matter almost alone.

## 5

The movement culminating in the "New History" was not so much a product of pragmatic ways of thinking as a parallel development. Its leader was a colleague and friend of Dewey's at Columbia, James Harvey Robinson, whose course on the history of the intellectual class in Europe influenced historical teaching throughout the country. Robinson insisted that for the understanding and writing of history two things were essential which Dewey had also stressed as basic for understanding the advance of philosophy.

First was the genetic method. "In its amplest meaning," Robinson wrote, "history includes every trace and vestige of everything that man has done or thought since first he appeared on the earth." But history in that sense is impossible; most events of the past have vanished beyond recall, and of those that remain on record only a fraction are worth recalling. On what principle, then, is history to select its material? Robinson answers: "The one thing that it ought to do, and has not yet effectively done, is to help us to understand our fellows and the problems and prospects of mankind." And how is it to work toward such understanding? Certainly not by the old drum-and-trumpet tales; certainly not by making history biographic with Carlyle, or nationalistic with Bancroft, or propagandist with the Marxians, or even, with Freeman, by identifying it with "past politics." History is rather "the study of how man has come to be as he is and to believe as he does." What we should seek in the past is the causal explanation of the present. The method of the historian should be the genetic method; as another member of the group, Harry Elmer Barnes, put it, "Evolution should be to the historian what dynamics is to the physicist." Every important institution and event of our own day is only the last bead on a thread that runs back continuously into the past. The business of the historian is to seize that thread and follow it backward wherever it leads.

If he does so, he will be led in strange directions. Instead of following the track of royal genealogies, he will be taken into regions that would have seemed to the classical historian too dim and perhaps too sordid to invite exploration. The sanitary arrangements in Rome may have had more to do with its fall than the character of its emperors; the wages of medieval workingmen may have thrown more light on the crusades than religion itself; one of the new historians, Charles A. Beard, shocked his readers by arguing with much force that the American Constitution was set up by the propertied classes to give security to their own position. The lines of historic causation thus run out into medicine, economics, and psychology, into geography, statistics, and law; indeed there is no detail of the civilization he is studying which the historian can dismiss beforehand as irrelevant. The first point of the new history was that the past must causally explain the present. The second point was that if such explanation was to be achieved, the historian must leave the beaten tracks and get out into the alleys and hedgerows of the civilization he is studying; he must know its disease rates and death rates, the state of its coinage and the state of its housing, as well as its battles and princely marriages. It would be impossible for him to explain how the family, the church, and present social divisions came to be what they are without entering into the conditions of past life with a fullness seldom even attempted by earlier historians.

The most disquieting part of the new history was its account of human beliefs. People have generally regarded their beliefs as resting on reasons, and they have held this not less of beliefs about ultimate matters of philosophy and religion than of beliefs about everyday concerns. The new historians agreed with Dewey in holding that these larger beliefs generally spring from causes rather than reasons. They are accepted because others accept them, and these others accept them ultimately because they help to allay fear, or because they bolster self-respect, or because they justify one's own position and conduct. In short, they are not rational; they are only rationalizations. While Dewey was elaborating this theory for metaphysics in his *Reconstruction in Philosophy* (1920), Robinson was doing it for religion and social beliefs in his widely read *The Mind in the Making* (1921). These books were the more influential because there were at the time a wave of popular interest in Freudianism and a new burst of activity on the part of the anthropologists; Franz Boas, R. H. Lowie, Alexander Goldenweiser, Clark Wissler, and Margaret Mead were producing a row of interesting volumes on the formation of primitive customs and beliefs. An able book showing the influence of Robinson and Dewey, and written by a pupil of both, was John Herman Randall's *The Making of the Modern Mind* (1926), which was widely used as a textbook in American colleges. It undertook to show that the successive world views from Dante to Marx and Hegel, far from being examples of pure thought, working under the exclusive control of logic, were molded in numberless ways by the social conditions and technical knowledge of the time.

6

Of course all this was bound to create apprehension among those who took their religious beliefs seriously. For such beliefs were supposed to rest either on a revelation which could not conceivably mislead or upon reasoning that led to firm objective truth, and if they were now to be set down as by-products of the wish to believe, controlled not by the evidence but by non-rational pulls and pushes, then to put it plainly they were illusions, and all religion rested on something very like a mirage.

To the formidable challenge of this relativism, religious writers responded in various ways. Some of them, the humanists, accepted the new line of argument and sought to elaborate a religion virtually devoid of creed. At the opposite extreme, some sought to defend their orthodoxy by throwing doubts on reason itself. Catholics and Fundamentalists reiterated their traditional positions. And between the two extremes stood the religious liberals, troubled and divided.

The philosophical humanists—not to be confused with the literary neo-humanists discussed elsewhere in this work—included some academic teachers of wide influence, Dewey, Max Otto, Roy W. Sellars, Eustace Haydon, and Shailer Mathews. But the most effective writer among them was not a professed philosopher or theologian, but a journalist, Walter Lippmann. In his youth a precocious student at Harvard, gifted with a graceful and facile style, Lippmann burst into print in defense of socialism almost instantly upon graduation and continued to produce a stream of readable books on politics, religion, and international affairs while writing a daily column for the newspapers. His history was one of slow movement from the red end of the spectrum to a position approaching conservatism, first in politics, then in religion. His statement of the humanist outlook was made in mid-career in his *Preface to Morals* (1929).

In this book Lippmann holds that the entire framework of traditional theology has collapsed. The dogmas of a personal deity, of the incarnation and the atonement, the fall, original sin, the resurrection, the last coming, and the final judgment, have all been eaten away by the "acids of modernity."

It is not so much that they have been formally refuted as that in the bleak light of the modern world, with its scientific atmosphere, they have lost their plausibility and withered away. Lippmann views their disappearance complacently enough. What concerns him more is that for many centuries theological beliefs have provided the sanction and sustenance for moral idealism; men's hopes, their moral seriousness, the set of values that have guided their lives, have come in very large part from their religion. What will happen to this moral fruitage if the religious roots are pulled up? Can the godless naturalism that is superseding the old religion provide a rich enough soil for high-principled and generous living?

Lippmann thinks it can. The connection between moral idealism and religious belief he considered historical rather than logical. If men rate pleasure above pain, love above hate, and beauty above ugliness, it is because they, or the best of them, have seen that this order of value holds in the nature of things; there is nothing subjective or capricious about such judgment; pronouncements from on high may corroborate it, but they did not originate it; it rests on man's own authentic insight. And this insight is wholly independent of his creeds. With the disappearance of his creeds, he must review the case, dismiss the moral with the theological lumber, and retain only what his own perception can validate. In this process he will lose much that he prized, for he can no longer rely on the friendliness of the universe nor look forward with the old confidence to a life that endures; his life on earth is presumably his all. But it remains as true as before that some ways of living are noble and some debased, and there is no reason at all why a cultivated and disinterested mind should not find in purely mundane goods an end that can enlist its wholehearted devotion. That devotion will in truth be more stable than it was, because it does not now spring from precarious theological commitments, but is rational and free.

There was a cogency in this humanism that found a large response in the minds of thoughtful Americans and disturbed the peace of the orthodox. What were orthodox believers to do in the face of this continuing encroachment by the scientific and rational spirit? They could of course announce that the Church had spoken, that revelation and true reason could never disagree, and that if they seemed to disagree, it was not true reason that was speaking. This line was taken by a considerable body of neo-scholastics, but it was not widely persuasive. Many Protestant theologians were convinced that if religion threw down the gage to modern science and philosophy, with reason as its only weapon, the case was as good as lost beforehand; and the slow retreat of theology for the past three centuries seemed to them good evidence that they were right. To base faith on reason was in fairness to admit that it might be overthrown by reason. They held that a wholly different strategy must therefore be adopted. Faith must be cut loose from reason altogether. The believer may assure himself that in faith he has a certainty which reason can neither generate nor destroy, and which science therefore cannot endanger. His faith is a rock deep-based in nonrational reality, against which the shallow waves of intellectualism may beat noisily, but will always beat in vain.

This theology did not come in the first instance from America. It was the product of a line of European thought that began with the strange Danish genius, Kierkegaard, was developed in Germany by Karl Barth and Emil Brunner, and was imported into this country, with modifications, by Paul Tillich, Wilhelm Pauck, and the brothers Reinhold and Richard Niebuhr. In its purity, as represented by Barth, it is a bold attempt to turn the tables on all the pretensions of reason. God is; he reveals himself through the incarnation and the Bible; our contact with him is the most certain and the most significant thing in human life. Yet he remains, and must remain, an inscrutable mystery. There is nothing we can say of him that is true, not even, in the ordinary sense, that he exists, or is interested in us, or is good, for every attempt of our feeble thought to figure to ourselves his nature must fall infinitely short of its object. The philosopher cannot know him. Neither can the mystic, since his experience, however exalted, is shot through with finite passion and prepossession. No saint, not even the Christ who was a human being, can really embody his will, for God's ways are not as our ways, and he stands over against all we know or feel or aspire to as something "absolutely other."

How then make contact with him? The Barthians say frankly that we cannot—"There is no way from man to God." But God in his infinite power can come to man. And for reasons beyond our knowing he does come to some men, in the sense that he gives them grace to see, by a sort of supernatural insight, that in this or that passage of scripture, through this or that favored human vessel, perhaps oneself, the word of God is spoken. It is by no merit or effort of one's own that this insight is achieved, and when it comes, it is incommunicable to any other. Nevertheless it is certain. Those who have it have also a detachment from human vicissitude that they could not gain from the profoundest of human philosophies and of course a peace that "the world" cannot give.

Among American writers sympathetic with this theology, the most impressive was Reinhold Niebuhr, one of the few American thinkers who have been invited to the distinguished Gifford lectureship in Scotland. In the lectures he delivered in Edinburgh in 1939, published in two volumes as *The Nature and Destiny of Man* (1941–1943), he softened somewhat the sharpness of Barth's antithesis between the natural and the supernatural. Man himself is supernatural, in the sense that he has in him a power of looking before and after, and a power of judging his own thought and conduct, which cannot be derived from the natural order. History is the record of the conflict between his two natures. If history is tragic, it is because of human sin; and the root of human sin is pride, the refusal of the "creature" to judge of his creatureliness by the divine standard within him and the setting up instead of some "idol" of the natural man—some philosophy supposed to be final, or some pitiful social scheme with which Utopia is to be ushered in. Both idealism and naturalism are rejected by Niebuhr as thus idolatrous.

Fortunately Niebuhr's preoccupation with sin and his melancholy view of human achievement did not prevent his taking a vigorous part in social advance. He described his own history as a movement to the right in theology and to the left in politics, and he was an inexhaustible fountainhead of politically liberal books and articles. It says much for their content that these were widely read, for while he was a powerful speaker, his writing is graceless and heavily Teutonic. The same judgment would apply to the writing of many others of this school. There are those who think this fact symptomatic. If one holds that reason at its best is a murky rushlight, one has less motive for nursing it along into greater clearness than if one takes it, with all its feebleness and flickering, as the best illumination we can hope to have.

Between the humanists on the one hand and the neosupernaturalists on the other stood the bulk of liberal Protestants, divided after their manner into innumerable sects and schools. Among these schools a distinctively American one was personalism, whose speculative leader was Edgar Sheffield Brightman of Boston. Brightman's idealism held that the world is a society of persons of all degrees of development, with God, the divine person, presiding over all. His *Philosophy of Religion* (1940) made a bold and significant attack on the problem of evil by contending that God must be thought of as finite and limited in power rather than omnipotent, and as struggling against a nonrational factor in his own nature, somewhat akin to sensation in man.

Another school which is well-nigh perennial and whose thought cuts across all sects is that of mysticism. Its American leader in the first half of the century was Rufus Jones, the most considerable thinker that American Quakerism has produced. In his *Studies in Mystical Religion* (1909), *New Studies in Mystical Religion* (1927), *Some Exponents of Mystical Religion* (1930), and many other works, he developed a religious philosophy which was essentially that of Emerson. Human minds are fragments of an Oversoul, and so far as they succeed in embodying the great values—truth, beauty, goodness—it may be said of them literally that the divine mind is finding expression through them. Rufus Jones' service to his public lay not so much, however, in speculative acuteness or originality as in his advocacy of a practical mysticism, simple and somewhat homespun, yet elevated and serene, of which Americans of other days had caught attractive glimpses in Woolman and Whittier.

If Rufus Jones is to be described as a moralist rather than a dialectician, the same could be said with more obvious truth of another spokesman of liberalism, Harry Emerson Fosdick. In the great church built for him on Riverside Drive, New York, Fosdick remained during the twenties and thirties the most eloquent voice in the American pulpit. Misty and fluid in his theology, like so many other liberal Protestants who were the victims of their own groping honesty, he was inclined to elide the deeper difficulties in his sermons in order to deal more directly with the personal problems of his hearers; but he did this with such moral discernment and rhetorical skill, not only in the pulpit and on the radio where his audiences were enormous, but also in his many books, as to give him membership in that distinguished succession of American preachers which descends through Horace Bushnell, Henry Ward Beecher, and Phillips Brooks.

### 7

Thus in education, law, history, and religion, much the same "acids of modernity" were eating at the foundations of traditional American idealism. It will be recalled that both the naturalism of Santayana and the pragmatism of Dewey were reactions against the philosophy that held the stage at the turn of the century. Among the American thinkers who led the revolt against nineteenth century idealism, none have ranked with Santayana in literary stature or with Dewey in originality. But if success is measured by effectiveness in undermining an enemy, the most successful recent philosophers have been neither materialists nor pragmatists, but realists. There have been two schools of these, each of which has stated its case in a collaborative volume. *The New Realism* (1912) represents the extreme point in the anti-idealist movement. The idealists had held that the shapes and sizes, colors and sounds, of ordinary experience are all mental, in the sense that if there were no perceiver, they would not exist. The new realists sought to maintain the exact opposite, that they were all nonmental. What the mind contributed was only the act of attention, the beam of the flashlight that lit up the figures on nature's tapestry; the qualities and relations attended to were out there waiting to be perceived. This sounds at first like the merest common sense. But it soon appeared that if taken seriously, the view involved some very odd consequences. If what I see is always nonmental, then when I see converging tracks and spoons bent in water, these too are nonmental; the illusions of hypnotism and the snakes of the delirious toper are really out there, as truly as the Great Pyramid. And then the common sense of a moment ago begins to seem almost insane.

For the new realists such considerations proved in the end disastrous; they were the rock on which the school disintegrated. The six authors of the volume, unable to agree on how the problem of error was to be met, went their several ways. One of them, Walter B. Pitkin, abandoned technical philosophy altogether, devoting himself to fiction and to the popular applications of philosophy and science; his *Life Begins at Forty* (1932) achieved an extraordinary popular success. Another, William Pepperell Montague, remained in his Columbia classroom and produced much less, but the essays and volumes he did produce, notably *The Ways of Knowing* (1925), are models of lucid exposition. The member of the original six who reached the widest scholarly audience was Ralph Barton Perry. His *General Theory of Value* (1926) is the most ambitious work in its field that has yet appeared in this country; his vigorous defenses of democracy during both world wars made him a very useful public servant; and his massive *The Thought and Character of William James* (1935), partly by reason of its subject, but partly also because of the depth and sympathy of its interpretation, may be put down roundly as one of the best biographies in the language.

The other realist manifesto, *Essays in Critical Realism* (1920), attempted to introduce saving qualifications into the doctrine that the earlier volume had sought, with no great success, to render credible. In the enthusiasm of its first reaction against idealism, the earlier group had been led to maintain that the objects of delusion and dream were as independent of perception as tables and chairs. The second group reversed the argument. They said that tables and chairs, as directly perceived, were of precisely the same stuff as dreams; in ordinary life we take their shapes and sizes to belong to things out there, and sometimes they almost certainly do, or at least qualities like them do. But of this we can never be wholly sure; in the end we must fall back on "animal faith." This latter doctrine and phrase were contributed by Santayana, whose name turns up among the seven authors. Of the remaining six, the most notable was Arthur O. Lovejoy. Lovejoy was little known to the larger public, but his chief book, *The Revolt Against Dualism* (1930), is one of the most competent pieces of technical philosophizing yet produced by an American, and is also noteworthy for its style which, though intricate and subtle, is also remarkably clear; and his later work *The Great Chain of Being* (1936) is a classic study of the evolution of a concept. Lovejoy here provided a new technique for literary history by wedding philosophy to historical method.

8

It would be a mistake to infer that by all this belaboring the idealists were pommeled into silence or acquiescence. Few of them found plausible the naturalism of Santayana, with its tendency to belittle the part of mind in the conduct of life; most of them dismissed pragmatism as a somewhat freakish passing fashion; and as for realism, the more thoughtful of them had long been realists anyhow, if that meant believing in an outer world. What they insisted on, as against the naturalists, was that this outer frame of things was spiritual, and as against the pragmatists, that it was the business of reason to trace its structure, and not merely to serve as a biological tool.

The most effective spokesman of this impenitent idealism was William Ernest Hocking, who inherited Royce's mantle at Harvard. Hocking was a Middle Westerner of great physical and mental vitality, who, after serving a youthful apprenticeship in railway engineering, made a pilgrimage to New England, fell under the spell of Royce and Palmer in Cambridge and later of Husserl in Germany, abandoned the Spencerian naturalism which was his first love, and moved on, as it seemed inevitably, to distinguished chairs at Yale and Harvard, and to the Hibbert and Gifford lectureships abroad. Hocking has suffered somewhat in concentration from the great range of his interests, which extend from logic and psychology to ethics, politics, and world religion, on all of which he wrote illuminatingly.

The central movement of his thought, however, is metaphysical. The business of reflection, he holds, is to understand its world. Now understanding proceeds through the linking of meanings. In mathematics, for example, it consists in seeing how one meaning, a triangle perhaps, implies another meaning, say the equality of its angles to a straight line. And meanings are ideal. The mathematician's triangle and line are not things that can be sensed, like red patches, nor are they material things in space. So of all the meanings with which the reasoner deals. Still, though they are ideal, they are not ideas merely: they do not live in our heads or minds alone; the mathematician discovers his relations, he does not invent them. What is more, the man who is trying to understand always assumes these relations to be intelligible, for unless they are, understanding would be out of the question. It is the first principle of Hocking's philosophy that for serious thinkers the world must be taken as a systematic whole of meaning, set to their understanding to construe. This is what he means by idealism.

So far there is nothing new; this is the view of all the great idealists from Plato down. Perhaps Hocking's most original addition was one made in his first major work, *The Meaning of God in Human Experience* (1912), in which he showed the importance of this outlook for the religious life. Religious experience is very largely feeling. Now feeling is "idea in process of being born." Our first intimation that an argument is unsound is normally a feeling of distrust; if analysis comes at all, it comes later; and where we are dealing not with abstractions but with concrete things and above all with persons, our analytic reason may never succeed in overtaking this advance guard of feeling. Nowhere does it fall so far behind as in religion. For religion, particularly in its purest form as mysticism, is an attempt to adjust oneself, not to this or that part of one's surroundings, but to the whole. The philosopher too is seeking such adjustment. But the mystic is the scout and pioneer of the philosophic enterprise; he does not know as the philosopher knows; he has not attained the end of the road; but his feeling is an "anticipated attainment" which the philosopher must take seriously. Indeed we should all take it seriously. It is one of Hocking's favorite doctrines that life, to achieve its best, must proceed by rhythm or alternation between vision and detail, life on the plains being rendered more meaningful by occasional withdrawals into the hills, and worship being saved from emptiness by embodiment in action.

Hocking's idealism was thus at a far remove from the frigid intellectualism of some of his predecessors. He remained close to fact; he was aware at every turn of the practical bearing of theory. It is significant that he was chosen by the American churches to head a commission of inquiry into their foreign missions, and that, with his colleagues, he wrote an admirably sane and large-spirited report, holding that in religious matters the process of enlightenment must proceed from east to west as well as from west to east. It is significant too that he was chosen as the leading member of a group of writers commissioned by the Armed Forces Institute to write a textbook on philosophy intelligible to men in camp and on shipboard (*Preface to Philosophy,* 1945). His style is singularly free from technicality and pedantry. Though a little discursive and lacking in emphasis, it is simple, clear, and flowing, with a command over example and analogy that could be exhibited only by a fertile mind.

Hocking did not, like Dewey, have a recognized school of disciples. This was due in part to the accidents of the time. Idealism, by 1910, had ceased to be a new thing, and idealists, however important the fresh insights they achieved, had to be content with a somewhat perfunctory attention, once the class label was attached to them. The great new event in the intellectual realm after the First World War was the recharting of physics, and therefore in a sense of all natural science, through the work of such frontiersmen as Einstein and Planck. This was an event which few idealists, nourished as they were on the humanities rather than on the sciences, were prepared to understand. And the younger philosophers wanted to understand it; they were impatient with thinkers who failed to take account of it, and they turned eagerly to those who were at home in the new science and competent to interpret it.

Preeminent among these were two visiting Cambridge mathematicians, Bertrand Russell and Alfred North Whitehead. Russell's visits to this country, though numerous, were temporary. Whitehead came to stay. Though his transplantation occurred at an age when most men would begin to think of retirement, he took so happily to the new environment, did so much of his important writing in America, and from his chair at Harvard achieved so large an influence on American thought that any review of the literature of ideas in this country must take account of it.

Whitehead came into philosophy from a profound study of mathematics and physics. His thought begins by eliminating one of the chief units with which previous philosophers had worked, and substituting another more in accord with the new science. He replaces substances by events. Einstein had shown that we cannot state precisely the place of anything without a reference to time; this holds equally of a stroke of lightning and of the Sphinx; both really are events, one short, the other relatively long. All things are in truth events; the universe is made of them. At present the most nearly elementary events with which we can work are the protons and electrons of physics.

The problem of the philosopher is not, therefore, to discover the stuff or substance of which things are made, but to find the laws or patterns in accordance with which events influence each other. Here Whitehead had some arresting things to say. Most physicists are mechanists in the sense that when they are explaining why iron filings leap to a magnet or why the earth goes round the sun, they would deny that purpose had anything to do with the matter. With this Whitehead disagreed. Every event, he held, is an activity which is essentially an urge, an appetition, an endeavor after greater fullness of being. And such an appetition is not a dead mechanical affair. It is a process best conceived in terms of sentience or experience. Thus in the foundations of his system there was a startling reversion to something very like idealism.

The resemblance is continued in his curious theory of "prehensions." Every event, he pointed out, is more influenced by some events in its environment than by others; the filings will leap to the magnet, for example, but not to a stick of wood. This is not totally blind; an elective affinity is involved; in the singling out of the magnet as a means by which their own activity may be furthered, the filings are showing something obscurely akin to man's selection of food and drink as a means of supporting life. Whenever one event acts upon or is influenced by another, it is "prehending" it.

And to prehend it is in the last resort to feel it. Let us now suppose that an event, or a group of events, such as an iron filing, displays a stable pattern of reactions to selected other events; we call such a patterned group of activities a "thing." Things are thus settled ways in which one set of events feels other sets of events.

It follows that to understand anything in isolation is a contradiction in terms. To understand what a cell in the nervous system is we must see how it interacts with other cells in that system. But of course that system itself must be understood in the same way; it, too, is a unit which is what it is because it maintains a fixed pattern of interactions with the organism as a whole, of which it is an integral part. And how understand the organism? By the same process again. The organism as a whole must be understood through its own design of interactions with a still larger environment.

Where is this to end? Are we to infer that according to Whitehead every cell in the body, every drop of water in the sea, is a pattern within a larger pattern, and that none of these can be fully made out except by discussing its place in the all-comprehensive structure of the universe? That seems to be what he meant by calling his world view "the philosophy of organism." If everything in the universe is seeking to maintain and perfect its own little structure, it is also maintaining, conjointly with everything else, an all-inclusive cosmic structure; and this structure it is the business of philosophy to disclose. Whitehead believed that the time had come for philosophers to leave the minutiae of analysis and take to speculation again in the grand style. And he was convinced that if they were to do so in earnest, the pattern that would gradually disclose itself would prove to be a rational pattern. He was moved by "the trust that the ultimate natures of things lie together in a harmony which excludes mere arbitrariness." The universal pressure toward rationality within the world of events is what Whitehead meant by God; God is "the poet of the world, with tender patience leading it by his vision of truth, beauty and goodness."

A man who thinks and writes in this vein is obviously not afraid to let himself go; if Whitehead was an acute mathematician, it is clear that he was also on occasion the dreamer of dreams. His writing is lighted up with epigrammatic flashes of insight. Unfortunately that writing is extremely uneven. Reading him is like listening to Coleridge's conversation as reported by Carlyle; one endures stretches of dreary obscurity for the sake of coming, as one ultimately and abruptly does, on "glorious islets of the blest and the intelligible." Among the chief sources of difficulty are his habits of coining words of his own: "prehension," "concrescence," "ingression," "concretion," not always clearly defined or even used in a single sense, and of giving familiar words and phrases—"object," "potentiality," "feeling"—new and strange significations. Unhappily these difficulties are at their worst in his major work, *Process and Reality* (1929); they are felt less in such semi-popular books as *Science and the Modern World* (1925), *Religion in the Making* (1926), and *The Aims of Education* (1929). Whitehead had probably a more profound mind than that of Russell, with whom he collaborated to produce one of the most impressive achievements of modern thought, *Principia Mathematica* (1910–1913). He was unfortunately far below Russell in that gift which is so peculiarly grateful in a philosopher, lucidity.

There is a sense in which the interval between these two remarkable co-workers is the interval between the beginning and end of the period under our review. Russell, like the naturalists, pragmatists, and realists who began the revolt against idealism, was suspicious of high flights of speculation, and inclined to think that all advance in thought must be by the scientific analysis of particular problems. Perhaps it was because Whitehead had given unquestionable proof of his prowess in such analysis that he commanded so much respect when he broke loose from it and began to paint again with the wide brushes and the full sweep of the great speculative periods. Dewey rose from reading *Process and Reality* with "the feeling that somehow the seventeenth century has got the better of the twentieth." Indeed the wheel of thought had come almost full circle in his own lifetime, moving from the whole-hearted metaphysics of idealism that was dominant in his youth to another metaphysics, equally wholehearted but more firmly grounded in science. Whether Dewey's own philosophy, which was so central to the period we have been studying, will appear to later historians of this highly irregular century as a peak between two valleys or a valley between two peaks it is perhaps safest to allow the future to decide.

# 77. A CYCLE OF FICTION

THESE currents of speculative thought found expression, of course, in the fiction, the drama, and the poetry of the years since 1925; but only when the despair of a "lost generation" is probed to its sources can they be recognized as providing the rationale of a literary era. It is not always easy to relate the specific work of art to its underlying inspiration—especially in so close a view. Artists are rarely philosophers or critics in the strict sense. But so much is evident: the literary work of these decades, taken as a whole, shows a more persistent search for values and a more competent control of forms than did that of the preceding decades.

If the weakness as well as the charm of the generation of the twenties lay in its indifference to its own past (for it was just then cutting its ties with the Progressive Movement in politics that had nourished it), there was at any rate a solid basis for its claims. Those were good years for American fiction. Chicago had been the center of the earlier days of the movement, and Dreiser and Sandburg and Sherwood Anderson, among others, had helped to establish its earlier tone—that initial revolt of the solid Midwest against both the pulpit and the stockyards. But now, as the literary current flowed east to New York and the "Little Renaissance" matured, its members seemed to represent every nook and corner of the country, from the Harvard of Dos Passos to the Michigan woods of Hemingway and the California coast of Robinson Jeffers. The South, too, was about to produce a whole host of Fugitives and Agrarians. Among the novelists and short-story writers Kay Boyle, like F. Scott Fitzgerald, came from Minnesota, Evelyn Scott and T. S. Stribling from Tennessee, Glenway Wescott from Wisconsin, Dorothy Parker from New Jersey, Joseph Hergesheimer from Pennsylvania, and James Branch Cabell of course—not to mention Ellen Glasgow or Pearl Buck—from Virginia.

Furthermore, the regional spread of this talent was matched by the variety of technical innovations it was using to commemorate the "Life of Realization." The ingenious new poets were not the only writers then continuously experimenting with the structure, the diction, the rhythms and the visual effects of their medium; for sheer technical virtuosity Elinor Wylie was

1296

to be matched in prose by Katherine Anne Porter, and T. S. Eliot by William Faulkner. This was the age of the craftsmen, and the complex interior monologue, for example, with its shifting elements of time and place and its purely personal framework of association, became a staple of the new novels. Between subjectivity and relativity all was flux for a while, and soon a novel which had a plot and related events in something like the normal order that events often take in life, a novel in which space was not time and time was not psychological, was almost a discovery in itself.

The sources of the new technique appeared to be chiefly European, and, among the Europeans, as Edmund Wilson suggested in *Axel's Castle* (1931), they were particularly the French symbolists and their heirs—although Proust and Yeats and Joyce led back in turn to Freud and Einstein. It was Gertrude Stein who was a chief intermediary for the Paris branch of the Lost Generation; yet it is interesting to notice that the cadences of Miss Stein's writing, mannered and self-conscious as they were and eventually pointing toward a sort of literary cubism or post-impressionism, had curious echoes of Midwestern talk. In Chicago, the urban center of the New American industrialism, Sherwood Anderson devoted his middle years to recalling the slow recurrent rhythms of the Ohio towns at the turn of the century—a language that was also at the base of Hemingway's. Those later "plain," "flat" tones, so laconic and ambiguous, brought to perfection a native style that had evolved from Thoreau to Twain. Like Ring Lardner, Anderson was aware of all the delicate grammatical intricacies and tonal gradations of the American language in its current forms, so thoroughly recorded by H. L. Mencken. These authors were joined in their determination to break the short story of fabricated action and a trick end. In such writers the most advanced European technical experimentation met a rich source of native material. As no other group of contemporary writers seemed more anxious to perfect their craft, so no other group had so much opportunity to do it.

It was the twenties, too, that had broken down the distinctions between schools of writing by producing outstanding individuals. Everybody was famous then, as Zelda Fitzgerald declared in *Save Me the Waltz,* and people were not concerned about the proletariat in a world where it was always teatime or "three o'clock in the morning"; while it was almost comic, again, to find H. L. Mencken, hot from denouncing the barren spirit of America, now complaining about the schools of fiction writing that were swarming in the land, and the hundred thousand secondhand Coronas that were rattling and jingling in ten thousand remote and lonely hamlets. By the time of *Prejudices: Fourth Series,* in 1924, even Mencken had to concede that the native literary spectacle had taken on an exhilarating aspect—that, in short, leadership in the arts "may eventually transfer itself from the eastern shore of the Atlantic to the western shore," since

no longer imitative and timorous, as most of their predecessors were, these youngsters are attempting a first-hand examination of the national scene, and making an effort to represent it in terms that are wholly American. They are the pioneers of a literature that, whatever its defects in the abstract, will at least be a faithful reflection of the national life. . . . In England the novel subsides into formulae, the drama is submerged in artificialities, and even poetry, despite occasional revolts, moves toward scholarliness and emptiness. But in America, since the war, all three show the artless and superabundant energy of little children. They lack, only too often, manner and urbanity; it is no wonder they are often shocking to pedants. But there is the breath of life in them, and that life is nearer its beginning than its end.

2

As early as 1924, F. Scott Fitzgerald had already given evidence that there was another aspect to all this glittering native pageantry. His *This Side of Paradise* was the generation's masculine primer, just as Edna Millay's *A Few Figs from Thistles* was the feminine, and as Ernest Hemingway's *The Sun Also Rises* was a second reader for both sexes. Irregular in exposition, broken in context, Fitzgerald's first novel set forth the apparently authentic observations of a typical young person of the period. "A chield's amang you taking notes"—and he printed them also.

Born in 1896, in St. Paul, Minnesota, Fitzgerald had gone to Princeton, "largely because of the Triangle Club," and had started work on *This Side of Paradise* (1920) during the week ends of his service with the armed forces in 1917. With the success of his first novel his "days of struggle were over," or at any rate the festive days had arrived. These were Fitzgerald's party days; the parties of *The Great Gatsby*; the big parties, as Edmund Wilson remarked, at which Fitzgerald's people "go off like fireworks and which are likely to leave them in pieces." This was the New York of the early twenties, of orchids and plush, which had "all the iridescence of the beginning of the world" with its young and disillusioned children who watched twilight fall, over cocktails at the Biltmore, and dawn strike the window of Childs' restaurant in Fifty-ninth Street. No other places were possible, for no other voices could whisper to the young Fitzgerald—and it was his gift to endow these rather unreal creatures with a peculiarly touching reality.

One took for granted the restlessness of these hotel children, their conviction that all Gods were dead, "all wars fought, all faiths in man shaken," their distaste for "the crude, vulgar air of Western civilization," their contempt for the "aliens" and the "masses" who contributed to "the heavy scent of latest America." And yet, triumphant as they were in their almost insatiable demands for wealth and glamour, the "visions of horror" also pursued these glittering narcissists of the Jazz Age. The sense of dark dissolution and of death "diffusively brooding" over *This Side of Paradise* and *The Beautiful and Damned* (1922)—over this whole lucent postwar panorama from absinthe to yachts—is at the center of Fitzgerald's work. Two of the four novels after *This Side of Paradise* attempt to deal with it, while it seems to form the hidden basis of the other two—and it splits his career in half. The corrosive vein in Fitzgerald's writing, the cry of suffering, the reverberations of the crack-up—these destructive accents become all too familiar and find their ultimate expression in those rich ruins and in those fugitives from justice who form the central group of *Tender Is the Night* (1934).

The true nature of that "misty tragedy played far behind the veil" which preoccupies the young Fitzgerald's mind remains obscure, although it was unquestionably sexual in origin. Fitzgerald's work, like Poe's, is colored by the imagery of incest. *Tender Is the Night,* psychologically perhaps the most interesting of all Fitzgerald's novels, deals directly with this theme, but, as the later Fitzgerald said about his friend Ring Lardner, "he had agreed with himself to speak only a small portion of his mind." What is certain, at any rate, is that he could never quite come to grips with the central inner conflict of his writing, and he moved to his outward and cultural studies of the American financial aristocracy at the cost of suppressing rather than resolving this problem.

It was not a complete defeat. Just as Fitzgerald had had "the conviction of the inevitability of failure" from the start, so at the end he had the insight of failure. During his entire later career, he devoted himself to his craft with something of the fanatical devotion of an anchorite expecting the collapse of the world, and here he reached a fulfillment that was not altogether granted to him elsewhere. And if *The Great Gatsby* fades a little with its last falling cadence, what an eloquent cadence it is! This is a deft and delicate tale, from the opening passages on the Buchanans' Long Island Georgian mansion, framed by its half-acre of deep, pungent roses, to the trip through the valley of ashes and the final passage on Gatsby's dream which had always been behind him—"somewhere back in that vast obscurity beyond the city, where the dark fields of the republic rolled on under the night." In the story of Jay Gatsby's illusion Fitzgerald caught the story of an age's illusion too, just as "The Diamond As Big As the Ritz" was a notable parable of our American ruling class, as "May Day" had all the faintly bitter fragrance of the age of wealth, and as *The Last Tycoon,* unfinished as it is, was still the closest an American novelist had come to the truth about Hollywood.

3

At various times Fitzgerald and Hemingway were in Paris together, when Fitzgerald had already achieved his early success, and even a certain notoriety. Gertrude Stein was said to have said that he had more talent than all the rest of the Lost Generation put together, while the younger man was still writing those early "sketches." Meanwhile, with "rather the aspect of an Eton-Oxford husky-ish young captain of a midland regiment of His Britannic Majesty," Hemingway pranced, as Ford Madox Ford tells us, among the young Americans from the limitless prairies who "leapt, released, on Paris."

Just as Fitzgerald had commented briefly on St. Paul, and as T. S. Eliot had passed lightly over St. Louis, Hemingway, a doctor's son born in Oak Park, Illinois, in 1898, had very early announced his verdict on commerce in the United States: "Let Hartman Feather *Your* Nest." He chose instead the Indians and the Michigan Woods—the idyllic scenes of youth in his first book, *In Our Time* (1925), that are contrasted so sharply with scenes from the First World War. He had been a reporter for the Kansas City *Star,* he had served with the Italian Arditi and had been wounded—and here his early experiences seemed to fuse: the flat yet equivocal Western tones, as well as the "innocence" of the provincial, were linked to that mode of "reporting" which, heightened by some altogether personal process of artistry, was to alter the rhythms of our contemporary prose. Perhaps, too, no other contemporary writer brought his readers so many vivid and almost unbearable impressions of the human temperament under the pressures of war. In a sense the war was made for him, and in a variety of stories—"In Another Country," "A Way You'll Never Be," "A Simple Enquiry," as well as in *A Farewell to Arms*—made the war his own.

In *The Sun Also Rises* (1926) the quality of this plain, factual recording of things became a little clearer. For it was only in a novel that a Lost Generation could feel its plight with such intensity and live out its fate with such meticulous perfection. Many tried but few could approach the disenchantment of Hemingway's little group of pleasure lovers, or seem quite so cunningly and even diabolically frustrated. He began to seem like a little more than another modern "realist," and, in the bulk of his work done between 1927 and 1937, the terms of Hemingway's "separate peace" were written out. For, while Scott Fitzgerald had largely allowed his own Western countryside to slip by, and had then walked a sort of intellectual tightrope between the élite and the masses, Hemingway had actually renounced his own society, as he stated in *The Green Hills of Africa* (1935), and he was through serving time "for society, democracy and the other things." America had been a good country, but "we had made a bloody mess of it and I would go, now, somewhere else as we had always had the right to go somewhere else and as we had always gone. You could always come back."

Such was the framework for the decade of dark stories collected in *Men Without Women* (1927) and *Winner Take Nothing* (1933). Some of them were notable, as were also certain sections of his rhapsody on the Spanish bull ring, *Death in the Afternoon* (1932), however much one might feel that there was something amiss in this safari of annihilation. For it was a curious world that Hemingway had taken to exploring: the world of the matador and the kudu in which the central trinity was the hunter, the hunted, and death; a world of deep and always fatally irrational feelings, in which the intellect pointed only to the method of destruction, and which was marked only by an increasing sense of dissolution, until all forms of action as well as all modes of thinking became merely another sort of opiate; a nihilistic spiritual world that reached its own perfection in such of his "first forty-nine" stories as "The Gambler, the Nun, and the Radio" ("Bread was the opium of the people") and "A Clean Well-Lighted Place." "What did he fear? It was not fear or dread. It was a nothing that he knew too well. *It was all a nothing and a man was a nothing too.*" Moreover, through the cheapened and coarsened texture of *To Have and Have Not*, in 1937, this all-consuming nihilism seemed to strike at last at the source of its own projection. Here, if only temporarily, Hemingway relinquished what had been his special gift among the American moderns: the gift of compassion which had modulated and given a kind of final harmony to the continuous play of the wounded psyche.

This was a step removed from the blind optimism of an earlier age of innocence; at times indeed it touched on a blind negation almost without parallel in the national letters, unless one finds it in Stephen Crane. But it is interesting to compare the increasing bitterness of Ring Lardner's work over the same period, the loss of that "abundant good humor" commented on in a previous chapter, and the almost continual omens and portents of disaster that also mark H. L. Mencken's work. Before passing a final judgment on Hemingway's "animalism" and "cynicism" it is well to remember that, if his researches into the darker instincts are limited intellectually, they are emotionally and aesthetically rewarding, and that the whole body of his work deals with a subject inadequately represented or almost misrepresented in our tradition, even in Melville and Hawthorne and Poe. In fact the best of these novels and stories—and the later stories like "The Snows of Kilimanjaro" and "The Short Happy Life of Francis Macomber" are among the best—are already part of the country's permanent literary heritage; whatever we may say about their shortcomings will not much affect their status. As Hemingway receded ever deeper into this interior sphere of the irrational death urges, he seemed to be drawing ever closer to the "real" world between two wars. For his portraits of a primitive and animal dignity in the face of suffering anticipated the dominant emotional pattern of this world, and described the last human heritage of thousands of similarly isolated and despairing individuals in the face of all the refinements of civilized viciousness.

## 4

Though *To Have and Have Not* was set in the Florida resort towns of the depression years, there was to be a still later development in the cycle of Hemingway's withdrawal and return. Meanwhile we are concerned with a very different sort of writer. If Hemingway dealt with the buried depths and the recessive impulses, John Dos Passos was the embodiment of the rational artist in our tradition—the conscious, moral, and progressive critic of our communal habits; and it is curious that both of these Americans should have started at a similar psychological and even geographical point. In the early Dos Passos, just as in the later Hemingway, there is the same central evocation of a detached and remote observer drifting on the tides of social renunciation. A grandson of a Portuguese immigrant, the young Dos Passos also found in republican Spain an apparent antidote to commerce under Harding and Coolidge: the Spain of Hemingway's fiestas and anarchists and ice-cold *horchata*. It was from a Spanish revolutionary writer, too, Pío Baroja, that Dos Passos gained his early intellectual concepts.

While Hemingway's *Death in the Afternoon,* in 1932, was still fixed on the matador, Dos Passos' *Rosinante to the Road Again,* as early as 1922, was already discussing the masses. And it was in Chicago, where Dos Passos was born in 1896, that his central trilogy, *U.S.A.*, would open: in the city which was the heart, or at any rate the nervous cortex, of the new American industrialism whose urban and strident rhythms also dominate Dos Passos' first major novel. In *Manhattan Transfer* (1925), too, we notice the early forms of those technical devices that would distinguish the later trilogy: the use of popular songs, of newspaper headlines, of the speech of the people as against the speech of the scholars, and of the actual figures from Woodrow Wilson to King C. Gillette—all these sociological indices which are fused into the panoramic view of our city culture, and, in *U.S.A.* itself, our national culture.

For the real "hero" of the trilogy—*The 42nd Parallel* (1930), *1919* (1932), and *The Big Money* (1936)—is of course the United States. Thus Dos Passos invented a series of technical devices in an attempt to widen the bounds of the novel: the "Newsreels," which form a running account of the actual events, as well as the crimes, fads, and follies of our society; the "Biographies" which form the record of our special personalities from Debs, "lover of mankind," who opens the trilogy, to Insull, manipulator of "power superpower," who closes it some fifteen hundred pages later; the "Novels" which form, by contrast, the record of the ordinary citizens in the great trading Republic of the West; and "The Camera Eye" which forms, as it were, the personal diary of the novelist as he writes the novel, the record of his shifting emotions in the face of this national scene which he is recording so brilliantly. These devices not only catch the more intricate patterns of industrialized society but also include all the real elements of the pattern by a stretching of every artistic resource to record "Nature." And while the aim was almost impossible the attempt was to a large degree successful.

Before Dos Passos, a score of American writers—including Norris, Fuller, Herrick, and Dreiser—had dealt with separate manifestations of the new industrialism, or in a series of novels had attempted to relate these manifestations. Of course the French from Balzac on were in a sense even closer to Dos Passos' aims, while Jules Romains suggested, in a later note, that the panoramic novel was *his* patent. But no one else had attempted to bring everything together at one moment and to set all the complexities of that "moment"—extending from the Promise of the American Century in 1900 to the Crash of 1929—within so sharp a focus; and perhaps none of them had understood so clearly the nuances of their own historical scene.

For Dos Passos was among the best informed and the most learned of the moderns—and this set him apart in a tradition that had been marked at once by its freedom from and ignorance of "ideas." And yet, though the exposition in *U.S.A.* was brilliant and its picture of American life was full and varied, the novelist's conclusion was simple, and not encouraging. Filled as the three volumes were with achievements of urban power in the land of power, the "Newsreels" became ever more sensational and chaotic, while the "Biographies" of our national heroes formed only the record of their disinheritance, the "Novels" recounted only the disintegration of these average lives, from the obscure merchant seaman Joe Williams to the publicity wizard J. Ward Moorehouse; and the reflections of the author in "The Camera Eye" became in turn increasingly desolate. Thus the immense national energy which had built up such a remarkable society within so short a period had apparently become centrifugal: the elaborate system was shaking itself apart. In fact, just as each novel of the trilogy was better than its predecessor, each was more despairing, and *The Big Money,* resembling in some respects Hemingway's *To Have and Have Not,* is a sort of apotheosis of stale horrors.

In one sense the basic view of life in *U.S.A.* defeats itself, for, if Dos Passos' people are really what he seems to think they are, there would be little value in the social revolution which is his central hope of redemption. A revolution implies the release of human traits which the older social order has been inhibiting. But what is there, in these grasping and empty American personages, left to release? The total picture is one of inherent human

weakness rather than of chained power, of barely restrained human viciousness rather than of an inhibited human grandeur. Indeed *The Big Money*
records the twilight of Dos Passos' radical hopes too, and here the revolutionary heroes who should perhaps reveal the promise of life most fully,
show it least, while whatever vision of Paradise Lost lay behind the trilogy
has turned into a sort of second-rate inferno. His two later novels, also
possessing related episodes (*The Adventures of a Young Man,* 1939, and
*Number One,* 1943) do not recover any of the vision.

5

As the literary paths of Dos Passos and Hemingway had separated in the
early twenties, only to meet again in a common view of the time, another
major figure was to carry this view forward in a rather special sense but in
an even more extravagant form.

Born in 1897, a year later than Dos Passos and Fitzgerald and a year earlier
than Hemingway, the young William Faulkner shared in the common experience of his generation: he joined the Canadian Flying Corps and served with
the R.A.F. in France. In him, too, the variety of its origins helped to explain
the variety of the American genius. Faulkner was heir to a family of Southern
governors, statesmen, and other public figures; early in his childhood he went
to live in Oxford, Mississippi, and it was his home almost uninterruptedly
thereafter. Perhaps these facts tell us more than those on Faulkner's European
experience: this Southern home that is uninterrupted except by visions of
ghouls, and these ancestral halls in which echo only the sobs of the possessed
and the demented. Faulkner built his work on an even grander scale than
Dos Passos. He related even his minor personages with one another, he
elaborated their genealogy from generation to generation, he gave them a
countryside: a deep land of Baptists, of brothels, of attic secrets, of swamps
and shadows. "Jefferson," Mississippi, is the capital of this world which
reaches backward in time to the origins of Southern culture and forward to
the horrid prophecies of its extinction, and which ranges down in social strata
from dying landed aristocracy, the Sartoris and Compson families, to the new
commercial oligarchy of the Snopeses; down to the poor-white Bundrens of
*As I Lay Dying,* to the pervert Popeye of *Sanctuary,* and to the Negro Christmas of *Light in August,* turned brute again by the society which had raised
him from the animal.

It is typical of Faulkner's meteoric talent that the three years between 1929
and 1932 contain two of his major works, *The Sound and the Fury* and
*Light in August.* Both novels are highly experimental in form. As a matter
of fact, all of Faulkner's big novels are marked by a technical experimentation
which adds to an already formidable ambiguity of content. *Light in August*

(1932), probably the most easily comprehensible to the average reader, seems to be written as an objective narrative; but it holds tale within tale and its meaning becomes clear only if you follow the story of Lena, the poor-white mountain girl—and a Faulknerian symbol of a rather appalling, blind, lower-class sexual fertility—to the story of Hightower, isolated, sterile, living in his memories of the Old South. Underneath, is the story of the New South: the murder in Jefferson, Mississippi, and the love affair of the northern spinster, Miss Joanna Burden, with the mulatto Christmas. Here finally Faulkner gives expression not only to the most bitter and profound cultural problem of the South, but to its dominant cultural phobia; and the nightmarish quality is matched only, perhaps, by one's sense of its reality in the haunted minds of the central figures.

The Faulknerian dialectic, which became reasonably clear in *Light in August,* had already been suggested in *The Sound and the Fury* (1929). The earlier novel is even more complex in its technique. It is an outstanding example of the interior monologue in our letters; and the skill of its architecture —the style moves from almost complete obscurity to the statement of prosaic fact—is evident in the use of the unifying symbols: the circus tickets, the river, the broken watch, the tolling clock, and, indeed, all the manifestations of dissolving time that pervade the novel. It is very different from *Light in August* in tone. In the Compson children, Faulkner caught the torment of childhood at the moment it reaches maturity—at the moment, that is, of the realization of sin and evil, the moment of the "Fall." Thus the "incestuous" love of Quentin Compson for his sister Caddy, which forms the central theme and provides the most eloquent passages of the novel, and which Faulkner handles with a peculiarly touching naïveté, is incestuous merely because these legitimate feelings of childhood—in a sense, the only true feelings of childhood—are judged from outside, from an adult framework of values. Indeed, filled as the tale is with all the pathetic devices and drives and tensions of infancy, and the intimations of those other lawless and poignant affections which color the better—or the worse—part of our lives, *The Sound and the Fury* is matched by few novels in its evocations of infantile origins. In spite of being specialized in form, rather self-consciously limited in appeal, it was a landmark of the new literature.

But the childhood here revealed is in a sense a double one. The drama of innocence and corruption takes place within a larger framework: there is the conflict, again, of a decaying landed aristocracy with the rising commercial classes. Avaricious and bigoted, the Jason Compson of *The Sound and the Fury* is the protagonist of the new economic order which, in effect, closes the novel. And, by contrast with Jason's "practicality," even the idiot Benjy Compson, whose obscure moaning and slobbering opens the novel, is an intelligible hero.

At least that is what Faulkner seemed to suggest, as he compared the youth of his culture with its misbegotten maturity. In the series of grotesque legends which followed, *As I Lay Dying* (1930), *These 13* (1931), *Sanctuary* (1931), and his later novels and tales, Faulkner dealt with the New South—with this modern stage, on which strut only those modern personages whose milieu is a cold and calculating corruption, whose single instinct is a lust for power, and whose lares and penates are the Faulknerian "Snopeses." It was only in *Absalom, Absalom!* in 1936, that Faulkner seemed to regain something of the tone of *The Sound and the Fury*; but there again he was treating the rise and decay of a landed aristocracy—and there, too, Quentin Compson proclaimed that he did not hate the South. " 'I dont hate it,' he said. *I dont hate it* he thought, panting in the cold air, the iron New England dark; *I dont. I dont! I dont hate it! I dont hate it!*"

With William Faulkner, the cultural pattern of isolation, of revolt, and of denial, the heritage of the American twenties lasting over and fully forming the American novelist of the 1930's reached an extreme. Here the two main elements of the pattern—the solitary and desperate individual of Hemingway's work, the acrid and despairing critique of contemporary society in Dos Passos' work—are given fullest expression, while even the shimmering flappers of Fitzgerald become a type of Faulknerian incubus. Indeed, the "misty tragedy" played far behind the veil becomes rather more explicit, and the sense of latent horror in the earlier evocation of the Jazz Age becomes acute. There is no denying Faulkner's real achievement. In the scope of his scene and the dimensions of his portraiture, in the complexity and subtlety of his emotions, as well as in the vivid and complex prose style, he is perhaps, as Gide remarked, "*the* most important of the stars in this new constellation." Nor is this Mississippi symbolist quite so esoteric as he may seem at first; for his picture of the Mississippi Valley and its people is the work of a realist even when, with the Representative Rankins, the Snopeses go to Washington. Those who praise Faulkner indiscriminately, *Sanctuary* as well as *The Sound and the Fury,* are in a sense unaware of how good Faulkner can be, and to what degree the history of this remarkable talent is also the history of its dissipation. The increasing stress on technical virtuosity, the sacrifice of content for effect, and of effect for shock—these, too, show the destructive element at work.

For this entire literary movement of the American twenties, fresh and promising, varied in talent and bold in achievement, seems to end almost everywhere on a note of negation and of exhaustion. Winesburg, Ohio, gave way to New York, and New York to Paris and Capri, and Capri to the Wasteland. This was the last resort, the true home of these innovators and rebels.

"My nerves are bad to-night. Yes, bad. Stay with me,
"Speak to me. Why do you never speak. Speak.
"What are you thinking of? What thinking? What? . . ."

I think we are in rats' alley
Where the dead men lost their bones.

So spoke the American poet of the twenties, T. S. Eliot, the poet from Sherwood Anderson's Middle West who turned East for his salvation to England, who turned still East. And the dominant note of aridity in Eliot, the evocation of a land without water, of rock and no water, found its echoes in the Gopher Prairie of Sinclair Lewis, the Manhattan Transfer of Dos Passos, the clean well lighted places of Ernest Hemingway, the Long Island suburbs of Fitzgerald, and even in the "George C. Tilyou smile" that floated above the spandangled bananas of Henry Miller's American Steeplechase, as well as in the deep and nightmarish shadows of Faulkner's Mississippi.

So, too, H. L. Mencken's own *Notes on Democracy,* which appeared in the middle twenties, marked what was probably a low ebb of the democratic belief in America. Here also, the first sense of gusto in Mencken's work was followed by a sense of black despair. Was the postwar malaise due primarily to the First World War itself? In a certain sense; but not in the sense that has usually been attributed to it. For what Mencken was tracing here, and what all these writers were describing in one form or another, may be more intimately related to "Faulkner's War"—it is, of course, the effect of the industrial change which began shortly after the Civil War: that age of disillusion foreshadowed in the gloomy Whitman and the dark Twain, whose impact colors the work of such figures of the "Middle Generation" as Dreiser, Cather, Glasgow, and Sinclair Lewis. As for the Lost Generation itself, its typical figure, Scott Fitzgerald, never saw action abroad, and Mencken himself, in some respects the worst war casualty of them all, was not in the Army. One notices, too, the curiously remote quality of the war novels of some of the writers who did see action: from the John Andrews of Dos Passos' *Three Soldiers* (1921), who devours *La Tentation de Saint Antoine* "as if the book were a drug in which he could drink deep forgetfulness of himself," or the still earlier Martin Howe of *One Man's Initiation* (1920), dreaming of his Gothic abbey, to the narrator of E. E. Cummings' *The Enormous Room* (1922), who prefers his prison camp to the outside world.

The First World War, which was after all a lesser war among our wars, and lasted barely two years out of the one hundred fifty of the Republic's history, completed the consolidation of the new industrialism in American life. It marked the triumph of the cartels, and the end of the older forms of agrarian democracy, if not, in fact, of free capitalism itself. Its extraordinary and disproportionate influence on the writing of a whole generation, now indeed lost, must be evaluated as the effect of this underlying cultural process. The war was the immediate cause; but the new economic order was the true cause of their discontent: this new money society which at the moment of its ascendance, seemed to render futile or grotesque the entire progressive movement, from the muckrakers to the trust busters, and from the Populist reforms to the New Freedom. This was the *causa sine qua non* of their despair. Whatever they suffered in a war which they had already felt was not their own, they sensed very early that they had lost the peace. And all the other revolts —against the Victorian gentility, against the Anglo-Saxon taboos, against the bourgeois virtues—were contained in the framework of this revolt.

In the forms of their opposition were they really, as they were later branded, the "Irresponsibles"? Certainly they had the limitations as well as the charms of youth; they had cultural innocence and ignorance. In their narrow range of values, too, and in their uneasy prejudices, in their fevered stress on pleasure and in the extremes of their despair, they often reflected the society they had repudiated: it shortly became clear that the "Aesthetic Man" was as dangerous a fiction as the "Economic Man." They, too, were living on borrowed time, and sometimes they believed it was eternity. But, without the solid affection for home and homeland that had marked the middle generation, in their unremitting devotion to their craft, at least, they carried forward an essential part of the older American life. Far more than some of their critics, they all sensed the real pressures of the period, and often they gave eloquent expression to the historical moment, as in *The Big Money:*

they have clubbed us off the streets   they are stronger   they are rich   they hire and fire the politicians the newspapereditors the old judges the small men with reputations the collegepresidents the wardheelers (listen businessmen collegepresidents judges   America will not forget her betrayers) they hire the men with guns the uniforms the policecars the patrolwagons

all right you have won. . . .
America our nation has been beaten by strangers who have turned our language inside out who have taken the clean words our fathers spoke and made them slimy and foul

their hired men sit on the judge's bench they sit back with their feet on the tables under the dome of the State House they are ignorant of our beliefs they have the dollars the guns the armed forces the powerplants

they have built the electricchair and hired the executioner to throw the switch

all right we are two nations

6

While the meaning of the lost generation became plain in the words of Dos Passos, the phrase itself was given a final twist by a new literary figure, who applied it to "those men of advanced middle age who still speak the language that was spoken before 1929, and who know no other. These men indubitably *are* lost. But I am not one of them." But with Thomas Wolfe, of course, we come to still another "younger generation," those who were raised on internal crisis. The impact of the depression years—"the unending repercussions of these scenes of suffering, violence, oppression, hunger, cold, and filth and poverty going on unheeded in a world in which the rich were still rotten with their wealth"—left a scar upon their lives, but a conviction in their souls. Since Wolfe was a primary figure among these new writers, his career may be used to summarize the entire shift of values that occurred in the thirties.

In Faulkner and Wolfe, too, were represented two poles of the modern South. Born in 1900, in Asheville, North Carolina, and descended from hill people, Wolfe was also caught up in the web of Southern emotionalism so pervasive in Faulkner's work. But while Faulkner seems to work steadily backward, Wolfe's movement is continuously forward; while the older writer explored the dissolving reaches of memory, the younger came to face the dimensions of the future. And while Faulkner marked the final full expression of the aesthetic nihilism that evolved out of the American twenties, Wolfe became perhaps the central spokesman for the artistic beliefs of the 1930's.

In a sense Wolfe's four huge novels, reaching well over a million words, may be considered as a single novel (or perhaps the beginning of a novel, since Wolfe rewrote the childhood episodes of the first volume in a later volume, and this, too, he considered still not a true beginning, but merely "something which led up to the true beginning"). *Look Homeward, Angel* (1929) deals with the early life of the Southern protagonist. *Of Time and the River* (1935) deals with his Northern adventures and first contact with the life of wealth and culture and sensibility: that life "so beautiful and right and good" toward which, as the young Wolfe felt, "all the myriads of the earth aspire"—or at least all the myriads of the American earth. For this was also the vision of a Mark Twain in Boston, and a Henry James in London, of Dreiser in New York, Cather in Nebraska, and Scott Fitzgerald on Long Island: this is the perennial fable in the national letters of the Provincial and the Magic City. And both *The Web and the Rock* (1939) and *You Can't Go Home Again* (1940) deal with the realization of this vision—and its final inadequacy—and with still another and a new beginning.

Moreover, this huge novel, multiformed and sometimes inchoate as it was, with its alterations always in progress, formed a central document of the period. Just as Dos Passos reinvigorated the naturalistic novel by means of the symbolist techniques, so Wolfe regenerated the whole tradition of native realism through the electric charge of curiosity, of lyricism, of anger and protest, and perhaps even of pure excitement which he put into it. In fact, he probably carried sheer energy to its highest pitch in the national letters, and this energy became matter. The emotional force of *Look Homeward, Angel,* for example, was materialized in its panorama of the general Southern scene, and, for all the obvious adolescent excesses and limitations of Wolfe's first novel, in the notable central portraits of the novel: those of Oliver Gant and Eliza Gant. Characters: that was one of Wolfe's plain contributions to the American novel—characters who, for all their idiosyncrasies, were by no means merely "eccentrics." It is interesting, too, that the weakest point of a national tradition based on "individualism" and the democratic character should be its indifference to individuals who are neither tycoons nor criminal cases—its indifference, in short, to character. Furthermore, the central conflict of the Gants, between Eliza's outrageous lust for property and Oliver's insatiable hunger for experience—a conflict that is not lacking in the American mind itself—became the central theme of the tetralogy.

The "Fame" which is sought by the artist-hero in *Of Time and the River* is nothing more than a barely sublimated form of Eliza's materialism. And the remarkable quality of Wolfe's unending evocations, descriptions, and evaluations of New York in *The Web and the Rock* is that he catches at once the fascination of the "Enfabled Rock" for the provincial mind, and the provincial's realization that this is not enough. Perhaps no other American has done so well with the first enchantments and terrors of the city. Both here and in *You Can't Go Home Again* Wolfe went, as Scott Fitzgerald never quite could go, beyond the whole glamorous pageantry of "that distant Babylon, cloud-capped and rosy-hued there in the smoke of his imagination."

There was never much doubt as to just whom Wolfe was talking about in these patently autobiographical novels; but the change of his hero's name from Eugene Gant to George Webber was more than a mere change of name. The mature Wolfe was no longer primarily concerned with one young man, however gifted, but with all young men; and not merely with his own experiences in society but with society's experience; not with the "superior individual" of Mencken and Fitzgerald but with Sherwood Anderson's "the general." So it was necessary to return and reevaluate his hero's youth and education—in fact to create a new youth and education. And in the world of the mountain grills in *The Web and the Rock,* or in the microcosm of Libya Hill during the boom and the bust of *You Can't Go Home Again,*

Wolfe did just that, while in the archetypal portrait of Judge Rumford Bland (one of his most memorable brief portraits) he seemed to present a local cousin of the Eumenides. Just as Wolfe's hero had been forced to renounce Esther Jack, the great lady of his provincial fantasies, since "love was not enough," he could now understand both the stature and the failure of the contemporary American writer, Lloyd McHarg, since "fame was not enough." And in the history of the Federal Weight and Scales Company, or in the portrait of "Mr. Jack at Morn," he displayed a notable increase in his satirical power. As a matter of fact, Wolfe would have been, and to a degree already was, a major social satirist.

Still, was it now claimed that he had lost his lyrical gift, by some of those who had earlier claimed that his only gift was the lyric? Probably he had done nothing more eloquent in his earlier works than the passages on New York ("Smoke-blue by morning in the chasmed slant, on quickening the tempo of the rapid steps, up to the pinnacles of noon") and on the rustle of the leaves across America:

*'Promised, promised, promised, promised, promised,'* say the leaves across America. . . . And everywhere, through the immortal dark, something moving in the night, and something stirring in the hearts of men, and something crying in their wild unuttered blood, the wild, unuttered tongues of its huge prophecies—so soon the morning, soon the morning: O America.

Nor had he done anything less rhetorical than the final words to that New York editor whom he had molded into his "Fox": "Man was born to live, to suffer, and to die, and what befalls him is a tragic lot. There is no denying this in the final end. *But we must, dear Fox, deny it all along the way.*" Where were the provincial accents now? Certainly the path that Wolfe took led him through all the heartbreaking detours that mark our literature from Melville to Dreiser. In July, 1938, after having delivered a new manuscript of more than a million words, he became ill with pneumonia. He died that September.

If he was ignorant and superstitious as the hill folks were, and stumbled into many gargantuan pitfalls—some those of his own making too—he had the persistence and cunning as well as the long legs of the hill people, and he walked with the mountain walk.

7

To some members of that original younger generation that was now the older generation, the Wolfean pilgrimage hardly seemed inspiring. "The stuff about the *Great Vital Heart of America,*" said Scott Fitzgerald in *The Crack Up* (1945), "is just simply corny." This little interchange of letters between Fitzgerald, as a sort of spokesman for the twenties, and Wolfe, for the thirties, forms an interesting footnote to our literary history. Maybe "corn" was a partial antidote to absinthe; at any rate there were many new literary figures who took up and supported Tom Wolfe's notions in one form or another. In a similar development over the same period, John Steinbeck moved from the primitive folk and the mystics of *To a God Unknown* (1933) and *Tortilla Flat* (1935) to the labor organizers of *In Dubious Battle* (1936). As the early tales, collected in *The Long Valley* (1938), had suggested, he was the most gifted of the writers surrounding Wolfe, and *Grapes of Wrath,* in 1939, confirmed his position in the new decade. It was chiefly an emotional facility and simplification of experience that kept Steinbeck's whole achievement from being as impressive as it was arresting. Nevertheless the story of the Okies' westward trek toward a New World—recalling as it did the historical meaning of the frontier in times of social crisis, even though the frontier was now an economic one—was a big and life-giving book. Similarly, Hemingway would soon announce his own return to a common humanity in *For Whom the Bell Tolls* (1940), while Dos Passos would take another look at the white pillars of the Republic in *The Ground We Stand On* (1941), and Fitzgerald himself would select, as the hero of *The Last Tycoon* (1941), a typical member of those odorous "aliens," a man who had moved up from the impoverished "masses" whom the earlier chronicler of the Jazz Age had described as "swarming like rats, chattering like apes, smelling like all hell . . . monkeys!"

It was indeed a new age, all over again—and even Edna Millay would desert her shining castles built upon the sand and beat a drum for mutual aid, while Muriel Rukeyser would voice the hopes of those other poets too young to see their funerals "in pantomime nightly before uneasy beds." Only William Faulkner remained an unreconstructed rebel. Furthermore, just as T. S. Eliot had earlier moved to England, W. H. Auden, perhaps the most gifted of the younger English poets, now moved to the United States. The obscure law of polarity seemed to be at work here as elsewhere. American literature, in its abrupt but rhythmic alternations between the opposing poles of the individual and of society, reflects the deeper process of cultural growth—the familiar oppositions of experiment and reaction—and the literary reaction in the thirties was historically almost inevitable. But the abrupt change of values in the new decade was more immediately connected, of course, with the financial crash of 1929—the sudden collapse of what Dos Passos had called "the great machine they slaved for" and what had seemed so recently more adamant, more unshakable than ever. In the stress of such quick and catastrophic change a Tom Wolfe might take up Sherwood Anderson's search for "the right place and the right people," while Steinbeck would carry forward the social criticism and something of the tone of Frank Norris and Jack London. And just as the larger literary figures carry within them both poles of the historical process, and are always classicists and romanticists together, so they seem at once more original as individuals and more deeply representative of their culture. Yet it was true also that the internal crisis had come as swiftly and unexpectedly upon the majority of the new writers as the First World War upon their predecessors. Under the new pressures, they were as guilty, in another mold, of the same excesses. They cut themselves off as completely from the twenties as the writers of the middle twenties had from the Progressive Movement of the 1900's. As a matter of fact, some of these New Dealers had hardly heard of the New Freedom, and believed that they were the first to initiate social progress in the United States—and they were not all New Dealers. Just as the new movement was primarily sociological in its orientation, some of its typical exponents, including Albert Maltz and Albert Halper, Leane Zugsmith, Fielding Burke, and even, it was rumored, Dorothy Parker (and also the talented mystery writer Dashiell Hammett), were avowed radicals; along with the revolutionary idealism they brought in revolutionary zealotry; very often the dogma got in the way of craft, and moral conviction became a substitute for artistic imagination. To some of these writers, indeed, the "Masses" became as formidable an abstraction as the "Individual" had been in the twenties; for a while, with the customary national intensity, it seemed that the age of the poets had been followed by the age of the pamphleteers. In America, as Sinclair Lewis remarked, a pendulum is not a pendulum; it is a piston.

This was part of the price of the American tradition under the stress of change—and in a world in crisis; but still, by contrast with the foreign scene, our own excesses were on the whole more ludicrous than vicious. By contrast with Dachau or Le Vernet, the Federal Writers' Project of the Work Projects Administration had even a certain grandeur—abused and vilified as it was—while in an extraordinary burst of studies, charts, reports, guidebooks, picture books, movies, plays, operas, and histories, these artistic leaf rakers on the "W. P. and A." brought forth an invaluable body of source material on the native scene. Their work, and a further group of related studies, such as Constance Rourke's *American Humor,* Carl Sandburg's *Lincoln,* and Van Wyck Brooks' *The Flowering of New England,* suddenly reestablished our sense of historical continuity, and if only through the Indians and the Negroes we seemed to gain a sort of racial unconscious, too. Many of these new journalists, historians, novelists, poets, and playwrights—and just as the Federal Writers' Project uncovered a richer past, so they helped to produce a richer present—also skipped the delicacies of their craft. If their work was sometimes crude, on the whole it was solid, and it could be built on. One of the best novels about the depression years, Ira Wolfert's *Tucker's People*, which appeared in the early forties, had been written during the thirties, and put away to mellow. Meanwhile a decade which saw, in addition to the works already mentioned, the plays of Clifford Odets or of Lillian Hellman, the movies of Pare Lorentz, and the popular historical novels of Walter Edmonds along with the tales of such an isolated and tragic figure as Hans Otto Storm —that decade was neither so extreme nor so barren as some critics have implied.

Nor was the break between periods and traditions, sharp as it seemed, altogether complete. The "nonpolitical" Southern Agrarians and Fugitives and their heirs went on their way unperturbed—although the members of the group, in their intense concern with purely "literary" values, and in their withdrawal from the more acute socio-economic issues of the decade, seemed to leave behind them the human problems as well, and to appear in their way quite as occult as the theoreticians of the class struggle. Essentially conservative also, such other Southern writers as Elizabeth Madox Roberts continued to display the virtues of a dissolving genteel tradition, which, by a greater boldness or a larger talent, Katherine Anne Porter had just escaped, and which, in the clinical morbidity of Evelyn Scott's work, or in that of Robert Penn Warren, seemed to be turning in upon itself. Yet all these writers were in one respect or another conservators of traditional values, and Willa Cather, who had by no means stopped writing over this period, or the Virginia radical of the nineties, Ellen Glasgow, who even put on a fresh burst of energy. In another area, near Park Avenue and Fifty-second Street, such a writer as John O'Hara continued to analyze the mores of the emancipated speakeasy set, and the polish of his phrases no less than the tone of his conversations recalled something of the lost elegance of the 1920's; in the neighborhood of Hollywood, too, James M. Cain brought the use of dialogue to a high gloss. And when such other skillful technicians and ex-expatriates as Kay Boyle, Glenway Wescott, and Frederic Prokosch turned their craft to the various phases of the world crisis it refreshed the entire tradition of sensibility.

The new "affirmation" of the American thirties, moreover, was not always accompanied by the vague sweetness and light that pervaded the tales of William Saroyan or by the rather murky violence of Edward Dahlberg's novels. In the middle ground also, along with Wolfe and Steinbeck, though not yet so firmly established, were writers like James T. Farrell and, a little later, Richard Wright. Considered as one of the most powerful and promising American novelists in the forties, Wright was also a leading representative of an established and versatile group of contemporary Negro writers and writers on Negro themes, including W. E. B. DuBois, James Weldon Johnson, Countee Cullen, and Claude McKay among the fiction writers; Roi Ottley, Zora Neale Hurston, Adam Clayton Powell, Chester Himes, Edwin Peeples, St. Clair Drake, and Horace Cayton, among a host of younger critics, poets, publicists, novelists, and scholars.

Both Farrell and Wright were working in the older and perhaps stronger naturalistic mold of Dreiser, although Wright, whose first important short story, "Big Boy Leaves Home," appeared in 1936, was still in a more formative stage. And, while Farrell relied chiefly on a cumulative effect of boredom with and disgust for the lives of his lower middle-class Irish people, and Wright relied on a cumulative effect of disgust for and horror at the existences of his Southern Negroes, both novelists had undoubted power. Their moral integrity, too, their determination to uncover all the unending viciousness and corruption of their environment—and perhaps the daily and hourly degradation of Farrell's people was as bad in the end as the moments of horror which marked the story of Wright's people—gave their work its solidity.

The limitations of Wright and Farrell, moreover, were just as revealing as their merits. In their work could be seen the real points of stress of contemporary American society—economic, racial, cultural; shaped by the pressures of the raw industrial cities in Farrell's novels, and by the blight of a diseased hinterland in Wright's. Here was the underlying social pattern that bound together both the aesthetic revolt of the twenties and the aesthetic conversion of the thirties. Showing the harsh prejudices and deep phobias of their milieu, these novelists also showed, through their own concentrated bitterness, through their refusal to accept even the catharsis of expression—through their indifference to the necessity of catharsis, the one reward of his art which the artist can always have, and which he can hardly afford not to have—they also showed, only too clearly, the harm that was already done. Thus Danny O'Neill, the "hero" of Farrell's tetralogy—and if Farrell's range was narrow, his architectonic concepts were certainly massive—was less convincing than Studs Lonigan, the "villain" of his earlier trilogy. The novelist's accent on personal emancipation hardly matched his earlier tones of blind cultural disintegration. Similarly, while Wright's autobiography, *Black Boy* (1945), was more moderate in tone than his earlier novel, *Native Son,* it was probably even more merciless in its impact—for the horrors one could tolerate in the life of a fictional hero, one could hardly accept in the actual life of an ordinary citizen.

No, those "latent atavistic urges" which a Thomas Wolfe saw everywhere around him in the disordered social arrangement of his time, as well as the Nazi Germany which exploited those urges, would not be eliminated by the liquidation of the German General Staff or by the atomization of Tokyo. They were strongly rooted also in the land of equal hope, and the imminence of a national future almost without limits seemed to revive all the fear and cruelty of the past. The Second World War also demonstrated the latent resources of a democratic order, since an average townsman from Abilene, Kansas, could become an outstanding military figure, while a patrician descendant of the Dutch landlords in the Hudson River Valley would best embody the common beliefs of the peoples of the world. These underlying cultural pressures still determined the shape of American life on the brink of another postwar era—and the shape of its literature—and whether the new age would burst in splendor or in terror.

# 78. AN AMERICAN DRAMA

Iɴ a previous chapter devoted chiefly to Eugene O'Neill, both the state of play writing and the general theatrical situation between 1915 and 1925 were discussed. The story is resumed at the end of that period, when three noncommercial "art theaters" testified to a widespread conviction that a "new" drama both could and should be brought to birth. However, except for O'Neill, no permanently important playwright was introduced through any one of these three theaters until the Theater Guild produced Elmer Rice's *The Adding Machine* in 1923. During the four or five years following that event, Rice was joined by various other "new American playwrights" destined to sustain their reputations through a series of plays, and it soon became evident that the new American drama—under discussion for at least ten years—was now a reality. The season of 1924–1925 * was especially notable for *What Price Glory* by Maxwell Anderson and Laurence Stallings, *They Knew What They Wanted* by Sidney Howard, and *Processional* by John Howard Lawson.

The fact that *What Price Glory,* the most sensationally successful of these plays, was produced by Arthur Hopkins, technically a "commercial" producer, should serve to remind one that the "new drama," once it had actually come into existence, was by no means monopolized by the "art theaters." Indeed, it came more and more to be taken up by Broadway until there soon ceased to be any clear distinction between what was possible in an art theater and what was possible in a commercial theater. Thus, the new American drama had hardly begun to exist before it ceased to be the property of any coterie, and it was never at any time written exclusively by men who thought of themselves as belonging to any one group. Some of the most successful and esteemed playwrights would themselves have found it impossible to say how much they owed to the stimulus of the experimental producers of exotic drama and how much to certain predecessors in the American theater.

Long arguments have raged over the question whether the English drama of Shaw and Galsworthy owed more to Ibsen than to Tom Robertson. An equally long and equally futile one might be conducted concerning the

* Dates in this chapter refer to first production rather than to first publication.

relative importance to the new American playwrights of the European tradition and of that native one which had for decades been slowly evolving through James A. Herne, Charles Hoyt, Clyde Fitch, William Vaughn Moody, George M. Cohan, and the rest. Undoubtedly the most violent stimulus was provided by the revolutionary dramatists of Europe, and undoubtedly the "little theaters" contributed greatly to the playwrights' awareness of possible new horizons in the theater. But even as early as the season of 1924–1925, the three outstandingly successful plays mentioned above were the work of men who were less the disciples of any playwright, native or foreign, and less members of any theatrical cult, than they were simply talented writers eager to reach an American public for plays they found it in themselves to write.

When *What Price Glory* and *They Knew What They Wanted* appeared the names of the three authors responsible meant nothing to the average playgoer, although Anderson and Howard had each recently produced a first play without achieving commercial success. Both of the new works were theoretically shocking since the first treated in a frankly ribald spirit certain incidents in the lives of soldiers fighting the First World War, and the second had as its sympathetic heroine a young waitress whom a middle-aged Italian winegrower was willing to marry despite his knowledge of the fact that she was soon to bear an illegitimate child by a lover who had deserted her. Both plays were enthusiastically received, and it is evident that the large audiences which saw them were not actually shocked as the early audiences of Ibsen and Shaw had been; the reason is simply that by 1924 much of what had formerly seemed dangerously paradoxical had been assimilated not only by the intellectual but also by the whole sophisticated public. The two plays were not preaching a new doctrine. What they actually did was tell, for the first time on the American stage, dramatically interesting stories looked at from the point of view of the 1920's rather than from that of the mid-nineteenth century.

The same thing may be said of many of the other characteristic plays of the period. Laurence Stallings, coauthor of *What Price Glory,* abandoned play writing after failing to repeat his first success; but *Saturday's Children* (1927) and *Gypsy* (1929) by his collaborator, Maxwell Anderson, as well as *Lucky Sam McCarver* (1925), *Ned McCobb's Daughter* (1926) and *The Silver Cord* (1926), all by Sidney Howard, were comedies or light dramas which, without being directly didactic, told remarkably various stories always from the point of view of what may be called libertarian humanism—one conspicuous element in which is a protest in the name of common sense and kindliness against conventional respectability.

Some of these plays involved also an element which was the most important one in others of the time; namely, satire directed against materialism and the gospel of success, both of which libertarian humanism despised as aspects of Philistinism. Thus George Kelly's *The Show-Off* (1924) is a rather bitter satire in which the central figure, a blustering vulgarian, actually succeeds through a fluke in "pulling off the big deal" he has always dreamed of; and the long series of popular farces from *Dulcy* (1921) to *Once in a Lifetime* (1930), which George Kaufman wrote with various collaborators, represent a somewhat more frankly popular exploitation of the same theme.

Early in its career the Theater Guild, besides popularizing Shaw on the American stage, had produced the work of Molnár and other central European dramatists whose "Continental" treatment of the comedy of sex was widely regarded as a corrective to Puritanism. In *The Road to Rome* (1927) Robert Sherwood responded to the influence of Shaw by writing an amusing pseudohistorical comedy somewhat in the manner of *Caesar and Cleopatra,* and then, in 1931, achieved with *Reunion in Vienna* a comedy so perfectly in the Continental tradition that it might easily pass as a translation.

With the exception of *Reunion in Vienna,* none of the typical plays of the twenties so far mentioned exhibit foreign influence as their primary inspiration. Neither, of course, do Hatcher Hughes' *Hell-Bent fer Heaven* (1924) and Paul Green's *In Abraham's Bosom* (1926)—two folk plays, which are certainly among the best representatives of a genre that did not flourish as many supposed it would. On the other hand two plays held in high esteem both by critics and by a large public—Elmer Rice's *The Adding Machine* (1923) and John Howard Lawson's *Processional* (1925)—were directly inspired by those same expressionistic experiments which influenced O'Neill's *The Hairy Ape. The Adding Machine* is a theatrically effective exposition of a nihilistic fable concerning a certain "Mr. Zero," who remains hopelessly insignificant even after he has been transported to heaven. *Processional* professed (not too convincingly) to owe its method to vaudeville and the comic strip rather than to the European expressionists, and its rather vaguely but amusingly stated theme—that the true spirit of America is to be found in the exuberance of popular music and dancing rather than in the mouthings of its politicians or preachers—fitted well the mood of the moment.

To audiences of the time it seemed that all these plays were alike at least in that they were characterized by a sincere forthrightness, a realistically honest facing of the facts, and a liberal attitude toward moral questions. The present-day reader, particularly if he happens to be young enough to know the twenties only as a historical epoch, is more likely to be struck by the almost complete absence in these supposedly serious plays of any reference to what he has come to regard as the only serious problems, those of politics and economics. The explanation of this seemingly curious fact is that, theatrically at least, the twenties, though commonly described as years of disillusion (and so pictured by the novelists), were fundamentally optimistic and self-confident.

No doubt this fundamental self-confidence was hardly compatible with the current disillusion concerning the results of the great war from which America had just emerged. No doubt it was hardly less compatible with the contempt freely expressed for the exuberant materialism of those who were proclaiming the new age in which everyone was to get richer and richer without limit or pause. But no foreign enemy was feared, the normal expectation of the young adult was that he would find in the world a place ready to receive him in the trade or profession of his choice, and it was generally believed that advancing liberalism in the moral realm was gradually making possible for the first time not only the good but also the rich life. Only the most frivolous of youth really deserved to have the age in which they lived labeled "the jazz age." It was also quite as truly the age in which the drama, like many novels, poems, and essays, exhibited, even when the form was satiric and protestant, a fundamental confidence that a world which had grown secure and prosperous might rather easily be made beautiful and happy also.

This attitude of confidence produced a multitude of plays and stimulated experiments with both form and ideas. Only the four most influential trends can here be considered, with a single playwright representing each, as judgment of literature so nearly contemporary must always be arbitrary and largely personal. These four trends were: (a) Maxwell Anderson's experiments with tragedy which, unlike those of O'Neill, assume that verse is necessary if the highest effects are to be achieved; (b) S. N. Behrman's development of a comic style not wholly different from that of his predecessor Rachel Crothers or his contemporary Philip Barry, but seeming to be more consciously aware of the problem of adapting conceptions of the nature of comedy to the circumstances of American life; (c) the work of Clifford Odets as representing the most successful cultivation of the play intended to further a definite political and social ideology; and (d) the attempt on the part of several otherwise diverse writers to develop a dramatic form in which symbolism and fantasy definitely replace the realistic method.

2

Poetic tragedy found a convinced advocate in Maxwell Anderson. Born in 1888, he had written more than a score of produced plays before 1945. Among the earliest of these were *What Price Glory* (with Laurence Stallings) and several light comedy-dramas; but suddenly in 1930 he revealed an entirely new style in the formal tragedy in verse, *Elizabeth the Queen*. Though from time to time thereafter he wrote pieces in several different manners, it is probably with the formal tragedy, frequently historical in subject but in some instances dealing with a contemporary situation, that his name is most often associated. Plays of this kind include, besides the first just mentioned, *Mary of Scotland* (1933), *Valley Forge* (1934), *Winterset* (1935), *Key Largo* (1939), and *The Eve of St. Mark* (1942).

Maxwell Anderson was the only conspicuously successful dramatist except O'Neill who persistently attempted tragedy during the first four decades of the twentieth century; but the parallel between him and the author of *Mourning Becomes Electra* cannot be drawn any further. While the style and methods of O'Neill have been at times almost freakishly unconventional and his plays more fundamentally than superficially in the great tradition, Anderson began by choosing subjects which would have been regarded as suitable by any writer of tragedies since Elizabethan times and by treating them in a manner which may have been quite unfamiliar to the average playgoer but was actually closer to Bulwer Lytton or George Henry Boker than to any of Anderson's contemporaries or immediate predecessors. That these plays were theatrically effective is sufficiently proved by their popularity with large audiences despite the prejudice against verse in the contemporary theater. Two serious criticisms were made with considerable show of justification; one was that, by choosing traditional subjects and treating them in a traditional manner, Anderson created something which could be more accurately described as a theatrically successful pastiche than as a genuinely modern tragedy; the other was that his verse, while speciously poetic, was too often inflated, banal, and monotonous.

To the second of these criticisms it might be replied that at least the verse was theatrically practicable, that a contemporary audience could understand and would accept it, while—to take as an example one of the few other modern plays in verse to receive professional production—T. S. Eliot's *Murder in the Cathedral* proved to be in many passages extremely difficult to follow. The other serious charge Anderson himself met when he produced *Winterset* in 1935 and demonstrated that he could treat a modern theme in the manner which he had previously reserved for historical tragedies.

The subject was obviously suggested by the Sacco-Vanzetti case. Seven years before *Winterset* appeared Anderson had collaborated with Harold Hickerson on a play called *Gods of the Lightning,* in which the same famous case had been literally—one might almost say journalistically—treated in one of the earliest American attempts "to make art a weapon" after a fashion which was to be widely advocated in the early thirties. *Winterset* seems, on the other hand, to be a conscious effort to draw the distinction between the journalistic and artistic treatment of a contemporary subject and an equally conscious effort to demonstrate that such a subject can be made the basis of a formal tragedy.

Long before the play begins, a radical agitator has been railroaded to death by a court which shared the popular determination to fix the guilt of murder upon a man whom it had other reasons to hate. More recently a college professor, reopening the case, has pointed the finger of suspicion at a gangster just released from prison, and thus a ghost has been raised to plague those who had had a part in the now almost forgotten events. The key to the mystery is held by a young witness lost in the obscurity of the lower depths, and upon him converge all those most deeply concerned: the actual murderer, determined at all costs to prevent the truth from coming to light; the outcast son of the man who paid the penalty for the crime he did not commit; and, finally, the presiding judge, now driven out of his wits by the unsuccessful effort to convince himself that he had done only what duty compelled him to do. Obviously there is in all this no lack of exciting action or of opportunities for direct sociopolitical argument. But both are subordinated, as they would be in a classical tragedy, to a brooding and poetic treatment of the themes which the action suggests; namely, the nature of guilt and of justice, and the meaning of revenge. If *Gods of the Lightning* constitutes what Anderson had, as a citizen, to say about the Sacco-Vanzetti case, *Winterset* is what he had, as a poet, to say about the same thing.

This play was markedly less successful in the commercial theater than several of the author's more conventional poetic tragedies, and some spectators raised the rather curious objection that "gangsters don't speak verse." Since the appropriateness or inappropriateness of elevated speech depends (as Shakespeare will sufficiently demonstrate) not upon the speaker's social or even intellectual status but upon the success of his creator in endowing him with an intensity of feeling for the expression of which the best utterance is none too good, this objection seems frivolous enough. It can be more reasonably alleged that the irregular blank verse of *Winterset* sometimes exhibits the characteristic turgidity of its author; but, for all this, there are reasons for maintaining not only that *Winterset* is its author's best play, but also that it is a striking and original one.

Anderson's subsequent plays include pieces as diverse as *The Masque of Kings* (1937), a romantic tragedy about Rudolph of Austria; the extremely popular, but not very original, fantastic comedy *The Star Wagon*; a romantic verse comedy, *High Tor*; a musical comedy, *Knickerbocker Holiday*; and a patriotic war play, *The Eve of St. Mark*. They also include *Key Largo* (1939), the only other piece which suggests obvious comparison with *Winterset*. Like the latter, it was not among the author's most conspicuous commercial successes, and it perhaps comes less close to the full realization of its intentions than *Winterset.* The situation is nevertheless a powerful one, and the central character—an ex-soldier trying to justify himself for a failure to perform a duty at the cost of his life—has an obvious relation to the judge in *Winterset.* Success was far more easily won by Anderson than it was by O'Neill. His originality is far less absolute; he generally seemed less eccentric to ordinary audiences, and either instinctively or through conscious design he adapted himself to the requirements of the modern stage instead of demanding, as O'Neill did, that the stage should adapt itself to him. The important fact that both have attempted to revive formal tragedy in the modern theater makes a comparison between them inevitable; but in every respect except this large general aim they seem to differ: Anderson showed, for example, the verbal facility which O'Neill so conspicuously lacked. Nevertheless, Anderson is to be ranked among the five or six most considerable playwrights of the two decades following 1925, and he represents one aspect of a movement which seemed, at least until the war arrested artistic development, likely to achieve something toward which the American drama had been struggling ever since the earliest of the "new playwrights" began to cultivate a "new drama"; namely, plays richer and more intense than the mere problem play can ever be.

## 3

At least at the beginning of his career, S. N. Behrman seemed to have dedicated himself to comedy as O'Neill did to tragedy, and pure comedy has been only somewhat less rare than genuine tragedy in the American theater. Sentimental folk drama tinged with comedy, and farce or melodrama tinged with sentiment had, of course, long provided one of the most popular genres. One may trace it from before the days of *David Harum* down through George M. Cohan's long series of plays with music and Winchell Smith's somewhat more sophisticated versions of the sentimental comedy which began in 1906 with *Brewster's Millions* and continued to achieve monotonously enormous successes until *"Lightnin'"* (1918) broke all previous records for length of run. But pure comedies—plays in which the comic spirit is recognized as something with which sentimentalism is fundamentally incompatible —had been so rare that when one has mentioned Langdon Mitchell's *The New York Idea* (1906) and Jesse Lynch Williams' very Shavian *Why Marry?* (1917) one has named the chief early examples. Behrman's *The Second Man* (1927) was, on the other hand, a drawing-room comedy which took as its theme the nature of the comic spirit here manifesting itself as the voice of a "second man" who whispers the witty counsels of common sense to the hero. As comedy it was "pure," both in the sense that it admitted no admixture of sentiment and in the sense that it so concerned generalized human nature rather than local conditions or customs as to seem almost abstract.

Two years later, Philip Barry, who had been producing plays at frequent intervals since 1923, turned aside from the rather whimsical style which had seemed his most characteristic one, to present in *Holiday* (1928) a witty drawing-room comedy somewhat closer than most of his previous works to high comedy in the usually accepted sense of that term; and two of his subsequent plays, *The Animal Kingdom* (1932) and *Bright Star* (1935), give him some claim to share with Behrman the distinction of being the most accomplished writer of comedy at once pure and smart. But in his writing he seemed to be a somewhat divided personality, so far from having dedicated himself to comedy that he could, on the one hand, revel in the rather cloudy mysticism of *Hotel Universe* (1930) and *Here Come the Clowns* (1938) and, on the other, purvey to an appreciative public the romanticism of *The Philadelphia Story* (1939). The result is that the impression produced by an attempt to consider his work as a whole is somewhat blurred and that, therefore, he seems less fit than Behrman to stand as our ablest exponent of the comic spirit.

Behrman was born in Worcester, Massachusetts, in 1893. Nothing in the quite ordinary details of his career—Clark University, Professor Baker's course in dramatic composition, work on the New York *Times,* and then as a theatrical press agent—helps to explain how he achieved at one bound the complete maturity of his powers and a mastery of the essential spirit of comedy. Nevertheless *The Second Man,* his first independent play, is as finished as anything he subsequently achieved.

His next important works, *Brief Moment* (1931) and *Biography* (1932), continued to cultivate the manner which he had just established. The hero of the first is a typical inhabitant of that intellectual world which its denizens have liked to call the Wasteland. But instead of gesturing magniloquently in the void and attempting to turn his predicament into tragedy despite the obvious absence of the necessary exaltation, he is content to analyze the situation intellectually and then to compensate for the absence of ecstasy by the cultivation of that grace and wit which no one can be too sophisticated to achieve. *Biography* is another vehicle for a comment made by the comic spirit upon one of the predicaments of modern life. Its heroine is a mediocre but successful portrait painter with a genius for comely living. Her dilemma arises out of the apparent necessity of choosing between two men, the one a likable but abandoned opportunist in public life, the other a fanatical revolutionary idealist. Her ultimate determination to choose neither is essentially a defense of her right to be a spectator and to cultivate the spectator's virtue—detached tolerance. The revolutionist says everything which can be said against her attitude. He denounces it as, at bottom, only a compound of indolence and cowardice, which parades as superiority when it is really responsible for the world's injustices. But the heroine sticks to her contention that neutrality is right for her. She may be useless while many persons less reasonable and less amiable than she are useful. But wit and tolerance are forms of beauty and, as such, provide their own excuse for being.

Such plays as these are obviously artificial, both in the sense that they deal with an artificial and privileged section of society and in the sense that the characters themselves are less real persons than idealized embodiments of intelligence and wit. Such actions as are represented could not take place, and such solutions to the problems presented could not seem valid except in a world fundamentally stable and comfortable because, as is usual in high comedy, all difficulties arise within the framework of the play itself and are solvable by common sense. If such a world seemed to many to exist during the twenties, it was already disappearing by the time *Biography* came to be performed, and the author himself soon felt the necessity of acknowledging in his plays the existence of forces with which the comic spirit is not capable of dealing. But instead of executing a complete about-face, as some of his playwriting contemporaries did, and attempting a kind of writing for which he had no gift, he devoted himself to exploring in dramatic terms the question whether the comic spirit could, while abandoning all attempt to present itself as a complete philosophy of life, nevertheless demonstrate that it had something to add to the discussions in which everyone was being compelled, willy-nilly, to take some part.

In *Rain from Heaven* (1934) we have what is basically the same situation as that in *Biography,* a wise and witty woman being brought into conflict with two men, each of whom is capable of a certain fanaticism incomprehensible to her. But in the earlier play, neither the Communist nor the practical politician is more than potentially dangerous; each is operating so nearly in a vacuum that the clash between them is chiefly a clash of temperaments and ideologies. In *Rain from Heaven,* on the other hand, another sort of crisis is near. One man, an aviator, is a popular American hero of the moment, being exploited by his brother in the interest of a vague Fascist scheme; the other is a German refugee. The scene has been moved to England, to an atmosphere charged with the possibility of proximate conflict. If the heroine elects again to remain to some extent "above the battle," there is, as there was not in *Biography,* a real battle to remain above. The exponent of the comic spirit is forced to approve the refugee's most uncomic decision to return to fight in his own homeland a dangerous battle over a matter of principle. When she attempts to defend the importance of "understanding" as opposed to even heroic passion, he replies that while you are trying to understand your enemy that enemy will kill you; and to this retort she can answer only that,

however useless people of her sort may seem now, some of them will somehow survive the storm and play a part in reestablishing the only kind of world
worth having.

Had Behrman happened to live in a more stable society he would doubtless
have written comedies more strictly in the great comic tradition than his later
plays. As it is, *Rain from Heaven* established a pattern into which his best
subsequent works—*End of Summer* (1936), *Wine of Choice* (1938), and *No
Time for Comedy* (1939)—tended to fall. Faced with the problem of writing
comedy in an atmosphere which many are ready to say makes comedy either
impossible or impertinent, he thus invented something which might not
improperly be called the comedy of illumination. This type of play touches
upon the graver issues of the moment, but it differs from the Shavian problem
comedy in two important respects: first, in its avoidance of Shaw's tendency to
beg the question in order to favor one side of the debate; and second, in its
persistent sympathy with those embodiments of the comic spirit who are
described by one of their enemies as "inhibited by scruple and emasculated
by charm." Behrman's wit enables him to make discussion really illuminating
and hence to write comedies which are neither merely didactic nor merely
trivial. Of the time in which he was fated to live, one may imagine that he has
often said: "O cursed spite, that ever I was born to set it right!" Yet he wrote
important comedies in an age which seemed to make them impossible.

4

In spite of the tendency of playwrights like Anderson and Behrman to
treat the issues of the moment with full seriousness, the play intended to
further a definite political and social ideology was slow in taking shape.
During the twenties, the epoch dominated by libertarian humanism, the Communist party was of course beginning to be heard of. But even to its members
revolution probably seemed pretty remote and the never widely attended
Communist-inspired plays which began to be produced at the New Playwrights' Theater—housed first in Fifty-third Street, later in Cherry Lane—
were extravagant and dilettantish rather than grim. Outside the definite Communist group, criticism of society meant usually a criticism of morals, manners, and tastes, not a criticism of political or economic institutions. If American life was denounced in the theater, as it often was, it was denounced as
crass, puritanical, unsophisticated, and nonintellectual rather than as capitalistic or fascist. Even political dissidence had little tendency to crystallize
into doctrine. Plays like *The Adding Machine* or *The Hairy Ape* were somewhat baffled considerations of the spiritual poverty of the underprivileged
rather than revolutionary protests, and a change in point of view did not
come until the crash of 1929. The depression which followed aroused wide-

spread doubt concerning the adequacy of libertarian humanism as a philosophy of life.

Both Anderson and Behrman responded somewhat to the changed atmosphere though neither changed fundamentally either his convictions or his style. Most of the other established playwrights, except O'Neill, reacted much more violently to the shock by attempting a fundamental reorientation plainly evident in their plays. Thus Elmer Rice, who had just before written in *Street Scene* a completely nonpolitical though completely sympathetic tragedy-melodrama about life in the slums, came out with a series of propagandistic plays; John Howard Lawson, who had celebrated America's exuberant health in *Processional,* turned to a Marxian denunciation of American decadence in *Gentlewoman* (1934) as well as in other didactic dramas; and Sidney Howard, who had produced a whole series of studies in manners and morals, wrote *The Ghost of Yankee Doodle* (1937). Inevitably, any new insurgent group was a political group, and the Theater Union, definitely committed to the propaganda play, was (or at least tried to be) for the new age what the Washington Square and the Provincetown Players had been for the old.

It would probably be pretty generally agreed that, except in the cases of O'Neill, Anderson, and Behrman, the work done by the established group under the new dispensation was less successful than that which it had done in the twenties. Of such newly emerging playwrights as George Sklar, Paul Peters, and Marc Blitzstein, on the other hand, much was promised. "Art is a weapon" became a frequently heard slogan, and for a time the theatrical scene seemed all but dominated by the Theater Union, by the somewhat less exclusively political but still definitely leftish Group Theater, and, finally, by the various units of the Federal Theater which sponsored the technique of the Living Newspaper as permitting the most direct treatment of social problems in theatrical form. None of these three institutions survives, none had a history comparable to that of the Provincetown or Washington Square Players. Of the new playwrights who arose to supply them with plays only one, Clifford Odets, made a notable place in the theater, and even he migrated to Hollywood in the forties. However truncated his career seems to have been, he deserves serious attention in any study of the recent American drama.

Though born in Philadelphia, Odets was educated in the public schools of New York City. While still quite young he joined a junior acting company originally sponsored by the Theater Guild and soon to become the independent Group Theater. He never achieved any prominence as an actor, but like most of the Group members he began to take an interest in the current discussion of social problems; and early in 1935 the Group filled out a short bill by the production of his brief tour de force called *Waiting for Lefty*. The public reaction was extremely favorable, and about six weeks later the Group offered his first full-length play, *Awake and Sing*.

*Waiting for Lefty* is ingenious and forthright rather than impressive as play writing. The stage is assumed to be the platform at a labor union meeting, and the audience to be the assembled members of the union. A proposed strike of taxi drivers is under discussion, "plants" in the audience arise to interrupt or protest, and flashbacks present scenes from the lives of various persons concerned. Word finally comes that the "Lefty" for whom all are waiting has been killed, and the action ends with the cry of "Strike! Strike!" Characterization is in simple black and white, much of the didacticism is crude as well as blatant; but at least *Waiting for Lefty,* unlike most plays offered as "weapons," might actually serve effectively as such. It was perhaps a recognition of this fact that aroused enthusiasm for the new author.

*Awake and Sing* exhibits virtues of quite a different kind. It is said to have been begun before its author's conversion to Marxism, and to have been hastily provided with the concluding scene in which a "revolutionary" moral is drawn. In any event, the general effect is dramatic rather than didactic and most reviewers recognized immediately an interesting new talent. The scene is a Bronx tenement. Most of the characters are part of a struggling Jewish family, the various members of which are held together by intense loyalties even though a clash of conflicting ideals and desires is going on in an atmosphere embittered by poverty. The milieu is certainly not unfamiliar on the stage, but it has seldom been described so vividly, so compassionately, or with so striking a combination of emotional intimacy and intellectual detachment. Ostensibly the moral is a revolutionist's moral, for the play ends when the young son of the family frees himself from his obsession with a purely personal rebellion against the poverty which separates him from his girl and determines to throw himself into the class struggle. Actually the subject is less this specific protest and rebellion than the persistent and many-sided rebellion of human nature against everything that thwarts it.

Odets was soon publicly claiming kinship with Chekhov, and a comparison between the two is less grotesque than it might seem. Chekhov's decaying aristocrats are at the opposite end of the social scale from the proletarians of *Awake and Sing,* but they are astonishingly like them in their self-centered absorption in the bitterness of their individual frustrations. It may very well be that Odets learned from the Russian his most striking stylistic trick, the writing of brisk colloquial dialogue in which much appears to be irrelevant or random, though all is actually very much to the point. His characters, like most of Chekhov's, reveal themselves by their very inability to communicate with their fellows; and, again like the characters of Chekhov, they cannot communicate because each is too absorbed in his own misery even to recognize the similar state of all around him.

It was certainly not from Chekhov that Odets learned a certain fierce faith in his people. Other historians of the oppressed have pictured them as dumb, brutalized, inarticulate, and despairing; but his characters all lead vivid lives within the limitations which Fate (or the injustices of our society) has imposed upon them, and this fact not only makes the best of his plays exciting but also redeems them from fundamental pessimism, however calamitous the outward events recorded may be. Moreover his implied faith that the human spirit is never defeated is by no means so identical with his faith in the Marxian doctrine as he would perhaps have liked to believe. In *Awake and Sing,* the young son who turns revolutionist is directing his determination into one channel; but the play strikingly demonstrates that the same determination may be directed into any one of many channels. Perhaps this young man's aim is, for the moment, the most intelligent and useful one. But the real secret of mankind's success, the real hope for its future, does not lie in anything so specific as one crusade or one determination. It lies in the persistence of man's passion, his unwillingness to accept defeat for his desires. He can go on indefinitely insisting that he will be happy and free, tirelessly protesting against the fact that he is not; and if, by chance, one generation does surrender there is always another wanting the old things with a young determination to have them. Odets' characters are ignorant and crude; but his play is exhilarating despite its tragedies, because he makes it so clear that people like this are going to go right on demanding of life more than it will give them.

During the same year which saw the first production of *Awake and Sing,* the Group Theater produced two other plays by the same author: *Till the Day I Die,* an undistinguished if earnest drama of Nazi brutality; and *Paradise Lost,* which Odets professed to regard as his most important work, but which to most critics seemed a highly doctrinaire, rather than convincing, study of American society in the process of a disintegration closely in accord with the pattern laid down in Marxian prophecy. Possibly because neither of these plays achieved great success, *Golden Boy* (1937) attempted, not wholly in vain, to tell in terms of the popular theater a story capable of conveying to the attentive a moral for the politically radical; and it was not until the following year that *Rocket to the Moon* again gave convincing demonstration of the fact that its author was a man of more than mediocre talents.

Many critics have insisted that *Awake and Sing* is Odets' best play; but *Rocket to the Moon* is at least comparable in merit though somewhat different in method as well as tone. Once more the scene is that of lower middle-class American life, and the principal characters are again distinguished by the intensity of their rebellion. But the story is more that of a few individuals than that of a loosely connected group, and there is nothing explicitly doctrinaire in the emphasis upon poverty as a dominant fact in their lives. The failure of an arrestingly presented situation to work itself out to any conclusion as striking as that which the exposition seems to promise, leaves the play somewhat less than completely satisfactory, but does not prevent it from being absorbing and impressive. On the other hand, neither *Night Music* (1940) nor *Clash by Night* (1941) was commercially successful, and neither adds to Odets' reputation, although the second reveals flashes of the dramatic power which made both *Rocket to the Moon* and *Awake and Sing* memorable.

After the outbreak of the Second World War, most radicals, including finally even the members of the Communist Party, became convinced that it was advisable to form with "capitalism" a "united front" against the Axis powers. One result was an effective dampening of their enthusiasm for revolutionary social criticism, and the "revolutionary theater" as a recognizable entity rapidly dissolved. Many new plays of social import were written, and audiences became larger than at any time since the twenties; but between 1939 and 1945 no one kind of play was persistently cultivated, and no new theatrical movement became discernible.

Many of the most successful pieces were adapted from popular novels, apparently because original plays did not appear in sufficient number to keep the theaters filled; and, while certain writers continued to use the stage to comment upon the war or its implications, their comments were usually either patriotic melodrama or the defense of some specific ideological line—which inevitably made them less works of the imagination than sheer polemics. Thus Robert Sherwood's *There Shall Be No Night* (1940) was widely praised for its statement of the case of Finland against Russia. Yet its author evidently regarded it as above all a work of propaganda and, when the political situation changed, revised the piece to provide new heroes and new villains.

Lillian Hellman's plays, despite the critical acclaim and popular success which some of them have won, have a propagandistic element which makes it difficult to take her artistic pretensions with full seriousness. She began with a powerful drama centering in a malicious child and called *The Children's Hour* (1934). Soon she devoted herself exclusively to social themes, first with *The Little Foxes* (1939), whose raison d'être is an implied criticism of capitalist society, and then with *Watch on the Rhine* (1941), in which violent condemnation of Nazi Germany is the main motivating idea. Both of these plays, like *The Searching Wind,* which was produced after the German invasion of Russia, exhibit considerable theatrical dexterity but suffer from the extent to which they appear to be limited by immediate political considerations. *Another Part of the Forest* (1947) deals with the same family as *The Little Foxes* and is theatrically the most dextrous of her plays.

5

When the modern drama was born in Europe the assumption was commonly made that naturalism was its normal method. In America, however, during the three decades after the founding of the Provincetown and the Washington Square Players, there was a strong tendency in an opposite direction, and even the Broadway audiences showed a willingness to accept fantasy, symbolism, poetry, and other deviations from the literal. This is surprising enough when one considers the supposed contemporary devotion to doctrinaire realism, or even when one remembers that the sentimental plays which dominated the late nineteenth and early twentieth century stages were usually presented in pseudorealistic terms. The least artistically self-conscious of audiences, during the second quarter of the twentieth century, accepted without surprise settings and methods of staging which would have seemed merely laughable to members of an earlier generation who had complacently accepted the box set and the convention of the fourth wall as the ultimate in theatrical art. What is much more important, general popular audiences accept, almost as readily, plays in which the imagination is given freer play than is possible in any work which confines itself to actuality.

Of the five modern dramatists given most extended consideration in this history, three, O'Neill, Anderson, and Saroyan, could not by any stretch of the term be called exclusively or even primarily realists. Marc Connelly's Negro fantasy *The Green Pastures* was tremendously successful in 1930, and Thornton Wilder's New England allegory *Our Town* won the Pulitzer Prize in 1938. Even the left-wing drama, though professing to be so practical in its implications, tended toward the expressionism cultivated by the earliest of the Communist-inspired groups and by John Howard Lawson in his *Processional* or, like many of the productions of the Theater Union and the Federal Theater, employed a symbolism which at times approaches the simple and directly translatable allegory of the old morality play. Moreover, a surprising number of isolated plays, presented in the commercial theater and directed, often with conspicuous success, toward a general audience, were frankly unrealistic and nonrepresentational; among them were *Our Town, On Borrowed Time, The Skin of Our Teeth,* and *The Glass Menagerie.* Moreover *Harvey,* winner of the Pulitzer Prize and one of the most successful plays of the 1944–1945 season, is realistic in method but highly fanciful in content. These sensational and sometimes merely eccentric deviations from the literal are possibly less significant as symptoms than the fact that O'Neill won success in formal tragedy or that Maxwell Anderson revived verse as the language of a genuinely popular play; but the various phenomena are not unrelated, and the ingenuities of the spectacularly nonrepresentational plays call unmistakable attention to a trend.

Among the symbolic plays which achieved conspicuous success during the forties, Thornton Wilder's extravaganza *The Skin of Our Teeth* (1942) and Mary Chase's engaging farce-comedy *Harvey* (1944) deserve special mention; but of the new playwrights who emerged between the debut of Odets and the middle of the forties only one, William Saroyan, has written often enough as well as originally enough to establish even a tentative claim to inclusion in any permanent list of American dramatists.

Saroyan's many plays are whimsical and symbolic to the extreme, yet he is only incidentally a playwright. For that matter he is also incidentally a novelist or short-story writer since he must be classed as a romantic egotist who lets himself go on paper. The fact nevertheless remains that he is gifted with an original vein of humor, sentiment, and fantasy which is delightful to those who can repress the irritation provoked by his adolescent pose of bumptious self-confidence. Born of poor Armenian parents in Fresno, California, he worked at various odd jobs, including that of messenger boy for a telegraph company; and in one of the many prose sketches which compose his spiritual—though presumably not factual—autobiography, he has described how a Mormon missionary converted him in the course of a few minutes to that "acceptance of the universe" which he has never lost. To the astonishment of a public accustomed to assuming that all serious young writers are bitter, disillusioned, despairing, and misanthropic, he volubly proclaimed his delight in a world so full to overflowing with a number of things that we should all be happy as kings if we would only, like him, relax, believe everything, and love the "beautiful people" all about us.

Of his several plays, only two, *My Heart's in the Highlands* (1939) and *The Time of Your Life* (1939), achieved any sort of conspicuous success; the second of these won the Pulitzer Prize and enjoyed a long run. Both are, however, a great deal more entertaining than any description is likely to seem, and both are perhaps best understood in the light of the author's complaint that the chief defect of American plays has been the lack of any "play" in them. *My Heart's in the Highlands* concerns a fantastically improvident and unsuccessful poet whose chief difficulty—getting something to eat for himself and his young son—is temporarily solved by the appearance of an old man who plays so sweetly on the bugle that the neighbors bring a tribute of eggs, fruits, and vegetables. In *The Time of Your Life,* a mysterious habitué of a waterfront saloon acts as deus ex machina in the lives of a group of fantastic unfortunates, and helps to rid the world of the only really ill disposed person in either play.

Inevitably the political- and the social-minded objected that such plays, far from being representative of reality, are merely fantasies, peopled by various projections of Saroyan's own personality who live in a daydream of their own. They are not impressed by such sly understatements as that at the end of *My Heart's in the Highlands,* where the poet's son brings the play to an end by remarking, "Don't say anything now but there is something wrong somewhere." Neither are they impressed by Saroyan's pervading implication that it is men who make "the system" rather than the other way around, and that if men were only happier they would make a better world to be happy in.

Technically the objection most often raised to Saroyan's plays is that, like his stories, they lack continuity, form, or unity. There is no doubt that they do, or that his later and less successful pieces like *The Beautiful People* and *Love's Old Sweet Song* were even looser and more inconclusive than the others. There is, however, a legitimate question whether or not the critics were wise when they urged upon the author a tighter theatrical form. Such form as he did achieve in *The Time of Your Life* was artificially imposed from without, and the more loosely written *My Heart's in the Highlands* is probably the better play of the two. The truth seems to be that Saroyan has composed daydreams, and that he is most convincing when the form is most dreamlike. The old man who plays the bugle does not come from anywhere. Like the Mock Turtle or Humpty Dumpty in *Alice,* he is simply there to be looked at before we pass on; and when, finally, he is "explained" as a fugitive from a home for superannuated actors, the explanation makes him less, rather than more, satisfactory—for reasons that are plainly Aristotelian. When he appears, asking for a drink of water and complaining that though he is present in California, his heart is as always in the Highlands, he is an example of the probable impossibility. As a runaway from an old men's home he is merely an example of the improbably possible. A good half-dozen of the fantastic personages in *The Time of Your Life* are similarly amusing, pathetic, and at least suggestive of certain realities which they do not literally imitate; and Saroyan is probably one of those authors who must be allowed, for good or ill, to go his own unorthodox way.

Saroyan is far too eccentric, both as a personality and as a writer, to be taken as typical of anything except himself. The fact that the theater of his day found some place for him does, however, serve to indicate how extremely eclectic that theater had become.

6

The revolution in the American theater which characterizes the twentieth century began when a group of new writers presented on the stage various stories told against the background of that new sophistication which not only the American intellectual but also a considerable part of the American population had somewhat self-consciously acquired from many sources, including more than a few European dramatists. Drama tended to remain up to date by treating themes current at any particular moment, and by treating them from current points of view rather than with the safe conventionality of most nineteenth century dramatists who, on the whole, were far more timid than essayists or writers of fiction. But this up-to-dateness, this topicality, imposes limitations even though it is, in itself and to a certain extent, a virtue. The brightly contemporary is often the transitory and journalistic, and most of the obviously outstanding dramatists were less topical than the general run, so that O'Neill wrote tragedy and Behrman wrote comedy while lesser men were inclined to stick closer to some immediate topic of the time.

Perhaps, then, the experiments with fantasy and symbolism and poetry so characteristic of the middle forties indicate a growing dissatisfaction of playwright and public alike with the limitations of a realistic treatment of current topics, and an obvious effort to gain intensity by exploring further methods not merely realistic and subject matter not essentially topical. On the whole, the novelists of these years were more successful than the dramatists in exploiting such subject matter, and the poets developed more highly experimental forms. But the drama, occupying a middle position, shared with writing unrestricted by the exigencies of stage and audience the creative vitality of the period, and the national theater was not wholly inhospitable to what the best playwrights could make of it.

# 79. POETRY — F. O. Matthiesson (Harvard)

Aᴍᴇʀɪᴄᴀɴ poetry in these years furnished the most serious evidence of a cleavage between what we have learned to call mass civilization and minority culture. Ignored for the most part by the large number of readers who hearkened to the novelists and playwrights, there were nevertheless more expert practitioners of the craft of verse during the twenty-five years before 1940 than during any other generation in our history. If we accept the proposition advanced by one of them, "Artists are the antennae of the race," the most sensitive registers of our spiritual and social well-being or malaise, we cannot ignore the poets' evidence, even though much of it may be disturbing. Indeed, in the view of the most influential poet of the 1920's, T. S. Eliot, one characteristic of authentic poetry, whether by Blake or by Æschylus, "is merely a peculiar honesty, which, in a world too frightened to be honest, is peculiarly terrifying."

Eliot's own career raises at once many of the most controversial issues. In some accounts of American literature he is omitted altogether on the ground that he lived in England during most of his maturity and became a British subject in 1927. Yet his work can no more be divorced from its American background than that of Henry James; and at a time when many European artists—including W. H. Auden, the leading English poet of his generation—are becoming American citizens, we must recognize that much of the future of art can only be international. Almost as controversial, however, is the value of Eliot's work, regardless of what country it belongs to. By 1940 he had already lived through two cycles of taste. In the early 1920's he was hailed as a revolutionary by the young survivors of the war, by "the lost generation" who read in him their feeling of the breakdown of tradition and their sense of being thereby liberated, if only into despair. But when he found his way out of the pit inhabited by "the hollow men" by means of a return to formal religion, he was dismissed by many of his followers as a reactionary. Yet his preoccupations, from first to last, show a singular consistency.

2

Before we can see his career in any perspective we must reckon with that of the craftsman to whom he dedicated *The Waste Land,* calling him, in

1335

Dante's phrase, "il migglior fabbro." The fact that Ezra Pound became an accused traitor can easily blind us to his previous services to modern art. In 1916, when the renaissance inaugurated by Harriet Monroe's magazine *Poetry* was still new Sandburg remarked that Pound "has done most of living men to incite new impulses in poetry." The propagandist for the Imagist movement in London, he had abandoned it when Miss Lowell took it over and transformed it into what he called "Amygism." He then moved on to further blasts and instigations. But his career antedated his appointment as the original European correspondent for *Poetry*. It might be said to have been officially inaugurated on that occasion in 1909 when he read aloud to his Soho friends his sestina, "Altaforte," and, according to a witness, "the entire café trembled."

The young American who could adapt one of the most delicate of Romance verse forms had just then begun his siege of London. His ancestors had been in America since the seventeenth century. His grandfather had moved from upper New York State to engage in the lumber business in Wisconsin. The poet himself had been born in Idaho, though his father soon returned East and became assayer at the United States Mint in Philadelphia. After graduating from Hamilton College and taking his Master's degree at the University of Pennsylvania (1906), Pound spent a year abroad in further preparation as a teacher of Romance languages. But his one appointment, at Wabash College, ended after four months with the mutual recognition that he was too much "the Latin Quarter type." He departed again for Europe to work on a doctoral thesis on Lope de Vega, but by the time he had printed, in a hundred copies in Venice, his first book of poems *A Lume Spento* (1908), the thesis had been dropped, and he had decided to remain abroad.

Pound's earliest poetry is saturated with medieval literature, with Provençal and Italian verse forms, with Arnaut Daniel and Guido Cavalcanti, whom he adapted freely. In the preface to his first book of criticism, *The Spirit of Romance* (1910), which was devoted to these same authors, Pound delivered several propositions by which he was able to abide throughout his work:

What we need is a literary scholarship, which will weigh Theocritus and Mr. Yeats with one balance . . . and will give praise to beauty before referring to an almanack. . . . Art is a fluid moving above or over the minds of men. . . . Art is a joyous thing. Its happiness antedates even Whistler; apropos of which I would in all seriousness plead for a greater levity, a more befitting levity in our study of the arts.

He had found our current attitude toward the arts particularly grim and barren, and said that when he left this country "there was no one in America whose work was of the slightest interest for a serious artist." His own attitude had been affected by the Pre-Raphaelites and the English aestheticism of the nineties; but he made his bridge from medieval to modern poetry mainly by way of his enthusiasms for Browning and Yeats. The fusion that Pound contrived between such seeming opposites is suggested by the title of his second book of verse—a title he also used for later collections—*Personae*. The word means "masks of the actor," which suggests Yeats' doctrine that the poet must objectify his emotions through finding his Mask or Anti-Self. It also suggests Pound's direct inheritance from Browning's *Men and Women*. Much of his work was to be monologue, in which, like Browning, he was concerned with "verse as speech"; but his technique is far more indebted to Yeats who, alone among his older contemporaries, was sufficiently concerned also with "verse as song." Pound's double gift of the musical phrase and the speaking voice is what challenged the admiration of so many other practitioners.

What he had to say was always less impressive. His view of his function was adumbrated in "Grace Before Song," the opening poem of his first book:

> As bright white drops upon a leaden sea,
> Grant so my songs to this grey folk may be.

To the first issue of *Poetry* he contributed "To Whistler, American," whom he hailed as "our first great," a sustaining force to the new generation:

> You and Abe Lincoln from that mass of dolts
> Show us there's chance at least of winning through.

But the masks Pound adopted were far less varied than Browning's. In "Altaforte" he was a medieval warrior; but he seemed far more in character in his guise of the faun in "Tenzone" or as the by then traditional Bohemian in "The Garret." In the course of his defense of Imagism, he defined an image as "that which presents an intellectual and emotional complex in an instant of time." Some of his best and shortest poems do precisely that, for instance his two-line "L'Art, 1910," in which he imitated the compression of the newly discovered Japanese poetry to convey another joyous discovery, that of the newest French painters:

> Green arsenic smeared on an egg-white cloth,
> Crushed strawberries! Come, let us feast our eyes.

In *Lustra* (1916), whose title was borrowed from the offerings made by the censors "for the sins of the whole people," he devoted a dozen or more poems to the discussion of the role of his own work. He was at his best when he was most light-handed, when he declared that his "chansons" had made "a considerable stir in Chicago," that they had been praised because they were really "twenty years behind the times," and concluded that their emotions were "those of a maître de café."

By then he had begun to make his most lasting contribution. He spoke of his translations as "but more elaborate masks," and demonstrated the accuracy of that statement with great fertility. His version of "The Seafarer" (1912), as subsequent poets recognized, was no mere tour de force; it reopened the possibilities for alliterative verse. On the basis of such poems as "The River Merchant's Wife" and "Exile's Letter" in *Cathay* (1915), Eliot declared Pound to be "the inventor of Chinese poetry for our time." Of course Pound did not know Chinese, and expressed his great indebtedness to the manuscripts of the late American scholar Ernest Fenollosa, for whose labors the poet gained wider recognition. When Pound produced his "Homage to Sextus Propertius" (1918) other scholars took him to task for inaccuracies in rendering the Latin; but his "more elaborate masks" are never strict translations. They are his most successful original poems.

That may be seen most clearly by contrasting his living version of the corruptions of Augustan Rome with "Mœurs Contemporaines" (1915), wherein his attempt to satirize his own surroundings seems thin and even smarty. In his discussions of the theory of poetry Pound may put an undue stress upon the importance of the "inventors," the discoverers of "a particular process" of technique, but it is natural for a man to exaggerate his own forte. When he had a subject matter provided for him, and could devote all his attention to his metrical and verbal inventions, he produced work of solidity as well as brilliance. When his masks were simply variants of himself, he often betrayed a human emptiness. The one great exception is *Hugh Selwyn Mauberley* (1920), where he was sustained by a major emotion, his reaction against the war, and was also challenged by Eliot's first dramatic monologues on the same theme. *Mauberley* is Pound's nearest approach to a criticism of his age. Its hatred of the futility of war is unforgettable, though Pound was far from being able to envisage any positive social goals. His versification is at its most accomplished here. He and Eliot had agreed to tighten up their verse by basing some experiments on the stanzas of Gautier, and when Pound let himself go again after this discipline, he created, in the flowing lines of his "Envoi," a masterpiece of subtle music.

In one of the last poems of this series he wrote as an epitaph:

> "I was
> And I no more exist;
> Here drifted
> An hedonist."

Though it may not have been apparent at the time, the Ezra Pound period was really over, the period in which he had been at the vortex of creative activity, had championed new poets as different as Frost and Eliot, and had helped to find an audience for Joyce and Lawrence. *Mauberley* was his farewell to London. He settled in Paris for four years and then went on to Rapallo. He kept up his interest in music, but was presently to be distracted by economics. In the meantime he had begun to publish his *Cantos,* the single poem with which he was concerned after *Mauberley.*

Two master craftsmen of the age spoke of the *Cantos* with great respect. Eliot cited them as the chief evidence that Pound's poetry "is an inexhaustible reference book of verse forms." Yeats accepted, at the end of the twenties, Pound's contention that when "the hundredth canto is finished," the whole would "display a structure like that of a Bach fugue." Certain recurrent themes, the Homeric descent into hell, one of Ovid's metamorphoses of men into beasts, passages from the history of Renaissance and Chinese courts and the American Revolution are meant to be counterpointed against passages dealing with the modern world to compose a musical pattern and to display persistent continuities between past and present. Pound kept repeating that "an epic poem is a poem including history," but neglected to remember that an epic poem also builds upon a narrative structure. On the basis of the seventy-one cantos that had been issued by 1940, it seems no longer necessary to believe that the whole could be more than the sum of the parts. And the parts are best described in the opening line of the eighth Canto, "these fragments you have shelved," a variant of the phrase Eliot used at the close of *The Waste Land.* Pound also revealed his initial conception in a sentence subsequently excised from the second Canto:

> the "modern world"
> Needs such a grab-bag to stuff all its thought in.

He further denoted his content as

> the usual subjects
> Of conversation between intelligent men,

and there is no denying the virtuosity of the sustained speaking voice, even though it divagated into seemingly endless monologue, and often left the reader dazzled by the surface texture of the language, but with the sensation that it was hardly saying anything.

Perhaps it would have been better if it had continued so, or if Pound had remembered his earlier declaration that he was "against all forms of oppression." But in the years of the slump he grew concerned with the problem of the distribution of wealth, and became a convert to Social Credit, which appealed as a panacea to several literary men. He perceived sharply the abuses of finance capitalism, though he seems never to have been greatly concerned with any poverty except that of the artist. He was increasingly isolated in Italy, less and less in touch with the actual state of society in either England or America. As a result of his interest in Chinese literature he began to believe that he could think in "ideograms," and worked out several fantastic equivalents, such as that if Jefferson had been alive in 1933 he would have acted as Mussolini had done. He also seems to have equated Fascist order with Confucian order, and to have allowed his hatred of "usury" to become a hatred of "international Jewry." He became a catastrophic instance of what can happen when the artist loses all foothold in his society. From the familiar position of the Bohemian thumbing his nose at the bourgeois he drifted to the point where, in pathological insecurity, he was obsessed with the question of monetary control to the exclusion of everything else. With no adequate equipment to judge such matters, he deludedly accepted Mussolini's kind of control as the answer. When the war came he was not a turncoat. He broadcast for the Fascists the same crackbrained ideas he had been expressing in prose and verse for more than a decade. But now they rendered him subject to the charge of the gravest crime in a nation's laws. Pound was finally brought back to America as a prisoner in 1945, and escaped trial only on the ground that his irresponsible judgment gave evidence of "a paranoid state."

3

Eliot arrived in London after the outbreak of the First World War. Like Pound he came abroad as a student engaged with a doctoral thesis; but his background and equipment were very different. Born in St. Louis, where his clergyman grandfather had been the pioneer in carrying the Unitarian church to that part of the Middle West, Eliot had studied philosophy at Harvard, and had also been influenced by Irving Babbitt's reaffirmation of classicism. He had spent a year at the Sorbonne, where he had listened to lectures by Bergson, and was in Germany when war was declared. He completed his thesis on F. H. Bradley's idealism, but did not return to Harvard to take his degree. His first published poem "The Love Song of J. Alfred Prufrock," appeared in *Poetry* in 1915; but his growing preoccupation with literary tradition as a necessary sustenance for mature art led him to settle in England. What he valued in tradition was represented by such a line of poet-critics as Dryden, Johnson, Coleridge, and Arnold, and he had found in his America, outside the special climate of the university, no living interest in any such succession.

His first book, *Prufrock and Other Observations* (1917), displayed a poetic orientation all his own. His chief masters were the Jacobean metaphysical poets and the French symbolists, not so unlikely a starting point for an American poet as might appear, since a taste for Donne and Herbert had been deeply rooted in New England from Emerson through Emily Dickinson, and Baudelaire and his followers had been inspired by Poe. The witty and ironic conversational tones of Eliot's earliest poems are most akin, among the symbolists, to Laforgue, but a graver spirit than Laforgue's can already be discerned beneath the surface of what seemed to most of its first readers to be a mocking vers de société. The epigraph to "Prufrock" was taken from Dante, about whom Pound had also been enthusiastic. But their divergence of interest in this master was the same as it was regarding Henry James. In both cases Pound was primarily occupied with pointing out the technical excellences. Eliot penetrated more deeply into the meaning of the texts. His predominant interest is suggested in his remark that James' "real progenitor" is Hawthorne, and that the essential quality common to both these Americans is their "profound sensitiveness to good and evil."

A much firmer critic than Pound, Eliot was to teach, through both his verse and his prose, a way of seeing and feeling to a younger generation. Pound may first have stimulated him to realize that the authors of the past and present should be judged with equal eyes, that a sense of the past is not "of what is dead, but of what is already living." But Eliot's ethical values gave him far more insight into the meaning of history, just as his projection of spiritual struggles endowed his monologues with a dramatic tension quite missing in Pound's. As a result his Prufrock, Sweeney, and Gerontion, sparely drawn as they were, became some of the most living characters of their time. Prufrock, the fastidious and futile middle-aged product of the genteel tradition, and Sweeney, the tough Irishman "assured of certain certainties," are Eliot's chief response to the decadent Boston he knew as a young man, when the gulf between Back Bay and the common life of the South End was so great as to cause him to say that the former's "society" was "quite uncivilized, but refined beyond the point of civilization."

In "Gerontion" (1920), the leading poem in his second book, Eliot presented, through the *persona* of the old man, the mood of disillusion most symptomatic of the postwar era. He also produced one of the most significant examples of his dramatic method. This poem makes clear why he believed that Baudelaire, by using "the imagery of the sordid life of a great metropolis" and by raising it "to the first intensity," had "created a mode of release and expression for other men." Such a belief divides Eliot sharply from the generation of Frost. Eliot did not see man in the country but in the city. He did not see the self-assured Emersonian individual, but men in a chaotic society consumed with doubt. He had been attracted to the metaphysicals because their poetry had also sprung out of self-consciousness, out of the need to express not merely lyric feeling, but likewise the "hard precision" of thought. While reflecting on the achievement of the school of Donne, he made one of the most revelatory statements of his own aims:

> It is not a permanent necessity that poets should be interested in philosophy, or in any other subject. We can only say that it appears likely that poets in our civilization, as it exists at present, must be *difficult*. Our civilization comprehends great variety and complexity, and this variety and complexity, playing upon a refined sensibility, must produce various and complex results.

Such, in his view, were the compelling grounds for devising the compressed, elliptical, and allusive method of his dramatic monologues. Only in such a way could he suggest the real fusion between feeling and thought in living brains, and, at the same time, pass beyond the too narrowly personal masks of Pound to portraits of a more general and more significant relevance.

He was not interested in experimentation for its own sake, since he noted, while discussing Wordsworth, that "any radical change in poetic form is likely to be the symptom of some very much deeper change in society and the individual." The imagists were on a false track in their attempted loosening of form, since "no *vers* is *libre* for the man who wants to do a good job," and since "the very life of verse" consists in the "constant evasion and recognition of regularity," in the precarious balance between monotony and flux. He had thought as persistently about the question of language, and held that it was the poet's responsibility to be as aware as possible of the historical weight of connotation behind the words he was using, and to master a diction that could range from the most erudite to the most colloquial, as the mind of the educated man must range.

As he extended his technical resources from "Gerontion" to *The Waste Land* (1922), he also demonstrated what he meant by a poet's "sense of his own age." This is something very different from a sense of journalistic surfaces, since it involves a recognition of the permanent no less than of the changing. As an inheritor of the nineteenth century's determination to repossess all of history, modern man could often have the feeling, as Eliot remarked in Joyce, "of everything happening at once." The duty of the critic was to train himself to the point where he could embrace the whole of literature since Homer as having "a simultaneous existence" in his mind, and composing "a simultaneous order." The philosophical historian must discern the phenomenon of cyclical recurrence, and thus the contemporaneity of various cultures. But such an extension of knowledge could become an oppressive burden if it left man with the feeling of "being too conscious, and conscious of too much." As Gerontion had cried out in a memorable line, "After such knowledge, what forgiveness?" Eliot had been profoundly impressed by Frazer's *Golden Bough,* but he had realized that the effect of comparative anthropology is both a freeing and a destruction, that taboos are removed but sanctions wither.

He gave voice to this awareness in *The Waste Land,* the most ambitious long poem of the period. Its structure is the opposite of the diffusion of the *Cantos,* since Eliot attempted to compress the essence of an epic into a poem of hardly more than four hundred lines. He omitted logical connectives, and the reader must find his way through this "music of ideas" in a way somewhat analogous to associating recurrent themes in a symphony. Eliot was much attacked for this method, though it was in deliberate keeping with his reasons for believing why modern poetry must be difficult. In the effort to give further coherence to his structure he borrowed a device from Henry James, and introduced Tiresias, the prophet who had "foresuffered all," as a central observer who *"sees,* in fact, the substance of the poem." *The Waste Land* may not succeed as a whole, it may exist simply as a succession of dramatic lyrics. But it interpenetrates the present and the past, it manages to treat on the same plane modern London and the world of primitive myth, and to probe thereby at the root causes of cultural decay. In discerning the imaginative possibilities in the use of myth, Eliot was at one with the leading creative minds of the age. He knew that he had found "a way of controlling, of ordering, of giving a shape and a significance to the immense panorama of futility and anarchy that is contemporary history."

Eliot could envisage the modern metropolis as an Inferno more affectingly than Pound could in the *Cantos,* since, as he observed, Pound's "is a Hell for the *other people,* the people we read about in the newspapers, not for oneself and one's friends." This complacency, this lack of feeling implicated in the struggle with evil, necessarily rendered much of Pound's observation of human beings "trivial and accidental." Eliot's peculiar intensity comes from his conviction that poetry must spring out of suffering. What excited the first appreciators of *The Waste Land* were its astonishing juxtapositions, its sudden transitions from the witty to the serious, its bewildering variety of literary allusions, its passages of satire and its passages of lyric beauty, and its unfailing expertness in phrasing. Few recognized sufficiently, even when Eliot reached the pit of his Inferno in "The Hollow Men" (1925), how terrifying an exposure he was making of the emptiness of life without belief, or that his main theme was how much of modern life is merely death. That his overwhelming sense of the need for redemption must finally transform Eliot into a religious poet was not apparent to many at that time.

4

The most striking evidence of Eliot's pervasive influence upon even the most vigorous younger imagination of the 1920's is provided by Hart Crane's *The Bridge* (1930). Crane's short life is a record of the disintegration that can result from modern rootlessness. Born in Garrettsville, Ohio, the son of well-to-do but incompatible parents, his high-strung nervous system was to display in its instability lasting scars from the tensions between them. No one seems to have paid much attention to his education, and he was allowed to be on his own in New York in 1916, nominally preparing for college, but actually immersing himself in the new poetry. He was soon to declare that he considered Pound second only to Yeats among living poets in English, and was then to share in the contemporary excitement about the symbolists and the Elizabethan dramatists, with a particular taste for Rimbaud and Marlowe.

His first poems, collected in *White Buildings* (1926), reveal the extent to which he had been affected by the French poets' experiments with handling language plastically, with the "color" and weight" no less than the sound of words. He spoke of wanting to capture the "illogical impingements" of connotations, and of depending only upon "the logic of metaphor." He aimed to express the kind of heightened consciousness that he evoked in "Wine Menagerie," the ecstasy that hovered between music and drunkenness. The resulting poems were very dense and obscure, though some of them, like his elegy "Praise for an Urn," were sustained by a compelling rhetoric. In his series of "Voyages" this rhetoric took on a deep sonority in response to his feeling for the sea and for Melville.

In "The Marriage of Faustus and Helen" (1922–1923) he showed the effect of Eliot's interpenetration of past and present by recasting the myth in jazz rhythms, in what he called a "symphonic" form. But he was already concerned with "an almost complete reverse" of Eliot's direction. Instead of disillusion and renunciation he was bent upon "a more positive goal," and he defied his skeptical generation by affirming his belief in "ecstatic vision." *The Bridge,* upon which he worked intermittently for half a dozen years, was designed to be his most important refutation of *The Waste Land.* Convinced of the necessity for poets to repossess the amplitude of myth, his was to be "the myth of America" from our earliest history. The content of his poem was to be an "organic panorama, showing the continuous and living evidence of the past in the inmost vital substance of the present," and its title was meant to suggest an equally vital span into the future. His declared master was Whitman, since Crane wanted an expansive identification with our life in order to be able to make his "mystical synthesis."

But his immense difficulty in finishing this poem, and the stylistic inequality between its parts, betray how much of it was a mere act of will and not a product of his deepest consciousness. His awareness of American history was hardly more than of a romantic spectacle. He had taken the leap from the time of "Powhatan's daughter" into modern New York with nothing to sustain him. What affirmation could he make when he knew only the breakdown of his family, and no community except a shifting metropolis? Cast off by his father, who disapproved of his being a poet, he often had lived on the ragged edge of poverty. Partly in consequence of his early emotional insecurity, he was a homosexual. Unlike Rimbaud, as Allen Tate remarked, Crane did not cultivate "derangement"; his disorder was ingrained and almost inescapable. No matter how strong his admiration for Whitman, his tortured sensibility was far more akin to Poe's, whose ghost he invoked in his hallucinated passage portraying the subway.

He knew that the modern poet needs "gigantic assimilative capacities," and he struggled hard over his structure. But he came to depend more and more on an exaltation difficult to capture. He managed to possess it during some summer weeks in the Caribbean in 1926. "I feel an absolute music in the air again," he said, "and some tremendous rondure floating somewhere." He attained his single fullest interval of production, but was again dispersed as soon as he got back to New York. *The Bridge,* when finally published, was far less of a whole than *The Waste Land.* It veered from passages of the purest poetic energy, as in the proem to Brooklyn Bridge, "The Harbor Dawn" and "The River," to other passages of sentimental tawdriness. In one of the most perceptive essays by one of our poets about another, Tate, while recognizing Crane's immense gifts, pointed out his utter failure to rise, in his conclusion, "Atlantis," to the passage from the *Paradiso* which is his source. Crane's failure was that of the romantic ego to find any sanctions outside itself. His "vision" had degenerated into sensationalism.

With the depression Crane did not share in the growing social and economic interests of many of his friends. He felt those interests to be largely a substitute for creative work. But he was unable to settle to anything sustained. He went to Mexico on a fellowship, but he dissipated there even more heavily. On the boat home, after a year with nothing done, and following a night of drinking, he committed suicide by jumping overboard. He felt, in his terrible violent restlessness, that he had reached a dead end. But despite his disintegration he had never given up his belief that "a real work of art" is "simply a communication between man and man, a bond of understanding and human enlightenment." In such lyric passages as his evocation of the Mississippi, at the close of "The River," he had attained his "absolute music," and an eloquence which has been rivaled in magnificence by few American poets.

Diametrically opposed to Crane's promiscuous immersion in the modern city are the exponents of Southern regionalism. As Tate argued: "Only a return to the provinces, to the small self-contained centers of life, will put the all-destroying abstraction, America, safely to rest." Such a line of argument separates the Nashville agrarians from Middle Western regionalists like Sandburg and Lindsay, who were largely followers of Whitman. Another feature, which distinguishes them from any recent talents in New England, is that for many years, beginning with their magazine the *Fugitive* (1922–1925), they worked together as a group and issued such joint pronouncements as *I'll Take My Stand* (1930). Some of the values that they held in common were their preference for the concrete and the localized as against the abstract and the generalized; and when they spoke in philosophical terms they dwelt on the necessity to offset the domination of a dehumanized scientific rationalism by the richer resources of imagination. Their politics were devoted to the preservation of tradition, and seeing the local menaced by the national, particularly through industrialization, they protested against the machine and against money values as the causes of modern rootlessness. Tate called himself a "reactionary," and some of the less clear minds of the group, taking their stand even against the racial reforms of the New Deal, drifted dangerously close to native Fascism.

Wholly free from such implications is John Crowe Ransom, who as a teacher of literature at Vanderbilt University was the moving force behind the *Fugitive*. Ransom is a poet of very limited production, the bulk of whose verse appeared in *Chills and Fever* (1924) and *Two Gentlemen in Bonds* (1927). If he could have managed to write poetry of so much suavity and elegance in any previous period of our history, he would be known by now as the kind of artist of whom we have had too few, the minor poet, not of promise but of a remarkably integrated and mature performance within his limitations. He is a serious wit in a sense akin to the seventeenth century poets, though he seems to have shaped his style independently of their revival, and to have received the impetus for his character studies rather from Hardy's *Satires of Circumstance*. He reflected on how a living tradition may make its adjustment to the Southern past in poems like "Antique Harvesters," where his diction is properly both slightly archaic and conversational. But his main theme is that of the divided sensibility, torn between reason and imagination, between science and faith. As he says in "Man Without Sense of Direction," he concentrates primarily on portraying the kind of character "who cannot fathom nor perform his nature." To the exposure of such states of consciousness he brings his most distinguishing gift, an irony which, as R. P. Warren pointed out, differs basically from all our familiar variants of romantic irony, since it is not used as a means of escape from an individual's predicament. Ransom's irony, in its experienced acceptance of human limitations, is an inheritance from Socratic irony, and is a device for gaining knowledge by offsetting any abstract ideal against a concrete actual. His poems, avoiding thereby any oversimplified statements, possess a remarkable fullness of body.

Allen Tate, growing up in the period when Eliot's criticism was making its first impact, shows in much of his verse the kind of intellectualization from which Eliot's richer lyrical impulse saved him, the intellectualization of a mind in which the analytical function outruns the creative. Despite Tate's objection to the limiting abstractness of so much modern knowledge, many of his poems are conceived very abstractly. He indicates his kinship with Ransom in remarking: "I often think of my poems as commentaries on those human situations from which there is no escape." In "The Last Days of Alice" he presents his version of the difficulty of belief in a mathematician's age; in "The Wolves" he probes to the sources of recent neurotic fear. In his best known poem, "Ode to the Confederate Dead," he deliberately contrasts the "active faith" of the Southern past with the contemporary "solipsism . . . that denotes the failure of the human personality to function properly in nature and society." Despite too numerous echoes of Eliot and Valéry, Tate's structure and rhythm have attained here a rare elevation and dignity.

If Tate's poetry reveals the results of tastes formed closely upon Eliot's, that of Robert Penn Warren, the youngest of the Fugitive group, furnishes the fullest evidence of what it meant to begin writing verse when the metaphysical poets had just been revived as a central influence upon creative activity. Some of Warren's early poems, especially "The Garden" and "Love's Parable," are thorough responses to the possibilities of reintroducing techniques like those of Marvell. Warren paid the price of his preoccupation with intellectual complexity by sacrificing almost any audience for his poetry except other poets and critics. But just after 1940 he was to start breaking away from such tight organization as he had used in poems of great moral weight like "Original Sin" and "Terror." In his "Ballad of Billie Potts" he renewed his approach to Southern history and made an attempt to combine what Yeats called "the poetry of the folk" and "the poetry of the coteries."

## 5

The diversity of the poetry of this time and the impossibility of arranging it into any single pattern may be sufficiently indicated by noting that Robinson Jeffers was born only a year before both Ransom and Eliot. His purposes are as far removed from either of theirs as the six thousand miles that separate Carmel and London. Born in Pittsburgh, the son of a Presbyterian theologian, he was educated partly in Europe, and manifested a range of intellectual curiosity by making some study of medicine, forestry, and zoology in various institutions on the Pacific coast. His first volume of poems, *Flagons and Apples* (1912), is as conventionally romantic as it sounds. He registered no response to any of the new poetic movements, and not until a dozen years later, in his narrative poem *Tamar,* did he find a voice of his own. In *The Tower Beyond Tragedy, Roan Stallion* (1925), and *The Women at Point Sur* (1927), he established both his content and his philosophy.

The plots of his long poems are of an unrelieved violence, presenting incest, rape, and murder, usually against the background of the bare California headlands and valleys. He chose this material deliberately. He insisted that since the First World War physical violence was no longer "anachronistic" in our lives; and he justified his treatment of sexual perversions on the ground that he wanted to "strip everything but its natural ugliness from the unmorality." Beyond that he developed his stories to present a thesis: "There is no health for the individual whose attention is taken up with his own mind and processes; equally there is no health for the society that is always introverted on its own members." That thesis would seem to rest on a basic confusion between psychology and politics, since the normal way for an individual to escape from excessive introversion is through a more outgoing interest in human society. But Jeffers holds, "Humanity is the mold to break away from, the atom to be split," and he carries his inhumanity to the point of announcing that "the unsocial birds are a greater race." In the light of such views it is no wonder that he possesses very little ability to represent dramatic action, since his characters exist only as symbols and stereotypes.

Some of his shorter poems are far more moving, since he has a broad descriptive mastery of his spectacular coast of granite and cypress, and his other interest in the exact processes of science enables him to give almost clinical accounts of moments of death—of man as well as of the "nobler" hawk. The form that he devised may superficially suggest Whitman, but though he believes that "a tidal recurrence is the one essential quality of the speech of poetry," he went far beyond Whitman in his understanding of the possibilities of accentual prosody, and of the "quantitative" value of his unstressed syllables. His handling of such verse, though monotonous in long stretches, is capable of passages of a grave majesty.

His view of the future of America is at the opposite pole from Whitman's. Jeffers' admirers have often spoken of him as universal, as beyond the restrictions of time or place, but he may best be understood as a peculiar kind of regionalist, a spokesman for the "continent's end" when the frontier movement was over, and the poet was aware of the oppressively luxuriant growth of Los Angeles and Hollywood. "Ascent to the Sierras," "Haunted Country," and "Apology for Bad Dreams" all offset primitive and austere nature against an overrich and soft civilization. In "Shine, Perishing Republic" (1926) he already dwelt on the decadence of American society, and revealed the extent to which he had been influenced by Spengler. With the depression and the advance of Fascism, he merely kept repeating that "civilization is a transient sickness." He declared that we had gutted and exploited a continent in our reckless western onrush, and that we deserved no better fate than to be oppressed by an imperialistic Caesar. He believed that in such times an individual must "isolate himself morally to a certain extent or else degenerate too." From his tower retreat at Carmel he averred that he was merely a "neutral" recorder of social decay. But he scorned the city proletariat, and insisted on the futility of any radical social reform. His irrationality also drove him to the length of announcing, despite his lifelong pacifism, that he preferred the greater dignity of "blind war" to any economic planning. In "Rearmament" he betrayed the unconscious worship of force to which his acceptance of Spengler had brought him by celebrating the "beauty" in "the disastrous rhythm . . . of the dream-led masses down the dark mountain."

## 6

In the years just at the end of the First World War when college undergraduates were more excited about contemporary American poetry than they had ever been before, such sinister thoughts were farthest from their minds. The popular taste of the twenties can be best caught in Edna St. Vincent Millay and Stephen Vincent Benét. Miss Millay's "Renascence" (1912) heralded her arrival at Vassar from Maine, and already contained the essence of what was to make her popular: an innocent freshness toward nature, which is none the less compounded out of the attitudes of the English romantic poets. She was soon to add the gamin boldness of the Greenwich Village Bohemian, and her quatrain about the candle burning at both its ends was hailed by the young anti-Victorians as their "Psalm of Life."

Her audience was increased by *Second April* (1921) and *The Harp-Weaver* (1923), and she was praised particularly by those who disliked the new intellectual poetry. The critical division over her work may be observed in the reception accorded *Fatal Interview* (1931). Some did not hesitate to liken this sonnet sequence to Shakespeare's. Others, upon more exacting scrutiny, insisted that even the most striking of these sonnets, such as "O sleep forever in the Latmian cave," did not wholly escape incoherence of feeling and blurred syntax. The fairest comparison for Miss Millay's qualities and limitations would be with the posthumous sonnet sequence by Elinor Wylie in *Angels and Earthly Creatures* (1929). Turning seriously to poetry only during the last decade of her life, Mrs. Wylie demonstrated how a romantic sensibility could be strengthened and purified by a taste for the metaphysicals, whereas, despite the phrase from Donne that forms her title, Miss Millay's sonnets remain enthusiastically but loosely Keatsian. Mrs. Wylie was the more mature craftsman, even though her personal distinction may have caused her friends to exaggerate her original force. As Morton Zabel said in reviewing her work: "In literature, as in life, there is room only for a few important experiences, but for many amenities." Her rewarding amenity is her deft and delicate control of her traditional medium, in contrast with most of Edna Millay's work. Miss Millay is at her best when freest from any emulation of other writers, in a poem like "The Return" (1934), the simplest kind of personal lyric. When she tried to go beyond lyrics, she showed little skill—though she produced, to be sure, in *The King's Henchman* (1926), a workmanlike libretto for an opera. She shared generously in the protest against the execution of Sacco and Vanzetti, but the poems she wrote on that occasion are hardly memorable. When she sought, under the growing pressures of the late thirties, to stir up an awareness of international problems, she fell into thin sentiment and hackneyed phrases.

Stephen Benét, as the son of an army officer, was brought up in various parts of the United States, and absorbed an interest in the American scene and its historical background. His precocious first poems gave evidence of another absorption, in the literary ballad as handled by William Morris and other late nineteenth century poets. He was to fuse these two interests in some of his best work, ballads using the material of American folklore and humor, of which "William Sycamore" (1923) is probably the most notable. Like Edna Millay he was also to participate in the gay revolt against the Victorians, particularly in the ebullience of "For All Blasphemers."

In *John Brown's Body* (1928) he solidified his gifts and produced the most widely read long poem of the period. In the view of some readers this work established Benét as the first national poet of the dimensions called for by Whitman; but Harriet Monroe characterized it as "a cinema epic." Composed within a couple of years, this full-length novel in a variety of verse forms testifies to its author's technical facility, as well as to his gusto for the personalities of the Civil War. But there are many slack pages, his fictional plots are rather expected, and most of his characters are two-dimensional. Such a work raises the problem of popular art in modern society. Benét's talents have not been considered as of anything like the first order by many other poets; and *John Brown's Body* has kept its largest following among readers under twenty. But such an audience is not to be scorned in a democracy, and Benét's share in reviving the bright colors of our heroic legends puts him squarely in the succession from Longfellow and Lindsay. The most striking defect of this poem is in its passages of reflection, which skip over grave problems with a delusive jauntiness. Benét had grown to understand more of our history when he wrote his "Ode to Walt Whitman" against the background of the depression; and in "Litany for Dictatorships" (1936) and "Nightmare at Noon" (1940), he looked ahead, much more affectingly than Miss Millay, to the menace of the war. In *Western Star,* the first section of a long poem on which he had been working for some years at his death, he still manifested the same warm feeling for the American land, if little advance in technique beyond his first attempted epic.

Archibald MacLeish, who was at Yale just ahead of Benét, performed another serviceable function by being a kind of middleman of taste between the experimenters and the general public. Reading his work from *The Pot of Earth* (1925) down to *America Was Promises* (1939) is to be presented with a chronicle of the dominant new influences in that period. He began writing verse as an undergraduate, but he dated his own poetic career from 1923, when he gave up the practice of law and went to live in France. At that time he reflected Eliot's interest in *The Golden Bough,* particularly in the theme of cyclical death and rebirth. He also utilized Eliot's technique of sudden contrasts to convey the broken rhythm of contemporary existence. A few years later, in "Land's End," he was bringing to American readers the wide-space imagery of Perse's *Anabase.* He demonstrated how much he had learned from Pound's versification in *Conquistador* (1932), and in its most successful portion, "Bernál Diaz' Preface to His Book," he extended the world-weary attitude of Gerontion. But he had returned to America by the end of the twenties, and was soon responding to the new mood of social protest. His *Frescoes for Mr. Rockefeller's City* (1933) was dedicated to Sandburg, and in *Public Speech* and his radio play, *The Fall of the City,* he caught up some of the tones and accents of the younger poets, particularly Auden. MacLeish was characterized throughout these years by generous enthusiasms, as well as by a sensitive ear, but he was too suggestible to possess a style quite his own. The conspicuous exception was in some of his short lyrics, like "The Too Late Born," or "You, Andrew Marvell," authentic expressions of his own elegiac emotion.

## 7

The period to which MacLeish served as a barometer was notable for a great deal more experimentation than can even be suggested here. Indeed, a leading aim of such an experimentalist as E. E. Cummings is to make it impossible to describe one of his poems or to do anything less than respond to its unique essence. His idiosyncratic treatment of punctuation and typography, which either excited or distracted his first readers, is his way of catching the eye and compelling attention. His content is actually very simple. He is a lyricist of romantic love, who is also a romantic anarchist in the New England tradition, and believes that a poem is an inspired moment breaking through the bars of syntax. His preoccupations hardly vary from the time of *Tulips and Chimneys* (1923). "Mostpeople" are frozen into conventional death, whereas "there's nothing as something as one"; the individual alone is alive, and that life is freshened by love, by "wonderful one times one." In his fleeting attention to "manunkin" in the mass Cummings strikes a note of colloquial satire against some of its misleaders, particularly the advertiser and the warmonger.

Conrad Aiken, at Harvard with Eliot, is an experimentalist of a different sort from Cummings. His poems are not designed to startle and shock the reader into an awareness of life's potential freshness. On the contrary, Aiken lulls the reader with a seductive music, and transports him into the dreamworld of Freudian fantasy. He was skeptical from the outset of Amy Lowell's Imagists because of their lack of emotional force, and took exception to their content as merely "the semi-precious in experience." But his own double concern with music and psychology served unwittingly to rob most of his many long poems of any great energy. In evoking "the melody of chaos" his series of *Preludes* risked what Yvor Winters has called "the fallacy of imitative form." Their lines tended to deliquesce into a murmuring indefiniteness of language, into a realm where the consciousness is blurred and "the maelstrom has us all." Aiken escaped from this dilemma through the more concrete imagery of some of his poetry dealing with the impact of the city upon the sensitive observer. In "Discordants" and "Senlin" he was writing poems of this sort at the same time as Eliot's earliest work; and he returned to this genre, with very seasoned technical resources, in *Brownstone Eclogues,* at the beginning of the forties.

Two other experimentalists whose importance cannot be more than stated were both friends of Pound when he was a student at the University of Pennsylvania. William Carlos Williams was then in the medical school, while Marianne Moore was an undergraduate at Bryn Mawr. Williams, of mixed English, French, Spanish, and Jewish extraction, was to make his living as a doctor, mainly to the working class in Rutherford, New Jersey. That fact had a considerable effect on his work. Very responsive at first to the Imagists, he grew to see that their kind of poetry fell short because it lacked "structural necessity." Even more significant, his sensual delight, like Lawrence's, soon became grounded in the homeliest images of our common life. He defined "the classic" as "the local fully realized, words marked by a place"; and, diverging farthest from Pound, he added a warm sympathy with ordinary people to an ability to discover beauty in the midst of the impoverished and the sordid. Many—perhaps most—of his poems were far too casual, in the imagist mode which he never quite outgrew, but at his best, in "By the road to the contagious hospital" or "The Yachts," he reinforced his unfailingly vivid notations by impressive structures.

Marianne Moore drew attention to the genre to which her poetry belongs by calling one of her few books *Observations* (1924). When asked once what distinguished her, she answered: "Nothing; unless it is an exaggerated tendency to visualize; and on encountering manifestations of life—insects, lower animals, or human beings—to wonder if they are happy and what will become of them." She was called an "objectivist," as Williams had styled himself, and Kenneth Burke offered this definition for her kind of work: "In objectivism, though an object may be chosen for treatment because of its symbolic or subjective references, once it has been chosen it is to be studied in its own right." That helps account for the loving care with which she studied the jerboa or a fish or Peter the cat. She is feminine in a very rewarding sense, in that she makes no effort to be major.

Her versification, which was praised by both Eliot and Wallace Stevens, is like no one else's. She composes not by feet but by syllables: the result is not free verse but a formal, sometimes light, sometimes rigid pattern. She described her intentions by saying: "Over accent and over emphasis are to be avoided . . . and I feel that mathematics as we have it in music, can be of inestimable help to a poet." The danger in such deliberate work is always dryness, but Miss Moore devoted herself unremittingly to values. The titles of several of her poems, "When I Buy Pictures," "Critics and Connoisseurs," "Picking and Choosing," suggest how a poem for her is also an act of discrimination. In "Poetry" she indicated her desire to be, like Yeats, "a literalist of the imagination," and gave her best known definition of what authentic imagination must produce: "imaginary gardens with real toads in them."

Since the history of poetry is, in the last analysis, made up of poems and not of poets, no account of this period should fail to mention such impressive achievements as "The Ballad of a Strange Thing" (1927) by Phelps Putnam or "Ode to the Sea" (1937) by Howard Baker. Putnam was another New England romantic who projected, though he did not manage to complete, a highly personal handling of the American hero in search of experience. Baker, on the other hand, made the best fulfillment so far of the kind of classical revival sponsored by Yvor Winters at Stanford. His "Ode" may seem at first glance merely a formal exercise, but it cuts to the heart of our age when it proclaims: "Man is collective. Change is sure."

Such proclamations characterized the shift from the twenties into the thirties, but for the most part the new political and economic interests were more effectively expressed in novels and plays than in verse. Though Sandburg, as we have seen, made a renewed Whitmanesque affirmation in *The People, Yes,* no younger group emerged here at all comparable in quality to the new English poets surrounding Auden. Among the poets who began to be known in the thirties, Horace Gregory added to Crane's city a serious knowledge of our public issues, and Kenneth Fearing used the freest of rhythms for a harsh staccato satire, while Langston Hughes continued to contribute left-wing blues, and Muriel Rukeyser, among many others, brought warm social sympathies to an imperfect search for the proper form. In 1938 Delmore Schwartz produced *In Dreams Begin Responsibilities,* which was hailed as the most promising first book of the decade. Karl Shapiro, who was not to be generally known until after the outbreak of the Second World War, was by then just beginning to appear in the little magazines.

## 8

During the thirties Wallace Stevens had been cutting through all the conventional divisions between poetic generations, and was to prove himself another kind of artist of whom we have had too few instances in America, the one who is more fertile at sixty than at twenty-five. Stevens' life provides an extreme instance of the isolation of the American artist. Nearer to Frost than to Eliot in age, he studied at Harvard, and subsequently became an insurance lawyer in Hartford. He developed his talent apart from the stimulus of any group. His first poems did not appear in *Poetry* until he was thirty-five, and not until he was forty-four did he publish a book, *Harmonium* (1923). That unusual title, which signifies "a small reed organ," calls attention to Stevens' pervasive interest in music. He also spoke of "the essential gaudiness of poetry," and embodied in his lines an extraordinary brilliance of color, a flair for the exotic and the gorgeous, a fondness for ornamental words that he also relished for their unexpected connotations, a fondness too for "rosy chocolate and gilt umbrellas" and for "good, fat, guzzly fruit." His lushness was linked by some critics with the new material luxury of the twenties. He was also called "a dandy of eloquence" on the basis of such poems as "Le Monocle de mon oncle." The contrast with "Prufrock" is revelatory. Stevens once mentioned his debt to "the lightness, the grace, the sound and the color of the French," and he is more at his ease among such qualities than Eliot. His irony is much less stringent, and he did not feel the intellectual urgency that carried Eliot to the metaphysicals. Stevens also elaborated a rhetoric more traditionally formal in its periods than the dramatic speech Eliot wanted. His polish and elegance, again the attributes of the dandy, partly mask his graver concerns, but in "Sunday Morning" his epicureanism is aware of the problems encountered by modern man through the disappearance of the sanctions of the supernatural. His longest poem, "The Comedian As the Letter C" presents various stages of the artist in his struggles with reality.

He was to write very little during the next decade, and a reissue of *Harmonium* in the early thirties added hardly more than a dozen short poems. But with *Ideas of Order* (1935) he inaugurated a period of greatly increased productivity. Both the title and the contents of this new book puzzled some readers who had grown to expect from Stevens the heady flamboyance of "The Emperor of Ice Cream." But Horace Gregory had already discerned that Stevens was not merely a connoisseur of the senses, but also a trained observer of "the decadence that follows the rapid acquisition of wealth and power." Some of Stevens' longer meditations may betray by their diffuseness of structure and the inconclusiveness of their thought his lonely lack of interchange with other minds; but poems like "The Men That Are Falling" poise his matured resources against the growing menace of disorder.

His most persistent subject is the opposition between bare reality and what the imagination can make of it, a subject which he shares in part with Williams. But Stevens had thought more deeply upon the nature of art and celebrated

> The magnificent cause of being,
> The imagination, the one reality
> In this imagined world.

He worked out the implications of that paradox most thoroughly in *The Man with the Blue Guitar* (1937). By suggesting the example of Picasso, he insisted that art, even when seeming to distort reality, may actually bring us to a heightened awareness of it. Standing himself apart from political movements, Stevens made the nature of art the content of many poems, and thought of the activity of the poet as demanding resistance to pressures from without, pressures of too unrelieved fact. He knew that "a violent order is disorder," and he held that the imagination is in a sense an escape, but an escape to our proper domain. He believed that the poet's role "is to help people to lead their lives," but that he does so by transforming them into epicures, since the poet is a lover "of the world he contemplates and thereby enriches." When the greatest violence broke in 1939, Stevens went on to probe what basis for any humanism remained in his "Examination of the Hero in a Time of War." The contours of that examination were still to be extended, but whatever his resolved philosophy, Stevens had established himself as a poet of "the ultimate elegance: the imagined land." As the thirties drew to their close, he was increasingly regarded by younger poets as the man of richest sensibility who was writing poetry in America at that time.

Meanwhile Eliot had been running counter to the most widespread tendencies of the age, ever since he announced his conversion to Anglo-

Catholicism near the end of the twenties. The reasons for his decision were revealed indirectly in some remarks he made about Pascal:

I can think of no Christian writer, not Newman even, more to be commended to those who doubt, but who have the mind to conceive, and the sensibility to feel, the disorder, the futility, the meaninglessness, the mystery of life and suffering, and who can only find peace through a satisfaction of the whole being.

His declared position, at the same time, as "a royalist in politics," had far less reputable sanctions, since it seems to have been strongly affected by Charles Maurras and *L'Action française,* later to be thoroughly discredited for fascist sympathies. Eliot's discussion of politics was never very coherent, though his spiritual depth saved him from Pound's disasters. Some badly chosen sentences in *After Strange Gods* (1934) veered close to anti-Semitism, but after the rise of Hitler to power Eliot regarded the ethically inert and negative society of the democracies as better at least than positive evil. He made no more telling observation upon the relation of the individual to society than a comment on "the Catholic paradox: society is for the salvation of the individual and the individual must be sacrificed to society. Communism is merely a heresy, but a heresy is better than nothing."

Eliot's later poems, from *Ash Wednesday* (1930) through the *Four Quartets,* which were inaugurated by "Burnt Norton" in 1935, must be judged like any other poems, not on the basis of whether we accept or reject their theology, but of whether they have conveyed in moving rhythms the sense that, whatever their author's final beliefs, he is here reflecting perceptively and persuasively on human nature as we know it. By any such test, *Ash Wednesday* may well prove to be his most integrated long poem, as it certainly is a remarkable musical whole. Its themes are not calculated for popularity. They do not give voice to easy affirmation. Their realm is that of a Purgatorio, where suffering is made more acute by doubt, by "stops and steps of the mind" between skepticism and assurance. But their integrity to actual experience allows them to fulfill what Eliot believes to be one of the most valuable services of poetry, its power to make us "a little more aware of the deeper unnamed feelings which form the substratum of our being, to which we rarely penetrate; for our lives are mostly an evasion of ourselves."

In *Four Quartets* (1943) he illustrated his conviction that "the use of recurrent themes is as natural to poetry as to music." Looking back now over the past generation, he here finds our poetry to have been most characterized by its "search for a proper modern colloquial idiom." But he holds that we may be nearing another stage: "When we reach a point at which the poetic idiom can be stabilized, then a period of musical elaboration can follow." The

Quartets undertake such elaboration in a very different style from the witty paradoxes and conceits with which he formerly emulated the metaphysicals. Here he balances passages of meditative declaration against formal lyrics. His early work was difficult in its form, these poems are difficult in their thought. Their logic is sufficiently straightforward, but they present the reader with discourse largely unfamiliar to a secular age. The poet's reflections on time and memory return to his interest in Bergson, but Eliot is primarily occupied with the Christian conception of how man lives both "in and out of time," of how he is immersed in the flux and yet can penetrate to the eternal by apprehending timeless existence within time and above it. No less central to his mind is the doctrine of Incarnation, of God become man through the Savior, since Eliot holds that the nineteenth century substitution of Deification, of man becoming God through his own potentialities, led ineluctably through hero worship to dictatorship. Eliot had now found a more solid basis for his politics, as he demonstrated in his play, *Murder in the Cathedral* (1935), where he contrasted Christian law with violent usurpation of the fascist kind. It was easy to say that Eliot's religious poems were not widely representative of the age; but in a period of breakdown, moving into the shadow of war, they constituted some of the most sustained, if most somber, devotional poetry since the seventeenth century.

# 80. SUMMARY IN CRITICISM

THE function of literary criticism is perhaps rather to analyze and define the forces already at work in a living literature than to provide the impetus for new work. Yet, if it is good criticism, it should do both of these things, and the existence of an active, almost an organized, literary criticism in the years from 1925 to 1945—a criticism in working harmony with the best of contemporary creative writing—is perhaps the most convincing evidence of the ultimate importance of American literature during those years.

The writers of this criticism, no less than their fellow workers among novelists and poets, were continuators in several distinct lines of intention and method that had already declared themselves by 1925. Even though they yielded some of the larger conceptions of literature and art to specializations of technique, analysis, and social and moral thought, they retained the persistent Emersonian hope of a "liberation" for American literature as it had been revived in the decade 1910–1920 by such pioneers of the modern movement as Brooks, Bourne, and Mencken. They did not abandon the idea of the "new" —of aesthetic innovation, of moral and intellectual revision, of social and political adventure—so insistent in the first flush of literary radicalism in the earlier period. The conditions of 1915, however disturbed or distanced by ominous and destructive events, were still the conditions of 1945, and they were still shaping the literature and the criticism of that later day.

2

The description of modern literary criticism must therefore begin with recapitulation. The hazardous task of allocating a distinct character to the product of each of the three decades between 1915 and 1945 may be simplified as follows. The years from 1915 to 1925 were, as we have seen in an earlier chapter, devoted primarily to an attack on tradition, on conservatism, and on those vested interests—call them Idealism, Puritanism, "the genteel tradition," sentimentality, or whatever shibboleth was convenient at the time—that represented the time-lag, the forces of reaction, the "demon of the absolute," to the younger forces of insurgence and rebellion. It was a decade not only of a "new poetry," a "new novel," and a "new drama," but of a "new criticism" whose exponents fell generally into two groups: the realists and iconoclasts led by Brooks, Bourne, Mencken, Lewis Mumford, Ludwig Lewisohn, and Max Eastman; and the aesthetic rebels who, stepping forward from the ground prepared by Santayana, Huneker, Lewis Gates, and J. E. Spingarn, were now led by Ezra Pound and T. S. Eliot. The two groups differed in their artistic and technical principles, but they were allied in their resistance to a common enemy. They were fortunate in having the support of a new generation of American writers. They were, step by step, accompanied in the demonstration and defense of their tenets by actual literary production. They were able to carry through to successful public vindication the efforts of creative artists who were sharing their battle and reinforcing their attack. Yet in spite of their spirit of revolt and their apparent total newness, the presence in their thought and in their programs of some part of the traditional American idealism is as unmistakable as is the use of skeptical rather than prophetic, controversial rather than inspirational, methods of reestablishing it.

By the middle of the twenties, the campaign of these pioneers was generally won, both critically and popularly. A new sensibility was established in American writing. A new enthusiasm, in that decade of excited enthusiasms, had spread the contagion of irreverence, of realism, of "debunking," and of a fresh aesthetic spirit across the country. The first phase of modern criticism was an established event, with the *American Mercury* under Mencken's editorship its popular mouthpiece, the *Dial* its most important aesthetic journal, the *Nation* and the *New Republic* its chief weekly defenders, and writers of acceptably classic stature—Dreiser, Cather, Lewis, Robinson, Sandburg, Anderson, Pound, and Eliot—the witnesses to its variety and its vitality.

The following decade, dating roughly from 1925 to 1935 or a little beyond (some may prefer to date it from October, 1929, to September, 1939, for historical convenience), shows the altered character which any movement assumes when it has emerged from the heat of first encounters and begins to rest on established claims and achievements. Then, with immediate objectives gained, it meets its opposition on more serious terms and comes to grips with a more sober and serious challenge. Inevitably, this decade showed a sharper dividing of forces than the one which preceded it. It was obliged to put its claims to proof, and to subject its defiance to the tests of more serious issues in the moral and social realities of experience. It was a decade that brought forward a new kind of argument, and it was marked by at least two great controversies that took on the character of public, even political, contention.

The first of these controversies was the battle between the Humanists and the Realists. This conflict, already gathering strength during the preceding fifteen years, broke out in full mobilization in 1930 when Irving Babbitt and Paul Elmer More, accompanied by lieutenants like Norman Foerster, Robert Shafer, Gorham Munson, and Prosser Hall Frye, led the defense of traditional and conservative moral values, while a large phalanx of modernist critics—Edmund Wilson, Burton Rascoe, Malcolm Cowley, Kenneth Burke, Allen Tate, R. P. Blackmur, Lewis Mumford—reconciled their differences by defending the critical and creative insurgence.

For several years around 1930 the opposition of these two schools of literature filled the journals and magazines of America; their hostility was presented in full scale in the two anthologies which appeared in that year: *Humanism and America,* defending the Humanist position, and *The Critique of Humanism,* which stated the resistance. In these two books the two lines of thought that had descended from the nineteenth century were fully displayed: the ethical and moral arguments that had their roots in religious orthodoxy, on the one side; the social realism and liberal emancipation of Emerson's and Whitman's lineage, combined now with aesthetic rebellion, on the other. No public controversy in the entire history of American criticism has ever presented the divided inheritance of American literature more expressly. The Humanist controversy was the testing ground of a major antithesis, a radical division, in American beliefs. It acted as a climax of a long-prepared rivalry of forces in the native culture. It served as a watershed of critical energies and ideas. And when it was over, when the heat and considerable smoke of the hostilities had cleared from the air, there was no longer any possibility of mistaking the fundamental hiatus in contemporary critical thought, or of failing to recognize that when a new impulse asserted itself in American literature, the divided forces would find themselves not cleanly and simply divided, but complexly and inextricably involved in their purposes.

Curiously, an issue such as the Humanist controversy raised does not permit liberalism or insurgence to retain their earlier advantages. It insists on a consolidation of beliefs and arguments on both sides. After the Humanist orthodoxy had been checked and repudiated by the defenders of liberalism, these liberals themselves were propelled toward a solidification of their faith and toward an orthodoxy or dogmatism of their own. It was no longer permitted to espouse a free experimental realism, an enthusiastic democratic socialism, a negative skepticism, or an uninhibited iconoclasm such as had been possible in the days of Brooks and Mencken. It became necessary to show a more positive faith, an explicit program of social and realistic action; and this came to hand, during the thirties, in the tenets of Marxism. Thus the second major controversy of the thirties came into being, with Marxism and the dialectic materialism as its doctrine, and the world-wide economic depression and political disturbance of that decade as its incitement toward applying the responsibilities of literature to an immediate program of political action.

3

The Marxist position of these critics had been prepared, in the United States, during the preceding quarter-century. Forerunners like Thorstein Veblen, Floyd Dell, Upton Sinclair, Max Eastman, and V. F. Calverton had been active for fully three decades. Journals like the *Masses,* its successors the *Liberator* and the *New Masses,* were its chief organs, with newspapers like the *New Leader* and the *Socialist Call* carrying on the defense of socialist claims in both political and literary fields, and with more specialized organs like the *Partisan Review, Science and Society,* and *Politics* soon to represent the scholarly and sectarian positions which Marxist radicalism generated.

The necessity in criticism of socialist claims was nothing new. But it now appeared that the pioneers in this movement in the earlier years of the twentieth century had submitted too easily to the "malady" of the humanitarian ideal to satisfy their inheritors. They had accepted "the promise of American life" in too mystical and Whitmanian a spirit, compromising too easily with the hopes of rugged individualism or democratic culture, and holding aloof from committal to positive beliefs. The nineteenth and early twentieth century reformers most acceptable to American thinking had been acceptable because they left their revolutionary ardors at a mid-point of compromise, and stopped short of imposing the technical and forcible reforms of economic socialism. They were still adherents to the thinking of Whitman, Emerson, Howells, Henry George, and Edward Bellamy—the meliorists or gradualists of an older tradition. Books like Veblen's *The Theory of the Leisure Class* (1899), Upton Sinclair's *The Industrial Republic* (1907), V. F. Calverton's *The Newer Spirit* (1925) and *The Liberation of American Literature* (1932) asserted a more positive line of action. In 1931 Eastman's *The Literary Mind: Its Place in an Age of Science* joined science with socialism in disputing the liberal and aesthetic leniency of the foregoing generation.

But even more positive statements of socialist and communist orthodoxy now appeared. They came in Michael Gold's contributions to the *New Masses*; in Calverton's journal, the *Modern Monthly*; in the columns of the *New Republic* during its phase of Marxist sympathies. Malcolm Cowley's book of 1934, *Exile's Return,* described the conversion of an American expatriate, who had taken refuge in Paris in the years of the "lost generation," to social and economic realities. Joseph Freeman wrote a typical record of political conversion in his *American Testament* (1936). Waldo Frank wrote *The Re-Discovery of America* (1929) in terms of a discovery of the economic imperatives underlying cultural optimism. A series of American Writers' Congresses were staged in New York under the Marxist (or, as was claimed by dissidents, under Stalinist) auspices of the League of American Writers in 1935, 1937, and 1939. The division between Stalinists and Trotskyists became a major cleavage among Marxist radicals. Granville Hicks' book, *The Great Tradition* (1933, revised 1935), addressed itself to the task of bringing the later literary history of America into line with the Marxist propositions and historical claims. And a wide variety of critics, as often disagreeing as agreeing in their specific methods or allegiances, followed the Marxist line: Hicks, Gold, Edwin Berry Burgum, Joshua Kunitz, and Newton Arvin in general agreement with the official Communist position of that moment; Edmund Wilson, Kenneth Burke, Philip Rahv, James T. Farrell, Dwight Macdonald, William Phillips, and the contributors to the *Partisan Review* in terms of increasing dissent from the party program as its authoritarian and Stalinist dominance became increasingly apparent. When Bernard Smith published his *Forces in American Criticism* in 1939, he undertook, on a cue provided by Hicks' *Great Tradition,* to assess the whole American critical tradition in expressly Marxist terms, and thereby provided an occasion for disputing the value of economic or political "force" as a criterion of criticism that was to be further enhanced by a major historical event in the autumn of that year.

Critical controversy was now at active grips with party politics. The systematic form of the materialist dialectic taxed the defenders of the aesthetic approach to literature with matching its logic and consistency. Propaganda in literature became a continuous issue of debate. The economic and political distress of the times forced an agreement even among fiercely contending critical parties on the practical and moral ends of literature, spurred a critical examination of these ends, and established more firmly than ever before in American thought the necessity of seeing what constitutes the truth and integrity of a work of literature before it can hope to produce a desired effect in social or moral regeneration.

Obviously these benefits of dispute and responsibility soon became offset by corresponding evils. Critical activity became distracted by false simplifications and partisan bias. Its exponents readily substituted personal abuse for sober thinking and propaganda for logic. There appeared a heated warfare of terms and premises, in which debates over the "function" of art, "utility," "ideology," "mass consciousness," "bourgeois" values against "proletarian," and "autonomy" versus "propaganda," badly hindered the mere communication of intelligence about these issues, and permitted the discipline of realistic logic to lapse into dilemma and confusion. Hicks' book on *The Great Tradition* became a special and typical center of dispute. Its coherence of argument and its graphic dramatization of American social history were rendered suspect by the facility with which it accepted or dismissed the writers of American literature according to the degree to which they satisfied his highly simplified proposition on the interdependence of literature and economic law. This book was the particular stimulus that aroused another writer of Marxist sympathies, James T. Farrell, to write his *Note on Literary Criticism* (1936), in which he scored the lapses in valid argument and appreciation among the critics of the Left, reproved the dogmatists, and sketched the necessary corrections and qualifications of literal Marxism that were needed to preserve its values and methods for legitimate literary study.

Perhaps the central issue raised by Marxism was the issue of economic determinism as a conditioning force and value-principle in literature—a determinism that became a purely mechanical routine in the writings of dogmatic and inflexible believers. Max Eastman, of the older Socialist guard, published in 1934 his two studies called *Artists in Uniform: A Study of Literature and Bureaucratism* and *Art and the Life of Action,* both of them issuing from his own disillusionment with orthodox Marxism and Stalinism, and both serving as warnings against the official coercion of art in the service of the political state, of which Stalinism no less than totalitarian Fascism was, in his view, guilty. Younger defenders of Marxist thought—Rahv, Phillips, Farrell, Macdonald—sounded their warnings against the regimentation of art in a too literal Marxist spirit. Edmund Wilson, in an essay on "Marxism and Literature" (included in his collection *The Triple Thinkers* in 1938), refuted the Marxist orthodoxy among critics in a series of analyzed propositions. The old resistance of the individual to mass action or compulsion, so characteristic a trait of American political and literary liberalism, asserted itself with increasing emphasis.

Three statements made during the thirties illustrate this gradual correction of social and political extremism in criticism. One appeared in Newton Arvin's essay on "Individualism and American Writers":

The case for a proletarian literature is not always cogently stated or wisely defended—any more than the case against it. One must insist that to adopt the proletarian point of view does not mean, for a novelist, to deal solely with economic conflicts, or, for a poet, to be a voice only for protest, momentous as both these things are and *implicit* as they are bound to be. That a truly proletarian literature, for us in America at least, would mean a break with the mood of self-pity, with the cult of romantic separatism, with sickly subjectivism and melodramatic misanthropy—this much is almost too clear to deserve stating. But the duty of the critic is certainly not to file an order for a particular sort of fiction or poetry before the event; his duty is to clarify, as best he can, the circumstances in which fiction and poetry must take shape, and to rationalize their manifestations when they arrive. For the moment the important thing is that American criticism should define its position: in the midst of so much confusion, so much wasted effort, so much hesitation, this will itself be an advance.

Another appeared in Joseph Freeman's statement in 1935, in the anthology called *Proletarian Literature in America:*

No party resolution, no government decree, can product art, or transform an agitator into a poet. A party card does not automatically endow a communist with artistic genius. Whatever it is that makes an artist, as distinguished from a scientist or man of action, it is something beyond the power of anyone to produce deliberately. But once the artist is there, once there is the man with the specific sensibility, the mind, the emotions, the images, the gift of language which makes the creative writer, he is not a creature in a vacuum.

A third was provided by Rahv and Phillips:

Unfortunately many misguided enthusiasts of revolution, effacing their own experience, take for their subject-matter the public philosophy as such, or attempt to adorn with rhetorical language conventionalized patterns of feeling and action. What they don't see is that these patterns are, in the final analysis, just as impersonal as the philosophy itself. . . . If there is to be an ever-fresh balance between the accent of the poet and the attitude he shares with other people, he must understand the connection between what is *real* to him as an individual and what is *real* to him as a partisan of some given philosophy.

The climax of ten years of Marxist controversy in American criticism arrived in the summer of 1939, when Stalin made his pact with Hitler on the eve of the outbreak of the Second World War in September. This event proved to be a violent and crucial test for those who had subscribed to the orthodox letter of the collaboration and interdependence of literature and political action. It provided, in fact, a date as crucial in the history of American critical thought as the Humanist controversy of 1930, the appearance of Van Wyck Brooks' *America's Coming-of-Age* in 1915, or, indeed, Emerson's Phi Beta Kappa address in 1837.

For some of the faithful the event had its logic and its explanation in the political ambiguities and cynicism of the preceding decade. But for many it meant a betrayal of faith, and the speed with which they resigned from the Communist Party or the Marxist cause (Granville Hicks, in his letter of resignation, provided the classic case of repudiation and eventual atonement to the American liberal principle) was perhaps in direct proportion to the obedient and blinkered docility of too many original conversions. Certain sympathizers whose ideas had been strongly stamped by the entire social-political issue— Edmund Wilson and Kenneth Burke chief among them—kept their minds flexible and receptive, and continued to adapt the Marxist analysis to their methods of formal analysis or social interpretation. But others were faced by absolute alternatives: repudiation or acceptance. Eloquence and mandatory dogmatism went out of the critical controversy swiftly. A more sober and considered critical balance was enforced among the thoughtful. Communism, during the succeeding years of the forties, was obliged, as a critical policy, to come to terms not only with historical and political fact but with aesthetic necessity and merit. Compromise, conciliation, and a sounder proportion of values asserted their usefulness, indeed their inevitability, in any literary program which is at all observant of the disparities that are bound to exist between theory and practice in art. Those disparities—the fact of them, but also the need of controlling or disciplining this wayward fact through a knowledge of aesthetic theory and of the recalcitrance of creative expression to theoretical abstractions—had meanwhile become the concern of another branch of American criticism, whose disputes provided a line of development that both corrected and paralleled that of Marxism in the criticism of the thirties.

4

If the political and social critics of the thirties can be described as descendants of an American line that brought the ideas of Emerson into conjunction with the claims of economic realism, the new aesthetic critics who were their contemporaries are recognizable as heirs of a similarly twofold evolution in American literary thought. It is an evolution whose salient traits appear in the concept of poetic "purity" as Poe sponsored it, and in the "moral necessity" of art as Henry James defined it. Whatever prominence these conceptions had arrived at in postclassical criticism in Europe, whatever hostilities or alliances they had engendered there during the nineteenth century, whatever actual indebtedness to the European masters these two American critics and their contemporaries showed, it was an expression definably American that they gave to their principles, and it is a peculiarly American version of the aesthetic-moralistic dualism that descended to their followers in the twentieth century. Aestheticism in the United States has always been more consciously and explicitly international in its tenets than the rival strain of social-realistic theory. The native defenders of artistic autonomy or privilege—Poe, Motley, Lowell, James, Brownell, Santayana, Gates, Huneker, Spingarn—have always invoked European precept or example more readily than exponents of social or humanitarian ideals, and some of them have taken their working principles directly from European sources: Coleridge, Schopenhauer, Arnold, Pater, France, or Croce. This continued to be the case when Ezra Pound and T. S.

Eliot appeared on the scene around 1915 as sponsors of a new aesthetic approach to literary problems. But it proved inevitable that even the most extreme of these defenders of the aesthetic principle in the United States should arrive at a dualism of art and morality that carries the accent of an essentially American alliance of forces—an alliance that makes Pound and Eliot, as much as Henry James himself, unmistakably American characters when we consider them in the role of critic.

It is necessary to bring the critical work of James into any valid picture of contemporary American criticism. Not only was his final and greatest critical writing (the prefaces he wrote to his own books in 1907–1909) done in this century; but his importance as a critic was first fully recognized and assessed in America after the collection of these prefaces into book form as *The Art of the Novel* in 1934. His rank as a craftsman and creative thinker emerged in full scale only after his death in 1916, when his criticism was first read and studied; and it finally touched the thought of almost every serious American writer only by the time of the revival that accompanied the centenary of his birth in 1943. Pound and Eliot took him as their major American preceptor around 1915 as frankly as the social realists of that day took Emerson, Whitman, or Howells as theirs. This office of James' has increased during the ensuing three decades until today he holds almost undisputed rank as the greatest American school-maker in matters of formal craftsmanship and aesthetic discipline.

It was James who first saw clearly the modern creative problem in its two essential aspects: its oppression by social conflict and theories of scientific and moral determinism, and its acute subtilization by the defenses which the aesthetic techniques of the modern sensibility had set up against these oppressions. He saw modern criticism confronting the task of reconciling the real with the aesthetic, human experience in "its unprejudiced identity" with the form and laws of art. That task was nowhere more urgent than in America, and during the 1880's, when James still had the ambition of becoming the "American Balzac," he formulated his working principles as a critic. His critical doctrine showed three principal clauses. He argued for subtlety and plasticity in the critic's sympathy as a first condition. As a second, he demanded a tireless study of the vital experience upon which all art is based and its use as a test of material validity, since for him all art was "in basis moral." And he required finally a knowledge of how the intelligence of the artist stamps this material with its unmistakable impression of form and language, since that imprint constituted for James the "quality of mind" for which he looked in any valid work of art.

He defended the mean in both art and criticism. He had an American's native suspicion of cults and dogmas. He looked upon Gautier's "art for art" as an absurdity and upon Zola's naturalism as a "treacherous ideal." To him, aesthetic quality was as indispensable as realistic documentation; but to insist on the one without the other, or upon either without the harmonizing presence of a moral conception, was futile. Criticism must begin where a work of imagination begins: with experience tangibly perceived.

To lend himself, to project himself and steep himself, to feel and feel till he understands, and to understand so well that he can say, and to have perception at the pitch of passion and expression as embracing as the air, to be infinitely curious and incorrigibly patient, and yet plastic and inflammable and determinable, patient, stooping to conquer and yet serving to direct—these are fine chances for an active mind, chances to add the idea of independent beauty to the conception of success. . . . Just in proportion as he reacts and reciprocates and penetrates, is the critic a valuable instrument.

This was his plea for training in critical sensibility—a pioneer formulation of the impressionist principle. It alone leads the critic directly into contact with the work of art and with art's own sources. But we must not make the mistake of confusing what James said with what Pater taught, or with what later American exponents of French impressionism like Huneker, or of Crocean expressionism like Spingarn, advocated. Impressionism was at that time almost as unknown in America as it had been exaggerated in Europe, and it had a service to perform in bringing critics back to an intimate sense of art (as Lewis Gates, Huneker, and finally Eliot were to show). But James had no intention of subscribing literally to its methods. He was too thoroughly bred in ethical seriousness. When he declared, in *Partial Portraits* (1888), that "the deepest quality of a work of art will always be the quality of the mind of the producer," he meant that in both art and criticism "the moral sense and the artistic sense lie very close together." Only their combination will supply the abstract operations of the intellect with the vitality of a union that makes such "quality" possible. "The critic's judgment," he repeated, "being in the last analysis an estimate of the artist's quality of mind, is at once moral and aesthetic." The persistent linking of these terms runs like a motif through James' essays. To separate the moral from the aesthetic is to rob either of its vital complement. Genuine "unity of mind" exists in such "fusions and interrelations," with "every part of the stuff encircled in every other." That is the secret of aesthetic form, a writer's ultimate aim and achievement, just as its elucidation is the secret of the critic's success, his highest responsibility. These precepts stayed with James from his critical coming-of-age until he finally assayed his own achievement by their light when he wrote the prefaces for the New York Edition of his tales in the last decade of his life. They remain the clue to his role in modern American writing and to his part in the aesthetic thought that came to rival the social-realistic and the Humanist-moral schools in American criticism after 1925.

The exponents of aestheticism found themselves, in 1930, in a position somewhere midway between Humanism and Realism, and they continued to hold that difficult medial ground when Humanism gave way to moral dogmatism and Realism to Marxism, in the ensuing fifteen years. The aesthetic schools of the twenties had been obliged, in the face of both Humanism and the Marxist challenge, to consolidate their forces and to commit themselves to more positive ends and beliefs than had been allowed in the freer days of artistic experiment and rebellion. Where the realist critics of that earlier decade had moved toward social and economic values, the aesthetic critics now began to move toward values that may be variously defined as moral, ethical, and in some cases explicitly theological but, in any case, as formal and intellectual, as against the impressionism of the eclectic sensibility that had been the general rule when Santayana, Huneker, or the early Pound and Eliot dominated the scene. When Eliot in 1928, in the foreword to his book of essays called *For Launcelot Andrewes,* announced himself as a classicist in literature, a royalist in politics, and an Anglo-Catholic in religion, he startled many of his former admirers into repudiating his leadership; but actually he was only arriving at certain commitments which had been implicit in his New England heritage, his European sympathies, his historical principles, and his classical and formalist leanings (particularly as derived from T. E. Hulme, the English philosophical writer) from the beginning of his career. His announcement was symptomatic.

The aesthete, as much as the realist, was searching for a positive doctrine by which to confirm his faith in the discipline of art and intellect, an orthodoxy with which to buttress his identification of individual experience with the imperatives of moral responsibility and historical tradition. Eliot's books after 1930 indicated by their very titles the extra-aesthetic values to which he dedicated himself: *The Use of Poetry and the Use of Criticism* (1933), *After Strange Gods: A Primer of Modern Heresy* (1934), *Essays Ancient and Modern* (correlating traditional with modern standards in morals and art) (1936), *The Idea of a Christian Society* (1939), *The Classics and the Man of Letters* (1942), *The Man of Letters and the Future of Europe* (1944). His earlier argument that modern society would benefit by the establishment of a critical dictatorship, an élite of the intelligent, had (despite its echo of Matthew Arnold) ominous possibilities in an age of coercive cultural policies, but Eliot has been concerned to keep that principle both cautious and tentative in its practical application, while insisting that it be serious and responsible in its literary and moral workings. In the absence, among English-speaking countries, of a positively orthodox Christian or Thomistic school of aesthetics such as Jacques Maritain and Etienne Gilson were fostering in France, Eliot came to stand as the foremost representative of the league between aesthetic and moral ideas which has offered itself as one central synthesis of the critical forces of our century. His loyalty to the literary standard, despite his preoccupation with religious and ethical problems, was also explicitly emphasized in 1935, in his essay on "Religion and Literature," when he asserted that "the 'greatness' of literature cannot be determined solely by literary standards; though we must remember that whether it is literature or not can be determined only by literary standards."

To bring criticism into active collaboration with values, to assert the indispensability of technical and aesthetic evidences as the basis of genuine critical judgment, have thus become paramount in Eliot's critical work, making him, perhaps above every other practitioner, the dominating influence in aesthetic analysis after 1925—a major force among critics as diverse as Edmund Wilson, Kenneth Burke, John Crowe Ransom, Allen Tate, and R. P. Blackmur. But immediately behind Eliot in this effort stood, as a personal mentor, another American poet whose office as a critical school-maker is important in these developments. It was "active criticism" that Ezra Pound went abroad to study when he left America in 1907, beginning a thirty-five-year career in England, France, and Italy. In the early days of his apprenticeship Pound stood for a militantly aesthetic standard in experimentation, a rescue of art from the academic formulae and discreet moralism into which it had fallen in the United States of his youth. He was drawn toward critics and editors like Henry James, Rémy de Gourmont, W. B. Yeats, Ford Madox Hueffer, and T. E. Hulme—men who made less pretense of organizing a philosophic system out of their tastes and appreciations than of refreshing and extending these by constant study of the problems of form and style. He put himself to school, as poet and critic, among the experimental masters of the past and the nonconformist teachers of the present. On an eclectic principle he studied the Latin lyrists, the balladists of Provence and medieval Italy, the Elizabethan translators, the French symbolists, and the Chinese manuscripts he inherited from Ernest Fenollosa, all with the same zest he gave to the teachings of Gourmont in Paris or Hulme in London. His enthusiasm was so contagious that he himself was soon recognized as a leader in innovation and critical pedagogy.

From Gourmont he heard those conversations on style and aesthetic form which were expressed in an aphorism (later to be employed as an epigraph by Eliot) that gives focal expression to the liaison now set up between impressionism and the new formalism: "Ériger en lois ses impressions personnelles, c'est le grand effort d'un homme s'il est sincère." From Hulme he took up a protest against the romantic, the sentimental, the formally vague and subjective, the relative and the abstract, which the author of the fragmentary *Speculations* offered as his prophecy of a classical revival in modern literature.

This principle of form, however, had little to do with the revival of Aristotelian laws which was to appear in England and America among certain critics after 1930. When Eliot somewhat later (in *The Sacred Wood* in 1920) said, "One must be firmly distrustful of accepting Aristotle in a canonical spirit; this is to lose the whole living force of him," he was following Hulme's and Pound's directive. Pound gained his chief stimulation from his contemptuous opposition to the degenerate romanticism of late Victorian and Edwardian writers. For that reason he made a necessity of experiment, and his career became a continuous participation in unconventionality—in Imagism, in Vorticism, in the aesthetic laboratories of Paris, in Objectivism, in fact in any activity that satisfied his demand for freshness, exploration, invention, novelty. He repudiated critical systems: "Systems become tyrannies overnight." Despite his later political and economic alliances (Social Credit, Jeffersonian aristocratic thought, or later the political authoritarianism which came curiously to attract numerous modern writers and which led, in Pound's case, to his admiration of Fascism in Italy and to his eventual indictment as a traitor to his native country in the War of 1941–1945), Pound's purposes, in his best years as critic, were never primarily moral, except in the sense that aesthetic discipline demands an integrity beyond the formality of practical ethics. His book titles indicate his motives: *Instigations* (1920), *Irritations* (1922), *How to Read* (1931), *The A.B.C. of Reading* (1934), *Make It New* (1935). All these were writen less to persuade than to irritate and thus to apply the authority of creative literature itself as a critical instrument. When Pound defined his "categories" of criticism, he opposed the ineffectuality of abstract dogma with the dynamic value of the actual literary text.

Pound brought criticism back to an active study of texts more directly and unequivocally than impressionism aimed to do, and with none of the complexities of scientific method or formal analysis that I. A. Richards or the formalists after 1930 were to employ. His arguments suffered as much as his style from his exaggerated iconoclasm. His classifications often failed to classify, and his preferences were likely to confuse discrimination. But Pound's work, for all its violence, haphazardness, and shock tactics, had the virtues that go with these offenses: it was direct, energetic, experimental, seminal. It showed, in the years between 1910 and 1930, a virtue to which academic criticism and often social criticism cannot usually pretend: it was useful to writers. And in his role as a teacher of writers Pound's service was greatest, and his importance to aesthetic thought in the immediately future years second only to Eliot's.

The disciplining of the aesthetic experience, its substancing in moral values, which Eliot and Pound promoted, was to resort to other methods during the thirties. One of these appeared in the mature work of Yvor Winters, whose efforts to analyze the form of modern poetry, to define its processes, to find a critical methodology for them, and to rescue poetry from the disorder and confusion of aimless experimentation, led him toward more and more severely classical principles, these being partly influenced by the arguments of Irving Babbitt, partly by a personal contempt for the abuses and anti-intellectual tendencies of artistic experiments based on psychological and amoral motives —his dissension from the Humanist position being indicated, however, by his judgment on Babbitt: "His analysis of literary principles appears to me to be gravely vitiated by an almost complete ignorance of the manner in which the moral intelligence actually gets into poetry."

Another large-scale attempt to bring formal analysis into a working collaboration with social and human values appeared in the work of Kenneth Burke. Burke undertook a widely explorative study of literary form by using any technique that came to his hand—semantic research, psychological method, social analysis, structural analysis: projects that entailed investigations in the problems of communication, perception, agency, and instrumentation which culminated in books like *The Philosophy of Literary Form* (1941) and *A Grammar of Motives* (1945).

Still another method of aesthetic investigation appeared in the essays of R. P. Blackmur (*The Double Agent*, 1935; *The Expense of Greatness*, 1940), who, combining a naturalistic motive derived from Santayana with an analytical procedure comparable to that of I. A. Richards and William Empson in England, but always with overt indebtedness to James and Eliot, brought the evaluation of literary quality and effects down to a minute dissection of the style, form, diction, and structure in the poets and prose writers he studied.

A still more prominent case of aestheticism joining forces with a moral conception of literature appeared in the writers of the Southern school—the Regionalists and Traditionalists who had first appeared as early as 1922 in the pages of the magazine called the *Fugitive* in Nashville, Tennessee, and who then, during the thirtiees and forties, under the leadership of John Crowe Ransom and Allen Tate, included such critics as Cleanth Brooks, Robert Penn Warren, Donald Davidson, Randall Jarrell, and had as their organs the *Southern Review* (1935–1942), the *Kenyon Review* (beginning in 1939), and the renovated *Sewanee Review* (beginning in 1944). Here again the obligation of literary analysis to historical and moral tradition was asserted, specifically, in terms of the Southern inheritance in American life—an order of society based on classical conceptions of authority, value, and the aristocratic principle of intelligence, now posed anew against the competitive, aggressive, and experimental standards of the North. The essays of Tate and Ransom submitted their literary findings to the responsibility that a critic faces when he attempts to reconcile modernity or innovation with the formal order implicit in tradition. Tate called his first volume of essays *Reactionary Essays* (1936), indicating by that title the positive standard he made of a principle usually associated by modernists with inhibition and conservative negation; he called his second book of criticism *Reason in Madness* (1941), making its theme the opposition of moral order to eclectic license or utilitarian materialism in contemporary literature. And when Ransom announced the focal ambition of his work in the title of a characteristic essay, "Wanted: An Ontological Criticism," he showed himself to desiderate in modern art and criticism a metaphysic based on a total comprehension of reality, connecting literature with the essential nature, properties, and relations of things in their fullest possible coherence of mind and moral continuity.

Less committed to a conscious program of technique or moral values than these men was Edmund Wilson, one of the earliest disciples of the new criticism in the twenties, and continuing in 1946 to be one of the most influential practitioners of criticism in America. Wilson began as a student of the historical methods of nineteenth century French critics like Sainte-Beuve, Taine, Renan, and Anatole France. He wrote his brilliant first book of criticism, *Axel's Castle* (1931), a study of the Symbolist tradition in modern literature, as a study of "the productions of men of genius in the setting of the conditions that have shaped them." He took, in his future work, whatever he found valuable from the social and Marxist schools short of their dogmatic conclusions; from Freud and psychoanalysis his increasingly emphasized clue to effective expression in the psychic disability or social maladjustment of the artist; and from historical processes a drama of forces that continuously enlivens his reading of texts through his appreciation of the vitality and dynamism of social and moral experience (*The Triple Thinkers*, 1938; *To the Finland Station*, 1940; *The Wound and the Bow*, 1941).

It was the thoroughness of their stylistic investigations, the insight of their studies of literary patterns and structures, that lifted the best of these critics above the irresponsible conjurings of the impressionists, that made them conscious of what is involved in the creative process, and so brought them to resist, with a morality and orthodoxy of their own, the mechanism of social and political formulae. In them, the aesthetic procedure was at once rationalized and corrected, and utilitarian critical methods were revealed in their routine of inflexible prejudice and ineptitude. In them, moreover, the Marxist schools of the thirties found their most formidable resistance. This resistance was sometimes carried out so stubbornly and uncompromisingly that it led one chronicler, Alfred Kazin in *On Native Grounds* (1942), to describe the hostility of orthodoxies which he witnessed around him as "Criticism at the Poles." This resistance indicated a profound and fundamental division in the critical forces of the thirties, and it made that decade memorable for the decisions and commitments which will characterize it for future historians

## 5

This brings us to the latest phase of our survey: the criticism of the middle forties, which may be described as a movement toward assimilation and synthesis, an attempted compromise of methods, an effort to strike a reasonable balance and proportion among the values which thirty years of literary insurgence and critical research have turned up. Those three decades began, as we have seen, with protest and rebellion. They continued with experimentation and a free exploring of the techniques and resources of literature. Then they fell into doctrinaire schools and a hostile opposition of critical forces—liberals against traditionalists, realists against idealists, rebels against academicians, socialists against aesthetes, experimenters against dogmatists, with methods of argument or analysis borrowed from every possible field of modern research—semantics, the new psychologies of Freud and Jung, Marxism, theology, anthropology, history, sociology, philosophy. Now, perhaps, the moment had arrived for a more difficult task than is possible to sectarians, extremists, or insurgents; namely, the undertaking of a whole view of literature which admits the possible benefits of diverse intellectual and critical disciplines but insists on keeping the central integrity of literature intact, and holds in view the unity of art with the total sum of human experience and its moral values.

# 81. AMERICAN BOOKS ABROAD

THERE is the same difficulty in writing a history of American literature during the twentieth century that there is in picturing an object a few inches from the eyes: both are too close to be in focus. The observer of natural objects can change his position, but the historian who deals with contemporary life and letters has not the same privilege, being part of the process he is trying to describe. Not only his judgments but his selection of facts for record will have to be revised in later years. It can scarcely be doubted, however, on the evidence of the foregoing chapters, that a literary movement of power and character existed in the United States after about 1910, with its origins going back to the nineties. Nothing like it had occurred in our literature since the mid-years of the past century, when Emerson, Melville, and Whitman were in their prime.

The early statement of N. P. Willis, "The Atlantic is to us a century," applies with the same half-truth to the reverse of the situation he had in mind, for distance in space has somewhat the same effect as distance in time. Crossing the oceans is still a means by which the historian can step back to gain perspective. He can observe what happens when contemporary American writers are judged by the critical standards of other nations, and he can thereby reach another estimate of their importance; at the very least, he can learn to question local judgments.

It is not easy to follow American books around the world, especially since war and national jealousies have added the censorship of facts to our own capacity for disregarding them. For a long time any report from abroad is certain to be uneven and incomplete; yet we know enough already to reach a few suggestive conclusions. Perhaps the first of these is that American literature acquired a different international status during the last half-century; that it came to be regarded in Europe, in Latin America, and in the Orient as one of the major living world literatures. A second conclusion might be that the American writers most widely read on other continents are, in general, not the same as those most highly esteemed by our own critics. A third conclusion—among many others—is that the history of American books abroad has as many local variants as there are civilized countries,

As a general rule, American literary influence has followed one of two paths. Either it started in England, spread outward through the British Dominions (except Canada, which was influenced directly), and moved northeastward through Germany to Scandinavia; or else—for a smaller number of authors—it started in France, traveled eastward to the Slavic countries (though Russia after the Revolution followed her own taste in American books), then spread southward through the Mediterranean and finally southwestward to Latin America, which accepted the Paris standards rather than those of London or Madrid. Whitman and Poe are examples from our classical period of authors whose books followed these separate paths. Poe was so warmly adopted by the French that he came to be regarded as one of their Symbolist poets; and it was largely in Baudelaire's French translation that his stories were read in Eastern Europe and Latin America before the Slavic and Spanish worlds made sometimes very effective translations of their own. Whitman, on the other hand, had enthusiastic French and Latin American disciples, just as Poe had German disciples; but in the Latin countries there was never the wide popular audience for *Leaves of Grass* that existed in England and Germany.

The northern path is the one likely to be followed by sound historical romances, humorous works, and realistic novels conceived on a large scale; in a word, by books distinguished for scope as opposed to depth, for human warmth as opposed to emotional fire, for reasonableness as opposed to bitter logic. To list a few contemporary names, it is the path followed by the works of Dreiser, Hergesheimer, Lewis, Willa Cather, and Pearl Buck (all of whom were also published in France, though without being really naturalized there). Books that followed the southern path were more likely to be narrow, technically inventive (rather than polished), lyrical, intense, and even extravagant: they were, for example, the novels of Hemingway, Dos Passos (studied for his technical innovations), Faulkner (most highly praised of all), Erskine Caldwell, and John Steinbeck (except for his epical *Grapes of Wrath,* which was read in all countries). In both cases, it was the unsophisticated violence of American life that appealed to Europeans.

There were other books that followed both paths. Usually they were novels dealing with the wilderness, slavery, or the misdeeds of big business—in other words, with native American material that seemed fascinating and wildly foreign to Europeans of all nations. The Leatherstocking Tales, *Evangeline* (studied in both French and German schools), *Uncle Tom's Cabin, Tales of the Argonauts* (Bret Harte during his lifetime was more popular in the Latin countries than Mark Twain), *The Call of the Wild, The Jungle,* and *Gone with the Wind* are some of the books enjoyed almost universally.

2

England had welcomed the American writers of the classical period, and continued to read them for some time after they had begun to be neglected by the American public. In a middle-class English home about the year 1900, Emerson would stand on the shelves next to Carlyle, Longfellow next to Tennyson (with signs of being more frequently read) and Lowell next to Matthew Arnold. The new generation rejected them all, the Bostonians along with the native Victorians. To the younger English intellectuals of the time, the only transatlantic authors worth reading, except Whitman and Thoreau, were the new social realists, from Garland through Norris to Upton Sinclair. Dreiser's *Sister Carrie* was a critical success in London, when published there in 1901, although it had been arousing such a bitterly quiet condemnation in New York that the author—till then a successful journalist—found that his articles were being rejected by all the magazines.

The English were usually hospitable to American writers as persons, often more hospitable than they were to imported books. During the 1890's, there was a large American literary colony in what was still called the mother country: it included the aging Bret Harte, Henry James, Harold Frederic, Pearl Craigie from Boston (who wrote under the name John Oliver Hobbes), Howard Sturgis (author of the fine but neglected *Belchamber*), Henry Harland (who founded and edited the *Yellow Book*), and, for his last two years, Stephen Crane. Most of these authors had a more appreciative public in England than in the United States; for example, Bret Harte's new books continued to be read in their English editions long after most Americans had forgotten that he was still a living author. Stephen Crane, who could not complain of being neglected at home, could justly complain of being pursued there by scandals that the English found beneath their notice. Henry James, with no larger audience in London than in New York, at least found more of the happy few to understand his work. The same hospitality in later years would be shown to Ezra Pound, Conrad Aiken, Hilda Doolittle ("H. D."), and T. S. Eliot, the last of whom became a British subject in 1927, like James in 1915.

At the turn of the century, some of the larger American magazines were printing English editions; that of *Harper's* was edited by Andrew Lang and had a British circulation of 100,000. Many American books crossed the Atlantic. In the October, 1904, issue of *World's Work*, Chalmers Roberts broadly asserted that ten American books were being published in England where one had been published twenty years before. He was not surprised by the fondness of the English public for the genteel writings of James Lane Allen, a phenomenon remarked upon by many critics. What amazed him was the

English success of American rural novels like *David Harum, Eben Holden,* and *Mrs. Wiggs of the Cabbage Patch,* all of which he described as being "intensely foreign and full of detail quite unintelligible to the average Briton."

Shortly after 1910, however, the British public showed signs of losing interest in American fiction, except for commodities like the works of Zane Grey and Edgar Rice Burroughs (who afterward claimed that the globe-girdling adventures of Tarzan had been translated into fifty-six languages). American magazines discontinued their London editions. As for the serious American novelists, English critics learned to say that they were ten or twenty or fifty years behind the times. A few critics, however, had begun to discover the new American poets—Robinson, Masters, Sandburg, Lindsay—sometimes before they were known in the United States; for example, Robert Frost had his first two books published in London.

There were new American novelists, too, but they had few English readers during the First World War; one of its effects was to keep the two countries apart intellectually, even after they became allies. In 1920 the English publisher of *Main Street* was so little impressed by Sinclair Lewis' American success that he began by merely importing a few hundred sets of printer's sheets; it was not until later that he had the novel printed in England. *Main Street* was never popular there, although it was more generally liked in Australia, which, more than New Zealand, makes its own choice of American books. *Babbitt,* however, was the English best seller of 1922; and when its author next visited London he was received like the general of an Allied army. "England," Lewis told his hosts, with his redheaded gift for speaking his mind, "can no longer be the mother country to American literature, any more than she can be the mother country to American politics or American life." The English listened, protested, argued with one another, and came to believe that Lewis was right.

*Babbitt* was the beginning of a new era, during which American books were not only read but imitated. On their different literary levels, Hemingway, Edmund Wilson, James Thurber, Damon Runyon, and Dashiell Hammett each had English disciples, who sometimes improved on their various models. Graham Greene, for example, wrote English gangster novels that had a psychological depth lacking in his American precursors, except Hemingway. A younger Englishman, Peter Cheyney, stuck to his models closely, so much so that one of his stories was included (1945) in a French anthology of the new American writing. The editor had learned of Cheyney's nationality before the volume went to press, but had kept him with the others because of his American style. By this time, however, styles and influences were flying back and forth across the Atlantic; and the English imitators of the

American hard-boiled novelists—Graham Greene especially—were finding American imitators in their turn. Among poets the transatlantic relations were even closer. T. S. Eliot was the strongest early influence on the new English poets of the thirties such as Auden (before he came to live in the States), Spender, and MacNeice; while Auden in turn set the tone for American poets in the forties.

The American vogue continued year after year. In 1938 an English publisher reported that all the novels since *Babbitt* with a sale of more than 100,000 copies in England had been of American origin. American magazines were also read: especially *Time* (which had two English imitations), the *Reader's Digest* (with an English edition), and the *New Yorker,* which, in the brighter circles, was quoted more often than *Punch.* In 1942 one-quarter of the new trade books listed in English publishers' catalogues had been written in the States. By 1946, however, the percentage of transatlantic imports was beginning to decline.

### 3

In France it was still growing. Not only were the French translating or planning to translate dozens of the more prominent American novelists and the plays of Eugene O'Neill; they were also discovering and publishing, in the midst of a paper shortage, American books that had been largely neglected at home; for example, the fantastic *Miss Lonelyhearts,* by Nathanael West, which had been published here in 1933 and had promptly gone out of print. At the same time they showed a renewed interest in the American classics. The first French translation of *Moby Dick* appeared during the German occupation, together with a somewhat fictionalized biography of Melville by Jean Giono; and a translation of *The Scarlet Letter* was published in 1946.

The French had read most of the American classical authors when they first appeared, but had forgotten them sooner than the English. There were a few striking exceptions: notably Cooper and Poe, who were carried over bodily into French literature and remain an integral part of it. Among the Americans writing at the turn of the century, Henry James had a few careful French readers, and exercised a still undetermined influence on Marcel Proust. Jack London had a wider public; he inherited the French popularity of Bret Harte. Edith Wharton, who lived in France, had most of her books translated; they were praised in the terms that are usually applied to estimable but unexciting French novels. Most of the other living American writers were little known even in Paris; and their country was regarded, in general, as the literary home of cowboys, miners, trappers, and the inimitable Nick Carter, whose weekly adventures were then appearing in France, as in fifteen other foreign countries.

The First World War, which tended to separate us intellectually from the English, thus marking the end of what might be called the second colonial period in American letters, was an occasion for renewing old literary ties with the French. Much has been written about the flight of American writers to Paris during the twenties; it is not so generally known that there was a smaller but influential movement of French writers and scholars in the opposite direction. The migration began under French government auspices, with professors from the Sorbonne encouraged to make American tours and lecture at American universities. They were shortly followed by a selected group of French postgraduate students, some of whom carried home with them a wide knowledge of American authors. Chairs of American Civilization and Literature were founded at several of the French universities: at Paris (where Charles Cestre was the incumbent), Grenoble, Lille, Aix-Marseille, and elsewhere. French students working in the field produced what is probably the largest group of scholarly studies of American literature that exists in any foreign language.

But interest in American culture was also growing in a quite different circle, that of the younger avant-garde writers. Finding not much hope in Europe after the war, they were looking for new material, new ideas, new ways of life. A sort of romantic Americanism became the vogue among them after 1920: they were connoisseurs of American films, especially Westerns, they read the advertisements in the *Saturday Evening Post,* they dreamed of living in a New York skyscraper (though few of them, in life, got beyond making a single brief voyage), and they even dressed in what they thought was the American fashion, wearing belts instead of suspenders and shaving their upper lips; whereas the young Americans who were running off to France in those years were connoisseurs of French books and French wines and liked to wear little French mustaches. These were superficial signs on both sides, but they were an indication of tastes that proved to be lasting. The young American writers were deeply influenced by French literature in the Symbolist tradition; the young French writers were looking for American books that would express the picturesque qualities they found in American life; and when the books began to appear in translation, after 1930, they seized upon them enthusiastically.

The *Index Translationum,* published for eight years by the Institute of Intellectual Cooperation of the League of Nations, lists the titles and authors of all the books translated into the major European languages between 1932 and 1940. During that period there were 332 French translations of American books in the field of general literature. Jack London stands at the head of the list with twenty-seven titles, and James Oliver Curwood follows with twenty; both these adventure-story writers were old favorites with the French public, although their day was passing. Sinclair Lewis and Edgar Allan Poe have fourteen titles each; Ellery Queen has ten detective stories; Pearl Buck has nine of her books; Edgar Rice Burroughs, Louis Bromfield, and Henry James all have seven. Farther down the list are the new authors that the younger generation was reading: William Faulkner with five titles, Ernest Hemingway and Dashiell Hammett with four, John Dos Passos and Erskine Caldwell with three. None of these last reached the broadest French public, but all of them had what Lewis and Bromfield and Pearl Buck failed to achieve, that is, a direct influence on the style and content of the new French writing.

Faulkner, comparatively little known at home, had gained an amazingly deep and lasting French reputation. André Gide called him "one of the most important, perhaps *the* most important, of the stars in this new constellation"; and Jean-Paul Sartre was more extreme in his praise: "For young writers in France," he said in 1945, "Faulkner is a god." Many French critics were disturbed by what seemed to them the completely foreign quality of the new American novelists. The newspaper man in Gide's *Imaginary Interviews* says:

I grant you Hemingway, since he is the most European of them all. As for the others, I have to confess that their strangeness appals me. I thought I would go mad with pain and horror when I read Faulkner's *Sanctuary* and his *Light in August*. Dos Passos makes me suffocate. I laugh, it is true, when reading Caldwell's *Journeyman* or *God's Little Acre,* but I laugh on the wrong side of my mouth. . . . If one believes what they are saying, the American cities and countrysides must offer a foretaste of hell.

But if one believes what Flaubert said a hundred years ago French cities also must have been an abode of the damned. All these American novelists, except possibly Caldwell, were students of Flaubert; they had been applying methods learned from him to American materials. Now their books were being studied in turn by Flaubert's countrymen.

### 4

Most of the other European countries followed either the French or the British pattern in their choice of American books. A novel that was a best seller in England, like Kenneth Roberts' *Northwest Passage,* would also be a best seller in Germany and Scandinavia. An author admired by the French for his intensity or his technical discoveries would also be admired by other Latin nations. Almost everywhere there was a lack of interest in American literature during the years after 1900 and a birth or rebirth of interest at some moment after 1920. This new interest appeared earlier in the northern countries, because they liked Dreiser and Lewis, and later in the Latin countries, which showed more interest in younger writers like Hemingway and Faulkner. There were, however, national variations in the two general patterns; and in Russia after the Revolution the variations were so wide as to form a new pattern of their own.

Germany between 1890 and 1945 was another special case that has to be considered in some detail. In the Kaiser's Germany, Mark Twain had been by far the most popular American author; there were exactly 100 translations of his various works between 1890 and 1913. After him came Anna Katharine Green, the early detective-story writer, with eighty-one translations; then Bret Harte, Frances Hodgson Burnett, F. Marion Crawford, and Lew Wallace, the author of *Ben-Hur*. More than half the novels of American origin translated into German during the twenty-four years before the First World War were the work of these six writers. The most admired American poet was Walt Whitman, although his greatest popularity would come later, during the early years of the Weimar Republic. Emerson was the favorite American essayist.

After the war, the Germans were eager for books that dealt with American industry, the power by which they felt they had been defeated, and especially eager for anything that dealt with Henry Ford. What they looked for in American books was information first of all, but they were better pleased if the information was presented critically; therefore they liked Theodore Dreiser (who was for several years the most popular American author in the public libraries), Sinclair Lewis, Upton Sinclair, and, in general, all the critical realists. Hemingway was admired by the younger German writers who would later go into exile, but most of them were puzzled by his habit of understatement. When a German novelist wants to convey sadness or mild regret, he is likely to say that he was overwhelmed by waves of intolerable grief. When Hemingway wants to imply that his hero was overwhelmed by waves of intolerable grief, as at the end of *A Farewell to Arms,* he says that he "walked back to the hotel in the rain"; and the Germans did not know what to make of it. Thomas Wolfe, who never used a little word when he could find three big ones, was an author more to their taste. *Look Homeward, Angel* appealed to young people of all political faiths, before and after Hitler's coming to power. There were good as well as sinister qualities in the German youth movement, and some of the better ones were mirrored at a distance in Wolfe's hero.

The strength of the Socialist and Communist parties under the Weimar Republic helped to create a public for American authors with radical sympathies: not only for Upton Sinclair and Jack London, but also for John Dos Passos, whose books at one time had a larger circulation in Germany than in the United States. Another writer admired by the German radicals was Agnes Smedley, whose autobiography, *Daughter of Earth,* is comparatively little known in her own country, although it has been translated into fourteen languages. In Germany, where it was called *Eine Frau Allein,* it was especially popular among women seeking courage to lead independent lives. Miss Smedley's various books on the Chinese Revolution were also widely read until 1933, when they were all withdrawn from circulation. It was the same with Dreiser, Sinclair, Dos Passos, and Hemingway, none of whose works appeared in Germany between 1933 and 1946; they were the best known of the many American authors who suffered from Hitler's burning of the books.

Some of Sinclair Lewis' novels were also burned, but his new novels continued to be published in spite of his having written the anti-Nazi *It Can't Happen Here.* The *Index Translationum* shows that five of his novels were translated into German between 1932 and 1940. There were eight translations of Pearl Buck during the same period, more than of any other serious American author; perhaps her work was thought to be politically harmless because it dealt with China and, unlike Agnes Smedley's, made no plea for the Chinese Communists. Very few American books were published in Hitler's Germany if they dealt with contemporary Europe or America in any thoughtful fashion, no matter whether their authors were radical or conservative. The German public was still curious about our literature, but was offered, in general, only romance, adventure, mystery, and sentiment.

The *Index Translationum* lists 297 German translations from American originals in the field of general literature, a figure not far from the French total of 332. There is, however, a difference in quality. Nearly half the German list consists of Westerns and detective stories, with Max Brand, a mass purveyor of cowboy fiction, standing at the head of it with twenty-six titles. Historical romances were popular as an escape from daily life under a dictatorship: *Anthony Adverse, Northwest Passage,* and especially *Gone with the Wind,* which by 1941 had achieved the huge German sale of 360,693 copies; then it disappeared from the bookstores with the demand for it still unsatisfied. *Grapes of Wrath* was circulated with official approval after Pearl Harbor, presumably on the ground that its picture of the Okies would serve as anti-American propaganda. Instead, what it proved to most of its readers was that American peasants at their most destitute could travel about the country in automobiles, and that American writers were free to speak their minds in epical novels, at a time when German literature was being stifled. American books were read hungrily after the war ended, although few were available. *Daughter of Earth* was republished and even serialized in a Berlin newspaper; Thornton Wilder's *The Skin of Our Teeth* was the hit of the German theaters.

## 5

In Sweden, and the other Scandinavian countries, there was not much interest in American literature before the middle twenties, although there was great interest in a few American writers. Mark Twain in particular enjoyed the same popularity as in Germany. The chief librarian of the Royal Swedish Library, Mr. O. H. Wieselgren, said in a letter that he was given the Swedish translation of *Huckleberry Finn* as a birthday present when he was ten years old.

I read the book [he continued] so that I learned it by heart. . . . *The Jungle,* by Upton Sinclair, was translated in 1906. Sinclair since that time has been very widely read, and his social views have a great importance for the working class in our country. *The Harbor,* by Ernest Poole, was translated in 1915 and met with great interest. But the most admired of all American authors in Sweden has been and is still Jack London. His first books came in translation in 1909–10, and since that time he has appeared in innumerable editions. In public libraries he is still the most sought-for American author.

Interest in American literature, as opposed to interest in particular writers, began with the visit to the United States of the influential critic G. Ruben Berg. On his return to Sweden in 1925, he published *Moderne Amerikaner,* in which he gave an account of the new authors who had appeared since 1910, with much space devoted to Sinclair Lewis. Most of the authors he mentioned were translated into Swedish during the years that followed, and in 1930 Lewis was the first American to win the Nobel Prize for literature, which is awarded by the Swedish Academy. Eugene O'Neill was the second, in 1936; he had always acknowledged his debt to Strindberg, and his plays were even more popular in Strindberg's country than in the rest of Europe. Pearl Buck, who won the prize in 1938, was also particularly liked in Sweden. Ten of her books appeared there between 1932 and 1940, more than were translated from any other American author during the years covered by the *Index Translationum.* In all, the *Index* lists 213 American books in the field of general literature that were published in Sweden: a curious selection from new and half-forgotten authors, with Louisa May Alcott rubbing elbows with Dashiell Hammett. "The 'hard-boiled' literature plays an important role for our younger authors," Mr. Wieselgren notes. "I think no literature has during the last decade been more important and more read here than the American."

The last statement would also apply to Norway and Denmark. In the latter country, Pearl Buck was the most popular American author from 1932 to 1939 (except for best sellers like *Anthony Adverse* and *Gone with the Wind*), but Hemingway and Steinbeck had succeeded her by 1940. Holland, however, was in a different situation. Sheltered from transatlantic winds by the British Isles, it received most of its American books indirectly, after they had first become popular in London. In general it made no distinction between British and American literature.

Under Mussolini the Italian censorship was in theory not very strict; the only two American novelists whose works are known to have been forbidden were Hemingway (after his description of the Italian retreat in *A Farewell to Arms*) and Upton Sinclair, whose books were removed by decree from public libraries. Still, the whole effect of Fascist policy was to discourage, in a quiet way, the translation of authors from the democratic countries. The Italian public heard little about the new American literature and, like the Dutch public, it made no sharp distinction between American books and English books—usually preferring the latter, just as it preferred French books to either. Even after the liberation, when the Italians set to work translating the foreign works they had missed for the previous twenty years, there were not many American authors in the early publishers' lists (Steinbeck, Vincent Sheean, Kenneth Roberts); more attention was paid to the new French and English poets and the classical Russian novelists.

In Spain, American books and American movies had a brief vogue under the Republic. There was a time when the younger Spanish poets, probably influenced by their French colleagues, wrote nostalgically about gangsters and skyscrapers and in some cases made pilgrimages to New York; that was also the time when the news stands in Barcelona and Madrid were full of American magazines; but the vogue ended with the civil war. American books were suspect in Franco's Spain; even *Gone with the Wind* was not published there until 1943.

6

But *Gone with the Wind*, which eventually appeared in all the other European countries and was read by both sides during the early years of the Second World War, was never published in Soviet Russia. In their choice of American books for translation, the Russians followed a pattern of their own, one that began to be discernible even before their Revolution. From the beginning they liked American books if they were realistic or humorous or heroic in treatment, if they were democratic in sentiment, if they dealt with life in a great city or, still better, with adventures on the frontier, and if the characters were representative of the American masses. Cooper was the first American author to win lasting favor in Russia; then came Harriet Beecher Stowe; then Bret Harte and Mark Twain; and then, in 1910, Jack London, whose popularity increased when he was universally regarded as a socialist writer after the 1917 Revolution—he was the author whom Krupskaya, Lenin's widow, read to her husband on his deathbed.

After 1918 there was a State Publishing House in Russia; but there were also commercial publishers until 1928, and they competed for books by American writers. Of these Jack London was still the most widely read: from 1918 to 1929 there were six editions of his collected works in twelve to thirty-volume sets. Upton Sinclair was almost as popular, his books being regarded as a mine of information about capitalistic society. There was such a scramble for the right to publish them that Lunacharsky, the People's Commissar of Education, put an end to it in 1925 by officially designating Sinclair as a Soviet classic, thus putting him on the same pinnacle as Tolstoy and Pushkin, and, incidentally, vesting the Russian copyright to his books in the State Publishing House.

O. Henry was another favorite, not only with the masses but also with many of the Soviet writers, who studied him for his technique (so that stories with an O. Henry twist were being published in Russia at a time when American short-story writers were imitating Chekhov). James Oliver Curwood was enough like London in his themes and settings to be liked for the same reasons; there were forty-two editions of his separate novels between 1925 and 1927. Other American authors published at about the same time were Sherwood Anderson (studied by serious Russian writers), Sinclair Lewis, Booth Tarkington (*Penrod*), Edna Ferber (*So Big* and *Show Boat*), Rex Beach, and Zane Grey. During all this period the general popularity of American books continued to increase. In six months of 1912, there had been seven American authors published in Russia as against twenty-two English authors; in six months of 1928, there were forty-two Americans and thirty-seven Englishmen.

In 1928, at the beginning of the first Five Year Plan, the state took over the whole Russian publishing trade. There was a change in the character of the books selected for translation: Rex Beach, Zane Grey, and other popular entertainers disappeared from the lists of the state-controlled publishing houses. In their place came several proletarian novelists of the American depression years: Michael Gold, Jack Conroy, Albert Halper, all of whom reached a Russian audience several times as large as their audience at home. A complete edition of Dreiser's works was published in 1930; it was called the literary event of the year. Dos Passos was the most widely read American author, in literary circles, from 1932 to 1934; at one time the Organization

Committee of Soviet Writers conducted a formal discussion of his work that
lasted for three heated and dialectical evenings. From 1935 to 1939 or later,
Hemingway occupied a similar position; he too was the subject of an organized discussion by Soviet writers, and his technical influence on them
seems to have been more extensive and more lasting than that of Dos Passos
(whose books, incidentally, continued to be published in Russia in spite of
the strongly anti-Communist position which he took after 1935).

Hemingway was translated in full; and all his books reached a wide
audience except *For Whom the Bell Tolls,* which had been set in type when
the publishers became worried by a long passage attacking André Marty by
name. Marty, the French Communist leader, was at that time a refugee in
Russia, and a publishing house controlled by the state did not like to be put
in the position of endorsing what it regarded as a slander against him. The
result was that the volume never went to press, although the proof sheets were
read attentively by most of the writers in Moscow. Erskine Caldwell and
John Steinbeck are two other widely translated Americans whom the Russian
writers admired. At the same time both men reached the general public,
which also liked Pearl Buck, Richard Wright's *Native Son,* and, during the
war years, John Hersey's *A Bell for Adano.*

Control of the publishing industry by the Soviet state kept many books
out of Russia and promises to keep out many others during the postwar years
of international tension. It also led to the translation of books with more
political than commercial appeal; but apparently it had no deep effect on the
literary preferences of the Russian people. They continued to like the American authors whom they liked from the beginning; and in general the state-
controlled publishers supplied them with the books they demanded. The
Russians are fond of exact figures: when they say that Jack London has been
the most popular of all American authors in the Soviet Union, they support
the statement by adding that his various books have been printed in 567
Russian editions, of which 10,367,000 copies were sold between 1918 and 1943.
Mark Twain comes after him at a distance, with 3,100,000 copies sold during
the same period, and Upton Sinclair comes third, with 2,700,000. In the
twenty-five years that followed the Russian Revolution, there were 217 American authors translated into Russian—again the exact figure, furnished by the
State Publishing House—and the total sale of their translated books was
36,788,900 copies.

7

There were not so many of our authors published in Latin America and,
until the Second World War, their appearance was subject to long delays.

They had to make a double voyage across the Atlantic before reaching Argentina or Brazil; they traveled by way of Paris, and few of their books were admitted without a French visa of critical or popular approval. As in France, some of our Western and Northwestern story writers found a public easily: Rex Beach, James Oliver Curwood, Zane Grey. But the only serious North American author who exercised a direct influence in America Hispaña during the twenties was Waldo Frank. He lectured in all the capitals from Mexico City to Buenos Aires, he spoke a fluent literary Spanish, and he attacked Yankee imperialism while defending—and introducing to a sympathetic audience—the rebel American writers.

Early in 1941, a student of inter-American affairs went through a collection of the catalogues issued by Spanish-language publishers, almost all of whom have their headquarters in Santiago de Chile, Buenos Aires, or Mexico City. He found that they listed seven translations from Waldo Frank, more than from any other living North American writer. There were five translations from Sinclair Lewis, four from Steinbeck, and two each from Dos Passos and Upton Sinclair (though Sinclair had seven other books issued by smaller, chiefly socialistic, publishers who printed no catalogues); also the student found translations of best-selling novels like *The Good Earth, The Bridge of San Luis Rey, A Farewell to Arms,* and *Gone with the Wind*— in all, forty-three volumes from our current literature, exclusive of technical works, Westerns, and detective stories. He would have found many more North American books if he had examined the lists of the same publishers five years later, for there was a new interest in our literature after Pearl Harbor.

In part this interest resulted from the wartime activities of the Office of Inter-American Affairs, which sent several of our writers on lecture tours of South America and subsidized the publication of North American books that would not otherwise have appeared by paying for their translation into Spanish and Portuguese. Most of the books it subsidized were technical or historical; but the Office of Inter-American Affairs also arranged for the publication in Spanish of a two-volume anthology of contemporary North American writing, carefully edited by John Peale Bishop and Allen Tate. There would have been a growing interest in our literature without such encouragement, for the Latin Americans were excited by our entrance into the war, they were receiving very few books from Europe, and they were hearing from many unofficial sources about the younger North American novelists and poets. Hemingway, Faulkner, Steinbeck, Katherine Anne Porter, and Hart Crane were among those admired by the Argentinian and Brazilian intellectuals.

It is hard to gather accurate information about American literature in the Orient, where, generally speaking, the laws of international copyright are not enforced. In Japan before the Second World War, they did not even exist, as regards American books: a treaty negotiated under the first Roosevelt gave the Japanese permission to translate any American work without notifying the author. Not even squatter's right was recognized, and there was nothing to prevent five Japanese publishers from presenting five differently garbled translations of the same novel, as happened in the case of *Gone with the Wind*. Of three Japanese versions of Whitman, who had a large following, only one is said to have had any literary merit. Poe also—his fiction rather than his verse—was inaccurately rendered and widely read.

After 1930 the ruling clique in Japan tried hard to discourage "decadent" American influences, including the new American fiction; but Japanese publishers kept racing to press with competing versions of American best sellers. *Main Street* was a success in Japan; so too was Pearl Buck's *The Good Earth*, which was followed by translations of her later books (even those like *The Patriot* in which she condemned the Japanese invasion of China); while *Gone with the Wind* was the greatest success of all, having a sale in its various translations of more than half a million copies. At least twenty-four books by Upton Sinclair were translated into Japanese. A correspondent told him in 1931, "A term now often on the lips of people interested in modern literature is *Sinkurea Jidai,* which means 'The Sinclair Era.'" Many of the American proletarian novelists who flourished in the thirties had larger sales in Japanese, as in Russian, than they had in their own language; and the censors at first were rather easy-going. Leafing through the proof sheets of translations about to be published, they looked chiefly for Japanese equivalents of three words, "revolution," "people's," and "social." If the dangerous words were present, at first they merely deleted them before approving the book for publication; but later they deleted the whole chapters in which they appeared and, still later, they began throwing the translators and publishers into jail. Hidemi Ozaki, who had translated Agnes Smedley's *Daughter of Earth,* was hanged in November, 1944, long after some of Sinclair's translators had preceded him to the scaffold. *Sinkurea Jidai* had ended.

There was also a Sinclair era in China, where at least seventeen of his books had been published by 1930. Six more were then in process of translation, but nobody in this country, it would seem, knows whether they appeared. In China the business of publishing foreign books is not only piratical, as it has been in Japan, but also completely unorganized. Any bookstore in Shanghai is likely to issue its own translations without notifying its rivals, let alone the American authors. Some of these authors have been widely read. There were, for example, at least three translations of *The Good Earth,* one of which was cut and garbled; the other two were widely discussed in the

Chinese press, where some of the reviewers—a minority, as might be expected—thought that Mrs. Buck had presented a true picture. *Gone with the Wind* appeared in one or more unauthorized translations. Lao Shaw, the author of *Rickshaw Boy,* reported for the Chinese writers born after 1910 that their chosen American author was Eugene O'Neill, who was also most influential with the educated public as a whole. Other favorites were Steinbeck and Saroyan.

In India the educated classes read many or most of their American books in the British colonial editions. Whitman, with what might be called his profound smattering of Eastern philosophy, has always had followers there; the greatest of these was Rabindranath Tagore. Gandhi read Thoreau, who contributed to his philosophy of nonviolent resistance; also, according to his nephew Narainadas Gandhi, he read "most if not all" of Upton Sinclair. No study has been made of recent translations into the various Indian languages; but it is known that *The Good Earth* was rendered at least into Bengali, and possibly into others as well, while various books by Sinclair have appeared in Bengali, Hindi, Gujarati, Tamil, Urdu, Telegu, Marathi, and Singhalese.

Beyond a doubt, Sinclair is the most widely translated novelist of the twentieth century not read for pure entertainment. By 1938 there had been 713 translations of his various books, which had then been published in forty-seven languages and thirty-nine countries. There are several reasons for Sinclair's international popularity. Shortly after he wrote *The Jungle,* which traveled round the world within two years of its American publication in 1906, he was adopted as a favorite author by the international working-class movement in both its main branches, the Menshevik and the Bolshevik, later the Social Democratic and the Communist. But his books were also read by the middle classes in most of the countries where they were allowed to circulate, partly because they all told straightforward, rapidly moving stories, but chiefly because each of his novels, besides being a story, was a well documented journalistic survey of some aspect of American life: an industry, a city, a political movement, or a celebrated trial. The world-wide interest in Upton Sinclair was also an interest in America as a whole.

8

From any survey of American books abroad, however incomplete it may be, we gain a somewhat different picture of American literature at home. We learn, for example, that it has been richer and more varied than most of us had suspected from merely reading our choice of each season's new fiction or factual reporting. The export of American literary works has not been standardized, like that of Detroit automobiles; instead each country has been choosing the American books that met its particular tastes. Sometimes these books have been the work of authors little known in the United States who achieved their widest fame in Europe or Asia. Sometimes American writers have been adopted and, as it were, given honorary citizenship by the different countries to which their minds appealed; so that Faulkner in France, Hemingway in Russia (like Jack London and Mark Twain before him), O'Neill and Pearl Buck in Scandinavia, Thomas Wolfe in Germany, Waldo Frank in Latin America, and Upton Sinclair in many parts of the world, but especially in the Orient, have come to be regarded as almost native authors.

At the same time, there are some American books that have swept across the world without pausing at national boundaries. Not a few of them were critical of American standards, and the reason for their popularity is not hard to explain: foreign readers like to be told that not everything is perfect in the land of the jukebox and the low-priced automobile. Most of the universally read books, however, were either adventure stories (a commercialized branch of fiction in which our writers have a long tradition of technical skill), or they were epical novels on the scale of *Gone with the Wind* and *Grapes of Wrath*—it did not matter, apparently, whether they dealt with the past or the present, from a conservative or a radical point of view, so long as they filled a canvas as big as the top of a covered wagon, and so long as they told a story that everyone could follow.

Story, or narrative, according to the English critic Lovat Dickson, is one of two qualities that distinguish recent American fiction. "To the outside observer," he said, "it seemed suddenly to become characteristic of all American entertainment and to mark it off quite sharply from the English equivalent. Story suddenly became of first-rate importance, and appreciation of narrative became a marked American characteristic." The other quality Dickson mentioned was gusto. "Today it seems to us in England," he said, "the essential, distinctive, and enviable quality of American fiction. Somewhere and somehow, in the American novel towards the end of the post-war decade, solemnity was miraculously shed and in its place appeared a new virility as mysteriously and suddenly as the works of Fielding, Sterne, and Smollett had appeared in eighteenth-century England."

French critics were more impressed by other qualities of American fiction (or by the same qualities under different names): they mentioned its intensity and singleness of emotion, its earthy dialogue, its delight in physical violence, and what they called its "pure exteriority," a term they applied to the practice common among American novelists of presenting character in terms of speech and action, without auctorial comments, as if they were writing for the stage. Russian and Czech critics were deeply impressed by the technical discoveries of our novelists, whom they studied very much as

American writers used to study Flaubert. Critics of all nations felt that they were dealing with a unified body of work. For that is our second impression after a survey of American books abroad: besides being immensely varied, they also possess a family resemblance that has not always been recognized at home. "American," said one French critic, "is not so much a nationality as a style."

During the first half of this century, the position of American literature in foreign countries has been completely transformed. It was still regarded, before 1900, as a department of English literature, a sort of branch factory that tried to duplicate the products of the parent firm. After 1930 it came to be regarded as one of the great world literatures in its own right, and perhaps, as regards contemporary work, the greatest of them all. But this transformed position was not merely a secondary result of the growth in economic and military power of the American nation; it was also an independent development that testified to a change in the literature itself. Europeans were not slow to recognize that there had been a literary revival here after 1910; and they showed the same hospitality to the new writers of the interwar period that they had shown, a century before, to the writers of the New York and New England renaissance.

# TABLE OF AUTHORS

*Editor's Note:* Most of the chapters in these volumes are the work of single contributors; a few are collaborations. In many cases, sentences and paragraphs have been added, usually at the beginnings and ends of chapters, to tie the book together and to emphasize dominant themes; occasionally passages designed for one chapter have found a more logical place in another; and extreme variations in style have been somewhat modified. Differences of opinion among authors have been allowed to stand.

Preface: the Editors and Associates
Address to the Reader: Henry Seidel Canby; the Editors and Associates

# INDEX

# 1418

567, 608, 610, 681; *Atalantis,* 312; *Beauchampe,* 312; *Charlemont,* 312; *Count Julian,* 312; *Guy Rivers,* 311, 312, 681; *Martin Faber,* 312; *The Partisan,* 312; *Pelayo, a Story of the Goth,* 312; *The Yemassee,* 312
Sinclair, Upton, 978, *995–999,* 1118, 1361, 1375, 1381, 1382, 1383, 1384, 1385, 1386, 1387, 1388, 1389; *American Outpost,* 998; *Boston,* 998; *Dragon's Teeth,* 998; *The Jungle,* 996–997, 1118, 1375, 1383; *Love's Pilgrimage,* 997; *Manassas,* 996; *Oil!,* 998; *World's End,* 998
Single tax, 795, 973, 978–979
Singmaster, Elsie, 684
Skinner, Otis, 1001, 1007, 1012
Sklar, George, 1327
Slavery, 85, 226, 227, 293, 301, 504–506, 511, 545, 563–568, 575–577, 583–584, 608–609. *See also* Civil War
Slick, Sam (Thomas Chandler Haliburton), 561, 734–735
Slosson, Annie Trumbull, 844
*Smart, Set,* 1078, 1144
Smedley, Agnes, 1382, 1383, 1388
Smith, Bernard, 1362
Smith, Charles Henry, 571, 744
Smith, Elihu Hubbard, 129, 168, 181
Smith, Elizabeth Oakes, 282
Smith, F. Hopkinson, 832, 988
Smith, Jedediah S., 777
Smith, John, 3, 7, 10, *32–33,* 44, 48, 187
Smith, Seba, 651, 732–733
Smith, William (1727–1803), 87, *96,* 97–98
Smith, William (1728–1793), 89–90
Smith, Winchell, 1005
Smithsonian Institution, 230, 647, 682
Social debate and fiction, 986–999
Social gospel, 649, 795, 951
Socialism and Socialization, 895, 896, 950, 969, 970, 971, 973, 977, 984, 1107, 1108, 1255, 1256, 1270–1272. *See also* Communism; Industrialism; Labor movement; Single tax; Social Security
Social Security, 1254, 1257–1259
Sociology, 980
Songs, 648, 707–715
Sothern, E. H., 1007
South, The, 38, 40, 41, 48, 49–52, *306–320,* 504, 510, 512, *607–617,* 641, 684–687, 791, 848–859, 949, 1216, 1256, 1257, 1304–1306, 1309, 1314, *1346–1347,* 1371
*South Carolina Gazette,* 22

*Southern and Western Monthly Magazine and Review,* 317
*Southern Literary Messenger,* 309, 310, 313, 314, 316, 317, 318, 326, 327, 328, 774
*Southern Quarterly Review,* 317
*Southern Review,* (1828–1832), 308, 311, 608
*Southern Review* (1935–1942), 1371
Southey, Robert, 296
Spalding, John Lancaster, 970–971
Spanish influence. *See* Foreign attitudes and influences; Folk-literature
Spanish-American literature, 25–26, 659, 678, 687–688
Spargo, John, 1111, 1255
Sparks, Jared, *285,* 286, 527, 645
*Spectator,* 624
Spelling, American, 670, 674
Spencer, Herbert, 790, 947, 970, 974, 978, 980, 1018, 1021
Spender, Stephen, 1378
Spenser, Edmund, 420
Spingarn, J. E., 1137, *1154–1156,* 1359, 1365, 1367
*Spirit of the Times,* 739, 741, 866
Springfield *Republican,* 770, 828
Stallings, Laurence, 1243, 1317, 1318
Standard Oil Company, 979
Standish, Myles, 35
Stanton, Daniel, 84
Stanton, Elizabeth Cady, 503
Stedman, Edmund Clarence, 524, 795, 809, 811, 812, 813, 814, *815–818,* 819, 825, 900, 1136, 1157; *American Anthology,* 815; *Blameless Prince,* 825; *The Nature and Elements of Poetry,* 815, 816–817; *Victorian Anthology,* 815; *Victorian Poets,* 815, 816
Steele, Richard, 19, 151
Steele, Wilbur Daniel, 1239
Steere, Richard, 65
Steffens, Lincoln, 993, 1125
Stein, Gertrude, 1297, 1300
Stein, Kurt M., 683
Steinbeck, John, 688, 1256, 1265, *1312,* 1314, 1375, 1382, 1384, 1386, 1387, 1390; *Grapes of Wrath,* 1256, 1312, 1382, 1390
Stephens, Alexander H., 558
Sterling, James, 52
Stevens, Thaddeus, 508
Stevens, Wallace, 1120, 1174, *1354–1355;* *Harmonium,* 1354; *Ideas of Order,* 1355; *The Man with the Blue Guitar,* 1355
Stevenson, Robert Louis, 832, 1008
Stewart, Charles S., 444